Microsoft® Office XP

Resource Kit

PUBLISHED BY
Microsoft Press
A Division of Microsoft Corporation
One Microsoft Way
Redmond, Washington 98052-6399

Copyright © 2001 by Microsoft Corporation

All rights reserved. No part of the contents of this book may be reproduced or transmitted in any form or by any means without the written permission of the publisher.

Library of Congress Cataloging-in-Publication Data
Microsoft Office XP Resource Kit / Microsoft Corporation.
    p. cm.
    Includes index.
    ISBN 0-7356-1403-2
    1. Microsoft Office. 2. Business-Computer programs. I. Microsoft Corporation.

HF5548.4.M525 M539   2001
005.369--dc21   2001030414

Printed and bound in the United States of America.

2 3 4 5 6 7 8 9   QWT   6 5 4 3 2 1

Distributed in Canada by Penguin Books Canada Limited.

A CIP catalogue record for this book is available from the British Library.

Microsoft Press books are available through booksellers and distributors worldwide. For further information about international editions, contact your local Microsoft Corporation office or contact Microsoft Press International directly at fax (425) 936-7329. Visit our Web site at mspress.microsoft.com. Send comments to *rkinput@microsoft.com*.

Active Desktop, Active Directory, ActiveX, Authenticode, BackOffice, FoxPro, FrontPage, Hotmail, IntelliMirror, IntelliMouse, JScript, Microsoft, Microsoft Press, MSDN, MSN, NetShow, Outlook, PhotoDraw, PivotTable, PowerPoint, SharePoint Team Services, Verdana, Visual Basic, Visual FoxPro, Visual Interdev, Visual SourceSafe, Windows, and Windows NT are either registered trademarks or trademarks of Microsoft Corporation in the United States and/or other countries. Macintosh, QuickTime, and TrueType are registered trademarks of Apple Computer, Inc. Kodak and FlashPix are trademarks of Kodak and the Kodak corporate symbol is a trademark of Kodak used under license. NetWare and intraNetWare are registered trademarks of Novell. Solstice Network Client is a trademark of Sun Microsystems. Unicode is a registered trademark of Unicode, Inc. Other product and company names mentioned herein may be the trademarks of their respective owners.

Unless otherwise noted, the example companies, organizations, products, people, and events depicted herein are fictitious. No association with any real company, organization, product, person, or event is intended or should be inferred.

Acquisitions Editor: Juliana Aldous
Project Editor: Maureen Williams Zimmerman

Body Part No. X08-22432

This book and its online version on the World Wide Web were produced by members of the Office Product Unit of Microsoft Corporation.

Project Lead

Randy Holbrook

Writers

Michael L. Cook, Gary Ericson, Mark Gillis, Jennifer Morison Hendrix, Samantha J.W. Robertson, Stacia Snapp

Editor

Stanley K. McKenzie

Program Managers

Paul C. Barr, Gordon Hardy, Darrin Hatakeda, Kristi Minietta, C. Scott Walker

Designers

Carr Pierce, Jim St. George

Indexer

Diana Rain

Production

Donalee Edwards, Jarrah Juarez, Erik Olson, Richard Parke, Penny Parks

Toolbox Contributors

David Chicks, Gordon Church, Maria-Nancy Domini, James Elder, Lucas Forschler, Lutz Gerhard, David Gerlt, Steve Greenberg, John Guin, Robert Hill, Bill Hunter, Mike Marcelais, Stephan Mueller, Chris Pearo, Matt Pearson, Jonathan Phillips, Matt Ruhlen, Helen Todd, Brian Trenbeath, Janny Wong, Jixin Wu, Rong Yang

Contents

PART 1   Getting Started

CHAPTER 1   Office XP Resource Kit 3
   Welcome 3
   What's New in the Office XP Resource Kit 10
   Options for Acquiring Office 17
   Web Sites of Interest to Administrators 19

CHAPTER 2   Collaboration with Office 21
   Introducing Microsoft's SharePoint Team Services 21
   Introducing Office XP Workgroup Strategies 23
   Microsoft Web Solutions 24

CHAPTER 3   Deployment Prerequisites 27
   Office XP System Requirements 27
   Upgrading Reference 47

PART 2   Deployment

CHAPTER 4   Overview of Setup 55
   Setup Components 55
   Tasks Handled by Setup 61
   Installations That Require Elevated Privileges 72

CHAPTER 5   Installing and Customizing Office 77
   Creating an Administrative Installation Point 77
   Customizing the Office Installation 83
   Customizing How Setup Runs 94
   Customizing Office Features and Shortcuts 102
   Customizing User-defined Settings 114

Contents

    Including Additional Packages in the Office Installation 129

    Customizing Removal Behavior 135

    Distributing Office to Users' Computers 141

    Deploying a Service Release 156

CHAPTER 6 Deploying on Windows 2000 . . . . **163**

    Deployment Issues Specific to Windows 2000 163

    Using Windows 2000 Software Installation 165

CHAPTER 7 Deploying on Windows NT 4.0 . . . . **189**

    Deployment Issues Specific to Windows NT 4.0 189

    Using Windows Installer Shortcuts with Office 190

PART 3 Maintenance

CHAPTER 8 Maintaining an Installation **195**

    Repairing Office Installations 195

    Changing Feature Installation States 197

    Changing User Settings After Installation 202

    Removing Applications or Features After Installation 205

    Reporting Office Application Crashes 214

    Using the Office Profile Wizard 225

CHAPTER 9 Using System Policies **235**

    Understanding System Policies 235

    How to Set System Policies 240

    Office System Policies 255

    Working with Difficult Policies 267

CHAPTER 10 Administering Security **289**

    Protecting Office Documents 289

    Running Office in a Secure Environment 306

    Office Macro Security Settings 308

    Security Settings and Related System Policies 312

    Microsoft Office Tools on the Web Security Scenarios 323

CHAPTER 11 Creating Custom Help **327**
    Customizing Error Messages 327
    Creating Custom Help Topics 341
    Making Custom Help Content Accessible 347

PART 4 Worldwide Deployment

CHAPTER 12 Planning an International Deployment **363**
    Preparing for an International Deployment 363
    International Deployment Scenarios 365
    Localized Versions of Office XP 370

CHAPTER 13 Deploying Office Internationally **373**
    Deploying Office with the Multilingual User Interface Pack 373
    Sample Customizations for Office with the Multilingual User Interface Pack 389
    Installing Proofing Tools 398
    Customizing Language Features 401

CHAPTER 14 Upgrading International Installations **407**
    Upgrading Your MultiLanguage Pack Installation 407
    Upgrading with Input Method Editors 408
    Sharing Files Across Language Versions 409

CHAPTER 15 Maintaining International Installations **425**
    Unicode Support and Multilingual Documents 425
    Taking Advantage of Unicode Support 427
    Changing Language Settings 431
    Removing Multilingual User Interface Files 433
    Managing Language Settings for Each Application 433

CHAPTER 16 Preparing Users' Computers for International Use **443**
    Choosing an Operating System 443
    Choosing a Web Browser 449
    Administering Fonts 451
    Printing Documents 455

Contents

PART 5 Messaging

CHAPTER 17 Planning for Outlook 459
Planning an Outlook Deployment 459
Choosing Among E-mail Servers 463
Determining When to Install Outlook 463

CHAPTER 18 Deploying Outlook 467
Options for Installing Outlook 467
Customizing an Outlook Installation 470
Customizing Profiles with an Outlook Profile File 477

CHAPTER 19 Special Outlook Deployment Scenarios 481
Ensuring a Quiet Installation and Startup 481
Installing in a Terminal Services Environment 484
Installing Before or After Office 485
Configuring Outlook for Roaming Users 497

CHAPTER 20 Upgrading to Outlook 2002 503
Planning an Upgrade 503
Upgrading from Previous Versions 504
Upgrading From Older Versions of Messaging Clients 505
Upgrading from Schedule+ 509
Sharing Information with Other Versions or Applications 511
Upgrading to Outlook 2002 Security 520
Reverting to a Previous Installation 522

CHAPTER 21 Maintaining an Outlook Installation 523
Updating Outlook Profiles 523
Locating and Configuring Outlook Settings 526
Using Automatic Message Encoding 529
Unicode Support 532

CHAPTER 22 Administering Outlook Security 535
Outlook 2002 Security Model 535
Secure E-mail Messaging 546

Appendix

Toolbox **551**

    Answer Wizard Builder 552

    CMW File Viewer 552

    Corporate Error Reporting 553

    Custom Installation Wizard 553

    Custom Maintenance Wizard 554

    HTML Help Workshop 555

    MST File Viewer 556

    OEM Tools 557

    Office Converter Pack 558

    OPS File Viewer 558

    Outlook Security Features Administrative Package 559

    Package Definition Files 559

    PowerPoint Viewer 560

    Profile Wizard 560

    Removal Wizard 561

    Setup INI Customization Wizard 562

    Supplemental Documentation 562

    System Policy Editor and Templates 565

Glossary **567**

Index **575**

PART 1

Getting Started

Chapter 1   Office XP Resource Kit   3

Chapter 2   Collaboration with Office   21

Chapter 3   Deployment Prerequisites   27

CHAPTER 1

Office XP Resource Kit

The Microsoft Office XP Resource Kit brings together the tools, information, and examples you need to customize and deploy Microsoft Office XP throughout your organization. Designed for the information technology (IT) professional, the Office XP Resource Kit provides comprehensive information about deployment strategies, international support, and messaging services. In addition, the Office Resource Kit tools have been updated to help you configure, secure, and manage your installations more quickly and efficiently.

In this chapter

Welcome   3

What's New in the Office XP Resource Kit   10

Options for Acquiring Office   17

Web Sites of Interest to Administrators   19

Welcome

The Microsoft® Office XP Resource Kit is designed for administrators, information technology (IT) professionals, and support staff who deploy and support Microsoft Office XP. The Office Resource Kit features a comprehensive set of tools to assist you with installation, configuration, and maintenance, as well as in-depth documentation on strategies and techniques that you can use to support Office XP within your organization.

For Office XP, the Resource Kit has been updated with improved tools and the latest information on deployment and administrative support. Some areas of the kit have been expanded, such as topics related to platform strategies, messaging, and worldwide support. Topics in other areas, such as migration and compatibility, have been greatly reduced, due to strong improvements in the product itself. Overall, the Office Resource Kit focuses on helping you get your organization up and running with Office XP in less time than ever.

A significant part of the Office Resource Kit is the ongoing support provided on the Office Resource Kit Web site. The Web site includes all of the information provided with the book, plus articles on emerging technologies, strategies, and issues. Current versions of all tools and support files are provided in the Office Resource Kit Toolbox, along with administrative update files for any Office XP service releases offered at a later date.

Office XP Resource Kit documentation

Online versions of the Office XP Resource Kit are available on the World Wide Web and with Enterprise editions of Office XP. The printed book is available through your local bookseller, online bookstores, or directly from Microsoft Press®. Included with this book is a CD that contains an electronic copy of the Office XP Resource Kit book, the Office Resource Kit tools, reference information, and supplementary documents.

To learn more about buying the book, visit the Microsoft Press Web site at http://mspress.microsoft.com. For Office XP product support information, visit the Microsoft Product Support Services site, at http://support.microsoft.com, which provides links to support phone numbers, online support requests, and worldwide support resources, as well as other helpful resources. For information about how to install the contents of the CD, see the orkcd.txt file on the CD.

Documentation for the Microsoft Office XP Resource Kit is organized into five parts and an Appendix.

Part 1: Getting Started

Getting Started covers the basic information you need to know to start planning for an Office XP deployment. Here, you will find details on system requirements and upgrading from previous versions, as well as a comprehensive list of new features included in the Office Resource Kit itself. This section also highlights the new collaboration services provided with Office XP through Microsoft's SharePoint™ Team Services technology.

Part 2: Deployment

At the heart of the Office Resource Kit are the tools and information designed to help you configure and deploy Office XP within your organization. The Deployment section provides extensive information on using the deployment tools, covering the basic installation scenarios along with specific information on platform issues, customization, and distribution. New areas covered in the Office XP Resource Kit include deployment strategies for Microsoft Windows® 2000, background information on how Setup runs, and instructions on how to deploy a service release.

Part 3: Maintenance

The Maintenance section describes many of the tools and strategies you can use to manage security and lower the total cost of ownership for Office XP. The topics on system policies, for example, explain how you can enforce settings and restrictions on users' computers to maintain the overall stability of their systems. The broad security section describes how to protect documents and safeguard your systems from viruses. Individual topics cover areas such as changing features or user settings, repairing an installation, and using the Office Profile Wizard to migrate settings and templates between computers. Finally, the topics on Custom Help show you how to integrate your organization's own support information into the Office XP Help environment.

Part 4: Worldwide Deployment

International organizations can use the Office XP Resource Kit to plan for multinational deployments. Topics describe how to implement international dictionaries and proofing tools, as well as how to use Unicode® support to open documents across different language versions of the product. The Worldwide Deployment section focuses on the Microsoft Office Multilingual User Interface Pack, which allows users to change the language of the user interface and the online Help system. Other features include sample customizations for multilingual deployments, along with information on Input Method Editors (IMEs), upgrading scenarios, and font support.

Part 5: Messaging

Fast and secure messaging is vital to any organization, and the Office XP Resource Kit covers what you need to know to plan, deploy, and maintain your messaging clients. Along with the standard deployment scenarios, the topics cover special cases such as quiet installations, roaming configurations, and deployment on Windows Terminal Services. The upgrading section covers upgrades from both previous and older versions of messaging clients, as well as Schedule+ migration and information on the Web protocol. Throughout the topics, a strong focus on security issues gives you the perspective you need to ensure the integrity of your systems.

Appendix

Summary information on all tools provided with the Office XP Resource Kit is provided in the Toolbox. Also included in the Office Resource Kit is a glossary of terms used throughout the topics, as well as a comprehensive index.

Documentation conventions in the Office Resource Kit

The following terms and text formats are used in the Office Resource Kit.

Convention	Meaning
Bold	Indicates the actual properties, commands, words, or characters that you type, view, or click in the user interface.
Italic	In procedures, command lines, or syntax, italic characters indicate a placeholder for information or parameters that you must provide. For example, if the procedure asks you to type a file name, you type the actual name of a file.
Path\File name	Indicates a Windows file system path or registry key — for example, the file Templates\Normal.dot. Unless otherwise indicated, you can use a mixture of uppercase and lowercase characters when you type paths and file names.
`Monospace`	Represents examples of code text.

Office XP Resource Kit Toolbox

The Office Resource Kit contains tools that help you to customize, configure, and deploy Office XP within your organization. If you have the Office XP Resource Kit CD or an Enterprise edition of Office XP, you can install the core tools and support documents through one integrated Setup program. The tools are also available separately from the download site of the Office Resource Kit Web site.

The following table summarizes the key tools that are installed by default when you run the Office Resource Kit Setup program. For information about specific tools, see the Toolbox.

Tool name	Description
Answer Wizard Builder	Enables you to build your own Answer Wizard content that contains information specific to your organization.
CMW File Viewer	Displays the contents of a CMW file created by the Custom Maintenance Wizard in a readable text format in Notepad.

Tool name (cont'd)	Description
Corporate Error Reporting	Enables you to manage the DW.exe crash-reporting tool. (DW.exe is a feedback tool used to analyze and develop fixes for crashes on users' computers.)
Custom Installation Wizard	Allows you to create a unique Windows Installer transform (MST file) for every installation scenario you need, without altering the original Windows Installer package (MSI file).
Custom Maintenance Wizard	Enables you to change settings, installation states, and other options after Office has been initially deployed.
Microsoft Internet Explorer Administration Kit 5	Lets you customize, distribute, and maintain Internet Explorer 5 from one central location.
Office Removal Wizard	Lets you maintain a fine level of control over which files are removed from a user's system.
OPS File Viewer	Displays the contents of an OPS file created by the Profile Wizard in a readable text format in Notepad.
Profile Wizard	Helps you to create and save a default user profile, including standard locations for files and templates.
Setup INI Customization Wizard	Provides a convenient way to enter information into the correct section of the settings file, create a command line that includes the **/settings** option, and specify a custom INI file.
System Management Server Package Definition Files	Used by Microsoft Systems Management Server to install Office 2000 applications remotely.
System Policy Editor and Templates	Allows you to set and control the user interface and behavior of an application.
MST File Viewer	Displays changes you make to a Windows Installer package (MSI file) in a readable text format in Notepad.

The Office Resource Kit also includes several tools that are not installed by default from the Setup program. These tools are available from the Office Resource Kit or Office Enterprise CD, or online from the Office Resource Kit Web site. For more information on installing the supplemental tools, see the Toolbox.

Tool name	Description
HTML Help	Use the HTML Help Workshop to create Help topics that provide information and assistance specific to your organization.
OEM tools	Support utilities designed for original equipment manufacturers (OEMs) that enable you to reset the source, user data, and other information after Office has been installed on a computer.
Office Converter Pack	A collection of add-ins, converters, and filters designed to help you migrate files generated by third-party products and early versions of Microsoft Office to Office XP.
Outlook Security features administrative template	Enables administrators to modify the default security settings of the Outlook® Security features.
PowerPoint Viewer	Enables you to share PowerPoint® 97, PowerPoint 2000, and PowerPoint 2002 presentations with users who do not have PowerPoint installed on their systems.

Supplemental documentation

The Office XP Resource Kit includes a number of supplemental documents that provide detailed information on such areas as registry settings, international settings, and the Office XP file list. The supplemental documents are installed by default when you run the Office Resource Kit Setup program, and they are also available online from the Office Resource Kit Web site. The following table summarizes the supplemental documents. For more information, see the Toolbox.

Document file name	Description
Cfgquiet.ini	Contains default settings for the Microsoft Office Server Extension log file.
Filelist.xls	Lists all files provided with Office XP.
Formats.doc	Lists supported data formats and installed OLE DB providers.
IE5feats.xls	Notes the Office XP features that degrade with previous versions of Microsoft Internet Explorer.
Opc.doc	Explains the syntax in files used by the Removal Wizard so that administrators can customize the removal of applications.
Regkey.xls	Lists default registry key values.
Setupref.doc	Lists Office Setup command-line options, properties, and settings file formats.
Stopword.doc	Contains the list of words not indexed by the Find Fast utility.
Webent.xls	Lists all entry points to the Web from within Office and describes how to disable them.
Intlimit.xls	Lists the limitations of plug-in language compatibility by component.
Multilpk.xls	Lists components of the Office Multilingual User Interface Pack and Office Proofing Tools by language.
Wwfeatre.xls	Lists the effect of various language settings on each Office application.
Wwsuppt.xls	Lists support, by language of operating system, of different language features of Office applications.

What's New in the Office XP Resource Kit

The installation process for Microsoft Office XP has been significantly improved over previous versions of Microsoft Office. Along with an improved Setup process, new tools and enhancements to existing tools provide the best means for managing the deployment of Office XP within a corporate environment.

Many improvements and corrections in this version of the Office Resource Kit are in response to top issues reported by Microsoft Product Support Services. The first thing you may notice is the number of changes made to core tools such as the Custom Installation Wizard, Custom Maintenance Wizard, and the Office Profile Wizard. The inclusion of a new tool, Corporate Error Reporting, is probably the most significant addition to the Office Resource Kit.

The following sections discuss the improvements to existing tools and addition of new tools to the Office Resource Kit.

Custom Installation Wizard

Several enhancements are visible in the latest release of the Custom Installation Wizard (Custwiz.exe), including the improvements mentioned the following sections.

New wizard pages

There are several new pages available in the Custom Installation Wizard, but the following two pages offer advantages not previously available:

- **Change Office User Settings**

    Similar to the Office Profile Wizard, you can customize specific menu settings to either display or not display, and also to set defaults to these settings.

- **Specify Security Settings**

    Due to the increased demand for tighter security with templates, documents, workbooks, etc., the ability to set and configure macro security, ActiveX® controls, and password security is now available through the wizard.

Enhanced user interface

Several changes were made to the Custom Installation Wizard to make it easier to use — not the least of which was improvements to the names and descriptive text for controls and labels in the user interface.

New installation state — Not Available, Hidden, Locked

To help administrators enforce an installation state that a user cannot change, the **Not Available, Hidden, Locked** installation state is provided to curb the ability of users to change the configuration administrators have set for applications and their features.

New options on the Set Feature Installation States page

Due to new installation capabilities and requests from administrators, the following capabilities have been added to control how Office is installed:

- **Do not Migrate Previous Installation State**

  A feature of Setup.exe and Windows Installer allows previously installed applications to be removed and new applications to install using the same settings from the previous installation. Enabling the option **Do not Migrate Previous Installation State**, you can disable that feature of Setup.exe or Windows Installer.

- **Disable Installed on First Use**

  The option **Disable Installed on First Use** turns off the ability of Windows Installer to advertise an application on the user's computer with a shortcut.

- **Disable Run from Network**

  The option **Disable Run from Network** turns off the ability of Windows Installer to install applications using the **Run From Network** installation state for the selected feature in the feature tree.

Ability to install Visual Basic as a feature of Office

You'll need to see the online help for the Custom Installation Wizard (Custom10.hlp) for specifics about this enhancement. Visual Basic® for Applications is a sensitive component of Office, and as such requires extra understanding by administrators. See the Help available from the **Set Feature Installation States** page or the **Specify Office Security Settings** page of the wizard for detailed information.

Ability to remove files with a transform

You can now remove files from a user's computer by using a transform. Previously, you could only add files with a transform.

Ability to remove registry entries with a transform

You can now remove registry branches, keys, or values from a user's computer by using a transform. Previously, you could only add them in the transform.

New properties in the Modify Setup Properties page

There are several new properties you can configure. It is advised you read the document Setupref.doc available with the Office Resource Kit for information on all the properties you can use. Setupref.doc is installed by default when you run the Office XP Resource Kit Setup program.

Easier-to-navigate Outlook customization pages

There are several new customization options available in the wizard for Outlook. One important one is the ability to create an Outlook profile file (PRF file).

Ability to create an Outlook PRF file

You can now create a PRF file for use with the installation of Outlook. You can create the initial instance of a PRF file from the Custom Installation Wizard and then perform further customization to this PRF file manually using a text editor like Notepad or Wordpad.

Enhanced Help

Available from the Custom Installation Wizard, Custom Maintenance Wizard, and Profile Wizard is an integrated Help file. This file contains the core information you will need to use these tools to help you configure Office, including property information, Setup.ini information, and a "special issues" section.

New format for MST and MSI files

Due to the differences in the previous release of Office 2000 and the enhancements to Office XP, there is a new MSI file format. This change also forced a change to the MST file format. Because of these changes, you cannot use the previous release of the Custom Installation Wizard with the new file formats; you must use the new release of the wizard.

Customize Internet Explorer 5 Installation Options page appears only when customizing the OSP.msi

Due to the new method of installing Office and upgrading system files, there is a corresponding update to how Office-related components are installed — specifically, how Microsoft Internet Explorer 5 is installed and how you customize it for your use. See the related sections in the Office Resource Kit and online Help available with the wizards for further information.

Custom Maintenance Wizard

Unlike the previous release, the extensively updated version of the Custom Maintenance Wizard (Maintwiz.exe) can help ease the task of maintaining Office XP. Several elements of the Custom Maintenance Wizard have been added or enhanced, including the following:

- New pages

    Several new pages in the Custom Maintenance Wizard mirror pages in the Custom Installation Wizard, including the following:

    - **Specify New Organization Name**
    - **Change Office User Settings**
    - **Add/Remove Files**
    - **Add/Remove Registry Entries**
    - **Identify Additional Servers**
    - **Specify Security Settings**
    - Outlook customization pages

- Enhanced user interface

    The upgrades to the Custom Maintenance Wizard user interface make it easier to use. Since it mirrors the behavior and capabilities of the Custom Installation Wizard, if you understand how one works, you understand the other. More meaningful option labels, descriptive text, and the customization workflow through the wizard provide easier use and understanding of the customization process.

- Enhanced online Help

    Much-improved online Help makes it easier to find answers to your questions about using the Custom Maintenance Wizard. Since it is integrated with the Help for the Custom Installation Wizard, you can view the Help available in the Custom Installation Wizard by using the Help index, or contents page, in the Custom Maintenance Wizard.

- Ability to create an Outlook profile file (PRF file)

    As with the Custom Installation Wizard, you can use the Custom Maintenance Wizard to create an Outlook profile file (PRF file).

- Ability to change the **Not Available, Hidden, Locked** installation state set with the Custom Installation Wizard

    The **Not Available, Hidden, Locked** installation state can be changed by the administrator, if required — but only by using the Custom Maintenance Wizard.

Corporate Error Reporting

An important, new feature of Office is the ability for Microsoft to learn from crashes encountered during the use of Office applications by users. A new error-reporting tool, DW.exe, allows relevant system crash data to be sent to Microsoft. The information is added to a database that developers review and use to produce work-arounds and fixes that can be posted immediately to the Internet. The Corporate Error Reporting tool (Cer.exe) allows administrators to redirect crash data to a local crash-reporting server and select information they wish to block from, or report to, Microsoft.

For more information, see the online Help available with CER.exe, or see "Reporting Office Application Crashes" in Chapter 8, "Maintaining an Installation."

Save My Settings Wizard

A new tool for users, the Save My Settings Wizard (Proflwiz.exe) is the end-user version of the Profile Wizard. The Save My Settings Wizard allows users to do the following:

- Save their current Office configuration plus supporting files on a Web server for three months for free.

- Restore only settings related to a selected application or applications, instead of being forced to restore an entire configuration.

Office Profile Wizard

The Office Profile Wizard is capable of doing all the things it could do for Microsoft Office 2000 — and more. Improvements include the following:

- New Profile Wizard INI files

  The INI files used to create OPS files using the Profile Wizard are different this time around because of all the new features, registry branches, registry keys, registry values, and files used by Office XP. These new files include OPW10usr.ini (available with Office, not the Resource Kit), ResetO10.ini, and OPW10adm.ini.

- Ability to selectively save or restore settings for specific Office applications

  Just like the Save My Settings Wizard, the Profile Wizard can now restore the configuration settings for any selected application or applications.

- Ability to manage most user-interface settings of the wizard through command-line parameters

  You can now set the Profile Wizard to use and set almost all user-interface options through the command line.

Setup.exe

Setup.exe is much smarter this time around. It knows when to install and use System Files Update files, chained files, and properties. Improvements include the following:

- New Setup.ini format

    The enhanced Setup.ini file format allows much more flexibility for administrators to add more programs to the Setup process. For more information, see the document Setupref.doc, which is installed by default when you run the Office XP Resource Kit Setup program, or the next section below titled "Setup INI Customization Wizard."

- New method of chaining installations

    Chaining can now only be accomplished through the Setup.ini file. The much-improved capability of the Setup.exe to read the Setup.ini file is valuable to administrators who need better control of installing supporting applications after Office is installed.

- Altered MSI naming convention

    The MSI file names have all changed for Office XP.

- New tool to help manage the Setup.ini file

    For more information, see the section below titled "Setup INI Customization Wizard."

- New method of upgrading system files on users' computers by using the System Files Update package (OSP.msi)

    Setup.exe can now determine whether to install the System Files Update to allow the operating system to support Office XP. If the operating system already has the sufficient files, the System Files Update is not installed.

Setup INI Customization Wizard

The Setup INI Customization Wizard (Iniwiz.exe) provides an easy way to add information to the Setup.ini file. You can then make final customizations to the Setup.ini file using a text editor such as Notepad. The wizard performs the following functions:

- Provides an easy method of customizing the Setup.ini file

    If you have had to customize the Setup.ini file in the past, you will recognize the value this wizard adds to the Office Resource Kit tool set.

- Provides an easy method of specifying MSI and MST files for an administrative installation point

You can add MSI and MST file references into the Setup.ini file by using the wizard.

- Takes the guess work out of setting up a series of chained installations

    Chained installations were difficult and confusing to accomplish with prior versions of the Custom Installation Wizard. Through the use of the Setup INI Customization Wizard, you can put the necessary information into the Setup.ini file easily, and then perform the final touches by using a text editor.

Windows Installer

Windows Installer has been improved to handle more tasks than in previous versions. You can choose from several new properties to perform special customization tasks. For more information, see the Custom10.hlp file or the document Setupref.doc, which is installed by default when you run the Office XP Resource Kit Setup program.

With Windows Installer, you can install a new application and still use the settings of the old application. If you do not want this capability, use the Custom Installation Wizard or a command-line option with Setup.exe to disable the **Migrate Previous Installation State** option of Windows Installer.

Removal Wizard

The Removal Wizard (Offcln.exe) is a valuable tool that helps administrators remove prior versions of many Microsoft applications. The Removal Wizard includes the following improvements:

- New OPC file system layout for managing file removal

    If you have made changes to OPC files in the past, you will definitely want to check out the new formatting and layout of the OPC files. For more information, see the document Opc.doc, which is installed by default when you run the Office XP Resource Kit Setup program.

- New capabilities of deleting international files

    You can now customize a special OPC file located in a folder labeled the same as the LCID used by any Office application currently on the computer with that LCID. Add localization-specific file names, keys, or folders to this file.

System Policy Editor

The System Policy Editor (Poledit.exe) has not changed since the prior release. However, because of new products and changes to existing products, all the policy templates have been updated, and several new policies have been added to the policy templates. You can examine these templates by using the System Policy Editor.

Answer Wizard Builder

The Answer Wizard Builder (Awbuild.exe) has been upgraded. Most of the changes are internal to the functions used to generate probabilities for Answer Wizard search results.

Troubleshooting tools

New troubleshooting tools have been provided so that administrators can read in plain text the contents of the transform (MST file), maintenance configuration file (CMW file), and profile settings file (OPS file). The viewers include the following:

- MST File Viewer

    The MST File Viewer (MSTview.exe) displays in text format the contents of any transform created with the Office XP Custom Installation Wizard.

- CMW File Viewer

    The CMW File Viewer (CMWview.exe) displays in text format the contents of any configuration maintenance file created with the Office XP Custom Maintenance Wizard.

- OPS File Viewer

    The OPS File Viewer (OPSview.exe) displays in text format the contents of any profile settings file (OPS file) created with the Office XP Profile Wizard or Save My Settings Wizard.

Options for Acquiring Office

If your organization is in the planning stages for Microsoft Office XP, you may want to explore the different options for purchasing or licensing the product. While Office XP is available worldwide through retail outlets, businesses and organizations can benefit from participating in volume licensing programs designed especially to meet their needs.

A new option for small businesses and individuals is the Office XP subscription program, which offers a lower entry cost, yet provides the full power of Office for a specified duration. Other organizations may also want to consider licensing Office XP as a client application running on Microsoft Windows Terminal Services.

Licensing programs

Microsoft Volume Licensing programs offer more flexibility, greater value, and easier license management for organizations than the purchase of a retail packaged product. By acquiring a license, you are granted permission to legally copy and redistribute Office XP within your organization. Licensees are eligible for a range of extra services, upgrades, and other benefits, depending upon the terms of their agreements.

Different licensing programs are available, depending upon your requirements and the size of your organization. For more information on volume licensing programs, contact your software reseller or see the Microsoft Business Licensing Web site at http://www.microsoft.com/business/licensing.

Subscription programs

The Office XP subscription enables customers to acquire software for a specified period of time. The subscription license provides a lower initial cost of acquiring Office XP, yet provides full use of all features, tools, and capabilities for the term of the subscription. Additionally, the subscription license entitles active subscribers to automatic upgrades of Microsoft Office, ensuring that customers always have the latest version of Microsoft Office running on their computers. Microsoft Office subscription is available for Office Professional and Office Small Business suites.

Office XP as a client on Windows Terminal Services

The terminal services technology of Microsoft Windows 2000 Server can deliver the Windows 2000 desktop, as well as Office XP, to virtually any desktop computing device, including those that cannot run Windows. When a user runs Office XP through Windows Terminal Services, all of the application execution takes place on the server—only the keyboard, mouse, and display information are transmitted over the network to the client computer.

If you elect to deploy Office XP as a client on Windows Terminal Services, you will need to acquire one license for each client computer that makes use of the Office applications.

For more information about Office XP licensing on Windows Terminal Services, see the Licensing Office for Terminal Server Web site at http://www.microsoft.com/ntserver/terminalserver/exec/EOMAP/OfficeandTSE.asp.

Web Sites of Interest to Administrators

Microsoft provides several Web sites that feature information and tools designed to address the needs of administrators. The following sites might be of special interest to those of you who deploy and support Microsoft Office XP.

Microsoft Office home page

This Microsoft Office home page, at http://www.microsoft.com/office/, provides overview information about the Microsoft family of products. The site includes feature guides, evaluation information, deployment support, and links to a wide range of resources designed to help you get the most out of your applications. You can click Site Index on the home page to view an index of all Microsoft sites related to recent Office products and solutions.

Microsoft Office Web site

The Microsoft Office Web site, at http://office.microsoft.com/, serves as a gateway to dozens of specialized sites that address solutions, strategies, and support issues for the Microsoft Office family of products. The site provides links to such areas as the Templates Gallery, the Office Assistance Center, and Office Update, as well as related sites covering platform, developer, and international issues.

Office Resource Kit

The Office Resource Kit Web site, at http://www.microsoft.com/office/ork/, provides the complete set of content and tools featured in the Office Resource Kit. The site is updated frequently to keep you current on topics such as service releases, security issues, and strategies and tactics for deployment. Links to previous editions of the Office Resource Kit for Office 2000 and Office 97/98 are included at the bottom of the left pane of the site's home page.

Microsoft Product Support Services

The Microsoft Product Support Services site, at http://support.microsoft.com/, provides links to such resources as the searchable Knowledge Base, the Download Center, and the Customer Support site. You'll also find links to support phone numbers, online support requests, and worldwide support resources.

MSDN Office Developer Center

The Office Developer Web site, at http://msdn.microsoft.com/office/, features articles, tools, and tips for creating programmable solutions using Microsoft Office XP. Topics focus on such areas as data access, automation, and developing applications with Office components and Visual Basic® for Applications.

Microsoft Windows

The Microsoft Windows site, at http://www.microsoft.com/windows/, provides links to information on both present and past versions of the Windows family of products. Within the site, you can browse to the Windows 2000 Home Page to discover resources such as the Technical Library, the Windows resource kits, and other support information.

Microsoft BackOffice Server

The Microsoft BackOffice Server Web site, at http://www.microsoft.com/backofficeserver/, provides information on this comprehensive server suite for the Microsoft Windows® 2000 operating system. The site includes deployment and support information on Microsoft Exchange 2000 Server and Microsoft SQL Server™ 2000, as well as the many other components included with BackOffice® Server.

Microsoft TechNet

Microsoft TechNet, at http://www.microsoft.com/technet/, is a general information and community resource for administrators and information technology (IT) professionals. TechNet contains a wealth of information about planning, evaluating, deploying, maintaining, and supporting a range of IT systems.

Office Sites Worldwide

International customers can visit the Office Sites Worldwide site, at http://www.microsoft.com/office/worldwide.htm, to find links to localized Microsoft Office sites around the world.

CHAPTER 2

Collaboration with Office

Microsoft Office XP enables new ways of working by including new technologies meant to foster team collaboration. For example, SharePoint Team Services from Microsoft is a technology that allows teams to communicate by using special Web sites with built-in features such as document libraries and lists. Several features in Office XP, such as the new Search feature, also help users work in new ways.

In this chapter

Introducing Microsoft's SharePoint Team Services   21

Introducing Office XP Workgroup Strategies   23

Microsoft Web Solutions   24

Introducing Microsoft's SharePoint Team Services

Many features of Microsoft Office XP were created in an effort to help teams work together and get things done. One way to work together as a team is by using a Web site to communicate. You can use Office XP to interact with a new technology, Microsoft's SharePoint™ Team Services, to improve your team communications. Your Office XP applications, including Microsoft FrontPage® 2002, Microsoft Word 2002, Microsoft Excel 2002, and Microsoft Outlook® 2002 can work with SharePoint Team Services to help you communicate and share information as a team over an intranet or the Internet.

Features available in SharePoint Team Services

Microsoft's SharePoint Team Services includes many features to help your team communicate and collaborate. All of these features are available with SharePoint Team Services and with Web sites based upon SharePoint Team Services. Some of the team features in SharePoint Team Services include:

- Prebuilt list functionality to help you track special events, contact information, and announcements

  As well, you can easily create and customize your own lists.

- Document libraries to help store, organize, and find documents on your Web site
- Surveys to help your team contribute to important decisions and graphically see how team members are voting
- Discussion boards, Web document discussions, and subscriptions to help your team communicate about important ideas and receive automatic e-mail notifications when pages or discussions have changed

In addition to the new team-related features, SharePoint Team Services provides new features geared to provide a good experience for Web server administrators. For administrators, SharePoint Team Services includes features such as:

- Improved permissions through finer-grained roles and rights

    Control the permissions granted to each user of your site. Assign users to one of several standard roles, or for even more flexibility, create your own custom roles by selecting individual rights.

- Better remote administration

    All Web site administration tasks can be performed remotely by using either HTML-based administration pages or the command line.

- New usage analysis reports

    Find out which pages in your site are generating the most interest, where users were referred to your site, which pages are slow to load, which pages and graphics are not being used, and which pages have not been updated recently.

Installing SharePoint Team Services

You can install SharePoint Team Services on computers that use Microsoft Windows® 2000 Professional, Server, or Advanced Server editions. For more information about installing SharePoint Team Services, see the "SharePoint Team Services Administrator's Guide." Information about the guide is provided in this topic on the Office Resource Kit Web site at http://www.microsoft.com/office/ork/.

> **Note** The SharePoint Team Services Administrator's Guide also covers FrontPage Server Extensions 2002, which are also included with Office XP. For more information about FrontPage Server Extensions 2002, see the "SharePoint Team Services Administrator's Guide." Information about the guide is provided in this topic on the Office Resource Kit Web site at http://www.microsoft.com/office/ork/.

Introducing Office XP Workgroup Strategies

New features in Microsoft Office XP make it easier than ever for users to find the information they need and share it with each other. Many of these features take advantage of network and Internet technologies, and rely on an intranet or the Internet to store or retrieve information. Office XP, by including these features, extends the reach of individuals and teams as they communicate about projects and ideas and share information.

Among the new workgroup features included in Office XP are:

- Network places and Web folders

    Users can store information easily in folders that reside on network, Web, FTP, or Microsoft Exchange 2000 servers. After users create a shortcut to a network place, they can copy, save, or manage folders and files from within Network Places as if they were working on their local computer.

- Save My Settings Wizard

    Users can save and transport their custom Office user configuration. They can save their settings to a Microsoft Web server and take them with them to a new computer whenever necessary.

- Communities on the Web

    Users can create online communities to share information about projects with team members, or to share personal information with friends and family.

- Office Web Components and Web queries

    Users can integrate data from Microsoft Excel or Microsoft Access, and include charts and pivot tables in HTML documents. Users can post data as static, or keep data synchronized with Web queries.

- Search

    Users can find what they need when they need it with Office XP Search, which is part of the new task pane in every Office XP application. Users can search through files on their computer, items in Microsoft Outlook, or on their network.

As an administrator, you want to know exactly what type of information is being shared, and how. And, you may want control over where that information is shared. For example, the new search features in Office XP allow users to search on their local hard drives, on a network drive, on an intranet, or even on the Internet. As an administrator, you can change settings that allow searching on any internal resources (such as the network or intranet) but block searching on the Internet.

Most of these features are installed by default when you install Office XP. As an Office XP administrator, there are certain things you can control about how these features are installed and used. For more information, see the topics under Workgroup Technologies on the Office XP Resource Kit Web site at http://microsoft.com/office/ork.

Microsoft Web Solutions

Microsoft has several products that help you work in a Web environment — from simple solutions for creating single Web pages, to prebuilt Web sites with integrated team tools, all the way to large, dynamic sites that take advantage of the latest Web technologies.

Web solutions in Office

Microsoft Office XP includes several tools that help you work with HTML pages, and create and manage Web sites. If you are looking to create single Web pages or individual Web sites, the following, easy-to-use Office XP products can help you:

- Microsoft Word 2002, Microsoft Excel 2002, Microsoft Access 2002, Microsoft PowerPoint® 2002

    Allow authoring of individual Web pages. Available as stand-alone products or with Office XP.

- Microsoft Publisher 2002

    Helps users author simple, small Web sites. Available as a stand-alone product or with the Small Business edition of Office XP.

- Microsoft FrontPage 2002

    Powerful tool that enables users to author simple or full-featured Web sites. Available as a stand-alone product or with the Professional with FrontPage edition of Office XP.

- FrontPage Server Extensions 2002

    Web server application used to host FrontPage 2002 Web sites. Available with FrontPage 2002 and Office XP.

Web solutions outside of Office

Outside of Office, there are several other Web-application solutions available from Microsoft. These solutions allow professional Web site developers to create powerful, dynamic, and comprehensive Web site solutions for their customers, or to create large-scale intranet solutions for their organizations. Among these products are:

- Microsoft's SharePoint Team Services

    New Web technology used to host SharePoint Team Web sites.

- Microsoft Visual Interdev® 6.0

    Helps developers create dynamic Web sites. Includes support for Active Server Pages and Dynamic HTML, and includes integrated database design and programming tools.

- Microsoft Commerce Server 2000

    A comprehensive Internet commerce server that enables you to engage customer, transact business, and analyze commerce Web sites.

Microsoft Web platforms

To support these Web solutions and to provide Web site hosting, Microsoft offers several products that make up the Web platform. The first part of the platform is the operating system. Newer Microsoft Web solutions are built to take advantage of the following Microsoft operating systems:

- Microsoft Windows NT®

    The Workstation edition for hosting a single Web site, and Server edition for hosting multiple sites

- Microsoft Windows 2000

    Professional edition for hosting a single Web site, and Server edition for hosting multiple sites.

Some Web solutions (such as for single Web pages or Web sites hosted by an ISP) require only support from the operating system. Most Web solutions, however, require additional software support. For example, to use Microsoft's SharePoint Team Services or FrontPage Server Extensions 2002, you need one or more of the following:

- Microsoft Internet Information Services (IIS)

    IIS provides background Web site processes for Microsoft's SharePoint Team Services. IIS is part of the operating system for Microsoft Windows 2000. You must have IIS to use SharePoint Team Services.

- Microsoft SQL Server or Microsoft Data Engine (MSDE)

    SQL Server™ and MSDE provide the database server support for Web sites based upon SharePoint Team Services. SQL Server is the preferred solution for larger sites or multiple sites on one server, while MSDE supports small, individual sites. You must have either SQL Server or MSDE to use many features of SharePoint Team Services.

CHAPTER 3

Deployment Prerequisites

You can deploy Microsoft Office XP in a variety of configurations and environments. System requirements vary depending upon the Office suite that you are deploying — and in some cases, you might choose to upgrade the operating system when you deploy the applications. If you are upgrading from a previous version of Office, consistent file formats make the transition to Office XP applications straightforward and simple for users.

In this chapter

Office XP System Requirements   27

Upgrading Reference   47

Office XP System Requirements

The system requirements for Microsoft Office XP depend upon the Office suite you are installing and upon whether you are deploying the software on a client computer, an administrative server, or a Windows Terminal Services server. A stand-alone computer will run well with the minimum requirements, for example, while an administrative server supporting thousands of desktops will require more processor power, memory, and hard-disk capacity.

> **Note**   None of the Office XP suites will run on the Microsoft Windows® 3.x, Microsoft Windows NT® 3.5x, or Microsoft Windows 95 operating systems. If your computers are currently running one of these operating systems, you must upgrade the operating system before installing Office XP.

The following sections present recommendations on the minimum system requirements for the different Office XP suites.

Office XP and Internet Explorer

All versions of Office XP require an installation of Microsoft Internet Explorer to be on the computer because Office applications take advantage of services provided by the browser. Office uses these Internet Explorer services behind the scenes, however, so there is no requirement that Internet Explorer be set as the default browser on the computer.

By default, Office XP installs Internet Explorer 5.01 at the same time as it installs the System Files Update. (Office will not install Internet Explorer on Microsoft Windows 2000, Microsoft Windows Millennium Edition (Windows Me), or higher operating system versions since those operating systems already have Internet Explorer 5.01 or above.) If you prefer to stay with an earlier version of Internet Explorer, you can turn off the default installation through Setup or the Custom

Installation Wizard. Office XP requires as a minimum Internet Explorer 4.01 with Service Pack 1 (the version first released with Windows 98). Any later version of Internet Explorer will work correctly with Office XP.

> **Note** If you are running Office XP on Windows NT 4.0 with Service Pack 6, you should confirm that Internet Explorer has been upgraded to at least version 4.01 with Service Pack 1.

If you are currently running Windows 2000 on your computers, and you want to upgrade to Internet Explorer 5.5 at the same time as you upgrade to Office XP, you must upgrade the browser separately from your Office XP deployment; the installation of the these two products cannot be chained together. Internet Explorer 5.5 can be deployed either before or after you deploy Office XP.

Office XP product suites

Office XP is available in several product suites, each of which contains a different collection of applications and services. Any of the suites can be installed on stand-alone computers or deployed throughout your organization from an administrative installation point.

The following sections describe the system requirements for each suite.

Microsoft Office XP Standard

Microsoft Office XP Standard includes the following applications:

- Microsoft Excel
- Microsoft Word
- Microsoft Outlook®
- Microsoft PowerPoint®

Core system requirements

To use Microsoft Office XP Standard, users' computers must meet the following requirements:

Processor Pentium 133 MHz or higher processor required for all operating systems.

Operating system Microsoft Windows 98, Microsoft Windows 98 Second Edition, or Windows Millennium Edition; Microsoft Windows NT 4.0 with Service Pack 6 or greater; Microsoft Windows 2000. The recommended operating system is Windows 2000 Professional.

On systems running Windows NT 4.0 with Service Pack 6, the version of Internet Explorer must be upgraded to at least Internet Explorer 4.01 with Service Pack 1.

Memory Memory requirements for Office Standard depend upon the operating system used with the computer. Operating system RAM requirements assume default Windows installations; running additional utilities or applications may require additional RAM.

- For Windows 98 and Microsoft Windows 98 Second Edition, 24 MB of RAM for the operating system, plus an additional 8 MB of RAM for each application running simultaneously.

- For Windows Millennium Edition and Windows NT Workstation or Server 4.0 or later, 32 MB of RAM for the operating system, plus an additional 8 MB of RAM for each application running simultaneously.

- For Windows 2000 Professional, 64 MB of RAM recommended minimum. For Windows 2000 Server or Advanced Server, 256 MB of RAM recommended minimum. In addition, you should have 8 MB of RAM for each application running simultaneously.

Hard-disk space Numbers indicate typical installation; your hard-disk usage will vary depending on the configuration. Custom installation choices may require more or less hard-disk space.

- 210 MB of available hard-disk space is required for the default configuration of Office XP Standard.

- Users without Windows 2000, Windows Millennium Edition, or Office 2000 SR-1 will need an extra 50 MB of hard-disk space for the System Files Update.

- On computers where Office XP is installed on a different drive than the operating system, the operating system drive should have 115 MB of available hard-disk space.

- For international deployments, you should allow an extra 50 MB of hard-disk space for each additional language interface you install.

Registry space Under Windows NT and Windows 2000, at least 4 MB of space must be available in the registry.

Disk drives CD-ROM drive.

Monitor VGA or higher-resolution monitor; Super VGA recommended.

Pointing device Microsoft Mouse, Microsoft IntelliMouse®, or compatible pointing device.

Additional requirements for specific features

Some Office XP Standard features have additional requirements:

Modem 9600 baud modem; 14,400 or higher baud recommended.

Multimedia Multimedia computer required for sound and other multimedia effects. A hardware-accelerated video card or MMX processor will provide improved graphical rendering performance.

E-mail Microsoft Exchange, Internet SMTP/POP3, IMAP4, or other MAPI-compliant messaging software.

Collaboration Microsoft Exchange Server required for certain advanced collaboration functionality in Microsoft Outlook.

Internet Some Internet functionality may require Internet access via a 14,400 or higher baud modem and payment of a separate fee to a service provider; local charges may apply.

Speech recognition Speech recognition technologies require a higher level of hardware support for the computer, as well as a microphone.

- For all operating systems, the recommended hardware requirements increase to a Pentium 400 MHz or higher processor and 128 MB of RAM.
- The recommended microphone is a high-quality, close-talk USB microphone that conforms to PC99 System Design Guide standards. If you are using a USB microphone, a sound card is not required, as audio processing is handled by the device itself.
- If you are using a conventional microphone, the unit should be a high quality close-talk headset that places the microphone within four inches of the speaker's mouth. Conventional microphones should also conform to PC99 System Design Guide standards. A conventional microphone requires a sound card in the computer.

Handwriting Graphics tablet recommended for handwriting features.

PowerPoint broadcasts Windows Media Encoder–compatible video camera for broadcasts including video; Microsoft Exchange Chat server to enable chats during live broadcasts; Microsoft Windows Media Server to enable multicasts of live broadcasts to more than 10 audience members.

Microsoft Office XP Small Business

Microsoft Office XP Small Business includes the following applications:

- Microsoft Excel
- Microsoft Word
- Microsoft Outlook
- Microsoft Publisher

Core system requirements

To use Microsoft Office XP Small Business, users' computers must meet the following requirements:

Processor Pentium 133 MHz or higher processor required for all operating systems.

Operating system Microsoft Windows 98, Microsoft Windows 98 Second Edition, or Windows Millennium Edition; Microsoft Windows NT 4.0 with Service Pack 6 or greater; Microsoft Windows 2000. The recommended operating system is Windows 2000 Professional.

On systems running Windows NT 4.0 with Service Pack 6, the version of Internet Explorer must be upgraded to at least Internet Explorer 4.01 with Service Pack 1.

Memory Memory requirements for Office Small Business depend upon the operating system used with the computer. Operating system RAM requirements assume default Windows installations; running additional utilities or applications may require additional RAM.

- For Windows 98 and Microsoft Windows 98 Second Edition, 24 MB of RAM for the operating system, plus an additional 8 MB of RAM for each application running simultaneously.

- For Windows Millennium Edition and Windows NT Workstation or Server 4.0 or later, 32 MB of RAM for the operating system, plus an additional 8 MB of RAM for each application running simultaneously.

- For Windows 2000 Professional, 64 MB of RAM recommended minimum. For Windows 2000 Server or Advanced Server, 256 MB of RAM recommended minimum. In addition, you should have 8 MB of RAM for each application running simultaneously.

Hard-disk space   Numbers indicate typical installation; your hard-disk usage will vary depending on the configuration. Custom installation choices may require more or less hard-disk space.

- 280 MB of available hard-disk space is required for the default configuration of Office XP Small Business.

- Users without Windows 2000, Windows Millennium Edition, or Office 2000 SR-1 will need an extra 50 MB of hard-disk space for the System Files Update.

- On computers where Office XP is installed on a different drive than the operating system, the operating system drive should have 115 MB of available hard-disk space.

- For international deployments, you should allow an extra 50 MB of hard-disk space for each additional language interface you install.

Registry space   Under Windows NT and Windows 2000, at least 4 MB of space must be available in the registry.

Disk drives   CD-ROM drive.

Monitor   VGA or higher-resolution monitor; Super VGA recommended.

Pointing device   Microsoft Mouse, Microsoft IntelliMouse, or compatible pointing device.

Additional requirements for specific features

Some Office XP Small Business features have additional requirements:

Modem   9600 baud modem; 14,400 or higher baud recommended.

Multimedia   Multimedia computer required for sound and other multimedia effects. A hardware-accelerated video card or MMX processor will provide improved graphical rendering performance.

E-mail   Microsoft Exchange, Internet SMTP/POP3, IMAP4, or other MAPI-compliant messaging software.

Collaboration   Microsoft Exchange Server required for certain advanced collaboration functionality in Microsoft Outlook.

Internet   Some Internet functionality may require Internet access via a 14,400 or higher baud modem and payment of a separate fee to a service provider; local charges may apply.

Speech recognition Speech recognition technologies require a higher level of hardware support for the computer, as well as a microphone.

- For all operating systems, the recommended hardware requirements increase to a Pentium 400 MHz or higher processor and 128 MB of RAM.
- The recommended microphone is a high-quality, close-talk USB microphone that conforms to PC99 System Design Guide standards. If you are using a USB microphone, a sound card is not required, as audio processing is handled by the device itself.
- If you are using a conventional microphone, the unit should be a high quality close-talk headset that places the microphone within four inches of the speaker's mouth. Conventional microphones should also conform to PC99 System Design Guide standards. A conventional microphone requires a sound card in the computer.

Handwriting Graphics tablet recommended for handwriting features.

PowerPoint broadcasts Windows Media Encoder–compatible video camera for broadcasts including video; Microsoft Exchange Chat server to enable chats during live broadcasts; Microsoft Windows Media Server to enable multicasts of live broadcasts to more than 10 audience members.

Microsoft Office XP Professional

Microsoft Office XP Professional includes the following applications:

- Microsoft Excel
- Microsoft Word
- Microsoft Outlook
- Microsoft PowerPoint
- Microsoft Access

Core system requirements

To use Microsoft Office XP Professional, users' computers must meet the following requirements:

Processor Pentium 133 MHz or higher processor required for all operating systems.

Operating system Microsoft Windows 98, Microsoft Windows 98 Second Edition, or Windows Millennium Edition; Microsoft Windows NT 4.0 with Service Pack 6 or greater; Microsoft Windows 2000. The recommended operating system is Windows 2000 Professional.

On systems running Windows NT 4.0 with Service Pack 6, the version of Internet Explorer must be upgraded to at least Internet Explorer 4.01 with Service Pack 1.

Memory Memory requirements for Office Professional depend upon the operating system used with the computer. Operating system RAM requirements assume default Windows installations; running additional utilities or applications may require additional RAM.

- For Windows 98 and Microsoft Windows 98 Second Edition, 24 MB of RAM for the operating system, plus an additional 8 MB of RAM for each application running simultaneously.

- For Windows Millennium Edition and Windows NT Workstation or Server 4.0 or later, 32 MB of RAM for the operating system, plus an additional 8 MB of RAM for each application running simultaneously.

- For Windows 2000 Professional, 64 MB of RAM recommended minimum. For Windows 2000 Server or Advanced Server, 256 MB of RAM recommended minimum. In addition, you should have 8 MB of RAM for each application running simultaneously.

Hard-disk space   Numbers indicate typical installation; your hard-disk usage will vary depending on the configuration. Custom installation choices may require more or less hard-disk space.

- 245 MB of available hard-disk space is required for the default configuration of Office XP Professional.

- Users without Windows 2000, Windows Millennium Edition, or Office 2000 SR-1 will need an extra 50 MB of hard-disk space for the System Files Update.

- On computers where Office XP is installed on a different drive than the operating system, the operating system drive should have 115 MB of available hard-disk space.

- For international deployments, you should allow an extra 50 MB of hard-disk space for each additional language interface you install.

Registry space   Under Windows NT and Windows 2000, at least 4 MB of space must be available in the registry.

Disk drives   CD-ROM drive.

Monitor   VGA or higher-resolution monitor; Super VGA recommended.

Pointing device   Microsoft Mouse, Microsoft IntelliMouse, or compatible pointing device.

Additional requirements for specific features

Some Office XP Professional features have additional requirements:

Modem   9600 baud modem; 14,400 or higher baud recommended.

Multimedia   Multimedia computer required for sound and other multimedia effects. A hardware-accelerated video card or MMX processor will provide improved graphical rendering performance.

E-mail   Microsoft Exchange, Internet SMTP/POP3, IMAP4, or other MAPI-compliant messaging software.

Collaboration   Microsoft Exchange Server required for certain advanced collaboration functionality in Microsoft Outlook.

Internet   Some Internet functionality may require Internet access via a 14,400 or higher baud modem and payment of a separate fee to a service provider; local charges may apply.

Speech recognition   Speech recognition technologies require a higher level of hardware support for the computer, as well as a microphone.

- For all operating systems, the recommended hardware requirements increase to a Pentium 400 MHz or higher processor and 128 MB of RAM.
- The recommended microphone is a high-quality, close-talk USB microphone that conforms to PC99 System Design Guide standards. If you are using a USB microphone, a sound card is not required, as audio processing is handled by the device itself.
- If you are using a conventional microphone, the unit should be a high quality close-talk headset that places the microphone within four inches of the speaker's mouth. Conventional microphones should also conform to PC99 System Design Guide standards. A conventional microphone requires a sound card in the computer.

Handwriting   Graphics tablet recommended for handwriting features.

PowerPoint broadcasts   Windows Media Encoder–compatible video camera for broadcasts including video; Microsoft Exchange Chat server to enable chats during live broadcasts; Microsoft Windows Media Server to enable multicasts of live broadcasts to more than 10 audience members.

Microsoft Office XP Professional with FrontPage

Microsoft Office XP Professional with FrontPage includes the following applications:

- Microsoft Excel
- Microsoft Word
- Microsoft Outlook
- Microsoft PowerPoint
- Microsoft Access
- Microsoft FrontPage

Core system requirements

To use Microsoft Office XP Professional with FrontPage, users' computers must meet the following requirements:

Processor   Pentium 133 MHz or higher processor required for all operating systems.

Operating system   Microsoft Windows 98, Microsoft Windows 98 Second Edition, or Windows Millennium Edition; Microsoft Windows NT 4.0 with Service Pack 6 or greater; Microsoft Windows 2000. The recommended operating system is Windows 2000 Professional.

On systems running Windows NT 4.0 with Service Pack 6, the version of Internet Explorer must be upgraded to at least Internet Explorer 4.01 with Service Pack 1.

Memory Memory requirements for Office Professional with FrontPage depend upon the operating system used with the computer. Operating system RAM requirements assume default Windows installations; running additional utilities or applications may require additional RAM.

- For Windows 98 and Microsoft Windows 98 Second Edition, 24 MB of RAM for the operating system, plus an additional 8 MB of RAM for each application running simultaneously.
- For Windows Millennium Edition and Windows NT Workstation or Server 4.0 or later, 32 MB of RAM for the operating system, plus an additional 8 MB of RAM for each application running simultaneously.
- For Windows 2000 Professional, 64 MB of RAM recommended minimum. For Windows 2000 Server or Advanced Server, 256 MB of RAM recommended minimum. In addition, you should have 8 MB of RAM for each application running simultaneously.

Hard-disk space Numbers indicate typical installation; your hard-disk usage will vary depending on the configuration. Custom installation choices may require more or less hard-disk space.

- 285 MB of available hard-disk space is required for the default configuration of Office XP Professional with FrontPage.
- Users without Windows 2000, Windows Millennium Edition, or Office 2000 SR-1 will need an extra 50 MB of hard-disk space for the System Files Update.
- On computers where Office XP is installed on a different drive than the operating system, the operating system drive should have 115 MB of available hard-disk space.
- For international deployments, you should allow an extra 50 MB of hard-disk space for each additional language interface you install.

For optimal performance, an additional 100 MB of available hard-disk space is recommended for use by the Windows swap file.

Registry space Under Windows NT and Windows 2000, at least 4 MB of space must be available in the registry.

Disk drives CD-ROM drive.

Monitor VGA or higher-resolution monitor; Super VGA recommended.

Pointing device Microsoft Mouse, Microsoft IntelliMouse, or compatible pointing device.

> **Notes** If you are deploying Microsoft's SharePoint™ Team Services or FrontPage Server Extensions, the system requirements may differ from the items specified above. For more information, see the system requirements section in the appropriate documentation:
>
> For SharePoint Team Services system requirements, see the "SharePoint Team Services Administrator's Guide." Information about the guide is provided in this topic on the Office Resource Kit Web site at http://www.microsoft.com/office/ork/.
>
> For FrontPage Server Extension system requirements, see the "SharePoint Team Services Administrator's Guide." Information about the guide is provided in this topic on the Office Resource Kit Web site at http://www.microsoft.com/office/ork/.

Additional requirements for specific features

Some Office XP Professional with FrontPage features have additional requirements:

Modem   9600 baud modem; 14,400 or higher baud recommended.

Multimedia   Multimedia computer required for sound and other multimedia effects. A hardware-accelerated video card or MMX processor will provide improved graphical rendering performance.

E-mail   Microsoft Exchange, Internet SMTP/POP3, IMAP4, or other MAPI-compliant messaging software.

Collaboration   Microsoft Exchange Server required for certain advanced collaboration functionality in Microsoft Outlook.

Internet   Some Internet functionality may require Internet access via a 14,400 or higher baud modem and payment of a separate fee to a service provider; local charges may apply.

Speech recognition   Speech recognition technologies require a higher level of hardware support for the computer, as well as a microphone.

- For all operating systems, the recommended hardware requirements increase to a Pentium 400 MHz or higher processor and 128 MB of RAM.

- The recommended microphone is a high-quality, close-talk USB microphone that conforms to PC99 System Design Guide standards. If you are using a USB microphone, a sound card is not required, as audio processing is handled by the device itself.

- If you are using a conventional microphone, the unit should be a high quality close-talk headset that places the microphone within four inches of the speaker's mouth. Conventional microphones should also conform to PC99 System Design Guide standards. A conventional microphone requires a sound card in the computer.

Handwriting   Graphics tablet recommended for handwriting features.

PowerPoint broadcasts   Windows Media Encoder–compatible video camera for broadcasts including video; Microsoft Exchange Chat server to enable chats during live broadcasts; Microsoft Windows Media Server to enable multicasts of live broadcasts to more than 10 audience members.

Microsoft Office XP Developer

Microsoft Office XP Developer includes two CDs: Microsoft Office XP Professional with FrontPage and Microsoft Office XP Developer Tools. Features and components included with the Developer Tools include the following:

- Microsoft Visual Basic® for Applications (VBA) tools, including Code Librarian, Packaging Wizard, and productivity add-ins

- Workflow Designer for Exchange

- Workflow Designer for SQL Server™

- Microsoft Visual SourceSafe™ for Windows 7.0
- MSDE (Microsoft Data Engine) and MDAC (Microsoft Data Access Components)
- Microsoft Access 2002 Runtime
- Replication Manager
- Microsoft Answer Wizard Builder
- MSDN Library
- HTML Help Workshop

While the system requirements for Office XP Professional with FrontPage are the same as described above, some of the Developer Tools components present different requirements. The following sections describe the specific requirements for Office XP Developer Tools.

Complete information about Office Developer Tools is available on the Microsoft Office Web site at http://microsoft.com/office/developer.

Core system requirements

To use Microsoft Office Developer, your computer must meet the following requirements:

Processor   Pentium 133 MHz or higher processor required for all operating systems.

Operating system   Microsoft Windows 98, Microsoft Windows 98 Second Edition, or Windows Millennium Edition; Microsoft Windows NT 4.0 with Service Pack 6 or greater; Microsoft Windows 2000. The recommended operating system is Windows 2000 Professional.

On systems running Windows NT 4.0 with Service Pack 6, the version of Internet Explorer must be upgraded to at least Internet Explorer 4.01 with Service Pack 1.

Memory   Memory requirements for Office XP Developer depend upon the operating system used with the computer. Operating system RAM requirements assume default Windows installations, and running additional utilities or applications may require additional RAM.

- For Windows 98, Microsoft Windows 98 Second Edition, and Windows Millennium Edition, a minimum of 32 MB of RAM for the operating system; 64 MB is recommended. In addition, you should have 8 MB of RAM for each application running simultaneously.
- For Windows NT Workstation 4.0 or later with Service Pack 6, a minimum of 32 MB of RAM for the operating system; 64 MB is recommended. In addition, you should have 8 MB of RAM for each application running simultaneously.
- For Windows 2000 Professional, a minimum of 64 MB of RAM for the operating system; 96 MB is recommended. In addition, you should have 8 MB of RAM for each application running simultaneously.
- For Windows 2000 Server, 128 MB of RAM minimum, 256 MB is recommended.

Hard-disk space Numbers indicate typical installation; your hard-disk usage will vary depending on the configuration. Custom installation choices may require more or less hard-disk space.

- 445 MB of available hard-disk space is required for the default configuration of Office XP Developer (285 MB for Microsoft Office XP Professional with FrontPage, plus 160 MB for the Developer Tools).
- In addition, hard-disk space is required for the Microsoft Office Developer system component update. The space required depends upon the operating system:
    - 120 MB of hard-disk space is required on Windows NT 4.0 or later.
    - 50 MB of hard-disk space is required on Windows 98, Microsoft Windows 98 Second Edition, or Windows Millennium Edition.
    - 230 MB of hard-disk space is required on Windows 2000.
- Users without Windows 2000, Windows Millennium Edition, or Office 2000 SR-1 will need an extra 50 MB of hard-disk space for the System Files Update.
- On computers where Office XP is installed on a different drive than the operating system, the operating system drive should have 115 MB of available hard-disk space.
- For international deployments, you should allow an extra 50 MB of hard-disk space for each additional language interface you install.

Registry space Under Windows NT and Windows 2000, at least 4 MB of space must be available in the registry.

Disk drives CD-ROM or DVD drive.

Monitor Super VGA 800x600 256 color is the recommended minimum.

Pointing device Microsoft Mouse, Microsoft IntelliMouse, or compatible pointing device.

Workflow Service for SQL Server system requirements

The Workflow Service included with Office XP Developer can be used to develop workflow on 7.0, SQL Server 2000, or Exchange Server 2000. The minimum system requirements for any of these servers are as follows:

Processor Pentium I 166 MHz or compatible processor minimum; Pentium II 266 or greater recommended.

Operating system Windows 2000 server family.

Memory 128 MB of RAM minimum; 256 MB of RAM recommended.

Additional requirements for specific features

Some Office XP Developer features have additional requirements:

Modem   9600 baud modem; 14,400 or higher baud recommended.

Multimedia   Multimedia computer required for sound and other multimedia effects. A hardware-accelerated video card or MMX processor will provide improved graphical rendering performance.

E-mail   Microsoft Exchange, Internet SMTP/POP3, IMAP4, or other MAPI-compliant messaging software.

Collaboration   Microsoft Exchange Server required for certain advanced collaboration functionality in Microsoft Outlook.

Internet   Some Internet functionality may require Internet access via a 14,400 or higher baud modem and payment of a separate fee to a service provider; local charges may apply.

Speech recognition   Speech recognition technologies require a higher level of hardware support for the computer, as well as a microphone.

- For all operating systems, the recommended hardware requirements increase to a Pentium 400 MHz or higher processor and 128 MB of RAM.

- The recommended microphone is a high-quality, close-talk USB microphone that conforms to PC99 System Design Guide standards. If you are using a USB microphone, a sound card is not required, as audio processing is handled by the device itself.

- If you are using a conventional microphone, the unit should be a high quality close-talk headset that places the microphone within four inches of the speaker's mouth. Conventional microphones should also conform to PC99 System Design Guide standards. A conventional microphone requires a sound card in the computer.

Handwriting   Graphics tablet recommended for handwriting features.

PowerPoint broadcasts   Windows Media Encoder–compatible video camera for broadcasts including video; Microsoft Exchange Chat server to enable chats during live broadcasts; Microsoft Windows Media Server to enable multicasts of live broadcasts to more than 10 audience members.

Enterprise editions of Office XP

In addition to the core applications, Enterprise editions of Office XP contain tools and functionality designed to support the deployment and support of Microsoft Office in organizations. Additional features of the Enterprise editions include the Office Resource Kit and built-in support for Microsoft Office Multilingual User Interface Packs.

The system requirements for a given Enterprise edition are the same as for the associated regular edition. For example, the requirements for Office XP Professional Enterprise are the same as for Office XP Professional.

The following Enterprise editions are available for Office XP:

- Office Standard — Enterprise edition
- Office Small Business — Enterprise edition
- Office Professional — Enterprise edition
- Office Professional with FrontPage — Enterprise edition

Notes If you are deploying Microsoft's SharePoint Team Services or FrontPage Server Extensions, the system requirements may differ from the items specified above. For more information, see the system requirements section in the appropriate documentation:

For SharePoint Team Services system requirements, see the "SharePoint Team Services Administrator's Guide." Information about the guide is provided in this topic on the Office Resource Kit Web site at http://www.microsoft.com/office/ork/.

For FrontPage Server Extension system requirements, see the "SharePoint Team Services Administrator's Guide." Information about the guide is provided in this topic on the Office Resource Kit Web site at http://www.microsoft.com/office/ork/.

Stand-alone Office XP applications

If you deploy a single Office XP application, such as Outlook or Word, the core requirements for the processor, RAM, and operating system will be the same as for the suites listed above. The hard-disk space requirements for a single application will be less than for a complete suite.

The following table lists the requirements for installing a single application on a computer. Because the applications in an Office suite share many files, the installation of a single application includes many files that would only be installed once for a complete suite. If you install multiple stand-alone applications, the footprint for the succeeding ones will usually be less than 40 MB.

Stand-alone product	Hard-disk space required
Word	150 MB
Excel	140 MB
Outlook	135 MB
PowerPoint	115 MB
Access	170 MB
FrontPage	165 MB
Publisher	180 MB
Microsoft Data Engine (MSDE)	100 MB

The hard-disk space numbers indicate typical installation; your hard-disk usage will vary depending on the configuration. Custom installation choices may require more or less hard-disk space.

- Users without Windows 2000, Windows Millennium Edition, or Office 2000 SR-1 will need an extra 50 MB of hard-disk space for the System Files Update.
- On computers where Office XP is installed on a different drive than the operating system, the operating system drive should have 115 MB of available hard-disk space.
- For international deployments, you should allow an extra 50 MB of hard-disk space for each additional language interface you install.

Office administrative platform

If you are planning to deploy Office XP in an organization, the most efficient approach is to create an administrative installation point on a network server. The administrative installation point contains all of the Office XP application files, plus the configuration information and other resources you specify. Users connect to the share and run Setup to install a customized version of Office XP on their computers.

Microsoft Office XP supports most widely available network operating systems and network clients for file and printing services. Office XP has been tested with the following network servers and clients.

Microsoft network operating systems and clients

Microsoft Office XP supports the following Microsoft network servers and clients:

Supported network servers

- Microsoft Windows 2000 Server, including support for Microsoft Gateway Service for NetWare and Services for The Macintosh
- Microsoft Windows NT Server 4.0 with Service Pack 6 or later, including support for Microsoft Gateway Service for NetWare and Services for The Macintosh

Supported network clients

- Microsoft Windows 98, Windows 98 Second Edition, or Windows Millennium Edition with Client for Microsoft Networks
- Microsoft Windows NT Workstation 4.0 with Service Pack 6 or later
- Microsoft Windows 2000 Professional
- Novell network operating systems and clients

Novell network servers and clients

Supported network servers

- Novell NetWare® 3.12 with year 2000 updates
- Novell NetWare 4.11 with year 2000 updates
- Novell intraNetWare® 4.11 with Support Pack 5b and year 2000 updates
- Novell NetWare 5.1

Supported Novell network clients

- Microsoft Windows 98, Windows 98 Second Edition, or Windows Millennium Edition with Novell intraNetWare client 2.5
- Microsoft Windows NT 4.0 Workstation with Service Pack 6 or later and Novell intraNetWare client version 4.30.410
- Microsoft Windows 2000 Professional and Novell intraNetWare client version 4.30.410

Supported Microsoft network clients

- Microsoft Windows 98, Windows 98 Second Edition, or Windows Millennium Edition and Client for NetWare Networks with Service for NetWare Directory Services
- Microsoft Windows NT Workstation 4.0 with Service Pack 6 or later and Client Service for NetWare
- Microsoft Windows 2000 Professional and Client Service for NetWare

Banyan network operating systems and clients

Microsoft Office XP supports the following Banyan network servers and clients.

Supported network servers

- Banyan VINES 6.4
- Banyan VINES 8.5

    Note Banyan VINES 6.x does not support long file names. Banyan VINES 7.x or later does support long file names. Also, Banyan requires upgrading to VINES 8.5 for year 2000 support.

Supported network clients

- Microsoft Windows 98, Windows 98 Second Edition, or Windows Millennium Edition and Banyan VINES Enterprise Client 8.52 for Windows 95
- Microsoft Windows NT Workstation 4.0 with Service Pack 6 or later
- Microsoft Windows 2000 Professional and Banyan VINES Enterprise Client 8.56 for Windows NT

UNIX NFS clients

Microsoft Office XP supports the following UNIX NFS clients:

- Microsoft Windows 98, Windows 98 Second Edition, or Windows Millennium Edition and Sun Microsystems Solstice Network Client™ versions 3.1 and 3.2
- Microsoft Windows NT Workstation 4.0 with Service Pack 6 or later and Sun Microsystems Solstice Network Client versions 3.1 and 3.2
- Microsoft Windows 2000 Professional and Sun Microsystems Solstice Network Client versions 3.1 and 3.2
- Microsoft Windows 98, Windows 98 Second Edition, or Windows Millennium Edition and FTP Network Access Suite 3.0
- Windows NT Workstation 4.0 with Service Pack 6 or later and FTP Network Access Suite 3.0
- Microsoft Windows 2000 Professional and FTP Network Access Suite 3.0

> **Note** Microsoft Office 2000 testing is performed for Sun Microsystems Solaris 2.4 NFS services and Microsoft NT Services for NFS. Record locking in shared Microsoft Access database files (MDB) is not supported. Use of drive aliases is required for NFS client support.

IBM network operating systems and clients

Microsoft Office XP supports the following IBM network servers and clients.

Supported network servers

- IBM OS/2 Warp LanServer 4.1.1

Supported network clients

- Microsoft Windows 98, Windows 98 Second Edition, or Windows Millennium Edition and IBM Network Client 4.1
- Microsoft Windows NT Workstation 4.0 with Service Pack 6 or later and IBM Network Client 4.2.2
- Microsoft Windows 2000 Professional and IBM Network Client 4.2.2

Digital network operating systems and clients

Microsoft Office XP supports the following Digital network servers and clients:

Supported network servers

- Digital Pathworks 5.0E for OpenVMS
- Digital OpenVMS v6.2 for Alpha

Supported network clients

- Microsoft Windows 98, Windows 98 Second Edition, or Windows Millennium Edition and Digital Pathworks 32 version 7.0
- Microsoft Windows NT Workstation 4.0 with Service Pack 6 or later and Digital Pathworks 32 version 7.0
- Microsoft Windows 2000 Professional and Digital Pathworks 32 version 7.0

Note Record locking in shared Microsoft Access database files (MDB) is not supported.

LANtastic peer-to-peer network operating systems

Microsoft Office XP supports the following Artisoft LANtastic peer-to-peer networking software:

- Microsoft Windows 98, Windows 98 Second Edition, or Windows Millennium Edition and Artisoft LANtastic 7.0

Office XP and Windows Terminal Services

Windows Terminal Services is a technology that lets you run Office XP applications remotely on a Windows-based server from a client computer over a network connection. When Terminal Services is enabled, administrators do not have to install Office XP on each client computer. Instead, the application is installed once on the server, and the clients gain access to Office XP through terminal emulation.

When a user runs an application on a client computer using Terminal Services, all of the application execution takes place on the server. Only the keyboard, mouse, and display information is transmitted over the network. Each user is restricted to his or her individual session, which is managed transparently by the server operating system.

For the Windows 2000 platform, Terminal Services is an optional service available on the standard server, advanced server, and datacenter server versions. For the Windows NT 4.0 platform, remote services are supported with Windows NT Server 4.0, Terminal Server Edition.

Note Licensing is required when deploying a Terminal Services–enabled server as an application server. Each client, regardless of the type of operating system and protocol used to connect to Terminal Services, must have the Terminal Services Client Access License (CAL) as well as a Windows 2000 Server CAL. Each copy of Windows 2000 Professional includes a Terminal Services CAL, but not a Windows 2000 Server CAL. Customers with servers using earlier versions of Microsoft Windows NT, or with client computers using other operating systems, must purchase a Terminal Services CAL and a Windows 2000 Server CAL, or the appropriate upgrade licenses.

Core system requirements for Terminal Services

The following sections list the system requirements for Windows 2000 and Windows NT 4.0 servers running Terminal Services.

Windows 2000 Server

Processor   Pentium 133 MHz or higher processor. Windows 2000 Server supports up to four CPUs on one machine.

Memory   256 MB of RAM recommended minimum (128 MB minimum supported; 4 gigabytes (GB) maximum).

Hard-disk space   2 GB hard disk with a minimum of 1 GB free space. (Additional free hard-disk space is required if you are installing over a network.)

Disk drives   CD-ROM or DVD drive.

Monitor   VGA or higher-resolution monitor; Super VGA recommended.

Pointing device   Microsoft Mouse, Microsoft IntelliMouse, or compatible pointing device.

Windows 2000 Advanced Server

Processor   Pentium 133 MHz or higher processor. Windows 2000 Advanced Server supports up to eight CPUs on one machine.

Memory   256 MB of RAM recommended minimum (128 MB minimum supported; 8 GB maximum).

Hard-disk space   2 GB hard disk with a minimum of 1 GB free space. (Additional free hard-disk space is required if you are installing over a network.)

Disk drives   CD-ROM or DVD drive.

Monitor   VGA or higher-resolution monitor; Super VGA recommended.

Pointing device   Microsoft Mouse, Microsoft IntelliMouse, or compatible pointing device.

Windows 2000 Datacenter Server

Processor   Pentium III Xeon processors or higher. 8-way capable or higher server (supports up to 32-way).

Memory   256 MB of RAM recommended minimum.

Hard disk space   2 GB hard disk with a minimum of 1 GB free space. (Additional free hard-disk space is required if you are installing over a network.)

Disk drives   CD-ROM or DVD drive.

Monitor   VGA or higher-resolution monitor; Super VGA recommended.

Pointing device   Microsoft Mouse, Microsoft IntelliMouse, or compatible pointing device.

Windows NT Server 4.0 with Service Pack 6 or later, Terminal Server Edition

Processor   Pentium 133 or higher processor.

Memory   32 MB of RAM minimum, plus 4 to 8 additional MB for each client connecting to the service.

Hard disk space   2 GB hard disk with a minimum of 1 GB free space. (Additional free hard-disk space is required if you are installing over a network.)

Disk drives   CD-ROM or DVD drive.

Monitor   VGA or higher-resolution monitor; Super VGA recommended.

Pointing device   Microsoft Mouse, Microsoft IntelliMouse, or compatible pointing device.

Core system requirements for client computers

Client computers use the Terminal Services Client software to manage communications between the client and the server running Office XP through Terminal Services. Each user that runs an application on Windows Terminal Server opens a separate instance of the application on the server, and all customizations are stored in a per-user storage area.

Client platforms that support Windows Terminal Services include the following:

- 32-bit Windows-based PCs running Windows 95, Windows 98, Windows 98 Second Edition, Windows Millennium Edition, Windows NT 3.51, Windows NT 4.0, or Windows 2000 Professional
- 16-bit Windows-based PCs running Windows for Workgroups 3.11 with MS TCP/IP-32
- Windows CE–based terminals
- Windows CE–based Handheld Professional devices (H/PC Pro)
- Third-party software vendors such as Citrix provide clients for non-Windows platforms such as the Apple Macintosh, MS-DOS, and UNIX

For more information about requirements and applications for Windows Terminal Services, see your Windows documentation.

Upgrading Reference

Upgrading to Microsoft Office XP from a previous version of Office is a straightforward process. The file formats for Microsoft Word, Microsoft Excel, and Microsoft PowerPoint have not changed since Office 97, and users upgrading from these versions do not need to convert any files. Microsoft Outlook 2002 users can continue to use data files and address books created in Outlook 2000. Microsoft Access 2002 users can work with databases in two file formats — Access 2000 and an enhanced Access 2002 format.

For organizations upgrading from Office 4.*x* or Office 95, Office XP Setup includes converters that automatically open and save Word documents, Excel workbooks, and PowerPoint presentations in the current format. In addition, Setup includes converters that allow users to import files from other applications, such as Lotus 1-2-3 and WordPerfect, and save those files in the appropriate Office XP file format.

If you do not have a converter that you need, or if you are switching to Office from a competitive product for which there is no installed converter, additional text converters and graphics filters are available separately in the Microsoft Office Converter Pack.

> **Note** Because the file formats for Word, Excel, and PowerPoint have remained unchanged since Office 97, several Office 97 text converters can convert legacy files to the Office 97–2002 format. These tools are available in the Microsoft Office 97/98 Resource Kit at http://www.microsoft.com/office/ork/home.htm.

Converting Word, Excel, and PowerPoint documents

If your organization upgrades in stages, then users might need to share files across versions until all users have installed Office XP. Even after the upgrade, Office XP users might need to open files from outside contacts that use another version of Office or another application.

In mixed environments, converters make it more efficient to manage files in the following ways:

- Users of an older version of Office can open documents created in Office XP without losing data.

- Office XP users can open and save documents in other file formats and continue to exchange information with all their colleagues.

- Office XP users can import images into their documents or export images to other file formats.

Install the Microsoft Office Converter Pack

The Office Converter Pack includes text converters and add-ins for the following Office applications:

- Word 2000, 97, 95, and 6.0
- Excel 2000, 97, 95, and 5.0
- PowerPoint 2000, 97, 95, and 4.0

These converters and filters are already installed with Office XP. Users of applications from Office 95 and Office 4.*x*, however, must install them from the Office Converter Pack before they can open documents saved in the Office 97–2002 file format. In addition, the Office Converter Pack includes converters and filters for a variety of other applications, including WordPerfect, Lotus 1-2-3, and Freelance Graphics.

You deploy the Office Converter Pack separately from both the Office XP installation and the Office XP Resource Kit core Setup program. The converters install on the following versions of Microsoft Windows:

- Microsoft Windows 3.1
- Microsoft Windows 95
- Microsoft Windows NT 4.0
- Microsoft Windows 95 and 98
- Microsoft Windows Millennium Edition
- Microsoft Windows 2000

You can install the Office Converter Pack with a full user interface and allow users to select the converters they want. Or you can customize the Convpack.ini and select the converters you want to install without user interaction. Converters are installed only for applications that Setup detects on the user's computer.

> **Toolbox** The Office XP Resource Kit includes two versions of the Microsoft Office Converter Pack. Use the self-extracting Convpack.exe to start Setup directly from the Office Resource Kit Web site or CD. If you are installing on a 16-bit version of Windows or if you want to customize the INI file, use Cnvpck16.exe to copy the files to your hard disk.

Locate converters and graphics filters

The following text converters and graphics filters are available for importing or exporting files in other file formats.

Word converters

Text converter	Location
Lotus AmiPro 3.x for Windows (import only)	Microsoft Office Converter Pack
Borland dBASE II, III, III+, and IV (import only)	Microsoft Office Converter Pack
Microsoft Excel (import only)	Microsoft Office Converter Pack
Microsoft FoxPro® 2.6 (import only)	Microsoft Office Converter Pack
HTML	Microsoft Office Converter Pack
Lotus 1-2-3 (import only)	Microsoft Office Converter Pack
RFT-DCA	Microsoft Office Converter Pack
Text with Layout	Microsoft Office Converter Pack
Recover Text (import only)	Microsoft Office Converter Pack
Microsoft Word 97–2002 (import only)	Microsoft Office Converter Pack
Word 6.0/95 Binary and RTF (export only)	Microsoft Office Converter Pack
Word 6.0/95 RTF Converter (export only)	Microsoft Office Converter Pack
Microsoft Word 3.x – 6.0 for MS-DOS	Microsoft Office Converter Pack
Microsoft Word for the Macintosh	Microsoft Office Converter Pack
WordPerfect 4.x	Microsoft Office Converter Pack
WordPerfect 5.x	Microsoft Office Converter Pack
WordPerfect 6.0 – 7.0 (import only)	Microsoft Office Converter Pack
WordStar 3.3 – 7.0 for MS-DOS and WordStar 1.0 – 2.0 for Windows	Microsoft Office Converter Pack
Microsoft Works 3.0 and 5.0 for Windows	Microsoft Office Converter Pack
Microsoft Windows Write 3.x	Microsoft Office Converter Pack
Word 97 Converter for Word 6.0 or 95 (import only)	Office 97/98 Resource Kit
Conversion Fonts for WordPerfect	Office 97/98 Resource Kit

Excel converters

Text converter cont'd	Location
HTML Add-in	Microsoft Office Converter Pack
Lotus 1-2-3	Microsoft Office Converter Pack
Quattro Pro 7 Add-in	Microsoft Office Converter Pack

PowerPoint converters

Text converter	Location
PowerPoint 95	Microsoft Office Converter Pack
PowerPoint 97–2002	Microsoft Office Converter Pack
HTML	Microsoft Office Converter Pack
Harvard Graphics 2.3 – 3.0 for MS-DOS	Microsoft Office Converter Pack
Freeland Graphics 4.0 for MS-DOS and 1.0 – 2.1 for Windows	Microsoft Office Converter Pack
PowerPoint 97 Translator for PowerPoint 4.0	Office 97/98 Resource Kit
PowerPoint 97 Batch Converter	Office 97/98 Resource Kit
PowerPoint Viewer 97	Office 97/98 Resource Kit

The Office Converter Pack also includes the following graphics filters for importing or exporting images:

- Bitmap (BMP)
- CorelDRAW (CDR)
- Computer Graphics Metafile (CGM)
- Micrografx Designer and Draw (DRW)
- AutoCAD (DXF)
- Windows Enhanced Metafile (EMF)
- Encapsulated Postscript (EPS)
- Flash Pix® (FPX)
- Graphics Interchange Format (GIF)
- Hewlett Packard Graphics Language (HPGL)
- JPEG File Interchange Format (JPEG)
- Kodak® Photo CD (PCD)

- PC Paintbrush (PCX)
- Macintosh PICT (PICT)
- Portable Network Graphics (PNG)
- Truevision Targa (TGA)
- Tag Image File Format (TIFF)
- Windows Metafile (WMF)
- WordPerfect Graphics (WPG)

Upgrading to Outlook 2002

The Outlook 2000 file format has not changed in Outlook 2002; users' PST files are automatically converted with no loss of data when you upgrade to Outlook 2002. However, Outlook 2002 does offer users some optional upgrades. For more information about upgrading to Outlook 2002, see Chapter 20, "Upgrading to Outlook 2002."

Upgrading to Access 2002

When your organization upgrades to Microsoft Access 2002, you do not need to convert Access 2000 databases to Access 2002; users of Access 2002 can continue to use the existing databases with no loss of functionality. The converse is not true: Access 2000 users cannot use a database saved in the new Access 2002 format.

If you are upgrading to Access 2002 in stages, Access 2000 provides a common file format for all users and an easier upgrade path from Access 97. You can convert Access 97 databases to Access 2000 or split them into front-end and back-end databases, which are accessible to all users.

If all the users in your organization have upgraded to Access 2002, then you can take advantage of the faster performance, better forward compatibility, and new features of Access 2002. You can also use Access 2002 to design a database and then save it in the Access 2000 file format; however, some functionality is lost when the database is opened in Access 2000.

> **Important** After you convert a database to the Access 2002 file format, the database is no longer accessible to users of any previous version, including Access 2000. Do not begin using the new file format until you are certain that all users have upgraded to Access 2002.

For more information about converting or enabling Access 97 databases, see the Microsoft Office 2000 Resource Kit on the Web at http://www.microsoft.com/office/ork.

For more information about upgrading to Access 2002, see the topic "Upgrading to Access 2002" on the Office Resource Kit Web site at http://www.microsoft.com/office/ork.

Additional upgrading resources

The following sources provide additional information and tips for managing an upgrade to Office XP.

For information about ...	See this source
Upgrading from a previous localized version or from the Office 2000 MultiLanguage Pack	*Office XP Resource Kit*: Chapter 14, "Upgrading International Installations"
Sharing files across language versions	*Office XP Resource Kit*: Chapter 14, "Upgrading International Installations"
Moving files from the Macintosh operating system to Windows	*Office 2000 Resource Kit*: Chapter 10, "Planning Your Move to Office 2000"
Contents of the Office Converter Pack and procedures for distributing converters	*Office 2000 Resource Kit*: Chapter 10, "Planning Your Move to Office 2000"
Application-specific upgrading issues for Access, Excel, FrontPage, Outlook, PowerPoint, and Word	*Office 2000 Resource Kit*: Chapter 11, "Office 2000 Upgrading Reference"
Conversion behavior between Office 97 applications and previous versions or competitive products (relevant for Word, Excel, and PowerPoint)	*Office 97/98 Resource Kit*: Part 3, "Upgrading to Microsoft Office"
Additional upgrading resources for Office XP	Microsoft Office Web site at http://www.officeupdate.microsoft.com/

PART 2
Deployment

Chapter 4   Overview of Setup   55

Chapter 5   Installing and Customizing Office   77

Chapter 6   Deploying on Windows 2000   163

Chapter 7   Deploying on Windows NT 4.0   189

CHAPTER 4

Overview of Setup

Microsoft Office XP uses Windows Installer technology, just as Office 2000 did. But the Setup program for Office XP has been enhanced. Setup now coordinates the entire installation process, including system file updates, core Office installation, and installation of chained packages. In addition, Setup automatically detects when Office is being installed from a Web server.

In this chapter

Setup Components   55

Tasks Handled by Setup   61

Installations That Require Elevated Privileges   72

Setup Components

You use the Microsoft Office XP Setup program (Setup.exe) to do the following:

- Create an administrative installation point for users to install Office over the network.
- Install Office and related packages on users' computers.
- Make changes to the installation in maintenance mode after Office XP is installed.

Like Microsoft Office 2000 Setup, Office XP Setup calls Windows Installer to install Office features; however, Office XP Setup manages more of the installation process.

For example, on computers running Microsoft Windows NT® 4.0 and Microsoft Windows® 98, Setup automatically checks for the required versions of shared and system files on the user's computer and updates the files from the System Files Update before installing Office. Setup can also coordinate installations of multiple chained packages through the Setup settings file (Setup.ini).

Setup program

Office XP Setup manages and coordinates the installation process from beginning to end. Setup spans required restarts and does not terminate until the last chained package is installed. Tasks performed by Setup include the following:

- Detecting and installing required system files, including restarting and resuming if necessary.
- Installing the core Office XP product.

- Installing chained packages specified in the Setup settings file.
- Detecting an HTTP source and installing Office from a Web server.

Setup.exe makes successive calls to Windows Installer (Msiexec.exe) to perform the installation of each package listed in the Setup.ini file. All command-line options documented in the Microsoft Office XP Resource Kit are defined for Setup.exe, which passes appropriate options to Msiexec.exe.

Setup settings file

Setup.exe reads the Setup settings file (Setup.ini) and writes tasks to the registry based on the information contained in the settings file. You can customize Setup.ini, or create your own custom INI files, to control many aspects of the installation process. Setup.ini is located in the Files\Setup folder on the administrative installation point. When you use the Setup INI Customization Wizard to specify your modifications, the wizard automatically writes the information in the appropriate sections of the INI file.

> **Toolbox** The Setup INI Customization Wizard is installed by default when you run the Office XP Resource Kit Setup program. Use the wizard to modify the Setup settings file, customize the installation process, and automatically generate the correct command line. For more information on the Setup INI Customization Wizard, see "Setup INI Customization Wizard" in the Toolbox.

For Office XP, the Setup settings file contains more information than previous versions and includes several new sections:

- [Product] section

    Contains the product code, product name, and version number. Setup uses this information to determine whether Office XP is installed.

- [MSI], [MST], and [Options] sections

    Contain information about the core Office package (MSI file) and any transform (MST file) to apply, as well as property settings for the core Office installation. For example, you can specify a value for the **COMPANYNAME** property in the [Options] section.

- [Display] section

    Contains settings for the user interface displayed during Setup. These settings override default values and apply to the entire installation process, including the System Files Update.

- [Logging] section

    Contains the logging mode to use for each portion of the installation process, as well as the location and naming scheme for log files.

- [Installer] section

    Contains Windows Installer information, including minimum version and path to Instmsi.exe or Instmsiw.exe (the program that installs or upgrades Windows Installer).

- [SystemPack] section

  Contains information about the System Files Update package, as well as some property settings to apply. For example, you can enter **DISPLAY=Basic** to display only simple progress indicators during the System Files Update installation, even if you set the core Office installation to run with a full user interface.

- [SystemPackOptions] section

  Contains custom settings and properties to pass to the System Files Update installation. For example, you can enter **TRANSFORMS=Custom.mst** to apply a transform to the System Files Update package.

- [SystemPack_DetectionFileList] section

  Lists all the shared and system files and version numbers that Setup checks during the detection process.

- [ChainedInstall_*n*] sections

  Contain information about chained packages and any transforms to apply. You can chain as many additional packages as you want and apply a transform to each one. These sections of Setup.ini are useful when you want to include multiple Office Multilingual User Interface Packs (MUI Packs) in an Office installation.

Windows Installer

Windows Installer (which includes Msiexec.exe) installs Office XP by using a dynamic-link library file (Msi.dll) to read the Windows Installer package (MSI file), apply a Windows Installer transform (MST file), incorporate command-line options supplied by Setup.exe, and install programs and files on users' computers.

When a user selects a feature to install during Office Setup, Windows Installer identifies a corresponding set of components to copy to the computer. Each component consists of a unique set of files, programs, dynamic-link libraries, and registry entries that work together as a unit.

Windows Installer uses two types of files to install Office XP and related products: packages (MSI files) and transforms (MST files). A Windows Installer package is a relational database that contains all the information necessary to install a product. The MSI file associates components with features. It also contains information about the installation process itself, such as installation sequence, destination folder paths, system dependencies, installation options, and properties that control the installation process.

Like a Windows Installer package, a Windows Installer transform is a relational database that contains information about components, features, and Setup properties. A transform is based on a particular package and contains the modifications to apply to that package during installation. When you use the Custom Installation Wizard to create a transform, the wizard compares the original MSI file and the MSI file with all your customizations incorporated. The differences are recorded in an MST file; the original package is never altered.

Office XP requires Windows Installer 1.1. The new version contains a number of improvements over Windows Installer 1.0, including better support for upgrading to a new version of a previously installed package.

If Windows Installer 1.0 is present on the computer, Setup automatically updates the program. If Windows Installer is not present on the computer, Setup calls Instmsi.exe (Windows 98) or Instmsiw.exe (Windows NT 4.0) to install it. Both the Microsoft Windows 2000 and Microsoft Windows Millennium Edition (Windows Me) operating systems include Windows Installer 1.1. If you are installing Office XP on one of these operating systems, no Windows Installer update is required.

Office XP packages

The Office XP package includes all the core applications and shared features. The core package also includes Input Method Editors (IMEs) for Korean, Japanese, and Simplified and Traditional Chinese. After Office is installed, Windows Installer continues to use the original package to add or remove features or to replace missing or damaged files. When you set Office features to be installed on first use, Windows Installer uses the package to copy the files the first time the user activates a feature.

The following Office XP technologies or features are not included in the core MSI file; these features require a separate installation:

- Microsoft's SharePoint™ Team Services
- Office Web Components
- Microsoft Data Engine (MSDE)
- Microsoft Office XP Resource Kit (Enterprise editions only)

The following table lists MSI files for Office XP and related products.

Product or Technology	Package (MSI file)
Office XP Professional with FrontPage	Proplus.msi
Office XP Professional	Pro.msi
Office XP Standard	Standard.msi
Office XP Small Business	Smbus.msi
System Files Update	Files\Osp\<LCID>\Osp.msi
Multilingual User Interface Pack Wizard	Lpkwiz.msi
Office Multilingual User Interface Packs	<LCID>/Lpk.msi.

Product or Technology	Package (MSI file)
SharePoint Team Services	Ows.msi
Office Web Components	Owc10.msi
Microsoft Data Engine (MSDE)	MSDE2000\Setup\Sqlrun01.msi
Access Runtime	Accessrt.msi
Microsoft Office XP Resource Kit (Enterprise editions only)	Ork\Ork.msi

For more information about the available editions of Office XP, see "Office XP System Requirements" in Chapter 3, "Deployment Prerequisites."

System Files Update

Office XP requires minimum versions of a set of dynamic-link library (DLL) files and other shared and system files. Before installing Office XP under Windows NT 4.0 and Windows 98, Setup verifies that these key system files are up-to-date and, if they are not, updates them automatically from the System Files Update before proceeding with the rest of the installation.

The release versions of Windows 2000 and Windows Me include an equivalent or better level of the key system files required for Office XP. Under Windows 2000 or Windows Me, you cannot install the System Files Update or run Internet Explorer Setup from the System Files Update. The **/spforce** command-line option has no effect on these operating systems.

If you are upgrading from Office 2000 Service Release 1 under Windows 98 or Windows NT 4.0 and you have Microsoft Internet Explorer 5.01 or later, then your system files are also up-to-date. In these cases, you can install Office XP without installing the System Files Update.

> **Note** During the installation of the Office XP package, Setup copies some files to the Systems folder on the user's computer. Unlike the files in the System Files Update package, these files do not update the operating system. They include dynamic-link library (DLL) files required by legacy applications and other shared files that the operating system looks for in the Systems folder. The workbook Filelist.xls lists these files. Filelist.xls is installed by default when you run the Office Resource Kit Setup program. For more information, see "Supplemental Documentation" in the Toolbox.

The System Files Update is a separate package (MSI file). If required, it is installed automatically with the Office XP package, but you customize it in a separate transform applied to the Osp.msi package. Key system files and components in the System Files Update include the following:

- Internet Explorer 5.01
- HTML Help
- Microsoft Data Access Components 2.5

- Microsoft Visual Basic® for Applications Runtime
- Microsoft Visual C Runtime
- Microsoft Foundation Class 4.2

   Tip The Setup settings file (Setup.ini) includes a list of the system and shared files that Setup checks before installing Office XP, along with minimum required version numbers. Setup.ini is located in the Files/Setup folder on the administrative installation point; you can find the file list in the [SystemPack_DetectionFileList] section of Setup.ini.

Internet Explorer 5

The minimum version of Internet Explorer required by Office XP is Internet Explorer 4.01 Service Pack 1. By default, the System Files Update includes a typical installation of Internet Explorer version 5.01. Under Windows NT 4.0 and Windows 98, any earlier version of Internet Explorer automatically triggers the System Files Update installation.

The following table lists the versions of Internet Explorer included with recent versions of Windows and Office.

Product	Internet Explorer
Windows 98 (release version)	Internet Explorer 4.01 Service Pack 1
Windows 98 Second Edition	Internet Explorer 5.0
Office 2000 (release version)	Internet Explorer 5.0
Office 2000 Service Release 1	Internet Explorer 5.01
Office XP	Internet Explorer 5.01
Windows 2000 (release version)	Internet Explorer 5.01
Windows Me	Internet Explorer 5.5

During an Office XP installation, administrators have several options for determining which version (if any) of Internet Explorer is installed on users' computers. For example, you can do one of the following:

- Run the System Files Update installation with a full user interface to give users the choice of installing or upgrading to Internet Explorer 5.
- Run the System Files Update installation silently and set the **NOIE** property to **True** to install only a required subset of Internet Explorer– and Microsoft Windows–related components.

Note Because the System Files Update installation does not run on Windows 2000 or Windows Me, you cannot update Internet Explorer during your Office XP installation on these operating systems. Instead, deploy the desired version of Internet Explorer separately before you install Office XP.

Office Multilingual User Interface Packs

Each language in the Office Multilingual User Interface Pack is installed as a separate package (Lpk.msi). The packages are stored in parallel folders on the Multilingual User Interface Pack CD: <LCID>\Lpk.msi. If you run Setup without user interaction, you can chain any number of MUI Packs to the core Office XP installation by adding them to the Setup settings file.

Alternatively, if you run Setup with a full user interface, you can include the Multilingual User Interface Pack Wizard (Lpkwiz.msi). Unlike most Windows Installer packages, this wizard cannot be customized or advertised by using the **/jm** command-line option or the software installation services in Windows 2000. Instead, Setup calls the wizard to display a list of all the languages available on the administrative image, and users select the languages they need. The wizard coordinates the installation of the selected MUI Packs.

See also

For more information about deploying MUI Packs in an international organization, see "Deploying Office with the Multilingual User Interface Pack" in Chapter 13, "Deploying Office Internationally."

For more information about Windows Installer, including online Help and other documentation, see the Platform SDK Components for Windows Installer (MSI) Developers page on the MSDN Web site at http://msdn.microsoft.com/downloads/sdks/platform/wininst.asp.

Tasks Handled by Setup

The Microsoft Office XP Setup program manages all the tasks associated with an Office XP installation, including system file updates, installation of chained packages, and required restarts. The Setup.exe thread spans and coordinates multiple installations and terminates only after the last chained package is installed, as shown in the following diagram.

Setup Sequence of Events

1. Performs required initialization tasks
2. Detects and installs the System Files Update (if required)
3. Restarts the computer and resumes (if required)
4. Installs the Office XP package
5. Installs chained packages
6. Completes

How Setup handles key tasks

You run Setup by double-clicking **setup.exe** on the Office XP CD or at the root of the administrative installation point. If Office XP is not installed on the computer, you can also run Setup by inserting the Office XP CD or by typing the following command line:

```
setup.exe [display settings] [logging settings] [options]
```

The following sections describe the sequence of events during Setup in more detail.

Initializing the installation process

When Setup starts, it first verifies that it is running on one of the following supported operating systems:

- Microsoft Windows 2000
- Microsoft Windows Millennium Edition (Windows Me)
- Microsoft Windows NT 4.0 Service Pack 6a
- Microsoft Windows 98

Any other version of Windows (including Microsoft Windows 95) generates an error message and causes Setup to exit.

Next, Setup reads the Setup settings file — Setup.ini or a custom INI file specified with the **/settings** command-line option. Most of the instructions for running the installation process are contained in the Setup settings file, including the display settings that Setup passes to Windows Installer before starting the installation process.

At this point in the process, Setup.exe also detects whether it is running from a Web server and, if so, sets the **URLPATH** property to **<http path>** in calls to Windows Installer.

Installing the packages

Setup.exe calls Windows Installer (Msiexec.exe) to install the System Files Update, the core Office XP package, and any chained packages. During the calls, Setup passes command-line options and properties to Windows Installer.

> **Toolbox** The Office XP Resource Kit includes a document named Setupref.doc that defines the Windows Installer command-line options most commonly used during Office Setup. Setupref.doc is installed by default when you run the Office Resource Kit Setup program. For more information, see "Supplemental Documentation" in the Toolbox.

Setup.exe recognizes all command-line options from Microsoft Office 2000, as well as the new options listed in the following table.

Option	Value	Description
/settings	<path>	Use the custom INI file at this location instead of default Setup.ini.
/webinstall	<URL>	Set **URLPATH** to install from a Web server.
/nosp	None	Override System Files Update detection and do not install the System Files Update.
/spforce	None	Install the System Files Update even if the detection process determines that it is not required.
/sponly	None	Install only the System Files Update; do not chain the Office XP package.
/noreboot	None	Do not restart the computer at the end of the installation.

Important Do not run Msiexec.exe directly. Instead, always run Setup.exe to install Office and related packages. Running Setup.exe ensures that all system verifications are performed.

You must have elevated privileges to install Office XP under Windows NT 4.0 or Windows 2000. Installing the System Files Update requires administrator rights both before and after the computer restarts. For more information, see "Installations That Require Elevated Privileges" later in this chapter.

Installing the System Files Update

Users installing Office XP under Windows 2000 or Windows Me already have the required versions of key system files, so Setup skips the System Files Update detection phase and does not call Windows Installer to install the package. (You cannot use **/spforce** to install the System Files Update on these operating systems.)

Under Windows NT 4.0 and Windows 98, users who are upgrading from Microsoft Office 2000 Service Release 1 and who have Microsoft Internet Explorer 5.01 or later also have up-to-date system files. Before proceeding with the Office XP installation, however, Setup.exe checks whether the System Files Update has been installed, and if not, determines whether it is required.

The [SystemPack_DetectionFileList] section of Setup.ini lists approximately 100 files that Setup checks during the detection process, as well as the minimum versions required. If the computer passes this test, Setup.exe moves on to the Office XP installation. All files checked, even those that meet the minimum version requirement, are recorded in the Setup log file.

If the computer fails the test, Setup.exe calls Windows Installer (Msiexec.exe) to install the System Files Update package (Osp.msi) with the following command line:

```
msiexec [display settings] [logging settings] [options] /i <Osp.msi>
```

Tip The Setup settings file (Setup.ini) includes a list of the system and shared files that Setup checks before installing Office XP, along with minimum required version numbers. Setup.ini is located in the Files/Setup folder on the administrative installation point; you can find the file list in the [SystemPack_DetectionFileList] section of Setup.ini.

By default, Setup.exe passes the Office display settings to Msiexec.exe. However, you can set the display level for the System Files Update to a different value by using the Setup INI Customization Wizard or by setting the **DISPLAY** property in the [SystemPack] section of Setup.ini. You can also add other property-value pairs specific to the System Files Update package in the [SystemPackOptions] section — including setting the **NOIE** property or specifying a transform (MST file) to apply.

When the System Files Update installation is complete, Setup.exe restarts the computer and proceeds to the core Office installation. You cannot advertise the System Files Update by using the **/jm** command-line option; the package must be installed locally. To advertise Office XP features, however, you must have the required level of system and shared files.

Note During the installation of the Office XP package, Setup copies some files to the Systems folder on the user's computer. Unlike the files in the System Files Update package, these files do not update the operating system. They include dynamic-link library (DLL) files required by legacy applications and other shared files that the operating system looks for in the Systems folder. The workbook Filelist.xls lists these files. Filelist.xls is installed by default when you run the Office Resource Kit Setup program. For more information, see "Supplemental Documentation" in the Toolbox.

Installing Internet Explorer

During the System Files Update detection (which occurs only on computers running under Windows 98 or Windows NT 4.0), Setup.exe determines which version of Internet Explorer is present on the computer. Internet Explorer 4.01 Service Pack 1 is the minimum version supported by Office XP. By default, however, any version earlier than Internet Explorer 5.01 triggers an installation of the System Files Update.

If you do not install Internet Explorer 5.01 (that is, if the administrator sets the **NOIE** property to **True** or if the user chooses not to upgrade), then Setup does not update the default Web browser or install Internet Explorer shortcuts. However, Setup still calls Internet Explorer Setup to install the subset of Internet Explorer– and Microsoft Windows–related components required by Office XP applications. If the System Files Update calls Internet Explorer Setup to install any component, then you must restart the computer at the end of the System Files Update installation.

At the end of the installation, whether or not Internet Explorer is upgraded to version 5.01, the user's system files are at least equivalent to the level in Office 2000 Service Release 1. All Office XP features function normally, except for some advanced and Web-related features, including the following:

- Integration features between SharePoint Team Services and Office XP.
- **Speech** command (**Tools** menu)
- Microsoft Data Access pages
- Microsoft Publisher **Publish as Website** command (**Tools** menu)
- Outlook feature that allows users to add an HTTP Hotmail® account.

Toolbox The Office XP Resource Kit includes a spreadsheet named IE5Feats.xls that lists all Office XP features that depend on Internet Explorer 5 for full functionality and describes their behavior when Internet Explorer 5 or 4.01 is not installed. IE5Feats.xls is installed by default when you run the Office XP Resource Kit Setup program. For more information on IE5Feats.xls, see "Supplemental Documentation" in the Toolbox.

The logic that Setup uses to determine when and how to upgrade or install Internet Explorer is described in more detail in the following tables.

If the administrator takes no action, then Setup installs or upgrades Internet Explorer as follows.

Existing version of Internet Explorer	Installation behavior
No Internet Explorer or earlier than Internet Explorer 4.01 Service Pack 1	Setup installs or presents users with the choice of typical Internet Explorer 5.01 (default), minimum Internet Explorer 5.01, or Windows Web Browsing Components only.
Internet Explorer 4.01 Service Pack 1 or later, but not Internet Explorer 5.0	Setup installs or presents users with the choice of typical Internet Explorer 5.01 (default), minimum Internet Explorer 5.01, or no upgrade.
Internet Explorer 5.0 or later, but not Internet Explorer 5.01	Setup upgrades to Internet Explorer 5.01 behind the scenes; users are not presented with a choice.

If you set the **NOIE** property to **True** (or if the user chooses not to upgrade), then Setup installs or upgrades Internet Explorer as follows.

Existing version of Internet Explorer	Installation behavior
No Internet Explorer or earlier than Internet Explorer 4.01 Service Pack 1	Windows Web Browsing Components are installed automatically.
Internet Explorer 4.01 Service Pack 1 or later, but not Internet Explorer 5.0	Internet Explorer is not upgraded to version 5.01, but Setup installs a subset of required components, including HTML Help.
Internet Explorer 5.0 or later, but not Internet Explorer 5.01	Internet Explorer is not upgraded to version 5.01, but Setup installs a subset of required components, including HTML Help.

Under Windows 98 and Windows NT 4.0, you can upgrade to Internet Explorer 5.5 by replacing the Osp/<LCID>/IE5 folder on your administration installation point with the Internet Explorer 5.5 folder. Then add **/spforce** to the command line or Setup.ini to ensure that the System Files Update installation is triggered. If you customize the Internet Explorer 5.5 package before installing it, then you must use the updated Internet Explorer Administration Kit for Internet Explorer 5.5.

Because the System Files Update installation does not run under Windows 2000 or Windows Me, you cannot use the **/spforce** command-line option to install or upgrade Internet Explorer during Office XP Setup. On these operating systems, you must deploy Internet Explorer 5.5 separately, before you install Office XP.

Note The Internet Explorer 5.*x* user interface identifies all versions as Internet Explorer 5. The specific version number of Internet Explorer 5.01 is listed in the [SystemPack_DetectionFileList] section of Setup.ini.

For more information about customizing and installing Internet Explorer, see the Internet Explorer Administration Kit Web site at http://www.microsoft.com/windows/ieak/en/corp/.

Installing Office XP

Setup.exe calls Windows Installer to install the core Office XP package by using the following command line:

```
msiexec [display settings] [logging settings] [options] /i <Proplus.msi>
```

The name and location of the package is specified in the [MSI] section of Setup.ini; the path defaults to the location of Setup.exe or **URLPATH**. You can specify a transform to apply and other property-value pairs on the command line or in the Setup settings file.

Note By using the Custom Installation Wizard, you can create a transform that specifies additional programs — for example, the Profile Wizard (Prflwiz.exe) — to run at the end of the Office XP installation. These programs are started by the core Office XP installation, before Setup calls Msiexec.exe to install any chained packages.

Installing chained packages

Office XP Setup handles installation of multiple chained packages, which are listed in the [ChainedInstall_1] to [ChainedInstall_*n*] sections of the Setup settings file. The following example shows the syntax used in Setup.ini:

```
[ChainedInstall_1]
PATH=\\server\share\<LCID>\Lpk.msi
CMDLINE=SOURCELIST=\\server2\share\<LCID>
DISPLAY=Basic
MST=Custom.mst
```

When the core Office XP installation is complete, Setup makes a series of calls to Windows Installer to install each chained package. For more information about chaining additional packages and setting properties for chained installations, see "Including Additional Packages in the Office Installation" in Chapter 5, "Installing and Customizing Office."

Installing Multilingual User Interface Packs

You can include Office Multilingual User Interface Packs (MUI Packs) on the same administrative image as Office XP, or you can choose a different location. (The Office Multilingual User Interface Pack Setup program is named LpkSetup.exe to allow you to use the same administrative installation point.) To chain individual MUI Packs directly to your Office XP installation, add the Lpk.msi files to the [ChainedInstall_*n*] sections of the Setup settings file. In this case, Setup.exe writes tasks to the registry for each package.

To take advantage of the Multilingual User Interface Pack Wizard user interface, you use LpkSetup.exe to run Lpkwiz.msi instead. When users select the languages they want during the installation process, Lpkwiz.msi writes the corresponding tasks to the registry for Setup.exe to install the MUI Packs.

When installing the MUI Packs, Setup automatically matches installation states of the MUI Pack features with those of the corresponding Office XP features. For example, if you install Office XP with Microsoft Access set to **Not Available**, then LpkSetup.exe automatically leaves Access out of the installation for each MUI Pack.

If you take advantage of these intelligent default settings, you do not need to create a separate transform to customize your MUI Pack installations. If you want to customize MUI Pack features differently, however, you can create a transform and override the default Setup behavior by setting the **NOFEATURESTATEMIGRATION** property to **True**.

Passing options and properties to Windows Installer

Setup uses command-line options and properties to control the installation process. Most global command-line options, such as **/qb**, are passed to Windows Installer for all the tasks that Setup handles. Others, such as **/nosp**, affect the behavior of Setup itself. Some command-line options, such as **PIDKEY** or **INSTALLLOCATION**, are passed only during the call to install Office XP.

The default values for Setup properties are defined in the package (MSI file), but you can customize your Office installation by specifying new values. For example, you can use the **COMPANYNAME** property to define the default organization name that Setup uses during installation.

In general, Setup properties are passed only during the call to install Office. (**NOIE** is an exception: that property is also passed during the call to install the System Files Update.) To override this behavior and pass a property to a package other than Office XP, you must specify the property in the relevant section of the Setup settings file and not on the command line. For example, you can install Office XP with a full user interface, but install the System Files Update silently by setting the **DISPLAY** property to **None** in the [SystemPack] section of Setup.ini.

Public and private properties

There are two types of Setup properties:

- Public property names are all uppercase and can specified on the command line, in the Setup settings file, or on the **Modify Setup Properties** page of the Custom Installation Wizard.

- Private property names are a mix of uppercase and lowercase letters and can be specified only on the **Modify Setup Properties** page of the Custom Installation Wizard.

If you enter a property name on the command line or in Setup.ini, Setup assumes that it is a public property and converts the name to all uppercase letters. When you enter a property name in the Custom Installation Wizard, you must enter the name exactly as it is defined, in all uppercase or in mixed-case letters. With few exceptions, all properties that you can use for managing the installation process are public properties.

Restarting the computer

Setup.exe restarts the computer under two circumstances:

- To complete the installation of a package (forced reboot)

    Setup resumes automatically after the computer restarts. Note that you cannot begin installing a new Windows Installer package until the previous installation is complete, including any forced reboots.

- To replace files in use (requested reboot)

    You can use the **/noreboot** command-line option to suppress requested reboots.

The Office XP package may end with a requested reboot if core Office files are in use during the installation; a forced reboot is never required. Installation of the System Files Update under Windows NT 4.0 or Windows 98 usually requires a forced reboot, except under the following conditions:

- The user chooses not to update Internet Explorer and all required Internet Explorer–related components are up-to-date.

    - and -

    Updated versions of Oleaut32.dll, Ole32.dll, and Odbc32.dll already exist on the computer.

Creating a log file

Both Office XP Setup and Windows Installer generate log files during the installation process. You cannot set options for the Setup log file; however, Windows Installer allows you to set a number of logging options that apply to each package that it installs during Office XP Setup. Note that any logging options you set apply to all log files created by Windows Installer during the Office XP installation.

You can also specify the name and path for log files. By default, Setup creates a log file in the %Temp% folder on each user's computer. Windows Installer creates a log file for each package that it installs, appends the task number to the log file name, and stores it in the same location. For example, %Temp%\<*SetupLogFile*>_Task(0001).txt is the name of the log file for the first package installed by Setup.

What Setup does behind the scenes

After Setup starts, it reads the Setup.ini file and writes information to the Windows registry that defines the entire installation sequence, as shown in the following diagram. If Windows Installer 1.1 is not present on the computer, Setup calls Instmsi.exe (Windows 98) or Instmsiw.exe (Windows NT 4.0) to install it.

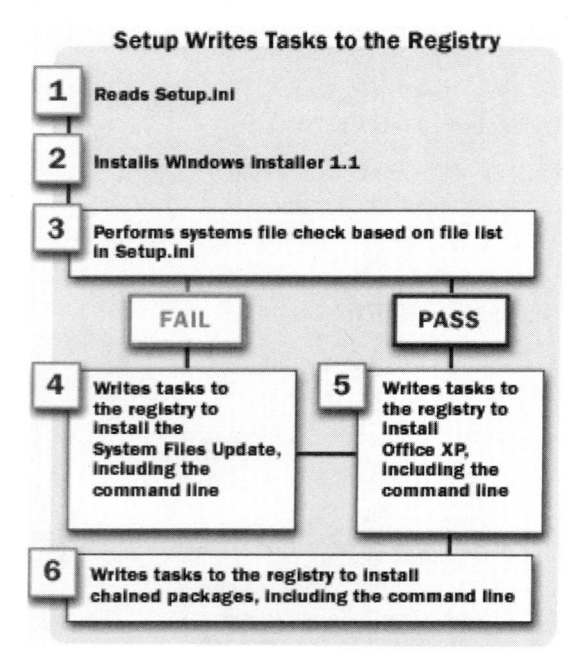

Setup Writes Tasks to the Registry

1. Reads Setup.ini
2. Installs Windows Installer 1.1
3. Performs systems file check based on file list in Setup.ini
   - FAIL → 4. Writes tasks to the registry to install the System Files Update, including the command line
   - PASS → 5. Writes tasks to the registry to install Office XP, including the command line
6. Writes tasks to the registry to install chained packages, including the command line

Then Setup executes each set of tasks in order, as shown in the following diagram.

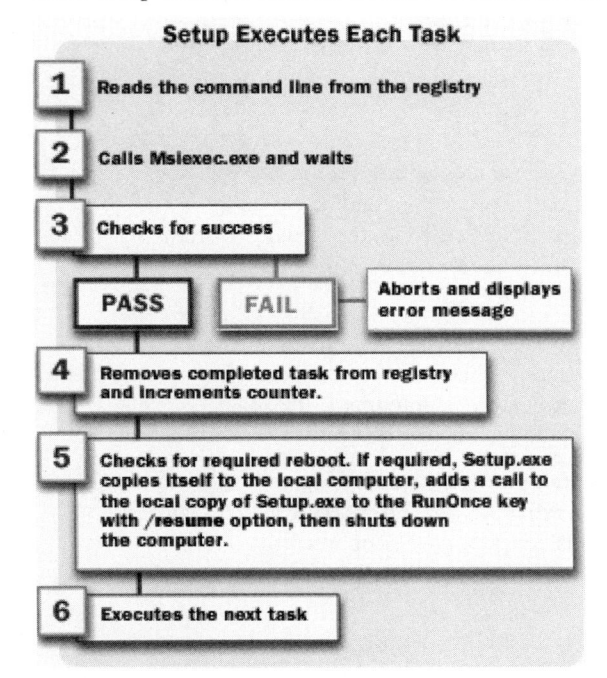

Setup Executes Each Task

1. Reads the command line from the registry
2. Calls Msiexec.exe and waits
3. Checks for success
   - PASS
   - FAIL → Aborts and displays error message
4. Removes completed task from registry and increments counter.
5. Checks for required reboot. If required, Setup.exe copies itself to the local computer, adds a call to the local copy of Setup.exe to the RunOnce key with /resume option, then shuts down the computer.
6. Executes the next task

Note On Windows 98, Setup.exe updates Windows Installer immediately after the forced reboot for the System Files Update, and adds an additional call to Instmsi.exe to the RunOnce key. This step reduces the number of restarts required to install Office XP under Windows 98.

Installations That Require Elevated Privileges

In Microsoft Windows NT 4.0 and Microsoft Windows 2000 environments, different groups of users have different levels of rights and permissions. In these environments, default users have limited access to system areas of the computer. Because Microsoft Office XP Setup updates system files and writes to system areas of the Windows registry, you must have administrator rights to the computer to install Microsoft Office XP.

Users without administrator rights cannot install Office XP. To install Office on computers where users lack administrator rights, you must run Setup with elevated privileges. After Office is installed, users without administrator rights can run all installed features, including installing features on demand, provided the initial installation was performed in an elevated context.

Under Windows NT 4.0 and Windows 2000, power users cannot install Office XP without elevated privileges. Elevated privileges are not required under Microsoft Windows 98 or Microsoft Windows Millennium Edition because these operating systems consider each user an administrator of the computer.

There are four methods of elevating the Office installation:

- Log on to the computer as an administrator and install Office XP.
- Assign, publish, or advertise Office applications.

    You use Windows 2000 software installation, a feature of IntelliMirror® management technology, to assign or publish Office XP. Under Windows NT 4.0 or Windows 2000, you can also log on to the computer as an administrator and run Setup with the **/jm** command-line option to advertise Office.

- Set a Windows Installer system policy that allows all Windows Installer applications to run with elevated privileges.
- Use Microsoft Systems Management Server in an administrative context to deploy Office.

Because all of the core Office XP products are installed as Windows Installer packages, any of the preceding methods grants users elevated privileges and allows them to install Office and any chained packages. When the initial installation is performed with elevated privileges, all subsequent installations — including install on demand and automatic repair of features — are also elevated.

> **Note** Under Windows NT 4.0, you cannot install the System Files Update merely by elevating the installation. Instead, you must log on to the computer with administrator rights when you begin the System Files Update installation, and log on again after the computer restarts to complete the installation. Alternatively, you can create a Systems Management Server script to elevate the installation.

Logging on as an administrator

You automatically install Office XP, the System Files Update, and the MUI Packs from the Office Multilingual User Interface Pack (MUI Pack) with elevated privileges if you log on to a computer with an account that has administrator rights. However, this method requires that all users have administrator rights or that an administrator visits every computer.

Under Windows 2000, you can also give users an administrator name and password and have them use the **Run as** command to install Office XP or the Multilingual User Interface Pack in an elevated context. If you create a shortcut to Setup.exe, you can include command-line options to customize the installation.

To create a shortcut to Setup.exe for users to run as administrators

1. Create a shortcut to Office XP Setup.exe.
2. Right-click the shortcut and then click **Properties**.
3. On the **Shortcut** tab, enter your command line in the **Target** box.

   To specify a custom INI file, use the **/settings** option; to apply a transform, use the **TRANSFORMS** property.
4. Select the Run as a different user check box, and then click OK.

You must distribute this shortcut with the domain, name, and password of an administrator account. The following procedure outlines the steps users must take.

To start Office XP Setup as an administrator (Windows 2000)

1. Press SHIFT and right-click **setup.exe** and then click **Run** as.
2. Click **Run the program as the following user**.
3. Enter the user name, password, and domain of the administrator account.

Setting a Windows Installer system policy

You can enable elevated privileges on a user's computer by setting a Windows Installer system policy. The **Always install with elevated privileges** policy allows a user without administrator rights to install any Windows Installer package (with the exception of the System Files Update).

> **Note** You must set the **Always install with elevated privileges** policy both per computer and per user to enable elevated privileges for installing Office XP.

To enable elevated privileges by policy (Windows 2000)

1. On the **Start** menu, point to **Programs**, point to **Administrative Tools**, and then click **Active Directory Users and Computers**.
2. In the console tree, right-click the domain or organizational unit for which you want to set the policy.
3. Click **Properties**, and then click the **Group Policy** tab.
4. Select a Group Policy Object in the **Group Policy Objects Links** box and click **Edit**.
5. Open the Local Computer Policy\Administrative Templates\Windows Installer folder.
6. In the details pane, double-click the **Always install with elevated privileges** policy.
7. In the **Group Policy Property** dialog box, enable the policy, select the check box to turn the setting on, and then click **OK**.
8. Open the User Configuration\Administrative Templates\Windows Installer folder and repeat Steps 6 and 7.

Under Windows NT 4.0, you can use the System Policy Editor and Windows Installer policy template file (Instlr11.adm) to set the **Always install with elevated privileges** policy. You must set the policy for the computer and for each user. For more information about setting system policies in Office XP, see "Understanding System Policies" in Chapter 9, "Using System Policies."

If you choose not use the Group Policy Editor or the System Policy Editor, you can specify the same setting on each computer by changing a value in the Windows registry.

To enable elevated privileges in the Windows registry

1. On the **Start** menu, click **Run** and type **regedit** to open the Registry Editor.
2. Find or create the following subkey in the Windows registry:

    HKEY_LOCAL_MACHINE\Software\Policies\Microsoft\Windows\Installer

3. In the Installer subkey, set the value of **AlwaysInstallElevated** to **1**.
4. Find or create the following subkey in the Windows registry:

    HKEY_CURRENT_USER\Software\Policies\Microsoft\Windows\Installer

5. In the Installer subkey, set the value of **AlwaysInstallElevated** to **1**.
6. Repeat Steps 5 and 6 for each user of the computer.

When you install Office XP from the Office CD, installing features on demand requires administrator rights each time a feature is installed. This scenario is the only exception to persistent administrator rights after an initial installation with elevated privileges.

To allow users to install features on demand from the Office XP CD, you must set the Windows Installer system policy **Enable user to use media source while elevated**. For more information about installing from the Office XP CD or a customized copy of the compressed Office CD, see "Distributing Office to Users' Computers" in Chapter 5, "Installing and Customizing Office."

Caution When you set the **Always install with elevated privileges** or **Enable user to use media source while elevated** policy, any Windows Installer package installed by any user can make changes to system areas. This state can leave the computer vulnerable to viruses.

Assigning, publishing, or advertising Office XP

If all the computers in your organization run under Windows 2000, you can elevate the Office installation by using IntelliMirror technology to assign or publish Office XP and the MUI Packs. Because Windows 2000 already provides the necessary level of system files, the System Files Update is not required.

Alternatively, if you are running Windows NT 4.0 or if you are not using Windows 2000 software installation, you can advertise Office XP by logging on as an administrator and then running Setup with the **/jm** option. If you also include a Windows Installer transform (MST file) to customize the installation, use the **/t** command-line option to specify the MST file. For example:

```
setup.exe /jm proplus.msi /t office.mst
```

When you advertise Office XP in this way, Windows Installer shortcuts for each application appear on the **Start** menu, and a minimal set of core Office files and components is installed on the computer. When a user clicks a shortcut or opens a file associated with an Office application, Windows Installer runs with elevated privileges to install the application, regardless of how the user logged on. After Office is advertised, users can also run Setup from an administrative installation point and install Office with elevated privileges.

Note that Windows NT 4.0 does not support Windows Installer shortcuts without an updated version of the Windows shell. The updated shell is included with Internet Explorer 4.01 Service Pack 1 or later. Even without the updated shell and Windows Installer shortcuts, however, core Office files and components are installed on the computer, and Windows Installer considers the initial installation complete. Users can subsequently run Office XP Setup from the administrative installation point and install with elevated privileges.

Like Office XP, the MUI Packs in the Office Multilingual User Interface Pack are Windows Installer packages, and you can advertise them to grant users elevated privileges when installing them. However, you must be logged on as an administrator when you advertise a package. Because the System Files Update cannot be advertised, advertising Office XP on Windows NT 4.0 fully installs the System Files Update on the local computer when the update is required.

See also

For more information about assigning or publishing Office XP, see "Using Windows 2000 Software Installation" in Chapter 6, "Deploying on Windows 2000."

For more information about advertising Office, see "Distributing Office to Users' Computers" in Chapter 5, "Installing and Customizing Office."

By using a Systems Management Server script, you can install Office in an elevated context. For more information, see the Microsoft Systems Management Server Web site at http://www.microsoft.com/smsmgmt/default.asp.

CHAPTER 5

Installing and Customizing Office

Deploying Microsoft Office XP from an administrative installation point gives you the most flexibility and control over the installation process. After you install the files on a network share, you can determine how much users interact with Setup and which Office features are available to them. You can specify default settings for most options, and even chain additional Windows Installer packages to the Office installation. Users can run Setup from the network or the Office CD, or you can distribute Office by using a hard-disk image or management services tool such as Microsoft Systems Management Server.

In this chapter

Creating an Administrative Installation Point   77

Customizing the Office Installation   83

Customizing How Setup Runs   94

Customizing Office Features and Shortcuts   102

Customizing User-defined Settings   114

Including Additional Packages in the Office Installation   129

Customizing Removal Behavior   135

Distributing Office to Users' Computers   141

Deploying a Service Release   156

Creating an Administrative Installation Point

The most common method of deploying a customized version of Microsoft Office XP to a large number of users is to create an administrative installation point on a network server and have users run Setup from there. This method provides several advantages over installing Office from the Office XP CD, and allows you to do the following:

- Manage one set of Office files from a central location.
- Create a standard Office configuration for all users.
- Take advantage of flexible installation options.

    For example, set Office features to be installed on first use, or deploy the Office XP package through Microsoft Windows® 2000 software installation, or use Systems Management Server to install Office.

- Manage controlled upgrades of Office in the future.

Running administrative Setup for Office XP

To distribute Office from a network server, you must first install Office on an administrative installation point by running Setup with the **/a** command-line option. Then you can customize your Office configuration before running Setup on users' computers.

To create an administrative installation point for Office

1. Create a share on a network server for the administrative installation point.

    The network share must have at least 650 megabytes (MB) of available hard-disk space.

2. On a computer that has write access to the share, connect to the server share.

    The computer must be running a supported operating system: Microsoft Windows 2000 or later, Microsoft Windows NT® 4.0 Service Pack 6a, Microsoft Windows Millennium Edition (Windows Me), or Microsoft Windows 98.

3. On the **Start** menu, click **Run**, and then click **Browse**.
4. On the Office XP CD, double-click **setup.exe** and add **/a** to the command line.
5. Enter the organization name that you want to define for all users who install Office from this administrative installation point.
6. Enter the server and share you created as the installation location.
7. Enter the 25-character product key and click **Next**.

    You must enter a valid product key when you create the administrative installation point; users who install Office XP from this administrative image do not need to enter the product key when they install Office XP or start an Office XP application for the first time.

8. Accept the end-user license agreement and click **Install**.

    By accepting the agreement here, you are accepting on behalf of all users who install Office from this administrative installation point.

Setup copies the files from the Office XP CD to the administrative installation point, extracts the compressed cabinet (CAB) files, and creates a hierarchy of folders in the root folder of the share. The System Files Update is automatically included during an administrative installation.

Note When you install Office XP under Windows 2000 and you set features to run from the network (**Run from Network** or **Run All from Network**), you must create your administrative installation point in a subfolder on the share; for example, \\server\share\admin_install_point\setup.exe. If Setup.exe is stored at the root of the share, Office XP features do not run properly.

The following table identifies the location of key files on the Office XP administrative image.

File	Location
Setup.exe	Root of the administrative image
Office XP MSI file	Root of the administrative image
System Files Update MSI file	Files\Osp\<LCID>
Setup.ini	Files\Setup

Setup also modifies the Windows Installer package for Office, identifying it as an administrative installation package and setting the **ProductID** and **COMPANYNAME** properties accordingly. After you create the administrative installation point, you make the share available to users by providing them with read access.

When users run Setup to install Office, any Office features that are installed to run from the network use this administrative installation point as the source of Office files, and Offices runs the features over the network from this server. Similarly, for features that are set to be installed on first use, Office copies files from this server when needed. If you install features in one of these two states, then you must keep this network server available to users.

Important When laptop users install Office from an administrative installation point, they must continue to use the network share as the source for tasks such as repairing features and installing on demand. Because files are compressed on the Office XP CD, they cannot use the CD as the source unless they installed from the CD.

When users install Office from the administrative installation point, Setup uses the organization name that you specify as the default. In the Office Custom Installation Wizard, you can create a Windows Installer transform (MST file) that modifies the organization name during installation. This flexibility allows you to create different organization names for different groups of users in your organization.

You can specify the organization name on the **Specify Default Path and Organization** page of the wizard, or set the **COMPANYNAME** property on the **Modify Setup Properties** page. You can also specify an organization name on the Setup command line or in the Setup settings file (Setup.ini), but in this case you must leave the organization name blank when you create the administrative installation point.

Toolbox The Office XP Resource Kit includes the Custom Installation Wizard as part of the core tool set. The Custom Installation Wizard is installed by default when you run the Office XP Resource Kit Setup program. For more information on the wizard, see "Custom Installation Wizard" in the Toolbox.

Replicating the administrative image

In many organizations, it makes sense to create multiple administrative installation points from which users can install Office — and to which Windows Installer can connect to install or repair Office features. As long as you use relative paths for any customizations that include paths, you can copy the complete folder hierarchy and files from one administrative installation point to multiple servers. If you copy the folders, then each new administrative image that you create has the same default organization name specified in Setup.

You list the paths to the servers that contain replicated administrative installation points on the **Identify Additional Servers** page of the Custom Installation Wizard.

Including additional files in the Office XP image

Not all the products on the Office XP CD are included when you run Setup in administrative mode. However, you can install these Office XP–related products separately — or you can copy them to your administrative installation point to simplify file management and replication of the administrative image. When users run Office XP Setup, these additional products can be included in the core Office XP installation.

The administrative installation point is also a logical place to store custom files that you create, including transforms (MST files) and Setup settings files (INI files). If you are planning a staged deployment and you create a configuration maintenance file (CMW file) to use after your initial deployment, you can store the CMW file on your administrative installation point, too.

Microsoft SQL Server 2000 Desktop Engine

The Microsoft SQL Server™ 2000 Desktop Engine (MSDE 2000) allows you to use a local computer as a data source for a SQL Server database, as well as take advantage of enhanced features in Microsoft Access 2002. MSDE 2000 is included in the following Office XP suites:

- Microsoft Office XP Professional
- Microsoft Office XP Professional with FrontPage (Enterprise and Select editions)
- Microsoft Office XP Developer
- Microsoft Access 2002 (Enterprise edition)

The Office CD includes an MSDE 2000 folder, but MSDE 2000 is not included when you run administrative Setup. Instead, you must copy the entire MSDE2000 folder from the Office CD to the root of the administrative installation point and install MSDE from there. The MSDE2000 folder contains the MSDE package (SqlRun01.msi) and a separate Setup program (Setup.exe). MSDE 2000 Setup installs MSDE 2000 on users' computers as an instance of the SQL Server 2000 Desktop Engine.

To customize the MSDE installation, you modify the Setup.ini file in the MSDE2000 folder. For example, you can set the **DISPLAY** property to **None** to install MSDE 2000 silently, or you can specify a unique value for the **INSTANCENAME** property. For detailed instructions about installing and customizing MSDE 2000, see the Readme.txt file in the MSDE2000 folder.

MSDE 2000 requires Microsoft Internet Explorer 5.0 and administrator rights to install; it does not support advertisement with the **/jm** switch or the IntelliMirror® technology software installation features of Windows 2000. MSDE 2000 installs Microsoft Data Access (MDAC) version 2.6. (Office XP installs only MDAC 2.5.) When MSDE Setup installs MDAC 2.6, the user must restart the computer to complete the installation.

For more information about MSDE 2000 and Office XP, see the resources on the Technical Information page of the Microsoft SQL Server Web site at http://www.microsoft.com/SQL/techinfo.

Office Web Components

Office XP Web Components are a set of Active X® controls — including Chart, Spreadsheet, and PivotTable® components — that can be used for data analysis and reporting. You can insert Office Web Components into Web pages from Microsoft FrontPage® 2002 or by using tools such as Visual Basic® for Applications. Microsoft Excel 2002 can also save Web pages that include Office Web Components.

Office Web Components are included in the core Office XP package as well as the stand-alone editions of Excel, Microsoft Access, and FrontPage. A separate Office Web Components package (Owc10.msi) is also included on the Office XP CD. Customers who want to develop solutions that include Office Web Components before deploying Office XP can install the Office Web Components package separately.

To deploy Office Web Components without installing Office XP

- Run the Office Web Components Setup program from the Office XP CD or from an Office XP administrative installation point.

    The Office Web Components Setup.exe is located in the Files\Owc folder on both the Office XP CD and the Office XP administrative installation point.

You can also create a separate administrative installation point for Office Web Components, but the procedure differs slightly from the one you use for Office XP.

To create an administrative installation point for Office Web Components

1. At the command prompt, type **msiexec.exe /a owc.msi**.
2. When prompted, enter a location for the administrative installation point.

3. Copy the System Files Update from the root of the CD to the root of the administrative installation point.

   The System Files Update is located in the Files\Osp\<lcid> folder.

If you want to customize the Office Web Components installation, modify the Office Web Components Setup.ini file, which is located in the Files\Owc folder. For example, to install Office Web Components silently, set the **DISPLAY** property to **None** in the [Options] section of Setup.ini.

For more information about designing solutions with Office Web Components or about using the controls in documents, see the Office Web Components Help file.

Microsoft's SharePoint Team Services and FrontPage Server Extensions 2002

Microsoft's SharePoint™ Team Services and FrontPage Server Extensions 2002 allow you to create and manage Web sites. SharePoint Team Services includes prebuilt team Web sites for team communication. The SharePoint Team Services package (Ows.msi) includes the components for both SharePoint Team Services and FrontPage Server Extensions 2002. No additional client components are required, beyond your usual installation of Internet Explorer 4.0 or later or Netscape Navigator 4 or later.

SharePoint Team Services and FrontPage Server Extensions 2002 are available with the Standard, Professional, Professional with FrontPage, and Enterprise editions of Office XP. They are also available in the stand-alone edition of FrontPage 2002. However, the SharePoint Team Services package is not included when you run Setup to create an Office XP administrative installation point. Instead, you must install SharePoint Team Services separately from the SharePt folder on the Office XP or FrontPage 2002 CD to a computer acting as a Web server.

SharePoint Team Services is supported on the following operating systems:

- Microsoft Windows 2000 Professional, Server, or Advanced Server edition with Microsoft Internet Information Server (IIS) 5.0 or later with the World Wide Web service installed (Windows 2000 Server only).

FrontPage Server Extensions 2002 are supported on the following operating systems:

- Microsoft Windows 2000 Professional, Server, or Advanced Server edition with Microsoft Internet Information Server (IIS) 5.0 or later with the World Wide Web service installed (Windows 2000 Server only).

- Microsoft Windows NT Workstation 4.0 with Service Pack 5 or later and Microsoft Internet Information Server (IIS) 4.0 or later (to support a single virtual server).

- Microsoft Windows NT Server 4.0 with Service Pack 5 or later and IIS 4.0 or later with the World Wide Web service installed (to support multiple virtual servers). Microsoft IIS 4.0 is available with the Windows NT 4.0 Option Pack.

Note On the Windows operating system, the security features of SharePoint Team Services and FrontPage Server Extensions 2002 require the NTFS file system. Windows NT 4.0 includes a conversion utility (Convert.exe) that you can use to convert an existing file allocation table (FAT) volume to NTFS without losing data.

For more information about installing SharePoint Team Services and FrontPage Server Extensions 2002, see the "SharePoint Team Services Administrator's Guide." Information about the guide is provided in this topic on the Office Resource Kit Web site at http://www.microsoft.com/office/ork/.

System Files Update language versions

The Microsoft Office Multilingual User Interface Pack includes multiple language versions of the System Files Update. You can copy the language versions you need to the Files\Osp folder on the administrative installation point. By default, Setup installs the language version that matches the language of the operating system; otherwise, Setup installs the English version.

Internet Explorer 5.5 or later

Office XP includes Internet Explorer 5.01, which is located in the Files\Osp\<LCID>\IE5 folder on the administrative installation point. To install Internet Explorer 5.5 on computers running Windows NT 4.0 or Windows 98, replace the IE5 folder with a folder that contains the configuration you want. The alternate version is installed during the System Files Update portion of the Office XP installation.

Note Because the System Files Update detection and installation process does not run under Windows 2000 or Windows Me, you must deploy Internet Explorer 5.5 separately, before you deploy Office XP, on these operating systems. For more information, see the Internet Explorer Web site at http://www.microsoft.com/windows/ie/default.htm.

Microsoft Office XP Resource Kit

The Microsoft Office XP Resource Kit is included in all Enterprise editions of Office XP. You can copy the ORK folder to the administrative installation point and run Setup.exe from that folder to install Office Resource Kit tools and documentation on your computer.

Customizing the Office Installation

After you create an administrative installation point for Microsoft Office XP, you can make extensive customizations before installing Office on users' computers. You can also customize many aspects of the installation process itself, as shown in the following diagram.

Customizing the Installation Process

1. Performs required initialization tasks
- Customize the way Setup runs, including logging mode and display settings

2. Detects and installs the System Files Update
- Customize Internet Explorer
- Override default display or logging settings for the System Files Update
- Set properties for the System Files Update, including forcing or skipping the installation

3. Restarts the computer and resumes

4. Installs the Office XP package
- Set Office feature installation states
- Customize default Office settings
- Add files or shortcuts
- Customize removal behavior
- Turn on Setup Error Reporting to report Setup failures directly to Microsoft

5. Installs chained packages
- Chain MUI Packs to the Office installation
- Customize and chain other Windows Installer packages

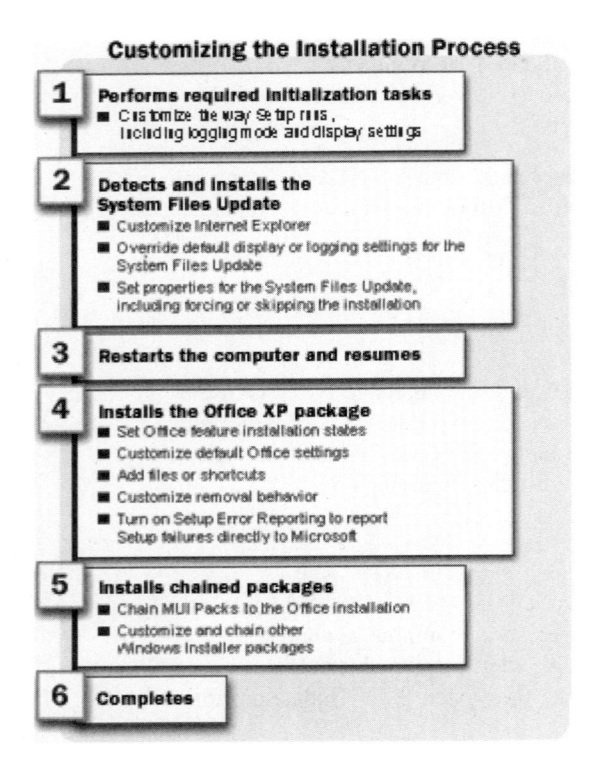

6. Completes

Many of the customizations you make to an Office XP installation can be accomplished by one of several methods:

- Specifying options on the command line.
- Modifying the Setup.ini file with the Setup INI Customization Wizard.
- Creating a transform (MST file) with the Custom Installation Wizard.
- Creating a profile settings file (OPS file) with the Profile Wizard.
- Running the Removal Wizard during or after the Office XP installation.

The following table shows packages (MSI files) related to Office that you can customize, and it provides recommended methods for different types of customizations.

Customization	MSI file	Command line	INI file	MST file	OPS file	Removal Wizard
Setup process (display, logging, installation location, organization name, and so on)	Proplus.msi	x	x	x		
Internet Explorer installation and settings	Osp.msi	x	x	x		
Office features, added files, and shortcuts	Proplus.msi			x		
Security settings	Proplus.msi			x	x	
Outlook settings	Proplus.msi			x	x	
Other user settings	Proplus.msi			x	x	
Removal options	Proplus.msi			x		x
Language settings	Lpk.msi			x		
Chained packages	*Chained*.msi	x				

Toolbox The Office XP Resource Kit core tool set includes the Custom Installation Wizard, Setup INI Customization Wizard, Profile Wizard, and Removal Wizard. These tools are installed by default when you run the Office Resource Kit Setup program. For more information, see the Toolbox.

Working with Setup properties

Setup properties control many aspects of the installation process, including the following:

- Display settings, logging options, and other properties used by Setup to manage the installation process.
- Properties that customize button labels and descriptive text in the Setup user interface.
- Properties that control how Office features are installed.
- Properties that determine how Microsoft Outlook® and Microsoft Internet Explorer are installed with Office.

The default values for Setup properties are defined in the Windows Installer package (MSI file). You can specify new values on the command line, in Setup.ini, or on the **Modify Setup Properties** page of the Custom Installation Wizard. During the installation, Setup passes all Setup property values to Windows Installer.

Most properties are passed only during the call to install Office XP, except for the following:

- Global display settings (**/q**option) are passed to every installation included with Office.

    For example, when you specify **/qb** on the command line, Setup displays simple progress indicators and error messages throughout the entire installation. To install the System Files Update silently, or to install Microsoft Office Multilingual User Interface (MUI) Pack files with a full user interface, you must set other properties in the Setup.ini file.

- **NOIE** is passed during the call to install the System Files Update.

    When **NOIE** is set to **True**, then Setup does not install or give the user the option to install Internet Explorer 5.01.

- When specified on the command line, **SOURCELIST** is passed to the System Files Update and any chained packages.

    Toolbox You can find detailed information about Setup command-line options and properties in Setupref.doc, which is installed by default when you run the Office XP Resource Kit Setup program. This document also describes the format of the Setup settings file. For more information, see "Supplemental Documentation" in the Toolbox.

For more information about Windows Installer, including online Help and other documentation, see the Platform SDK Components for Windows Installer (MSI) Developers page on the MSDN Web site at http://msdn.microsoft.com/downloads/sdks/platform/wininst.asp.

Specifying options on the command line

When you run Setup, you can use command-line options to change some of the parameters that Setup uses to install Office. By using command-line options, you can do the following:

- Identify the package (MSI file) and transform (MST file) to use.
- Specify a custom Setup settings file (INI file) to use.
- Direct Setup to run in quiet mode.
- Set Windows Installer logging options.
- Change default values of Setup properties.

For example, you can enter the following options on the command line:

```
setup.exe /qb+ /l* %temp%\office10.txt COMPANYNAME='Northwind Traders'
```

This command line customizes Setup in the following ways:

- Setup does not prompt the user for information, but displays progress indicators and a completion message when it installs Office (**/qb+**).

- Windows Installer logs all information and any error messages (**/l***) for Setup.exe to the file C:\Temp\Office10.txt on the user's computer.

    Logging information for the System Files Update is recorded in C:\Temp\Office10_Task(0001).txt; logging information for the Office XP package is recorded in C:\Temp\ Office10_Task(0002).txt.

- Setup sets the default organization name to Northwind Traders.

- Because no custom INI or MST file is specified, Setup installs the same Office features that it would if the user clicked **Install Now** in the Setup user interface.

When to use command-line options

The Setup command line is most useful when you have few customizations to make, or when you want to create several different installations quickly. You can use one custom INI file or apply the same MST file to install a basic Office XP configuration to everyone, but define different command lines for targeted groups of users.

For example, you can have your Engineering and Accounting departments install the same set of Office XP features and settings, but specify unique organization names. In the administrative installation point, you create two shortcuts that have the following command lines:

```
setup.exe /q /settings Custom.ini COMPANYNAME='Engineering Department'
setup.exe /q /settings Custom.ini COMPANYNAME='Accounting Department'
```

Command-line options are also useful if you use Microsoft Systems Management Server or another systems management tool to create multiple deployment packages, each of which requires a different command line.

> **Tip** Any settings that you can specify on the command line can also be added to Setup.ini — including the command line itself. For extensive or complex customizations, use Setup.ini to make the installation process easier to track and troubleshoot.

How to distribute command-line options

When users double-click **setup.exe** on the administrative installation point, Setup runs with no command-line options. To apply your custom command-line options, users must click **Run** on the Windows **Start** menu and enter the path to Setup.exe, along with your command-line options.

To simplify this process, you can create in MS-DOS a batch file that runs Setup.exe with your command-line options. Or you can create a Windows shortcut and add your custom options to the command-line box. Users double-click the batch file or shortcut to run the Setup command line that you have defined. You can store the batch file or shortcut in the root folder of the administrative installation point.

If you run Setup from a network logon script or through a systems management tool (such as Systems Management Server), you can add your custom options to the Setup command line in the script or deployment package.

Customizing the Setup settings file

Before applying the values specified on the command line, Setup reads the properties specified in the Setup settings file (Setup.ini), where you can set all the properties that you can on the command line. For example, you can:

- Identify the MSI and MST files to use in the [MSI] and [MST] sections.
- Direct Setup to run in quiet mode in the [Display] section.
- Set logging options for Windows Installer and Office XP Setup in the [Logging] section
- Change the default values of Setup properties in the [Options] section.

The Setup.ini file for Office XP also contains several new sections that allow you to specify settings that you cannot add to the command line. For example:

- Customize the System Files Update separately from Office XP in the [SystemPack] and [SystemPackOptions] sections.
- Chain multiple Windows Installer packages, including MUI Packs, to your core Office installation in the [ChainedInstall_n] sections.

In most sections of Setup.ini, including the [Options] and [SystemPackOptions] sections, you use the syntax **PROPERTY=value** to specify custom property values. In the [ChainedInstall_n] sections, you can set the **DISPLAY** and **MST** values with this syntax; however, you must use the **CMDLINE** property to add other options to the command line that Setup passes to Windows Installer for a chained package.

The Office XP Resource Kit includes a new tool — the Setup INI Customization Wizard (Iniwiz.exe) — that provides a convenient user interface for creating or modifying custom Setup settings files. The wizard automatically enters the settings that you select into the correct section of the settings file, and it creates a command line that includes the **/settings** option and specifies your custom INI file.

> **Toolbox** The Office Resource Kit core tool set includes the Setup INI Customization Wizard, which is installed by default when you run the Office Resource Kit Setup program. For more information, see "Setup INI Customization Wizard" in the Toolbox.

When to use a custom INI file

Because the Setup settings file organizes Setup options in an easy-to-read format, it is more convenient to use than long or complex command lines. If you use Setup.ini to set most Setup properties, then you can reserve the command line for specific and targeted modifications, or changes that you need to make late in the deployment process.

If you want to chain MUI Packs from the Office Multilingual User Interface Pack or chain other Windows Installer packages to your core Office XP installation, then you must enter the MSI files by adding the name and path in the Setup INI Customization Wizard or in the [ChainedInstall_n] section of Setup.ini.

Other scenarios in which the Setup settings file is the best customization method to use include the following:

- You want users to run Setup.exe directly from the administrative installation point, instead of creating a batch file or shortcut to install a customized version of Office XP.

- You want to override global display settings (that is, the display settings specified for Office XP) and set unique display settings for the System Files Update or other chained packages.

    For example, if you are installing Office XP with a full user interface, but you want to install an MUI Pack with a basic user interface, you can enter **Display=Basic** in the [ChainedInstall_n] section for the Multilingual User Interface Pack package. You can also select the Lpk.msi file in the Setup INI Customization Wizard and set the **Display setting** to **Basic**.

- You want to set additional options for the System Files Update or a chained package, such as specifying a transform to apply.

How to use the Setup INI Customization Wizard

The Setup INI Customization Wizard provides a convenient user interface for creating custom versions of the Setup settings file. The wizard also helps prevent you from inadvertently specifying conflicting settings and automatically generates a Setup command line that includes the **/settings** switch and the name and path to your custom INI file.

Before you can use the Setup INI Customization Wizard, you must create an Office XP administrative installation point. Your custom INI file must be based on an existing INI file, such as the Setup.ini file for Office XP.

To create a custom Setup.ini file

1. Enter the path to your Office XP administrative installation point and click **Next**.

   The wizard searches the specified network share for a Setup.ini file.

2. Select an INI file from the administrative installation point on which to base your custom INI file, or click **Browse** to go to a different location, and then click **Next**.

3. Under **Logging**, select a logging mode and enter a name for the log file or template.

   Click **Default** to use the logging mode specified in the INI file; click **Verbose** to use all logging options. Note that verbose logging creates very large log files.

4. Under **Display**, select a default display setting and click **Next**.

   The wizard searches the administrative installation point for additional packages (MSI files) that you can chain to the Office installation.

5. Select the check boxes next to the packages that you want to include in your custom INI file, add packages or programs (EXE files) stored in another location, and then click **Next**.

6. Use the arrow keys to determine the order in which you want Setup.exe to install the chained packages.

   The System Files Update package is always installed first (if required), followed by the Office XP package. You can change the order in which subsequent chained packages are installed.

7. Select each package, specify the options you want for that package, and click **Next**.

   For each package you can specify an MST file and a unique display setting, as well as additional property values.

8. To add additional property-value pairs to your custom INI file, select a package, click **Advanced Properties**, enter the properties and values you want, and then click **Next**.

   The wizard displays a summary of the changes to save in the custom INI file.

9. Click **Save As** and enter a name and path for your INI file.

   The wizard supplies you with a sample Setup command line that specifies your custom INI file with the **/settings** option.

10. Click **Finish** to exit the wizard.

    Note Do not overwrite the original Setup.ini file. If you want Setup to use your custom INI file, copy Setup.exe and rename it to match the name of your custom INI file. In this case, Setup uses your custom INI file by default, and you do not need to use the **/settings** option.

How to distribute a custom INI file

When you edit the default Setup settings file (Setup.ini), users can run Setup without using command-line options to install Office with your customizations.

To create multiple custom installations that use different Setup options, you can create several custom INI files that have different names and store them in the root folder of the administrative installation point. Users specify the name of a settings file by using the **/settings** Setup command-line option. You can simplify this process by creating an MS-DOS batch file or Windows shortcut that contains the appropriate **/settings** command-line option.

> **Note** If your custom INI file is stored in any location other than the folder that contains Setup.exe, you must include the relative or absolute path with the **/settings** option. For example:
>
> `Setup.exe /settings \\server\share\files\setup\off10eng.ini`

If you run Setup from a network logon script or through a systems management tool (such as Systems Management Server), then you must edit the Setup command line in the script or deployment package to refer to the appropriate settings file by using the **/settings** option.

You can create multiple custom INI files for different groups of users. For example, you might want to deploy the French and Spanish Language Packs with Office to your Accounting department, but give users in your Engineering department their choice of languages in the Multilingual User Interface Pack Wizard. In this case, you can create two custom INI files: one that chains the French and Spanish Lpk.msi packages, and another that chains the Lpkwiz.msi package. Users in each department run Setup by using one of the following command lines:

`setup.exe /settings off10act.ini`
`setup.exe /settings off10eng.ini`

> **Note** When you create a custom INI file, you can also specify options on the Setup command line. If you specify a command-line option that conflicts with a value in the INI file, Setup uses the command-line option.

Storing values in a transform

When you install Office XP from an administrative installation point, you can customize the Office XP configuration that is installed on users' computer by applying a Windows Installer transform (MST file). Many of the customizations that you make in Setup.ini or on the command line can also be made in a transform, but some tasks are better handled in a transform. For example, a transform is typically used to set default installation states for Office XP features or to specify default application settings.

You create a Windows Installer transform by using the Office Custom Installation Wizard. The transform contains the changes that you want to make to the Windows Installer package (MSI file). When you apply the transform during the installation, your modifications become the default settings for anyone who runs Setup from your administrative installation point. If you run Setup in quiet mode (with no user interaction), your selections define precisely how Office is installed on users' computers.

Toolbox   The Office XP Resource Kit core tool set includes the Custom Installation Wizard, which is installed by default when you run the Office Resource Kit Setup program. The wizard includes a detailed Help file. For more information, see "Custom Installation Wizard" in the Toolbox.

When to use a transform

A Windows Installer transform is most useful when you want to make extensive customizations, particularly customizations that you cannot readily make by using the Setup command line or Setup settings file. By creating multiple transforms, you can also install different Office XP configurations to different groups of users from the same administrative installation point.

When you create a transform, the Custom Installation Wizard allows you to do the following:

- Define the path where Office is installed on users' computers.
- Define the default installation state for all Office XP applications and features.

  For example, you can install Microsoft Word on the local computer, but set Microsoft PowerPoint® to be installed on demand or run from the network. You can also hide and lock features so that users cannot make changes after Office XP is installed.

- Add your own files and registry entries to Setup so that they are installed with Office.
- Modify Office application shortcuts, specifying where they are installed and customizing their properties.
- Define a list of servers for Office to use if the primary administrative installation point is unavailable.
- Specify other products to install or programs to run on users' computers after Setup is completed.
- Configure Microsoft Outlook.

  For example, specify a default user profile.

- Specify which previous versions of Office are removed.

You can create transforms for other chained Windows Installer packages, including the MUI Packs and the System Files Update. By using the Microsoft Internet Explorer Administration Kit (which you can call from the Custom Installation Wizard), you can also customize how Internet Explorer is installed on users' computers during the System Files Update installation.

Note   Office XP Setup automatically matches MUI Pack feature installation states to the corresponding features in the core English version of Office. If you specify different installation states for MUI Pack features in a transform, you must set the **NOFEATURESTATEMIGRATION** property to **True** to override the default matching behavior.

How to apply a transform during Office installation

For users to install Office with your customizations, you must specify the name and path to the transform by setting the **TRANSFORMS** property on the command line or by adding an entry to the appropriate section of the Setup settings file.

For example, to direct Setup to use the transform Custom.mst (stored in the same folder as Setup.exe), you use the following Setup command line:

```
setup.exe TRANSFORMS=custom.mst
```

You can also specify a transform in the Setup INI Customization Wizard. In the **Transform (MST file) to apply during installation** box, select the Office XP package and enter <*path*> **Custom.mst**. This step adds the following entry to the [MST] section of Setup.ini:

```
MST1=Custom.mst
```

On the same page of the wizard, you can select other packages that you added to the installation — including the System Files Update and chained packages — and specify a transform. The wizard records this information in the appropriate sections of Setup.ini. (Note that the property used to specify a transform for the System Files Update differs from other packages included in Setup.ini.) For example:

```
[SystemPackOptions]
TRANSFORMS=SystemPack.mst
[ChainedInstall_1]
MST=French.mst
```

> **Note** If you misspell the **TRANSFORMS** option on the command line as **TRANSFORM** (singular), then Setup automatically corrects it during the call to Windows Installer. However, if you enter **TRANSFORM=** in the [SystemPackOptions] section of Setup.ini, then the incorrect option is passed to Windows Installer, but your transform is not applied. You can avoid this error by using the Setup INI Customization Wizard to specify a transform for the System Files Update.

If you create unique transforms for different groups of users, you must specify — on the command line or in Setup.ini — which transform to use. For example, users in your Accounting department might need all the add-ins included with Microsoft Excel, and users in the Engineering department might need a custom set of Microsoft Access features. In this scenario, you can create different transforms that specify different feature installation states for Excel and Access features, and then create two shortcuts on the administrative installation point by using the following command lines:

```
setup.exe TRANSFORMS=off10eng.mst
setup.exe TRANSFORMS=off10act.mst
```

> **Note** You can apply a transform only when Office is initially installed. To make changes to an Office configuration after Office is installed, you must use the Custom Maintenance Wizard. For more information, see "Changing Feature Installation States" in Chapter 8, "Maintaining an Installation."

Resolving conflicting Setup options

Office XP offers many ways to customize an Office XP installation, and using a combination of methods can result in conflicting settings. If you specify different values for the same Setup options on the Setup command line, in the Setup settings file, and in a transform, then Setup uses the following rules to determine which value to use:

- If you set an option in the Custom Installation Wizard that corresponds to a Setup property, the wizard sets the corresponding property automatically in the MST file.

    For example, if you select the **Upgrade to Internet Explorer 5** option on the **Customize Internet Explorer 5 Installation Options** page, the wizard sets the **NOIE** property to **False**.

- If you modify a Setup property on the **Modify Setup Properties** page of the Custom Installation Wizard, this setting overrides any corresponding options that you set on previous pages of the wizard. Your modified Setup property is written to the MST file.

- If you set options (including Setup properties) in the Setup settings file that conflict with options in the transform, then the values in the INI file take precedence over the transform.

- If you set options on the command line, those settings take precedence over any conflicting values in either the INI file or the transform.

Customizing How Setup Runs

You can always run Setup interactively to install Microsoft Office XP — or allow users to run Setup interactively. However, by using command-line options or setting values for Setup properties in the Setup settings file (Setup.ini) or in a transform (MST file), you can customize the way Setup installs Office XP throughout your organization.

You can set most properties that control the behavior of Setup in one of three locations, listed in order of precedence:

- On the command line
- In the Setup settings file (Setup.ini)
- On the **Modify Setup Properties** page of the Custom Installation Wizard, which stores your settings in a transform (MST file)

    Note that settings specified on the **Modify Setup Properties** page override any corresponding settings specified on previous pages of the wizard.

    Toolbox   The Office XP Resource Kit core tool set includes the Custom Installation Wizard and Setup INI Customization Wizard. These wizards are installed by default when you run the Office Resource Kit Setup program. For more information, see "Custom Installation Wizard" or "Setup INI Customization Wizard" in the Toolbox.

Display settings

When you distribute Office XP throughout an organization, you can determine how much of the Setup user interface is displayed to users. You can allow users to interact fully with Setup and make choices that differ from the defaults you specify, or you can run Setup silently so that your configuration of Office is installed with no questions asked. You can even set different display settings for different portions of the installation process.

The following display settings are available:

- **None**

    No user interface is displayed; Office is installed silently.

- **Basic**

    Only simple progress indicators and error messages are displayed. To display only progress indicators, append a minus sign to the command-line option (**/qb-**).

- **Reduced**

    Full progress indicators and error messages are displayed, but Setup collects no information from the user.

- **Full**

    All dialog boxes and messages are displayed to the user, and the user can enter information during the Setup process.

When you run Office XP Setup silently or with only the basic user interface, you can also determine whether users see a completion message when the installation is finished. A completion notice is displayed only when Setup does not have to restart the computer to complete the installation.

You set all these display options on the command line by using the **/q** switch or in the [Display] section of Setup.ini, as shown in the following table. In the Setup INI Customization Wizard, you select a value for the **DISPLAY** property in the **Default display setting** box.

Display setting	Command-line option	Setup.ini value
None	/q or /qn	DISPLAY=None
Basic	/qb or /qb-	DISPLAY=Basic
Reduced	/qr	DISPLAY=Reduced
Full	/qf	DISPLAY=Full
Completion message on	+ (e.g., /qn+ or /qb+)	COMPLETIONNOTICE=Yes

Display settings like the **/q***option* are passed globally to every installation. For example, if you set this option on the command line or in the [Display] section of Setup.ini, all Office XP–related installations, including chained Office Multilingual User Interface Packs and the System Files Update, are installed with the same level of user interface, unless you set a different display setting for just those packages.

> **Toolbox** You can find detailed information about Setup options and properties in Setupref.doc, which is installed by default when you run the Office XP Resource Kit Setup program. This document also describes the format of the Setup settings file. For more information, see "Supplemental Documentation" in the Toolbox.

Install Office quietly

By default, Setup installs Office XP with a full user interface and displays a completion notice at the end of the installation. In many large organizations, however, it is more efficient to install Office without any user interaction. In this case, the recommended setting is **/qb-**, which installs Office as follows:

- Progress indicators are displayed during the installation.
- Error messages and other modal dialog boxes are not displayed.
- Setup restarts the computer automatically, if a restart is required (for example, when Internet Explorer is installed).
- Setup displays a completion notice when the installation is finished.

When you run Office XP Setup with a basic or reduced display, users can still click the **Cancel** button to stop the installation process. However, if you set the **NOCANCEL** property to **True**, then the **Cancel** button is displayed but is unavailable. Users know that the installation is occurring and they know when it is complete, but they cannot interrupt the process.

You can install Office XP with no user interface whatsoever by using the **/qn** option or setting the **DISPLAY** property to **None**. If you are using a deployment tool such as Microsoft Systems Management Server to run the installation when users are not logged on, then you must use this display setting.

Set unique display settings for other packages

In some circumstances, you might want to specify different display options for different packages installed with Office XP. You must use Setup.ini to override global display settings set on the command line or in the [Display] section of Setup.ini.

For example, if you install Office XP with a full user interface, you can install the System Files Update quietly to ensure that system files and Internet Explorer are updated the same way for every user. In this case, you enter the following in the [SystemPack] section of Setup.ini:

```
[SystemPack]
DISPLAY=Basic
```

Similarly, if you install Office XP quietly, but you want users to choose their MUI Packs in the Multilingual User Interface Pack Wizard, you can specify a full user interface for each chained MUI Pack package in the appropriate section of Setup.ini. For example:

```
[ChainedInstall_1]
DISPLAY=Full
```

You can modify display settings for all chained packages at once by using the Setup INI Customization Wizard. The wizard adds the correct entries to the correct sections of the INI file and helps prevent you from inadvertently specifying conflicting settings.

To modify display settings by using the Setup INI Customization Wizard

1. Start the Setup INI Customization Wizard and enter information about your administrative installation point, Setup settings file, and packages to include in the installation.
2. Select the package for which you want to change display settings and select a new value in the **Display setting** box.

   Note If you specify a display setting on the command line, that setting overrides any display settings specified in any section of Setup.ini.

Customize the Setup user interface

When you run Office XP Setup with a full user interface, you can customize some of the text and buttons that users see by setting properties on the command line, in Setup.ini, or on the **Modify Setup Properties** page of the Custom Installation Wizard.

For example, if a user selects the **Customize** option, Setup prompts the user for the installation location and then displays a list of Office applications or a hierarchy of Office features so that the user can select an installation state for each one. You can change descriptive text for the **Customize** option. For example, if you have omitted Microsoft Access from the installation, but you want to tell users how to install it for themselves, specify the following:

```
CUSTOMINSTALLDESCRIPTION="By default Access is not installed. Click
Customize to install Access on your computer."
```

You can also customize the descriptive text for the **Typical**, **Complete**, and **Run from Network** options. Similar properties customize the **Install Now** and **Upgrade Now** button labels and descriptive text. All of these properties are defined in the following table.

Property	Default value
TYPICALINSTALLTEXT	&Install Now
TYPICALUPGRADETEXT	&Upgrade Now
TYPICALINSTALLDESCRIPTION	Installs Microsoft Office with the default settings, including the most commonly used components.
TYPICALUPGRADEDESCRIPTION	Upgrades your Microsoft Office installation. Setup will remove your previous versions, and install based on your current configuration.
RUNFROMSOURCEINSTALLDESCRIPTION	Installs only the files that must be copied to your computer. Access to the installation source will be required to run Office.
CUSTOMINSTALLDESCRIPTION	Customize your Microsoft Office installation, selecting which Office applications and features to install on your computer.
COMPLETEINSTALLDESCRIPTION	Installs all of Microsoft Office on your computer, including all optional components and tools.

In Microsoft Windows 2000 only, you can also customize what users see in **Add/Remove Programs** when they run Office XP Setup in maintenance mode. For example, to prevent users from changing an installed Office configuration, you can set the Setup property **ARPMODIFY** to **True** in a transform. When users run Office XP Setup in maintenance mode, the **Change** button in **Add/Remove Programs** is unavailable.

Logging options

Both Office XP Setup and Windows Installer generate log files during the installation process. You cannot set options for the Setup log file; however, Windows Installer allows you to set a number of logging options that apply to each package that it installs during Office XP Setup. Note that any logging options you set apply to all log files created by Windows Installer during the Office XP installation.

You set Windows Installer logging options and specify a log file name on the command line by using the **/l** option. For example:

`/lv+ "Office Setup(*).txt"`

> **Note** If your custom log file name includes spaces, you must enclose it in quotation marks on the command line.

You can set the same options by specifying values in the [Logging] section of the Setup settings file. Valid logging options include the following.

Option	Information written to the log file
I	Information-only messages
W	Warning messages
E	Error messages
F	List of files in use
A	Start-of-action notification
R	Action data record, containing action-specific information
U	User-request messages
C	Initial user-interface parameters
M	Out-of-memory messages
p	Property table list, written in the form *property* = *value*
v	Verbose; includes debug messages
*	Turns on all options except **v**
+	Appends to the log file if it already exists

The default — and recommended — logging options are **piwae**. Verbose logging can slow the installation significantly and produce very large log files. Verbose logging is generally useful only to diagnose installation problems during the testing phase or after a failed installation.

In Setup.ini, you specify the same logging options by setting the **TYPE** property, and you determine a name for the log files by setting the **TEMPLATE** property. The following example shows the syntax used in Setup.ini:

```
[Logging]
TYPE= <options>
PATH=<path>
TEMPLATE=<file name>.txt
```

You must include the .txt file extension when you specify a Setup log file name. Appending an asterisk (*) to the file name results in a unique log file for each installation performed by Setup.exe. The same log file name is used for each Windows Installer log file, with the task number from Setup.ini appended to the file name. For example:

```
[Logging]
TYPE= v+
PATH=%Temp%
TEMPLATE=OfficeSetup(*).txt
```

These values create the following verbose log files during the installation process, append any new log files to the existing log files, and store them in the %Temp% folder on each user's computer. (%Temp% is the default location for log files.)

Log file	Description
OfficeSetup(0001).txt	Setup.exe log file
OfficeSetup(0001)_Task(0001).txt	System Files Update log file
OfficeSetup(0001)_Task(0002).txt	Office XP log file
OfficeSetup(0001)_Task(0003).txt	Log file for first chained package

The Setup INI Customization Wizard allows you to specify logging options for the entire installation. (You cannot set unique logging options for chained packages.)

To modify logging options by using the Setup INI Customization Wizard

1. Start the Setup INI Customization Wizard and enter information about your administrative installation point and Setup settings file.

2. In the **Logging mode** box, select **Default** or **Verbose**.

3. In the **Log file name or template** box, enter the name of the template file.

For more information about Windows Installer properties and options, see the Windows Installer section of the MSDN Online Library at http://msdn.microsoft.com/library/default.asp?URL=/library/psdk/msi/pref_9z1v.htm.

System Files Update options

Unless you are installing Office XP on Windows 2000 or Microsoft Windows Millennium Edition (Windows Me), Office XP Setup automatically checks to see whether key system and shared files are up-to-date, based on the file names and minimum versions listed in the [SystemPack_DetectionFileList] section of Setup.ini.

If the computer passes this test, Setup proceeds directly to the Office XP installation. If it fails this test, Setup calls Windows Installer to install the System Files Update and update the files — including installing Internet Explorer 5.01.

If you are installing Office XP on Microsoft Windows NT 4.0 or Microsoft Windows 98, you can control this default Setup behavior by using the following command-line options:

- **/nosp**

    Setup skips the detection process and does not install the System Files Update.

- **/spforce**

    Setup installs the System Files Update even if the computer passes the detection check.

- **/sponly**

    Setup installs the System Files Update but does not chain the Office XP package.

You can also set the **NOIE** property to **True** on the command line, in the [SystemPackOptions] section of the Setup settings file (Setup.ini), or on the **Modify Setup Properties** page of the Custom Installation Wizard. Setting **NOIE** to **True** prevents Setup from upgrading the computer to Internet Explorer 5.01, except for required components such as Windows Web Browsing Components and HTML Help.

> **Note** Because Windows 2000 and Windows Me already have the required level of system files, the System Files Update detection and installation process does not run on these operating systems, nor can you use **/spforce** or **/sponly** to trigger the System Files Update or upgrade Internet Explorer.

Installation location

By default, Setup installs Office XP in the Program Files\Microsoft Office\Office10 folder on each user's computer. You can change this location by specifying a different path for the **INSTALLLOCATION** property.

In the Office Custom Installation Wizard, you can specify a default value for the installation location on the **Specify Default Path and Organization** page. You can also specify the location by setting the **INSTALLLOCATION** property on the **Modify Setup Properties** page of the wizard, on the Setup command line, or in the Setup settings file.

> **Note** Unlike previous versions, Office XP is always installed in a version-specific folder. If you choose to retain a previous version of Office on the computer, you can specify the same custom location without overwriting any files.

Setup error messages and failure reporting

Office XP Setup allows you to customize the error messages that users see when they run Setup with a full or reduced user interface. For example, you can add text to the error message box that refers users to an internal support group. Specify a string value for the **SUPPORTERRORSTRING** property on the command line, in Setup.ini, or in a transform.

Microsoft Office Application Error Reporting (Dw.exe) also allows you to report Setup failures directly to Microsoft. By default, this feature is turned off when you create an administrative installation point. However, you can turn it back on by setting the **SETUPDW** property to **True**. Note that, unlike Application Error Reporting for application failures after installation, you cannot redirect Setup failure reporting to an internal Web site.

For more information on reporting application failures after installation, see "Reporting Office Application Crashes" in Chapter 8, "Maintaining an Installation."

Customizing Office Features and Shortcuts

When you install Microsoft Office XP from an administrative installation point, you can determine which applications and features are installed on users' computers, including how and when features are installed. You can also customize the way that Setup creates shortcuts for Office XP applications and even add your own custom files to the Office installation.

Selecting Office features

When running Office Setup interactively, users can choose which Office applications and features are installed by selecting options from the feature tree that Setup displays. Office features can be installed in any of the following states:

- Copied to the local hard disk
- Run from the network server
- Installed on first use, which means that Setup does not install the feature until the first time it is used
- Not installed, but accessible to users through **Add/Remove Programs** or the command line
- Not installed, not displayed during Setup, and not accessible to users after Office is installed

By using the Office Custom Installation Wizard, you can make these choices for users ahead of time. When users run Setup interactively, the installation states that you specify in the transform (MST file) appear as the default selections. When you run Setup quietly, your choices determine how the features are installed.

> **Toolbox** The Office XP Resource Kit includes the Custom Installation Wizard, which is installed by default when you run the Office Resource Kit Setup program. For information about specific options and settings, you can click the **Help** button on any page of the wizard. For more information, see "Custom Installation Wizard" in the Toolbox.

Set the installation state for features

The **Set Feature Installation States** page of the Custom Installation Wizard displays the same feature tree that users see when they select the **Customize** option during Setup. The feature tree is a hierarchy. Parent features contain child features, and child features can contain subordinate child features. For example, the **Microsoft Word for Windows** feature includes the child feature **Help**. The **Help** feature includes the child feature **Help for WordPerfect Users**.

When you click a feature in the feature tree, you can select one of the following installation states:

- **Run from My Computer**

   Setup copies files and writes registry entries and shortcuts associated with the feature to the user's hard disk, and the application or feature runs locally.

- **Run all from My Computer**

   Same as **Run from My Computer**, except that all child features belonging to the feature are also set to this state.

- **Run from Network**

   Setup leaves components for the feature on the administrative installation point, and the feature is run from there.

- **Run all from Network**

    Same as **Run from Network**, except that all child features belonging to the feature are also set to this state.

    Note that some child features do not support **Run from Network**; these child features are installed on the local computer.

- **Installed on First Use**

    Setup leave components for the feature and all its child features on the administrative installation point until the user first attempts to use the feature, at which time the components are automatically copied to the local hard disk.

    Note that some child features do not support **Installed on First Use**; these features are installed on the local computer.

- **Not Available**

    The components for the feature, and all of the child features belonging to the feature, are not installed on the computer.

- **Not Available, Hidden, and Locked**

    The components for the feature are not installed and the feature does not appear in the feature tree during Setup — nor can users install it by changing the state of the parent feature or by calling Windows Installer directly from the command line.

Not all installation states are available for every feature. For example, if a feature contains a component that cannot be run over the network, then **Run from Network** is not included in the list of available installation states.

When you change the installation state of a feature, Windows Installer may automatically change the installation state of a parent or child feature to match. If you set the **Help** feature to **Installed on First Use**, for example, but set the child feature **Help for WordPerfect Users** to **Run from My Computer**, then Setup installs the entire **Help** feature on the local hard disk.

> **Tip** If you run the Custom Installation Wizard (Custwiz.exe) with the **/x** command-line option, the wizard displays the feature tree fully expanded on the **Set Feature Installation States** page.

Hide or lock features during Setup

In addition to setting the installation state, you can right-click any feature on the **Set Feature Installation States** page and click **Hide** to hide the feature from the user. Setup does not display hidden features in the feature tree when users run Setup interactively; instead, the feature is installed behind the scenes according to the installation state that you have specified. When you hide a feature, all of the child features belonging to the feature are also hidden.

The best use of the **Hide** setting is to simplify the feature tree for users. For example, you might hide the **Office Tools** branch of the feature tree so that users do not have to decide which tools they need. Only the tools that you select are installed.

> **Note** When you edit the transform in the Custom Installation Wizard, you can reverse the **Hide** setting by right-clicking the feature and clicking **Unhide**. However, you cannot use the Custom Maintenance Wizard to expose a hidden feature after Office is installed.

Even if you set a feature to **Not Available** and hide it in the feature tree, users can still change the setting and install the feature by installing the parent feature or by running Office XP in maintenance mode. For example, if you set the **Help for WordPerfect Users** feature to **Not Available** and hide it, users can still install it by setting the parent **Help** feature to **Run All from My Computer**.

If you want to prevent users from installing hidden features, choose the **Not Available, Hidden, and Locked** installation state. In this case, the feature or application is not installed and is not available in maintenance mode. Users cannot install it by changing the state of the parent feature or by calling Windows Installer directly from the command line. The only way to change the **Not Available, Hidden, and Locked** installation state after Office XP is installed is to use the Custom Maintenance Wizard.

> **Toolbox** The Office XP Resource Kit includes the Custom Maintenance Wizard, which is installed by default when you run the Office Resource Kit Setup program. For more information, see "Custom Maintenance Wizard" in the Toolbox.

When users install Office, Setup does not display the feature tree by default. Clicking the **Customize** option displays a top-level list of Office applications. Users can select the check box next to an application to install a typical set of features. When you set an Office application to **Not Available, Hidden, and Locked**, the check box on this page remains visible but appears grayed out — users cannot select the application. To remove the check box altogether, set the **SKIPCHECKBOX** property to **True**.

For more information about changing feature installation states after Office XP is installed, see "Changing Feature Installation States" in Chapter 8, "Maintaining an Installation."

Disable installation states that rely on a network connection

Installing features on demand or running features over the network is not always efficient. Both of these installation states require a fast connection and reliable access to the administrative installation point on the network — which laptop users in the field might not always have.

The Custom Installation Wizard for Office XP includes two new options on the **Set Feature Installation States** page that disable these installation states and help ensure that users do not reset features to these states during Setup or in maintenance mode:

- **Disable Run from Network**

  When you select a feature in the feature tree and then select this check box, users are prevented from setting the feature to run from the network — the installation state does not appear in the list of options during initial Setup or in maintenance mode.

- **Disable Installed on First Use**

  When you select a feature in the feature tree and then select this check box, users are prevented from setting the feature to be installed on first use — the installation state does not appear in the list of options during initial Setup or in maintenance mode.

Child features do not inherit these settings from parent features. You must select each feature in the tree and set **Disable Run from Network** or **Disable Installed on First Use** for only that feature.

> **Note** The **Disable Run from Network** and **Disable Installed on First Use** properties remain in effect for as long as Office is installed on the user's computer. You cannot reverse these settings by using the Custom Maintenance Wizard.

Modify intelligent Setup behavior

To make an Office XP installation more efficient, Setup automatically sets default feature installation states in the following circumstances:

- When you upgrade to Office XP, Setup detects and matches feature installation states from the previous version.

  For example, if Microsoft Word 2000 is installed to run from the network, Setup installs Word 2002 to run from the network. If Microsoft Access 2000 is set to **Not Available**, Setup does not install Access 2002.

- When you install MUI Packs from the Office Multilingual User Interface Pack, Setup matches the feature installation states specified for the core version of Office.

  For example, if the core English version of Microsoft PowerPoint 2002 is set to be installed on demand, then Setup automatically sets international versions of PowerPoint 2002 features to **Installed on First Use**.

- When you install Office under Windows Terminal Services, Setup applies the most efficient installation state for each feature.

  For example, because the speech recognition feature does not run efficiently over most networks and might not be supported by all clients, Windows Terminal Services automatically changes the feature installation state from **Installed on First Use** to **Not Available**.

This intelligent Setup behavior works to your advantage in most situations. However, you can override Setup and specify your own default feature installation states in a transform by using one of the following two settings:

- **NOFEATURESTATEMIGRATION** property

  Setting this property to **True** for the Office XP package overrides intelligent Setup behavior for the entire package. Note that this property has no affect on Windows Terminal Services logic; you must override optional Windows Terminal Services installation states on a per-feature basis.

- **Do Not Migrate Previous Installation State** check box on the **Set Feature Installation States** page of the Custom Installation Wizard

  Selecting an Office XP feature in the feature tree and then selecting this check box overrides intelligent Setup behavior and enforces the installation state you set in the transform. (If you have already set the **NOFEATURESTATEMIGRATION** property for the entire package, then selecting this check box for a given feature has no effect.) Note that this setting has no effect on default feature installation state matching for MUI Pack features.

The following table summarizes the results of setting the property for an Office XP package or selecting the check box for a feature.

Package	Property set to True	Check box selected
Office	Default feature installation state migration is disabled for all of Office.	Does not apply the installation state from a previous version to the selected feature.
MUI Pack	Default feature installation state matching is disabled for the entire package.	Has no effect on default feature installation state matching.
Proofing Tools	Default feature installation state matching is disabled for the entire package.	Has no effect on default feature installation state matching.

The **NOFEATURESTATEMIGRATION** property has no effect on Windows Terminal Services logic. However, you can select the **Do Not Migrate Previous Installation State** check box to override default Windows Terminal Services settings for some features. For example, if your network and clients support the speech recognition feature, you can set that feature to **Run from My Computer** and select the **Do Not Migrate Previous Installation State** check box to enforce your setting.

> **Note** You cannot override all of the installation states set by default under Windows Terminal Services. For example, Windows Terminal Services does not allow any feature to be set to **Installed on First Use**.

Adding files to the installation

In addition to selecting what Office files are installed, Setup allows you to add your own files to the Office installation. You can deploy corporate templates, images, custom applications, or other files along with Office. On the **Add/Remove Files to the Installation** page of the Office Custom Installation Wizard, click **Add** to add a new file to the installation.

After you select one or more files to add, enter the destination path for the file or files in the **File Destination Path** dialog box. You can enter an absolute path on the user's computer, or you can select a path from the list. If you select a path, you can add a subfolder to it by appending a backslash (\) followed by the subfolder name. When you click **OK**, the wizard adds the file to the transform. Setup installs the file on the user's computer, in the folder you specified, when the user installs Office.

> **Note** Files that you add to the installation on this page are not removed if the user subsequently modifies the file or removes, repairs, or reinstalls Office.

After you add the file, you can add a shortcut for the file on the **Add, Modify, or Remove Shortcuts** page of the wizard. On that page, click **Add** — the file you added appears in the **Target** box. Because the file is copied into the transform, you must update the transform if the file changes later on.

To update the installation with modified files

1. On the **Create or Open the MST File** page, enter the name of the Windows Installer transform (MST file).
2. On the **Select the MST File to Save** page, enter the name of the MST file again.
3. Click **Next** until you reach the **Add/Remove Files to the Installation** page.
4. Select the file that has changed, and click **Remove**.
5. Click **Add**, and then enter the information for your modified file.

The Custom Installation Wizard also allows you to specify files to remove from users' computers when Office is installed. For example, you can have Setup delete custom templates designed for Word 97 or Word 2000 when you upgrade to Word 2002. Click the **Remove Files** tab to list files to remove.

For more information about adding or removing files by using a transform, see the Custom Installation Wizard Help file.

Customizing Office shortcuts

By using the Office Custom Installation Wizard, you can customize the shortcuts that Setup creates for Microsoft Office applications and files. You can control what shortcuts are installed, and you can also specify which folder the shortcut is stored in and what command-line options to use with the shortcut.

On the **Add, Modify, or Remove Shortcuts** page, the Custom Installation Wizard displays shortcuts for all the features that you selected on the **Set Feature Installation States** page.

An additional tab displays shortcuts for Office XP features that you did not set to be installed. Use the **Shortcuts Not Installed** tab to customize shortcuts for applications that you plan to install later. For example, if you omitted Access 2002 from your initial installation, you can use the Custom Maintenance Wizard to install Access later. Because the Custom Maintenance Wizard does not allow you to customize the way shortcuts are installed, however, you can customize Access shortcuts ahead of time in the transform.

Modify an existing shortcut

On the **Add, Modify, or Remove Shortcuts** page, you modify any existing shortcut by selecting the shortcut and clicking **Modify**. In the **Add/Modify Shortcut Entry** dialog box, you can make the following modifications:

- **Target**

  Change the application associated with the shortcut. The names in the list correspond to features that you selected on the **Set Feature Installation States** page of the wizard, plus any custom files that you added to the installation on the **Add Files to the Installation** page. You can add command-line options by appending a space and a list of options to the target name.

  For example, to customize the Microsoft Word shortcut to open a Word document as a template, select **<Microsoft Word>** and append the **/t** option as follows:

  ```
  <microsoft word> /t "c:\Tools\Accounting Forms.doc"
  ```

- **Location**

  Change the folder in which the shortcut is created by selecting a location from the list. You can specify a subfolder by appending a backslash (\) followed by the subfolder name.

For example, to install the Microsoft Word shortcut in the Microsoft Office XP subfolder in the Programs folder in the **Start** menu, select **<StartMenu\Programs>** and append the subfolder name as follows:

`<startmenu\programs>\Microsoft Office XP`

- **Name**

    Change the name of the shortcut by entering any string.

- **Start in**

    Change the starting folder for the application by entering a path. The path must be a valid path on the user's computer. If it is not a valid path, the user sees an error message when trying to use the shortcut.

- **Shortcut key**

    Associate a shortcut key with this shortcut by entering the shortcut key string in this box. Click the **Help** button in the wizard for a description of how to specify a shortcut key.

- **Run**

    Select how you want the application to run when the user double-clicks this shortcut. For example, if you want the application to run in a maximized window by default, then select **Maximized**.

- **Change Icon**

    Select a new icon for the shortcut.

Add or remove shortcuts

You can click **Add** to add a new shortcut for any file being installed by Setup. This step allows you to create duplicate shortcuts for the most frequently used Office applications on the user's computer. It also allows you to create shortcuts for custom files or applications that you add to the installation.

To remove a shortcut from the list, select the shortcut and click **Remove**.

Create Windows Installer shortcuts

Windows Installer shortcuts support automatic repair of Office features and allow you to advertise Office applications. Advertised applications are installed the first time a user clicks the shortcut or opens a file associated with the application. If the computer does not support Windows Installer shortcuts, then any feature set to **Installed on First Use** is installed on the local hard disk, and Setup creates a standard Windows shortcut.

By default, Setup creates Windows Installer shortcuts on any computer that supports them. The following operating systems support Windows Installer shortcuts:

- Microsoft Windows 2000 or later
- Microsoft Windows Millennium Edition (Windows Me)

- Microsoft Windows 98
- Microsoft Windows NT 4.0 Service Pack 6a, if you also install either Microsoft Internet Explorer 4.01 Service Pack 1 or Internet Explorer 5.01 with the Active Desktop® option.

In some circumstances, you might not want Setup to create Windows Installer shortcuts. For example, if you are deploying to roaming users who sometimes log on to computers that do not support Windows Installer shortcuts, you can circumvent the default behavior by clearing the **Create Windows Installer shortcuts if supported** check box on the **Add, Modify, or Remove Shortcuts** page.

For more information about updating Windows NT 4.0 to support Windows Installer shortcuts, see "Using Windows Installer Shortcuts with Office" in Chapter 7, "Deploying on Windows NT 4.0."

Migrate or clean up custom shortcuts from previous versions

Office users can create shortcuts with custom names or command-line options. For example, a custom shortcut might open a particular document whenever Word is started. In previous versions of Office, these shortcuts were left behind and broken when users upgraded to a new version of Office. When you upgrade to Office XP, however, Setup automatically migrates custom shortcuts to point to the corresponding Office XP application.

For example, if you create a shortcut to Word 2000 on the Desktop, Setup replaces it with a shortcut to Word 2002. If you associated a custom command line with the shortcut, Setup preserves that as well.

> **Note** Custom shortcuts for previous versions of Access are not updated to point to Access 2002 when you upgrade.

How Setup handles custom shortcut migration

Setup handles shortcut migration for each application separately. If you upgrade most of your applications to Office XP but retain Microsoft Excel 2000, for example, then all your shortcuts point to the correct versions — Office XP applications and Excel 2000.

If you install more than one version of the same application on your computer — for example, both Excel 2000 and Excel 2002 — then Setup updates all custom shortcuts to point to the Office XP application. (Default shortcuts from the previous version are left unchanged.) In this multiple-version scenario, you might later uninstall Office XP; however, your custom shortcuts are not migrated back to the previous version.

If you are installing Office XP in a multiple-version environment, and you do not want to update custom shortcuts to point to the new version, you can prevent Setup from upgrading existing custom shortcuts. Set the **DISABLESCMIGRATION** property to **True** in a transform or on the command line.

Setup handles migration of custom shortcuts in the following circumstances:

- When Office XP is first installed
- When an advertised Office XP application is installed
- When the installation state of an installed application is changed to **Not Available**

Setup searches the following locations for custom shortcuts:

- Desktop
- **Start** menu, including the **Programs** and **Microsoft Office Tools** submenus
- **Quick Launch** toolbar
- **Office XP Shortcut Bar**

You can specify additional custom shortcuts in other locations by editing the Oclncust.opc file in the Office folder. These shortcuts are migrated when Office is installed. In the OPC file, custom shortcuts are specified by using the following syntax:

```
SHORTCUT=<OPC directory token or drive letter and
colon>\<subdirectory>\<target file name> | <feature> | <version> |
<component> | <command line>
```

To remove a custom shortcut during the installation, you must specify only the target file name — Setup matches the target file name with any shortcut, regardless of the actual shortcut name (LNK file). For example, to remove any custom shortcut to Word in the Office subfolder of the StartMenu\Programs folder, add the following line to the Oclncust.opc file:

```
SHORTCUT=SYSMENUPROGRAMSDIR\Office\winword.exe
```

However, if you want Setup to automatically migrate this custom shortcut to point to Word 2002, add the following line instead:

```
SHORTCUT=SYSMENUPROGRAMSDIR\Office\
winword.exe|WORDFiles||Global_Word_Core
```

> **Note** When a custom Windows Installer shortcut that includes command-line options migrates to Office XP, the new shortcut becomes a normal Windows shortcut. The new shortcut no longer supports install-on-demand functionality, but users can modify the command line after the upgrade.

> **Toolbox** The Office XP Resource Kit includes a file named Opc.doc, which describes in more detail how to customize the OPC file. This file is installed by default when you run the Office Resource Kit Setup program. For more information, see "Supplemental Documentation" in the Toolbox.

How Setup cleans up custom shortcuts

Office XP removes custom shortcuts to Office XP applications more efficiently than past versions. For example, if a user copies a shortcut to Excel 2002 onto the Desktop and then removes Excel 2002 from the computer, Setup automatically removes that shortcut.

In addition to the default locations that Setup checks for custom shortcuts to remove, you can direct Setup to search additional folders for outdated custom shortcuts by setting the **CIWEXTRASHORTCUTDIRS** property in a transform or on the command line. You specify additional locations by using a list delimited by semicolons.

For example, to direct Setup to clean up custom shortcuts in the Startup and Favorites\My Office folders, specify the following:

```
CIWEXTRASHORTCUTDIRS=<StartMenu\Programs\Startup>; <Favorites>\My Office
```

When you specify additional folders, you can use any of the following location tokens, appending other path information to them:

- <Desktop>
- <StartMenu>
- <StartMenu\Programs>
- <StartMenu\Programs\Startup
- <ProgramFiles\Microsoft Office>
- <ApplicationData>
- <Favorites>
- <NetHood>

You can also specify additional locations by using a full path – for example, C:\Office\My Office. Wildcards — both asterisks (*) and question marks (?) — are supported. For example, the following setting causes Setup to search the Start Menu\Programs folder for all folders that include Office in the name:

```
CIWEXTRASHORTCUTDIRS=<StartMenu\Programs\*Office*
```

See also

The Help file in the Custom Installation Wizard contains detailed information about specifying installation options for Office features and shortcuts. For more information about selecting feature installation states, adding and removing files, or customizing shortcuts, click **Help** on the relevant page of the wizard.

Customizing User-defined Settings

Microsoft Office applications are highly customizable. Users can change how Office functions by setting options or adding custom templates or tools. For example, a sales department can create a custom template for invoices or a custom dictionary with industry-specific terms. Users can change everything from the screen resolution to the default file format for saving documents. Most of these user-defined settings are recorded as values in the Windows registry.

If you are an administrator in a large organization, you can customize user-defined settings and distribute a standard Microsoft Office XP configuration to all users. To do this, you first install Office XP on a test computer and then customize toolbars, settings, templates, custom dictionaries, and any other options. Then you run the Profile Wizard to create an Office profile settings file (OPS file) that captures all of these configuration options. If you add the OPS file to a transform (MST file), your customized settings are included when Office XP is installed on client computers.

The Custom Installation Wizard also allows you to customize user-defined settings directly in the transform. You can set user options and add or modify registry entries. You can even add the Profile Wizard to a transform and run it separately to distribute new default settings. When Office is installed, your customizations modify values in the Windows registry, and your settings appear as the defaults on users' computers.

Methods of customizing user settings

The method you choose to customize user-defined settings depends on the following:

- How extensively you want to configure Office XP.

    You can create a custom configuration for all of Office XP or preset just a few key options.

- How complex your deployment scenarios are.

    You can distribute the same custom settings to all the users in your organization, or you can configure Office XP applications differently to meet the needs of different groups of users.

- How and when you deploy Office XP applications.

    If you are staging your Office XP deployment, you can customize only the applications that you are installing at a given time. Or, if you have already deployed Office, you can distribute a standard configuration to all Office XP users.

- Whether you want to enforce your custom settings.

    Settings that you distribute through a transform (MST file) or Office profile settings file (OPS file) appear to users as the default settings — but users can choose different options for themselves. By contrast, using Office XP system policies ensures that your settings are always applied.

The following table lists typical scenarios for customizing user settings and the recommended methods and tools to use in each case.

Scenario	Method	Tool
Distribute a standard default Office XP configuration.	Add an OPS file to a transform.	Profile Wizard and Custom Installation Wizard (**Customize Default Application Settings** page)
Set just a few options or adjust your Office XP configuration without recreating the OPS file.	Add user settings to a transform.	Custom Installation Wizard (**Change Office User Settings** page)
Set default security levels and customize trusted sources list.	Specify security settings in a transform.	Custom Installation Wizard (**Specify Office Security Settings** page)
Set migration and e-mail options for Outlook.	Specify Outlook settings in a transform.	Custom Installation Wizard (**Outlook: Custom Default Settings** page)
Specify settings that are not captured in an OPS file.	Add registry values to a transform.	Custom Installation Wizard (**Add/Remove Registry Entries** page)
Distribute a default Office XP configuration but store one or more OPS files separately from the MST file.	Run the Profile Wizard during Setup.	Profile Wizard and Custom Installation Wizard (**Add Installations and Run Programs** page)
Preserve users' custom settings from a previous version instead of specifying new default settings.	Allow Setup to migrate settings from a previous version of Office.	Default Setup behavior

Scenario (cont'd)	Method	Tool
Set unique options for Office Multilingual User Interface Packs or other chained packages	Specify settings in the transform applied to the chained package.	Custom Installation Wizard and Setup INI Customization Wizard
Distribute a default Office XP configuration that overrides individual users' settings.	Run the Profile Wizard as a stand-alone tool after Office is installed.	Profile Wizard
Modify user settings after Office is installed.	Distribute a configuration maintenance file (CMW file) after Office is installed.	Custom Maintenance Wizard
Prevent users from modifying the options you set.	Set system policies.	System Policy Editor or Windows 2000 Group Policy snap-in

Resolving conflicting settings

Most customized user options correspond to entries in the Windows registry. If you define conflicting values for the same setting, Windows Installer must determine which value to use. In most cases, a setting applied later in the installation process overwrites any settings applied earlier.

Settings for user options are applied in the following order:

1. Settings in an OPS file included in a transform.
2. Settings specified in a transform.

    These settings can be entered on the **Change Office User Settings**, **Specify Office Security Settings**, or **Outlook: Custom Default Settings** pages of the Custom Installation Wizard.

3. Registry values specified in a transform.
4. Settings applied by running the Profile Wizard during Setup.
5. Settings that migrate from a previous version of Office.
6. Settings applied by using the Profile Wizard or Custom Maintenance Wizard after Office is installed.

    This precedence assumes that users have already started each Office XP application and any migrated settings have already been applied.

7. Settings managed through system policies.

Using the Office Profile Wizard

The Office Profile Wizard saves and restores user-defined settings in Office XP applications. Most user-defined settings can be stored in an Office user profile. When you run the Office Profile Wizard to save a user profile, you create an Office profile settings file (OPS file). Setup uses the OPS file to apply default settings when Office XP is installed.

Note If an OPS file contains settings for an application that is not installed, those settings are still written to the registry.

By design, the Profile Wizard excludes some settings, including user-specific information such as the user name and Most Recently Used file list (**File** menu). For example, the Profile Wizard does not capture the following Microsoft Outlook 2002 settings:

- Profile settings, including mail server configuration
- Storage settings, such as default delivery location and personal folder files (PST files)
- E-mail accounts and directories (**Tools|Options|Mail Setup|E-mail Accounts**)
- Send/Receive groups (**Tools|Options|Mail Setup|Send/Receive**)
- Customized views; for example, the fields displayed in the Inbox or another folder
- Outlook Bar shortcuts
- Auto-archive options set for a particular folder, which you set by right-clicking the folder, clicking **Properties**, and choosing options in the **AutoArchive** tab
- Delegate options (**Tools|Options|Delegates**)

In addition, the following Outlook 2002 settings are not captured in an OPS file:

- **Send Immediately when connected** check box (**Tools|Options|Mail Setup**)
- **When forwarding a message** option (**Tools|Options|Preferences|E-mail Options**)
- **Mark my comments with** option (**Tools|Options|Preferences|E-mail Options**)
- **Request secure receipt for all S/MIME signed messages** check box (**Tools|Options|Security**)
- **Show an additional time zone** check box (**Tools|Options|Preferences|Calendar Options|Time Zone**)
- **Automatically decline recurring meeting requests** check box (**Tools|Options|Preferences|Calendar Options|Resource Scheduling**)
- **Automatically decline conflicting meeting requests** check box (**Tools|Options|Preferences|Calendar Options|Resource Scheduling**)
- **Automatically accept meeting requests and process cancellations** check box (**Tools|Options|Preferences|Calendar Options|Resource Scheduling**)

Toolbox The Office XP Resource Kit includes the Office Profile Wizard, which is installed by default when you run the Office Resource Kit Setup program. The wizard includes a detailed Help file. For more information, see "Office Profile Wizard" in the Toolbox.

Add an OPS file to a transform

Adding an OPS file to a transform is a convenient way to deploy a collection of custom settings throughout your organization. Settings contained in the OPS file are implemented when users install Office, and those settings apply to every user who logs on using that computer. However, any other method of customizing user options — including specifying user settings elsewhere in the transform or choosing to migrate settings from a previous version of Office — overwrites default settings in the OPS file.

To customize default options for users in this way, follow these general steps:

1. Use the Profile Wizard to create an OPS file that contains your default settings for Office application options.
2. Use the Custom Installation Wizard to create a transform (MST file) that contains the OPS file.
3. Install Office XP on users' computers with your transform.

Create an OPS file

Before you create an OPS file, you must start each Office application on a test computer and set all the options you want for your users. You can set most options by using the **Options** command (**Tools** menu). To customize toolbars and menus, use the **Customize** command (**Tools** menu). After you have customized the Office applications, you run the Profile Wizard to save the settings to an OPS file.

To save settings to an OPS file

1. Run the Profile Wizard.
2. On the **Save or Restore Settings** page, select Save the settings from this machine, and enter the name and path for the OPS file.
3. Select the check boxes next to the Office XP applications you want to include in your OPS file.
4. Click **Finish**.

    The Profile Wizard saves the Office application settings on your computer to the OPS file.

    Tip For Office XP, the Profile Wizard allows you to save settings for only a selected application or group of applications. This feature is particularly useful when you are staging your Office XP deployment; you can limit the settings saved in the OPS file to only the applications that you are deploying at a given time.

Create a transform that contains your OPS file

You use the Custom Installation Wizard to create a transform that includes the OPS file.

To create a custom transform that contains the OPS file

1. Start the Custom Installation Wizard.
2. On the **Customize Default Application Settings** page, select **Get values from an existing settings profile**, and type the file name and path of the OPS file you created.

The Custom Installation Wizard creates a transform that contains your OPS file and any other customizations you have made.

> **Toolbox**   The Office XP Resource Kit includes the Custom Installation Wizard, which is installed by default when you run the Office Resource Kit Setup program. For more information, see "Custom Installation Wizard" in the Toolbox.

Allow Setup to migrate settings

By default, if a previous version of Office is installed on a user's computer, Windows Installer copies the previous application settings for that version to Office XP. Migrated settings are applied the first time each user starts an Office application, and the user's migrated settings overwrite any duplicate settings contained in an OPS file or added to the transform.

On the **Customize Default Application Settings** page of the Custom Installation Wizard you can modify this Setup behavior. If you are not including an OPS file in the installation, the wizard selects the **Migrate user settings** check box by default. When users install Office XP with your transform, Setup migrates relevant settings from a previous version. If you add an OPS file to the transform, the wizard clears the **Migrate user settings** check box and uses the values in your OPS file instead.

> **Note**   If you add an OPS file to the transform and also select the **Migrate user settings** check box, the settings from your OPS file are applied during the initial installation. However, the first time a user starts an Office application, Windows Installer migrates settings from a previous version of Office and overwrites any corresponding settings previously applied.

Run the Profile Wizard during Setup

Adding an OPS file to the MST file increases the size of the transform and also requires that you recreate the transform whenever you modify the OPS file. Alternatively, you can store the OPS file on a network server and direct Setup to run the Profile Wizard with your OPS file during Office XP installation.

Running the Profile Wizard during Setup applies a standard default Office XP configuration to users' computers. However, because the OPS file is stored separately, you can modify the configuration without changing the transform. You can also create different OPS files for different groups of users.

When you run the Profile Wizard separately, you can choose whether to apply the settings in the OPS file once per user (the recommended option) or once per computer. You can also specify whether user-defined options are returned to their original default settings before your customized settings are applied; this step ensures that all users begin with exactly the same Office XP configuration.

When you add Proflwiz.exe to a transform, the Profile Wizard runs after Office is installed, so settings from this OPS file overwrite any duplicate settings specified in the transform, including the following:

- Settings specified in an OPS file added to a transform
- Settings specified on the **Change Office User Settings** page
- Microsoft Outlook e-mail options specified on the **Outlook: Customize Default Settings** page
- Security levels specified on the **Specify Office Security Settings** page
- Registry entries added on the **Add/Remove Registry Entries** page

Distribute a standard Office user profile

When you add the Profile Wizard to a transform, it runs after Office XP is installed and applies default settings from the OPS file that you specify.

To run the Profile Wizard during Setup

1. Copy the Profile Wizard executable file (Proflwiz.exe) and your customized OPS file to the Office administrative installation point.
2. Start the Custom Installation Wizard.
3. On the **Add Installations and Run Programs** page, click **Add**.
4. In the **Target** box, type the file name and path to Proflwiz.exe, or click **Browse** to select the file.
5. In the **Arguments** box, add command-line options directing the Profile Wizard to apply the OPS file to the user's computer, and then click **OK**.
6. Choose **Run this program only once per machine** to apply your default settings the first time a user logs on.

    — or —

    Choose **Run this program once for each user** to apply your default settings to every user of the computer. Note that this option requires a connection to the network every time a new user logs on. See Help for a complete explanation of the settings for this wizard page.

For example, to run the Profile Wizard from the Profile subfolder in the Office administrative installation point, enter the following in the **Target** box:

\\server\share\admin_install_point\profile\proflwiz.exe

Then add the following command-line options to the **Arguments** box:

```
profile\newprofile.ops /r /q
```

These arguments run the Profile Wizard quietly (**/q**), reset all options to their original default settings (**/r**), and apply settings from the file Newprofile.ops (**profile\newprofile.ops**).

Distribute unique Office user profiles

Storing the OPS file separately allows you to create unique Office XP configurations for different groups of users. You can target unique OPS files to different groups in one of two ways:

- Create a standard user profile, create separate department profiles, and then substitute the department profiles for the standard profile during installation.

  This method is simpler — the appropriate OPS file is included in the transform and default settings are applied when Office is installed. However, it requires keeping track of multiple versions of the OPS file.

- Create a standard user profile, allow department administrators to create separate department profiles, and distribute both profiles during installation.

  This method allows department administrators to deploy Office XP without modifying the corporate installation and apply default settings by running the Profile Wizard during Setup. However, it requires that each department install Office from a separate administrative installation point.

Distribute a department-specific user profile

In this scenario, the corporate administrator first creates a default OPS file.

To create a standard corporate user profile

1. Install and configure Office XP on a test computer.
2. Run the Profile Wizard to create the default OPS file.
3. Start the Custom Installation Wizard and, on the **Customize Default Application Settings** page, add the default OPS file to the corporate transform.

Before Office is installed, each department administrator creates a new OPS file based on the standard corporate configuration.

To create a department-specific user profile

1. Using the corporate transform, install Office on a test computer.
2. Customize Office XP applications to suit the department needs.
3. Run the Profile Wizard to create a new department-specific OPS file.

4. Start the Custom Installation Wizard and, on the **Customize Default Application Settings** page, add the new OPS file to the department transform.

5. Using the department transform, install Office throughout the department.

Distribute both corporate and department settings

In this scenario, the corporate administrator customizes the Office XP installation to point to the Profile Wizard and OPS file with a relative path. Using a relative path allows each department to add the Profile Wizard and a department-specific OPS file to its own administrative installation point.

To customize the Office installation for department-specific user profiles

1. Install and configure Office XP on a test computer.

2. Run the Profile Wizard to create a default OPS file.

3. Start the Custom Installation Wizard and, on the **Customize Default Application Settings** page, add the default OPS file to the corporate transform.

4. On the **Add Installations and Run Programs** page, add the Profile Wizard as an application to be run at the end of the installation, and point to the Profile Wizard and OPS file with a relative path. Use the following syntax:

   OPW\Proflwiz.exe /r *Department*.ops /q

5. Create separate administrative installation points on the network for each department.

6. Create an OPW folder at each administrative installation point, and copy the Profile Wizard to that folder.

When Office is deployed, the individual department administrators update the Office installation with their own customized versions.

To install a department-specific user profile

1. Using the corporate transform, install Office on a test computer.

2. If the corporate administrator included an OPS file, this installation includes those settings.

3. Customize Office XP applications to suit the department needs.

4. Run the Profile Wizard to create an OPS file based on the new settings, and name the file *Department*.ops.

5. Copy the new *Department*.ops file to the OPW folder on the department administrative installation point.

6. Install Office XP on department computers.

When Office XP is installed, the settings in the corporate OPS file are included. Immediately following the installation, the Profile Wizard runs and the corporate settings are updated with the department administrator's changes.

Run the Profile Wizard after Office is installed

You can run the Profile Wizard as a stand-alone tool after you deploy Office XP. This method allows you to distribute a standard user profile that overwrites any other settings distributed through a transform, migrated by Windows Installer, or set by users.

Running the Profile Wizard separately also allows you to customize the process more precisely. For example, you can include only the settings you want to manage. This approach is very helpful when you deploy Office in stages and you want to customize each application separately at each stage of the process.

Customize the Profile Wizard

To customize the performance of the Profile Wizard, you edit the INI file (Opw10adm.ini). Open the file in Notepad or another text editor, and then add or delete references to settings that you want to include or exclude. You can include or exclude registry settings or Application Data folders, template files, and so on. You can also run the Profile Wizard from the command line with no loss in functionality. Every option available in the wizard has a corresponding command-line switch.

Tip You do not need to edit the Profile Wizard INI file to include or exclude Office applications. **On the Save or Restore Settings** page of the wizard, select the check boxes next to the applications for which you want to save settings.

For more information about customizing the Profile Wizard, editing the Profile Wizard INI file, or specifying command-line options for the Profile Wizard, see "Using the Office Profile Wizard," in Chapter 8, "Maintaining an Installation."

Preserve your customized settings

When Office is deployed in stages, it is easy to overwrite settings in previous user profiles. It is even easier to overwrite settings when you are not the only administrator installing Office applications. One way to control which settings are affected in a given deployment is to customize the Profile Wizard.

For example, you might invest time customizing Office XP in the lab. You run the Profile Wizard to capture your user profile settings. You do not configure Outlook because someone else is installing Outlook next month, but you do deploy Microsoft Excel, Microsoft Word, and Microsoft PowerPoint with a default user profile.

One month later, your colleague deploys Outlook. Like you, he customizes Office XP in the lab and uses the Profile Wizard to capture his user profile settings. But he does not customize the wizard to exclude settings for any of the other applications — the customized settings that you deployed and the customized settings that users have been working with for a month.

When your colleague installs Outlook, he accidentally changes your settings for Excel, Word, and PowerPoint. And, if he happens to use the **Reset to defaults** option, all of your OPS file settings are gone — along with any later user configurations — even if he did not explicitly change them in his profile.

You can avoid this scenario by selecting only the applications for which you want to save or restore settings when you run the Profile Wizard. On the **Save or Restore Settings** page of the wizard, select only the Office applications that you are deploying at any given time.

Specifying user settings in a transform

If you do not want to distribute an entire Office XP configuration, you can still customize selected user-defined options in a transform.

Add user settings to a transform

Most of the options captured by the Profile Wizard can also be set on the **Change Office User Settings** page of the Custom Installation Wizard. This method is useful for presetting just a few key options, or for modifying a default configuration without recreating the OPS file.

When users install Office with your transform, the settings you specify are applied to every user of the computer. However, only settings that differ from existing default settings are applied. Options that you set on this page of the wizard overwrite corresponding settings in an OPS file added to the transform.

Specify Outlook settings in a transform

Many Outlook options appear on the **Change Office User Settings** page, and you customize them the same way you customize options for any other Office XP application. However, the following Outlook settings require a different method.

Outlook profile information

You cannot define an Outlook profile by running the Profile Wizard, adding registry entries, or setting system policies. Instead, you must create or modify an Outlook profile on the **Outlook: Customize Default Profile** page of the Custom Installation Wizard. These settings are not overwritten by any other method of customizing user options.

Outlook e-mail settings

Several important Outlook settings appear on their own page of the Custom Installation Wizard. You specify default settings for the following options or items on the **Outlook: Customize Default Settings** page of the wizard:

- Whether to convert the personal address book (PAB file) to an Outlook Address Book
- Default e-mail editor
- Default e-mail format

For more information about customizing Outlook, see "Customizing an Outlook Installation" in Chapter 18, "Deploying Outlook."

Specify security settings in a transform

You can customize Office XP security settings in a transform or OPS file, but some security settings are implemented differently than other user-defined settings.

Security levels

Security levels — **High**, **Medium**, or **Low** — apply to each Office XP application. However, the default security level can be set in one of two areas of the Windows registry:

- HKEY_CURRENT_USER\Software\Microsoft\Office\10.0\<Application>\Security

  The **Level** value in this subkey is the security setting captured by the Profile Wizard when you create an OPS file or when you customize the setting on the **Specify Security Settings** page of the Custom Installation Wizard. It is applied once for each user of the computer.

- HKEY_LOCAL_MACHINE\Software\Microsoft\Office\10.0\<Application>\Security

  The **Level** value in this subkey is the security setting that applies to the local computer. This setting takes precedence over the per-user setting, regardless of how the per-user setting is customized. You can customize this setting on the **Change Office User Settings** page or the **Add/Remove Registry Entries** page of the Custom Installation Wizard.

For example, on the **Specify Security Settings** page, you can set the default security level for Microsoft Word to **Medium**. This step sets the **Level** value in the Security subkeys in the HKEY_CURRENT_USER branch to **2**. However, on the **Change Office User Settings** page, you can also set the **Level** value in the Security subkey in the HKEY_LOCAL_MACHINE branch to **3**. In this scenario, Word is installed on the computer with the default security level set to **High** for all users.

You can also set security levels by using system policies — a policy that applies to the security level in the HKEY_CURRENT_USER branch or another policy that applies to the HKEY_LOCAL_MACHINE branch. In this case, the security level set by policy for the local computer takes precedence over the policy for the current user.

Trusted sources

On the **Specify Security Settings** page of the Custom Installation Wizard, you can also customize the list of trusted sources on users' computers. You cannot customize trusted sources in an OPS file, on any other page of the Custom Installation Wizard, or through system policies.

For more information about configuring security settings for Office XP applications, see "Protecting Office Documents" in Chapter 10, "Administering Security."

Add registry values to a transform

Because most Office options correspond to entries in the Windows registry, you can customize those options by adding or modifying registry values in a transform. Setup applies your new default options when users install Office. Depending on which branch of the registry you customize, your settings are applied once per user (HKEY_CURRENT_USER) or once per computer (HKEY_LOCAL_MACHINE).

In addition, you can add registry settings to customize some options that cannot be set directly in the Office XP user interface and are not captured by the Profile Wizard in an OPS file. For example, you can include custom applications in Office Setup that require custom Windows registry settings.

After Office Setup is completed, Windows Installer copies the registry entries that you added to the transform to users' computers. Options that you set by adding or modifying registry entries override duplicate values that you set on other pages of the Custom Installation Wizard, including the following:

- Settings specified in an OPS file added to a transform
- Settings specified on the **Change Office User Settings** page
- Options on the **Outlook: Customize Default Settings** page
- Settings configured on the **Specify Office Security Settings** page

Add registry entries to a transform

You add or modify registry entries on the **Add Registry Entries** page of the Custom Installation Wizard. You need to know the complete path for each registry entry, as well as the value name and the data type for that entry.

To add Windows registry entries to a transform

1. Start the Custom Installation Wizard.
2. On the **Add Registry Entries** page, click **Add**.
3. In the **Root** box, select the portion of the registry you want to modify.

4. In the **Data type box**, enter a data type for the new entry.

5. In the remaining boxes, enter the full path for the registry entry you want to add, enter the value name and data, and click **OK**.

    For more information about how to enter these values, click the **Help** button.

Import a registry file into a transform

To add multiple registry entries to a transform, you can create a registry (.reg) file, and then use the **Add Registry Entries** page of the Custom Installation Wizard to import the registry file.

A registry file is a text file that contains a copy of a section of the Windows registry. If your computer already has the registry entries you want to copy to users' computers, then creating a registry file is an efficient way of distributing those entries.

To create a registry file

1. On the computer that has the registry entries you want to add to the installation, click **Run** on the **Start** menu and type **regedit**.

2. In the Registry Editor, select the portion of the registry tree that you want to copy.

3. On the **Registry** menu, click **Export Registry File**, and follow the instructions to export the selected portion of the registry tree to a registry file.

To import a registry file to a transform

1. Start the Custom Installation Wizard.

2. On the **Add Registry Entries** page, click **Import**.

3. Select the registry file you created, and click **Open**.

    The wizard adds the registry entries from the registry file to the list on the **Add Registry Entries** page. If the wizard encounters an entry in the registry file that is a duplicate of an entry already in the list, and the two entries contain different value data, then the wizard prompts you to select the entry you want to keep.

Specify settings for chained packages

You can specify default settings for packages that you chain to your Office XP installation. If you create a transform for a chained package, you can include an OPS file or set options on other pages of the Custom Installation Wizard that apply only to the chained package. Because Windows Installer installs chained packages after Office XP is installed, any conflicting settings in the chained package overwrite options set during the Office XP portion of the installation.

For example, you can set the default installation language to French in a transform applied to the Office XP installation. You can also chain the German Language Pack and apply a transform that sets the default language to German. In this scenario, Office XP installs with French as the default language; but the default language changes to German when the Language Pack is installed.

For more information about chaining packages to your Office XP installation, see "Including Additional Packages in the Office Installation" later in this chapter.

Modify settings by using the Custom Maintenance Wizard

You can apply a transform only during your initial installation of Office XP. If you want to make changes after Office XP is installed, you can use the Custom Maintenance Wizard to modify almost everything that you can set in the Custom Installation Wizard — including default user settings, security levels, Outlook settings, and registry keys.

The user interface of both wizards is very similar. For example, you specify new default settings on the **Change Office User Settings** page of the Custom Maintenance Wizard. However, you cannot use the Custom Maintenance Wizard to distribute a new OPS file; you must run the Profile Wizard separately.

For more information about using the Custom Maintenance Wizard to change user-defined settings, see "Changing User Settings After Installation" in Chapter 8, "Maintaining an Installation."

> **Toolbox** The Office XP Resource Kit includes the Custom Maintenance Wizard, which is installed by default when you run the Office Resource Kit Setup program. For more information, see "Custom Maintenance Wizard" in the Toolbox.

Modify settings by using system policies

When you install Office, you can modify registry values by using Windows system policies. System policy settings take effect when the user logs on to the network, and they override any duplicate values set during installation. Unlike default application settings set by means of an OPS file, system policies are not optional; if a user changes a setting set by policy, then Windows reinstates your setting the next time the user logs on.

For more information about setting Office XP system policies, see "Understanding System Policies" in Chapter 9, "Using System Policies."

> ### Office profiles and multiple languages
>
> Office user profiles generated by the Profile Wizard are independent of the operating system — including operating systems in other languages. For example, an OPS file created on Microsoft Windows 98 (U.S. English version) can be restored to a computer with Windows 2000 (Japanese version).
>
> However, Office user profiles are specific to a particular Office language version. For example, if you create an OPS file in the U.S. English version of Office XP, it cannot be restored to a computer with the German version of Office XP installed. There is some overlap between language families. For example, you can restore a U.S. English Office profile to an English or Australian version of Office XP.
>
> This Office language limitation exists because the different Office versions include localized folder names for the folders that contain the Office user profile information.

Including Additional Packages in the Office Installation

The Microsoft Office XP Setup program supports the chaining of additional packages (MSI files) or programs (EXE files) to the core Office XP installation. Chaining allows you to deploy Office XP and related applications in one seamless process.

A typical installation of Office follows this pattern: The System Files Update is always installed first, followed by the core Office XP package. Then Setup calls Windows Installer to install any number of chained packages in the order that you specify in the Setup settings file (Setup.ini). You customize chained packages by setting properties in Setup.ini or by creating a transform.

Specifying chained installations in Setup.ini

Setup reads the Setup.ini file at the start of the installation process and writes a set of tasks to the Windows registry to install each package listed in the [ChainedInstall_1] through [ChainedInstall_*n*] sections. By default, Setup passes to Windows Installer the command-line options and properties defined for Office XP; however, you can set unique properties for a chained package in Setup.ini.

For example, you can include Office Multilingual User Interface Packs (MUI Packs) in your Office XP installation by adding the appropriate Lpk.msi files to Setup.ini:

```
[ChainedInstall_1]
PATH=\\server\share\admin_install_point\1036\Lpk.msi
DISPLAY=None
MST=French.mst
CMDLINE=SOURCELIST=\\server2\share admin_install_point\1036
```

These lines add the French Language Pack to the Office XP installation. The French Language Pack is installed silently (regardless of the display setting specified for the Office XP installation), the customizations in the transform French.mst are applied, and an alternate source is identified for when the primary administrative installation point is unavailable.

Customize chained packages

In most sections of Setup.ini, including the [Options] and [SystemPackOptions] sections, you use the syntax **PROPERTY=value** to specify custom property values. In the [ChainedInstall_*n*] sections, you can set the **DISPLAY** and **MST** values with this syntax, along with several additional settings that customize the installation process. However, you must use the **CMDLINE** property to add other options to the command line that Setup passes to Windows Installer for the package.

You can set the following properties for chained packages in Setup.ini:

- **TASKNAME**=<*task_name*>

    Assigns a friendly name to the installation. Setup uses this name in the Setup log file.

- **TASKTYPE**=<*task_type*>

    Identifies whether the chained installation is an MSI file or EXE file.

    > **Note** If you edit Setup.ini directly, you must specify **TaskType=exe** to chain an executable file; the value **exe** is case-sensitive and must be all lowercase. The Setup INI Customization Wizard enters the correct value automatically when you add an EXE file to the Office installation.

- **PATH**=<*path_to_msi_or_exe*>

    Specifies the relative or full path to the MSI file or EXE file.

- **DISPLAY**=<*user interface display level*>

    Specifies a display setting for the chained installation. Use **Basic** to display only progress indicators; use **None** for a completely silent installation.

- **MST**=<*transform.mst*>

    Specifies the path and file name of a transform (MST file) to apply to the chained package.

- **CMDLINE**=<*command_line_options*>

    Specifies other property=value pairs or command-line options that Setup passes to Windows Installer during the call to install the chained package.

- **IGNORERETURNVALUE=[0|1]**

    To continue installing successive chained packages even if this installation fails, set this property to **1**.

- **REBOOT=[0|1]**

    To restart the computer after the installation completes, set this property to **1**.

Use the Setup INI Customization Wizard to add installations

Although you can modify Setup.ini manually in Notepad, the Setup INI Customization Wizard (Iniwiz.exe) provides a convenient interface for adding and customizing chained packages.

To add chained packages to Setup.ini

1. Install the package you want to chain on the Office XP administrative installation point or another network share.

2. Start the Setup INI Customization Wizard and enter the path to your Office XP administrative installation point.

   The wizard searches the specified network share for a Setup.ini file and all Windows Installer packages on the network share.

3. On the **Select MSI and EXE files to include in your INI file** page, select the check boxes next to the packages that you want to include in your custom INI file, or click **Browse** to add packages from another location, and then click **Next**.

4. Use the arrows to determine the order in which you want Setup.exe to install the chained packages.

5. On the **Specify options for each package in your INI file** page, select the chained package you want to customize and specify the options you want for that package.

   For each package you can specify an MST file and unique display settings, as well as additional property values.

6. To add additional property-value pairs to your custom INI file, select a package, click **Advanced Properties**, enter the properties and values you want, and then click **Next**.

The wizard enters all your customizations in the correct sections and with the correct syntax in the Setup.ini file. For example, if you set the **SOURCELIST** property to **\\server\share\admin_install_point2**, the wizard correctly enters the following line in the [ChainedInstall_*n*] section of Setup.ini:

```
CMDLINE=SOURCELIST=\\server\share\admin_install_point2
```

> **Toolbox** The Office XP Resource Kit includes the Setup INI Customization Wizard, which is installed by default when you run the Office Resource Kit Setup program. For more information, see "Setup INI Customization Wizard" in the Toolbox.

Requirements and limitations

The Setup program for Office XP is designed to support chaining of other Windows Installer packages and simple executable programs (EXE files). This chaining functionality makes it more efficient to deploy MUI Packs from the Multilingual User Interface Pack at the same time you deploy Office. However, chaining is not the best method to use in all circumstances, as described in the following sections.

Adding programs through the Custom Installation Wizard

The Custom Installation Wizard allows you to add installations and run programs during the Office XP installation. For example, you can run the Profile Wizard (Proflwiz.exe) to distribute custom settings at the end of the Office XP installation. However, you cannot use the **Add Installations and Run Programs** page of the Custom Installation Wizard to chain additional Windows Installer packages. If Windows Installer tries to start installation of a second package before it has completed installation of the first package, the entire installation process stops.

> **Toolbox** The Office XP Resource Kit includes the Customization Installation Wizard and the Profile Wizard, which are installed by default when you run the Office Resource Kit Setup program. For more information, see "Custom Installation Wizard" or "Office Profile Wizard" in the Toolbox.

Using Windows 2000 software installation services

Microsoft Windows 2000 software installation, a feature of IntelliMirror, works directly with the MSI file and bypasses Office XP Setup and the Setup.ini file when assigning or publishing packages. For this reason, you cannot use Setup.exe to chain Office XP installations when you assign or publish packages. Instead, Windows 2000 deploys Office XP, the Office Multilingual User Interface Pack, and other Office-related packages separately and in random order.

Restarting the computer after a chained installation

Office XP Setup does not support forced reboots for chained packages. In other words, you cannot chain a package that must restart the computer to complete its installation because restarting interrupts the Office XP Setup.exe thread and stops the installation process. To avoid this problem, Office Setup sets the **REBOOT** property to **REALLYSUPPRESS** by default for all but the last chained package.

You can, however, direct Setup.exe to restart the computer and then resume to complete a chained installation by setting the **REBOOT** property. For example, if you chain a Japanese Language Pack that includes an Input Method Editor (IME), you can set the **REBOOT** property to **1** in the [ChainedInstall_*n*] section of Setup.ini. (In the Setup INI Customization Wizard, select the **Restart computer after this package. Setup will resume after restart, and continue installation** check box.) This setting adds a task to the registry that directs Setup to restart the computer and then resume the Office XP installation.

Elevating installation of a chained package

If you chain a package that requires elevated privileges to install, you must take the same steps to elevate the installation that you do for Office XP. Setup.exe does not automatically install a chained package with administrator privileges when the Office XP installation is elevated. However, several of the methods that you use to elevate the Office XP installation also elevate any chained installations:

- If you use the **/jm** option to advertise Office XP, then every installation listed in Setup.ini is also advertised and therefore elevated.

- If you set the Windows system policy **Always install with elevated privileges**, then any user can install any Windows Installer package with elevated privileges.

- If you log on as an administrator when you begin the Office XP installation and do not log off or restart before it completes, then chained installations run with elevated privileges.

For more information about elevating the Office XP installation for users who are not administrators, see "Installations That Require Elevated Privileges," in Chapter 4, "Overview of Setup."

Chaining MUI Packs

Chaining is particularly useful for adding individual MUI Packs to the core Office XP installation. Each MUI Pack in the Office Multilingual User Interface Pack is installed as a separate Windows Installer package (Lpk.msi). To create an administrative installation point for all the MUI Packs, you run LpkSetup.exe with the **/a** option from the root of the MUI Pack CD. Alternatively, you can install individual MUI Packs by running Setup.exe from the appropriate LCID folder.

You can install MUI Packs on the same administrative installation point as Office XP or create a separate one. The folder structure for each MUI Pack is parallel:

\\server\share\admin_install_point\<LCID>\Lpk.msi

After you install the MUI Packs on the administrative installation point, you edit the Office XP Setup.ini file to chain them to the core Office XP installation. You can set a new display setting, specify a transform to apply, and set other properties that apply only to the MUI Pack installation. The wizard enters the correct information into the [ChainedInstall_n] section of Setup.ini.

To chain MUI Packs to the Office XP installation

1. Start the Setup INI Customization Wizard.
2. On the Select MSI and EXE files to include in your INI file page, select the check boxes next to the MUI Packs you want to chain.

   –or–

   If you installed the MUI Packs on a different administrative installation point, enter the name and path of each Lpk.msi file you want to add.

3. On the **Specify options for each package in your INI file** page, select an Lpk.msi, enter the name and path of a transform, and select a display setting.

   For example, even if you are installing Office XP with a full user interface, you can select **Basic** to install the MUI Packs quietly.

4. Click **Advanced Properties** and add values for any other properties you want to set for the MUI Pack installation.

For example, the **NOFEATURESTATEMIGRATION** property cancels the custom action that matches installation states for MUI Pack feature states to corresponding Office feature installation states. When you specify a different installation state for MUI Pack features in the transform, enter the following property-value pair in the Setup INI Customization Wizard:

NOFEATURESTATEMIGRATION=True

Chaining the Media Content CD

Another Office-related package that you can chain to the Office XP installation is for Microsoft Office XP Media Content, which includes the Microsoft Clip Organizer and a library of clip art and other media files that users can insert in Office documents.

The Media Content CD is included with the following Office 2000 suites:

- Microsoft Office XP Standard
- Microsoft Office XP Professional
- Microsoft Office XP Professional with FrontPage (Enterprise and Select editions)
- Microsoft Office XP Small Business
- Microsoft Office XP Developer

You install Media Content on users' computers the same way you install Office. A default installation copies only the Microsoft Clip Organizer (a collection of catalog files) on the local hard disk and leaves the media files (or clips) to run from the source. Instead of deploying Media Content separately, however, you can use the Setup INI Customization Wizard to chain the Media Content package (Cag.msi) to the Office XP installation.

To chain Media Content to the Office XP installation

1. Copy the Media Content CD to the Office XP administrative installation point.
2. Start the Setup INI Customization Wizard.
3. On the Select MSI and EXE files to include in your INI file page, select the check box next to the Cag.msi package, which is located at the root of the Media Content CD.
4. On the Specify options for each package in your INI file page, select the Cag.msi and specify any options you want.

   For example, to install the Media Content quietly and prevent users from installing the media files on their local hard disks, select the **Basic** display setting.

Unlike the Office XP CD, the Media Content CD is not compressed. If you use the default setting and leave media files to run from the source, users can get media files from either the CD or the CD image on the network. Unless you change the setting, the Media Content uses the same installation location as Office XP and is installed in the same folder on users' hard disks.

> **Note** You cannot use the **/jm** command-line option to advertise the Media Content package or use Windows 2000 software installation (IntelliMirror) to assign or publish Media Content.

Customizing Removal Behavior

When you upgrade to Microsoft Office XP, the Removal Wizard (Offcln.exe) removes unnecessary or obsolete components from previously installed versions of Office and related applications. The wizard components run behind the scenes during Setup, but you can also run the Removal Wizard on its own.

Both the wizard and the Office Setup program use the same logic and the same text file (OPC file) to detect and remove unneeded or obsolete files and settings from users' computers. You can determine which previous versions of Office applications are removed by selecting options in a transform. You can also customize the OPC file so that only the files and components that you specify are removed.

> **Toolbox** The Office XP Resource Kit includes the same stand-alone Removal Wizard (Offcln.exe) that is included with Office XP. The Removal Wizard is installed by default when you run the Office Resource Kit Setup program. For more information, see "Removal Wizard" in the Toolbox.

Removal Wizard components (which are used by both the wizard and Setup) include the following files:

- Offcln.exe

    Provides the user interface that lets you run the wizard as a stand-alone utility; located in the \Files\Pfiles\MSOffice\Office10 folder on the administrative installation point. The wizard is also available in the Office XP Resource Kit.

- Oclean.dll

    Used by the stand-alone Removal Wizard and Setup to carry out instructions in the OPC files and clean up the user's hard disk.

- Oclncore.opc

    Global OPC file for Office XP; located in the \Files\Pfiles\MSOffice\Office10 folder on the administrative installation point. This file specifies files, registry entries, INI file settings, and shortcuts associated with all components in the core English version of Office XP.

- Oclnintl.opc

    Satellite OPC file for each language version of Office XP; located in the LCID subfolders. Specifies files, registry entries, INI file settings, and shortcuts associated with a particular language version of Office XP.

- Oclncust.opc

    Template file for adding additional content to be deleted by the Removal Wizard, including all content that was commented out in previous versions of the wizard; located in the \Files\Pfiles\MSOffice\Office10 folder on the administrative installation point. Modify this file if you want to delete additional files or registry keys.

Removing previous versions during Setup

When users install Office XP, Setup detects files, settings, and shortcuts from previously installed versions of Office and removes them. When you run Setup in quiet mode (**/q**), default Setup behavior removes all previous versions of Office applications that are also included in the version of Office XP that you are installing. For example, if you are installing the stand-alone version of Word 2002 over Microsoft Office 2000 Premium, only Word 2000 is removed by default during the update process. If you run Setup with a full user interface, users can choose which previous versions to remove.

Setup can detect and remove the following versions of Office and Office-related products:

- Microsoft Office 4.*x*, Office 95, Office 97, Office 2000
- Microsoft Outlook 97, Outlook 98, Outlook 2000 (does not include Outlook Express)
- Microsoft FrontPage 1.1, FrontPage 97, FrontPage 98, FrontPage 2000
- Microsoft Publisher 2.0, Publisher 95, Publisher 97, Publisher 98, Publisher 2000
- Microsoft Project 4.0, Project 95, Project 97, Project 98, Project 2000
- Microsoft Office 2000 MultiLanguage Packs

  Language packs are removed by default only if all other Office 2000 applications are also being removed.

- Obsolete files, including orphaned files, registry settings, **Start** menu shortcuts, and INI file settings used by any previously installed edition of Office applications.

  Note Setup does not remove documents or other user files from the user's hard disk.

Setup also detects the following as candidates for removal:

- Incompletely installed or uninstalled components that leave unusable files on the hard disk
- Files that begin with the tilde (~) character

Finally, Setup detects and can remove temporary files, which are defined as files found in any of the following folders:

- Windows temporary folder (Windows\Temp or Windows\Tmp)
- Folders identified by the MS-DOS environment variable **%TEMP%** or **%TMP%**
- MS-DOS temporary folder (*drive*:\Temp or *drive*:\Tmp); Setup searches every drive on the computer.

Setup removes files according to instructions contained in the global OPC file (Oclncore.opc) plus any language-specific OPC files (Oclnintl.opc) that you add to the LCID subfolders on your administrative installation point.

For example, a user might have a French version of Microsoft Word and an English version of Microsoft Excel. The global OPC file cleans up all components included in the core English version of Office. If you add the Oclnintl.opc file to the 1036 subfolder, then Setup also removes components unique to the French version of Office.

Note Because Setup recognizes components at the application level, the removal process detects and removes stand-alone versions of applications such as Word and Excel. If all the core applications are removed, Setup also removes shared components such as Office Binder and Equation Editor.

Removing Small Business Tools

Office XP does not include the Microsoft Small Business Tools programs (Small Business Customer Manager, Business Planner, Direct Mail Manager, and Financial Manager) that were part of Microsoft Office 2000 Premium Edition. If you are upgrading from Office 2000, Small Business Tools components are not removed by default.

If you want Office XP Setup to remove Small Business Tools during the installation, set the following properties on the command line, in Setup.ini, or in a transform:

- **OPCREMOVESBT2000**

    Setting this property to **1** allows Office XP Setup to remove Small Business Tools from users' computers.

- **OPCREMOVESBTTEXT**

    Setting this property to a string value — for example, "**&Small Business Tools**" — adds a check box to the **Remove Previous Versions** page of Setup so that users can choose to remove Small Business Tools the same way they remove any other previous-version Office application.

Customizing the removal process

There are several ways that you can specify how the Setup program for Office or the Removal Wizard cleans up users' computers:

- In the Custom Installation Wizard, specify which Office components to remove on the **Remove Previous Versions** page.

- Customize the OPC file used by Setup to include or exclude additional files or registry entries during the removal process. When users run Setup, your custom removal routine runs automatically.

- Create your own OPC file and run the Removal Wizard with a command-line option that specifies your custom OPC file.

    Toolbox The Office XP Resource Kit includes the Custom Installation Wizard, which is installed by default when you run the Office Resource Kit Setup program. For more information, see "Custom Installation Wizard" in the Toolbox.

Customize removal behavior in a transform

You can use the Custom Installation Wizard to customize removal behavior during Office XP Setup. On the **Remove Previous Versions** page of the wizard, you specify exactly which previous versions of each application are removed from users' computers. In this case, Setup does not display the **Remove Previous Versions** page to users during the installation — the instructions in the transform are carried out regardless of the display setting.

> **Note** When you remove previous applications during Setup, the Removal Wizard always runs in safe mode.

Customize the OPC file used by Setup

Setup follows the instructions in the global OPC file and any language-specific OPC files to determine which components to remove. The OPC files identify files, registry entries, INI file entries, and **Start** menu items that were installed or modified by previously installed versions of Office and Office-related products. The OPC file also contains rules that describe which of these files or entries to remove, where they are located, and under what conditions they can be deleted.

By editing the default OPC file or by creating a custom OPC file, you can specify which components to remove from the users' computers. You can also use the OPC file to remove non-Office components, such as custom applications. To add components to the removal list, customize the Oclncust.opc file. To exclude components from removal, you must edit the default Oclncore.opc file.

> **Toolbox** The Office XP Resource Kit includes a document named Opc.doc, which contains information about the syntax of the OPC file and instructions for modifying it. Opc.doc is installed by default when you run the Office Resource Kit Setup program. For more information, see "Supplemental Documentation" in the Toolbox.

Run the Removal Wizard separately

After Setup removes files and settings from previously installed versions of Office or Office components, other unneeded files might remain on users' computers. For example, font files and dynamic-link library (DLL) files might not be removed. You can run the Removal Wizard as a stand-alone utility to remove all Office-related files from users' computers.

Situations in which it makes sense to run the Removal Wizard as a stand-alone utility include the following:

- Before you upgrade to Office XP, to clean up existing Office-related files.
- When you stage your upgrade to Office XP applications.

    For example, if you upgrade to Word 2002 before upgrading to the rest of Office XP, you can remove previously installed versions of only Word.

- When upgrading to Office XP, replaces the need for a custom application on users' computers. You can use the wizard to remove the custom application.

  Note On the Microsoft Windows 2000 and Microsoft Windows NT 4.0 operating systems, you must have administrator rights to run the Removal Wizard. If a user does not have administrator rights, you must log on as an administrator and run the wizard with the proper permissions.

You can run the Removal Wizard in one of three modes, depending on the degree to which you want to clean up users' hard disks:

- Aggressive mode

  Removes all Office-related components, including components shared by more than one Office application. Before installing Office XP, you might run the wizard in aggressive mode for users who are upgrading from a variety of Office versions. In aggressive mode, the wizard marks all items listed in the OPC file for removal.

- Safe mode

  Removes only components that are no longer needed. Components deleted in safe mode are not being used by any application. In safe mode, the wizard marks items listed in the OPC file for removal only if it does not detect a corresponding application.

- Safe mode with user discretion

  Runs in safe mode, but allows users to select which detected applications to keep and which to delete.

  Caution Never run the Removal Wizard in aggressive mode after you install Office XP. The wizard might remove shared components that are needed by other applications installed on the computer.

The final page of the Removal Wizard lists all files scheduled for removal. This list is accurate for all Office applications from Microsoft Office 97 or earlier. However, because the Removal Wizard relies on Windows Installer to manage removal of files associated with a particular application, the list might be incomplete for Office 2000. This behavior results in a cleaner and safer removal of Office 2000 files, even though the list in the Removal Wizard might be incomplete.

Using command-line options with the Removal Wizard

Creating a custom OPC file and running the Removal Wizard with command-line options gives you the greatest amount of flexibility. To run the Removal Wizard with command-line options, click **Run** on the **Start** menu, and then type **Offcln.exe** followed by the command-line options you want.

Removal Wizard command-line options use the following syntax:

Offcln.exe [/a | /s [/q[/r]] [/l][!][*logfile*]]] [*directory*]

These command-line options are defined in the following table.

Option	Definition
/a	Indicates aggressive mode; the Removal Wizard removes files associated with all previously installed versions of Office and Office-related applications. When you use this command-line option, the wizard does not allow you to select which files to keep.
/s	Indicates safe mode; the Removal Wizard removes only those files for which it does not detect an associated application. When you use this command-line option, the wizard does not allow you to select which files to keep.
/q	Indicates quiet mode; the Removal Wizard runs without prompting the user for information or displaying progress indicators. The wizard does not restart the user's computer; therefore, changes might not be completed until the user restarts the computer.
/r	Used with the /q option to restart the computer automatically if necessary. The user has no opportunity to save files before the computer restarts.
/l*logfile*	Generates a log with the file name *logfile*. If no log file name is specified, the Removal Wizard creates a default log file, Offcln9.log, in the current folder of the wizard.
/l!*logfile*	Generates a log file in the same manner as /l, but the Removal Wizard does not perform the removal process. This option is useful to test the Removal Wizard before running it to remove files.
directory	Specifies the folder that contains the files used by the Removal Wizard: Oclncore.opc, Oclncust.opc, and <LCID>\Oclnintl.opc files. By default, the Removal Wizard searches the same folder that contains Offcln.exe.

For example, you can enter the following command line:

```
Offcln.exe /a /q /r /l
```

This command line does the following on users' computers:

- Removes all files from previously installed versions of Office (**/a**)
- Runs the Removal Wizard without user intervention (**/q**)
- Restarts the computer automatically if needed (**/r**)
- Creates the default log file (**/l**)

> **Tip** The Removal Wizard returns a code to indicate whether the wizard ran with any errors. If you create a batch file to run the wizard, you can include error-checking code so that the wizard returns **0** to indicate that errors occurred or returns **1** to indicate that no errors occurred.

Running the Removal Wizard with a custom OPC file

When you run the Removal Wizard separately, you can create a custom OPC file that controls the removal process. For example, suppose you want to remove an internal company tool that is being replaced by Office XP functionality. The internal tool, Chart.exe, resides on users' computers in the folder C:\Program Files\Internal\Chart. In addition, the folder contains support files — Chartsub.dll, Chartprt.dat, and Readme.txt.

The following procedure shows you how to modify the OPC file to accomplish all these aims.

To modify the Oclncust.opc for a custom removal routine

1. Create a backup copy of the default Oclncust.opc file.
2. Open Oclncust.opc in a text editor.

   In Microsoft Windows 98, this file is too large for Notepad, but it can be edited in WordPad.
3. Add the following lines:

   [SAFE] "Internal charting tool"

   C:\program files\internal\chart\chart.exe

   C:\program files\internal\chart\chartsub.dll

   C:\program files\internal\chart\chartprt.dat

   C:\program files\internal\chart\readme.txt

   These entries direct the wizard to always delete files in the [SAFE] section and specify the name and location of the files to delete.
4. Save and close Oclncust.opc.

   Tip Test your customized OPC file on a computer by using the **/l!***logfile* command-line option. This step generates a log of the files that will be deleted by your customized OPC file without actually removing any files.

Distributing Office to Users' Computers

After you create an administrative installation point and customize your Microsoft Office XP configuration, users can install Office from the network. You can use any of the following methods to distribute Office to users:

- Have users run Setup from the administrative installation point using the command-line options, Setup settings file, or transform that you specify.
- Assign or publish Office to users or computers (Microsoft Windows 2000).

- Advertise Office on users' computers (Windows 2000 or Microsoft Windows NT 4.0).
- Create and distribute a custom CD based on the Office XP CD.
- Create a hard-disk image and replicate it on users' computers.
- Use a systems management tool, such as Microsoft Systems Management Server, to install Office.

Running Setup from an administrative installation point

When users double-click **setup.exe** on the administrative installation point, Setup runs with no command-line options. To apply your customizations, users must click **Run** on the Windows **Start** menu and enter the path to Setup.exe, along with the appropriate command-line options. For example, the command line must include the **/settings** option to specify a custom Setup settings file or the **TRANSFORMS** property to specify a transform MST file.

To ensure that Office XP is installed with the correct customizations, you can create in MS-DOS a batch file that runs Setup.exe with your command-line options. Or you can create a Windows shortcut and add options to the command-line box. Users double-click the batch file or shortcut to run the Setup command line that you have defined. You can distribute the batch file or shortcut to users in an e-mail message.

Unless you choose to install Office XP quietly, the Setup user interface guides users through the following steps to install Office on their computers:

1. Update system files.
2. Enter user information.
3. Select installation mode and location.
4. Select installation options for Office features.
5. Select previous versions of Office to keep.

Most of the customizations that you specify on the command line, in the Setup settings file, or in a transform appear as defaults in the Setup interface; however, users can modify your choices when they run Setup interactively. To prevent users from changing the configuration during the installation, run Setup in quiet mode. For information about installing Office XP quietly, see "Customizing How Setup Runs" earlier in this chapter.

Update system files

On Microsoft Windows 98 and Windows NT 4.0, Setup first checks to see whether the computer has the required versions of key system and shared files. If the computer fails this test, Setup starts the System Files Update installation and displays a list of components that need to be updated.

The next page of Setup gives users the option of upgrading to Microsoft Internet Explorer 5. If users choose not to upgrade, Setup calls Internet Explorer Setup to install a subset of Internet Explorer– and Windows-related components (such as HTML Help) that are required by Office XP applications.

You can install the System Files Update quietly, even if you run Setup with a full user interface. In this case, system files and Internet Explorer are updated based on the settings that you specify on the command line, in the Setup settings file, or in a transform applied to the System Files Update package. After updating system files and installing Internet Explorer, Setup restarts the computer before starting the Office XP installation.

> **Note** If a computer already has Internet Explorer 5.0 installed, then Setup upgrades to version 5.01 behind the scenes, without offering the user the option of upgrading. If the **NOIE** property is set to **True**, then Setup installs only the subset of Internet Explorer– and Windows-related components required by Office XP applications.

Enter user information

User information appears on users' computers in the **About** box (**Help** menu) in Office applications. When a user installs Office from an administrative installation point, Setup uses the organization name you specify without prompting the user.

> **Note** Because you must enter the product key from the Office CD when you create an administrative installation point, users are not prompted for a product key during the installation.

Accept end-user license agreement

When users install Office XP from the CD, Setup displays an end-user license agreement page. When users install Office from the administrative installation point, however, the license agreement that you accepted when you created the administrative installation point applies, and users do not see this page of Setup.

Select installation mode and location

After they enter the required user information, users select the type of installation to perform and the location to install Office on the next page in Setup.

Installation mode

Users can select one of the following installation options:

- **Install Now**

    Automatically installs the most frequently used Office features in the default installation location and skips the remaining pages of Setup.

- **Upgrade Now**

    Automatically upgrades to Office XP and skips the remaining pages of Setup. This option removes all previous versions of Office applications and installs Office XP features based on the user's current configuration.

- **Custom**

    Allows the user to configure all aspects of the Office installation on the remaining pages of Setup.

- **Complete**

    Installs all Office features locally on the user's computer. This option requires the most disk space but ensures that users do not need access to the Office XP CD or an administrative installation point on the network later.

- **Run from Network**

    Installs all Office features to run over the network; only components that must be installed locally are copied to the user's computer. This option requires access to the network to run any Office application.

    Note Office XP Setup does not include the option to run from the Office XP CD.

By using the Custom Installation Wizard, you can create a Windows Installer transform (MST file) that specifies the default features installed by Setup when the user clicks **Install Now**. You can also change the button labels and descriptive text on this page by setting the properties described in the following table.

Property	Default value
TYPICALINSTALLTEXT	&Install Now
TYPICALUPGRADETEXT	&Upgrade Now
TYPICALINSTALLDESCRIPTION	Installs Microsoft Office with the default settings, including the most commonly used components.
TYPICALUPGRADEDESCRIPTION	Upgrades your Microsoft Office installation. Setup will remove your previous versions and install based on your current configuration.

Property (cont'd)	Default value
RUNFROMSOURCEINSTALLDESCRIPTION	Installs only the files that must copied to your computer. Access to the installation source will be required to run Office.
CUSTOMINSTALLDESCRIPTION	Customize your Microsoft Office installation, selecting which Office applications and features to install on your computer.
COMPLETEINSTALLDESCRIPTION	Installs all of Microsoft Office on your computer, including all optional components and tools.

For example, if few users in your organization work with databases, you might omit Microsoft Access from a typical installation by setting its installation state to **Not Available** in the transform. To alert the minority of users who might need Access, however, you can change the description of the **Custom** option by setting the following property:

```
CUSTOMINSTALLDESCRIPTION="To install Microsoft Access, choose this option
and select the Microsoft Access check box."
```

Installation location

On this page of Setup, users can also enter the path to the installation location they want. The default location is Program Files\Microsoft Office\Office10.

You can specify a default value for the installation location on the **Specify Default Path and Organization** page of the Office Custom Installation Wizard. You can also specify the location by setting the **INSTALLLOCATION** property on the command line, in the Setup settings file, or on the **Modify Setup Properties** page of the Custom Installation Wizard.

Select installation options for Office features

When users choose the **Custom** installation mode, Setup displays a list of all the applications included in the suite. Users select the check boxes next to the applications they want, and Setup installs a typical set of features for each one.

Alternatively, users can select **Choose detailed installation options for each application** to further customize their Office XP configuration. In this case, Setup displays the Office feature tree and allows users to set an installation state for each feature. The installation states you specify in a transform are set by default, but users can modify them. Features that you have hidden or locked or installation states that you have disabled are not displayed.

The following feature installation states are normally available to users during Setup:

- **Run from My Computer**

    Setup copies files and writes registry entries and shortcuts associated with the feature to the user's hard disk, and the application or feature runs locally.

- **Run all from My Computer**

    Same as **Run from My Computer**, except that all child features belonging to the feature are also set to this state.

- **Run from Network**

    Setup leaves components for the feature on the administrative installation point, and the feature is run from there.

- **Run all from Network**

    Same as **Run from Network**, except that all child features belonging to the feature are also set to this state.

- **Installed on First Use**

    Setup leaves components for the feature and all its child features on the administrative installation point until the user attempts to use the feature for the first time, at which time the components are automatically copied to the local hard disk.

- **Not Available**

    The components for the feature, and all of the child features belonging to this feature, are not installed on the computer.

For more information about customizing what users see in the feature tree, see "Customizing Office Features and Shortcuts" earlier in this chapter. You can also find detailed information about setting installation states in a transform by clicking **Help** on the **Set Feature Installation States** page of the Custom Installation Wizard.

For information about using the Custom Maintenance Wizard to modify feature installation states after Office is installed, see "Changing Feature Installation States" in Chapter 8, "Maintaining an Installation."

Select previous versions of Office to keep

If the user is upgrading from a previous version of Office, Setup displays a list of all the Office applications currently installed — applications that Setup removes when it installs Office XP. Users can choose to keep all or some previous-version applications on the computer.

Because Office XP is always installed in a version-specific folder, users can choose to keep previous versions without overwriting any files. However, Setup does redefine system settings, such as file types and shortcuts, to point to the Office XP applications.

On the **Keep Previous Versions** page of the Office Custom Installation Wizard, you can specify default settings for this Setup page, or even hide the page from users altogether. The wizard also includes an option to remove obsolete files, shortcuts, and registry settings left over from previous versions.

Assigning or publishing Office

If all the computers in your organization run under Windows 2000, you can use a set of Windows 2000–based technologies known collectively as IntelliMirror to install and manage Office XP by policy. IntelliMirror includes a software installation and maintenance feature that allows an administrator to centrally manage software installation, repairs, updates, and removal.

> **Note** Before you can use Windows 2000 software installation, you must set up an Active Directory™ and Group Policy structure. You manage Office XP applications within a Group Policy object (GPO), which is associated with a particular Active Directory container – a site, domain, or organizational unit.

There are three ways to install and manage Office XP applications by using Group Policy and Windows 2000 software installation:

- Assign Office to computers

    Office is installed on the computer the next time the computer starts. Users can repair Office applications on the computer, but only an administrator can remove applications.

- Assign Office to users

    Office is available to all users in the designated group the next time they log on. Each Office application is installed the first time a user clicks the associated shortcut on the **Start** menu or opens a file associated with that Office application.

- Publish Office to users

    Office is available to all users in the designated group the next time they log on. Users install Office through **Add/Remove Programs** in Control Panel or by opening an Office document. (Under Windows 2000, you cannot publish an application to a computer.)

With any of these methods, Office XP is installed from your administrative installation point; however, Windows 2000 works directly with the MSI files and bypasses Setup.exe and the Setup settings file. To customize the installation you must apply a transform (MST file) when you assign or publish the Office package (MSI file). Note that you can apply only one transform to a given installation of the Office XP package.

> **Important** Transforms are applied when Office is assigned or published. You cannot reapply a transform after Office is installed, nor can you use the Custom Maintenance Wizard to make changes. If you need to modify a managed Office installation, you must remove and then reinstall Office with a new transform.

For more information about using software installation to assign or publish Office XP, see "Using Windows 2000 Software Installation" in Chapter 6, "Deploying on Windows 2000."

Advertising Office

Under Windows NT 4.0 and Windows 2000, you can advertise Office XP by logging on as an administrator and then running Setup with the **/jm** option. If you also include a Windows Installer transform (MST file) to customize the installation, you use the **/t** command-line option to specify the MST file. For example:

```
setup.exe /jm proplus.msi /t office.mst
```

> **Note** When you use the **/t** command-line option to specify a transform, you must insert a space between the option and the transform name to ensure that the transform is correctly applied.

In many organizations, advertising is a quick and efficient means of making Office XP available to users. Advertising is similar to assigning Office XP under Windows 2000, in that all Office applications and features are installed on demand. However, you can advertise only to computers, and advertising does not provide the same management capabilities as Windows 2000 software installation.

When you advertise Office XP in this way, Windows Installer shortcuts for each application appear on the **Start** menu, and a minimal set of core Office files and components is installed on the computer. When a user clicks a shortcut or opens a file associated with an Office application, Windows Installer installs the feature or application from the administrative installation point. After Office is advertised, users can also run Setup directly from an administrative installation point to install Office.

Windows NT 4.0 does not support Windows Installer shortcuts without the Windows Desktop Update, which is an updated version of the Windows shell. The Windows Desktop Update is included with Internet Explorer 4.01 Service Pack 1 or later, but it is not installed by default. Without the updated shell and Windows Installer shortcuts, core Office files and components are installed on the computer, and users can subsequently run Office XP Setup from the administrative installation point.

Like core Office XP, the MUI Packs in the Office Multilingual User Interface Pack are Windows Installer packages, and you can advertise them on users' computers. However, the System Files Update cannot be advertised. Advertising Office XP on Windows NT 4.0 fully installs the System Files Update on the local computer when the System Files Update is required and then restarts the computer before advertising other packages.

For more information about installing Office XP and updating the Windows shell on Windows NT 4.0, see "Using Windows Installer Shortcuts with Office" in Chapter 7, "Deploying on Windows NT 4.0."

Installing Office XP on Windows NT 4.0 or Windows 2000 requires elevated privileges. For more information, see "Installations That Require Elevated Privileges" in Chapter 4, "Overview of Setup."

Distributing a custom CD

If you have users who cannot install or run Microsoft Office over the network, you can distribute a customized version of Office to them by creating copies of the Office XP CD. This option requires that you have the capability to create and distribute CDs.

For example, traveling users who have limited access to the network might install Office XP from a CD. Because many less frequently used features in Office XP are set to **Installed on First Use** by default, these users might find that they need an additional feature when their Office XP CD is back at the office and out of reach. You can ensure that the source is always available by providing customized copies of the Office XP CD.

> **Important** You must obtain the proper user licenses before copying, modifying, or distributing a customized version of the Office XP CD. For more information about volume licensing programs, contact your software reseller or see the Microsoft Business Licensing Web site at http://www.microsoft.com/business/licensing.

Copy the Office XP CD

Office XP source files are compressed in a cabinet (CAB) file to fit onto the Office XP CD. You copy the compressed CAB file to a network share before customizing and duplicating it. In this scenario, you do not run Setup to create an administrative installation point; instead, you copy the compressed files directly to the network share.

Unlike the process of running Setup with the **/a** option — which expands the compressed files on the administration installation point — the files in the CD image remain compressed. Nor does copying the CD enter the product key or accept the end-user license agreement automatically on behalf of all users who install Office XP from this network share.

After you copy the contents of the Office XP CD to a network share, however, the process of customizing an Office CD image is similar to the process of customizing an administrative installation point. For example, you can use the Custom Installation Wizard and Setup INI Customization Wizard as long as you point the wizards to the MSI file on the compressed image. You can also customize files that reside outside the Office XP CAB file, such as the OPC file used by Setup or the Removal Wizard to remove previous versions.

To create a customized copy of the Office XP CD

1. Insert the Office XP CD into your CD-ROM drive.
2. In Windows Explorer, select all the folders on the CD.

    Be sure to display all hidden files so that you see the entire contents of the Office XP CD.

3. Copy the CD contents to a network share; the complete CD image for Office XP Professional with FrontPage requires approximately 460 MB of space.

   You can reduce the amount of space required by omitting unneeded folders such as the ORK, SharePt, and MSDE2000 folders. If all your users are running Windows 2000 or Windows Millennium Edition (Windows Me), you can also omit the OSP folder. The CAB file and core Office XP MSI file require approximately 230 MB of free space.

4. Customize the CD image by creating one or more transforms and modifying Setup.ini.

   For example, to avoid making users enter the correct product key from the Office XP CD case, set the **PIDKEY** property in the transform, and specify the transform in the [MST] section of Setup.ini. You cannot accept the end-user license agreement, but if you specify a quiet display setting, users do not see that page during Setup.

5. Copy the image on your hard disk onto a CD and distribute copies to users.

   The volume label of the CDs you create must match the volume label of the Office XP CD for Setup to run properly from the custom CDs.

The CDs that you create can be used in the same way as the original Office CD, except that Setup runs with your modifications. When users install Office by using your custom CD, however, they cannot use the network as an alternate source for installing on demand, repairing features, or running Setup in maintenance mode. They must use a compressed CD or CD image on the network as a back-up source. Similarly, if users install Office XP from an administrative installation point, then they cannot use the compressed Office XP CD or your customized copy as a source.

If all your users are running Windows 2000 or Windows Me or later, you may be able to omit the OPS folder and create a CD that contains a customized version of the uncompressed Office administrative image, as described in the following section. In this case, users can use the administrative image and your custom CD interchangeably as a source.

> **Tip** If the original Office XP source is unavailable and you must use a different type of source, you can reinstall Office by running Setup with the **/fv** option. This option allows Setup to use a new source, but you cannot return to your original source without repeating the reinstallation process.

For more information about customizing the Setup process or your Office XP configuration, see "Customizing the Office Installation" earlier in this chapter.

Copy a portion of the Office XP administrative installation point

When you create an administrative installation point, the compressed CAB file on the Office XP CD is expanded. You cannot copy the entire administrative installation point onto a custom CD to distribute to users — the expanded files take up too much space. However, in some cases you can copy a portion of the administrative image onto a CD and distribute it to users.

For example, running Setup in administrative mode does not copy the ORK, SharePt, or MSDE2000 folders to the network share, which reduces the disk-space requirement. If all the users in your organization are running Windows Me or Windows 2000 or later, then they do not need the System Files Update to install Office XP. You can remove the OSP folder from the administrative image, freeing up even more space. After you customize Office XP the way you want it, you can copy the administrative image onto one custom CD, which can then be copied and distributed to users.

In this scenario, the custom CD functions as an interchangeable equivalent to the administrative installation point on the network. Because the files are uncompressed, users can rely on either the custom CD or the network as a source. In addition, users are not prompted to enter a product key or accept the end-user license agreement when they install Office from the CD, because you entered that information for them when you created the administrative installation point.

Creating a hard-disk image

Some organizations deploy a complete user system at one time, including Microsoft Windows software, device drivers, Office applications, and custom settings. In this scenario, you install the entire system onto a test computer, and then you create an image of the hard disk to copy to users' computers.

Installing Office with a complete user system is almost as fast as installing Office by itself. It is a particularly efficient way to configure new computers or to restore a computer to its original state. When you distribute the hard-disk image to users, everything on the computer is replaced by your custom configuration, so users must back up any documents or other files they want to keep.

Customize Office on the administrative installation point

To create the hard-disk image, you begin by running Office XP Setup with the **/a** option to create an administrative installation point. You can use the Custom Installation Wizard to create a transform and the Setup INI Customization Wizard to modify Setup.ini, just as you do when you customize Office XP in any other network installation scenario. In addition, you must take several steps to exclude user-specific information from the hard-disk image.

To customize Office XP for a hard-disk image

1. Run Setup with the **/a** option to create an Office XP administrative installation point.
2. If you are including MUI Packs in your installation, run LpkSetup.exe with the **/a** option and install them on the same administrative installation point or a different network share.
3. Start the Custom Installation Wizard.
4. On the **Customize Default User Settings** page, specify the name and path of any OPS file you have created.
5. On the Set **Feature Installation States** page, set installation states for each Office application.

6. On the **Modify Setup Properties** page, set the following properties:
   - **NOUSERNAME=True**
   - **ENTERPRISE_IMAGE=True**
7. If you are **installing** Outlook 2002, choose to create a new Outlook profile on the **Outlook: Customize Default Profile** page, and configure the profile on subsequent pages of the wizard.
8. Make any **additional** customizations and save the transform.
9. Start the Setup INI **Customization** Wizard and specify the transform you created, along with any other modifications you want to make to Setup.ini.

   For example, add MUI Packs to the ChainedInstall_n sections of Setup.ini.
10. Save the custom INI file and copy the command line it generates.

Specifying Setup properties

You must set the following Setup properties to ensure that your Office XP configuration installs properly on users' computers:

- **NOUSERNAME=True**

   Prevents Setup from defining a user name during installation. This setting allows users to enter their own user names the first time they run an Office application.

- **ENTERPRISE_IMAGE=True**

   Prevents Setup from creating a digital license identification based on the hardware components of the test computer. This setting allows Setup to generate a unique digital license identification on each client computer the first time Office is started, instead of when Office XP is initially installed.

Including an OPS file

You can use the Profile Wizard to configure user settings and add an OPS file to your transform. However, you must install Office XP and the MUI Packs on a separate test computer before you start any Office applications to configure user options and capture the settings. If you start any Office applications on the computer you intend to image, then user- and computer-specific settings are included in the hard-disk image.

To customize users settings on the Office XP image by using an OPS file

1. Before you create a transform, install Office from the administrative installation point to a test computer.
2. On the test computer, run the Office applications and modify application settings, and then close all the Office applications.
3. Start the Profile Wizard.

4. On the **Save or Restore Settings page, click Save the settings from this machine.**
5. **Enter the file name and** path for the OPS file, and click **Finish**.
6. When you create the transform, enter the file name and path of the OPS file on the **Customize Default User Settings** page of the Custom Installation Wizard.

Install Office on a clean test computer

The next step is to install Office XP from the administrative installation point onto a clean client computer — one that already has the Windows configuration you want and one that has never had Office XP or any previous version of Office installed. This installation becomes the model for your hard-disk image.

After you have installed and configured all the system software on the test computer, run Office Setup to install Office from the administrative installation point. If you have not already done so in the transform or Setup.ini file, set the **NOUSERNAME** and **ENTERPRISE_IMAGE** properties on the Setup command line.

To install Office on the test computer

1. On the Start menu, click **Run**.
2. Enter the name and path to Office Setup.

    You can copy and paste the command line generated by the Setup INI Customization Wizard.

3. If you have not already done so, set the **NOUSERNAME** and **ENTERPRISE_IMAGE** properties on the command line; for example:

    ```
    \\server\share\admin_install_point\setup.exe NOUSERNAME=True ENTERPRISE_IMAGE=True
    ```

4. Unless you want all users who receive the hard-disk image to use your administrative installation point as a source for installing, repairing, or removing Office features, reset the source list to point to the Office CD or another network share.

    Caution To prevent user-specific information from appearing on the hard-disk image, do not start any Office applications on the test computer. After you install Office on the test computer, you can make additional modifications to the configuration. However, starting an Office application writes user-specific information to the Windows registry, which is then duplicated to all users.

Distribute the hard-disk image

Before you distribute your hard-disk image, install it on a client computer and make sure that Office XP applications are installed and configured correctly. Then you can use any one of a number of tools to create copies of the hard-disk image.

The Windows 2000 operating system includes several new or improved technologies for automating installation of Windows 2000 Professional on client computers through hard-disk imaging. Two of these technologies allow you to include Office XP in the hard-disk image that installs Windows 2000 Professional:

- SysPrep 1.1

    Prepares the hard disk on the test computer for duplicating to other computers and then runs a third-party disk-imaging process. SysPrep can copy the hard-disk image to client computers that have different hardware application layers (HALs) and different Plug and Play device drivers. SysPrep is fast — the hard-disk image can be packaged and compressed; only the files required for the specific configuration are included.

- Remote Installation Services (RIS)

    Installs both Windows 2000 and Office XP remotely on client computers. You can set up new computers and new users without on-site technical support, and recover more quickly from computer failures. RIS requires adequate network capacity and the Active Directory directory service.

Use Remote Installation Services (Windows 2000)

Remote OS Installation, which is based on RIS, is an optional service in Windows 2000 Server. It provides a mechanism for computers to connect to a network server during the initial startup process, while the server controls a local installation of Windows 2000 Professional.

If all the computers in your organization are running under Windows 2000, you can use remote installation services to copy a preconfigured hard-disk image — with standardized versions of both Windows 2000 Professional and Office XP — to client computers. RIS also requires that you have Active Directory and a Group Policy structure set up.

This method can significantly reduce deployment time. A remote installation of Windows and Office together takes only slightly longer than a remote installation of Windows by itself. When clients download the disk image, Office XP is fully installed on the local computer — and not merely advertised.

> **Note** If you want users to receive a managed Office installation, you must use the Software Installation snap-in to assign Office to the test computer before creating your disk image.

When used together, Remote OS Installation and other Windows 2000 management services offer the following benefits:

- More efficient and cost-effective setup of new computers
- Dynamic configuration and repair of both Windows 2000 and Office XP
- Easier recovery from computer failures

If the computer fails, you can quickly restore Windows 2000 Professional (by using Remote OS) and restore the user's applications, data, and settings (by using IntelliMirror features).

To distribute Office XP by using RIS

1. Install and configure Windows 2000 Professional for your organization on a test computer.
2. Install and customize Office XP on an administrative installation point.
3. Install your customized version of Office XP from the administrative installation point to the test computer.
4. Run the Remote Installation Preparation Wizard (RIPrep.exe) from the RIS server that will receive the hard-disk image.

   Note Remote OS Installation works only in a homogenous Windows 2000 environment — Windows 2000 Server and Windows 2000 Professional clients. You cannot use it to install to clients running under Windows NT 4.0 or Windows 98.

For a detailed outline of the steps necessary to install, configure, and use Remote Installation Services (RIS), see the "Step-by-Step Guide to Remote OS Installation" on the Microsoft Windows 2000 Web site at http://www.microsoft.com/WINDOWS2000/library/planning/management/remotesteps.asp.

To find out how to create an installation image by using the Remote Installation Preparation Wizard, search for **Creating an installation image** in the Windows 2000 Server Help page on the Microsoft Windows 2000 Web site at http://windows.microsoft.com/windows2000/en/server/help/.

Using Microsoft Systems Management Server

Microsoft Systems Management Server (SMS) 2.0 provides a robust distribution model for deploying Office XP to client computers. If you are installing Office XP under any of the following circumstances, consider using SMS:

- You want more control over the timing of your Office XP installation.

  For example, you need to complete the installation during off hours, or you need to coordinate upgrades across multiple sites.

- You need advanced reporting and troubleshooting tools.

- You are deploying to users over slow network or dial-up connections.

- You are deploying to a mixture of Windows clients, including Windows 2000, Windows Me, Windows NT 4.0, and Windows 98.

Systems Management Server also gives you the flexibility to deploy non-Windows Installer packages and to target collections of users or computers based on advanced resource attributes (such as software or hardware inventory properties).

For more information about using Systems Management Server, see the Microsoft Systems Management Server Web site at http://www.microsoft.com/smsmgmt/default.asp.

For a comparison of software deployment features in Windows 2000 IntelliMirror, Remote OS Installation, and Systems Management Server 2.0, see the white paper "Software Deployment Using Windows 2000 and Systems Management Server 2.0" on the Windows 2000 Web site at http://www.microsoft.com/windows2000/library/planning/management/smsintell.asp.

Deploying a Service Release

Microsoft Office XP service releases are interim upgrades that are designed to improve the performance and reliability of your applications. While service releases are often developed in response to emerging issues, such as virus attacks, they may also contain bug fixes or updated features.

In considering whether to deploy a given service release, your first step should be to determine how the changes will benefit your organization. If a particular upgrade does not apply to how you use Office, you may elect to pass on that release. Deploying a service release is typically not required to maintain the functionality of your original installation.

Information on the changes and features offered by a specific service release is posted on the Microsoft Office Web site. Administrators and information technology (IT) professionals can refer to the Office Resource Kit Web site for details on administrative issues associated with a given release. If a particular service release has language dependencies, separate versions of the update will be made available for each language in which Office XP is released.

Administrative updates and standard updates

When Microsoft Office issues a service release, two separate versions of the update are made available — one for upgrading administrative installation points and the other for upgrading stand-alone computers. The administrative update is typically a larger file that provides full-file replacement for all changes contained in the update. In contrast, the standard update patches the existing files instead of replacing them. It is designed only for stand-alone computers and cannot be used to update an administrative installation point.

When you deploy an administrative update, Windows Installer performs a recache and reinstallation of the original version of Office. This process replaces the previously cached MSI file and overwrites any old files with the newer versions. By installing complete files, as opposed to patched files, the administrative update can correctly replace any files on the server that have been modified with Microsoft quick fix engineering (QFE) updates.

All updates are designed to make sure that your features retain their existing installation states, and that support files, such as transforms, continue to work as they did before. You can continue to use existing transforms (MST files) on an updated administrative image to reproduce the same customizations for new client installations.

By applying a service release to either an administrative installation point or a stand-alone version of Office XP, you create an upgraded version of the original product. The original product and the upgraded version cannot coexist as separate installations on the same computer.

Planning for a service release

For most organizations, the best way to deploy an Office service release is to create an updated image of the product on an administrative installation point. Local users can then connect to this share and update the version of Office installed on their computers.

If you are staging your upgrades over a period of time, you may need to maintain two administrative installation points during the process:

- The original share to serve as a source for clients who have not yet upgraded.

    Until they upgrade, some clients may need access to the original share for install on demand, automatic feature repair, and other services.

- An updated share from which clients can upgrade to the new service release.

If you need to create administrative installation points in multiple locations, you can copy the folder hierarchy and files from one administrative installation point to additional servers.

Upgrading an administrative installation point

While a standard update package provides a Setup program with dialog boxes and other interface support, you must install an administrative update from the command line. On the command line, you run Windows Installer along with options to specify the path to the updated MSI file and the name of the updated MSP file.

- The MSI file is the Windows Installer package file from your original administrative image.
- The MSP file is the Office administrative update file that contains information on the changes in the upgrade.

    The update instructs Windows Installer to add, update, or remove files in the administrative image.

Administrative update files for Office XP are made available on the Office Resource Kit Web site. The following procedures describe how to apply an update to an administrative installation point.

> **Note** Before you update an administrative installation point, make sure that no users are using the share. If a file on the share is in use during the upgrade process, a newer version of that file is not copied to the installation point.

To apply an update to an Office administrative installation point

1. Download the self-extracting executable file for the update from the Office Resource Kit Web site and double-click the file name to extract the MSP file.

Part 2   Deployment

2. Connect to the server share for your administrative installation point.

   You must have write access to the administrative installation point on the server and the appropriate privileges to carry out the task.

3. On the **Start** menu, click **Run** and then type the command line for Windows Installer with the appropriate options for your installation. Use the following syntax:

   `[start] msiexec /p [path\name of update MSP file] /a [path\name of MSI file] SHORTFILENAMES=TRUE /qb /L* [path\name of log file]`

If an update contains multiple MSP files, you will need to run the command line separately for each MSP file that you apply to the administrative installation point — you cannot reference multiple MSP files on the same command line.

The following table describes the command-line options.

Command-line option	Description
[start]	Required only for Windows 98 systems where **Msiexec** is not directly in the path.
Msiexec	Executable file name for Windows Installer.
/p	Enables Windows Installer to apply an update to an existing installation.
[path\name of update MSP file]	Path and file name of the MSP file for the update.
/a	Enables Windows Installer to perform an administrative installation of a product on a network share.
[path\name of MSI file]	Path and file name of the Windows Installer package for your original administrative image.
SHORTFILENAMES=TRUE	Directs Windows Installer to create all file names and folders with MS-DOS–compatible file names. Required when you run Windows Installer from the command line.
/qb	Sets the user interface to the basic level (simple progress and error handling).
/L*	Turns on logging and sets a path for the log file. The * flag causes the switch to log all information.
[path\name of log file]	Path and file name of the Windows Installer log file.

158   Microsoft Office XP Resource Kit

Updating client computers from an administrative installation point

After you update your administrative installation point, you need to perform a recache and reinstallation on existing client computers that use the administrative image. Any new client installations from the administrative installation point will automatically include the updated version of Office.

To update an existing client installation from an administrative installation point, run the following command line on the client computer:

```
start msiexec /i [path to updated .msi file on the administrative image]
REINSTALL=All REINSTALLMODE=vomus
```

You can run this command line by creating a logon script, distributing it as a batch file, deploying it via Systems Management Server, or using other means according to your practice. The options for this command line are as follows.

Command-line option	Description
[start]	Required only for Windows 98 systems where **Msiexec** is not directly in the path.
Msiexec	Executable file name for Windows Installer.
/I	Enables Windows Installer to apply an update to an existing installation.
[path to updated .msi file on the administrative image]	Path and file name of the Microsoft Installer (.MSI) file on the administrative installation point.
REINSTALL=ALL	Specifies whether you want to reinstall specific features or reinstall all applications on the administrative image.
REINSTALLMODE=vomus	Triggers the recache and reinstallation on the client computer.

Note If you originally installed Office XP on a client computer from an administrative installation point, you must follow the recache and reinstallation procedure described above to update that client. If you update the client directly by using a patch designed for stand-alone computers, the client and administrative images will become out-of-sync, which may cause future updates to fail.

Customizing Office XP while deploying a service release

If you want to modify your existing installations at the same time as you're deploying a service release, you must plan to carry out the two actions separately. For example, to make changes such as adding applications or changing the installation states of existing Office features, you should first deploy the service release, then proceed with the changes.

To make changes to an existing installation, you can run Office Setup in maintenance mode or take advantage of the Custom Maintenance Wizard to change installation states either before or after an update. For more information about the Custom Maintenance Wizard, see "Changing Feature Installation States" in Chapter 8, "Maintaining an Installation."

You cannot redeploy a transform (MST file) when you update an existing installation of Office. A transform can only be used to configure Office during the initial installation. If you try to apply a transform against existing installations, the transform is ignored and the existing settings are maintained.

Synchronizing independently updated client computers

If a client computer is upgraded independently of an administrative installation point, the computer may not recognize an administrative image after it has been updated. Further, its link to the original Office source is no longer usable. To synchronize an independently updated client computer to recognize an updated administrative image, run the following command line on the client computer:

[*path to updated administrative image*] **setup.exe /fvm** [*path to new MSI*]

If the client computer also independently upgraded Microsoft Internet Explorer, this update and resynchronization will not bring in any customizations from the Internet Explorer package on your administrative installation point. You must install Internet Explorer from your original image or other customized location again to update the client computer with your customizations.

Applying an administrative update under Windows 2000

If your administrative installation point and all of your client computers are running Microsoft Windows 2000, you can use IntelliMirror technology to manage the installation of an administrative update.

> **Note** Be sure to test all software updates in a controlled setting before modifying your administrative installation point or deploying the update throughout your organization.

To deploy a QFE fix or update under Windows 2000

1. Apply the updates (MSP files) to the original Office administrative installation point.

   You will need to run the command line separately for each MSP file that you apply to the administrative installation point; you cannot reference multiple MSP files on the same command line.

2. Open the Software Installation snap-in within the Group Policy Object (GPO) that you are using to manage the existing Office installation.

3. In the details pane, right-click the Office package, point to **All Tasks**, and click **Redeploy application**.

The next time the Group Policy Object is applied to the designated users or computers, the updated files are copied to their computers.

> **Note** You can redeploy a package only if it is being managed by Group Policy — that is, only if you originally installed it by using IntelliMirror software installation and maintenance or if you brought it into a managed state under Windows 2000.

Upgrading a stand-alone computer

If you need to update a stand-alone computer (one not associated with an administrative installation point), you can update the computer directly from the World Wide Web or from a CD. Updates for stand-alone computers are made available on release from the Microsoft Office Web site and through channels such as Enterprise Agreement, Select, and Microsoft Developer's Network.

When you run Setup for an Office service release, Setup first detects which Office applications and supporting components are installed on the computer, and then displays the appropriate upgrade options. As part of the Setup process, you must enter the product ID (PID) key from your original Office XP CD. Be sure to find your original CD case or product ID number before you start the upgrade.

As with all software installations and upgrades, you need to have the appropriate systems-level privileges on the computer in order to complete the upgrade.

> **Note** If you update a client computer independently of an administrative installation point on the same network, the client will no longer recognize the administrative image. Be sure to update client computers by using the procedures described in "Updating client computers from an administrative installation point," earlier in this topic.

To install an update on a stand-alone computer

1. Close all Windows-based applications.

   If you are installing the update from the World Wide Web, go to the appropriate download page on the Microsoft Office Web site.

   –or–

   If you are installing the update from a CD, insert the CD into the CD-ROM drive.

2. Run the Setup program for the update.

   To run the update with the default settings, double-click the **Download Now** link on the Web site. If you are installing from a CD, Setup will start automatically when you insert the disc into the drive.

   –or–

   To run the update with command-line options, click **Run** on the **Start** menu and type the path and update name with the appropriate options.

3. When the update starts and the license agreement dialog box is displayed, read the agreement and click **Yes** to continue the installation.
4. Follow the instructions on your screen to complete the upgrade.
5. Restart your computer after the installation is complete.

CHAPTER 6

Deploying on Windows 2000

Microsoft Windows 2000 offers significant advantages to organizations that deploy Microsoft Office XP. Windows 2000 already includes the required level of system files, so Setup skips that portion of the installation process. In addition, Windows 2000 offers new management tools that centralize installation, maintenance, and upgrades of applications. Under Windows 2000, you can even install Office remotely on new computers.

In this chapter

Deployment Issues Specific to Windows 2000   163

Using Windows 2000 Software Installation   165

Deployment Issues Specific to Windows 2000

Microsoft Windows® 2000 offers a number of benefits to organizations that are deploying Microsoft Office XP:

- Office XP requires the same level of system files as the release version of Windows 2000, so the System Files Update installation is not required.
- Windows 2000 offers management features that allow you to centrally install and manage Office applications on users' computers, while Windows 2000 automatically maintains the desired configuration.
- By using remote installation services (RIS), you can install customized configurations of both Windows 2000 and Office XP remotely on client computers.

Windows 2000 installation requirements

Requirements under Windows 2000 include the following:

- You must have elevated privileges to install Office XP under Windows 2000.

    For more information about elevating the Office XP installation, see "Installations That Require Elevated Privileges" in Chapter 4, "Overview of Setup."

Part 2 Deployment

- In order to use Windows 2000 software installation, all the computers in your organization must be running Windows 2000, and you must already have implemented an Active Directory™ directory service and Group Policy structure.

- Because Windows 2000 software installation works directly with the MSI file and bypasses Office XP Setup.exe and Setup.ini, all customizations must be made through a transform.

- Windows 2000 software installation deploys each package separately and in random order, so you cannot chain other packages to your Office XP installation.

  If you deploy Office Multilingual User Interface Packs at the same time as Office XP, set the **CHECKINSTALLORDER** property to **False** to ensure that the MUI Packs are installed even if Office XP is not.

- You cannot run the Systems File Update installation under Windows 2000.

  If you want to deploy Internet Explorer 5.5 or later, you must install it separately, before you install Office XP.

Using Windows 2000 software installation

You use a set of Windows 2000–based technologies known collectively as IntelliMirror® to install and manage Office XP by policy. IntelliMirror includes the software installation and maintenance feature, which allows an administrator to install, repair, update, or remove Office XP by using Group Policy.

There are three ways to install and manage Office XP applications by policy:

- Assign Office to computers

  Office is installed on the computer the next time the computer starts. Users can repair Office applications on the computer, but only an administrator can remove applications.

- Assign Office to users

  Office is available to all users in the designated group the next time they log on. Each Office application is installed the first time a user clicks the associated shortcut on the **Start** menu or opens a file associated with that Office application.

- Publish Office to users

  Office is available to all users in the designated group the next time they log on. Users install Office through **Add/Remove Programs** in Control Panel or by opening an Office document. (Note that under Windows 2000, you cannot publish an application to a computer.)

When you use the Windows 2000 software installation, you can specify a transform to apply at the time the Office XP package is assigned or published. When users run Office XP Setup in maintenance mode, Windows 2000 also allows you to customize the text and options that appear in **Add/Remove Programs** in Control Panel.

For example, to prevent users from changing an installed Office configuration, you can set the Setup property **ARPMODIFY** to **True** in the transform. When users run Office XP Setup in maintenance mode, the **Change** button in **Add/Remove Programs** is unavailable.

For more information about using Windows 2000 Group Policy and software installation tools to deploy Office XP, see "Using Windows 2000 Software Installation" later in this chapter.

> **Toolbox** The Office XP Resource Kit Toolbox includes a document named Setupref.doc that defines Setup properties that you can set for Office XP, including the properties that modify **Add/Remove Programs**. Setupref.doc is installed by default when you run the Office Resource Kit Setup program. For more information, see "Supplemental Documentation" in the Toolbox.

Using Remote Installation Services

Remote OS Installation, which is based on Remote Installation Services (RIS), is an optional service in Windows 2000 Server. It provides a mechanism for computers to connect to a network server during the initial startup process, while the server controls a local installation of Windows 2000 Professional.

If all the computers in your organization are running under Windows 2000, you can use remote installation services to copy a preconfigured hard-disk image — with standardized versions of both Windows 2000 Professional and Office XP — to client computers. RIS also requires that you have Active Directory and a Group Policy structure set up.

This method can significantly reduce deployment time. A remote installation of Windows and Office together takes only slightly longer than a remote installation of Windows by itself. When clients download the disk image, Office XP is fully installed on the local computer — and not merely advertised.

For more information about creating a hard-disk image for Office XP, see "Distributing Office to Users' Computers" in Chapter 5, "Installing and Customizing Office."

For a detailed outline of the steps necessary to install, configure, and use RIS, see the "Step-by-Step Guide to Remote OS Installation" on the Microsoft Windows 2000 Web site at http://www.microsoft.com/windows2000/library/planning/management/remotesteps.asp.

Using Windows 2000 Software Installation

Microsoft Windows 2000 provides new software installation and maintenance capabilities that make it faster, easier, and less expensive to deploy Microsoft Office XP in a homogenous Windows 2000 environment. Because many administrative tasks can be accomplished remotely or automatically, users require fewer on-site visits from technical support staff. And because users have persistent access to their applications, data, and settings, they can continue working without interruption.

When you use the software installation and maintenance features of Windows 2000 with Office XP, you can help ensure the following:

- Users have access to the Office applications they need to do their jobs whenever they log on to the network — and no matter which computer they use.
- Computers are equipped with essential applications, such as Microsoft Outlook® or virus protection software, whenever they start up.
- Office applications are automatically installed, updated, repaired, or removed according to the rules that you define.

Relying on Active Directory and Group Policy

In a Windows 2000–based network, the Active Directory™ directory service provides the framework for centralized administration of users and computers. Active Directory stores information about objects on the network, and makes this information easy for administrators and users to find and use.

Network objects in this context include users, computers, and printers — as well as domains, sites, and organizational units. A structured data store provides the basis for a logical, hierarchical organization of all directory information.

Active Directory makes it possible to manage all users, computers, and software on the network through administrator-defined policies, known as Group Policy in Windows 2000. A collection of Group Policy settings is contained in a Group Policy object (GPO), and the GPO is associated with an Active Directory container.

The Group Policy object can be applied at any level of the Active Directory hierarchy. You can set policies that apply to an entire site, a domain, or an individual organizational unit.

Group Policy options include the following:

- Registry-based settings, including Office XP system policies
- Scripts
- Microsoft Internet Explorer maintenance
- Folder redirection
- Security settings
- Remote installation services
- Software installation and maintenance

After you set up your Active Directory and Group Policy structure under Windows 2000, you use a set of Windows 2000–based technologies known collectively as IntelliMirror to install and manage Office XP by policy. IntelliMirror includes the following features:

- Software installation and maintenance

    Allows an administrator to centrally manage software installation, repairs, updates, and removal.

- User data management

    Supports mirroring of user data to the network and local copies of selected network data.

- User settings management

    Allows an administrator to centrally define settings for users and computers. Also includes mirroring of user settings to the network.

The deployment and management tools designed for Office XP — including the Custom Installation Wizard and Office XP policy template files — work with IntelliMirror. By using all these tools together, you can make a unique configuration of Office available to all users or computers in a given GPO, and then rely on Windows 2000 to maintain your software configuration automatically.

Using IntelliMirror to install Office

In Windows 2000, the IntelliMirror software installation and maintenance feature allows you to manage Office XP applications within a Group Policy object (GPO), which is associated with a particular Active Directory container — a site, domain, or organizational unit.

Within the GPO, you specify Group Policy settings to assign or publish Office to users or computers based on their Active Directory group memberships. You set policy definitions for Office XP once. After that, Windows 2000 applies them for you automatically.

There are three ways to install and manage Office XP applications by policy:

- Assign Office to computers

    Office is installed on the computer the next time the computer starts and is available to all users of the computer. Users can repair Office applications on the computer, but only an administrator can remove applications.

- Assign Office to users

    Office is available to all users in the designated group the next time each user logs on to a computer. Each Office application is installed the first time a user clicks the associated shortcut on the **Start** menu or opens a file associated with that Office application.

    Note After an assigned user installs Office, the applications are not necessarily available to subsequent users of the computer. Instead, each assigned user's Office configuration follows the user from computer to computer.

- Publish Office to users

    Office is available to all users in the designated group the next time they log on. Users install Office through **Add/Remove Programs** in Control Panel or by opening an Office document. (Note that under Windows 2000, you cannot publish an application to a computer.)

Avoiding installation conflicts

Do not assign Office to both a user and a computer. When assigned to a computer, Office applications are installed locally (based on settings in the transform). When assigned to a user, Office applications are advertised on the computer, but are not installed until the user activates them — one Windows Installer shortcut at a time.

Assigning Office to both users and computers can create conflicts in which Office applications appear to be installed locally but are actually only advertised.

In addition, if you assign Office to both users and computers and also apply different transforms, Windows 2000 automatically uninstalls and reinstalls Office every time the computer starts or the user logs on.

Assign Office to computers

Assigning Office to computers is the simplest way to use IntelliMirror to manage a package as large and complex as Office XP. With this method, Office is automatically installed the first time a designated computer is started and the software installation portion of Group Policy is applied.

Assigned applications are resilient under Windows 2000. If a user removes an Office application from the computer, Windows automatically reinstalls it the next time the computer starts.

Supporting knowledge workers with dedicated computers

If you are supporting a group of knowledge workers, each of whom uses a dedicated computer with consistent, high-speed connections to the network, you can assign Office to that group's computers. The next time users start up their computers, the entire Office package is installed. To minimize the amount of network traffic, you can apply a transform that installs a subset of Office features on the local computer.

Supporting shared computers

If users in your organization typically share computers, you can assign a standard Office configuration. For example, for bank tellers who work from different stations but still perform the same tasks, you can ensure that the same Office configuration is available to them no matter which computer they use.

Assigning to computers also minimizes potential conflicts when users who perform different jobs share the same computer. These users often need different sets of Office applications or features. By applying a transform when you assign Office, you can ensure that all the Office features required by all users are installed at the outset.

Assign Office to users

Assigning Office to users allows you to take advantage of additional IntelliMirror management features. This method ensures that users have access to the same Office configuration no matter where they are or which computer they use. Their Office installation is based on Group Policy — not fixed by their location.

When you assign Office to users, information about the software is advertised on users' computers in the Windows registry and on the **Start** menu or Desktop the next time the users log on. When a user clicks an Office application shortcut, Windows Installer retrieves the package from the administrative installation point, installs the application on the user's computer, and starts the application. If you choose to activate installation by file extension, clicking an Office document automatically installs the corresponding application in the same way.

Applications assigned to users are also resilient. If a user removes an assigned Office application from the computer, Windows automatically restores the registry information and Windows Installer shortcuts the next time the user logs on.

Supporting roaming users

In many organizations, users with unique job responsibilities roam from one computer to another. If you assign Office to users in this scenario, their Office configuration is available to them wherever they log on. You control which Office configuration is available to a given group of users by applying a transform when you assign the software to the GPO.

Individual Office applications and features are not installed until the user activates them by clicking a shortcut or opening a file. Because these users typically have consistent, high-speed network connections, the installation process takes little time.

> **Note** If roaming users in your organization do not have administrative privileges, and if they also share computers, then Office may not be installed correctly for every user on every computer. In this scenario, assign a standard Office configuration to every computer.

Targeting groups of users more precisely

Assigning to users allows you to target your Office installation more precisely. For example, you can assign Office to particular organizational units and apply a unique transform to each group.

Alternatively, you can assign Office to users at a higher level in the Active Directory hierarchy, and then filter the Group Policy settings through Windows 2000 security groups. Users who would otherwise inherit an Office installation through their Active Directory group memberships can be prevented from installing Office through their security group memberships.

Publish Office to users

When you publish Office to users, no information about the software is present in the registry or on the **Start** menu. However, users can click **Add/Remove Programs** in Control Panel and view a list of all software published to them.

If a user selects Office from this list, **Add/Remove Programs** retrieves information about the Office installation location from Active Directory, and Windows Installer installs the package on the computer and applies any transform that you have associated with the Office package.

If you plan to have users run Office Setup themselves (for example, if your organization routinely makes a variety of software applications available to users from an installation location on the network), consider publishing Office to users. In this case, users in the designated group can install Office from **Add/Remove Programs** anytime they choose.

Unlike assigned applications, published applications are not automatically reinstalled. If a user removes Office after installing it from **Add/Remove Programs**, the shortcuts and registry information are not automatically reapplied on the computer. However, the next time the user logs on to the network, Office is republished in **Add/Remove Programs**.

Apply a transform to customize Office

You control which Office applications and features are available to users by applying a transform (MST file) when you assign or publish the Office package (MSI file). Note that you can apply only one transform to a given installation of the Office XP package.

> **Important** Transforms are applied when Office is assigned or published. You cannot reapply a transform after Office is installed. If you need to modify a managed Office installation, you must remove and then reinstall Office with a new transform.

On the **Set Feature Installation States** page of the Custom Installation Wizard, you set installation options for individual Office applications or features.

For example, when you assign or publish Office, you can:

- Set an application to **Not Available** and hide it to prevent it from appearing on the **Start** menu or in **Add/Remove Programs**.

  If you want to hide an application and make it inaccessible to users, you can set the installation state to **Not Available, Hidden, Locked** — a new setting exposed in the Custom Installation Wizard. This setting is reversible when you use the Custom Maintenance Wizard.

- Set an application to **Run from Network** to store the source files on the network and allow users to run the application from there.

- Set an application to **Installed on My Computer** to install it locally.

  (This option applies only if you assign to computers or publish to users. When you assign to users, applications are not installed locally until a user clicks the Windows Installer shortcut.)

> **Toolbox** The Office XP Resource Kit includes the Custom Installation Wizard and Custom Maintenance Wizard, which are installed when you run the Office Resource Kit Setup program. For more information, see "Custom Installation Wizard" or "Custom Maintenance Wizard" in the Toolbox.

Installation scenarios

Suppose you want to make Office available to all users in the marketing department. Using Group Policy and IntelliMirror software installation, you can assign the package to either all the computers or all the users managed by the marketing GPO.

Assign to computers

In this scenario, Office applications are advertised on every computer managed by the marketing GPO. The first time the computer starts, Windows Installer installs the Office package locally (based on the feature installation states specified in the transform), and the applications are accessible to anyone who uses that computer.

A user can remove Office from this computer through **Add/Remove Programs** in Control Panel. However, the next time the computer is started, Office is reinstalled based on the Group Policy settings.

Assign to users

In this scenario, Office applications are advertised to every user in the marketing GPO. The next time each user logs on, the Windows registry is updated and the appropriate Windows Installer shortcuts appear on the **Start** menu.

Although Office is now available, the assigned applications are not installed. However, users in the marketing department probably start Outlook as soon as they log on. At that point, the following events occur:

- A background Windows service calls Windows Installer.
- The minimal set of files required to run Outlook is downloaded from a distribution point on the network and installed on the user's computer.
- Outlook starts.

If the user receives an e-mail message with an attached Word document and double-clicks the document shortcut, Windows Installer is called to install Word. If the user edits the document in Word and clicks **Help** for assistance, Windows Installer is called again to install the Help feature.

A user in marketing can delete an assigned Office application through **Add/Remove Programs** in Control Panel. But because the assigned Office application is managed under IntelliMirror, the installation information that advertises Office in the Windows registry and that adds shortcuts to the **Start** menu is immediately reapplied. The next time the user logs on, the application is assigned again without intervention from the administrator.

> **Tip** IntelliMirror tools can affect large groups of users, and inadvertent errors or conflicting settings can cause considerable inconvenience. Before you use IntelliMirror to install Office throughout your organization, it is highly recommended that you test your deployment scenario in a controlled setting.

How to assign or publish Office applications

Before you assign or publish Office XP in a Windows 2000–based environment, you must perform the following preliminary steps:

1. Plan and set up your Active Directory structure and Group Policy and security group memberships.

2. Determine which users need which configuration of Office.

    By default, Group Policy settings apply to all Active Directory containers lower in the hierarchy, so it is usually best to assign Office at the highest possible level. Then you can filter Group Policy through Windows 2000 security groups to target users more precisely.

3. Install Office on an administrative installation point by running Setup with the **/a** command-line option.

4. Use the Custom Installation Wizard to customize your Office installation, and store the transform (MST file) on the administrative installation point.

5. Give users read-access to the network share that contains the administrative installation point.

Then you are ready to use the Software Installation snap-in to assign or publish Office to users or computers.

Open the Software Installation snap-in

In Windows 2000, the Microsoft Management Console (MMC) provides a consistent interface for using administrative tools called snap-ins. After you set up Group Policy in your organization and install Office XP on an administrative installation point, you can use the Software Installation snap-in to specify Group Policy settings for users or computers managed by a particular GPO.

There are several ways to open the Software Installation snap-in, which is an extension of the Group Policy snap-in. If you are applying Group Policy to a domain or organizational unit (as opposed to a site), the best place to start is with the Active Directory Users and Computers snap-in.

To open the Software Installation snap-in

1. On the **Start** menu, point to **Programs**, point to **Administrative Tools**, and then click **Active Directory Users and Computers**.

2. In the console tree, right-click the domain or organizational unit for which you want to set Group Policy.

3. Click **Properties**, and then click the **Group Policy** tab.

4. To create a new GPO, click **New** and type a name for the GPO; then select the new GPO and click **Edit**.

   –or–

   To edit an existing GPO, select the GPO in the **Group Policy Objects Links** box and click **Edit**.

5. To assign or publish software to users, click the **User Configuration** node.

   –or–

   To assign software to computers, click the **Computer Configuration** node.

6. Expand the **Software Settings** node, and then click the Software Installation node to open the Software Installation snap-in.

The following illustration shows the Group Policy Software Installation snap-in for a GPO in which Office XP has been published to users.

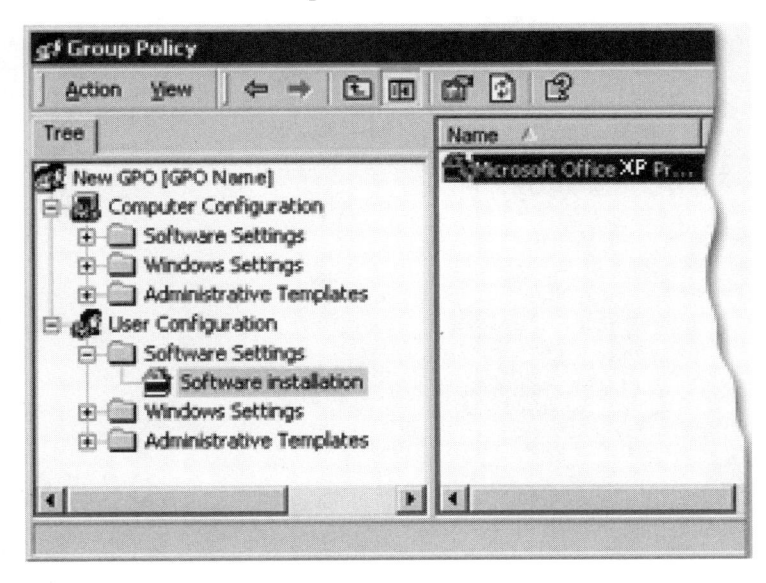

General tab

When you publish or assign the Office XP package, relevant information about the package is automatically displayed on the **General** tab.

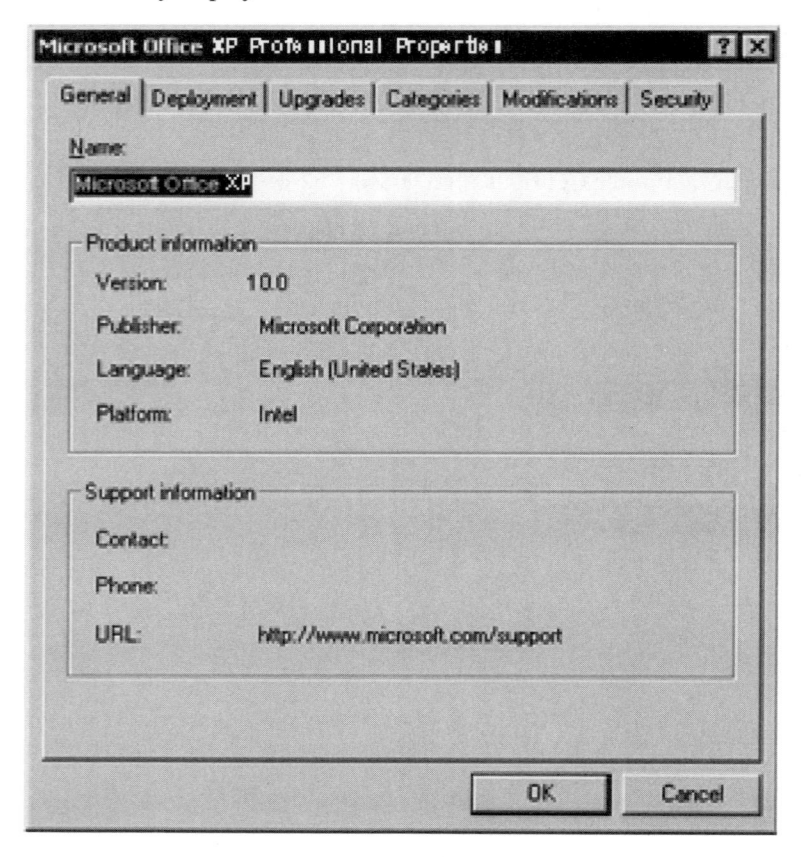

Deployment tab

On the **Deployment** tab, you specify whether to publish or assign Office XP. Note that if you open the snap-in under Computer Configuration, the **Published** option is unavailable.

Under **Deployment** options, select check boxes to specify when and how Office XP is installed on users' computers. You can set any of the following options:

- Install Office applications automatically when users open a file associated with an Office application. This setting is turned on by default.

    For example, if Excel is assigned to a user and the user double-clicks an Excel document, Windows 2000 installs Excel.

    > **Note** You cannot trigger an installation of Word by file association. In this case, double-clicking a Word document opens WordPad, instead of installing Word.

- Automatically remove Office when the computer or the user moves to another GPO that does not manage Office XP.

    Administrators can choose whether Office XP is removed in this circumstance, or whether the package remains installed but is no longer managed by Group Policy.

- Prevent assigned applications from appearing in **Add/Remove Programs** in Control Panel.

    You can set this option to hide critical applications from users and display only optional (published) applications. This option can also be useful when Office is assigned to multiple users who share one computer. It prevents one user from changing the Office configuration and removing an application required by another user. (You can achieve the same result by assigning Office to the computer, instead of to the users.)

Under **Installation user interface options**, you specify how much of Office Setup is displayed to users during the installation process. The recommended setting (and the default) is **Basic**, which installs Office quietly and requires no user interaction. (The Basic setting corresponds to the **/qb-** command-line option.)

> **Tip** If you want users to be able to choose an installation location for Office and set some Setup properties for themselves, you can use IntelliMirror and still run Setup with a full user interface. To give users this access, you set the Windows Installer system policy **Enable user control over installs**. In the Group Policy Editor, you find this policy in the Local Computer Policy\Computer Configuration\Administrative Templates\Windows Installer folder.

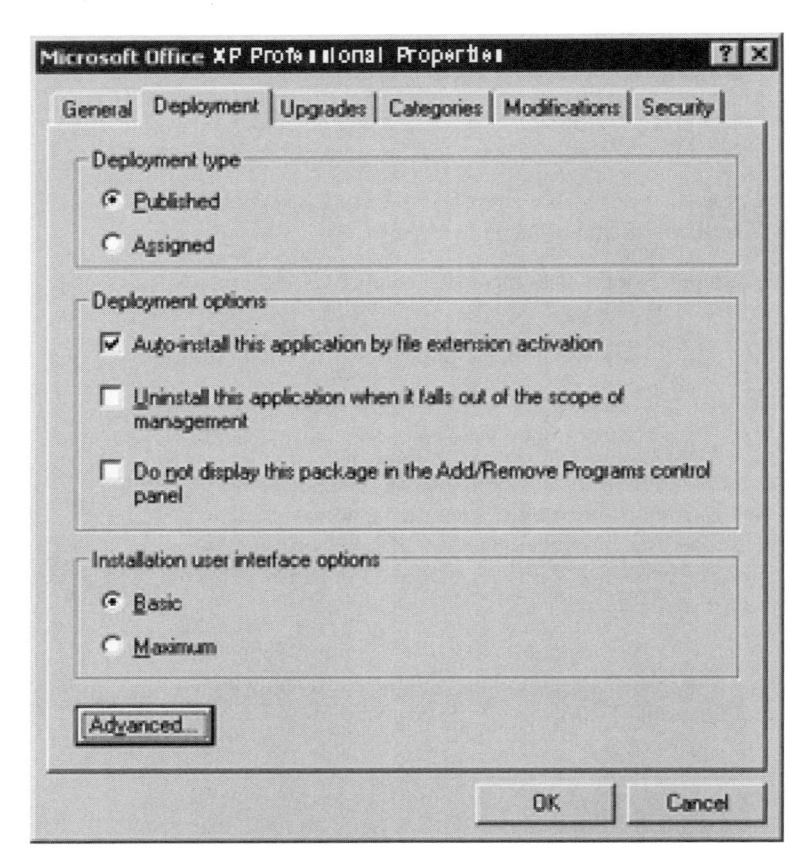

To set additional deployment options, click **Advanced**. In the **Advanced Deployment Options** dialog box, you can:

- Specify that Windows 2000 should install Office XP even if the Office installation language differs from the Windows 2000 installation language.

  Select this option if you are deploying Office XP with the Office Multilingual User Interface Pack (MUI Pack) on a computer where English is not the default language. This setting allows you to assign U.S. English Office (the core version) and then install the MUI Packs to add additional language support.

- Remove unmanaged Office installations when you deploy Office through Group Policy software installation and maintenance.

  If you have already deployed Office XP in your organization and are making the transition to Window 2000, select this option to remove and then reinstall Office in a managed state on users' computers. This scenario is described later in this chapter.

Upgrades tab

If you are already managing an Office XP installation under Windows 2000, you can use the **Upgrades** tab to deploy a new version of the product. This upgrade scenario is described later in this chapter.

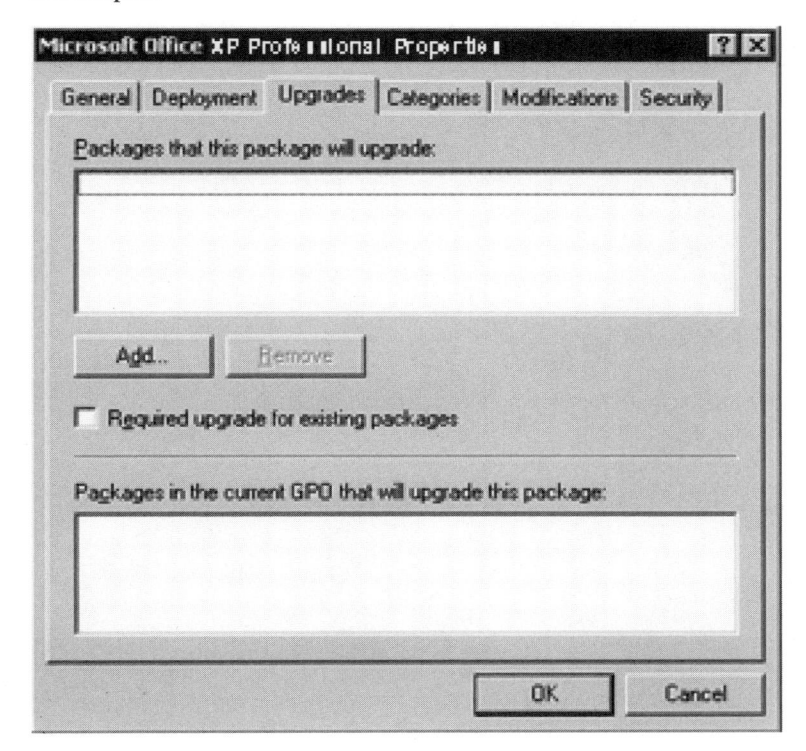

Categories tab

Associating Office XP with a category can make Office easier for users to find in **Add/Remove Programs** in Control Panel. However, you must already have set up categories for your organization in Active Directory. In that case, you can use the **Categories** tab to assign the new Office package to an available category.

Modifications tab

You use the **Modifications** tab to apply a transform (MST file) to your Office installation. Click **Add**, select your transform, and then click **Open** to add it to the **Modifications** tab.

Note that you can add multiple transforms, but you can apply only one transform to a given Office XP installation, and you can apply the transform only when you assign or publish Office. If you assign or publish the Office package to several GPOs, however, you can add a unique transform to each one.

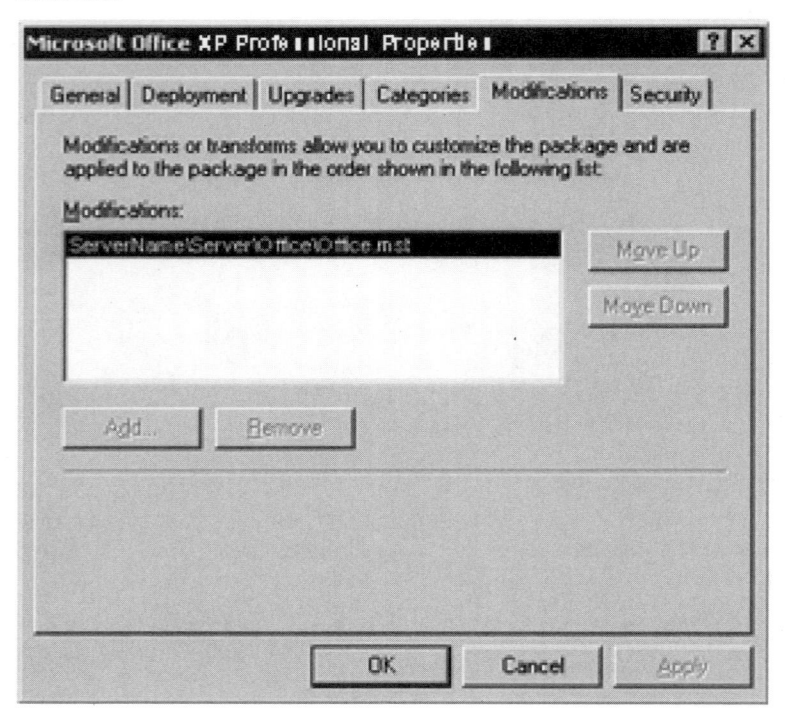

Security tab

The **Security** tab displays standard Windows 2000–based security options. You can fine-tune your Office deployment by filtering the Group Policy software installation settings through Windows 2000 access control lists (ACLs). To do this, click **Advanced**, and then click the **Permissions** tab.

Tips for managing Office XP through Group Policy

You can assign unique configurations of Office to different GPOs within your organization. For example, if the engineering and marketing departments are managed by separate GPOs, you can include Microsoft Access in the engineering transform, and substitute Microsoft PowerPoint® in the marketing transform.

In a properly designed Group Policy structure, Group Policy applies policies by precedence. As long as you give each transform a unique name, users receive the Office configuration designed for them.

Remember that you cannot change settings in a transform after you deploy Office through Group Policy. If you make changes to the installation later on — for example, if you try to apply a new transform — Windows 2000 automatically uninstalls Office and reinstates the configuration set by Group Policy. Nor can you use the Custom Maintenance Wizard to modify an installation being managed through Group Policy To change the Office configuration without uninstalling and reinstalling Office, you must use another deployment mechanism, such as Systems Management Server or a logon script, that can run a new command line.

How to maintain Office under Windows 2000

After you establish an Active Directory structure and install Office XP by using Group Policy, Windows 2000 maintains your installation automatically. But new organizational needs, upgrade schedules, or software updates might require some administrative intervention.

Bring an unmanaged installation into a managed state

In some circumstances, you may need to bring an unmanaged Office XP installation into a managed state under Windows 2000. Any installation scenario that does not use Group Policy and IntelliMirror software installation and maintenance results in an unmanaged Office installation.

For example, the following scenarios install Office in an unmanaged state:

- You upgrade to Office XP under Windows NT® 4.0, and subsequently upgrade your operating system to Windows 2000 Server and Windows 2000 Professional.
- You install Office XP by using Microsoft Systems Management Server — even in a homogenous Windows 2000 environment.
- You install Office XP by distributing hard-disk images on a CD.

The most straightforward method of making the transition to a managed state is to remove your original Office installation and reinstall Office from a new administrative installation point by using IntelliMirror software installation and maintenance — particularly if you upgrade to Windows 2000 after your initial Office XP deployment.

For example, suppose that you installed Office XP in an unmanaged state, and you are now installing an Office XP service release under Windows 2000. In this scenario, use the following procedure to assign the new Office XP package and remove the original unmanaged Office XP installation.

To reinstall Office XP in a managed state

1. Open the Software Installation snap-in for the target GPO and assign or publish the new Office XP package, as described earlier in this topic.

2. In the **Microsoft Office XP Properties** dialog box, click the **Deployment** tab, and then click **Advanced**.

3. Select the **Remove previous installs of this product for users, if the product was not installed by Group Policy–based Software Installation** check box, and click **OK**.

4. Configure any other options you want in the **Microsoft Office XP Properties** dialog box, and click **OK**.

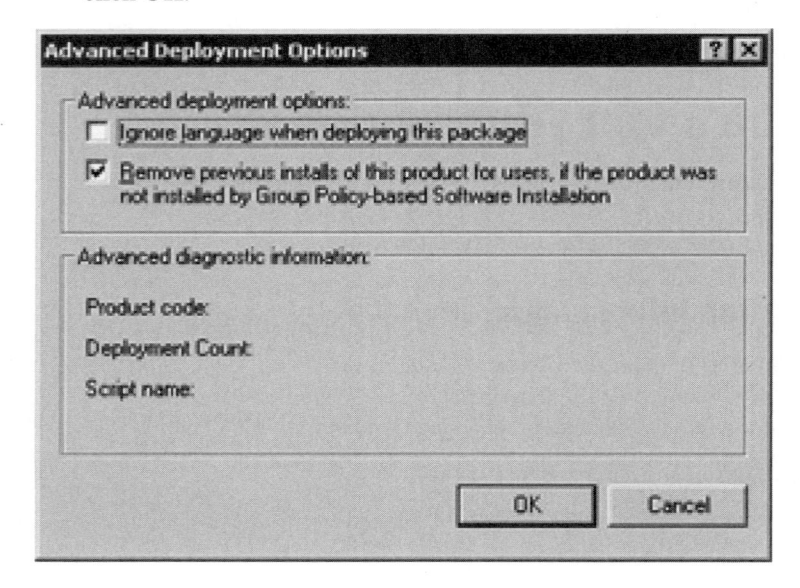

If you know that you will eventually manage Office XP by using IntelliMirror tools, you can install Office in such a way that you avoid having to remove and reinstall it later.

To bring Office into a managed state under Windows 2000

1. Create an administrative installation point for Office and install the Office package (MSI file) and transform (MST file) at that location.

2. Install Office on users' computers from this location by using Systems Management Server or any other distribution method.

3. Upgrade to Windows 2000 and create your Active Directory and Group Policy structure.
4. Using the same administrative installation point, assign Office XP to the appropriate GPO.

   You must use the identical package and transform from the original administrative installation point.
5. Move the computers that have your original Office configuration to the Active Directory container that includes the GPO from Step 4.

   The next time users start up their computers, Windows 2000 detects the Office configuration and manages the installation from that point forward.

   Caution If the Office configuration you assign by using Group Policy differs in any respect from your original Office installation, Windows 2000 automatically removes and reinstalls Office. You must use the same package (MSI file) and apply the same transform (MST file) with no modifications. IntelliMirror ensures that an approved Office configuration is installed on the computer, and it removes any installation that differs from that configuration — even if the differences are minor changes in the transform.

Distribute service releases and upgrades

After you complete your Office XP installation under Windows 2000, you may need to deploy updates to the original package. These updates include quick fix engineering (QFE) fixes and service releases. You can use IntelliMirror software and installation to manage these interim updates to Office XP, along with full-scale product upgrades.

Note Be sure to test all software updates in a controlled setting before modifying your administrative installation point or deploying the new version throughout your organization.

To deploy a QFE fix or service release

1. Apply the update or patch (MSP file) to the original Office administrative installation point.
2. Open the Software Installation snap-in within the Group Policy object (GPO) that you are using to manage the existing Office installation.
3. In the details pane, right-click the Office package, point to **All Tasks**, and click **Redeploy application**.

   The next time the Group Policy is applied to the designated users or computers, the Office XP MSI file is recached locally, and only the updated files are copied to users' computers.

   Note You can redeploy a package only if it is being managed by Group Policy — that is, only if you originally installed it by using IntelliMirror software installation and maintenance or if you brought it into a managed state under Windows 2000.

You can also use IntelliMirror to deploy future upgrades of Office — that is, a new package with a new product code.

To deploy a product upgrade

1. Install the new package (MSI file) and transform (MST file) on a new administrative installation point.

2. Open the Software Installation snap-in within the Group Policy object (GPO) that you are using to manage the existing Office installation.

3. In the details pane, right-click the original Office package, click **Properties**, and then click the **Upgrades** tab.

4. Click **Add**.

5. In the **Add Upgrade Package** dialog box, click **Browse** to locate the new Office package that you want to deploy, select it, and click **OK**.

6. To reinstall with the new version, click **Uninstall the existing package, then install upgrade package**, and click **OK**. This option completely removes the previous version and installs the new version as a new product on the computer.

   –or–

   To upgrade the existing Office installation, click **Package can upgrade over existing package**, and click **OK**.

   Note that if you are upgrading from Office 2000 and you have assigned Office to users, you must remove Office 2000 before you deploy the new package. For more information, see "Upgrade from Office 2000 to Office XP" later in this section.

7. On the **Upgrades** tab, select the **Required upgrade for existing packages** check box to make the upgrade mandatory for all users in the GPO.

8. Click **OK** to close the **Microsoft Office XP Properties** dialog box.

9. In the details pane, right-click the Office package, point to **All Tasks**, and click **Redeploy application**.

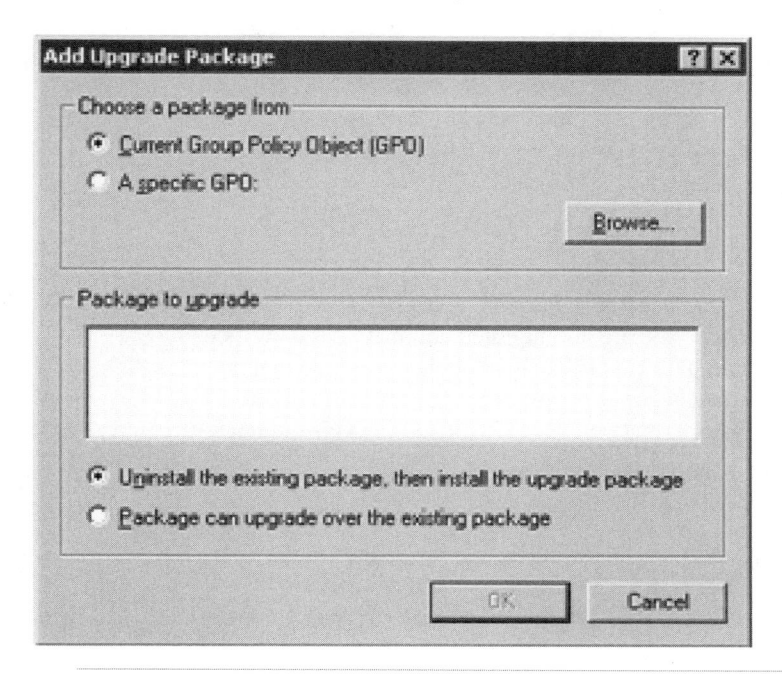

Important To avoid a series of removals and reinstallations when you upgrade, make sure that you create an upgrade relationship between the new package and all previous versions of the product on the **Upgrades** tab. For example, establish an upgrade relationship between Office XP and Office 2000.

Upgrade from Office 2000 to Office XP

If you are upgrading from a managed Office 2000 installation, you can use Group Policy and the options in the Software Installation snap-in to manage the transition to Office XP. You begin by creating an administrative installation point for Office XP and by creating any transforms you want to apply. Then you open the Software Installation snap-in in the GPO and add the new package. The steps you take after that depend upon whether you assign Office to computers or to users.

If you assign Office to computers, you get the most benefit from creating an upgrade relationship between Office 2000 and Office XP. On the **Upgrades** tab, choose the **Package can upgrade over existing package** option. This option allows you to take advantage of the upgrade logic built into Office XP Setup. For example:

- Office 2000 feature installation states are automatically migrated to Office XP.
- Only the files that need to be updated are copied to the user's computer.

If you assign Office to users, however, and you choose to upgrade over Office 2000, then the old applications and shortcuts might not be properly removed from users' computers. In this case, the recommended method is to remove Office 2000 before you deploy Office XP. When you deploy the Office XP package, select the **Uninstall the existing package, then install upgrade package** option on the **Upgrades** tab. This option completely removes the previous version and advertises Office XP as a new product on the computer.

> **Note** When you remove Office 2000 and then assign Office XP, users may experience a significant delay the first time they log on.

Because Office is not truly upgraded in this scenario, some automatic migration behavior does not happen. For example, users' settings from Office 2000 are not migrated automatically to Office XP. And Office XP Shortcut Bar shortcuts that reference Office 2000 applications may not be updated to point to Office XP applications. You can duplicate automatic migration behavior manually, however, by setting values in a transform that you apply to the Office XP installation.

To migrate user settings the first time an Office application is started

1. Start the Custom Installation Wizard.
2. On the **Add/Remove Registry Entries** page, add the following registry values to the HKEY_LOCAL_MACHINE\Software\Microsoft\Office\10.0\Common\Migration*Application* key, where *Application* is Office, Access, Excel, FrontPage, PowerPoint, or Word. (Outlook settings migrate automatically.)

Registry value	Registry data
Lang	**1033** (English) or another LCID
Path	'''' (empty)
UpgradeVersion	9

For example, to trigger migration of Office 2000 common settings, Word 2000 settings, and Excel 2000 settings, add the following registry keys and values in the Custom Installation Wizard:

- HKEY_LOCAL_MACHINE\Software\Microsoft\Office\10.0\Common\Migration\Office

    Lang = **1033**
    Path = ''''
    UpgradeVersion = 9

- HKEY_LOCAL_MACHINE\Software\Microsoft\Office\10.0\Common\Migration\Word

    Lang = **1033**
    Path = ''''
    UpgradeVersion = 9

- HKEY_LOCAL_MACHINE\Software\Microsoft\Office\10.0\Common\Migration\Excel

    Lang   = 1033

    Path   = ""

    UpgradeVersion = 9

Similarly, if you discover during testing that Office 2000 shortcuts are left on the Office XP Shortcut Bar, you can clean up users' outdated shortcuts by removing the corresponding LNK files in the transform.

To remove Office XP Shortcut Bar shortcuts that reference Office 2000 applications

1. Start the Custom Installation Wizard.
2. On the **Add/Remove Files** page, click the **Remove Files** tab.
3. Using the path <Application Data>\Microsoft\Office\Shortcut Bar, add the following files to the list of files to remove:
    - Microsoft Access.lnk
    - Microsoft Excel.lnk
    - Microsoft FrontPage.lnk
    - New Appointment.lnk
    - New Contact.lnk
    - New Journal Entry.lnk
    - New Message.lnk
    - New Note.lnk
    - New Task.lnk
    - Microsoft Outlook.lnk
    - Microsoft PowerPoint.lnk
    - Microsoft Word.lnk
    - Microsoft Binder.lnk
    - New Office Document.lnk
    - Open Office Document.lnk
    - Screen Saver.lnk

When to use other installation technologies

IntelliMirror software installation and maintenance offers significant benefits to organizations that are deploying Office XP and other applications under Windows 2000. Not only does IntelliMirror allow administrators to centrally manage software installation, it also allows them to maintain and preserve users' settings and files.

By itself, however, IntelliMirror is not the most efficient or cost-effective choice for deploying Office in all circumstances. For example, IntelliMirror does not provide the following:

- Support for clients running any version of Windows other than Windows 2000
- Hardware and software inventory and reporting
- A licensing mechanism
- Reports for failed installations
- Precise control over the timing of Office XP installations

Because assigned applications are installed on start up or on first use, all users might try to install new applications from the network on the first day of the work week. By contrast, users who do not regularly log off and on the network might not see assigned or published applications at all.

If you need additional capabilities, you can use either Windows 2000 remote installation services or Microsoft Systems Management Server 2.0 instead of, or in combination with, IntelliMirror software installation and maintenance.

See also

For a general introduction to the new management services in Windows 2000, see the documentation on the Management Services page of the Microsoft Windows 2000 Web site at http://www.microsoft.com/windows2000/library/technologies/management/default.asp.

For information about planning your Active Directory structure and setting up Group Policy, search for **Software Installation preparation checklist** in the Windows 2000 Server Help page, which available on the Microsoft Windows 2000 Web site at http://windows.microsoft.com/windows2000/en/server/help.

For more information about how Windows 2000 technologies and SMS work together, see "Understanding the Value of IntelliMirror, Remote OS Installation, and Systems Management Server" on the Microsoft Windows 2000 Web site at http://www.microsoft.com/windows2000/guide/server/solutions/valueim.asp.

The Windows 2000 Technical Library on the World Wide Web contains detailed step-by-step guides for using the new installation tools and technologies, including the following:

- "Step-by-Step Guide to Understanding the Group Policy Feature Set" at http://www.microsoft.com/windows2000/library/planning/management/groupsteps.asp.
- "Step-by-Step Guide to Software Installation and Maintenance" at http://www.microsoft.com/windows2000/library/planning/management/swinstall.asp. This guide includes examples of several Office installation scenarios.
- "Step-by-Step Guide to Remote OS Installation" at http://www.microsoft.com/windows2000/library/planning/management/remotesteps.asp.

CHAPTER 7

Deploying on Windows NT 4.0

You can install Microsoft Office XP on Windows NT 4.0 Service Pack 6a, but you must have the required level of system files. Setup automatically detects and updates these files during the installation. You can also advertise Office XP applications on Windows NT 4.0 and get install-on-demand functionality, provided that you also install the Windows Desktop Update.

In this chapter

Deployment Issues Specific to Windows NT 4.0   189

Using Windows Installer Shortcuts with Office   190

Deployment Issues Specific to Windows NT 4.0

The following deployment issues may affect installations of Microsoft Office XP on computers running Microsoft Windows NT® 4.0:

- You must have Windows NT 4.0 Service Pack 6a to support Office XP.
- Users installing Office XP on Windows NT 4.0 might not have the required versions of some system and shared files.

    Setup checks for required versions and installs the System Files Update when necessary.

- You must have elevated privileges to install Office XP under Windows NT 4.0.

    If you also install the System Files Update, you must log on with administrator rights both before and after the computer restarts.

- You advertise Office XP under Windows NT 4.0 by using the **/jm** command-line option.

    To use Windows Installer shortcuts and get install-on-demand functionality, however, you must install the Windows Desktop Update.

System Files Update

If you are upgrading to Office XP Service Release 1 and you have Microsoft Internet Explorer 5.01, then you do not need to install the System Files Update. However, Office XP Setup still runs the System Files Update detection process and records all file versions (even if they are up-to-date) in the log file.

For more information about the System Files Update, see "Setup Components" in Chapter 4, "Overview of Setup."

Elevated privileges

You must have elevated privileges to install Office XP under Windows NT 4.0. For more information about elevating the Office XP installation, see "Installations That Require Elevated Privileges" in Chapter 4, "Overview of Setup."

Windows Desktop Update

You can advertise Office XP by logging on as an administrator and then running Setup with the **/jm** option. When you advertise Office XP, Windows Installer shortcuts for each application appear on the **Start** menu, and a minimal set of core Office files and components is installed on the computer. When a user clicks a shortcut or opens a file associated with an Office application, Windows Installer installs the feature or application from the administrative installation point.

When you advertise Office XP or when you set one or more applications to **Installed on First Use**, Windows Installer shortcuts appear on the user's computer. However, Windows NT 4.0 does not support Windows Installer shortcuts without the Windows Desktop Update, which is an updated version of the Windows shell. For more information about enabling Windows Installer shortcuts, see "Using Windows Installer Shortcuts with Office" later in this chapter.

For more information about advertising Office, see "Distributing Office to Users' Computers" in Chapter 5, "Installing and Customizing Office."

Using Windows Installer Shortcuts with Office

In many organizations, advertising is a quick and efficient means of making Microsoft Office XP available to users. When you advertise Office XP, Windows Installer shortcuts for each application appear on the **Start** menu, and a minimal set of core Office files and components is installed on the computer. When a user clicks a shortcut or opens a file associated with an advertised application, Windows Installer fully installs the application from the source.

When you install Office XP under the Microsoft Windows® 2000 or Microsoft Windows NT 4.0 operating systems, you can advertise the entire Office package by logging on as an administrator and then running Setup with the **/jm** command-line option. On any supported operating system, you can advertise a single application by setting its installation state to **Installed on First Use** in a transform.

Advertising accomplishes the following:

- Ensures that users always have access to Office applications from the Windows **Start** menu, even if the applications are not yet installed locally.

- Provides application-level resiliency.

    If a user inadvertently deletes a required file (such as Winword.exe), Windows Installer automatically replaces the file when the user clicks the shortcut or tries to open a file associated with the application.

- Elevates the Office XP installation on Windows 2000 and Windows NT 4.0.

    After an administrator advertises Office XP, any user can run Setup from **Add/Remove Programs** to install Office.

Requirements for using Windows Installer shortcuts

By default, Microsoft Windows 98, Microsoft Windows Millennium Edition (Windows Me), and Windows 2000 support Windows Installer shortcuts. On Windows NT 4.0, however, you must install the Windows Desktop Update (an updated version of the Windows shell) before you can use Windows Installer shortcuts to trigger an installation of Office applications on demand.

Windows Desktop Update is included with the following versions of Microsoft Internet Explorer:

- Internet Explorer 4.01 Service Pack 1 or later with Active Desktop®

    You can turn off Active Desktop after the installation is complete, but you must install the files associated with Active Desktop to get the updated Windows shell components.

- Internet Explorer 5.01

    The updated shell components are included in Internet Explorer 5.01, but they are not installed by default. You must use the Custom Installation Wizard to create a transform that includes the Windows Desktop Update in the System Files Update installation.

If you do not have the updated Windows shell, you can still advertise Office XP under Windows NT 4.0. In this case, however, Windows Installer installs a minimal set of files and components for the application and creates regular Windows shortcuts, which point to a file on the local hard disk. Users can subsequently use **Add/Remove Programs** to run Office XP Setup from the administrative installation point to modify the installation. However, there is no support for install-on-demand functionality.

Toolbox The Office XP Resource Kit includes the Custom Installation Wizard. For more information, see "Custom Installation Wizard" in the Toolbox.

How to install the Windows Desktop Update with Office XP

You install the Windows Desktop Update during the System Files Update installation portion of the Office XP installation. (Note that you can install the System Files Update to get the updated Windows shell and choose not install Internet Explorer 5.01 as your default Web browser.) To include the Windows Desktop Update, you must customize the System Files Update package.

To install the Windows Desktop Update with Office XP

1. Start the Custom Installation Wizard.

2. On the **Open the MSI file** page, specify the System Files Update package; for example:

   \\server\share\admin_install_point\files\osp\1033\osp.msi

3. On the **Modify Setup Properties** page, select the **InstallDesktopUpdate** property and click **Modify**.

   This property is exposed only when you are creating a transform for the System Files Update package (Osp.msi). It is a private property; that is, you cannot set it on the command line — only in the transform. Note that setting this property automatically sets Internet Explorer options on other pages of the wizard.

4. In the **Value** box, select **Install Windows Desktop Update**.

5. Add the transform for the System Files Update package to the Office XP Setup.ini file; for example:

   ```
   [SystemPackOptions]
   TRANSFORMS=SystemPack.mst
   ```

Note The Internet Explorer Customization Wizard also includes the option **Would you like to install the shell update**. This option works only if you run the stand-alone version of the Internet Explorer Administration Kit to customize Internet Explorer. If you start the Internet Explorer Customization Wizard from the Custom Installation Wizard, you must set the **InstallDesktopUpdate** property to get the Windows Desktop Update.

Like Office XP, the language packs in the Office Multilingual User Interface Pack are Windows Installer packages, and you can advertise them on users' computers. However, the System Files Update cannot be advertised. Advertising Office XP on Windows NT 4.0 fully installs the System Files Update on the computer and restarts the computer before Office XP or any chained packages are advertised. Windows Installer shortcuts appear when the next user logs on.

PART 3
Maintenance

Chapter 8   Maintaining an Installation   195

Chapter 9   Using System Policies   235

Chapter 10   Administering Security   289

Chapter 11   Creating Custom Help   327

CHAPTER 8

Maintaining an Installation

After Microsoft Office XP is deployed to users, there are several tools and methods you can use to update, repair, and improve the configuration of Office to suit your company's needs. Many of these tools might be familiar to the experienced administrator, but some are new — such as Corporate Error Reporting, a tool that helps manage crash reporting. For both the new and experienced administrator, a review of the utilities and methods used to maintain an Office installation should be beneficial.

In this chapter

Repairing Office Installations   195

Changing Feature Installation States   197

Changing User Settings After Installation   202

Removing Applications or Features After Installation   205

Reporting Office Application Crashes   214

Using the Office Profile Wizard   225

Repairing Office Installations

Microsoft Office XP retains functionality introduced in Office 2000 to automatically detect and repair missing or corrupt files in Office applications. This functionality has helped administrators reduce the number of application failures caused when files are accidentally deleted or overwritten by older files.

Microsoft Office XP retains functionality introduced in Office 2000 to automatically detect and repair missing or corrupt files in Office applications. This functionality has helped administrators reduce the number of application failures caused when files are accidentally deleted or overwritten by older files.

Automatic repair feature of Office

The automatic repair of applications and features in Office is an important part of managing an Office installation. Office XP accomplishes this function by tracking important groupings of Office resources known as components — the files or registry entries necessary for an application to function properly. Lists of information about these components are stored with each Office installation in a Windows Installer package (MSI file).

Some of the files or registry entries are marked within Office as keypath resources. If a keypath of a component is found missing or corrupt when Office attempts to load it, Office will force the resources of that component to be restored from the original installation source, or administrative installation point.

The same technology that installs or removes files on a user's computer — Windows Installer — also performs the repairs. When Office fails to find or load a component, Windows Installer automatically attempts to repair the fault by using files from the administrative installation point. Office uses the cached MSI file local to the user's computer and reinstalls all missing or defective files or registry entries.

This repair process is conducted without user intervention or failure messages that occur with other application or file failures. A user might notice a slight delay in starting an application when the files and registry entries are replaced, but the application should resume functioning as normal.

Forcing an application repair

Users can force the repair of an application they think is corrupt. The **Detect and Repair** command (**Help** menu) in any Office XP application forces a review of all Office files associated with that application. If any components have missing or corrupt keypaths, new copies of files or registry settings are retrieved from the original installation source and copied to the proper locations on the users' computers. Registry entries are reset to default installation settings if required.

There are two options available on the **Detect and Repair** dialog, **Restore my shortcuts while repairing** and **Discard my customized settings and restore default settings**. Administrators have the option of disabling these two options through policy settings in the Office10.adm template (**Microsoft Office XP | Help | Detect and Repair...**).

Users can also repair an application by running Office XP Setup in maintenance mode (click **Add/Remove Programs** in Control Panel and select **support information**, then click **Repair**), or, if necessary, by uninstalling and then reinstalling Office XP.

Keypaths and components in Keypath.xls

The Microsoft Excel workbook Keypath.xls has a list of all the keypath files and registry values associated with Office XP features and components.

Keypath.xls lists Office XP features in alphabetical order. For each feature, the workbook includes the following information:

- Feature — Name of a feature used by Office in abbreviated form.
- Component — Components of a feature listed in alphabetical order.

  A component can be used by more than one feature.

- Component ID — Globally unique identifier (GUID) added to the Windows registry after a feature using the component is installed.

  In the registry, the GUID appears in a compressed format.

- Directory — Folder where the keypath file is stored (if the keypath is a file).

- Keypath — File or registry value used as an indicator for the component.

  Note In the Keypath column, some entries begin with the text **msorid**, which refers to ORAPI registry data. The Keypath.xls workbook does not provide the registry information for these entries.

Limitations of automatic repair

Office XP will not instruct Windows Installer to initiate a repair process in all circumstances. For example:

- When the Windows Desktop Update is not installed.

  To enable all the self-repair capabilities of Office XP, the Windows Desktop Update must be installed (the Microsoft Windows® 2000 and Windows Millennium Edition operating systems have this functionality by default). If necessary for Microsoft Windows NT® 4.0 or Windows 98 operating systems, the Desktop Update can be installed by creating a transform for the OSP.msi and setting the **InstallDesktopUpdate** property in the **Modify Setup Properties** page of the Custom Installation Wizard to **Install the Windows Desktop Update**.

- When a component contains more than one file or registry entry, and one of the corrupt or missing files or registry entries is not listed as a keypath.

  For example, the Global_Word_Intl component includes two resources — Ww10intl.dll (which is also marked as a keypath) and Email.dot (which is not marked as a keypath). If Ww10intl.dll is missing when Microsoft Word 2002 starts, then Global_Word_Intl is repaired automatically. However, if Email.dot is missing, no repair is triggered.

  Caution Do not intentionally corrupt or delete keypath resources to trigger a repair. If you suspect files are corrupt, click **Detect and Repair** from the **Help** menu of any Office application, rerun Office Setup in maintenance mode and use the **Repair Office** option, or uninstall and then reinstall Office XP completely.

Changing Feature Installation States

Changing the installation states of an application after it has been installed on a user's computer is easier in Microsoft Office XP than in Office 2000. By using the new tools in Office XP, namely the Custom Maintenance Wizard and the Office Profile Wizard, you can change a configuration without having to uninstall and reinstall the application.

Custom Installation Wizard and the Custom Maintenance Wizard

The Office XP Resource Kit contains wizards you can use to customize Office. The Custom Installation Wizard and the Custom Maintenance Wizard are the two main wizards and are similar in several ways. Each utility reads a Windows Installer package (MSI file) — the former to create a transform (MST file), the latter to create a configuration maintenance file (CMW file). Both wizards are used to change most of the same settings, installation states, and additional options; and both have similar dialogs and pages.

To easily differentiate between the Custom Installation Wizard and the Custom Maintenance Wizard, remember the following:

- The Custom Installation Wizard is used to customize settings before Office is installed.
- The Custom Maintenance Wizard is used to change settings after Office is installed.

If you want to apply changes to an installation on client computers, you must create a configuration maintenance file that is based upon the same MSI file used in the Office installation. For example, if you use the Custom Maintenance Wizard to create a transform based on the MSI file for Office Professional, you must use that MSI file when you use the Custom Maintenance Wizard to create a configuration maintenance file. If you use an MSI file different from the one used to install Office on a client computer, you cannot apply the changes from your CMW file.

Changing installation states

After you deploy a customized installation of an Office XP application, you may need to update installation options for applications and features, registry settings, files, and user settings. This need usually arises when you stage a deployment of Office, make changes to the structure of your organization when people move from one group to another, fine-tune the installation, or correct a mistake made during the initial deployment.

The Custom Maintenance Wizard helps you make changes to the deployed installation state of applications and features for an Office XP installation. For example, if you have installed most of Office XP Professional with FrontPage, you can use the Custom Maintenance Wizard to change the installation state of Microsoft Outlook® 2002 from **Not Available** to **Run from My Computer**.

To create a Custom Maintenance Wizard file

1. Start the Custom Maintenance Wizard.
2. On the **Open the MSI File** page, enter the path to the MSI file used to install Office.

3. If you are running the wizard for the first time, on the **Open the Custom Maintenance Wizard File** page, click **Do not open an existing Custom Maintenance Wizard file**.

   – or –

   To use an existing Custom Maintenance Wizard file, click **Open an existing Custom Maintenance Wizard file** and enter the path to the Custom Maintenance Wizard file.

   Note that the Office XP version of the Custom Maintenance Wizard can only use Custom Maintenance Wizard files created by the Office XP version of the Custom Maintenance Wizard.

4. On the Select the Custom Maintenance Wizard File to Save page, enter the path to the Custom Maintenance Wizard file where you want to save your new settings.

   If you are using an existing Custom Maintenance Wizard file, this file appears as the default.

5. On the **Set Feature Installation States** page, select new installation options for the features you want to change.

   Features are displayed in the same hierarchical tree used in the Custom Installation Wizard. However, there are a few minor differences you should know about. For assistance with this page of the Custom Maintenance Wizard, click the Help button.

   Tip When you run the Custom Maintenance Wizard, you can use the **/x** command-line option to completely expand the feature tree.

For more information about installation states and options, see the online Help in the Custom Maintenance Wizard or Custom Installation Wizard.

Updating a user's configuration

To update a user's installed feature configuration, run the Custom Maintenance Wizard on a user's computer from a command line. Use the **/c** command-line option and include the name of your Custom Maintenance Wizard file. For example:

```
maintwiz.exe /c <path>\MyConfig.cmw
```

Use of the **/c** command-line option runs the Custom Maintenance Wizard in **apply** mode. This causes the Custom Maintenance Wizard to take customizations saved in the Custom Maintenance Wizard file, and use Windows Installer to apply those changes to the installed edition of Office on the user's computer.

For users who are working on Windows NT 4.0 or Windows 2000 operating systems, you must place the configuration maintenance file (CMW file) in a subfolder under the root of the administrative installation point and name the subfolder CMW. If the CMW file is not placed in this subfolder, users will not be able to apply maintenance configuration changes. If you cannot create a subfolder named CMW, you can set the system policy **Allow CMW files at any location to be applied** in the System Policy Editor or Group Policy snap-in by using the Office10.adm policy template. By default, administrators of a local computer are allowed to run maintenance files from any location. Users with only user privileges on the local computer are restricted to the \CMW subfolder off the administrative installation point.

When applying a CMW file, a log file is automatically created. To change the way a log file is written, use the **/l** command-line option with the name of the log file to save and the logging options to use. For example:

```
maintwiz.exe /c <path>\MyConfig.cmw /lpiwae <path>\MyLogFile.log
```

To run the Custom Maintenance Wizard in quiet mode, append a **/q** to the command line. Quiet mode disables the user interface and runs the Custom Maintenance Wizard without the user's knowledge.

> **Note** Even when using a user interface mode that suppresses error dialogs, the errors are recorded in the log.

Removing Office from a user's computer and then reinstalling it will not remove customizations to Office user settings (for example **Tools | Options** settings in Microsoft Word) applied by a configuration maintenance (CMW file). Like other Office user settings, these settings are stored in the registry and are not removed when Office is removed. When Office is reinstalled, users will see the same personal configuration settings they had prior to the removal of Office.

How the Custom Maintenance Wizard affects Custom Installation Wizard settings

The previous release of the Custom Maintenance Wizard was able to change feature installation states but did not have the extensive capabilities available in the latest release available in the Office XP Resource Kit. The Custom Maintenance Wizard cannot override the following features and installation states set by the Custom Installation Wizard:

- **Disable Run from Network**

    This check box in the **Set Feature Installation States** page of the Custom Installation Wizard can be used to prevent the selected feature from using the **Run from Network** installation state. If selected, users are not able to select **Run from Network** during custom setup, or any time after installation in maintenance mode or with the Custom Maintenance Wizard.

- **Disable Installed on First Use**

    This check box in the **Set Feature Installation States** page of the Custom Installation Wizard can be used to prevent the selected feature from using the **Installed on First Use** installation state. If selected, users are not able to select **Installed on First Use** during custom setup, or any time after installation in maintenance mode or with the Custom Maintenance Wizard.

The new feature installation state **Not Available, Hidden, Locked** is available in both the Custom Installation Wizard and the Custom Maintenance Wizard. This installation state can be reversed by the Custom Maintenance Wizard at any time.

Changing installation states in the feature tree

The feature tree in the Custom Maintenance Wizard is displayed slightly different than the one in the Custom Installation Wizard. The Custom Maintenance Wizard feature tree includes an additional selection in the left-click menu, **Leave unchanged**. This is represented by a blue circle and indicates that no changes are made to the state of this feature on the client computer when the CMW file is applied. All the remaining feature installation options appearing in the drop-down menu are identical to those found in the Custom Installation Wizard feature tree and have the same effect if selected.

If you set the installation state for a child feature to **Run from My Computer**, **Run from Network**, or **Installed on First Use**, the Custom Maintenance Wizard sets the parent feature to one of these states as well. This ensures the child feature you selected will be changed to the state you requested. Since you do not always know the installation configuration of a user's computer, you may attempt to install a child feature of a parent feature that is not yet installed. If you attempt to do so, the Custom Maintenance Wizard will not install the child feature. This is a beneficial feature of the Custom Maintenance Wizard if you want those who do not have the parent feature installed to not receive the feature. This feature also allows you to use the same Custom Maintenance Wizard file by users who already have the parent feature installed. For example, if you deploy a CMW file that is customized to install some of the Microsoft Excel add-ins to all users, users who have Excel installed will get the add-ins installed, and users who do not have Excel installed will not get the add-ins installed.

> **Note** During initial deployment, you can disable **Run from Network** or **Installed on First Use**, using the check boxes in the **Properties** frame next to the feature tree shown in the Custom Installation Wizard. Because these changes are not reversible using the Custom Maintenance Wizard, if you choose to change a feature to a state you disallowed, the change is not made on the user's computer where a transform with this setting has been applied.

Hidden applications and features

When you hide an application or feature of Office using the Custom Installation Wizard (by using the right-click menu), the application or feature will not appear in the feature tree during Setup or when the user is in maintenance mode, which is accessible through the **Add/Remove Programs** utility of Control Panel.

However, though the application or feature is hidden from the user, a user can still implicitly install them by changing the feature state of the parent feature. For example, the Custom Installation Wizard can hide the Equation Editor and mark it as **Not Available**. The user can still install the Equation Editor by selecting Office Tools in maintenance mode by selecting **Run all from My Computer** or **Run all from Network**.

A stronger option, which makes it impossible for a user to install a hidden application or feature, is the **Not Available, Hidden, Locked** install state of both the Custom Installation Wizard and the Custom Maintenance Wizard. Once you have set this option, the only other way to install the hidden feature or application is with the Custom Maintenance Wizard by selecting another installation state.

Why hidden features remain hidden

When you update an Office installation by using the Custom Maintenance Wizard, you can change the installation state of a hidden feature. Unlike the Custom Installation Wizard, the Custom Maintenance Wizard does not provide for a **Hide** or **Unhide** feature.

It is not possible to display an application or feature in maintenance mode when that application or feature was set to **Hide** in the transform used to deploy Office. This is because the Custom Maintenance Wizard does not read the transform used to install Office on the user's computer.

Information regarding the Hide or Unhide state of an Office application or feature is stored only in a transform.

In order to unhide an application or feature so it will display in maintenance mode is to uninstall Office, create a new transform that displays the hidden feature, and then reinstall Office. For more information about how to hide or unhide features when creating a transform, click the **Help** button for the Custom Installation Wizard from the **Set Feature Installation States** page.

Changing User Settings After Installation

Once Microsoft Office XP is installed on a user's computer, the Custom Installation Wizard cannot be used to install new applications, features, user settings, or to make any changes to the installation. Furthermore, when an installation based upon a specific MSI file is complete, the Custom Installation Wizard cannot be used to make further customizations to that installation. You can still use the Custom Installation Wizard with other packages (MSI files) that support customization for other applications, providing the applications have not been installed on a users' computer.

If you want to change an existing installation, use the Custom Maintenance Wizard, the Office Profile Wizard, and system policies.

The Custom Maintenance Wizard is designed to change the feature settings you implemented with the Custom Installation Wizard, and install applications or features you left out of the initial deployment of Office.

The Office Profile Wizard can help you capture and distribute new application and feature settings in an Office profile settings file (OPS file), but the wizard cannot be used to install applications or features. If you apply an OPS file that includes registry settings or files that cannot be used by the Office applications and features installed on a user's computer, those registry settings or files are installed but ignored by Office.

The System Policy Editor and Group Policy snap-in for Windows 2000 allow you to use ADM templates provided with the Office Resource Kit to enforce system policies globally for users of Office on a network. By using system policies an administrator can quickly enforce a user configuration on users' computers when users, groups, or computers log on to the network.

Using the Custom Maintenance Wizard to change user settings

The Custom Maintenance Wizard allows administrators to configure and distribute applications, features, and settings to a user's computer. With the Custom Maintenance Wizard, you can:

- Change the installation state of applications and features associated with the installed edition of Office on the user's computer.
- Change security settings of applications.
- Change Microsoft Outlook profile settings.
- Specify various Office user settings (for example settings under **Tools | Options**).
- Add or remove registry settings.
- Add or remove files.
- Change the list of additional servers where additional administrative installation points exist.
- Change the organization name displayed in the splash screen or the Help About dialog

These advantages make using the Custom Maintenance Wizard preferable to using the Profile Wizard in most cases. You will need to copy the Custom Maintenance Wizard (maintwiz.exe) to the administrative installation point. Instructions for performing this task are included in the Help file.

Unlike the Custom Installation Wizard, which uses a transform to convey customizations through Setup.exe, the Custom Maintenance Wizard is run from, and applies a configuration maintenance file (CMW file) to, users' computers.

New to the Custom Maintenance Wizard is the ability to customize individual user's settings in Office. Administrators can create a configuration maintenance file (CMW file) using the **Change Office User Settings** page of the Custom Maintenance Wizard to change user settings associated with menu options and user interface settings — once the sole domain of the Profile Wizard. If you want to add or remove other files or registry settings, you will need to specify them in the **Add/Remove Files to the Installation** page or the **Add Registry Entries** page of the Custom Maintenance Wizard. An important feature of the **Change Office User Settings** page is the ability to change user settings stored in binary blobs in the registry. Previous to this release of the Office Resource Kit, it was hard to administer user settings individually. The Custom Maintenance Wizard now makes this possible.

Another advantage to using the **Change Office User Settings** page of the wizard is the ability to configure specific settings without having to install and configure Office on a test machine (as the Office Profile Wizard requires).

Applying a profile settings file after installing Office

The Office Profile Wizard can be used to apply settings captured in an OPS file after Office has been installed.

> **Note** After Office is installed, do not create a new transform with new profile settings file to apply to an existing installation of Office. Transforms are used in initial deployment only.

You copy the OPS file to the user's computer and allow the user to run proflwiz.exe in Save My Settings mode to apply the new settings. Or, you run the Profile Wizard from a batch file or shortcut that points to an OPS file on the administrative installation point or server share to which all users have access. You can even use Microsoft Systems Management Server (SMS) to force the Profile Wizard to apply the OPS file configuration changes.

Using the System Policy Editor to change user settings

Several user settings can be enforced by using the System Policy Editor. To review the possible settings, start the System Policy Editor and load the related Office application ADM templates. After the templates are loaded, create a new policy file. When the policy file is created, you can select either the **Default Computer** or **Default User** policy profiles to configure various policy settings. For example, select the **Default User** policy profile and look for **Microsoft Word 2002**. Examine the **Tools | Options** branch of the tree. There you'll find the policy branch **General**. Within the **General** policy branch, you will find **Recently used file list**. Here you can change the number of files presented in the File menu option drop down. You can change the policy to display a maximum of nine recently used files.

See also

For more information about applying user settings after an installation of Office, see "Using the Office Profile Wizard" in Chapter 8, "Maintaining an Installation."

For further examples of the contents of the ADM policy templates, see "Office System Policies" in Chapter 9, "Using System Policies."

For more information about setting system policies, see "How to Set System Policies" in Chapter 9, "Using System Policies."

Removing Applications or Features After Installation

Removing Microsoft Office XP applications, features, files, or registry settings after they are installed requires special tools provided as part of the Office XP Resource Kit. You can complete the task of removing an Office application or related files by using any of the following tools:

- Custom Maintenance Wizard

    The Custom Maintenance Wizard is the tool of choice if you want to remove part of an application or feature from a user's computer.

- Removal Wizard

    The Removal Wizard is best for removing previous versions of Office from a user's computer. You can also create a custom profile settings file (OPC file) to remove only those files and registry settings you select.

- Profile Wizard

    While it is not advised to use the Office Profile Wizard to remove an application, it can be used to remove files, folders, and registry settings. It works well removing small support files like templates, ActiveX® controls, batch files, utilities, and registry settings by placing instructions in the **…ResetToDefaults** sections of the INI file used to capture settings.

Using the Custom Maintenance Wizard to remove applications or features

The Custom Maintenance Wizard allows you to remove an Office application or feature by setting its installation state to **Not Available** or **Not Available, Hidden, Locked**. Using **Not Available, Hidden, Locked** provides an advantage over simply removing an application with the Removal Wizard: it ensures that a user cannot install the application at a later date.

For directions on how to set and change installation states for Office applications and features, see the Help for the **Set Feature Installation States** page of the Custom Maintenance Wizard.

Setting applications or features to Not Available

Setting an application or feature to **Not Available** with the Custom Maintenance Wizard removes the application from the user's computer. When **Not Available** is used, a user can still install the feature by starting the **Add/Remove Programs** utility from Control Panel and selecting **Add/Remove…** to add the application. Windows Installer then installs the application from the administrative installation point. The user has the option of changing the installation state of the application to **Run from My Computer**.

Part 3   Maintenance

Setting applications or features to Not Available, Hidden, Locked

Setting an application or feature to **Not Available, Hidden, Locked** with the Custom Maintenance Wizard removes the application from the user's computer. The user cannot defeat this installation state by running **Add/Remove Program** in Control Panel. The only way to change this installation state is by using the Custom Maintenance Wizard.

Using the Removal Wizard to remove applications

The Removal Wizard is one of the easiest wizards to use in the Office Resource Kit. It allows you to select different modes of removal and how aggressively it will perform a removal of older versions of Office applications. The following subjects are included in this section:

- Overview of the Removal Wizard
- Removal Wizard command-line options
- Components of the Removal Wizard
- Customizing the Oclncust.opc and Oclncore.opc files
- Running the Removal Wizard from a user's computer

Overview of the Removal Wizard

If you use the Removal Wizard without supplying any command-line options, the **Removal Options** page of the wizard presents three options:

- Remove only the files that I absolutely do not need.

    This option removes only the applications you will never need again. If you examine the OPC file used by the Removal Wizard, all the file groups marked with SAFE are removed. Anything marked RISKY is retained on the user's computer.

- Let me decide which Microsoft Office applications will be removed.

    This option allows you to choose which applications to remove by displaying the **Applications You Can Remove** page. This page has two list boxes. The **Applications to Keep** list box on the right displays the applications you can delete. By moving them to the **Applications to Remove** list box, you instruct the Removal Wizard to remove them from your computer.

- Completely remove all my previous versions of Microsoft Office applications.

    This option searches for all instances of Office applications — as well as shared and common files — to remove. This option can have adverse effects upon other Microsoft applications that are not being removed due to use of shared or common files with those applications that are being removed.

Administrators have the extra options of using the Removal Wizard to:

- Remove all existing Office files and registry settings prior to upgrading to Office XP.

  This capability is also available for setting in the Custom Installation Wizard so a transform will instruct Windows Installer to display the **Remove Applications** page when running the Setup user interface. This feature can also be set with a property when starting Setup.exe from a command line or by adding the property to the Setup.ini (see the document Setupref.doc supplied with the Office Resource Kit for a list of properties).

- Remove previous installations of a single version of an Office application.

  This is usually associated with staged deployment scenarios where one or two applications of Office XP are installed at a time while previous versions of other applications are still required by the user.

- Remove custom applications on a user's computer.

  You can modify the Oclncust.opc file to instruct the Removal Wizard to remove files and registry entries for custom applications.

  Note The Removal Wizard needs administrator permissions to run under Microsoft Windows NT 4.0 or Microsoft Windows 2000.

You can run the Removal Wizard in one of three modes, depending on the degree to which you want to clean up a user's hard disk:

- Aggressive

  If selected, the Removal Wizard removes all instances of existing Office applications from the computer, plus common and shared files and applications. From the command line, use the **/a** option, or select the **Completely remove all my previous versions of Microsoft Office applications** option from the **Removal Options** page of the wizard.

- Safe

  If selected, the Removal Wizard only removes the necessary Office applications and files necessary to provide a clean install environment for Office XP. From the command line, use the **/s** option, or select the **Remove only the files that I absolutely do not need** option from the **Removal Options** page of the wizard.

- Let me decide...

  This option requires running the Removal Wizard without the **/q** command-line option. This starts the user interface and allows users the ability to selectively remove only those applications they want removed from the computer. The only way to emulate this capability when using the **/q** command-line option is to modify the OPC files to remove only those applications and files you want removed. Setting dependency variables in the OPC file to KEEP or REMOVE is usually all that is required.

  Caution Running the Removal Wizard using the **/a** (aggressive mode) command-line option removes all instances of Office applications. If you plan on deploying Office in stages, you should modify the OPC files accordingly.

Removal Wizard command-line options

By using command-line options, you can set:

- The mode in which the Removal Wizard runs
- The OPC file it uses
- The log file it creates
- Whether to display the user interface

To run the Removal Wizard with command-line options, click **Run** on the **Start** menu, and then type **Offcln.exe** followed by the command-line options you want to use.

The Removal Wizard uses the following command-line options syntax:

```
Offcln.exe [/a | /s [/q [/r]] [/l[!][logfile]]] [directory]
```

/a   Aggressive mode; the Removal Wizard removes files associated with all previously installed versions of Office and Office-related applications. This option does not allow you to select which files to keep. You must use a customized OPC file if you want the wizard to remove only selected files.

/s   Safe mode; the Removal Wizard removes only those files marked as SAFE in the command section of the OPC file. This option does not allow you to select which files to keep. You must use a customized OPC file if you want the wizard to only remove specific files.

/q   Quiet mode; the Removal Wizard runs without prompting the user for information or displaying progress indicators. The wizard does not reboot the user's computer automatically; therefore, changes might not be completed until the user reboots the computer.

/r   Used together with the **/q** option, reboots the computer automatically if necessary. The user has no opportunity to save files before the computer reboots.

/l*logfile*   Creates a log with the file name *logfile*. If no log file name is specified, the Removal Wizard creates a default log file, Offcln.log, in the current folder of the wizard.

/l!*logfile*   Creates a log file in the same manner as **/l**, but the Removal Wizard does not perform the removal process. This option is useful for testing the Removal Wizard before running.

For example, the following command-line string runs the Removal Wizard in aggressive mode without user intervention, restarts the system automatically if needed, and creates a default log file:

```
Offcln.exe /a /q /r /l
```

directory   Instructs the Removal Wizard where to look for the Oclncore.opc. The requirement is for Oclncore.opc and Oclncust.opc to be in the same directory. Any LCID subdirectories (for example 1033 for English) found below the directory where these two files are found and the current language of the user interface with that LCID language is also found on the computer, the Removal Wizard will run the Oclnintl.opc found in the folder with the same LCID number.

The Removal Wizard uses a new method for loading and evaluating OPC files. In prior releases it would only open one OPC file. Now, it automatically opens three different OPC files. It loads the following OPC files in the following order:

- Oclncore.opc
- Oclncust.opc
- Oclnintl.opc

The Removal Wizard looks for the first two files in the same directory from which the Offcln.exe is run. It then looks for any LCID subdirectories for instances of an Oclnintl.opc for the language in which the Office Resource Kit was provided.

> **Note** The Removal Wizard provides a return code to indicate whether the wizard encountered any errors. If you use the Removal Wizard in a batch file, you can use this with conditional statements to provide branching to alternate actions in case you want a specific activity to occur if an error is encountered. The wizard returns **0** to indicate an error occurred or **1** to indicate no errors were encountered (success).

Components of the Removal Wizard

The Removal Wizard consists of several files, including templates and executable files.

OPC templates

The Removal Wizard includes the following template files:

- Oclncore.opc

    This template file is used by the Offcln.exe (Removal Wizard). It identifies files, registry settings, and shortcuts to remove from a target computer. This OPC file specifies the core resources of Office for removal. The Removal Wizard searches for this file first.

    You can customize this OPC file so only the files or registry settings you specify are removed. However, it is recommended that additions to an OPC file should be made in the Oclncust.opc. You should only comment out entries in the Oclncore.opc file by adding a semicolon to a line to ignore entries in the file, removing a semicolon to activate an instruction, or change the setting of the dependency variable to either KEEP, DETECT, or REMOVE.

- Oclncust.opc

    This template file contains removal information for non-typical installations. It is provided for administrators who need to customize their removal processes. Any customizations an administrator may need to make to a removal process should be made in this file. Almost all the necessary files an administrator may optionally remove are provided in this OPC file. An administrator only needs to uncomment them to force the removal of the file or registry entry. Optionally, you can add sections to this file, comment instructions, or add instructions as needed.

- Oclnintl.opc

    This template file is stored in the LCID subfolder of the Office Resource Kit install folder (for English, look in the 1033 folder). This special file contains a listing of those files and registry settings unique to a localized language. It is not advised to make any changes to this file. The English version of this file has no sections or instructions.

Executables

The Removal Wizard includes the following executable files:

- Oclean.dll — Dynamic Link Library file containing the core code for the Office Removal Wizard.
- Offcln.exe — Provides the user interface for running the wizard as a stand-alone utility.

Customizing the Oclncore.opc and Oclncust.opc files

The Oclncore.opc and Oclncust.opc files can be edited to specify which components the Removal Wizard will remove from a user's computer, including non-Office applications. Before editing these files, it is beneficial to understand the contents and structure of OPC files.

An OPC file is divided into two unmarked sections, definitions and commands. The definitions section is for dependency variables (defining variables also known as application tokens), which are used to point to groupings of files, registry settings, and INI file entries defined in the commands section. The commands section contains a reference to the dependency variable that instructs how those groupings are removed.

When the Removal Wizard runs, it reads the OPC file and, depending on the mode it runs in, performs the instructions it finds within the file.

The dependency variables are set only in the definitions section of the Oclncore.opc file. The Oclncust.opc has optional customization commands you can activate by removing comments.

Unlike the Office 2000 release of the Removal Wizard, the Office XP release uses three OPC files instead of one. These three files are read in the following order: Oclncore.opc, Oclncust.opc, and Oclnintl.opc. The files are cumulative. As each file is read, the dependency variables defined in the Oclncore.opc apply to all the subsequent OPC files read by the Removal Wizard.

Definitions section

The definitions section contains a declaration of a token known as a dependency variable (appears in capital letters) with a specific action it can have: KEEP, DETECT, or REMOVE.

> **Note** Do not attempt to add new dependency variables; they will not be recognized or used. Only the existing dependency variables listed in the Oclncore.opc are recognized by the Removal Wizard.

Example: WORD94=DETECT

Syntax: Dependency variable=action

Where action can be:

- KEEP — Synonyms are FALSE and EXIST.
- DETECT — Changes to KEEP or REMOVE, depending on whether the Removal Wizard is in aggressive or safe mode.
- REMOVE — Synonyms are TRUE and NOTEXIST

Commands section

The commands section contains a reference to the dependency variable that instructs how files, registry entries, shortcuts, menu items, shared dynamic-link library files (DLLs), and INI file entries are removed. The syntax of this section consists of SAFE or RISKY, followed by listed dependency variables listed in the definitions section.

An optional string can be added to the right of the [ ] block to define what the section is associated with. In the case of a custom application, no dependency variable exists in the definitions section and therefore is not required.

SAFE instructs the Removal Wizard to remove the listed contents whenever the Removal Wizard is run, and the dependency variable in the definitions section is set to either DETECT or REMOVE.

RISKY instructs the Removal Wizard to only remove the listed contents when the wizard is set to use aggressive mode and the dependency variable is set to either DETECT or REMOVE. When not run in aggressive mode and the dependency variable is set to DETECT, the contents of the section are not removed.

If a dependency variable is used in a command grouping and is set to KEEP, any instance within the commands section where the token is found is not executed, thereby KEEPing the application, feature, or utility associated with this token, regardless of whether the SAFE or RISKY instruction is found at the beginning of the section.

If the token is set to DETECT, the mode in which the Removal Wizard is running determines whether or not the commands found later in the OPC are executed. Modes are:

- Aggressive mode, where all applications (whether marked as RISKY or SAFE on their command section) are removed.
- Safe mode, where only command sections marked as SAFE are removed.

Customizing this file consists of any of the following actions:

- Setting a dependency variable to KEEP, DETECT, or REMOVE.
- Adding a comment instruction to a line using a semicolon at the beginning of the line.
- Removing a comment instruction from a line to activate it.

- Adding an instruction to a section to remove a file, registry entry, or INI file entry.
- Creating a new command section.

Creating a new command section takes the form of the following example:

```
[SAFE]
<registry entries to remove>
<files to remove>
<INI file entries to remove>
<shortcuts to remove>
<special actions>
<shared dll files to remove>
<menu items to remove>
```

For further information regarding the syntax and how to use or change an OPC file, see the OPC.doc Microsoft Word document supplied with the Office Resource Kit.

Though it is not recommended, there are instances where an administrator may need to make changes to the Oclncore.opc — specifically to the definitions section of the file where application tokens are set to either KEEP, REMOVE, or DETECT.

To modify the Oclncore.opc file

1. Create a copy of Oclncore.opc, and name it SafeCore.opc.
2. Open Oclncore.opc in a text editor.
3. Change any of the KEEP, REMOVE, or DETECT settings associated with dependency variables to the configuration you need for that application.
4. Uncomment any needed dependency variables listed in the SPECIAL CLEANUP OPERATIONS area within the definitions section and set them to either KEEP, REMOVE, or DETECT as appropriate for your configuration needs.

    This step may require adding a section to remove the files associated with the application if no section exists in either the Oclncore.opc or Oclncust.opc.

5. Comment any instructions you do not want to occur by adding a semicolon to the beginning of the line.
6. Save and close the Oclncore.opc.

The following procedure shows how to modify the Oclncust.opc file to create a custom OPC file.

To modify the Oclncust.opc file

1. Create a copy of Oclncust.opc, and name it SafeCust.opc.
2. Open Oclncust.opc in a text editor.
3. Remove any leading semicolon from a line that you want activated.

4. Add any required entry to a line where a file, registry entry, or INI file entry should be removed for that application.

5. To delete any registry, file, or INI file entry for a custom application, add lines similar to other entries.

   For example:
   ```
   [SAFE] "Internal charting tool"
   C:\program files\internal\chart\chart.exe
   C:\program files\internal\chart\chartsub.dll
   C:\program files\internal\chart\chartprt.dat
   C:\program files\internal\chart\readme.txt
   ```

   Adding a new entry with [SAFE] instructs the wizard to remove the registry entries, files, and INI file entries listed below this section whenever the wizard is run.

   Creating an entry with [RISKY] assures the registry entries, files, and INI file entries are removed only when the wizard is set to run in aggressive mode:
   ```
   [RISKY] "Stuff to remove only when we're being aggressive"
   HKLM\Software\Inhouse\accounting\specialaccounting\startup
   HKLM\Software\Inhouse\accounting\specialaccounting\MRU1
   HKLM\Software\Inhouse\accounting\specialaccounting\MRU2
   HKLM\Software\Inhouse\accounting\specialaccounting\MRU3
   HKLM\Software\Inhouse\accounting\specialaccounting\MRU4
   C:\program files\internal\accounting\SpecialAccounting.exe
   C:\program files\internal\accounting\SpecialAccounting.dll
   ```

6. Save and close Oclncust.opc.

Test your customized OPC file on a computer by using the **/l!***logfile* command-line option. This step creates a log of the files and registry entries it will delete when using your customized OPC file.

Running the Removal Wizard from a user's computer

To run your custom OPC file on a user's computer, copy Offcln.exe, Oclean.dll, Oclncust.opc, and Oclncore.opc to the administrative installation point. If you are running a localized version, copy the Oclnintl.opc to the appropriate subdirectory. The Removal Wizard evaluates the language the operating system is set to and uses the subdirectory (LCID number) of the LCID for that language posted on the administrative installation point.

To run the Removal Wizard provide a batch file or shortcut with the following command line and post to the administrative installation point, e-mail it to users, or use Systems Management Server (SMS) to enact your changes:

```
<path>\Offcln.exe /a /q /r
```

Using maintenance mode to repair features or applications

Access to maintenance mode is through the **Add/Remove Programs** utility of Control Panel. The **Add/Remove Programs** utility starts Windows Installer and, if necessary, changes the install configuration of the operating system to allow changes to registry branches and restricted folders.

When Windows Installer is in maintenance mode, and when it is set to use elevated privileges, users can make changes to their installation of Office. They have the option of opening the feature tree in Setup and changing the state of an application or feature to **Installed on First Use** or **Not Available**. Setting an application or feature to either of these two installation states removes all the files and registry settings associated with the feature or application (excluding user settings) from the computer.

Users can be restricted from running in maintenance mode by using system policy settings.

Using the Office Profile Wizard to remove files

It is possible to use the Office Profile Wizard to remove files and registry settings for a small application or utility on a user's computer, but the wizard should not be used to remove large applications. For more information on how to customize an INI file for the Profile Wizard, see "Using the Office Profile Wizard" in Chapter 8, "Maintaining an Installation." For further information about the Profile Wizard, see the Help in the Profile Wizard.

By modifying the **Reset to default** sections of the OPW10adm.ini file, you can remove files and registry settings. Add the path and file name plus any registry entries to remove to the appropriate sections of the file.

This is advantageous when you want to apply a user-setting customization and need to remove a small set of files or registry settings at the same time.

Reporting Office Application Crashes

The Microsoft Office XP Resource Kit includes a new utility, Corporate Error Reporting, that enables administrators to manage a new feature of Office, the DW.exe crash-reporting tool. DW.exe is a feedback tool used by Microsoft to analyze and develop fixes for instances of crashes on users' computers. DW.exe ships with all editions of Office and is installed by default with Office XP.

The advantage of DW.exe is how it can help increase the reliability of Office applications, tools, and features. When a crash is reported, the crash data Microsoft receives helps Microsoft analyze the problem and create a repair — without forcing the user to supply hard-to-obtain information.

DW.exe starts automatically whenever a crash is detected. The application that crashes is automatically shut down, and before relevant crash data can be lost, DW.exe captures user settings related to the crash from the registry and the current memory block where the application is running. DW.exe then packages the data and any supporting files — such as the file being worked on at the time of the crash, templates if needed, and any associated files in use by the application during the crash — and submits the information to Microsoft for analysis.

Corporate Error Reporting utility

Corporate Error Reporting is a tool for use by administrators to manage the cabinet files created by DW.exe. Corporate Error Reporting allows businesses to redirect crash reports to a file server within an organization instead of submitting the information directly to Microsoft crash-reporting servers over the Internet. When enough crash entries are collected, administrators can review the information and submit only the crash data they think is useful to Microsoft.

With Corporate Error Reporting administrators can review what types of crashes users are experiencing the most. The information can then be used in educating users on how to avoid problems or produce work-arounds to potential crash situations.

> **Note** See the CER.HLP file available with the Corporate Error Reporting tool for a complete listing of all the files, folder hierarchy, and notes associated with usage of the tool.

How Corporate Error Reporting works

Corporate Error Reporting consists of executable files (cer.exe and cerintll.dll), a File Folder Tree, registry settings, and reporting options. An administrator creates and configures the File Folder Tree to enable Corporate Error Reporting.

Crash data collected by DW.exe is stored in "buckets" within the File Folder Tree. These buckets are groupings of errors submitted by users with a roll up of their system's memory, metrics of the crash, and any supporting files necessary to determine the circumstances and causes of a crash. Corporate Error Reporting allows administrators the ability to change what Microsoft has set as being necessary information for reporting a crash.

If an administrator does not want to submit documents involved in a crash (such as documents with proprietary or limited corporate information), an administrator can block the submission of this crash data to Microsoft by setting a policy or changing a registry setting on the user's computer.

Redirecting a user's computer

You can use Corporate Error Reporting to redirect and configure a user's computer for reporting crash data. Redirecting a user's computer to an alternate location is simple. Change the URL in the registry entry **DWFileTreeRoot** to a different URL, drive alias, or UNC. Note that there must be a File Folder Tree at the location specified; if the File Folder Tree does not exist with the proper permissions and security, then DW.exe will not write crash-reporting data to the specified location or to Microsoft.

Configuring a crash-reporting server

The administrator creates a File Folder Tree for use with Corporate Error Reporting. To create a File Folder Tree, an administrator must have administrative privileges on the server where the File Folder Tree will be created. A crash-reporting server must have the following:

- Microsoft Windows NT 4.0 with Service Pack 6a or Windows 2000
- Internet Explorer 4.01 or higher
- 64 MB of RAM
- An NTFS-formatted disk drive with at least 2 to 8 GB of hard-disk space for the File Folder Tree

    The amount of disk space used by DW.exe is dependent on the number of crashes and the number of cabinet files collected, not on the number of users. If you increase the number of cabinet files collected per bucket beyond the defaults in either the Default or Selected Buckets' policy dialogs, DW.exe will use more disk space.

- At least a 200-megahertz (MHz) computer (recommended) that has access to the Internet

To establish a local crash-reporting server (recommended method)

1. Install the Office XP Resource Kit on the server where the File Folder Tree will be stored.
2. Create a File Folder Tree on a share accessible to users who will report crashes (see "Create a File Folder Tree" later in this chapter).
3. Configure Default and Selected Buckets' policy settings by using the Corporate Error Reporting menu options, **Default Policy** and **Selected Buckets' Policy** (**Edit** menu).
4. Set the **DWFileTreeRoot** registry setting on all users' computers with the UNC or drive alias where the root folder of the File Folder Tree is located.

    To set a registry setting on a user's computer, use either the System Policy Editor (load the Office10.ADM template) or add the registry setting to a transform using the **Add Registry Entries** page of the Custom Installation Wizard or the Custom Maintenance Wizard. It is also possible to capture the configuration of a user's computer by using the Profile Wizard and then propagate that configuration to all users with a customized OPS file.

Create a File Folder Tree

Before DW.exe can begin reporting crash data to a local crash-reporting server, an administrator must create a File Folder Tree in which to store crash information. Use the following procedure to establish a reporting share on a local file server.

> **Note** A File Folder Tree must be created on an NTFS-formatted drive to properly configure permissions and security settings.

Before you create a File Folder Tree, you should decide on what server configuration to use. The following will help you decide:

- You need a share with at least 2 GB of hard-disk space available on an NTFS-formatted drive.

    Regardless of company size, Corporate Error Reporting will not require a lot of extra space. However, you might need more space if you choose to track more than the default number of crash files. For most cases, 2 GB should properly handle all crashes for an entire corporation.

- If you prefer, you can create two or more crash-reporting file servers and direct different users to the one most appropriate (for example, Engineering, Accounting, Sales, etc.).

- If you create a single crash-reporting share, all users in the company will need access to that share.

    If the share is not accessible to all users, then you may need to create multiple crash-reporting servers. See the security settings in the table following the procedure for what permissions should be set for each folder to allow users access to the File Folder Tree.

To create a File Folder Tree

1. Create a folder on the drive beginning one folder below the root of the drive.

    You can give the folder any name you want, but FileFolderTree may be the easiest to remember.

2. Share this new folder on the server.

3. Under the folder you created and shared, create these folders: Cabs, Counts, Status.

    Example:

    <drive letter>\FileFolderTree\
              Cabs
              Counts
              Status

4. Set the security for each folder to the following.

Folder	For Windows 2000
Cabs	For Windows 2000, set **Allow inheritable permissions from parent to propagate to this object** to unchecked
	For Windows NT, set **Replace Permissions on Subdirectories** to unchecked (default) for the root or parent directory of this folder.
	Allow **List Folder Contents** to **Everyone**
	Allow **Write** to **Everyone**
Counts	For Windows 2000, set **Allow inheritable permissions from parent to propagate to this object** to unchecked
	For Windows NT, set **Replace Permissions on Subdirectories** to unchecked (default) for the root or parent directory of this folder.
	Allow **Read** to **Everyone**
	Allow **Write** to **Everyone**
Status	For Windows 2000, set **Allow inheritable permissions from parent to propagate to this object** to unchecked
	For Windows NT, set **Replace Permissions on Subdirectories** to unchecked (default) for the root or parent directory of this folder.
	Allow **Read** to **Everyone**
	Allow **List Folder Contents** to **Everyone**

The crash-reporting server is now ready for use by DW.exe and Corporate Error Reporting.

Configure policy settings

Both the Default and Selected Buckets' policy settings use the same policy entries. However, the effect of each is enforced at different levels of the File Folder Tree. The Default policy settings determine the default settings for the entire File Folder Tree. Setting these policies is easy and is usually all you need to begin reporting crash data in the File Folder Tree.

At some point you might need to limit the amount of reporting and the need for secondary data (associated files in a crash), or limit whether the supporting data can be referenced for the user to work around the problem. Enabling and setting the Selected Buckets' policy settings will override the Default policy settings and allow for special handling of specific types of crashes.

Default policy settings are saved in the policy.txt file found in the root folder of the File Folder Tree.

Selected Buckets' policy settings are set in the status.txt file found in the cabs folder branch of the File Folder Tree. These settings control policy settings of the individual cab folder (or bucket) in the Bucket View of Corporate Error Reporting you had selected when you set Selected Buckets' policy settings.

Distribute policy settings

If all users of your organization are installing Office XP for the first time, it is possible to change the following registry setting on their local computers to the file server configured for crash reporting:

HKCU\Software\Policies\Microsoft\Office\10.0\Common\DWFileTreeRoot

It should be a fully qualified URL, drive alias, or UNC and path to the File Folder Tree root directory. Setting this one registry entry to a local file server is all that is needed to enable the corporate solution.

Example:

\\server\share

It is highly recommended to make the root of the File Folder Tree the share point. Or, if needed, a folder path can be added after the \\server\share.

To add a policy to enforce redirection of DW.exe

1. Start the System Policy Editor.
2. Make sure the Office10.adm template is loaded.
3. Double-click the **Default User** profile icon.
4. Expand the **Microsoft Word 2002** node (click the plus (+) sign or double-click the **Microsoft Word 2002** text).
5. Expand the **Corporate Error Reporting** node.
6. Set the **Error reporting location** policy to checked.
7. Enter the UNC or drive letter plus any required path into the **Path** text box.
8. Click **OK**.

In situations where you do not wish to use system policies, it is possible to force a redirection of DW.exe using the following method:

To add a registry entry to redirect DW.exe using either the Custom Maintenance Wizard or Custom Installation Wizard

1. Start the wizard.
2. Navigate to the **Add/Remove Registry Entries** page.
3. In the **Add/Remove Registry Entries** page, click the **Add Registry Entry** tab, then click the **Add...** button.

4. Select the **HKEY_CURRENT_USER** node and **REG_SZ** data type from their respective drop-down combo boxes.

5. Enter **Software\Policies\Microsoft\Office\10.0\Common** in the **Key** text box.

6. Enter **DWFileTreeRoot** in the **Value name** text box

7. Enter the UNC or URL in the **Value data** text box.

8. Click **OK**.

Enforcing policy settings local to the crash-reporting server only requires setting policies in either the Policy.txt file (accessible through the **Default Policy** dialog box from the **Edit** menu) or, specific to a given bucket, in the status.txt file (accessible through the **Selected Buckets' Policy** dialog from the **Edit** menu). Redirecting users to the local crash-reporting file server requires the use of the System Policy Editor, which ships with the Office Resource Kit or is available with Windows NT Server 4.0 and above. Use the Office10.adm policy template and navigate to **Office XP | Corporate Error Reporting | Error Reporting Location** and set the check box to checked.

When users are redirected to the local crash-reporting file server, the policy settings within the File Folder Tree are used by DW.exe to manage how crash data is reported.

Security of crash data

Submitting the data from files associated with a crash (secondary data) increases the probability that Microsoft can find a solution to your crash faster. In many cases, it is impossible to isolate a crash-causing problem without more relevant data to explain the crash. If it all possible, allow secondary data to be submitted with crash data to Microsoft.

For many corporations, reporting secondary crash data is a sensitive subject, because there may be limited or proprietary data in the associated files, and because it may take extra time to send the data to Microsoft. Furthermore, reporting secondary data that is proprietary can be considered a breach of conduct or grounds for termination in some corporations.

With these critical issues in mind, Microsoft designed and developed Corporate Error Reporting as an intermediate point where administrators have a chance to collect, evaluate, and, if need be, block the submission of crash reports and secondary data to Microsoft.

How users know if data can be uploaded

DW.exe prompts all users when a crash occurs, asking them whether they want to report the crash. If secondary data is requested by DW.exe, users are asked if they are willing to upload the secondary files. If a user chooses not to upload the files, then only the core memory associated with a crash is placed in the cabinet file (along with other crash data).

Administrators also have the option of using expand.exe to open cabinet files and examine the contents prior to uploading. When crash data is reported by individuals or groups that have access to sensitive information, you might want to create a separate File Folder Tree for their reports. You can then expand each cabinet file that is submitted and examine it for any proprietary or limited data prior to uploading it to Microsoft.

Registry settings for DW.exe controlled by Corporate Error Reporting

All the registry entries vital to controlling the reporting of crash data are explained in this section. Most of these entries can be overridden with the **Default Policy** (policy.txt) or **Selected Buckets' Policy** (status.txt) dialog settings. However, some require deployment through a system policy or must be deployed to users through a transform (MST file), configuration maintenance file (CMW file), or Office profile settings file (OPS file).

The local copy of DW.exe running on a user's computer uses the registry entry **DWFileTreeRoot**. This registry entry is set with a system policy. When DW.exe runs, it evaluates the File Folder Tree it finds listed at this location. If the location is a valid File Folder Tree, then DW.exe reports to it. If the location is not valid, DW.exe will not report a crash. It is very important that the **DWFileTreeRoot** registry entry be specified correctly in order for any crash-reporting system to work correctly.

All customized registry entries for DW.exe must be in the following registry node:

HKEY_CURRENT_USER\Software\Policies\Microsoft\Office\10.0\Common\<value>

These custom registry entries for DW.exe are not created when Office XP is installed on a user's computer. These settings must be created by the administrator or present in either a Default or Selected Buckets' policy on the local crash-reporting server. The only exception to this is the **DWFileTreeRoot** registry entry. It must exist on a user's computer to redirect users to the local crash-reporting server.

DWFileTreeRoot registry entry

If any valid URL, drive alias, or UNC is present in the **DWFileTreeRoot** registry entry, DW.exe communicates with the corporate crash-reporting server instead of Microsoft's crash-reporting server. This setting must be a valid URL, drive alias, or UNC server-share combination on a local crash-reporting server where all users have write access. If the provided string is not a valid UNC path, DW.exe aborts. The specified path can also be a drive-letter alias to the network share. However, this drive letter must reference the same network and server share on all computers; otherwise you may encounter an error if DW.exe cannot connect to the File Folder Tree.

You can set the **DWFileTreeRoot** registry entry with one of the following values by using either the System Policy Editor, Custom Installation Wizard, Custom Maintenance Wizard, or Office Profile Wizard:

Null = go to the Internet (Microsoft server)
(string) = UNC to store crash information to (File Folder Tree root of local server)

DWTracking registry entry or Tracking policy

If any value is present in the **DWTracking** registry entry, it enables tracking of crashes to the File Folder Tree. If tracking is enabled, DW.exe writes user information for every crash to the log file crash.log. It also writes the same information to hits.log and associates each set of user data with a particular cabinet file.

You can set the **DWTracking** registry entry with one of the following values by using a Default or Selected Buckets' policy setting, the Custom Installation Wizard, Custom Maintenance Wizard, or the Profile Wizard:

null = no tracking
1 (non-zero - dword) = tracking enabled

DWNoExternalURL registry entry or NoExternalURL policy

If any value is present in the **DWNoExternalURL** registry entry, DW.exe will not connect to the Microsoft Web site from the DW.exe response dialog when users report a crash. Only internal URLs are displayed to users on the final response dialog when they report a crash.

You can set the **DWNoExternalURL** registry entry with one of the following values by using a Default or Selected Buckets' policy setting, the Custom Installation Wizard, Custom Maintenance Wizard, or Profile Wizard:

null = launch the Microsoft supplied URL found in the Response entry in the status.txt file
1 (non-zero - dword) = do not connect to the Microsoft supplied URL

DWNoFileCollection registry entry or NoFileCollection policy

If any value is present in the **DWNoFileCollection** registry entry, DW.exe will not send, or prompt the user, for any files requested by the Microsoft crash-reporting server.

You can set the **DWNoFileCollection** registry entry with one of the following values by using a Default or Selected Buckets' policy setting, the Custom Installation Wizard, Custom Maintenance Wizard, or Profile Wizard:

null = prompt the user for any files requested by Microsoft.
1 (non-zero - dword) = no file collection

DWNoSecondLevelCollection registry entry or NoSecondLevelCollection policy

If any value is present in the **DWNoSecondLevelCollection** registry entry, DW.exe will not send second-level data, or prompt the user for any supporting data, requested by Microsoft. Second-level data includes any files, file version information, Windows Management Instrumentation (WMI) queries, user registry settings, and current documents considered relevant to resolving the reason for the crash. These are never uploaded without explicit permission of the user.

You can set the **DWNoSecondLevelCollection** registry entry with one of the following values by using a Default or Selected Buckets' policy setting, the Custom Installation Wizard, Custom Maintenance Wizard, or Profile Wizard:

null = prompt the user for second level data
1 (non-zero - dword) = no collection (and no prompting of the user)

DWURLLaunch registry entry or URLLaunch policy

If the **DWURLLaunch** registry entry contains a URL (string), DW.exe provides a link pointing to the location where fixes or work-around information for a particular crash are stored. This is posted on the final DW.exe response dialog shown to users after they report a crash. Use this entry to redirect users to local fixes and work-arounds for a particular crash.

You can set the **DWURLLaunch** registry entry with one of the following values by using the Custom Installation Wizard, Custom Maintenance Wizard, or Profile Wizard:

null = no URL (an empty string)
(string) = URL to jump to for further information

DWNeverUpload registry entry

If the **DWNeverUpload** registry entry value is set to **1**, DW.exe never uploads data and never prompts the user. If this is set to **0**, DW.exe prompts the user before uploading.

You can set the **DWNeverUpload** registry entry with one of the following values by using the Custom Installation Wizard, Custom Maintenance Wizard, or Profile Wizard:

0 = Prompt
1 (non-zero - dword) = Never

DWReporteeName registry entry

If the **DWReporteeName** registry entry value is set to empty (**null**), the string "Microsoft" will appear in the user interface for any messages or dialogs informing the user where data is being sent regarding a crash. If this value is replaced with a string value, DW.exe replaces any references to Microsoft in the data reporting messages. Specifically, if a user receives the message "**Report problem to Microsoft**" from DW.exe when data is being redirected to a local crash-reporting server, it is best to change this entry to the name of your server or the department that is managing crashes. For example, setting this registry entry to "**corporate server \\Corp1\crashshare**" changes the previous message to "**Report problem to corporate server \\Corp1\crashshare**".

You can set the **DWReporteeName** registry entry with one of the following values by using the Custom Installation Wizard, Custom Maintenance Wizard, or Profile Wizard:

null = None, defaults to "Microsoft"
(string) = substitutes "Microsoft" with the specified string within the user interface

Reporting stored crash data to Microsoft

Perhaps one of the easiest tasks to perform in Corporate Error Reporting is to report stored crashes from the File Folder Tree. However, this task can also be the most time-consuming of features in the utility, depending upon the amount of data to report.

If you are part of a large corporation, you may prefer with large reports to export only the selected buckets instead of the entire File Folder Tree. If you are part of a small company with only a few crashes to report, you are probably safe to report all the buckets at once.

Quantity of reported data is the key factor in how long the process will take. It is highly recommended to begin the reporting process at the end of the day; using the evening to accomplish the upload can ensure full performance of your computer system by the morning.

To report all buckets in the current File Folder Tree

- Select **File, Export Buckets...**

To report only a select bucket or set of selected buckets

1. Hold the **Ctrl** key and click on each bucket in the Bucket View grid that you want to submit to Microsoft.
2. Select **File, Export Selected Buckets...**

If the Bucket ID does not exist in the File Folder Tree, DW.exe creates:

- The folder structure within the File Folder Tree to support the crash (a bucket)

    The folder structure within the File Folder Tree created by DW.exe is the concatenation of <File Folder Tree Root directory>\<Application name>\<Application Version>\<Module Name>\<Module Version>\<Memory offset>

- A mini-dump of the memory, then turning it into a file
- A collection of any registry keys, entries, documents, or related files, along with the mini-dump, into a cabinet file (cab)
- An instance of a cabinet file in the lowest leaf for the new bucket in the Cabs folder
- A hits.log file in the Cabs folder
- An identical folder structure created for the Cabs folder under the Counts folder
- A count.txt file in the Counts folder
- An identical folder structure created for the Cabs folder under the Status folder
- A status.txt file in the Status folder

Using the Office Profile Wizard

The Microsoft Office Profile Wizard is used to capture user settings and customizations of the Office user environment, and to migrate these settings and essential templates and support programs to other users' computers.

One of the best advantages the Profile Wizard offers is its ability to save the configuration of a user's computer and then restore that configuration at a later date — for example, when a user migrates to a new computer.

In order to use the Profile Wizard, an installation of Microsoft Office must exist on a computer. After Office is installed, the Profile Wizard can be used to capture the configuration of configurable user settings and files. With changes to the INI files used by the Profile Wizard, it is possible to instruct the wizard to capture custom files, templates, dictionaries, and other supporting files by adding them in the appropriate sections of the customized INI file you create.

Using the Office Profile Wizard to change user settings

The Office Profile Wizard is an administrative tool for capturing an Office user configuration from a user's computer to a profile settings file (OPS file). The Profile Wizard is also the Save My Settings Wizard for end users. The Save My Settings Wizard ships with Office; the Profile Wizard ships with the Office XP Resource Kit.

The Office Profile Wizard and the Save My Settings Wizard are the exact same application but use different interfaces. Each wizard is activated by a parameter setting on the command line. By default, the Save My Settings Wizard begins whenever you start proflwiz.exe; however, you have the option of including the **/u** command-line option to force the use of the non-administrative user interface. You must add the **/a** command-line option to start the Profile Wizard with the administrative user interface.

There are three INI files available for use with the wizard. These INI files instruct the Profile Wizard to capture registry settings and files from a user's computer. Each INI file is tailored for the uses stated below and can be modified with a text editor to add or remove registry settings or files from an OPS file.

- OPW10adm.ini

    Created as a starting point for administrators. This file is only available with the Office Resource Kit. You can use this INI file as a template for creating customized INI files.

- OPW10usr.ini

    Created for users. This is only available with Office and is designed for use with the Save My Settings Wizard user interface. This INI can also be used as a template for a customized INI file. If you customize this INI file you cannot use the Save to Web feature in the Save My Settings Wizard.

- ResetO10.ini

    Specifically used for resetting all configuration and user settings of Office to their default settings. This file is only available with the Office Resource Kit.

Resetting to defaults

The Office Profile Wizard includes an option to reset user settings to defaults. This option clears all custom user settings saved in the registry and related templates. Using the **Reset to default** option is critical to implementing a clean user configuration on a computer. If settings have previously been customized on a user's computer prior to applying an OPS file, those settings not customized in the OPS file are retained on the user's computer — a scenario that can lead to different configurations on user's computers because their previous settings were not cleared. Using the **Reset to defaults** option clears all user settings and then applies the configurations supplied in the OPS. This ensures all users will have the same configuration after the OPS file is applied.

Capturing user configuration settings

Any setting a user can configure within an application and retain from one session to the next can be saved to an OPS file by using the Profile Wizard. You can even instruct the Profile Wizard to pick up any specific files you need and include them in the OPS file by altering the INI file used by the wizard.

Before you create an OPS file, you must start each Office application and set all the custom user settings you want users to have. You can set most options by using the **Options** command (**Tools** menu). To customize toolbars and menus, use the **Customize** command (**Tools** menu). You can even distribute a customized dictionary by replacing the default dictionary or making changes to the existing dictionary.

After the Profile Wizard creates the OPS file, you can add it to a transform using the Custom Installation Wizard. You can then deploy Office XP using the transform with the embedded OPS file. This installs the default user configuration you created with the Profile Wizard to all users who install Office with that transform. If you create an OPS file for use with a transform, it is advised to use the OPW10adm.ini.

Applying user configuration settings from an OPS file

You can apply user configuration settings with the Profile Wizard using any of the following three methods.

- Run the Profile Wizard automatically at the end of the deployment process by specifying it in the **Add Installations and Run Programs** page of the Custom Installation Wizard.

- Embed the OPS file in a transform with the Custom Installation Wizard from the **Customize Default Application Settings** page.

- Manually run the Profile Wizard with the OPS file on the user's computer.

  Copy the OPS file to the user's computer and allow the user to run proflwiz.exe in Save My Settings mode to apply the user settings. Or, run the Profile Wizard from a batch file or shortcut that points to an OPS file on the administrative installation point (or server share to which all users have access). You can even use System Management Server (SMS) to force the Profile Wizard to apply the OPS file configuration changes.

Running Profile Wizard at the end of deployment

Running the Profile Wizard at the end of the deployment process occurs whether you embed the OPS file in the transform on the **Customize Default Applications Settings** page of the Custom Installation Wizard or if you specify the action in the **Add Installations and Run Programs** page of the Custom Installation Wizard. If you would rather not embed the OPS file in a transform on the **Customize Default Applications Settings** page, you can instruct the Custom Installation Wizard to run the Profile Wizard at the end of the deployment process by including the Profile Wizard executable plus command-line options in the **Add Installations and Run Programs** page. This process allows you to:

- Use the **Reset to defaults** option of the Profile Wizard.
- Modify an OPS file without having to change or update the transform.
- Apply the OPS file separate of the transform.
- Selectively restore settings to specific Office applications with command-line options. You can also do this through the user interface, but this method is only available when using the Profile Wizard in administrative mode.

To run the Profile Wizard at the end of the deployment process

1. Copy proflwiz.exe to the administrative installation point if it is not already there.

   You can place proflwiz.exe and related executable files into the same folder as Office Setup.exe, or you can create a subfolder for them.

2. Copy the OPS file you created to the administrative installation point.
3. Start the Custom Installation Wizard.
4. Navigate to the **Add Installations and Run Programs** page of the Custom Installation Wizard.
5. Click **Add...**
6. In the **Target** text box, enter **<path>\proflwiz.exe** or use the **Browse...** button to navigate to proflwiz.exe.
7. In the **Arguments** text box, enter **/r <path> <ops file name>**.

   /r instructs the Profile Wizard to Restore settings from the OPS file to the computer the Profile Wizard is running on. See the **Profile Wizard command-line options** topic in the Profile Wizard help for examples and definitions of all command-line options.

After Office is installed, Windows Installer starts all the applications you specify on the **Add Installations and Run Programs** page in the order in which you specify them.

Understanding the Reset to defaults option

Unexpected results can occur if the **Reset to defaults** option is not fully understood before you apply customizations in an OPS file. If the **Reset to defaults** check box is selected when you run the Profile Wizard to restore a user profile, all existing user configuration settings of Office XP are reset to their default states before the profile is applied. Your new settings, which are then applied, should be customized to enable Office XP to work as you intend.

Resetting all previous user settings is the default behavior of the wizard when not used in quiet mode (user interface is displayed). If you want to restore some settings in specific applications but retain others, you will need to edit the INI file used to capture the settings and clear the **Reset to defaults** check box in the wizard during the restore process.

> **Note** When running the Profile Wizard in quiet mode (**/q** command-line option), you can turn on this **Reset to defaults** feature of the Profile Wizard through the use of the **/d** command-line option.

Customizing the Reset to defaults feature of the Profile Wizard is controlled by modifying sections in the INI files. Changes to sections in the INI file ending with text "ResetToDefaults" will affect how the Profile Wizard manages the application of an OPS file. The INI file ResetO10.ini is a good example of what files and registry settings can be changed if you plan on making changes to any ResetToDefaults sections of an INI file.

Use of the **Reset to defaults** option is the same as specifying the **/d** command-line option. When selected, the Profile Wizard uses the ResetO10.ops file to apply changes to the user's computer. To review the changes this OPS file will make to a computer, examine the ResetO10.ini file.

When the ResetO10.ops file is applied to a user's computer, the following user settings are reset to their default install state:

- The Assistant character
- Most recently used (MRU) entries on the File Menu
- Size and position of application windows
- Menu and toolbar positions or customizations
- Office XP Shortcut Bar (if installed)
- Security level of all applications
- Settings for viewing data (such as the Calendar view in Outlook)

Within each Office application is an option to **Detect and Repair** (**Help** menu). Selecting this option and then setting the **Discard my customized settings and restore default settings** check box to checked is the same as running the Profile Wizard with the **/d** command-line option or selecting the **Reset to defaults** check box within the Profile Wizard.

Note When you use **Detect and Repair** with the **Discard my customized settings and restore default settings** check box selected, all added installations, the Outlook profile (if supplied), and all other user customizations are reapplied when Office is reinstalled using a previously applied transform. All installations and programs added in the **Add Installations and Run Programs** page of the Custom Installation Wizard are reapplied also.

Using the **Discard my customized settings and restore default settings** check box from any Office application affects the user settings and registry settings where a transform was used to install the application. This happens because transforms store a registry setting that controls reapplication of user content in the transform in this node.

After Office is reinstalled using a transform, the configuration maintenance files (CMW files) will automatically be reapplied the next time the user starts any Office application; Office is configured to its previous configuration without any user customizations. This process is equivalent to when a new user logs on to a multiuser machine and receives all the user customizations applied from the transform, or configuration maintenance files, that the administrator has applied.

Customizing a generic profile settings file

The OPW10adm.ini is used to create a generic profile settings file (OPS file). This file contains the most likely configuration changes administrators want to capture. However, not all administrators have the same needs. It is possible to use this file as a starting point for creating a customized OPS file.

In order to capture the customized user settings for Office, you must set most of the important options by using the **Options** command (**Tools** menu) from within each Office application. To customize toolbars and menus, use the **Customize** command (**Tools** menu). You can even distribute your own customized dictionary.

When you are ready to create an OPS file, perform the following steps.

To save settings to an OPS file

1. Run the Profile Wizard.
2. On the **Save or Restore Settings** page, select **Save the settings from this machine**, and enter the name and path for the OPS file in the **Settings File** text box.
3. Click **Finish**.

The Profile Wizard saves all the Office application settings from your computer as specified in the INI file, if you instructed the wizard to use a customized INI file on the command line, to the OPS file.

Note If you do not specify an INI file on the command line, the Profile Wizard uses the OPW10adm.ini by default if the Profile Wizard is being used in administrative mode, or the OPW10usr.ini if the Profile Wizard is being used in user mode. (If you are using the Save My Settings Wizard, see the Save My Settings Wizard online Help for more information.)

Defining environment variables for use with Windows 98

Environment variables are a feature of the operating system. Environment variables are used to set the configuration of an operating system. Environment variables can be accessed through special function calls in applications to determine what the contents of the variables are. This process is very similar to setting a string variable in a programming language and then gaining access to it from another program later on whenever it is needed. Since the operating system is always running, the environment variable is always accessible.

Unlike Microsoft Windows 2000 and Microsoft Windows NT, Microsoft Windows 98 does not have a USERPROFILE or USERNAME environment variable by default. You must create and define these environment variables manually so they resolve to the correct location for each user.

Note To view current environment variables on your computer, open a command prompt window and enter **SET** at the command line.

To create the USERPROFILE environment variable for Windows 98 clients, create a Windows NT logon script. Use the following command line in the logon script to create the USERPROFILE and USERNAME environment variables when a user logs on:

```
<path>\Winset.exe USERNAME=%USERNAME%
<path>\Winset.exe USERPROFILE=%windir%\Profiles\%USERNAME%
```

An environment variable can be created at any time by running the **SET** command from a command window; however, this method sets the variable only for as long as the window is active.

With Windows 98, you can create an environment variable in the autoexec.bat file, and retain the variable for as long as Windows 98 is running. If you prefer, you can perform the same step above by adding the following to all autoexec.bat files on users' computers:

SET USERNAME

SET USERPROFILE

Then, in the NT logon script, you can change the command lines referenced earlier to:

```
SET USERNAME=%USERNAME%
SET USERPROFILE=%windir%\Profiles\%USERNAME%
```

If user profiles are not enabled on the Windows 98 computer where the resulting OPS file is to be applied, you must also include the commands to create the Profiles folder and the USERNAME environment variable. In this case, use the following DOS commands from a batch file or manually enter them on the command line:

```
SET USERNAME
cd %windir%
md Profiles
md Profiles\"%USERNAME%"
```

Windows 2000 and Windows NT store user-related profile variables in the registry. When a user logs onto the computer the operating system recalls the related user settings from the registry and updates the USERPROFILE and USERNAME environment variables accordingly.

Restricting the contents of an OPS file

You can customize the Profile Wizard to include only the registry settings and files you want to include in an OPS file. This can be helpful when you deploy Microsoft Office XP in stages with a default user profile.

For example, you can roll out Microsoft Excel, Microsoft Word, and Microsoft PowerPoint® with one set of customizations, then at a later date roll out Microsoft Outlook and Microsoft Internet Explorer with different customizations. In this scenario, you can customize the Profile Wizard to save and distribute only the settings you need for each stage of your deployment. It is also possible to use command-line switches to restore only the settings you want for a specific application, even though an entire Office configuration is saved in the OPS file. See the Profile Wizard help for information on how to use the available command-line switches.

To customize the behavior of the Profile Wizard, you edit the OPW10adm.ini file. Open the file in Notepad or another text editor, and then add or delete references to settings you want to include or exclude. When you edit the OPW10adm.ini file, you can include or exclude specific applications, registry settings or Application Data folders, and template files.

Each section of the OPW10adm.ini or OPW10user.ini file contains comments documenting the usage and syntax for entries within that section. The default entries are designed to gather a complete set of user configuration data, including files containing user configuration settings and Windows registry values, for Office XP.

> **Note** Some settings in a user profile are shared among applications in Office XP. When you customize the OPW10adm.ini file for a staged deployment, make sure you change only non-shared settings or be sure you have tested the shared settings to make sure they work correctly for all applications before you deploy the Office profile settings (OPS file).

The new release of the Profile Wizard includes new capabilities that allow you to avoid making customizations to an INI file. The ability to selectively capture settings for an individual application instead of all applications can be achieved through the administrative interface or from the command line. This also applies to restoring settings for a select application from an OPS file that contains settings for all of Office. See the Profile Wizard Help (administrative mode) for more information on command-line options and capturing select user settings.

Editing the OPW10usr.ini and OPW10adm.ini files

While you can edit any of the INI files used by the Profile Wizard, editing the OPW10adm.ini or OPW10usr.ini is the best place to begin. The OPW10adm.ini is tailored for administrators who want to create generic OPS files for distribution to many users. The OPW10usr.ini is better suited for capturing and restoring the customizations of a specific user more completely. You can edit either of these files to make the Profile Wizard include or exclude additional files, folders, or registry subkeys and values.

> **Note** If an INI file is set to include a folder, that folder is created on a user's computer when the settings are restored from an OPS file whether there are any files for the folder or not.

Each INI file is divided into two pieces:

File/Folder Section

Registry Section

INI sections in the table below, which deals with files and folders, appear under the **File/Folder Section** of each INI file.

INI sections in the table below dealing with registry keys, entries, and values appear under the **Registry Section** of each INI file. For a full description of each INI section, including examples of syntax, see the INI file.

INI section	Contents
[IncludeFolderTrees]	All folders and subfolders for a select registry node. Files in these folders and subfolders are also included.
[IncludeIndividualFolders]	Include only a specific folder.
[IncludeIndividualFiles]	Include a specific file.
[ExcludeFiles]	Files to exclude from the user profile. Accepts wildcard characters in the file name (to exclude groups of files).
[FolderTreesToRemoveToResetToDefaults]	Folder trees to delete prior to writing data from the OPS file to the user's computer. Use this section with caution.
[IndividualFilesToRemoveToResetToDefaults]	Files to delete prior to writing data from the OPS file to the user's computer. Each folder must be explicitly specified.
[ExcludeFilesToRemoveToResetToDefaults]	New to Office XP, this allows you to keep specific files or groups of files normally removed during a **Reset to defaults** action.
[SubstituteEnvironmentVariables]	Environment variables to expand if found in a registry value with a data type of REG_EXPAND_SZ. See the **Creating a customized Generic profile settings file** for important information.
[IncludeRegistryTrees]	Include all Keys, subkeys, and values from the specified registry node.

INI section	Contents
[IncludeIndividualRegistryKeys]	Includes only a specific key and any associated values in the key.
[IncludeIndividualRegistryValues]	New to Office XP, includes only a specific key and a specific entry value.
[ExcludeRegistryTrees]	Any keys or subkeys in the specific node are excluded.
[ExcludeIndividualRegistryKeys]	Exclude a specific key.
[ExcludeIndividualRegistryValues]	Exclude a specific named value of a key.
[RegistryTreesToRemoveToResetToDefaults]	Registry node (and all subkeys) to delete prior to writing values from the OPS file to a user's computer.
[IndividualRegistryValuesToRemoveToResetToDefaults]	Specific registry entry values to delete prior to writing values from the OPS file to the user's computer.

Note When you use the Profile Wizard to restore the settings from the OPS file, and also instruct it to not use the **Reset to defaults** option, be aware that any customizations you have made to the sections ending with the text "...ResetToDefaults" are ignored. The instructions in the ResetToDefaults section of any INI file are always added to an OPS file when it is created, which means the instructions will take effect on the target computer, not on the computer where the configuration was obtained.

CHAPTER 9

Using System Policies

Using system policies is an effective way to enforce changes across a corporate network. With the addition of several new policies, enforcing changes has become easier. These topics provide information to help you create a policy file, set and enforce a policy, obtain hard-to-find information for complex policies, and posture a policy file on a domain controller. In large corporations, setting system policies may require research and testing before the policies are deployed to users.

In this chapter

Understanding System Policies   235

How to Set System Policies   240

Office System Policies   255

Working with Difficult Policies   267

Understanding System Policies

System policies allow you to enforce settings and restrictions on users' computers — one of the best forms of control an administrator can have over users' computers. The Microsoft Office policy templates (ADM files) describe all of the policy settings you can set for Office. These ADM files can be used with the System Policy Editor and Group Policy snap-in tools in Microsoft Windows® operating systems to apply policies to users' computers.

The System Policy Editor uses ADM templates, which come with the Microsoft Office XP Resource Kit and are in standard text format. The ADM files describe the policies available in Office XP. Each policy is a registry setting that Office will respect. ADM templates for respective Office applications must be loaded prior to configuring a policy for Office.

System policies can only be enabled and enforced on computers connected to a network whose primary domain controller is a Microsoft Windows NT® server or Microsoft Windows 2000 server.

What policies can do

System policies have several advantages. For instance, they enable an administrator to:

- Disable or enable most menu commands and corresponding toolbar buttons.
- Disable or enable shortcut keys.
- Specify settings for many dialog box items, including most of the options in the **Options** dialog box (**Tools** menu).
- Set Windows Installer to always install applications with elevated privileges.
- Disable patching of software by Windows Installer.
- Customize the shared Startup folder for all users.

There are also specific Office XP policies to support many of the new Office XP features listed here:

- Improved security policies

    Use system policies to control how Office uses Visual Basic for Applications and control the trust level of each Office application.

- The start working pane

    Use system policies to control when this pane is displayed, and add new links to it.

- Save My Settings Wizard

    Use system policies to control Internet access and where profile settings files (OPS files) are uploaded to.

- Language settings

    Set the list of languages you want users to see in the language settings utility.

    Note When you enforce the **Installed version of Microsoft Office** language policy (**Microsoft Office XP | Language settings | Enabled Languages**), you should also run a configuration maintenance file (CMW file) with the language changes you want to make. This will force Office applications to perform an optimization of their language configuration the next time each application is started.

- Collaboration

    Control exactly how Office applications should collaborate with the collaboration settings policies.

- Corporate Error Reporting tool

    Use system policies to disable the Corporate Error Reporting tool, control the content of the information uploaded, and customize dialogs that get displayed during error reporting.

- Web Archives

    Control exactly how users save Web Archives.

- Default encryption values for passwords

    Set the ability of a user to change encryption ciphers on or off.

    Set the default encryption cipher for all users.

Office XP policies

Office XP has enhanced and improved system policies.

As part of the support for policies in Office 2000 and Office XP, policies are consolidated in a separate subkey in the Windows registry: HKEY_CURRENT_USER\Software\Policies. In Office 97, policies were stored in application-specific Software subkeys, such as HKEY_CURRENT_USER\Software\Microsoft\Office\8.0\Word or HKEY_CURRENT_USER\Software\Microsoft\Office\8.0\Excel.

> **Note** Because policy configuration settings are stored in a different area of the registry for each release of Office, policy configuration settings from one release do not transfer to a new release. You are required to use the new policy templates to configure your policies for Office XP.

Safer policies

In Windows 2000, you can set an Access Control List (ACL) to lock the Policies subkey in the Windows registry. (The HKEY_CURRENT_USER policies branch is locked by default on Windows 2000). This step prevents users from changing a policy configuration setting by modifying security settings to nodes in their registry. Or, if you prefer, you can set security permissions manually using the regedt32 utility in both Windows 2000 and Windows NT 4.0 Service Pack 6a or later.

More Excel and Word policies

Most of the settings in the **Options** dialog box (**Tools** menu) in Microsoft Word and Microsoft Excel can be set through a policy, except for settings stored internal to the document, or for settings that are valid only for the current edit session.

Corporate Error Reporting tool policies

The new crash-reporting tool, Corporate Error Reporting, has policy settings you can set in the Office10.adm template. This new tool is a critical component of Microsoft Office. When used in a corporate setting, Corporate Error Reporting requires administrators to decide how they are going to use the crash-reporting data produced by Office applications, and how the reporting tool will be configured. For more information about the Corporate Error Reporting tool, see "Reporting Office Application Crashes" in Chapter 8, "Maintaining an Installation."

Overview of the System Policy Editor

System policy files are created by using the System Policy Editor. The editor requires the loading of ADM templates created for use with the System Policy Editor from the **Policy Template...** option (**Options** menu). When the ADM templates necessary for creating a policy file are loaded, selecting the **New Policy** option (**File** menu) creates two policy profiles. The **Default Computer** profile is for controlling policies associated with the HKEY_LOCAL_MACHINE registry node, and the **Default User** profile is for controlling policies associated with the HKEY_CURRENT_USER registry node.

After these two policy profiles are created, the administrator must make the necessary changes to enable and enforce policies on each computer connected to the network, or for each user who logs on to the network. Enabling a policy is accomplished by setting a leaf in the policy profile properties tree to checked. Disabling it is accomplished by setting it to unchecked (cleared). A setting of grayed is ignored by the System Policy Editor.

After creating a policy file, rename it and copy it to the NetLogon folder of the primary domain controller. If the policy is for use with Windows 98, name it config.pol. If the policy file is for NT-based operating systems (including Windows 2000), name it NTConfig.pol. When the file appears in this folder, the domain controller automatically activates and enforces the policy settings. When users log on to the network, the system policy file is read and enforced at the user's computer. Changes to an existing policy are automatically propagated to users the next time they log on to the network.

Because of subtle differences in how the Windows registry works for the Microsoft Windows 98, Microsoft Windows Millennium Edition, Microsoft Windows NT, and Microsoft Windows 2000 operating systems, you need to create groups of policies to enforce for each operating system. The System Policy Editor can be used with all of these Windows operating systems. The Group Policy snap-in can only be used with Windows 2000. See the Group Policy snap-in Help for information on how to activate policies using the Active Directory™ directory service in the Windows 2000 environment.

Using policy templates

Policy templates are the starting point for all policies. Find the ADM templates you need and then create a policy file based on the available policy settings within the templates. You can add several ADM files to the policy editor and set the entire configuration of a user's computer with just one policy file. For example, include the Office10.adm, Pub10.adm, Word10.adm, Excel10.adm, and Instlr11.adm files into the System Policy Editor using the **Policy Template...** menu option (**Options** menu). Then select **New Policy** from the **File** menu option. You should see **Default Computer** and **Default User** icons appear in the work area. **Default Computer** controls the HKLM (HKEY_LOCAL_MACHINE) registry entries, and **Default User** controls the HKCU (HKEY_CURRENT_USER) registry entries. Double-click the **Default User** icon. Then double-click **Windows Installer**. You will see the policy settings for Windows Installer.

A policy setting is tri-state: if the policy is checked, it is enforced; if the policy is empty (clear), it is not enforced (turned off); if the policy is grayed, it implies the registry setting is ignored on the user's computer. In other words, if the policy is set to grayed, and the policy is either set or not set on the user's computer, the registry entry is left alone on the user's computer.

> **Note** Part of the confusion for some users of the System Policy Editor is the tri-state logic implemented with each policy. Along with this tri-state logic is a second option to "activate" or "enforce" the policy. Even though the policy setting is checked, most instances require "enforcing" the policy by setting the **Check to enforce setting on; uncheck to enforce setting off** check box to checked in the work area at the bottom of the **Policy Properties** dialog.

Policy templates available with the Office Resource Kit

The following list includes all of the policy templates shipping with the Office XP Resource Kit. Those with the name of an Office application contain policy settings used exclusively with that application. The Office10.adm has policy settings related to more than one Office application (shared).

Access10.adm	Office10.adm
Excel10.adm	Outlk10.adm
FP10.adm	Ppt10.adm
GAL10.adm	Pub10.adm
Instlr11.adm	Word10.adm

To load Group Policy templates for Windows 2000, start the Group Policy snap-in. You may need to start the Microsoft Management Console and load the Group Policy snap-in before you can perform the following steps.

The Group Policy file gpedit.msc file is installed to the C:\WINNT\SYSTEM32 folder during a default install of Windows 2000. If you create a shortcut to this file using Windows Explorer, it will create a Group Policy shortcut on your Desktop.

To add a Windows 2000 ADM template to the Group Policy snap-in

1. Start Group Policy.
2. Select **Administrative Templates** from either the **Computer Configuration** or **User Configuration** branches.

    These two nodes of the Group Policy tree are parallel to the **Default Computer** and **Default User** policy profiles in the System Policy Editor.

3. Right-click on the **Administrative Templates** branch and select **All Tasks**.
4. Select **Add/Remove Templates...**
5. Click **Add...**
6. Load any or all of the ADM templates.

The new policy entries will appear within the appropriate branches of the Group Policy tree.

> **Note** The ADM template syntax for Group Policy snap-in is now a superset of the ADM template syntax used by the System Policy Editor. ADM templates created specifically for the Group Policy snap-in will not work with the System Policy Editor.

Office enforces system policies

When you set a policy to be turned off for an element of an application, such as a menu command or toolbar button, that element appears dimmed (grayed) in the user interface. Users will not be able to use or reset that option. With previous versions of Office, users could change a setting back to enabled, even if the element had been turned off by system policies.

Office now enforces and respects policy settings even if a user happens to edit a registry setting on the fly. When an Office application restarts, it reviews policies and reinforces settings, rather than having to wait for the user to log on again and revalidate the policy settings.

Special policy configurations

The System Policy Editor allows you to create policies for unique situations. You can create policies for one user, one computer, or a group of users. If you need to enforce a set of policies for one individual, you can create a policy for this user, and the policy will be applied when the user logs on. You can also create specific policies for more than one user, user group, a computer, default computers, and default users within one policy file. See the System Policy Editor Help for more information on creating special policy profiles. See the Group Policy snap-in Help for more information on configuring policies for Windows 2000.

> **Note** To see the exact registry setting controlled by a policy, you can view the ADM file with a text editor and examine the registry entry for that policy.

How to Set System Policies

System policies provide administrators the ability to control client desktops. Policies are special registry settings applied to users' computers when users log on to the network. The Microsoft Office XP Resource Kit includes system policy templates that describe the system policy settings available for Microsoft Office XP. The policy settings available in these policy templates enable administrators to do the following:

- Modify the user interface.

- Grant permissions to run or not run features of an application or utility.
- Restrict a user from customizing parts of the different Office applications.

> **Note** The System Policy Editor is the primary tool mentioned in this topic. However, the Group Policy snap-in is the suggested tool of choice for the Microsoft Windows 2000 operating system. Consult the Help available with the Group Policy snap-in for information on how to set policies, to propagate them with Active Directory™, and to create custom ADM templates.

Working with system policy templates

A system policy setting represents a controllable option or feature on a user's computer. Each system policy setting listed within an ADM template corresponds to one or more registry keys, value names, or value data. Policy templates are organized by the application they can control. Each registry key, value name, or value data is noted in standard ASCII text within the ADM template and lists the minimum or maximum values each entry can have, if applicable, and the registry key changed on the user's computer.

When you create a system policy file (*.pol) or a Group Policy Object (GPO), you use one or more policy templates loaded into either the System Policy Editor from the **Policy Templates...** menu option (**Options** menu) or the Group Policy snap-in (select either **Computer Configuration** or **User Configuration**, right-click **Administrative Templates**, then click **Add/Remove Templates...**). The Office XP Resource Kit includes the policy template files listed in the table below. These files list the policy settings you can control for each application.

> **Note** With the System Policy Editor you cannot add templates if your policy file is open, so be sure to add in all the templates you plan to use for the policy file you are working with prior to setting policies.

Template file name	Includes policies
Office10.adm	shared by Office XP components
Access10.adm	for Microsoft Access 2002
Excel10.adm	for Microsoft Excel 2002
Fp10.adm	for Microsoft FrontPage® 2002
Outlk10.adm	for Microsoft Outlook® 2002
Pub10.adm	for Microsoft Publisher 2002
Ppt10.adm	for Microsoft PowerPoint® 2002
Word10.adm	for Microsoft Word 2002
Gal10.adm	for Clip Organizer
Instlr11.adm	for Windows Installer 1.1

Policies in a template are organized into a hierarchy so they are easier to find. For applications with user-interface elements, the templates are organized to correspond to the user interface. For example, items usually found in the **Options** dialog box (**Tools** menu) are listed under **Tools | Options** in the template.

In some cases, however, the templates do not exactly match the user interface. Some Office settings appear in the **Options** dialog box (**Tools** menu) for each component. Corresponding policies are listed in the Office10.adm template. For example, the **Provide feedback with sound** option (under **Miscellaneous**) is common to Word, Excel, PowerPoint, and Access, so it is stored in the Office10.adm template rather than in the templates of the individual applications. Similarly, each component has a **Web Options** button on the **General** tab in the **Options** dialog box (**Tools** menu), so you can control the use of Office applications and their ability to access the Web. You can set a policy for these options by using the Office10.adm template. Look for the **Tools|Options|General|Web Options...** category in the Office10.adm rather than in each template for the individual applications.

> **Note** The System Policy Editor can also work with other Windows template files (Common.adm, Windows.adm, Winnt.adm, System.adm, etc.) and the Windows Installer template Instlr11.adm. These templates do not contain Office-related policies. Windows policy templates are useful for managing a workgroup, user, or a single computer. In the case of Windows Installer, the template provides both system and user policies. For more information, see the *Windows NT Server Resource Kit* or the *Windows NT Workstation Resource Kit*.

Before you enable a policy, you must load the policy template containing the policy you want to use.

The system policy templates contain individual system policy settings organized by category. For detailed information about the contents of each template, use a text editor and examine the contents of each ADM file to determine which registry settings are being changed.

> **Note** ADM templates created for use with the Group Policy snap-in cannot be read by the System Policy Editor. The syntax for the Group Policy snap-in ADM templates is a superset of the syntax used by the System Policy Editor and uses statements not recognized by the System Policy Editor.

Policy setting states

When you use the System Policy Editor, you will see that a policy can have one of three settings in the **Properties** dialog box:

- Selected (checked)

    When selected, a policy is enforced. For many policies, another check box in the work area of the **Properties** dialog for the policy indicates whether the setting is enforced as on or off. When a user logs on, the Windows registry changes to conform to the policy.

For example, in Excel you can set a policy to determine whether the **Formula** bar is visible in normal view. You enforce the policy by selecting the **Show Formula bar in Normal View** check box. Then you use the **Check to enforce setting on; uncheck to enforce setting off** check box to determine which way the setting is enforced (selecting the check box enforces the policy).

- Cleared (unchecked)

   When cleared, the policy is turned off. If it was enforced previously, the previously specified settings are removed from the Windows registry. When you clear a policy, the option returns either to the application default state or to whatever setting the user had specified before you set the policy.

   For example, if an Excel user has set the **Formula** bar to appear in normal view, and you apply a policy to turn off the **Formula** bar, that user no longer sees the **Formula** bar in normal view. If you then clear the policy, it reverts to the previous settings, so the user sees the **Formula** bar in normal view once again.

   Note It is advised to clear a policy setting if it has ever been enforced previously, to make sure it is turned off. Settings from a policy remain in effect until the setting is cleared.

- Unavailable (grayed)

   System policies can be changed to an unavailable state. A grayed check box indicates the setting is not configured or is being ignored by the policy setting enforcement code in the logon process. Note that registry settings are neither set nor removed by the logon process. When you first create a system policy, all of the settings are set to the unavailable (grayed) state. If you have configured a policy and distributed the policy file and need to turn it off, use the clear setting to disable the policy.

   Note The unavailable state does not disable a previously enforced policy setting. Only the clear setting of a policy forces a change to the registry entry associated with this policy.

By using the Group Policy snap-in available with Windows 2000, you can give a policy one of three settings in the **Properties** dialog:

- Not Configured

   This is the same as the **Unavailable** option in the System Policy Editor.

- Enabled

   This is the same as the **Selected** option in the System Policy Editor.

- Disabled

   This is the same as the **Cleared** option in the System Policy Editor.

All of the system policies for an application are listed in the corresponding policy template (ADM file).

Setting system policies for selected users or groups

You can set system policies to apply to a single user, a group of users, or for all users. You can also set policies for a single computer or for all computers. You make these choices in the System Policy Editor when you create policy profiles from the **Edit** menu. The **Edit** menu provides the ability to create a policy profile for a user, computer, or group.

Policies set by the Group Policy snap-in are stored in Registry.pol files. Policies for machine-related settings go in the GPT\Machine folder, while policies for user-related settings go in the GPT\User folder. For more information on how these files are propagated through Active Directory, see the Group Policy snap-in Help.

The policies you create and enforce from the Office10.adm policy template are set in the \Software\Policies\Microsoft\ node of each user's Windows registry.

Setting system policies for all users or all computers

You can configure a policy for all of the users in your domain by double-clicking the **Default User** icon in the System Policy Editor. You can also set a policy for all client computers in your domain by double-clicking the **Default Computer** icon. When you double-click one of these icons, the **Properties** dialog box opens, and you can set the policies for the user or computer you selected. You can set a policy for all users, for all computers, or for both. If you do not want to set a system policy for users or computers, you can select users or computers and press the delete key or select **Remove** (**Edit** menu).

> **Note** The full name of the **Properties** dialog box changes depending on the name of the icon you double-click in the main window of the System Policy Editor. The dialog box is generically referred to as the "**Properties** dialog box" in this topic.

Setting system policies for one user or one computer

You can set a policy for a specific user account by adding the user to the policy file. For example, if your network includes a Guest account, and you want to limit a guest user's access to options, you can create a system policy for the Guest account (considered a User and added in through the **Add User** option as **Guest**). Similarly, if all your guest users only use one computer, you can create a policy for that computer. See the Group Policy snap-in Help for information on how to set policies for a single user or computer.

> **Note** The user name or computer name you specify in the System Policy Editor must be recognized by the domain controller, otherwise the policy is never enforced. You cannot create new user names or computer names from within the System Policy Editor.

To add a user to a policy file

1. Start the System Policy Editor.
2. Create a new policy file or open an existing policy file.

3. Select **Edit**.

4. Select **Add User…**

5. Enter the UserID of the user you want to create a policy for into the text box in the **Add User** dialog and click **OK**.

   Since a user's settings are maintained in the HKCU, the resulting policy profile has the same options as the Default User policy profile.

To add a computer to a policy file

1. Start the System Policy Editor.

2. Create a new policy file or open an existing policy file.

3. Select **Edit**.

4. Select **Add Computer…**

5. Enter the machine name of the computer you want to create a policy for into the text box in the **Add Computer** dialog and click **OK**.

   A computer's settings are maintained in the HKLM registry node. The resulting policy profile has the same options as the Default Computer policy profile.

Setting system policies for a group

You can set policies for groups of users in your domain. For example, all of the users in your Accounting department may require the same options in Excel. If you create a Microsoft Windows NT user group for the Accounting department, you can control the options for all users in the Accounting group by setting a policy for them. See the Group Policy snap-in Help for information on how to set policies for a group.

> **Note** The group name you specify in the System Policy Editor must be recognized by the domain controller. You cannot create new groups from within the System Policy Editor.

Some users are members of more than one group. To avoid potential conflicts between policies enabled for these groups, you can prioritize the different groups so policies are applied in a particular order. When a user who is a member of several groups logs on, the policy settings from the highest priority group are read in last so these settings take precedence over the settings from lower-priority groups.

To create a group policy

1. Start the System Policy Editor.

2. Create a new policy file or open an existing policy file.

3. Select **Edit**.

4. Select **Add Group...**

5. Enter the Group name of the group you want to create a policy for into the text box in the **Add Group** dialog and click **OK**.

   Since a group is a collection of users, a group receives the same policy profile settings as used by users, HKCU. The resulting policy profile has the same options as the Default User policy profile.

Sometimes a user is a member of more than one group. To avoid potential conflicts between group policies, you can set relative priorities so group policies are applied in a specific order. To set priorities for a group, click **Group Priority** (**Options** menu) in the System Policy Editor.

Using system policies to disable user-interface items

Several system policies enable you to stop users from changing items in the user interface. By using these policies, you can disable menu commands, toolbar buttons, and shortcut keys so users cannot use or gain access to those features or options.

Disabling menu and toolbar items

System policies can disable menu commands and their corresponding toolbar buttons. When you disable a menu command and toolbar button through a policy, users cannot use that command or button.

A menu command disabled through a policy still appears on the menu, but it is grayed out and unavailable. Similarly, a toolbar button disabled through a policy appears on the toolbar as grayed out, but it is unavailable to users. It also displays the name of the toolbar button followed by "Disabled by your system administrator".

Several menu commands and toolbar buttons are listed in the **Predefined** category of each applications template. These include several commands administrators frequently disable, such as the **Hyperlink...** command (**Insert** menu) and the **Macro** command (**Tools** menu). If you want to disable any other command in an Office XP application (even predefined commands), use the **Custom** category or use either the Custom Installation Wizard or Custom Maintenance Wizard to modify settings on the **Specify User Configuration Settings** page of each wizard. To disable a menu command and toolbar button in the **Custom** category, enter the control ID for the item in the System Policy Editor. You can look up the control ID for any command or button using Visual Basic® for Applications (VBA). For more information about finding control IDs for menu commands, see "Working with Difficult Policies" in Chapter 9, "Using System Policies."

Disabling shortcut keys

Many Office commands have corresponding shortcut keys. When you disable the menu command and toolbar button through a policy, users can still press the shortcut key to run the command. To make the option completely unavailable, you must also disable the shortcut key.

For example, suppose you disable the **Hyperlink...** option (**Insert** menu) in Excel and a user knows the shortcut key for the command is CTRL+K. The user can still use the shortcut key to insert a hyperlink. To prevent users from inserting hyperlinks, disable the CTRL+K key combination, too.

To disable a shortcut key in the **Predefined** category of a policy template, select the shortcut key from the resulting list in the **Settings for Disable shortcut keys** work area. You can also disable any shortcut key by using the **Custom** category. To disable a shortcut key in the **Custom** category, look up the virtual key code for the registry entry corresponding to the shortcut key (see Help in the Custom Installation Wizard and search the index for **virtual key code**) and then enter the virtual key code (example: VK_T or VK_DOWN). If it is used with a modifier key (like Alt, Ctrl, Shift) enter the two as CTRL+VK_T. In situations where more than one modifier is used, combine them as CTRL+SHIFT+VK_T.

For more information about disabling shortcut keys and virtual key codes, see "Working with Difficult Policies" in Chapter 9, "Using System Policies."

Note Even when you disable both a menu command and its corresponding shortcut key, the command is still available through Visual Basic for Applications (VBA). This is by design, so you can create macros to use the command.

You can also disable the following: a predefined or custom menu, a toolbar item, and either a predefined or custom shortcut key.

Using environment variables in system policies

Windows 98, Windows NT 4.0, Windows Millennium Edition (Windows Me), and Windows 2000 all include the capability to use environment variables in the Windows registry to replace file names, paths, or other changeable values. Environment variables in the Windows registry use the **REG_EXPAND_SZ** data type.

For example, the **Default file location** policy for Excel 2002 allows the setting of a default path where users can store Excel files. If you want to store the Excel files of users under their user names on the network, you can use a network drive and the following environment variable:

X:\%USERNAME%\

When you distribute the policy, the environment variable is written to each user's registry. Office XP recognizes %USERNAME% as an environment variable and expands it to whatever the %USERNAME% variable is set to on the user's computer. For example, Office XP expands this example to X:\UserA\ for User A, X:\UserB\ for User B, and so on.

You can also use any other appropriately defined environment variable to set **Default file location** to a particular path or folder. Because Office XP recognizes the **REG_EXPAND_SZ** data type, you can use environment variables that exist by default in the operating system or variables you set on your own.

> **Note** Windows 98 does not create environment variables automatically. You must create and define variables manually so they resolve correctly for each user. For example, to create the %USERNAME% environment variable for Windows 98 clients, use a Windows NT logon script. To view the current environment variables you already have, open a command prompt (DOS window) and enter "SET".

You can use environment variables in place of directory paths or specific user information. For more information, see the *Windows NT Server 4.0 Resource Kit*.

System policies and the Windows registry

If you used the System Policy Editor to create a system policy file and then placed that file in the network logon directory on the primary domain controller server, when a user logs on to the network, the system policy file is downloaded to the user's computer. Before the user can begin to use his computer again, the Windows registry is updated to use the values specified in the system policy file.

If a change occurs to your organization that requires changing policy settings again, you can update each user's computer by placing an updated system policy file in the logon directory on the primary domain controller. The Windows registry for each client computer is updated when the user logs on.

Where the Windows registry stores policies

In previous versions of Office, system policies were stored in the Windows registry in application-specific subkeys under HKEY_CURRENT_USER\Software\Microsoft\Office. System policies for Office 2000 and Office XP are consolidated in the HKEY_CURRENT_USER\Software\Policies subkey.

The Policies subkey mirrors most of the HKEY_CURRENT_USER\Software\Microsoft\Office\10.0 subkey. Placing all of the system policies together in the same subkey prevents Windows registry errors and also makes it possible for administrators to lock the Policies subkey for Windows NT–based operating systems.

The following example shows the hierarchy of the Policies subkey in the Windows registry.

HKEY_CURRENT_USER
  Software
    Policies
      Microsoft
        Office
          10.0
            Access
            Common

Excel

FrontPage

Outlook

PowerPoint

Word

Locating a registry entry associated with a system policy

Each system policy in a policy template corresponds to one or more entries in the Windows registry. If you want to know which entries in the Windows registry correspond to a particular policy, you can open the policy template in a text editor, and then look for the policy.

The policy template files are divided into categories, and each category lists the Windows registry subkey with the entries for that category. Each policy entry in the template lists the Windows registry value name the policy affects and the specific Windows registry value data it sets when the policy is turned on or off.

For example, in the Word10.adm template, the following policy entry lists the Windows registry entries set when you disable the **Insert Hyperlink** shortcut key:

```
POLICY !!DisableShortcutKeys
KEYNAME Software\Policies\Microsoft\Office\10.0\Word _
\DisabledShortcutKeysCheckBoxes
    PART !!InsertHyperlinkKey CHECKBOX
    VALUENAME InsertHyperlink
    VALUEON 75,8
    VALUEOFF 0
    END PART
```

The double exclamation points (!!) in the template file indicate the text following it is a string variable and the variable is set at the bottom of the file. For example, if you see a line such as **!!InsertHyperlinkKey** in the template file, there is a section at the bottom of the file under [strings] where it is set:

```
[Strings]
InsertHyperlinkKey = "Ctrl+K (Insert | Hyperlink...)"
```

The following table lists the entries in the policy template files you can see when you open the files with a text editor.

Entry	Description
POLICY	Policy you are turning on or off. In the preceding example, the **Disable Shortcut Keys** policy includes several subpolicies, including the policy to turn off the **Insert Hyperlink** shortcut key.
KEYNAME	Affected registry subkey.
PART	Specific option you are setting with the policy. In the preceding example, there are several shortcut keys you can disable individually.
VALUENAME	Affected registry value.
VALUEON	Registry value data setting to indicate when this policy is turned on (for example, the **Insert Hyperlink** shortcut key is disabled).
VALUEOFF	Registry value data setting to indicate when this policy is turned off (for example, the **Insert Hyperlink** shortcut key is enabled).
;	Comment. Add a comment by placing a semicolon at the extreme left of a line.

Saving and distributing the policy file

After you set the policy values you want, you are ready to save and distribute the policy file. For Windows 98 clients, save the policy file as Config.pol. For Windows NT 4.0 or Windows 2000 clients, save the policy file as Ntconfig.pol. Then exit the System Policy Editor.

Next, you need to store the policy file on the network, where it can be downloaded to users' computers when they log on.

For networks running Windows NT Server, copy Config.pol or Ntconfig.pol to the Netlogon folder of the primary domain controller, as defined for your client computers. When your users next log on, the system policies are automatically downloaded to their computers and their registry settings are updated with the policy settings.

For Windows 2000 systems with Active Directory, no special posturing of the policy files (Registry.pol) is required on the primary domain controller. Active Directory manages the task for you. See the Group Policy snap-in Help for details on how to use the Group Policy snap-in.

Locking down user options in Office using system policies

The new administrative features in Microsoft Office XP include the ability to turn off options or features to which you do not want users to have access. Office XP provides the ability to lock down a specific configuration and control exactly how users interact with applications.

Locking down Office is accomplished primarily for registry settings on systems running Windows 98. Operating systems like Windows NT and Windows 2000 require setting permissions of registry branches, drives, or folders to lock down the configuration of the computer. Some settings related to locking down a system are controlled through the System Policy Editor and of these settings, they can all be set by using the Custom Installation Wizard or Custom Maintenance Wizard with either the **Set User Configuration Settings** page or the **Add/Remove Registry Entries** page. If a test computer is used, it is possible to capture a configuration of Office on the test computer and then distribute that configuration to all users using the Profile Wizard.

For more information on locking down a Windows NT or Windows 2000 operating system, see "Running Office in a Secure Environment" in Chapter 10, "Administering Security."

When to lock down an Office installation

There are several reasons for wanting to lock down a particular configuration of Office XP. The following scenarios illustrate a few of the more important reasons for locking down a configuration.

Keep important information accessible

If your organization has a high employee turnover rate, you might not want some employees to add password-protection to their files. When someone is replaced, your new employee will probably need access to all the previous user's files. Disabling password-protection on user files helps guarantee important customer information is always accessible.

Even organizations that do not have a high employee turnover face situations where many users need access to files on one workstation, and all of those users may need to store files in a specific folder or in a source file library management system like Microsoft Visual Source Safe. Setting a default directory where files are stored simplifies the user experience and adds a level of configuration control to the system.

Reduce support costs

If you are training employees who are computer novices, you can raise everyone's confidence level by locking down a uniform configuration of Office and disabling all user customization until users become more skilled. Enforcing default Office settings can help reduce training and support costs.

Create a consistent user environment

If you have shifts of employees sharing computers, you can make the transitions between shift changes easier by enforcing a consistent user interface on every computer. A consistent user experience is easier for all users when they can rely on settings and features being the same every time they use a computer.

Limit potential distractions of the Internet

Office XP includes built-in hyperlinks to sites on the World Wide Web where users can obtain more information about features of Office. However, if users do not normally use the Internet for their work duties, distracting them with the Web may not be beneficial to productivity. You can disable access to these URLs to reduce user distraction.

How to lock down options with system policies

System policies are organized by application when displayed within the System Policy Editor. Each application requires the loading of a related system policy template. Within the templates are categories for Office applications, such as **Tools | Options** or **Disable items in user interface**. Within these categories are individual policies. You enable a policy by selecting it in the System Policy Editor and setting it to checked (selected) and then enforcing the policy or adding extra parameters/values to the policy in the work area at the bottom of the properties dialog.

The following types of policies are useful for locking down options.

Disable command bar items

You can disable any menu command in an application, along with its corresponding toolbar button. To disable a standard command bar item, use the **Disable command bar buttons and menu items** policy in the **Predefined** category for a specific Office application. To disable any other command bar button, use the **Custom** category and enter the control ID for the user interface element.

When you disable an item on a menu or toolbar, that item still appears on the menu or toolbar; but the item is grayed, which means the corresponding command is unavailable. When a user points to a disabled toolbar button, the ScreenTip indicates the button has been disabled.

Prevent command bar customization

To enforce a consistent user interface across all of the computers in your organization, you can stop users from customizing menu bars or toolbars. To disable command bar customization, set the **Disable command bar buttons and menu items** policy to checked in the **Predefined** category and select the **Tools | Customize** check box.

Disable shortcut keys

Many users memorize the keyboard shortcuts for various menu commands and toolbar buttons. If you want to completely lock down an option, you must disable the shortcut key as well as the corresponding menu bar and toolbar items.

You can disable any shortcut key by using the **Disable shortcut keys** policy under the **Predefined** or **Custom** category. When a user presses a disabled shortcut key combination, the application does not respond.

> **Note** Even when you disable both a menu command and its corresponding shortcut key, the command is still available through Visual Basic for Applications. This is by design, so macros can be created to use the command.

Disable dialog box items

You can prevent users from changing options in dialog boxes by locking them down with a policy. For example, several of the options in the **Options** dialog box (**Tools** menu) for each application can be changed using a policy in the policy template. This allows you to easily disable an option you don't want users to change.

Disable Password Protection

Several of the applications in Office XP give users the ability to protect file content by setting a password. You can disable this feature by turning off the command-bar buttons and menu-bar items used to set passwords in Access, Excel, and Word by configuring a policy setting.

To disable password protection for Access, Excel, and Word

1. In the System Policy Editor, double-click the **Default User** icon.
2. In the **Properties** box, expand the application node (click the plus (+) sign) you want to change.
3. Expand the **Disable items in user interface** node.
4. Expand the **Predefined** node.
5. Set the **Disable command bar buttons and menu items** policy to checked.
6. For Access 2002, set the **Tools | Security | Set Database Password** check box to checked.

   For Excel 2002, set the **Tools | Protection**, **Tools | Protection | Protect Sheet**, **Tools | Protection | Protect Workbook** and **Tools | Protection | Protect and Share Workbook** check boxes to checked.

   For Word 2002, set the **Tools | Protect Document** check box to checked.

In Word 2002, PowerPoint 2002, and Excel 2002, users can still set passwords for a file by using the **Save As** command (**File** menu). Setting a policy to lock down the command-bar buttons and menu-bar items for password protection does not prevent users from taking advantage of this alternative.

For example, in Word, users can set a password for a document by clicking **Save As** on the **File** menu, and then in the **Save As** dialog box, clicking the **Tools** menu and then clicking **Security Options…**. The **Security** tab is displayed and includes two password options allowing users to set a password for the file: **Password to open** and **Password to modify**. Excel makes similar options available through the **Save As** command (**File** menu).

Disable built-in connections to the Web

Office XP includes several built-in references to URLs on the World Wide Web. For example, if a user queries the Office Assistant and it cannot find an answer, the user can click **None of the above, look for more help on the Web**. This starts a search across the Web to a Microsoft server with more information.

If you do not want users to use these built-in links to the Web, you can disable them with system policies. For example, you can prevent users from gaining access to the Web by not installing the feature that provides the access, or you can block the Web address using a firewall server.

> **Toolbox** The built-in Web connections in Office XP are listed in a spreadsheet called Webent.xls. The spreadsheet also identifies the connections you can disable and how to disable them. Webent.xls is installed by default when you run the Office Resource Kit Setup program. For more information, see "Supplemental Documentation" in the Toolbox.

For example, you can disable the **Office on the Web** hyperlinks within HTML Help by setting a policy in each of the templates for applications you want to limit. The following procedure shows how to disable this option for Excel.

To disable the Office on the Web connections in Excel

1. In the System Policy Editor, double-click the **Default User** (HKCU) icon.
2. In the **Default User Properties** dialog box, expand the **Microsoft Excel 2002** node (click the plus (+) sign to the left).
3. Expand the **Disable items in user interface** node.
4. Expand the **Predefined** node.
5. Set the **Disable command bar buttons and menu items** check box to checked.
6. Under **Settings for Disable command bar buttons and menu items**, set the **Help | Office on the Web** check box to checked.

You can redirect the Answer Wizard Web connections to a place on your own Internet or intranet site. For more information about customizing Web connections in the Answer Wizard, see "Making Custom Help Content Accessible" in Chapter 11, "Creating Custom Help."

Other policy settings related to disabling Web access are:

- Feedback URL (**Microsoft Office XP | Assistant | Help on the Web**)
- Office on the Web URL (**Microsoft Office XP | "Help | Office on the Web"**)
- Web Query dialog home page (**Microsoft Office XP | Shared paths**)
- Prevent users from uploading settings to the Internet (**Microsoft Office XP | Save My Settings Wizard**)
- Error reporting location (**Microsoft Office XP | Corporate Error Reporting**)
- Display Clips Online access from Clip Organizer (**Clip Organizer 2002**)

For more information on locking down the configuration of an operating system, see "Running Office in a Secure Environment" in Chapter 10, "Administering Security."

Enabling read and write access to Office documents on the web

With the requirement of many businesses to maintain documents on a Web site, a new policy was added to the Office10.adm template to allow users the ability to open a document directly from the Web site while in a browser. Through the use of the System Policy Editor you can easily create a policy file to enable this feature of Office.

To enable read and write access to Office documents on the Web

1. Start the System Policy Editor.
2. Make sure the Office10.adm template is loaded.
3. Create a new policy file or open an existing one.
4. In the **Default User Properties** dialog box, expand the **Microsoft Office XP** node (click the plus (+) sign to the left).
5. Expand the **Tools|Options|General|Web Options** node.
6. Expand the **Files** node.
7. Select the check box for the **Open Office documents as read/write while browsing** policy.

Office System Policies

Each system policies template (ADM template) available with the Microsoft Office XP Resource Kit provides a selection of customizable registry entries. Some of the settings you can change are listed in this topic. To see the possible range of values for these policies, open the ADM template with a text editor (such as Notepad) and examine the listed parameter boundaries, or run the System Policy Editor and examine the work area for each policy. For text boxes requesting file or path information where you must provide a string value, be sure to carefully provide the text using appropriate syntax.

Policies in the Office policy template

The Office10.adm template contains policy settings common to all of the Microsoft Office XP applications. You can use a text editor to open the template and examine the contents. Below is a sample of some of the policy settings you can set to customize a configuration of Office (entries in bold are policies):

Microsoft Office XP

    Security Settings

        Disable VBA for ALL Office applications
        Unsafe ActiveX Initialization

    Language Settings

        User Interface

        Display menus and dialog boxes in
        Display help in

        Enabled Languages

        Show controls and enable editing for

        Afrikaans
        Albanian
        Amharic
        ...

        Installed version of Microsoft Office

        Other

        Office on the Web language
        Prevent language tune-up from running
        Do not adjust defaults to user's locale
        Disallow Taiwan calendar

Policies in the Access policy template

Below are samples of some of the policy settings available in the Access10.adm template (entries in bold are policies):

Microsoft Access 2002

    Tools | Macro

        Security

        Trust all installed add-ins and templates

Customizable error messages

> **List of error messages to customize**

Disable items in user interface

> Predefined
>
> **Disable command bar buttons and menu items**
> **Disable shortcut keys**
>
> Custom
>
> **Disable command bar buttons and menu items**
> **Disable shortcut keys**

Miscellaneous

> **Do not prompt to convert older databases**
> **Custom Answer Wizard database path**

Policies in the Excel policy template

Below are samples of some of the policy settings available in the Excel10.adm template (entries in bold are policies):

Microsoft Excel 2002

> Tools | Macro
>
>> Record New Macro…
>>
>> **Store macro in Personal macro Workbook by default**
>>
>> Security
>>
>> **Security Level**
>> **Trust all installed add-ins and templates**
>> **Trust access to Visual Basic Project**
>>
>> Customizable error messages
>>
>> **List of error messages to customize**
>>
>> Data recovery
>>
>> **Do not show data extraction options when opening corrupt workbooks**
>>
>> **Assume structured storage format of workbook is intact when recovering data**
>>
>> **Corrupt formula conversion**
>>
>> Miscellaneous
>>
>> **Chart gallery path**
>> **Custom Answer Wizard database path**

Enable four-digit year display
Locally cache network file storages
Locally cache PivotTable reports
Automatic query refresh
OLAP PivotTable User Defined Function (UDF) security settings

Policies in the FrontPage policy template

Below are samples of some of the policy settings available in the Fp10.adm template (entries in bold are policies):

Microsoft FrontPage 2002

    Tools | Options…

        General

        Startup Task Pane

    New Page or Web Links

        Custom Link #1
        Custom Link #2
        Custom Link #3
        …

    Disable items in user interface

        Predefined

        Disable command bar buttons and menu items

        Custom

        Disable command bar buttons and menu items

Policies in the Outlook policy template

Below are samples of some of the policy settings available in the Outlk10.adm template (entries in bold are policies):

Microsoft Outlook 2002

    Tools | Macro

        Security…

        Security Level

    Instant Messaging

        Disable Instant Messaging in Outlook
        Installation URL

Customizable error messages

List of error messages to customize

Miscellaneous

NetMeeting
Data format for importing cc:Mail (DB8 only)
Junk e-mail filtering
Auto-repair of MAPI32.DLL
Convert PST stores to LST stores
Delete converted PST stores after xxx days or Outlook startups
Prevent users from adding HTTP e-mail accounts
Prevent users from making changes to Outlook profiles

Exchange settings

Exchange view information
Folder size display
OST Creation
Personal distribution lists (Exchange only)

Outlook Today settings

Outlook Today availability
URL for custom Outlook Today
Folders in the Messages section of Outlook Today

Folder Home Pages for Outlook special folders

Disable Folder Home Pages
Folder Home Page Security
Inbox Folder Home Page
Calendar Folder Home
Contacts Folder home Page
Deleted Items Folder home Page
Drafts Folder Home Page
...

Policies in the PowerPoint policy template

Below are samples of some of the policy settings available in the Ppt10.adm template (entries in bold are policies):

Office PowerPoint 2002

    Tools | AutoCorrect Options…

        AutoFormat as you type

        Replace straight quotes with smart quotes
        AutoFit title text to placeholder
        AutoFit body text to placeholder

    Tools | Options…

        Edit

        Replace straight quotes with smart quotes
        When selecting, automatically select entire word
        Use smart cut and paste
        Drag-and-drop text editing
        New charts take on PowerPoint font
        Maximum number of undos
        New animation effects
        Multiple masters
        Password protection
        Tools | Macro

        Security

        Security Level
        Trust all installed add-ins and templates
        Trust access to Visual Basic Project

    Disable items in user interface

        Predefined

        Disable command bar buttons and menu items
        Disable shortcut keys

        Custom

        Disable command bar buttons and menu items
        Disable shortcut keys

    Miscellaneous

        Custom Answer Wizard database path

Policies in the Publisher policy template

Below are samples of some of the policy settings available in the Pub10.adm template (entries in bold are policies):

Microsoft Publisher 2002

    Default File Locations

        Publication location
        Picture location

    Tools | Spelling

        Do not flag spelling errors in words containing mixed digits
        Do not flag spelling errors in words that look like URLs or e-mail addresses

        Use the user dictionary for spelling correction suggestions
        Arabic spelling options
        Hebrew spelling options

    Tools | Macro

        Security

        Security Level
        Trust all installed add-ins and templates

    Format

        Prompt user when reapplying a style

    Spelling

        Check spelling as you type
        Ignore words in UPPERCASE
        Show repeated words

    Miscellaneous

        Disable Tools | eServices
        Prevent web pages displayed in Publisher from accessing the Office object model

        Default Publisher direction
        Activate Input Sequence Checker
        Use type and replace
        Add double quotes in Hebrew alphabet numbering
        Convert wizards to right-to-left layout

Policies in the Word policy template

Below are samples of some of the policy settings available in the Word10.adm template (entries in bold are policies):

Microsoft Word 2002

    Tools |AutoCorrect

        AutoCorrect

        Correct TWo INitial CApitals
        Capitalize first letter of sentence
        Capitalize names of days
        Correct accidental usage of cAPS LOCK key
        Replace text as you type
        Correct keyboard setting

        AutoFormat as you type

        Replace as you type

        Straight quote with smart quotes
        Ordinals (1st) with superscript
        Fractions (1/2) with fraction character
        Symbol characters (-) with symbols
        "Bold" and _italic_ with real formatting
        Internet and network paths with hyperlinks
        Match parentheses
        Auto space
        Dash-like characters

        Apply as you type

        Headings
        Borders
        Tables
        Dates
        Automatic bulleted lists
        Automatic numbered lists
        First line indent
        Closings

Automatically as you type

Format beginning of list item like the one before it
Set left indent on tabs and backspace
Define styles based on your formatting
Insert memo closing
Launch Greetings Wizard
Insert closing

Policies in the Clip Organizer policy template

These are the policy settings available in the Gal10.adm template.

Microsoft Clip Organizer

Disable Clips Online access from Clip Organizer
Clip Organizer Online URL
Disable menu item: File | Open Clip In...
Disable menu item: File | Add Clips to Organizer | From Scanner or Camera
Disable menu item: File | Send to Mail Recipient (as Attachment)...
Disable menu item: Tools | Tools on the Web...
Hide 'My Collections'
Hide 'Office Collections'
Hide 'Shared Collections'
Hide 'Web Collections'
Prevent automatically importing clips
Prevent users from importing new clips
Prevent changes to primary collection
Enable preview of sound and motion on Terminal Server

Policies in the Windows Installer policy template

Below are the policy settings available in the Instlr11.adm template.

Windows Installer (HKCU)

Always install with elevated privileges
Search order
Disable rollback
Disable media source for any install

Windows Installer (HKLM)

> **Disable Windows Installer**
> **Always install with elevated privileges**
> **Disable rollback**
> **Disable browse dialog box for new source**
> **Disable patching**
> **Disable IE security prompt for Windows Installer scripts**
> **Enable user control over installs**
> **Enable user to browse for source while elevated**
> **Enable user to use media source while elevated**
> **Enable user to patch elevated products**
> **Allow remote Terminal Server installations**
> **Cache transforms in secure location on workstation**
> **Logging**

Office policies that accept environment variables

The following tables list Microsoft Office XP policies that accept environment variables, and the Windows registry entry that corresponds to each policy.

Office policies that accept environment variables

Policy name	Registry entry
Microsoft Office XP | Graph settings | Custom Answer Wizard database path	HKCU\Software\Policies\Microsoft\Office\10.0\Graph\AnswerWizard\AdminDatabase
Microsoft Office XP | Graph settings | Graph gallery path	HKCU\Software\Policies\Microsoft\Office\10.0\Graph\Options\GalleryPath
Microsoft Office XP | Shared paths | Workgroup templates path	HKCU\Software\Policies\Microsoft\Office\10.0\Common\General\SharedTemplates
Microsoft Office XP | Shared paths | Shared themes path	HKCU\Software\Policies\Microsoft\Office\10.0\Common\General\WorkgroupThemes

Policy name (cont'd)	Registry entry
Microsoft Office XP | Shared paths | Web Query dialog home page	HKCU\Software\Policies\Microsoft\Office\10.0\Common\General\WebQueryHomePage
Microsoft Office XP | Shared paths | "User queries path"	HKCU\Software\Policies\Microsoft\Office\10.0\Common\General\UserQueriesFolder
Microsoft Office XP | Shared paths | User templates path	HKCU\Software\Policies\Microsoft\Office\10.0\Common\General\UserTemplates
Microsoft Office XP | Save My Settings Wizard | Default location to store settings file (OPS)	HKCU\Software\Policies\Microsoft\Office\10.0\Common\General\settings\defaultOPSfile

Access policies that accept environment variables

Policy name	Registry entry
Microsoft Access 2002 | Miscellaneous | Custom Answer Wizard database path	HKCU\Software\Policies\Microsoft\Office\10.0\Access\AnswerWizard\AdminDatabase

Excel policies that accept environment variables

Policy name	Registry entry
Microsoft Excel 2002 | Miscellaneous | Custom Answer Wizard database path	HKCU\Software\Policies\Microsoft\Office\10.0\Excel\AnswerWizard\AdminDatabase
Microsoft Excel 2002 | "Tools | Options…" | General | Alternate startup file location	HKCU\Software\Policies\Microsoft\Office\10.0\Excel\Options\AltStartup
Microsoft Excel 2002 | "Tools | Options…" | General | Default file location	HKCU\Software\Policies\Microsoft\Office\10.0\Excel\Options\DefaultPath
Microsoft Excel 2002 | Miscellaneous | Chart gallery path	HKCU\Software\Policies\Microsoft\Office\10.0\Excel\Options\GalleryPath
Microsoft Excel 2002 | "Tools | Options…" | Save |AutoRecover save location	HKCU\Software\Policies\Microsoft\Office\10.0\Excel\Options\AutoRecoverPath

PowerPoint policies that accept environment variables

Policy name	Registry entry
Microsoft PowerPoint 2002	Miscellaneous	Custom Answer Wizard database path	HKCU\Software\Policies\Microsoft\Office\10.0\PowerPoint\AnswerWizard\AdminDatabase
Microsoft PowerPoint 2002	"Tools	Options…"	Save	Default file location	HKCU\Software\Policies\Microsoft\Office\10.0\PowerPoint\RecentFolderList\Default
Microsoft PowerPoint 2002	"Slide Show	Online Broadcast	Set Up and Schedule…"	Broadcast Settings	Recording - Save it in the following location	HKCU\Software\Policies\Microsoft\Office\10.0\PowerPoint\Broadcast\ArchiveLoc
Microsoft PowerPoint 2002	"Slide Show	Online Broadcast	Set Up and Schedule…"	Broadcast Settings	Other Broadcast Settings	Chat server URL	HKCU\Software\Policies\Microsoft\Office\10.0\PowerPoint\Broadcast\ChatURL
Microsoft PowerPoint 2002	Slide Show	Online Broadcast	Set Up and Schedule…"	Broadcast Settings	Other Broadcast Settings	Chat file CAB	HKCU\Software\Policies\Microsoft\Office\10.0\PowerPoint\Broadcast\ChatFile
Microsoft PowerPoint 2002	"Slide Show	Online Broadcast	Set Up and Schedule…"	Server Options	Shared file location	HKCU\Software\Policies\Microsoft\Office\10.0\PowerPoint\Broadcast\FileServerLoc
Microsoft PowerPoint 2002	"Slide Show	Online Broadcast	Set Up and Schedule…"	Server Options	The Server will access presentation files from	HKCU\Software\Policies\Microsoft\Office\10.0\PowerPoint\Broadcast\NetShow\NetShowFileLoc
Microsoft PowerPoint 2002	"Slide Show	Online Broadcast	Set Up and Schedule…"	Server Options	Other NetShow Settings	Location of audio ASD file	HKCU\Software\Policies\Microsoft\Office\10.0\PowerPoint\Broadcast\NetShow\Options\AudioAsd
Microsoft PowerPoint 2002	"Slide Show	Online Broadcast	Set Up and Schedule…"	Server Options	Other NetShow Settings	Location of video ASD file	HKCU\Software\Policies\Microsoft\Office\10.0\PowerPoint\Broadcast\NetShow\Options\VideoAsd
Microsoft PowerPoint 2002	"Slide Show	Online Broadcast	Set Up and Schedule…"	Server Options	Other NetShow Settings	Multicast address	HKCU\Software\Policies\Microsoft\Office\10.0\PowerPoint\Broadcast\NetShow\Options\MulticastAddress

Publisher policies that accept environment variables

Policy name	Registry entry
Microsoft Publisher 2002 | Default location | Publication location	HKCU\Software\Policies\Microsoft\Office\10.0\Publisher\Doc_Path
Microsoft Publisher 2002 | Default location | Picture location	HKCU\Software\Policies\Microsoft\Office\10.0\Publisher\Picture_Path

Word policies that accept environment variables

Policy name	Registry entry
Microsoft Word 2002 | Miscellaneous | Custom Answer Wizard database path	HKCU\Software\Policies\Microsoft\Office\10.0\Word\AnswerWizard\AdminDatabase
Microsoft Word 2002 | "Tools | Options…" | File Locations | AutoRecover files	HKCU\Software\Policies\Microsoft\Office\10.0\Word\Options\AUTOSAVE-PATH
Microsoft Word 2002 | "Tools | Options…" | File Locations | Documents	HKCU\Software\Policies\Microsoft\Office\10.0\Word\Options\DOC-PATH
Microsoft Word 2002 | "Tools | Options…" | File Locations | Clipart pictures	HKCU\Software\Policies\Microsoft\Office\10.0\Word\Options\PICTURE-PATH
Microsoft Word 2002 | "Tools | Options…" | File Locations | Startup	HKCU\Software\Policies\Microsoft\Office\10.0\Word\OptionsSTARTUP-PATH
Microsoft Word 2002 | "Tools | Options…" | File Locations | Tools	HKCU\Software\Policies\Microsoft\Office\10.0\Word\OptionsTOOLS-PATH

Working with Difficult Policies

System policies can be difficult to set if you do not know what the policy requires as input parameters, or if you cannot find the input data you need. Furthermore, some policies are confusing. Setting some system policies requires an understanding of the feature the policy controls, what allowable settings can be changed, and how a change will affect an application or feature. Some of the more complex policies are discussed in this section.

Setting a simple policy

In order to understand how to set complex policies, it might be helpful to review setting simple policies. Policies for Microsoft Word and Microsoft PowerPoint are used in this section.

As a form of shortcut notation, the following registry nodes are abbreviated.

HKEY_LOCAL_MACHINE to HKLM

HKEY_CURRENT_USER to HKCU

> **Note** Consult the Group Policy snap-in Help for information on how to set and enforce policies on Microsoft Windows 2000 operating systems. The processes of setting and enforcing policies using either the Group Policy snap-in or the System Policy Editor are very similar; however, there are differences in how the policy file is postured for use. Search for Active Directory in the Group Policy snap-in Help for enabling the Registry.pol files.

Allow background saves in Word

In Word, you can determine whether or not files can be saved in the background (automatically) while a user is working. If you want to enable this feature through a policy, you can enforce the **Allow background saves** policy.

To configure a policy to allow background saves in Word

1. Start the System Policy Editor.
2. Create a new policy file or open an existing policy file.
3. Double-click the **Default User** policy profile icon.
4. Expand the **Microsoft Word 2002** node (click the plus (+) sign or double-click **Microsoft Word 2002**).
5. Expand the **Tools | Options...** node.
6. Expand the **Save** node.
7. Set the **Allow background saves** check box to checked.
8. In the **Settings for Allow background saves** work area, set the **Check to enforce setting on; uncheck to enforce setting off** check box to checked.

If you create this policy and place it on your domain controller, when users log on to the network the logon process will automatically enforce the settings found in the policy file to their computer. It will use the information in the policy file to create the following string registry entry on users' computers:

HKCU\Software\Policies\Microsoft\Office\10.0\Word\Options

Value name: **BackgroundSave**

Data type   = **REG_SZ** (string)

Value data   = "0" | "1"

When Word starts, it examines this registry setting and checks to see if there is a value present. If the entry is "1", it sets background saves to on.

Changes to some policy settings may cause an update to the Normal.dot template if they are persistent or are related to application settings stored in the template.

Control the recently used file list in PowerPoint

In PowerPoint, you can control whether the user sees a list of recently used documents on the **File** menu and how many file names to display in the list. This list is technically referred to as the MRU — Most Recently Used file list. The following procedure shows how to configure a system policy to display five recently used files for all users in this list.

To configure a policy for the recently used file list in PowerPoint

1. Start the System Policy Editor.
2. Create a new policy file or open an existing policy file.
3. Double-click the **Default User** policy profile icon.
4. Expand the **Microsoft PowerPoint 2002** node (click the plus (+) sign or double-click **Microsoft PowerPoint 2002**).
5. Expand the **Tools | Options** node.
6. Expand the **General** node.
7. Set the **Recently used file list** check box to checked.
8. In the **Settings for Recently used file list** work area, set the **Enable recently used file list** check box to checked.
9. In the **Size of recently used file list** text box, select **5**.

   When you save and distribute this policy, all of your PowerPoint users will see a recently used file list of five files on the **File** menu.

If you create this policy and place it on your domain controller, and users log on to the network, their logon process will automatically enforce the settings found in the policy file to their computers. It will use the information in the policy file to create the following two DWORD registry entries on users' computers:

HKCU\Software\Policies\Microsoft\Office\10.0\PowerPoint\Options

Value name:	**MRUListActive**
Data type:	**REG_DWORD** (DWORD)
Value data:	**0	1**

HKCU\Software\Policies\Microsoft\Office\10.0\PowerPoint\Options

Value name:	**SizeOfMRUList**
Data type:	**REG_DWORD** (DWORD)
Value data:	**0 - 9**

When PowerPoint starts, it examines these registry settings and checks to see if there are values present. If the **MRUListActive** entry is **1**, it instructs PowerPoint to use the next **SizeOfMRUList** registry entry. The **SizeOfMRUList** can use a maximum value of **9** in the value entry.

Setting difficult policies

Some policies are difficult to set, requiring information that is not easy to find. For instance, you can disable any built-in or custom item on a menu or a toolbar. Some policy settings allow you to disable both the menu command and the corresponding toolbar button at the same time. The toolbars and menu commands that come with Microsoft Office applications "out of the box" are considered predefined. Any menus or commands you add after Office is installed are referred to as custom.

Disable a predefined menu command and toolbar button

Several predefined menu commands and toolbar buttons are available in the Predefined category of many Office application ADM templates. Predefined menu commands and toolbar buttons are considered to be the ones shipping with each application "out of the box". Those menu commands and toolbar buttons created by users or developers and added to the user interface of an Office application through the **Tools | Customize** dialog are considered custom.

To disable a predefined menu command and toolbar button with a policy

1. Start the System Policy Editor.
2. Create a new policy file or open an existing policy file.
3. Double-click the **Default User** policy profile icon.
4. Expand the Office application node (click the plus (+) sign or double-click the application name) that has the item you want to disable.
5. Expand the **Disable items in user interface** node.
6. Expand the **Predefined** node.
7. Set the **Disable command bar buttons and menu items** check box to checked.
8. In the **Settings for Disable command bar buttons and menu items** work area, set the check box for the menu command you want to enforce a policy setting for, to checked.

   For example, to disable the **Hyperlink** command (**Insert** menu) and the **Insert Hyperlink** button (**Standard** toolbar) in Microsoft Excel, set the **Insert | Hyperlink** check box to checked.

If you create this policy and place it on your domain controller and users log on to the network, their logon process will automatically enforce the settings found in the policy file on their computers. It will use the information in the policy file to create the following string registry entry on users' computers:

HKCU\Software\Policies\Microsoft\Office\10.0\Excel\DisabledCmdBarItemsCheckBoxes

Value name: **InsertHyperlink**
Data type: **REG_SZ** (string)
Value data: "**<control ID>**"

When Excel starts, it examines this registry setting and checks to see if there is a value present. If the entry is "**1576**", it turns the **Hyperlink** menu command off. If the value is later changed to "**0**", it turns the menu command back on. Actually, you can use any value name in this registry key and supply an appropriate control ID, and it will turn off the menu command.

Disable a custom menu command and toolbar button

In the following example, you will need to know the control ID of the menu command or toolbar button you want to disable. If you do not have access to the documentation that supplies the control IDs, you can run the example programs listed later in this topic to help you find the information if it is in the Word or Excel applications. In many cases, predefined menu commands across Office applications share the same control ID; therefore, you can try to turn off a menu command using the same control ID as found in another application if you are unable to find the control ID using the example programs listed later in this topic.

You can disable custom menu commands and toolbar buttons, even if they are not defined within a policy template. If you have the control ID, you can remove any menu command or toolbar within the application.

To disable a custom menu command and toolbar button with a policy

1. Start the System Policy Editor.
2. Create a new policy file or open an existing policy file.
3. Double-click the **Default User** policy profile icon.
4. Expand the Office application node (click the plus (+) sign or double-click the application name) that contains the item for which you want to configure a policy.
5. Expand the **Disable items in user interface** node.
6. Expand the **Custom** node.
7. Set the **Disable command bar buttons and menu items** check box to checked.
8. In the **Settings for command bar buttons and menu items** work area, click **Show**.
9. In the **Show Contents** box, click **Add**.
10. In the **Add Item** box, enter the control ID for the menu and toolbar item.

If you create this policy and place it on your domain controller, and users log on to the network, their logon process will automatically enforce the settings found in the policy file to their computer. It will use the information in the policy file to create the following string registry entry on the user's computer:

HKCU\Software\Policies\Microsoft\Office\10.0\Excel\DisabledCmdBarItemsList

Value name: **TCID**x

Data type: **REG_SZ** (string)

Value data: "**<control ID>**"

When Excel starts, it examines this registry setting and checks to see if there are values present. If the entry is "**3**", it turns the **Save** menu command off. If the value is later removed from the list, it turns the **Save** menu command back on.

This is a unique registry entry because it is a list of TCIDx entries. The x is incremented by 1 for each entry added to the list. Examples of possible TCIDx entries in the registry are:

TCID1 = "3"
TCID2 ="748"
TCID3 = "20"
TCID4 = "21"

Control IDs for menu commands and toolbar buttons

You can look up control IDs for any item on a menu or toolbar in Microsoft Office XP applications where the **CommandBars** collection is available by using Visual Basic for Applications (VBA). Supplying the control ID in a specific policy entry allows you to disable that menu command and toolbar button. You can either look up a single control ID or use a macro to find a series of control IDs.

> **Note** Menu commands and their corresponding toolbar buttons share the same control ID. For example, the control ID for both the **Save** command (**File** menu) and the **Save** button (**Standard** toolbar) in Microsoft Word is 3.

Finding a single control ID

You can use the **Immediate** window in VBA to look up the control ID for a single item on a menu if you know the name of the command bar it is on, the name of the control, and if necessary, the name of the sub control (if one exists). For example, the following command prints the control ID for the **Save As** command (**File** menu) to the Immediate window (directly below the command you enter). Start Microsoft Word, select **Tools**, select **Macros**, then select **Visual Basic Editor**. Enter the following command in the Immediate Window and press enter.

Example Code #1

```
? commandbars("menu bar").controls("file").controls("save as...").id
```

> **Note** For Microsoft Excel, use "worksheet menu bar" instead of "menu bar" in the previous command.

Example Code #2

Use the following code to find the names of all the command bars in any Office application (replace the **MsgBox** with **Print** to obtain a list of names):

```
For Each cbar In Application.CommandBars
MsgBox cbar.Name
Next
```

Example Code #3

Use the following code to find all the control captions and control IDs for controls on the "menu bar" in Word. Replace "menu bar" with any of the CommandBar names returned in the example code provided in example #2:

```
For Each ccntrl In Application.CommandBars("menu bar").Controls
MsgBox ccntrl.Caption & " = " & ccntrl.ID
Next
```

Example Code #4

Use the following code to find all the control captions and control IDs for sub-controls on the "menu bar — file" control in Word. Replace "menu bar" with any of the command-bar names returned in the example code provided in example #2 and the related control captions provided in the example code provided in example #3:

```
For Each csubcntrl In Application.CommandBars("menu bar") _
.Controls("file").Controls
msgbox csubcntrl.Caption & " = " & csubcntrl.ID
Next
```

Example Code #5

If you want to find the control IDs for all the items on a menu or toolbar, you can create a macro in VBA. For example, the following macro opens a series of message boxes to display the commands and corresponding control IDs for each item on the **File** menu for any Office XP application:

```
Sub EnumerateControls()
    Dim icbc As Integer
    Dim cbcs As CommandBarControls

Set cbcs = Application.CommandBars("Menu bar") _
.Controls("File").Controls
    For icbc = 1 To cbcs.Count
      MsgBox cbcs(icbc).Caption & " = " & cbcs(icbc).ID
    Next icbc
End Sub
```

Example Code #6

Based on all the previous code examples, the following code provides a Word document with all the possible command-bar names, controls within the command bar, all sub-controls and their control IDs for Microsoft Word:

```
Sub ListControls()
    For Each cb In Application.CommandBars
        Selection.TypeText Text:=cb.Name
        Selection.TypeParagraph
    For Each cntl In Application.CommandBars(cb.Name).Controls
        Selection.TypeText Text:=vbTab & cntl.Caption
        Selection.TypeParagraph
        On Error GoTo ErrJump1:
        For Each subcntl In Application.CommandBars(cb.Name) _
        .Controls(cntl.Caption).Controls
            Selection.TypeText Text:=vbTab & vbTab & subcntl.Caption & _
            " = " & subcntl.ID
        Selection.TypeParagraph
        Next
PastError:
    Next
  Next
```

274 Microsoft Office XP Resource Kit

```
GoTo bypass:
ErrJump1:
    Selection.TypeBackspace
    Selection.TypeText Text:=" = " & cntl.ID
    Selection.TypeParagraph
    Resume PastError:
bypass:
End Sub
```

Example Code #7

Here is the example code from #6 modified to work with Excel:

```
Sub ListControls()
Dim icbs As Integer
icbs = 1

    Columns("A:A").ColumnWidth = 18
    Columns("B:B").ColumnWidth = 21
    Columns("C:C").ColumnWidth = 23

    Range("A1").Select
    ActiveCell.FormulaR1C1 = "Command Bar"
    Range("B1").Select
    ActiveCell.FormulaR1C1 = "Control caption"
    Range("C1").Select
    ActiveCell.FormulaR1C1 = "Control caption or ID"
    Range("D1").Select
    ActiveCell.FormulaR1C1 = "Control ID"

    Rows("2:2").Select
    ActiveWindow.FreezePanes = True

    For Each cb In Application.CommandBars
        icbs = icbs + 1
        Range("A" & icbs).Select
        ActiveCell.FormulaR1C1 = cb.Name
```

```
                For Each cntl In Application.CommandBars(cb.Name).Controls
                    icbs = icbs + 1
                    Range("B" & icbs).Select
                    ActiveCell.FormulaR1C1 = cntl.Caption
                    On Error GoTo ErrJump1:
                    For Each subcntl In Application.CommandBars(cb.Name) _
                    .Controls(cntl.Caption).Controls
                        icbs = icbs + 1
                        Range("C" & icbs).Select
                        ActiveCell.FormulaR1C1 = subcntl.Caption
                        Range("D" & icbs).Select
                        ActiveCell.FormulaR1C1 = subcntl.ID
                    Next
PastError:
            Next
        Next
GoTo bypass:
ErrJump1:
        Range("C" & icbs).Select
        ActiveCell.FormulaR1C1 = cntl.ID
Resume PastError:
bypass:
End Sub
```

Disable shortcut keys

Disabling predefined (built-in) and custom shortcut keys for commands in Microsoft Office XP requires that you know how to enter the shortcut key ID into the policy editor.

Disable a predefined shortcut key

Several built-in shortcut keys are listed in the Predefined category of most application policy templates.

To disable a predefined shortcut key with a policy

1. Start the System Policy Editor.
2. Double-click the policy profile you want to work with.
3. Expand the Office application node (click the plus (+) sign or double-click the application name) that contains the built-in shortcut key you want to disable.

4. Expand the **Disable items in user interface** node.
5. Expand the **Predefined** node.
6. Set the **Disable shortcut keys** check box to checked.
7. In the **Settings for Disable shortcut keys** work area, set the check box next to the shortcut key you want to disable to checked.

   For example, click the **Ctrl+K (Insert | Hyperlink)** check box and set it to checked to disable the shortcut key for the **Hyperlink** command (**Insert** menu) in Word.

If you create this policy and place it on your domain controller, and users log on, their logon process will automatically enforce the settings found in the policy file to their computers. It will use the information in the policy file to create the following string registry entry on users' computers.

HKCU\Software\Policies\Microsoft\Office\10.0\Excel\DisabledShortcutKeysCheckBoxes

Value name:	**InsertHyperlink**
Data type:	**REG_SZ** (string)
Value data:	"**<virtual key code>,<key code modifier>**"

When Excel starts, it examines this registry setting and checks to see if there is a value present. If the entry is "**75,8**", it turns the **Hyperlink** shortcut key off. If the value is later changed to "**0**", it turns it back on. You can use any value name in this registry key and supply an appropriate shortcut key code combination, and the shortcut key will be turned off. See "Key codes for shortcut keys" later in this topic for more information on virtual key codes.

Disable a custom shortcut key

You can disable any custom shortcut key by using the System Policy Editor, even if the item is not listed in the policy template.

> **Note** In order to disable a custom shortcut key, you must know the key code for the shortcut key.

To disable a custom shortcut key with a policy

1. Start the System Policy Editor.
2. Double-click the policy profile you want to work with.
3. Expand the Office application (click the plus sign (+) or double-click the application name) that contains the custom shortcut key you want to disable.
4. Expand the **Disable items in user interface** node.
5. Expand the **Custom** node.
6. Set the **Disable shortcut keys** check box to checked.
7. In the **Settings for Disable shortcut keys** work area, click **Show**.

8. In the **Show Contents** box, click **Add...**.

9. In the **Add Item** box, type the key and modifier key values for the shortcut key by using the following syntax:

   key,modifier

   For example, to disable the shortcut key ALT+K, type **75,16**

If you create this policy and place it on your domain controller and users log on, their logon process will automatically enforce the settings found in the policy file to their computers. It will use the information in the policy file to create the following string registry entry on each users' computer:

KCU\Software\Policies\Microsoft\Office\10.0\Excel\DisabledShortcutKeysList

Value name:	**KeyMod*x***
Data type:	**REG_SZ** (string)
Value data:	"**75,16**"

When Excel starts, it examines this registry setting and checks to see if there is a value present. If the entry is "**77,12**", it turns the custom shortcut key off (in this case Ctrl + Shift + M). If the value is later changed to "**0**", it turns it back on. Actually, you can use any value name in this registry key and supply an appropriate shortcut key code combination and the shortcut key will be turned off.

This is a unique registry entry because it is a list of **KeyMod*x*** entries. The *x* is incremented by 1 for each entry in the list. Examples of **KeyMod*x*** entries in the registry are:

KeyMod1 = "72,0"
KeyMod2 = "74,4"
KeyMod3 = "81,8"
KeyMod4 = "69,12"
KeyMod5 = "70,16"
KeyMod6 = "73,20"
KeyMod7 = "78,24"
KeyMod8 = "88,28"

Key codes for shortcut keys

Each modifier key and alphanumeric key on a keyboard has an associated key code. You use these codes to identify the unique key you want to control.

In the System Policy Editor, disabling shortcut keys requires you know the key code for alphanumeric keys and modifier keys. Once you have discovered what these key codes are, use the following syntax in policies that disable shortcut keys:

key,modifier

where *key* is the key code of a key (for example, G = **71**) in Windows, and *modifier* is the value of either a modifier key (for example, ALT = **16**) or a combination of modifier keys in Windows (ALT + CTRL = **24**).

If you have multiple modifier keys for the shortcut key, you add the values of the modifier keys together to determine the actual modifier key code you will enter in the System Policy Editor (for example, ALT+SHIFT = 16 + 4 = **20**).

Use the following values to refer to keys in the System Policy Editor.

Key	Value
ALT	**16**
CONTROL	**8**
SHIFT	**4**
A – Z	A sequential number between **64** and **90**, where A = **65** and Z = **90**.

Note The System Policy Editor does not use the literal virtual key codes for ALT, CONTROL, and SHIFT. To refer to these keys in the Office environment, use the values of the modifier keys specified in the table.

If you are not sure what the key code of an entry on the keyboard is, use the following code in the Immediate window of the Visual Basic Editor:

```
MsgBox BuildKeyCode(wdKeyA)
```

Substitute the wdKeyA with wdKeyB, wdKeyC, etc., for each letter you want the key code to represent, or select the appropriate key from the list provided through the VBA editor when entering this command.

Example Code

This code provides you with a listing of all the shortcut keys in Word. This program is very helpful in showing what keys have shortcuts assigned to them and what the value of those keys are:

```
Function FindTheseKeys()
Dim IsValue As String
Dim IsValue2 As String
Dim I As Integer
Dim NoVal as Integer

Selection.TypeText Text:="Single key entries: Modifier value is 0"
Selection.TypeParagraph
For I = 1 To 254
    IsValue = FindKey(I).Command
    IsValue2 = KeyString(I)
```

```
        NoVal = PrintKey(IsValue, IsValue2, I)
Next I
Selection.TypeText Text:="Shift key entries: Modifier value is 4"
Selection.TypeParagraph
    For I = 1 To 254
    IsValue = FindKey(wdKeyShift, I).Command
    IsValue2 = KeyString(wdKeyShift, I)
    NoVal = PrintKey(IsValue, IsValue2, I)
Next I
Selection.TypeText Text:="Control key entries: Modifier value is 8"
Selection.TypeParagraph
For I = 1 To 254
    IsValue = FindKey(wdKeyControl, I).Command
    IsValue2 = KeyString(wdKeyControl, I)
    NoVal = PrintKey(IsValue, IsValue2, I)
Next I
Selection.TypeText Text:="Alt key entries: Modifier value is 16"
Selection.TypeParagraph
For I = 1 To 254
    IsValue = FindKey(wdKeyAlt, I).Command
    IsValue2 = KeyString(wdKeyAlt, I)
    NoVal = PrintKey(IsValue, IsValue2, I)
Next I
Selection.TypeText Text:="Shift + Control key entries: Modifier" & _
" value is 12"
Selection.TypeParagraph
For I = 1 To 254
    IsValue = FindKey(KeyCode:=BuildKeyCode(wdKeyShift, wdKeyControl, I)) _
    _.Command
    IsValue2 = KeyString(BuildKeyCode(wdKeyShift, wdKeyControl, I))
    NoVal = PrintKey(IsValue, IsValue2, I)
Next I
Selection.TypeText Text:="Shift + Alt key entries: Modifier value is 20"
Selection.TypeParagraph
For I = 1 To 254
```

```
    IsValue = FindKey(KeyCode:=BuildKeyCode(wdKeyShift, wdKeyAlt, I)) _
    .Command
    IsValue2 = KeyString(BuildKeyCode(wdKeyShift, wdKeyAlt, I))
    NoVal = PrintKey(IsValue, IsValue2, I)
Next I
Selection.TypeText Text:="Control + Alt key entries: Modifier value is 24"
Selection.TypeParagraph
For I = 1 To 254
    IsValue = FindKey(KeyCode:=BuildKeyCode(wdKeyControl, wdKeyAlt, I)) _
    .Command
    IsValue2 = KeyString(BuildKeyCode(wdKeyControl, wdKeyAlt, I))
    NoVal = PrintKey(IsValue, IsValue2, I)
Next I
End Function


Function PrintKey(IsValue As String, IsValue2 As String, I As Integer)
    If IsValue <> "" Then
        Selection.TypeText Text:=vbTab & "Key value is " & I & _
        " defined as " & IsValue2 & " = " & IsValue
        Selection.TypeParagraph
    End If
End Function
```

Getting a list of all commands for Word

Use the following code to create a listing of all the commands in Word. If you run this command in a Word macro, Word will create a listing of all the commands, keys, modifiers, and the menus in which they appear. Replace the **True** with **False**, and the listing will provide only the custom commands added to Word. This process creates a new document in Word. You can then review the document, add to it, or print it out. You can use this new document to help you create key codes.

```
Sub GetCommands()
Application.ListCommands ListAllCommands:=True
End Sub
```

Working with Outlook cryptography policies

Security is a crucial aspect of all applications. As part of the security for Microsoft Outlook, cryptography (encryption schemes) is supported and has policies you can enable by using either the Group Policy snap-in available with Windows 2000, or the System Policy Editor available with the Office Resource Kit.

Microsoft Outlook has unique security requirements because of its interface to the outside world through e-mail servers, and because of the type of secure communication many businesses and government agencies require. To support these security issues, Outlook includes cryptography and certificate validation for macros, ActiveX® controls, and documents. Outlook also has the ability to perform a Certificate Revocation List (CRL) check — much like what Microsoft Internet Explorer can perform when validating a certificate in order to use an executable. A policy is included in the Outlk10.adm to set this behavior. The policies presented below deal with cryptography. These policies, which are typically referred to as federal release features, are considered important for administrators to understand. In many cases, companies are required to use these policies in order to work with government agencies.

Retrieve a Certificate Revocation List (CRL)

Used to retrieve CRLs (Certificate Revocation Lists)

HKCU\Software\Policies\Microsoft\Office\10.0\Outlook\Security

Value name:	**UseCRLChasing**
Data type:	**REG_DWORD**
Value data:	**[0	1	2]**

Can be set to the following:

    0 - Use system Default

    1 - When online always retrieve the CRL

    2 - Never retrieve the CRL

This policy can slow the system down when it performs a CRL check. Use of this policy can adversely affect system performance.

Always Encrypt

Used to encrypt all e-mail messages.

HKCU\Software\Policies\Microsoft\Office\10.0\Outlook\Security

Value name:	**AlwaysEncrypt**
Data type:	**REG_DWORD**
Value data:	**[0	1]**

Set the AlwaysEncrypt key value to **1** to enable encryption on all e-mail messages. Within the System Policy Editor use the **Check to enforce setting on; uncheck to enforce setting off** option at the bottom of the policy dialog.

Always Sign

Used to sign all e-mail messages

HKCU\Software\Policies\Microsoft\Office\10.0\Outlook\Security

Value name:	**AlwaysSign**
Data type:	**REG_DWORD**
Value data:	[0	1]

Set the AlwaysSign key value to **1** to enable the signing of all e-mail messages created by a user. Within the System Policy Editor use the **Check to enforce setting on; uncheck to enforce setting off** option at the bottom of the policy dialog.

Clear Sign

Used to send all signed messages as clear signed messages.

HKCU\Software\Policies\Microsoft\Office\10.0\Outlook\Security

Value name:	**ClearSign**
Data type:	**REG_DWORD**
Value data:	[0	1]

Set the ClearSign key value to **1** to enable the sending of all signed messages as clear signed messages. Within the System Policy Editor use the **Check to enforce setting on; uncheck to enforce setting off** option at the bottom of the policy dialog.

Request Secure Receipts

Used to request a secure receipt for all S/MIME-signed messages.

HKCU\Software\Policies\Microsoft\Office\10.0\Outlook\Security

Value name:	**RequestSecureReceipt**
Data type:	**REG_DWORD**
Value data:	[0	1]

Set the RequestSecureReceipt key value to **1** to enable the sending of an acknowledgment from the recipient of an e-mail message. Within the System Policy Editor use the **Check to enforce setting on; uncheck to enforce setting off** option at the bottom of the policy dialog.

Force Security Label

Used to ensure all S/MIME-signed messages have a label.

HKCU\Software\Policies\Microsoft\Office\10.0\Outlook\Security

Value name:	**ForceSecurityLabel**
Data type:	**REG_DWORD**
Value data:	**[0	1]**

Set the ForceSecurityLabel to **1** to enable the labeling of all S/MIME messages that are signed. Enforces the labeling of all outgoing signed mail. It does not indicate what kind of label to use, only that one must be attached. Within the System Policy Editor use the **Check to enforce setting on; uncheck to enforce setting off** option at the bottom of the policy dialog.

Signature Status for no valid CRL

Used to indicate a missing CRL as a warning or error.

HKCU\Software\Policies\Microsoft\Office\10.0\Outlook\Security

Value name:	**SigStatusNoCRL**
Data type:	**REG_DWORD**
Value data:	**[0	1]**

Set the SigStatusNoCRL to either "warning" or "error" (**0** or **1**) to report missing CRLs as either a warning or an error. Default is to report it as a warning. Within the System Policy Editor use the **Check to enforce setting on; uncheck to enforce setting off** option at the bottom of the policy dialog.

Promote Errors as Warnings

Used to elevate errors to the same level as a warning so the error is reported as a warning to users.

HKCU\Software\Policies\Microsoft\Office\10.0\Outlook\Security

Value name:	**PromoteErrorsAsWarnings**
Data type:	**REG_DWORD**
Value data:	**[0	1]**

This policy controls whether level **2** errors are promoted to warnings to the user. Set the **PromoteErrorsAsWarnings** key value to **1** to promote errors to warnings, **0** to not promote them. Within the System Policy Editor use the **Check to enforce setting on; uncheck to enforce setting off** option at the bottom of the policy dialog.

Possible error 2 conditions are:

Unknown Signature Algorithm

No Signing Certification Found

Bad Attribute Sets

No Issuer Certificate Found

No CRL found

Out of Date Certificate

Root Trust Problem

Out of Date CTL

Publish to GAL

Used to allow access to the **Publish to GAL** button.

HKCU\Software\Policies\Microsoft\Office\10.0\Outlook\Security

Value name:	**PublishToGALDisabled**
Data type:	**REG_DWORD**
Value data:	**[0	1]**

Hides the **Publish to GAL** button in the user interface. Set the **PublishToGALDisabled** key value to **1** to disable the **Publish to GAL** button. Within the System Policy Editor, use the **Check to enforce setting on; uncheck to enforce setting off** option at the bottom of the policy dialog.

FIPS Mode

Run in FIPS compliant mode.

HKCU\Software\Policies\Microsoft\Office\10.0\Outlook\Security

Value name:	**FIPSMode**
Data type:	**REG_DWORD**
Value data:	**[0	1]**

Set the FIPSMode value key to **1** to enforce this setting. Within the System Policy Editor, use the **Check to enforce setting on; uncheck to enforce setting off** option at the bottom of the policy dialog.

Warn About Invalid signature

Used as a signature warning.

HKCU\Software\Policies\Microsoft\Office\10.0\Outlook\Security

Value name: **WarnAboutInvalid**

Data type: **REG_DWORD**

Value data: **[0 | 1 | 2]**

Set the WarnAboutInvalid value key to:

    0 - to let users decioa

    de if they want to be warned about invalid signatures

    1 - to always warn about invalid signatures

    2 - to never warn about invalid signatures

This policy provides the administrator the option of presenting users with a choice of whether or not they want to be warned, or if they should always or never be warned about any invalid received signatures.

Disable Continue button

Used to disable the **Continue** button on all encryption warning dialogs.

HKCU\Software\Policies\Microsoft\Office\10.0\Outlook\Security

Value name: **DisableContinueEncryption**

Data type: **REG_DWORD**

Value data: **[0 | 1]**

Hides the **continue** and **ignore errors** buttons for encryption problem dialogs so messages cannot be sent to recipients who are unable to decrypt them. Within the System Policy Editor use the **Check to enforce setting on; uncheck to enforce setting off** option at the bottom of the policy dialog.

Respond to Receipt Requests by senders

Used to acknowledge a response to a received e-mail.

HKCU\Software\Policies\Microsoft\Office\10.0\Outlook\Security

Value name: **RespondToReceiptRequests**

Data type: **REG_DWORD**

Value data: **[0 | 1 | 2 | 3]**

Handles an e-mail message in the following manner:

- **0** - Open message if receipt can't be sent
- **1** - Always prompt before sending receipt
- **2** - Never send secure receipts
- **3** – Do not open message if receipt can't be sent

Need Encryption String Message

Used to display a message if Outlook cannot find the Digital ID to decode a message.

HKCU\Software\Policies\Microsoft\Office\10.0\Outlook\Security

Value name:	**NeedEncryptionString**
Data type:	**REG_STRING**
Value data:	**[<error message>]**

This string should be less than 255 characters in length.

Displays a message to the user if Outlook is unable to find the digital ID for decoding the received message.

CHAPTER 10

Administering Security

Securing a corporation's work files from intentional corruption is a high priority for many administrators. The Microsoft Office development team has worked to provide ways to enforce and apply security to applications and data. Some of these new methods include an ability to control macro security levels through policies, set default encryption ciphers for all users through policies, install or uninstall Visual Basic for Applications as a feature of Office, protect Office documents with new encryption ciphers, disable access to the World Wide Web, and control the startup behavior of ActiveX controls.

In this chapter

Protecting Office Documents   289

Running Office in a Secure Environment   306

Office Macro Security Settings   308

Security Settings and Related System Policies   312

Microsoft Office Tools on the Web Security Scenarios   323

Protecting Office Documents

A chief concern of most businesses is to protect files and data against malicious attacks, such as tampering, espionage, and intentional destruction. If your work environment subjects your files to such threats, you should review the options that can help protect your data. The Custom Installation Wizard and Custom Maintenance Wizard allow the setting of some security options, but other options must be selected by each user in order to set the protection method, such as the use of passwords.

The following list presents the key features of security in Microsoft Office:

- Security settings for macros, trusted sources, and ActiveX® controls
- Password and encryption protection
- Privacy options
- Removing Visual Basic® for Applications (VBA)

Microsoft Office XP Resource Kit   289

> **Note** Security settings for Microsoft Outlook® 2002 are numerous and require specialized knowledge of mail servers, network servers, and links to external mail providers to properly configure Outlook for use by organizations. Administrators are advised to read "Outlook Security" in Chapter 22, "Messaging".

Office security settings

Microsoft Office provides methods for managing application and document security. Understanding how to set the following security-related features can help you establish a secure environment for users' applications and data:

- Macro security
- Certificate revocation
- Trusted sources
- ActiveX controls

Setting security properly helps limit the vulnerability of applications and data to malicious attacks. An additional security measure is the ability to require passwords for users who want access to document content in some applications.

All applications listed on the **Specify Office Security Settings** page of the Custom Installation Wizard and Custom Maintenance Wizard are available to receive security settings for macros, trusted sources, and ActiveX controls. Security settings can be changed to High, Medium, or Low, or remain at the default level.

> **Note** There is an issue administrators should consider when they use a transform to install different editions of Office or stand-alone versions of Office applications. If an administrator creates a transform for installing Microsoft Word in a staged deployment, the **Specify Office Security Settings** page allows an administrator the option of setting the default security level for Microsoft Excel (whether or not Excel is already installed on the user's computer) while also providing the option to customize stand-alone Word. If Excel is not installed, the security setting is ignored.

Macro security

Macro security is used to control the use of automatic or manual code embedded within a template associated with a document, or saved as part of the document itself. Setting macro security levels enables applications to:

- Run macros automatically when trusted
- Run macros only after user approval (prompted)
- Block macros because they are not trusted
- Run all macros without security enabled

Each of these security levels can be set by administrators and distributed to some or all users in an organization by using either the Custom Installation Wizard, Custom Maintenance Wizard, Office Profile Wizard, or the System Policy Editor.

Setting macro security levels in Office applications

Macro security for Microsoft Word, Excel, Microsoft Outlook, Microsoft Publisher, and Microsoft PowerPoint® can be set to High, Medium, or Low through the **Macro Security** dialog of the user interface. It is highly recommended to select High or Medium. Setting the security level to Low allows a macro or VBA program to run without the knowledge of the user.

You can only set the macro security level for Access with a policy setting or on the **Specify Office Security Settings** page of either the Custom Installation Wizard or the Custom Maintenance Wizard.

The basic definition of High, Medium, and Low security levels are:

- High security

    Macros must be signed by an acknowledged trusted source. Otherwise, macros in documents are automatically disabled without warning to the user when the documents are opened. All Office applications are installed with high security by default.

- Medium security

    Users are prompted to enable or disable macros in documents when the documents are opened.

- Low security

    No macro checking is performed when documents are opened, and no macro restrictions are imposed. This security level is not recommended because it will not protect against malicious programs.

Default installation settings for security can be controlled by using the **Specify Office Security Settings** page of either the Custom Installation Wizard or the Custom Maintenance Wizard.

To set the security level in Word, Excel, Outlook, or PowerPoint

1. On the **Tools** menu, point to **Macro**, and then click **Security**.
2. Click the **Security Level** tab and select a security level.

    Note You can also gain access to the security dialog from the **Tools | Options | Security** tab; then click the **Macro Security...** button.

Signing a macro

You can use Selfcert.exe to sign macros or templates you create for use within your organization. Selfcert.exe calls Makecert.exe; both programs are available with Office in the Office10 folder and are not available with the Office Resource Kit.

There are limitations to the deployment of Selfcert.exe certificates applied to a macro when macro security is set to High. Setting security to Low and then running the macro does not register the certificate in the trusted sources list. Security must be set to Medium or High before any certificates are posted to the list. In cases where security is set to High on all computers, a Selfcert.exe-signed macro can be deployed but cannot be run because it does not have a secure enough certificate. You must use a certificate issued by a Certificate Authority such as VeriSign® for a High security enabled environment.

One approach to deploying a macro in a High security environment is to send the source code (text) for the macro to users, instruct them how to paste it into a VBA editor, and then use Selfcert.exe to certify the code using their own local certificate.

Certificate revocation

By default, the certificate revocation check setting of Microsoft Internet Explorer is disabled. Because Office inherits this setting, Office will not check for certificate revocation. Administrators can turn the feature on; however, it can take a considerable amount of time to analyze whether a certificate has been revoked, because Internet Explorer has to check a database on the Internet. To enable this setting, select the **Check for publisher's certificate revocation** check box in the **Advanced** tab in the **Internet Options** dialog under the **Security** section of the tree view control.

Microsoft Outlook 2002 also uses certificate revocation for evaluating the certificate attached to any received files. For more information on the certificate revocation list (CRL) policy and policies associated with cryptography for Outlook, see "Working with Difficult Policies" in Chapter 9, "System Policies."

Trusted sources

Using trusted sources is a means of cataloging and allowing signed executables to run on users' computers. With this feature enabled, users can choose whether to allow executable code or programs to run from sources that can be identified or trusted.

Administrators have the option of turning the trusted sources feature off or enabling a list of trusted sources as a default. If this feature is selected, any future installable code (add-ins, applets, executables, etc.) is automatically copied to, or run from, the user's computer.

The trusted sources feature requires that a special embedded certificate be applied to an executable. This certificate includes a digital signature that identifies the source, providing assurance to the user because of the rigorous method required to apply a certificate and digital signature to an executable.

A digital signature is like a seal of approval. The signature ensures code is from the source listed in the certificate used to sign the code, and ensures the code has not been tampered with since the creators of the certificate signed it. A digital signature requires developers or creators of code to identify themselves and attach their name to the digital signature. In this way a digital signature can be used to prove that the data or code is really from the user or source that the digital signature claims it is from.

Specifying trusted sources in Office applications

When users open a document that contains digitally signed macros, they are prompted to choose whether to trust the source if the digital certificate has not previously been trusted and the security for their application is set to High or Medium. If they choose to trust the source, any document with a macro with that same digital certificate automatically runs the macro. If they accept to trust the digital signature from that source for all future macros, programs, or applets, any time a new macro, program, or applet is asked to run on the computer, the source is trusted and the macro, program, or applet is run automatically (without prompting), regardless of the security level set for the application.

> **Note** Office and Internet Explorer use separate trusted source lists within the registry. Therefore, accepting the certificate of an ActiveX program or Java applet in Internet Explorer does not mean it was accepted by Office and vice versa. For example, if you accept the certificate of an ActiveX control within Word, it is accepted for all Office applications, but not Internet Explorer.

You have the option to trust all currently installed add-ins and templates on a computer so that all files installed along with Microsoft Office or added to the Office templates folder are trusted even though the files are not signed.

> **Note** There is no direct way to preload the trusted source list. You must accept each certificate on a test computer by opening a document with a signed macro, running the applet from the Web, or running the compiled executable. Then use the Office Profile Wizard to capture the add-in and registry settings associated with the add-in.

To specify trusted sources in Word, Excel, Outlook, or PowerPoint

1. On the **Tools** menu, point to **Macro**, and then click **Security**.
2. To view or remove trusted sources, click the **Trusted Sources** tab.
3. To trust all add-ins and templates currently installed on the computer, select the **Trust all installed add-ins and templates** check box.

Though the **Security** dialog is available from Word, PowerPoint, Outlook, and Excel, it is not available in Access.

Adding trusted sources

You can add trusted sources by accepting the request to trust an applet or program the first time it attempts to run. Macro security must be set at Medium or High to force this request.

It is possible to add Microsoft to the list of trusted sources without accepting a request to trust the source by setting the **Add Microsoft to list of trusted sources** check box to checked in the **Specify Office Security Settings** page of the Custom Installation Wizard or the Custom Maintenance Wizard.

Administrators can block users from adding to the list of trusted sources by enforcing a policy. To block users from making any changes to the trusted source list, use the **default computer** policy profile and set the **Microsoft Office XP | Security Settings** policy of each application to checked (for example, **Word: Trust all installed add-ins and templates**). Unlike the setting of security options through the Custom Installation Wizard or Custom Maintenance Wizard, the use of a system policy forces the implementation of administrative settings on a user's computer each time the user logs on, resetting any changes the user may have made during a session with the application.

Regarding policy settings, if a list of trusted sources is added to the HKCU node of the registry, users can add trusted sources through the user interface of an application. However, if the list of trusted sources is stored in the HKLM node of the registry, then users cannot add to their list of trusted sources.

Presetting trusted sources for all users

To preset trusted sources on a user's computer, you use the Office Profile Wizard to save your security settings from a test computer where the sources are currently trusted. On a computer with Office XP installed, open Office documents with macros signed by the sources you want to trust so that the Office application can enter the certificates trust data into the registry. Choose to trust the sources as you open each document. Then, run Internet Explorer and open all the Web sites that contain applets you want users to have, and accept the certificates associated with the applets. Because Office and Internet Explorer use two separate trusted source lists, you must accept the certificate in at least one Office application and Internet Explorer to load the registry entries so you can propagate the changes with the Profile Wizard. If you have any special executables that work along with Office applications, run them and accept their digital certificates as well (if the executables are signed).

After you have saved the configurations you want in a profile settings file (OPS file), use the Custom Installation Wizard to include your OPS file in a transform on the administrative installation point. When users run Office Setup from the administrative installation point with this transform, the trusted sources you specified are set as trusted sources on users' computers. You can also apply an OPS file separately. For more information about applying a profile settings file (OPS file), see "Using the Office Profile Wizard" in Chapter 8, "Maintaining an Installation."

> **Tip** You can create a system policy to preset **Macro Security Levels** and to enable the **Trust all installed add-ins and templates** in each Office application. Review the list of Office applications you can set policies for in the **Default Computer** profile by using the Office10.adm policy template (**Microsoft Office XP | Security Settings**). There are also security settings you can enable for users within the **Default User** profile; however, you will need to examine each Office application node of the policy tree you have added ADM template files for in the System Policy Editor to know which settings can be configured.

To implement trusted sources, you can use:

- The Custom Installation Wizard and the Office Profile Wizard to preset security levels and trusted sources.
- The System Policy Editor to preset security levels and specify whether to trust installed add-ins and templates.
- The Custom Maintenance Wizard or the Profile Wizard to change the installed macro security configurations of Office applications.

You can also use a virus-scanning program in combination with security levels of Microsoft Office applications to reduce the probability of a macro virus infection introduced through a trusted source.

ActiveX

An ActiveX control is essentially a simple OLE or COM object. It is a self-registering program or control; that is, it adds registry entries for itself automatically at start up. An ActiveX control can be as simple as a text box and as complex as an entire dialog. ActiveX controls are used extensively with Web sites. Therefore, ActiveX is synonymous with Java, Netscape plug-ins, and scripting. However, the advantage of ActiveX over these other programming options is that ActiveX controls can also be used in applications written in different programming languages, including all of the Microsoft programming and database languages.

ActiveX controls facilitate distribution of specialized controls over networks and integration of those controls within Web browsers. This includes the ability of the control to identify itself to applications that use ActiveX controls.

ActiveX controls can be scripted from Web pages. This means you can create (or buy) an ActiveX control to provide a control for a user interface or graphics device interface (GDI) element. Once created, you can use a scripting language such as Visual Basic Scripting Edition (VBScript) or JavaScript™ to use the control. Your script instructs the control how to work.

ActiveX security settings

Two extra security settings exist for use with ActiveX controls:

- Initialize using control defaults

    User will be warned. This setting disables the ability of the control to use and save persistent data. It forces the control to run using the default settings, thereby reducing the probability of an errant setting causing a problem for the user. If this setting is enabled, the user is always warned that default settings are enabled for the control and any persistent data the control would normally store with the hosted document is discarded when this setting is activated and the document is being closed.

- Prompt user to use persisted data or control defaults

    When set, this security setting provides the user the option of saving the control with persistent data that can be used the next time the control is activated. Potentially, this can be used to introduce a virus.

Use of these settings, along with the **<do not configure>** setting in the Custom Installation Wizard or Custom Maintenance Wizard, provides users control over how the unsafe ActiveX controls run on their computers.

ActiveX and other programming options

If you have tried using Java or Visual Basic to draw on the screen using DirectX®, you know you cannot do it. The virtual machine environment created for these languages is not allowed access to the system's services — protecting the computer on which an applet is run from inadvertently downloading a virus that reads from or writes to the hard disk. To gain access to basic system services, create an ActiveX control using the Win32® API and C++.

Code signing

Because ActiveX allows access to basic system services, you need a special method to download a control for use without worrying it might be a malicious program. This method is provided by Authenticode, which allows an ActiveX developer the ability to digitally vouch for their code. This is known as code signing. Code signing allows users the ability to identify the author of any ActiveX control before allowing it to execute.

If you've used unsigned or unmarked ActiveX controls with Microsoft applications, you may have seen dialog boxes informing you that a control is not signed, the control is not safe for initializing, or the control is not safe for scripting. Or, if you set your security level at high rather than medium, the control did not load or display at all.

ActiveX controls that can automatically be downloaded over the Internet can do anything a regular program can do — including deletion of files or registry entries. Java addresses this problem by severely limiting what a Java applet can do. Java cannot, for instance, gain access to the computer's file system. ActiveX controls take a different approach: they demand positive identification of the author of the control, verification that the control was not modified since it was code signed, and confirmation that it is a safe control. Because of this approach, ActiveX controls can use the full power of the operating system safely.

If a user attempts to load an unregistered ActiveX control, the application checks to see if the control has been digitally signed.

If the application is set to use:

- High security, there is no option to use the ActiveX control if it is not signed.
- Medium security, users are asked whether or not they want to accept the digital signature of the control.

  If the signature is accepted, the control is loaded and run.

- Low security, the digital signature is ignored and the ActiveX program is run without an acceptance dialog box shown to the user.

Once the control is registered on the user's system, the control no longer invokes code-signing dialog boxes. After a control is installed, it is considered safe even if it was not signed originally.

Signing an ActiveX control

To sign a control, you'll need to obtain a certificate from a Certificate Authority such as VeriSign. Find directions for signing controls from VeriSign at http://digitalid.verisign.com. This link points to a server not under the control of Microsoft; therefore, it may change between the time this information is published and when you attempt to use it.

Determining if an ActiveX control is safe

Since the digital signing of an ActiveX control stays with the file, ActiveX controls marked as safe must be safe in all possible conditions. So a control marked as safe must be written to protect itself from any unpredictable results a script author might unintentionally create when scripting the control. While it is easy for a programmer to make a specific control safe, it is impossible to guarantee that the control is always safe when used with scripting created by another author.

If a control is marked as safe for initializing, the programmer who created it is claiming that no matter what values are used to initialize the control, it will not do anything to damage a user's system or compromise the user's security.

The developer of an ActiveX control should take extra care to ensure that a control is in fact safe before it is marked as safe. For instance, each ActiveX control should be verified that it:

- Does not manipulate the file system.
- Does not manipulate the registry (except to register and unregister itself).
- Does not over-index arrays or otherwise manipulate memory incorrectly, thereby causing a memory leak or corrupt memory region.
- Validates and corrects all input, including initialization, method parameters, and property set functions.
- Does not misuse any data about, or provided by, the user.
- Was tested in a variety of circumstances.

Password and encryption protection for Excel, Word, and PowerPoint files

Several features are available in Microsoft Excel, Microsoft Word, and Microsoft PowerPoint to protect files through passwords or encryption. These file-level security measures are in addition to any operating system-level security already set, such as permissions to a folder, a specific file, or an entire drive.

File encryption is one of the best ways to protect a document. When saved, the file is scrambled with an encryption code, making the contents of the document unreadable. However, this requires setting a password and remembering that password.

Setting password protection can be partially programmatically automated through VBA or can be disabled in situations where you do not want it available to users through a policy setting. However, hard-coding a password into a program is not a recommended practice and can lead to weakened security.

For example, the **SaveAs** method in VBA has four arguments it can use — **LockComments**, **Password**, **WritePassword**, or **ReadOnlyRecommended**. These arguments can allow a programmer to save a document with a password.

As a part of all good security and encryption methods, using strong password methods provides additional benefit to any attempted security attacks. Documentation regarding the implementation of strong password methods is available from http://www.microsoft.com/NTServer/security/deployment/planguide/password.asp.

Microsoft Access does not provide the same method of password and file encryption methods available with Excel, Word, and PowerPoint. For security, encryption, and password schemes for Microsoft Access, see "Secure a Microsoft Access project" and "Administering and Securing an Application - Securing a Database" from the **Contents** pane of Microsoft Access Help.

> **Note** To use encrypted documents in collaboration, you must clear the **Encrypt document properties** check box in the **Encryption Type** dialog (**Tools | Options | Security | Advanced...**). Clearing this check box is required because the routing information within the document must be unencrypted, thereby allowing the routing handling programs to use the routing data.

Protecting Excel workbooks

Microsoft Excel supports three levels of workbook file protection. The user who creates a workbook has read/write permission to a workbook and can control the level of protection. The three levels are:

- File open protection

    Excel requires the user to enter a password to open a workbook.

- File modify protection

    Excel requires the user to enter a password to open the workbook with read/write permission. The user can click **Read Only** at the prompt, and Excel opens the workbook in a read-only state.

- Read-only recommended protection

    Excel prompts the user to open the workbook in a read-only state. If the user clicks **No** at the prompt, Excel opens the workbook with read/write permission, unless the workbook has other password protection enabled.

Excel encrypts password-protected workbooks by using encryption routines. Because protected workbooks are encrypted, they are not indexed by Find Fast or by the Microsoft Office Server Extensions (OSE) search feature. Encryption is provided by various cryptographic methods available from the **Advanced** button on the **Security** dialog (**File | Save As** menu option). Default encryption can also be set for users by using a system policy.

In addition to protecting an entire workbook, you can also protect specific elements from unauthorized changes. This method is not as secure as using a password to protect the entire workbook because Excel does not use encryption when you protect only specific elements.

For example, hidden cells on a protected worksheet can be viewed if a user copies across a range on the protected worksheet that includes the hidden cells, opens a new workbook, pastes, and then uses the **Unhide** command to display the cells.

> **Tip** To ensure the strongest security on a workbook, use a password to protect the entire workbook.

You can protect the following elements of a workbook:

- Protect Sheet

    This allows the creator of the workbook the ability to protect a worksheet and the contents of locked cells. It also allows the creator of the file the option of restricting the following formatting capabilities by other users of the file:

    - Select locked cells
    - Select unlocked cells
    - Format cells
    - Format columns
    - Format rows
    - Insert columns
    - Insert rows
    - Insert hyperlinks
    - Delete columns
    - Delete rows
    - Sort
    - Use AutoFilter
    - Use PivotTable® reports
    - Edit objects
    - Edit scenarios

- Allow Users to Edit Ranges

    This provides the creator of a workbook the ability to let other users make changes to specific ranges in a worksheet. This method uses network security permissions so the creator can select a User ID of an individual and provide specific access rights to data within a range of a worksheet.

- Protect Workbook

    Allows the creator of a workbook the ability to protect the structure or windows of the workbook with a password. Protection of these two elements of a workbook are:

    - Structure of a workbook

        Worksheets and chart sheets in a protected workbook cannot be moved, deleted, hidden, unhidden, or renamed, and new sheets cannot be inserted.

    - Windows in a workbook

        Windows in a protected workbook cannot be moved, resized, hidden, unhidden, or closed. Windows in a protected workbook are sized and positioned the same way each time the workbook is opened.

- Cells or formulas on a worksheet, or items on a chart sheet

    Contents of protected cells on a worksheet cannot be edited. Protected items on a chart sheet cannot be modified (right-click on the cell of interest, select **Format Cells...**, then click the **Protection** tab). Use of this feature on a protected cell requires the worksheet it is part of to be protected.

    Tip You can also hide a formula so only the result of the formula appears in the cell.

- Graphic objects on a worksheet or chart sheet

    Protected graphic objects can be locked. This prevents the object or chart from being moved or edited. Requires the worksheet it is part of to be protected.

- Scenarios on a worksheet

    Definitions of protected scenarios cannot be changed (**Tools** menu, **Scenarios** option).

- Change histories of shared workbooks

    Protected change histories (track changes enabled) cannot be cleared by the user of a shared workbook or by the user of a merged copy of a workbook. Enabled by setting the **Sharing with track changes** check box in the **Protect Shared Workbook** dialog (**Tools | Protection | Protect and Share Workbook...** option) to checked.

Chapter 10 Administering Security

Caution If a user assigns password protection to a workbook and then forgets the password, it is impossible to perform the following activities:

- Open the workbook
- Gain access to the workbook's data from another workbook through a link
- Remove protection from the workbook
- Recover data from the workbook

You should advise users to keep a list of passwords and corresponding workbook, worksheet, and chart sheet names in a safe place.

Protecting Word documents

Microsoft Word supports three levels of document protection. The user who creates a document has read/write permission to a document and controls the protection level. These protection methods are accessed by selecting **File | Save as | Tools | Security**. The three levels of document protection are:

- File open protection

    Word requires the user to enter a password to open a document.

- File modify protection

    Word requires the user to enter a password to open the document with read/write permission. If the user clicks **Read Only** at the prompt, Word opens the document as read-only.

- Read-only recommended protection

    Word prompts the user to open the document as read-only. If the user clicks **No** at the prompt, Word opens the document with read/write permission, unless the document has other password protection.

Word encrypts password-protected documents by using encryption routines. Because protected documents are encrypted, they are not indexed by Find Fast or by the Microsoft Office Server Extensions (OSE) search feature. Encryption is provided by various cryptographic methods available from the **Advanced** button on the **Security** dialog (**File | Save As** menu option). Default encryption can also be set for users by using a system policy.

In addition to protecting an entire document, you can also protect specific elements from unauthorized changes. This method is not as secure as using a password to protect the entire document because Word does not use encryption when you protect only select elements. For example, field codes can be viewed in a text editor such as Notepad even if forms or sections of a document are protected.

Specific elements you can protect in a document are:

- Tracked changes

    Changes made to the document can be neither accepted nor rejected, and change tracking cannot be turned off.

- Comments

    Users can insert comments into the document but cannot change the content of the document.

- Forms

    Users can make changes only in form fields or unprotected sections of a document.

To protect tracked changes in a Word document

1. Open the document in Word.
2. Select the **Protect Document** menu option (**Tools** menu).
3. Select **Tracked changes**.
4. Add a password to the **Password** text box.
5. Save the document.

After setting any of these elements to protected status in the document, you can unprotect them at any time. To do so, select the **Unprotect** menu option (**Tools** menu) and provide the password used to set the protection.

> **Caution** If a user assigns password protection to a document and then forgets the password, it is impossible to perform the following activities:
>
> - Open the document
> - Gain access to the documents data from another document with a link
> - Remove protection from the document
> - Recover data from the document
>
> Advise users to keep a list of passwords and corresponding document names in a safe place.

Protecting PowerPoint presentations

Microsoft PowerPoint supports three levels of presentation file protection. The user who creates a presentation has read/write permission to a presentation and controls the protection level. The three levels of presentation protection are:

- File open protection

    PowerPoint requires the user to enter a password to open a presentation.

- File modify protection

    PowerPoint requires the user to enter a password to open the presentation with read/write permission. The user can click **Read Only** at the prompt, and PowerPoint opens the presentation as read-only.

- Read-only recommended protection

    PowerPoint prompts the user to open the presentation as read-only. If the user clicks **No** at the prompt, PowerPoint opens the presentation with read/write permission.

PowerPoint encrypts password-protected presentations by using encryption routines. Because protected presentations are encrypted, they are not indexed by Find Fast or by the Microsoft Office Server Extensions (OSE) search feature. Encryption is provided by various cryptographic methods available from the **Advanced** button on the **Security** dialog (**File | Save As** menu option). Default encryption can also be set for users by using a system policy.

Optionally, you can encrypt document properties, too. To do so, click the **Advanced...** button and set the **Encrypt document properties** check box to checked. This prevents people from opening the presentation using a text editor and viewing any clear text (ASCII text) in the presentation.

> **Caution** If a user assigns password protection to a presentation and then forgets the password, it is impossible to perform the following activities:
>
> - Open the presentation
> - Gain access to the presentation data from another presentation through a link
> - Remove protection from the presentation
> - Recover data from the presentation
>
> Advise users to keep a list of passwords in a safe place.

Password and encryption options

Password and encryption options have been moved to the new **Security** tab within the **Tools | Options** dialog. They can still be accessed from the **File Save | Tools | Security** option.

There are also new hot keys for these options. The groups and controls are:

File encryption options for this document

- Password to open
- Advanced...

File sharing options for this document

- Password to modify
- Read-only recommended
- Digital signatures...
- Protect Document...

> **Note** The use of the term **Digital signatures** is not the same as when used with code signing or certificates attached to executable code. In this instance, a Digital signature is the unique identifying element of an individual's mark on a document, like a legal and binding signature at the bottom of a page. When attached to a document, workbook, or presentation, it implies the user has signed the document and has validated its contents.

Privacy options

- Remove personal information from this file on save
- Warn before printing, saving, or sending a file that contains tracked changes or comments
- Store random number to improve merge accuracy

Macro security

- Macro Security...

Protect Document dialog

Within the **File sharing options for this document** section of the **Security** tab is a button to access the **Protect Document** dialog. This button provides the same functionality as the **Tools | Protect Document** menu option and the **File | Save As | Tools | Security | Protect** document button.

Privacy options

Privacy options help reduce the visibility of an author or editor of content in a file by removing all references in the document. Author and editor references are attached to tracking changes or comments and can identify who made a change or added a comment. The privacy features of Office can replace these references by adding a generic user name to each comment or tracking change.

Word 2002 uses three options to protect access to private information. The check boxes are grouped under **Privacy options** in the **Security** dialog. Not all Office applications take advantage of these features.

The first privacy check box, **Remove personal information from this file on save**, sets a document property. If a user has a document with comments and saves it, the author identifier for the current comments are removed.

The second privacy check box, **Warn before printing, saving or sending a file that contains tracked changes or comments**, sets a global property. The setting, which is **off** by default, causes a dialog to appear whenever a request to save, print, or e-mail a document containing markup (change tracking or comments) is issued.

The third privacy check box, **Store random number to improve accuracy**, sets a global property. The setting, which is **on** by default, determines whether the file to save will receive a stamp with the RSID number for a particular editing session. The RSID number is a harmless pseudo-random number that reveals no information about a document's authorship or origin. Word uses the RSID information, if present, to enhance the results of merging two versions of a document; but the RSID information is not required for a merge to succeed.

Removing Visual Basic for Applications

Visual Basic for Applications (VBA) is considered a security risk by some administrators. The risk, however, is not with VBA itself but with the problems that can be caused when VBA is intentionally used by individuals to disrupt or sabotage work.

For this reason, several companies have requested a version of Office that does not include VBA. To accommodate this request, Visual Basic for Applications has been made an installable feature of Office — that is, it can be removed by changing its installation state.

> **Note** Removing VBA does not protect against malicious programs that are written using another programming language and that are of a compiled format (EXE). It also does not remove the possibility of script-based executables from accomplishing the same goal.

Setting the install option for VBA to **Not Available** or **Not Available, Hidden, Locked** in the **Set Feature Installation States** page of the Custom Installation Wizard and Custom Maintenance Wizard turns off VBA; any other installation option turns on VBA.

Turning VBA off presents significant issues:

- Microsoft Access 2002 cannot be installed to a user's computer and is removed if it is already installed when VBA is turned off.
- **Office Tools on the Web** will not run.
- Macros will not run.
- All add-ins dependent on VBA will not run.

Turning off VBA keeps programs dependent on VBA from running, and it also turns off most add-ins and all macros within all applications for all users. It is highly recommended not to turn off VBA. Instead use the security features of Office to limit the potential for malicious attacks and possible damage to computer hardware or software. For more information, see the **Set Feature Installation States** page of the Custom Installation Wizard and select Help for further information.

In general, setting maximum-security settings for applications in Office protects against malicious attacks in all forms and allows organizations to retain VBA as an installed feature.

Changes to the File | Save As | Tools menu

The Word 2000 **Save As** dialog included a method of gaining access to the **Save** tab properties dialog. In Word 2002 this has changed. Instead of finding it through the **Tools | General Options** menu, it is now in the **Tools | Save Options** menu.

Running Office in a Secure Environment

The Microsoft Windows NT® and Microsoft Windows® 2000 operating systems can provide a secure working environment for multiple users. This security is achieved by allowing permission-restricted access to registry branches and folders on NTFS-formatted hard disks connected to the same computer running either of these operating systems. When this restrictive access is enabled on a system, it is known as locked down.

With a locked-down configuration, only someone with administrative permissions to the registry and system-related folders on the hard disk where the operating system resides can make changes to the configuration of the computer. By locking these areas so other users cannot make changes, you can freeze the configuration of the operating system and applications running on it, ensuring the same user experience for all users on the system.

Microsoft Windows 98 and Microsoft Windows Millennium Edition (Windows Me) do not provide for these security capabilities because they are single-user operating systems; therefore, an administrator can only freeze user options within Office through the use of system policies. For more information about setting system policies for Office, see "How to Set System Policies" in Chapter 9, "Using System Policies."

Locking down a system prevents users from:

- Installing new software
- Removing existing software
- Changing currently configured application settings
- Updating system files to different levels
- Viewing other users' files

The added restrictions an administrator imposes can create problems for some users, especially when the needs of the users require changes to the configuration of the applications on the computer. The need to add new software or adjust application settings may cause users some frustration, which can only be alleviated by reviewing the system configuration and making necessary changes at scheduled intervals by the administrator.

Locking down an Office configuration

Administrators have the capability to configure an Office installation on a user's computer and restrict user access to menu options. (These same restrictions can also be set by using system policies.) If the client computer is running Windows NT 4.0 or Windows 2000, there is an extra means of locking down that configuration by locking portions of the registry and folders or drives. The security design of Windows NT 4.0 and Windows 2000 provides administrators with the ability to lock the registry, or portions of the registry, with security and permission settings so users cannot make changes to registry settings. Locking the registry can be accomplished safely for the following registry branches:

- HKEY_LOCAL_MACHINE (HKLM)
- HKEY_CLASSES_ROOT (HKCR)
- HKEY_CURRENT_CONFIG (HKCC)

However, locking down the HKEY_USERS or HKEY_CURRENT_USER branches can present problems for some applications and should only be done by an experienced administrator after thorough testing of Office applications on a test computer.

Each customized installation of Office is unique and requires testing, especially if registry branches are going to be locked down. Users can encounter problems when applications they are using try to make changes to a locked portion of the registry.

To lock down the registry for systems running Windows NT 4.0 and Windows 2000, use the Registry Editor (regedt32.exe). Regedt32.exe is not available as a shortcut from the Start menu. You must run it by selecting **Start** and pointing to the **Run...** utility. Then enter **regedt32** in the **Open** combo box.

To lock down a branch of the registry with regedt32

1. Select the registry branch or node you want to lock down.
2. Select **Security**.
3. Select **Permissions**.
4. Add permissions for administrators of the computer to **Full Control**, if those permissions are not already present.
5. Set permissions for **Everyone** to **Read**.
6. Click **OK**.

Changes to permissions are enforced the moment you click **OK**.

In Windows 2000, you can also create an Access Control List (ACL) to lock the Policies subkey in the Windows registry. This option prevents users from changing a policy configuration setting by modifying security settings in the user's registry. See the Group Policy snap-in Help available with Windows 2000 for further information.

Windows NT 4.0 Terminal Server and Windows 2000 Terminal Services

Terminal Services is a term applied to operating systems that can provide remote multi-user access. These operating systems are available for use by more than one user simultaneously. Windows NT 4.0 Terminal Server and Windows 2000 Terminal Services are the current operating systems that can provide this capability. Since these operating systems allow multiple users to log onto the system at the same time through remote communication links, it creates potential configuration control issues if all users are allowed to make changes to the configuration of the computer at any time.

To avoid these possible configuration problems, Terminal Services locks down the two branches of the registry named HKEY_CURRENT_USER (HKCU) and HKEY_LOCAL_MACHINE (HKLM). These two branches of the registry must be locked to prevent all users, except administrators, from making changes to the registry. Implementing this restrictive action imposes control of the configuration of the operating system on the administrator.

The locking of registry branches forces administration of the system to become more frequent since users are not allowed to administrate the computer themselves. You should review and make necessary changes to the system on a scheduled basis. If you cannot perform the necessary review and maintenance of the Terminal Server, you should consider removing some of the restrictions or allow one user administrative access so that individual can manage the adding or removal of software depending on the needs of users.

Outlook and Terminal Services

Of all the Office applications, Microsoft Outlook and Microsoft Solution Designer are the most sensitive to a locked-down configuration. Administrators must consider how changes to forms, user e-mail profiles, and the use of roaming profiles can affect the registry prior to implementing changes. Each of these changes requires frequent interaction with locked-down portions of the registry. To properly allow for the usage of the major features of Outlook, you are advised to closely monitor the needs of users with regard to forms and e-mail profiles, which are stored primarily in registry entries. As needs change, the administrator must update the configuration of the system accordingly.

For more information about configuring Outlook, see "Installing in a Terminal Services Environment" in Chapter 19, "Special Outlook Deployment Scenarios."

Office Macro Security Settings

This topic discusses macro security settings for Microsoft Word, Microsoft Excel, Microsoft PowerPoint, and Microsoft Outlook. All macro security settings are the same for these applications. Even though macro security is the same among these applications, a review of how each security setting affects associated features in an application is recommended since disabling an ActiveX control, for example, in Outlook or Excel may limit functionality in each application to different degrees that are acceptable or unacceptable for users.

Macro security depends on a certificate being associated with the application's data file or executable code attached to a document, workbook, presentation, or e-mail message. The validation of this certificate requires legitimate authentication of the author who signed the certificate, and authentication of the digital signature created for the author. Attaching a certificate of authenticity to a file, executable, ActiveX control, dynamic-link library (DLL) file, etc., requires obtaining a certificate from a Certificate Authority such as VeriSign™. For more information about digital signatures and certificates, see "Protecting Office Documents" in Chapter 10, "Administering Security."

Use of the term macro also implies ActiveX controls, COM objects, OLE objects, and any executable that can be attached to a document, worksheet, e-mail message, etc., for Word, Excel, or PowerPoint. For Outlook, Microsoft Publisher, and Microsoft FrontPage®, the term macro is explicitly used for macros used by Visual Basic for Applications.

The security settings of Microsoft Internet Explorer are inherited by Microsoft Office applications that make calls to Internet addresses. Each application can optionally instruct the core Internet Explorer components to use different security settings when it makes the call to open the URL if required.

The Outlook **Security** dialog does not provide a method of setting the **Trust all installed add-ins and templates** check box in the **Trusted Source** tab as with other applications.

Anti-virus software

Under all security-setting levels, if anti-virus software compatible with the Microsoft Office 2000 or Microsoft Office XP anti-virus API is installed, and you open a document that contains macros, the anti-virus software scans the document for known viruses.

There are two types of anti-virus software you can use with Office. One type looks at the file as it arrives either from a disk or from over the network; the other type looks at the file whenever the file is opened by an application. Anti-virus software compatible with the Office anti-virus API examines a file when the file is being opened by the application. If the file is found to have a virus, the user is notified prior to the file being activated and displayed in the work area of the application. Virus software compatible with the Office anti-virus API and installed on the computer is noted at the bottom of the **Security** dialog of the application. If the computer does not have anti-virus software that is compatible with the API, "**No virus scanner installed.**" appears at the bottom of the **Security** dialog.

Macro security levels in Word, Excel, PowerPoint, and Outlook

The following list summarizes how macro-virus protection reacts to the different types of signed and unsigned macros encountered under each setting. Users can change these settings through the **Security Level** tab in the **Security** dialog box (**Tools** menu, **Macro** submenu).

In all cases **Low security** presents no prompt to the user, and macros are allowed to run. Any certificates attached to macros that are run under low security are not posted to the trusted source list for Office applications. Only when security is set to **Medium** or **High**, and a user agrees to trust a certificate, will a certificate be added to the trusted source list for Office. This list of security settings does not present the **Low Security** option since low security is the same for all cases.

- Unsigned macros

    High — Macros are disabled, and the document, workbook, presentation, or e-mail message is opened.

    Medium — User is prompted to enable or disable macros.

- Signed macros from a trusted source with a valid certificate

    High and Medium — Macros are enabled, and the document, workbook, presentation, or e-mail message is opened.

- Signed macros from an unknown source with a valid certificate

    High and Medium — A dialog box appears with information about the certificate. Users must then determine whether they should enable any macros based on the content of the certificate. To enable the macros, users must accept the certificate.

    Note A network administrator can lock the list of trusted sources and prevent a user from adding the certificate to the list, thereby disabling any macros associated with the document, workbook, presentation, or e-mail message.

- Signed macros from any source with an invalid certificate

    High and Medium — User is warned of a possible virus. Macros are disabled.

- Signed macros from any source, in which validation of the certificate is not possible because the public key is missing or an incompatible encryption method was used

    High — User is warned that certificate validation is not possible. Macros are disabled.

    Medium — User is warned that certificate validation is not possible. User is given the option to enable or disable macros.

- Signed macros from any source, in which the macro was signed after the certificate had expired or was revoked by the Certificate Authority

    High — User is warned that the certificate has expired or was revoked. Macros are disabled.

    Medium — User is warned that the certificate has expired or was revoked. User is given the option to enable or disable macros.

Programming-related security issue

Macro security prior to Office XP was not enabled — that is, security was set to Low — by Office applications started by an executable program making a call into the application object. Therefore, any macro would run when an application like Word opened a document and instructed it to run a macro, regardless of whether the macro was trusted or not. To address this issue of low security, a new security method was added to all VBA application objects called `AutomationSecurity`. This method can be used with the application object for each Office application.

Example:

`Application.AutomationSecurity=msoAutomationSecurityLow`

The values for use with this method are:

- msoAutomationSecurityLow

    Sets the macro security to Low for this application; macros run without checking their certificate for authenticity.

- msoAutomationSecurityByUI

    Sets the macro security to the same level as currently set in the user interface for the application (as found in the **Security** dialog).

- msoAutomationSecurityForceDisable

    Sets the macro security level to High; all macros must be from a trusted source in order to run.

For programmers who need to instruct Office applications to open files and run macros, it is recommended they set this method to `msoAutomationSecurityByUI` prior to opening a file to conform to the security level set for the application by the user. For instances where high security is required, use the `msoAutomationSecurityForceDisable` to disable the running of any macros.

High Security and Excel 4 (.xlm) macros

If you plan to use Excel 4 macros (.xlm) with Excel 2002, you need to add a registry entry to enable them if you also plan to use High Security. All Office applications are set to High Security by default when installed, unless a lower security level has been specified in a transform (MST file).

This registry entry is necessary because Excel .xlm macros cannot be digitally signed and, therefore, cannot load when High Security is enabled. (High Security requires a macro to be signed with a valid certificate from a trusted source.) Because some Excel add-ins were created using .xlm, you will need to add this registry entry to each user's computer to allow the macros to run.

To allow add-ins created from .xlm macros to run as exceptions under High Security in Excel 2002, add the following registry entry to each user's computer using a transform, configuration maintenance file (CMW file), or .reg file:

HKEY_LOCAL_MACHINE\SOFTWARE\Microsoft\Office\10.0\Excel\Security

Value name: **XLM**

Data type: **DWORD** (integer)

Value data: **[0 | 1]**

Creating and setting the **XLM** registry value to **1** allows users to load .xlm macros. Setting this value to **0** returns Excel 2002 to its default behavior of not allowing .xlm macros to run in High Security.

When this registry entry is added and set to **1**, users are warned about .xlm macros when they attempt to open a workbook and are given the option to open the workbook and enable the use of macros. End-users should run a virus check on any .xlm macro before they enable it. Even though .xlm macros are allowed through the High Security check, the High Security feature for all forms of macros (such as VBA macros) is still enabled.

Setting this registry entry allows for automatic and silent disabling of non-signed VBA macros; however, the .xlm macros are evaluated as if Excel was set to Medium Security. The administrator of the machine can force the running of signed and trusted VBA macros, but also allow exceptions for Excel 4 macros. If you set this registry entry, users should be educated about Excel 4 viruses and how they are enabled if a workbook is opened.

> **Note** Addition of this registry entry provides no indication through the user interface to the end user that the system is running a modified or reduced level of High Security.

Security Settings and Related System Policies

Security is an important subject for today's businesses. The increase in malicious hacking of corporate computers has forced businesses worldwide to develop better methods of protecting their data and systems. As a way to help administrators enable the security features of Microsoft Office XP, Microsoft has created system policies that force the use of security features and are available in the Office10.adm policy template.

> **Note** Removing registry keys in the HKEY_CURRENT_USER registry branch using the **Add/Remove Registry Entries** page of the Custom Installation Wizard does not work on Windows Terminal Server. However, adding registry keys using this page works as expected. It is possible to add and remove registry keys in the HKEY_CURRENT_USER registry branch for Windows Terminal Server systems using the **Add/Remove Registry Entries** page of the Custom Maintenance Wizard.

Security settings can be enforced in one of four registry areas within two branches of the registry — Local Machine (HKLM) and Current User (HKCU).

Local Machine (associated with the **Default Computer** policy profile in the System Policy Editor)

- HKLM\Software\Policies\Microsoft\…
- HKLM\Software\Microsoft\…

Current User (associated with the **Default User** policy profile in the System Policy Editor)

- HKCU\Software\Policies\Microsoft\…
- HKCU\Software\Microsoft\…

The content in this topic covers most of the concerns an administrator will have when viewing the **Specify Office Security Settings** page of either the Custom Installation Wizard or the Custom Maintenance Wizard. Most of these settings can also be set using a policy when the appropriate ADM template is added to the System Policy Editor or Group Policy snap-in with Microsoft Windows 2000.

Included in this topic are policy settings relevant to maintaining a secure user environment related to the operating system user interface.

Adding Microsoft to the trusted source list

The trusted source list is managed in four possible places within the registry. Policy settings are in the **Policies** node of the registry and are controlled by using the System Policy Editor. The first two registry key entry examples shown below can be set by using the **Specify Office Security Settings** page of the Custom Installation Wizard or the Custom Maintenance Wizard. Registry key examples:

HKLM\Software\Microsoft\VBA\Trusted

HKCU\Software\Microsoft\VBA\Trusted

HKLM\Software\Policies\Microsoft\VBA\Trusted

HKCU\Software\Policies\Microsoft\VBA\Trusted

Use of the HKLM key prevents users from modifying the trusted sources list.

By adding recognized value names and data to any of these keys instructs Office to trust or not trust sources. For example, adding **Microsoft Corporation** *nnnn* (where *nnnn* is a year) as a value name instructs Office to trust all sources with a digital signature from Microsoft. It is preferable to use the **Specify Office Security Settings** page of the Custom Installation Wizard or Custom Maintenance Wizard to propagate your request to trust Microsoft certificates, but if it is absolutely necessary, you can create a configuration maintenance file (CMW file) with the Custom Maintenance Wizard and then use the Custom Maintenance Wizard Viewer to view the contents of the file to identify the registry data value if the setting must be made manually.

You use the listed value name and data to populate the registry setting.

Value Name:	**Microsoft Corporation** *nnnn*
Data type:	**REG_BINARY**
Value data:	(data content provided by wizards)

Setting the value name of the key to **No source will be trusted. - your Administrator** forces Office to not trust any sources. Setting this key disallows the option to let users trust a source. This setting can be controlled by the Custom Installation Wizard and the Custom Maintenance Wizard with the check box **Ensure users cannot add trusted sources through Office** on the **Specify Office Security Settings** page.

Value Name:	**No source will be trusted. - your Administrator**
Data type:	**REG_BINARY**
Value data:	**(d3,0f,d6,00,91,21,bf,51,7e,60,48,a2,99,ba,25,00,b7,96,08,01)**

Use of the HKLM node only allows the use of what is in the list and does not allow users to add entries through the Office user interface (the Custom Installation Wizard and the Custom Maintenance Wizard do not use the HKCU node for this key).

Application Security key

Through the use of the application Security key, you can instruct Office to set macro security for each application or for the trusting of all installed add-ins. The basic key consists of the following, where <APP> can be any or all of the listed applications (Word, Microsoft , Microsoft Access, PowerPoint):

HKCU\Software\Microsoft\Office\10.0\<APP>\Security

The parallel keys as specified through a policy setting are:

HKLM\Software\Policies\Microsoft\Office\10.0\<APP>\Security

HKCU\Software\Policies\Microsoft\Office\10.0\<APP>\Security

The **Specify Office Security Settings** page of both the Custom Installation Wizard or Custom Maintenance Wizard contain the check box **Trust all installed add-ins and templates**. When this check box is set to checked, it creates the non-policy version of this key and adds the value **DontTrustInstalledFiles** to the key. When this policy is set to **1**, this registry value instructs the Office application listed in the <APP> portion of the key to trust all currently installed add-ins and templates (and their respective macros) within specific folders created by Office applications. It does not accept all currently installed add-ins and templates on the user's computer, only those installed by specific Microsoft applications.

If you use either HKLM or HKCU when setting a registry entry for a policy, you will prevent users from changing the setting.

>   Value name: **DontTrustInstalledFiles**
>
>   Data type: **REG_DWORD-**
>
>   Value data: 0   // Do not trust Installed Files

If you use the **Specify Office Security Settings** page of either the Custom Maintenance Wizard or the Custom Installation Wizard, and change the **Default Security Level** for an application, this process is the same as using the **Security** dialog available through the application's user interface. Use of this key sets the macro security level for each application specified in the <APP> portion of the key to the respective value data listed below.

<APP> = Word, Excel, Access, PowerPoint, Publisher, Outlook

>   Value name: **Level**
>
>   Data type: **REG_DWORD**
>
>   Value data: 1   // Low
>   2   // Medium
>   3   // High

Common Security key

Through the use of the common Security key, you can instruct Office to set ActiveX security for all applications. This key can be set through either the Custom Installation Wizard or the Custom Maintenance Wizard.

HKCU\Software\Microsoft\Common\Security

By using the System Policy Editor, you can set the equivalent key for Office applications.

HKLM\Software\Policies\Microsoft\Common\Security

HKCU\Software\Policies\Microsoft\Common\Security

The value name **UFIControls** can be set for any of these keys to the following values and respective actions:

Value name: **UFIControls**

Data type: **REG_DWORD**

Value Data:
1   // No warning.
2   // No warning (use safe mode if available)
3   // Alert. Do not load any UFI controls.
4   // Alert. Do not load any UFI controls (use safe mode if available)
5   // Prompt the user.
6   // Prompt the user (use safe mode if available)

See documentation on ActiveX control development for information on safe mode for ActiveX controls. Look for the following object and method: **IObjectSafetyImpl::SetInterfaceSafetyOptions**. The **IObjectSafety** interface allows a client to retrieve and set an object's safety levels. For example, a Web browser may call **IObjectSafety::SetInterfaceSafetyOptions** to make a control safe for initialization or safe for scripting.

The use of safe mode for an ActiveX control instructs it to run but not process data. This should force the control to read in the data but not change the data in any way or write it back out. However, not all controls are designed with a safe mode and therefore may process data even though you instructed the control to use safe mode.

Setting the **Unsafe ActiveX Initialization to** combo box to "**Initialize using control defaults. User will be warned.**" in either the Custom Installation Wizard or the Custom Maintenance Wizard adds the **UFIControls** value to the common security key and adds a data value of **3**.

Setting the **Unsafe ActiveX Initialization to** combo box to "**Prompt user to use persisted data or control defaults.**" in either the Custom Installation Wizard or the Custom Maintenance Wizard adds the **UFIControls** value to the common security key and adds a data value of **5**.

Configuring security-related system policies

This section includes samples of system policies for security-related configuration options of Office and related applications. Most of these policies do not affect security directly, nor do they directly change Office XP; however, they limit the exposure of critical portions of a network, operating system, or user interface to destructive changes by users. By setting these policies, an administrator can reduce the amount of data users must consider, or reduce the choices users must make while they interact with the system. As a result, productivity can increase by not having to support some features and by streamlining the user interface of the operating system. The policies in this section are available with the listed templates.

It is highly recommended for administrators to examine the policy templates for the operating systems with which their users are working. Several policies provide methods to control and enforce the configuration of the operating system and reduce the probability of a user creating a problem. These policies limit the access of users to features of the operating system they do not need to change.

Windows NT and Windows 2000

The following list of policy templates and system policies highlights some of the more important system policies you can use to limit the user environment in Microsoft Windows NT and Windows 2000 operating systems:

- common.adm - Shell | Restrictions
- common.adm - System | Restrictions
- winnt.adm - Windows NT Shell | Restrictions

Windows 2000–related system policies are also found in the conf.adm and system.adm policy templates.

common.adm - Shell | Restrictions

- Remove **Run** command from **Start** Menu
- Hide drives in My Computer
- No "Entire Network" in Network Neighborhood
- Remove Shut Down command from Start menu

common.adm - System | Restrictions

- Run only allowed Windows applications

winnt.adm - Windows NT Shell | Restrictions

- Remove the "Map Network Drive" and "Disconnect Network Drive" options

Windows 2000 only

The following list of policies highlights some of the more important system policies you can use to limit the user environment in the Windows 2000 operating system:

- system.adm - Administrative | Start Menu & Taskbar
- system.adm - Administrative | Windows Components | Windows Explorer | Common Open File Dialog

system.adm - Administrative | Start Menu & Taskbar

- Do not keep history of recently opened documents

system.adm - Administrative | Windows Components | Windows Explorer | Common Open File Dialog

- Hide the Common Dialog Places Bar
- Hide Common Dialog Back button
- Hide the drop-down list of recent files

Sample system policies explained

Provided in this section is an in-depth explanation of the policies presented earlier in this topic. Each explanation provides the registry key, value name, data type, and associated data necessary to enforce the policy.

Remove Run command from Start Menu

When this policy is enabled, Windows 2000 removes **Run** from the **Start** menu and disables launching the **Run** dialog by pressing the **Windows Key + R**.

If an application has a "run" function that allows users to start a program by typing in its name and path in a dialog, the application disables this functionality when this policy is enabled.

Template: common.adm

Path: Shell | Restrictions

HKCU\Software\Microsoft\Windows\CurrentVersion\Policies\Explorer

Value name:	**NoRun**
Data type:	**REG_DWORD**
Value data:	**0** // Display the Run option
	1 // Do not display the Run option

Hide drives in My Computer

When enabled, this policy removes the icons representing the selected disk drives from **My Computer**, **Windows Explorer**, **My Network Places,** and the Windows common dialogs.

All Office applications hide any of the listed drives when this policy is enabled. This includes any buttons, menu options, icons, or other visual representation of drives in Office applications. This does not prevent the user from accessing drives by manually entering drive letters in dialogs.

Template: common.adm

Path: Shell | Restrictions

HKCU\Software\Microsoft\Windows\CurrentVersion\Policies\Explorer

    Value name: **NoDrives**

    Data type: **REG_DWORD**

    Value data: **0**   // Display drives

                   1   // Do not display drives

No "Entire Network" in "My Network Places"

When enabled, this policy removes all computers outside of the user's workgroup or local domain from lists of network resources in **Windows Explorer** and **My Network Places**.

When this policy is enabled, applications that allow users to browse network resources must limit browsing functionality to a local workgroup or domain.

Template: common.adm

Path: Shell | Restrictions

HKCU\Software\Microsoft\Windows\CurrentVersion\Policies\Network

    Value name: **NoEntireNetwork**

    Data type: **REG_DWORD**

    Value data: **0**   // Show

                   1   // Remove

Remove Shut Down command from Start menu

This policy prevents the user from using the Windows user interface to shut down the system.

When this policy is enabled, applications that enable the user to shut down Windows must disable this capability.

Template: common.adm

Path: Shell | Restrictions

HKCU\Software\Microsoft\Windows\CurrentVersion\Policies\Explorer

    Value name: **NoClose**

    Data type: **REG_DWORD**

    Value data: **0**   // disabled

                     1   // enabled

Run only allowed Windows Applications

When this policy is enabled, users can only run applications listed in the value data field of this registry key. Applications with the ability to run and start other applications are also restricted to the applications appearing in this value data field.

This restriction does not apply when launching applications via OLE/COM/DCOM. If you use ShellExecuteEx, Windows 2000 will handle this automatically.

The only exception to this restriction is for OLE/DCOM where an installation of Microsoft Internet Explorer is displaying a file in its native format (Word, Excel, etc.) within the browser. Use the executable names (including extension) in the Data field separated by a semicolon.

Template: common.adm

Path: System | Restrictions

HKCU\Software\Microsoft\Windows\CurrentVersion\Policies\Explorer

    Value name: **RestrictRun**

    Data type: **REG_SZ** (string)

    Value data: **WinWord.exe;Excel.exe;PowerPnt.exe**

Remove "Map Network Drive" and "Disconnect Network Drive"

When this policy is enabled, users are prevented from using **Windows Explorer** and **My Network Places** to connect to other computers or to close existing connections.

When this policy is enabled, applications do not provide buttons, menu options, icons, or any other visual representation that enable a user to map to or disconnect from network drives.

Template: winnt.adm

Path: Windows NT Shell | Restrictions

HKCU\Software\Microsoft\Windows\CurrentVersion\Policies\Explorer\

    Value name: **NoNetConnectDisconnect**

    Data type: **REG_DWORD**

    Value data: **0**   // Display

                        1   // Remove

Do not keep history of recently opened documents

When this policy is enabled, the system does not save shortcuts to most recently used (MRU) documents in the **Start** menu.

When this policy is enabled, applications must not keep any MRU lists.

Template: system.adm

Path: Administrative | Start Menu & Taskbar

HKCU\Software\Microsoft\Windows\CurrentVersion\Policies\Explorer

    Value name: **NoRecentDocsHistory**

    Data type: **REG_DWORD**

    Value data: **0**   // Display shortcuts in MRU list

                        1   // Do not display shortcuts in MRU list

This policy affects Office applications in the following ways:

1. Do not show MRU lists while the policy is enabled.
2. Do not save new entries into MRU lists (freeze the list) while the policy is enabled, which means that after the policy is turned off, the MRU list will not contain any files used while the policy was on, but will contain files used before the policy was enabled.
3. If there is an MRU option in the **Options** dialog, it is grayed out while the policy is enabled.
4. After the policy is turned off, the user MRU settings and the application policy MRU settings are restored to the state before the policy was enabled.

    For example, if the number of MRU files was five (5) before the policy was enabled, it becomes zero (0) when the policy is turned on, and becomes five again when the policy is turned off.

5. If both the application MRU policy and the system MRU policy are enabled, the system policy setting is used.

Hide Common Dialog Places Bar

The places bar allows users to navigate via the common file open/file close dialog directly to the following locations:

- History folder
- Desktop
- My Documents
- My Computer
- My Network Places

When this policy is enabled, Windows 2000 removes the **Places Bar** from the Windows common dialog.

When this policy is set, applications that provide their own file open/file close dialogs must remove any equivalent functionality from the **Places Bar**. Applications using the Windows common dialog API automatically comply with this policy.

Template: system.adm

Path: Administrative | Windows Components | Windows Explorer | Common Open File Dialog

HKCU\Software\Microsoft\Windows\CurrentVersion\Policies\Comdlg32

> Value name: **NoPlaceBar**
>
> Data type: **REG_DWORD**
>
> Value data: **0**   // Display Places bar
>
>   **1**   // Do not display Places bar

Hide Common Dialog Back button

When this policy is enabled, Windows 2000 removes the **Back** button from the common dialog, preventing the user from browsing to the previous folder accessed from the dialog.

When this policy is set, applications with their own file open/file close dialogs must remove any **Back** button functionality from these dialogs. Applications using the Windows common dialog API automatically comply with this policy.

Template: system.adm

Path: Administrative | Windows Components | Windows Explorer | Common Open File Dialog

HKCU\Software\Microsoft\Windows\CurrentVersion\Policies\Comdlg32

    Value name: **NoBackButton**

    Data type: **REG_DWORD**

    Value data: **0** // Display back button

                        1 // Do not display back button

Hide the dropdown list of recent files

When this policy is enabled, Windows 2000 removes the MRU list from the common dialog.

When this policy is set, applications with their own file/open dialogs must not display an MRU list in these dialogs. Applications using the Windows common dialog API will automatically comply with this policy.

Template: system.adm

Path: Administrative | Windows Components | Windows Explorer | Common Open File Dialog

HKCU\Software\Microsoft\Windows\CurrentVersion\Policies\Comdlg32

    Value name: **NoFileMru**

    Data type: **REG_DWORD**

    Value data: **0** // Display MRU list

                        1 // Do not display MRU list

Microsoft Office Tools on the Web Security Scenarios

The following discussion presents several security problems that users might encounter when they use Office Tools on the Web, including tampering, system error, or interception by a hostile Web site. After each scenario is presented, the protection scheme devised by Microsoft is revealed, providing you the assurance that security issues have been addressed.

Taking users to a wrong Office Tools on the Web portal

Scenario: Users are taken to another Office Tools on the Web portal when they try to access Office Tools on the Web.

This scenario is usually caused by a virus that changes the registry or the contents of an executable on users' computers. The bogus Office Tools on the Web portal then begins causing problems to users' computers.

Protection scheme: There are several design elements to protect against the above scenario.

- The URL each application executes to go to the Office Tools on the Web portal is hard-coded into the executable of each application. Any attempt by hackers to change the registry entries on users' computers is useless.

- An administrator in a corporate environment can shut off the Office Tools on the Web feature for users.

  In this case, the administrator cannot point to another destination, which means administrators cannot develop their own intranet-based Office Tools on the Web portal.

- All Microsoft Office executables are specially encoded to protect against someone trying to patch the EXE and thereby alter the Office Tools on the Web URL.

  In this case, if someone tries to change the EXE, that EXE becomes non-functional. As a result, patching of an Office executable will not allow someone to hijack the Office Tools on the Web destination. If the executable is determined by Office to have been changed, the automatic repair feature of Office will replace it with a new copy.

Privacy of data exchange

Scenario: A hacker could possibly intercept Internet traffic and view the data a user is exchanging with the Microsoft Office Web site server while using Office Tools on the Web.

Protection scheme: Microsoft requires all Office Tools on the Web pages on the Microsoft Office Web site server to be secured by Secure Socket Layer (SSL) encryption. The resulting data stream appears as random characters, protecting the data exchange between a user and the Microsoft Office Web site server from eavesdroppers.

Abuse of object model by Office Tools on the Web providers

Scenario: The Web pages of an Office Tools on the Web provider could use the object model of an application to gather or alter more information than is necessary, thereby violating privacy of users.

Protection scheme: Office does not allow any Office Tools on the Web provider to connect directly to a user's live application. Only the pages hosted by the Microsoft Office Web site can connect directly to a user's live application. If the Microsoft Office Web site needs data or work from a third-party Office Tools on the Web provider, then the Microsoft Office Web site servers talk to those systems and then send the answers back to the user's computer.

Denial of Service attacks on the Microsoft Office Web site

Scenario: A hacker discovers the URL of the Office Tools on the Web portal and then bombards it with fake requests so that servers hosting the Microsoft Office Web site are overwhelmed and unable to respond to genuine user requests.

Protection scheme: This scenario presents a Microsoft Office Web site security issue. Microsoft relies on continuous monitoring of the site by the Web site administrators to detect and defend against such attacks.

Microsoft Office Web site domain name hijacked

Scenario: A hacker using an Internet Service Provider (ISP) hacks a Domain Name Server (DNS) so the hacked DNS points the user to a fake Office Tools on the Web portal instead of the real one. As a result, all the users who get DNS services from the hacked server end up connected to the fake Office Tools on the Web portal.

Protection scheme: This is a Microsoft Office Web site security issue. Microsoft relies on continuous monitoring by the Microsoft Office Web site Operations Team to detect and defend against such attacks.

Office Tools on the Web site has bad code

Scenario: Accidental or intentional Office Tools on the Web implementation code or Web pages are posted to the site. The code contains bad content or intentionally written to harm users' computers.

Protection scheme: This is a Microsoft Office Web site development and management issue. Prior to making any Office Tools on the Web page live, the Office Tools on the Web team will check content and code for the site so that:

- All code is thoroughly tested.
- All changes to code can be traced back to the author of the changes; that is, a system of code check-in is in place before code goes live.
- Office Tools on the Web code can be quickly rolled back to the last-known good state if any problems in a service are detected.

Bad frame on a page

Scenario: An Office Tools on the Web page is implemented using frames. One of the frames displays content or services available from a third-party source that uses access to the object model to accomplish its work.

Protection scheme: Access to the object model is managed in two ways:

1. In the operations policy, any third-party code that works with Office Tools on the Web is double-checked for malicious content.
2. In the design and implementation of Office Tools on the Web code, the currently active Office application knows which URL is being requested.

The shared Office Tools on the Web code detects this, whether the request is coming from a page or a frame, and is able to refuse execution of the request. This prevents exposure of the user to unauthorized URLs that might originate from a frame.

CHAPTER 11

Creating Custom Help

With Microsoft Office XP, you can expand the usefulness of built-in Help and error messages to include information unique to your organization. For instance, you can redirect users who encounter error messages to Web sites or files that provide solutions to their problems; and you can create custom Help topics and make them available through a seamless interface, just like built-in Help.

In this chapter

Customizing Error Messages   327

Creating Custom Help Topics   341

Making Custom Help Content Accessible   347

Customizing Error Messages

In Microsoft Office XP, you can customize error messages to provide additional information about an error. When users can find problem-solving information on their own, they are less likely to call your support staff.

Adding value to error messages

Error messages, or alerts, are displayed when a user attempts an action the computer cannot perform. For example, if a user tries to print a document on a network printer without first installing a printer driver, the error message "No printer available" is displayed. If the user does not know how to install a network printer, the user will probably click **OK** or **Cancel** and call the support staff for assistance.

In Office XP, you can extend error messages — that is, you can customize some error messages to direct users to more information about the error encountered. To do so, link a custom button in the error message box to additional information on a Web site. By pointing the user to comprehensive or updated information on a Web site, you potentially reduce user frustration and increase productivity.

For example, you can create a button in the "No printer available" error message box to connect users to an intranet site with instructions for installing a network printer.

Extending custom error messages on a network

Some Office XP error messages are extended by default, leading users directly to the Microsoft Office Web site. However, you can extend these error messages to point to a site on your intranet. Additionally, there are error messages that are not extended by default that you can also customize.

Whether you customize an error message or redirect a default error message, you must create Web pages with information for how users can either correct or understand the problem encountered. If you redirect a user to a Web page for each custom error, you must also provide an Active Server Pages (ASP pages) file that resides on the Web site to manage which Web page is displayed to a user.

Expanding the use of custom error messages

Linking a custom error message to a Web page that contains information for solving a problem is helpful to the user. But if you create your own Active Server Pages (ASP pages) file, you can apply custom solutions to benefit you and the support staff — not just the users.

If you create an ASP file to customize error messages, your technical support staff should benefit by:

- Receiving fewer calls for assistance

    Custom error messages can help reduce calls to the support staff. For example, you can link a "Server is down" error message to a Web page through an ASP file to analyze the occurrence of the error message and also include a segment of script code to notify the support staff that a user has probably experienced a possible network problem.

    When a server goes down, you can also link the error message to a Web page with status information about the server or the network. When the users see that you are working on the problem, they are less likely to flood the support staff with calls for technical assistance.

- Collecting valuable information about errors users encounter

    You can take custom error message routing a step further and create an ASP file to collect and forward information about error messages to the support staff through e-mail or a pager. This use of customized error messages keeps the support staff informed about current issues and helps them respond faster.

Suppose your organization has a system of Help pages in an intranet site, and you have linked error messages to those pages by using the **Help Desk** button in each error message box. With an ASP file you redirect users from the Help information on your intranet site to either a Web page or a generic Help site where the user can selectively browse for more information.

The following shows how an ASP script is used in extending error messages:

1. When a user encounters an error message, the user can click the **Help Desk** button for more information.

2. The ASP file checks the error message number, determines which Web page applies, and then redirects the user's browser to that Web page.

3. If the error message number does not match any of the predefined error message numbers listed in the ASP file, the ASP script can connect the user to a generic Help page for more information (see the `case else` script language usage).

> **Toolbox** You can look up detailed information about custom error messages (including error numbers and error categories) in the Microsoft Excel workbook Errormsg.xls. Errormsg.xls is installed by default when you run the Office Resource Kit Setup program. For more information, see "Supplemental Documentation" in the Toolbox.

Creating custom error messages

The task of creating and implementing your own custom error message consists of the following four steps:

1. Gather error numbers, globally unique identifiers (GUIDs) for each application, and country codes.
2. Create Web pages that are linked to your custom error message.
3. Create the ASP files for your custom error message.
4. Activate the custom error message.

> **Note** This process documents extending a custom error message through the use of ASP scripting. If you want to use a Common Gateway Interface (CGI) script, refer to the CGI reference manual for more information about CGI scripting.

At the end of this process, you have the following components:

- A functioning ASP page
- A Web page with information or help about your custom error message
- Updated Windows registries on users' computers
- Functioning custom error messages

Gathering information for custom error messages

The first step in extending an error message is to collect the following information:

- Error message number

  Each error message in an application has a number, which is stored in the registry. For example, error message number 2202 in Microsoft Access is "You must install a printer before you design, print, or preview." This number is not required if you plan to redirect all error messages to a single Web page.

- GUID

    A globally unique identifier (GUID) identifies the application to which the error message belongs. The GUID is required and can be found by adding the following line of code to either a macro, module, or running it directly from the Immediate Window of the Visual Basic Editor.

    `MsgBox Application.ProductCode`

    The GUID for each release of an Office application changes for each build. This means, the SR-1 release is going to be different than the original release of the product. If you implement custom error message handling, you may be required to update the ASP files if they identify the application that called it by the GUID it submits with the error it spawns.

- Country code (the LCID, or locale ID)

    If you plan to redirect error messages based on the current default language of Office, you must provide the LCID, which allows the ASP script to determine the locale of Office XP. This parameter is only necessary if you are in a multilingual environment. Find the LCID by running the following command from the Immediate Window in Visual Basic® for each application:

    `MsgBox Application.LanguageSettings.LanguageID(msoLanguageIDUI)`

    You can replace the `msoLanguageIDUI` with other parameters to find the language for the installed Help, EXE mode, previous install language, and the "installed" (default) language the application was installed to use. Usually, you want to test for the user interface language since that determines what language the user was working in when the error occurred. Testing for the Help language might be helpful for instances when the Help system is the "native" language spoken where the application is being used.

Toolbox You can look up detailed information about custom error messages (including error numbers and error categories) in the Microsoft Excel workbook Errormsg.xls. Errormsg.xls is installed by default when you run the Office Resource Kit Setup program. For more information, see "Supplemental Documentation" in the Toolbox.

Creating a Web page for custom error messages

You must create a Web page to provide users with custom information for error messages they encounter. For example, when a user encounters the "No printer found" error message and then clicks the button linked to the intranet Web site, you must have a Web page describing how to solve the printer error problem.

You can redirect multiple error messages to a single Web page if you need to. If properly created, you can use one Web page to handle multiple error messages and reduce the number of registry entries. A single Web page is also the best solution if you do not want to create an ASP script.

If you choose to implement an ASP script, place your Web pages on your server and put the ASP file in the root directory of the Web server to which you are pointing custom error messages.

> **Toolbox** For simple implementations of customizable error messages, such as a general question and answer page, start with the following sample Web pages: Alert.asp, Alert.htm, Alert2.asp, Alert2a.asp, and NYI.htm. These files are installed by default when you run the Office Resource Kit Setup program. For more information, see "Supplemental Documentation" in the Toolbox.

Creating an ASP file for custom error messages

When users click the custom button in an error message box, an Active Server Pages script directs their browsers to a Web page that provides information about the error and allows them to take action accordingly.

> **Tip** ASP files are designed to only run on Microsoft Windows® operating systems. For optimal performance, use Windows NT® Server 4.0 or later and Internet Information Server (IIS).

There are three ways to create or update an ASP file. You can:

- Use the ASP generator

    The ASP generator (an Excel workbook called Aspscrpt.xls) is the quickest and easiest way to create a generic ASP file. However, not all programming or scripting options are available, and the script cannot handle large numbers of error messages. You need Excel 97 or later to use the ASP generator.

- Modify a sample ASP script

    This method requires a minimal knowledge of Microsoft Visual Basic programming and is made easier if you use the Microsoft Script Editor available in Microsoft Word. This method allows for a quick start and the ability to use all programming and scripting options available for ASP scripts.

- Write your own script

    This method requires knowledge of Visual Basic programming language, ASP scripting, and the Microsoft Script Editor (though you can use a text editor if you prefer). It also requires extra development time and a more extensive knowledge of scripting and Visual Basic. It is advised to copy an existing ASP script to get started.

Use the ASP generator

If you are going to create ASP files for a small number of custom error messages, the simplest solution is to use the ASP generator (Aspscrpt.xls). The template requires information about each error message you are going to customize.

> **Toolbox** Use the Excel workbook Aspscrpt.xls (ASP generator) to create an ASP file for handling custom error messages. You need to know the error message number, GUID, and LCID for each custom error message, as noted in the "Gathering information for custom error messages" section earlier in this topic. Aspscrpt.xls is installed by default when you run the Office Resource Kit Setup program. For more information, see "Supplemental Documentation" in the Toolbox.

To use the ASP generator, you need the following:

- Excel 97 or later
- An intranet Web server running Windows NT Server 4.0 with Service Pack 6a or Windows 2000 Server
- The ASP extensions included with Windows NT Server 4.0 with Service Pack 6a or included with the Windows NT Server 4.0 Option Pack installed on the network computer
- The GUID for each application you want to trap and redirect error messages for. You can find the GUID for each application by running the following command from the Immediate Window of the Visual Basic Editor from each application:

    `MsgBox Application.ProductCode`

    Running this command displays the literal GUID you need to supply (including the brackets) to the ASP. Substitute the `MsgBox` command with either `Print` or `?` (question mark) to obtain a textual printout you can copy into your code.

- The LCID for each application

    Find the LCID by running the following command from the Immediate Window in Visual Basic for each application:

    `MsgBox Application.LanguageSettings.LanguageID(msoLanguageIDUI)`

    You can replace the `msoLanguageIDUI` with other parameters to find the language for the installed Help, EXE mode, previous install language, and the "installed" (default) language the application was installed to use.

To generate an ASP file

1. Start Excel, and open the file Aspscrpt.xls.
2. In the **Enter the default URL for error messages not listed below** text box, type the URL of the default Web page.

   The default Web page is a generic page used to handle all error messages without a unique Web page assigned to them.
3. In the **Enter the physical, or actual, path of the base URL** text box, type the path to the destination directory where the new ASP file is stored.
4. Fill in the LCID, Microsoft Installer GUID, Error Message Number, and URL to the Destination Web Page columns for any error messages you want to customize.
5. Click **Go**.

   The new ASP file is created and stored where you specified.

Modify a sample ASP script

If you plan to implement a larger number of custom error messages, you can modify a sample ASP script.

> **Toolbox** The Office Resource Kit includes sample ASP and HTML files to help you create a custom error message system. Create your own ASP and HTML files from the files Alert.asp, Alert.htm, Alert2.asp, Alert2a.asp, and NYI.htm. These sample files are installed by default when you run the Office Resource Kit Setup program. For more information, see "Supplemental Documentation" in the Toolbox.

Example Code #1

The following ASP code from the sample file Alert.asp handles four custom printer-related error messages (remember, the GUID used may not apply in your situation, so use `Msgbox Application.ProductCode` to be sure you are testing for the correct GUID):

```
<% response.expires=0
alertNum=request.queryString("alrt")
LCID=request.queryString("HelpLCID")
GUID=request.queryString("DCC")

select case (alertNum & GUID & LCID)
case "197573{00000409-78E1-11D2-B60F-006097C998E7}1033"   ' for Word
   response.redirect("http://helpdesk/office10alerts/printer.htm")
case "197574{00000409-78E1-11D2-B60F-006097C998E7}1033"   ' for Word
   response.redirect("http://helpdesk/office10alerts/printer.htm")
case "197575{00000409-78E1-11D2-B60F-006097C998E7}1033"   ' for Word
   response.redirect("http://helpdesk/office10alerts/printer.htm")
case "197576{00000409-78E1-11D2-B60F-006097C998E7}1033""  ' for Word
   response.redirect("http://helpdesk/office10alerts/printer.htm")
case else
   response.redirect(http://helpdesk/office10alerts/FAQ.htm)
end select %>
```

Example Code #2

The following script code may be easier to maintain for large numbers of custom error messages. The case structure allows you to group all the LCID messages together in one place. Then the script tests for all the GUIDs and then the error message number. This process might run slightly faster on most systems.

```
<% response.expires=0
alertNum=""&request.queryString("alrt")
LCID=request.queryString("HelpLCID")
GUID=request.queryString("DCC")

select case (LCID)
case "<insert LCID for Language here>"
    select case (GUID)
    case "<insert GUID for Word here>"
        select case (alertNum)
        case "197573"
            response.redirect("http://helpdesk/officealerts/wdprinter.htm")
        case "197574"
            response.redirect("http://helpdesk/officealerts/wdprinter.htm")
        case else
            response.redirect("http://helpdesk/officealerts/wdFAQ.htm")
        end select
case "<insert GUID for Excel here>"
    select case (alertNum)
    case "197573"
        response.redirect("http://helpdesk/officealerts/xlprinter.htm")
    case "197574"
        response.redirect("http://helpdesk/officealerts/xlprinter.htm")
    case else
        response.redirect("http://helpdesk/officealerts/xlFAQ.htm")
    end select
case else
    response.redirect("http://helpdesk/officealerts/catchall.htm")
end select
case else
    response.redirect("http://helpdesk/officealerts/NoSuchLCID.htm")
end select %>
```

To modify this sample script for your custom error messages, open the file in Microsoft FrontPage® or another ASP editor and substitute the GUID variables (everything within the double quotes after the `case` statement) with your own values.

The following values and variables are used in the sample ASP scripts:

- Error message ID number

    The number immediately after the word `case` is the error message ID number.

- GUID

    This 32-character number is the globally unique identifier (GUID). The ASP script uses this number to determine which application spawned the error message. There is only one GUID for each Office application. Use the `Application.ProductCode` command in Visual Basic to find the GUID for each application.

- LCID

    This number is used to identify the locale of Office XP. The LCID for the currently configured "default" language (**Tools** menu, **Language**, **Set Language…**, **Language** dialog) is the number supplied (regardless of the install language).

- response.redirect

    This function of the script language instructs the operating system to start the Web browser and display the Web page associated with the error message.

- case

    This is a programming-related function of the Visual Basic programming language. A case "statement" is similar to an "if" statement in most other programming languages. Whatever appears to the right of the case statement is considered the test condition of the information supplied in the `select case` function statement.

    If the information passed to the ASP file from the Office application that spawned an error message matches the information in the case statement, then the `response.redirect` action is initiated — in this case, the Web page assigned to an extended error message is displayed.

    All of the error messages in this sample script reference the same Web page. Any error messages not covered in a case statement are directed to the FAQ.htm Web page (the `case else` test condition is a catchall for any errors not tested for in previous case statements). A `case else` must ALWAYS be the last entry in the `select case` series of test conditions. You can easily add new case test conditions with `response.redirect` functions calling other Web pages by copying an existing entry and pasting it anywhere between the `select case` and `case else` statements. Then change the Web page called in the `response.redirect` function.

    Note Two additional sample scripts, Alert2.asp and Alert2a.asp, provide examples of how you can extend the functionality of the ASP file. Alert2.asp prompts users to enter an explanation of the error. After users type their feedback and click **Submit**, they are redirected to Alert2a.asp, which contains a message thanking them for their feedback.

Write your own ASP file from scratch

You can write your own ASP file by using the Microsoft Script Editor available in the Microsoft Word **Macro…** dialog (**Tools** menu) or JavaScript, both of which are supported by Windows NT Server and IIS. When you write your own ASP file, you can add the ability to capture information about an error and use it to perform more advanced actions.

For example, a custom ASP file can generate dynamic HTML or redirect a browser to go to a different page, depending on the values sent to the ASP file from the browser. It can also capture the values from an error message and write them to a log file. A network administrator can use the log file to help solve common network problems.

Activating custom error messages

You activate a custom error message by setting a registry entry that is recognized by each application. You can use any of the following tools to set a registry entry:

- Custom Installation Wizard (**Add Registry Entries** page)

    Be sure to use the correct error number and text.

- Custom Maintenance Wizard (**Add Registry Entries** page)

    Be sure to use the correct error number and text.

- Office Profile Wizard

    You can add the registry settings to a test computer and modify OPW10adm.ini to capture the settings and install them on a user's computer.

- System policy

    You can add a system policy using the template (ADM file) for each application. Look for the customizable error messages policy branch.

    Note When you enable custom error messages by using a system policy, the policy settings override any existing custom error messages registered in the HKEY_CURRENT_USER\Software\Microsoft\Office\10.0*Application* \CustomizableAlerts subkey.

To activate all custom error messages, add the following registry key to a user's registry if the key isn't already there:

HKEY_CURRENT_USER\Software\Microsoft\Office\10.0\Common\General \CustomizableAlertBaseURL

The error message number, GUID, and LCID are automatically appended to the URL by the application that spawned an error. This allows the ASP script to correctly route the user to the Web page that contains more information about an error. For the ASP file to function properly, append a question mark (?) to the end of the URL. This allows you to pass the error message number, GUID, and LCID as parameters for use within the ASP file. The following is an example of a base URL:

```
http://localhost/mypage.asp?
```

The default BaseURL shipping with Office XP is:

```
http://OfficeUpdate.Microsoft.com/office/redirect/fromOffice9/ExtendedAle
rts.htm?DPC=%ProductCode%&AppName=ApplicationName%&HelpLCID=%HelpLang%&UI
Lang=%UILang%&
```

If you choose to configure your ASP file to handle any additional parameters, such as the computer name, you will need to add an ampersand (&) to the end of the registry value string so the default parameters are added when the link is activated. The following is an example of a base URL query string:

```
http://localhost/mypage.asp?ComputerName=%CompName%&
```

When you change the URL, you can also update the custom button text that appears on the error dialog by using the following registry subkey:

HKEY_CURRENT_USER\Software\Microsoft\Office\10.0\Common\General
\CustomizableAlertDefaultButtonText

Adding text to this button should be short and include an ampersand (for a hotkey) that is not used elsewhere on the error dialog.

Activating a custom error message

If you want to enable a single error message, add an entry for the error message to the following registry subkey (substitute *Application* with Word, Excel, etc):

HKEY_CURRENT_USER\Software\Microsoft\Office\10.0*Application*\CustomizableAlerts

Each registry entry has a related name and value entry. The registry name is the numeric ID for the error message, and the registry value is the custom text you add for users to see on the custom button for the error message.

For example, to add a custom error message for error message number 46 (a printer error) in Word, you can change the following registry subkey:

HKEY_CURRENT_USER\Software\Microsoft\Office\10.0\Word\CustomizableAlerts

Value name:	**46**
Data type:	**REG_SZ** (string)
Value data:	"**<custom text>**"

Add custom text to the button similar to:

```
&Printer Help
```

The "&" allows use of the ALT+P shortcut key combination by the user to activate the custom error action.

Activating custom error messages with a system policy

Custom error messages activate when the correct value settings are entered into the Windows registry. Each computer on your network must be updated to activate custom error messages completely, after you have created an Active Server Pages file. You can activate one or all of the custom error messages by using the System Policy Editor.

Activate all error messages with a system policy

If you want to enable all custom error messages for all Office XP applications, use the System Policy Editor to set the following policy in the policy tree:

Microsoft Office XP | Customizable error messages | Base URL

Your new URL must point to the ASP page you created for the custom error messages. The error message number, GUID, and LCID are automatically appended to this base URL so the ASP script can correctly supply the defined HTML page. For the ASP file to function properly, you must type a question mark (?) at the end of the URL to submit the error message number, GUID, and LCID parameters to the ASP page. The following is an example of a base URL:

```
http://localhost/mypage.asp?
```

If you decide to create an ASP file to handle any additional parameters, such as the computer name, add an ampersand (&) to the end of the query string. The following is an example of a base URL with a parameter named CompName added:

```
http://localhost/mypage.asp?ComputerName=%CompName%&
```

Activate one error message with a system policy

If you want to activate a single error message, use the System Policy Editor to add an entry for the error message to the **List of error messages to customize** policy.

For example, to add a custom error message to Word, enforce the following policy:

Microsoft Word 2002 | Customizable error messages \ List of error messages to customize

In the **Settings for List of error messages to customize** work area, click the **Show** button. Click **Add...**, and then type the name and value for the error message. The name is the numeric ID for the error message, and the value is the text for the custom button for the error message (what the user sees on the button).

Removing or disabling custom error messages

You might decide to disable or remove one or more custom error messages. For example, if you do not want users to have access to the Internet and you do not want to redirect them to an intranet site, you can disable or remove all custom error messages.

You can use a system policy to disable or remove custom error messages. Setting a system policy to "clear" removes that selected policy from a user's computer when the policy file is implemented on the primary domain controller.

You can also use the Custom Maintenance Wizard to remove or disable custom error messages by navigating to the **Change Office User Settings** page and searching for the **Customizable error messages** entries within each application and setting them appropriately.

> **Note** If you disable a custom error message, the custom button in the error message box no longer appears. The error message will function as originally designed.

Disabling custom error messages for all applications

If you want to disable all custom error messages for all Office XP applications, delete the URL in the following registry subkey:

HKEY_CURRENT_USER\Software\Microsoft\Office\10.0\Common\General
\CustomizableAlertBaseURL

The **CustomizableAlertBaseURL** entry is the master switch for custom error messages. If a URL is not listed in this entry, none of the error messages in Office are customizable.

When you remove the URL, be sure to remove any custom button text from the associated registry subkey:

HKEY_CURRENT_USER\Software\Microsoft\Office\10.0\Common\General
\CustomizableAlertDefaultButtonText

Disabling custom error messages for a single application

If you want to disable all custom error messages for a single application, such as Microsoft Word, remove any customized error message listed in the following registry subkey:

HKEY_CURRENT_USER\Software\Microsoft\Office\10.0*Application*
\CustomizableAlerts

Removing a single custom error message

If you want to remove a single error message, delete the entry for that error message from the following registry subkey:

HKEY_CURRENT_USER\Software\Microsoft\Office\10.0*Application*
\CustomizableAlerts

Each registry entry consists of a name and a value. The name is the numeric ID for the error message, and the value is the text you added to change the text that appears on the custom button in the error message box.

For example, to remove a custom error message for error message number 46 (a printer error) in Word, you would delete the following registry value entry:

HKEY_CURRENT_USER\Software\Microsoft\Office\10.0\Word\CustomizableAlerts

Value Name: **46**

Disabling custom error messages after deploying Office

If you have already deployed Office XP, and you want to disable or remove custom error messages, you can use the System Policy Editor.

Disable all custom messages for all Office applications

If you want to disable all custom error messages for all Office XP applications, use the System Policy Editor to clear the following policy:

Microsoft Office XP   Customizable error messages | Base URL

Disable all custom messages for a single application

If you want to disable all custom error messages for a single application, such as Microsoft Word, use the System Policy Editor to clear the application's **List of error messages to customize** policy.

For example, to remove custom error messages from Word, you would follow the policy path **Default User | Microsoft Word 2002 | Customizable error messages** and clear the **List of error messages to customize** check box.

Remove a single custom error message

If you want to remove a single error message, remove the entry for that error message from the **List of error messages to customize** policy.

For example, to remove a specific custom error message from Word, use the following policy:

Microsoft Word 2002 | Customizable error messages | List of error messages to customize

In the **Settings for List of error messages to customize** area, click **Show**, and then select the **Value Name** and click the **Remove** button.

If you do not want to enable custom error messages for your organization, you can disable them by using the Office Custom Installation Wizard or Custom Maintenance Wizard to remove the URL entry from your users' registries.

The System Policy Editor is another tool you can use to disable custom error messages by removing the URL entry from your users' registries.

Creating Custom Help Topics

You can expand the scope of built-in Microsoft Office XP Help by using Microsoft HTML Help Workshop and the Microsoft Answer Wizard Builder to create and distribute custom Help topics. Users gain access to those topics by using the Office Help system and the Office Assistant.

Using Microsoft HTML Help Workshop

Help for applications can be created by using Microsoft HTML Help Workshop or an HTML text editor. The associated Help file available with HTML Help Workshop is an excellent source of information that explains what is required to create Help content. Included within the Help for HTML Help Workshop are several recommendations for how to configure your help project to best suit your needs, as well as the required steps you must take to create and call the Help from within an application. HTML Help Workshop can also be used to test your Web site or compiled Help, but if you prefer, you can use a Web browser to test and navigate that content.

Help content you create and compile with HTML Help Workshop is displayed by an Office application, or an application you have developed, by using the Microsoft HTML Help application that ships with Office. The HTML Help application can use either CHM files (compressed HTML Help metafile) or HTML content in a Web site as a source. Content destined for compilation by HTML Help Workshop can come from an HTML text editor, Microsoft FrontPage, Microsoft Word, or HTML Help Workshop itself. To compile help content into a CHM file, all you need to do is install HTML Help Workshop and perform the necessary steps to do a build.

To add custom Help to an existing Office application, you must create new Help topics and a new Answer Wizard (AW) file. Depending on the number of new topics you need to create, the effort required to create an additional help source and AW file can vary greatly. A few topics with very little cross-references or links is relatively easy. The more topics you add and the number of links you add to other sources or topics greatly increases the amount of effort necessary to create a complete, consistent, and stable Help source.

To modify an existing custom Help system (other than the Office Help system) for a custom-built application, you must have the original HTML files used to create the Help. Having these materials is required if you plan to delete any topics from the custom system and then recompile all topics into one CHM file. Access to the original Help source materials for an application is not required if you are only adding topics and creating a new AW file.

If you need to ignore some topics in your Help system, it is possible to selectively ignore topics by clearing the check box in the **Topics** frame for each topic in the Answer Wizard Builder. When set to unchecked, the topic is not included in the probability index and, therefore, never appears in the Office Assistant **What would you like to do?** dialog.

Customizing Help content for users

Microsoft Office XP allows you to create and distribute custom Help content for users. For instance, you can use custom Help to explain new features you have added to Office or instruct how to use a template or form. When a user asks the Office Assistant a question about a custom feature, applicable topics will appear in the search list generated by the Answer Wizard, and the topics will look like built-in Help.

Creating and distributing custom Help content for use in Office Help involves the following steps:

- Creating HTML-compatible Help files

    Custom Help topics can be HTML Help files that reside on a Web site, or compressed HTML (CHM) Help files that you distribute to users' computers or store on a network server. The Answer Wizard Builder analyzes the words contained in these files when it indexes your topics.

- Creating a custom Answer Wizard (AW) file

    The Microsoft Answer Wizard Builder stores your custom Help topics in a project file (AWB file) that is used to build an AW file — an index that is searched by the Answer Wizard in response to users' queries.

- Registering the custom Help files

    To make your custom Help content available to users, copy the new AW file to each user's computer and update each user's Windows registry for the AW file. The next time a user asks the Office Assistant a question, the custom Help content automatically becomes part of the Answer Wizard results list.

Creating custom Help content

Creating custom Help topics involves these steps:

- Choosing a custom Help file format (HTML or CHM files)

    Each file type has its advantages and disadvantages, depending upon your needs — namely, how you plan to store the Help files, and how often you plan to update them.

- Creating the custom HTML topics

    If you want to create, format, and link HTML Help topics, you can use any HTML editor. If you want to create CHM files, install Microsoft HTML Help Workshop and compile your custom Help. You have the option of compiling HTML pages into a CHM file when your custom Help is complete.

Choosing a Help file format

The format you choose for your Help files also depends on where you plan to store the files and how often you need to update the content. Custom Help topics can be stored on a user's computer, on a server, or hosted on a Web site. Each file type has its advantages and disadvantages, depending upon your needs.

Advantages of using HTML Help

HTML Help files can be stored on either a Web server or a network file share. If they are stored on either of these, the following advantages apply:

- You can update Help content in one place and not have to worry about deploying or updating it on individual computers.
- No hard-disk space is required on a user's computer.
- If you already have a Web-based Help site, you can use its contents to create the custom AW file.
- You do not have to register Web-based Help on each user's computer.
- HTML Help does not require a hosted Web site to display Help content.

Disadvantages to using HTML Help files include the following:

- If you use HTML Help files hosted on a Web site, users must have access to the Web.
- If a Web server is used to host the Help files, you must also maintain the Web server and site.
- If a Web server or network file server share is used, users might experience slow response times when they submit queries due to network traffic or Web site loading.

Advantages of using compressed HTML Help (CHM)

A CHM file is a compressed HTML Help metafile. You can take the equivalent of an entire Web site and compile it into a CHM. It uses a special technology to combine HTML files into one file with a special directory, index, and file structure similar to a compressed drive. A CHM file can only be read by the HTML Help system and Microsoft Internet Explorer. CHM files are created by HTML Help Workshop and require creating a special project and build area where you create and organize Help topics in HTML format.

Access to CHM files can be obtained through a network share or locally on a user's computer. CHM files offer the following advantages over other file types:

- CHM files can be compressed, taking up less hard-disk space and providing more portability than an entire Web site.
- Users get faster results when the CHM file is stored locally.

- A single CHM file can contain an entire Web site of HTML files.
- Users do not need access to the Web or the network.

If you use CHM Help files, you must deploy them to each client computer whenever you update the content.

Disadvantages to using CHM files include the following:

- You are required to register the CHM before it can be used.

    However, once it is registered, it does not need to be registered again.

- You are required to recompile the file every time a change is made to the Help system.
- You are required to redistribute the Help file each time a CHM file is modified.
- CHM files take up hard-disk space on the user's computer, if posted locally.

The rule of thumb for creating CHM files is based on how often your Help will change. If your Help changes frequently, it is probably better to leave your Help in HTML pages and post them on a file server where everyone can gain access to them, and where you can update them easily.

If your content rarely changes, you can create CHM files with Microsoft HTML Help Workshop. This compresses the HTML pages and makes a nice, portable single file for your Help system.

Creating custom Help topics

Once you choose what format you will use for your custom Help topics, you can begin creating your topics. Where you start the process of creating custom Help depends on what format your Help files are in. If you have CHM files or Help topics in WinHelp format, you can import them into HTML Help Workshop. If you have HTML Help topics already posted on a Web site, you can point the Answer Wizard Builder to the Web site.

Start with WinHelp sources

Many companies already have custom Help that exists in Windows Help format (winhlp or winhlp32). Microsoft HTML Help Workshop can automatically convert the source files for these to HTML.

After converting your source files, use HTML Help Workshop to create a CHM file from the new HTML files.

Follow the procedure below to convert the source files for an existing Winhelp Help system to HTML Help.

To convert an existing Help project to an HTML Help project

1. On the **File** menu, click **New**, and then click **Project**.
2. Select the **Convert WinHelp project** check box, and then click **Next**.
3. Specify the location of the existing Help project (.hpj) file you want to convert.
4. Specify a location and name for the new HTML Help project you are creating, click **Next**, and then click **Finish**.

Note All the files referenced by the existing Help project (.hpj) file must be in the locations specified or the conversion process will fail. HTML Help Workshop converts the entire project as defined in the WinHelp project file.

Start with HTML files

If your Help content is currently in HTML format, you can create an AW file by creating an Answer Wizard Builder project with the URL to the Web site or the drive where the HTML files are currently stored.

If you need to edit or update HTML files, modify them first by using an HTML editing tool (such as FrontPage) or HTML Help Workshop.

You can also use HTML Help Workshop to create a new CHM file based on existing HTML files. If you create a Help system with fairly static information, a CHM file is a good solution. If your Help information will change frequently, it is a good idea to post the HTML files on a server accessible by all users and direct the AW to use the files in that location.

Start with compressed HTML files

If users do not have access to the Web, intranet, or are frequently accessing Help from portable systems, you can use HTML Help Workshop to create CHM files and store them either on the network or local to the user's computer. You can use your existing CHM files with the Answer Wizard Builder or, if they need editing, modify them first by using HTML Help Workshop.

When using CHM files to create an Answer Wizard (AW) file, you have the option of not including topics in the results list. By doing so, the Answer Wizard ignores the topics you do not include in the result list. For more information, see "Making Custom Help Accessible" in Chapter 11, "Creating Custom Help."

Start from scratch

If you do not have any existing content, you can create your own Help topics in HTML Help Workshop or in any other HTML authoring tool (FrontPage, Word, text editors). Then use the Answer Wizard Builder to create the AW file from the HTML or CHM Help content.

For help in developing an HTML Help system, consult the Help for Microsoft HTML Help Workshop.

Making custom Help content look like built-in Help

If you want your custom Help to look like the built-in Office XP Help system, create HTML files using the two Microsoft cascading style sheets provided with the Office Resource Kit. Then add your custom Help content to the Answer Wizard with the Answer Wizard Builder. Accessing Help content through the Answer Wizard ensures your Help uses the same window definitions and functionality as Office Help.

> **Toolbox** HTML Help Workshop helps you create custom HTML Help content for use with the Office Help system. To help you create files that look like Office Help files, the Office Help cascading style sheet files are included. For more information on installing HTML Help Workshop, see "HTML Help Workshop" in the Toolbox.

The Office Resource Kit includes the two cascading style sheets Office10.css and startpag.css. The Office10.css is the main style sheet used for all basic Help topics. The startpag.css style sheet is used for the main start page for each Office application main Help (for example: **Help** menu, **Microsoft Word Help** option). Attach the appropriate cascading style sheet to each HTML file in your project, and use the defined styles when you format the Help text within each topic.

To view the HTML source for help files

1. Start an Office application.
2. Enter a question in the Office Assistant.
3. Right-click on the displayed Help file.
4. Select **View Source**.

The HTML source will display in the Notepad editor.

> **Note** To view the definitions for each style in a cascading style sheet file, open the file with a text editor. Each style is listed, along with the formatting specifications for that style, such as font and size.

To provide easy access to the style sheets, store each style sheet in the same folder where the HTML Help source files are stored and add the following code to the header in each HTML page:

```
<LINK rel=stylesheet type="text/css" href="Office10.css">
<LINK REL="stylesheet" HREF="startpag.css" type="text/css">
```

The user's Web browser determines which cascading style sheet file is used when the HTML page is opened.

Both Office10.css and startpag.css are for Microsoft Internet Explorer 4.02 or later.

Making Custom Help Content Accessible

Microsoft Office XP allows administrators the option to create and distribute Help topics unique to their organization, expanding the usefulness of an application's built-in Help. The Answer Wizard links custom Help to users through a natural language interface. When a user enters a question into the Office Assistant, the Answer Wizard returns a list of Help topics applicable to the question.

Requirements for building a custom Help system

The Answer Wizard uses an index (AW file) of your custom Help topics generated by the Answer Wizard Builder as the source for deriving answers to user questions. Before you can use the Answer Wizard tools, you must have a Help system in place. A Help system requires:

- One or more topics (each topic is only one HTML file)
- That all topics are stored in either a CHM file or the equivalent of an HTML Web site

So, to create a complete Help system, you must create a topic for each portion of the product users are trying to use, and then provide an answer for each of the major questions a user might ask about the product. After topics are documented and compiled into the help, you can then optionally assign user questions to each topic with the Answer Wizard Builder.

> **Note** The CHM file you use must have been compiled with all the Help topics (HTML files) one directory below where the CHM file is created. If the CHM file references all the files at the root of the project, the HTML Help will not find the Help content.

HTML Help is the utility used to display Help topics. HTML Help can use two types of files for Help topics, HTML files and CHM files (a CHM file is a compilation of HTML files in compressed format). A topic within a Help system is a single HTML file. Several HTML files configured similar to a Web site, or an Internet Information Server–hosted Web site, can be used as a Help system. HTML Help topics do not require a hosted Web site. The files only need to be arranged as if they are part of a Web site and do not require programs like Internet Information Server (IIS).

For more information on creating custom Help topics and choosing file formats, see "Creating Custom Help Topics" in Chapter 11, "Creating Custom Help."

Linking custom Help content to the Answer Wizard

If you want custom Help topics to be accessible from Office XP, you must first use the Answer Wizard Builder to create a project file (AWB file) where you store Help topic information. The Answer Wizard Builder then uses the project file to create an index (AW file) of your HTML Help topics. When users submit queries in Office Help, the Answer Wizard gathers the applicable information using the AW file and starts the HTML Help system that displays the information.

> **Note** Microsoft periodically publishes new AW files for download from the Microsoft Office Web site. The information in the AW files is based upon articles posted on the Microsoft Office Web site in response to customer feedback from Help on the Web, an Office feature. Each AW file is application-specific and replaces an existing AW file on the user's computer.

You can use the Answer Wizard Builder utility to add custom Help content to any application that uses the Office Assistant. However, the Answer Wizard Builder will only work on a computer that has Office XP installed.

Creating an Answer Wizard Builder project

The first step in making custom Help topics available to users is to create an Answer Wizard Builder (AWB) project file where information about your custom HTML Help topics is stored. You can then choose to assign user questions to custom Help topics to increase the searching power of the Answer Wizard.

To create an Answer Wizard Builder project

1. Click Start, point to Programs, point to **Microsoft Office Tools**, point to **Microsoft Office XP Resource Kit Tools**, and then click **Answer Wizard Builder**.

2. In the **Create a new Answer Wizard project** frame, click **CHM File** or **Web Site**.

   If you selected the **CHM File** option, enter the path to the CHM file in the text box. If you selected the **Web Site** option, enter the UNC or drive alias of the computer with a Web site and the share name of the drive where the Web files are stored (plus the path to a particular folder, if necessary) in the adjacent text box.

3. If you selected **Web Site,** add the **Virtual directory alias** (http://<URL>).

   The Virtual directory name is used by the Answer Wizard Builder as a dispatch string. The dispatch string is appended to the beginning of the HTML file name for the topics you select to be included in the AW file. This must be the location of the files in the Web site where Help is going to be called by the Answer Wizard. Leave this blank if you selected the **CHM File** option. You can use a drive letter or UNC if you prefer.

4. Optionally, you can set the language the Help file system was developed for (the default is English).

The Answer Wizard Builder parses the CHM or HTML files and populates the Answer Wizard project with the Help topic title information.

Refine Help responses with user questions

You can improve the searching power of the Answer Wizard by assigning user questions to each custom Help topic. Assigning questions refines the index, which allows the Answer Wizard to more accurately provide topics associated with a query.

The questions you assign should be specific to one topic and worded to reflect what a user might ask. Applying these guidelines will increase the probability that the Answer Wizard will return applicable topics. For example, you might select a topic about setting up a network printer and assign the question "What is the path to our department printer?"

> **Note** Adding user questions is optional and is not required for the Answer Wizard to function normally.

Guidelines for writing user questions

The questions you assign to Help topics are more useful if you follow these guidelines:

- For short Help topics, assigning two or three questions with different keywords is sufficient.
- For in-depth topics, assigning several questions with unique keywords provides a broader selection base for the Answer Wizard.
- Adding the topic title as a question adds no value.
- Rephrasing a question with the same words adds no value.

Examples of good question form (for a topic about formatting a paragraph) are:

- How do I select a paragraph?
- How do I format a paragraph?
- How do I change the hanging indent?
- How can I add space to the bottom of a paragraph?
- Where do I go to add blank space to the top of a paragraph?
- When aligning a paragraph, how do I set the left indent for the first line?

Adding a question to a topic

Refining the searching power of the Answer Wizard is easy but time consuming. Since the time required to refine the results is directly associated with how many questions you add and how quickly you add them, consider the amount of effort required to refine the answers from the wizard against the amount of increased benefit users will receive.

To add a question to a help topic

1. Start the Answer Wizard Builder.
2. Open an existing help project.
3. Select a topic from the **Topics** list.
4. Enter a question in the **Questions** text box.
5. Click **Add**.

   Repeat for each topic you want to add questions to and as many times as you feel necessary for a given topic.
6. Save the project.

When you are finished adding questions, build the AW file by selecting the **Build** option (**Tools** menu).

Building an Answer Wizard file

Once you have created an Answer Wizard Builder project file, use the Answer Wizard Builder to create an index (AW file) of your HTML Help topics. Because the Answer Wizard Builder uses a considerable amount of memory, you may want to close all other applications and run it on a separate workstation. It is not recommended to build AW files on a file server or Terminal Services enabled server.

To build a new custom Answer Wizard file

- In the Answer Wizard Builder, click the **Build** option (**Tools** menu).

   Tip Save the new AW file in the same folder where you saved the AWB project file.

When the build process completes, an AW file (with the same name as the project file) is available in the build directory.

Building an AW file is a time consuming process and can take many hours for large Help files. The speed of the processor on your computer and the amount of RAM available to the builder greatly affects the amount of time it takes to create the file.

   Note Answer Wizard Builder will only work on a computer where Office XP is installed.

Enabling custom Help

After you have created an index (AW file) of your Help topics, you need to make the file accessible to the user. Enabling custom Help requires knowing how the Office Help system is configured, and determining whether registry settings must be changed or new settings added.

To enable custom Help content and Answer Wizard files, you need to:

- Determine whether you are going to store the custom Help files on each user's computer or on a network share.

    Help files on a Web site do not need to be registered in the registry, but CHM files do. If you plan on redirecting users to Help on the Web, you need to change a registry setting for the URL.

- Deploy the custom Help files to each user's computer, or place the files on a network share.

    HTML Web pages are better suited for use on Web sites or network file servers. CHM files are best suited for use on a user's computer due to their smaller size and portability (though they will run just fine from a server). If the Help system is small and is not likely to change, CHM files are a good solution. If the Help content is subject to considerable change, use a Web-based solution.

- Update each user's Windows registry to point to the AW file created by the Answer Wizard Builder.

    There are separate registry entries for AW files and CHM files. You do not need to register regular HTML files.

    You can also store an AW file in any location as long as users have access to the location. Storing the AW file on a user's computer can improve access speed.

    Note If you make changes to an AW file or CHM file after it has been registered, you can replace the file with an updated version at any time. You do not need to register the file again, as long as you use the same file name and location.

You can use the Answer Wizard and custom Help with the following applications:

- Microsoft Access
- Microsoft Clip Organizer
- Microsoft Solution Designer
- Microsoft Excel
- Microsoft FrontPage
- Microsoft Graph
- Microsoft Outlook®
- Microsoft PhotoDraw®
- Microsoft PowerPoint®
- Microsoft Project
- Microsoft Publisher
- Microsoft Query
- Microsoft Word

Deploying custom Help with Office XP

If you have not yet deployed Office XP, you can use the Office Custom Installation Wizard to deploy the custom Help and AW files to each user's computer by:

- Adding the AW and CHM files to a transform using the **Add/Remove Files** page.
- Updating registries with paths to these new files with the **Add Registry Entries** page.

If you have already deployed Office XP, you have two options for deploying the custom AW and CHM files and correct registry settings to each user's computer:

- Custom Maintenance Wizard

  On the **Add/Remove Files** page, add the AW and CHM files. Then add the registry settings you need to activate the CHM and AW files to the **Add Registry Entries** page. Or go to the **Change Office User Settings** page and click the **Miscellaneous** entry for each application and add the AW file path and file name to the **Custom Answer Wizard database path** entry.

- Office Profile Wizard

  Using the Custom Installation Wizard, install Office to a test computer and configure all the user settings, Help, and any other supporting files to achieve a complete user configuration. Then use the Profile Wizard to capture those settings along with the necessary AW and CHM files. This may require making customizations to the OPW10adm.ini file to capture the AW and CHM files.

If you have deployed Office and have distributed the AW and CHM files accordingly, but have not registered the AW and CHM file to each user's computer, you can set the necessary registry settings on users' computers by using a system policy.

> **Tip** The easiest way to administer customized Help is to set up the custom Help content on a Web site, store the AW file on a network share, and then set the locations through system policies. By having everything stored on network servers, and having the file registration handled by system policies, you can avoid configuring the client computers individually. This method assumes users have a persistent network connection.

Register an Answer Wizard file

The Answer Wizard registry entry requires the use of the **REG_SZ** (string) data type. Create a unique name for the entry name and use the path where the AW file resides, including the AW file name, as the value.

The Answer Wizard subkeys are stored in the following location in the Windows registry:

HKEY_CURRENT_USER\Software\Microsoft\Office\10.0*ApplicationName*
\Answer Wizard

For example, if you create a new AW file called Plugins.aw for Word and place it in the C:\Program Files\Microsoft Office folder, add a new registry entry called **PluginsAW** to the following subkey:

HKEY_CURRENT_USER\Software\Microsoft\Office\10.0\Word\Answer Wizard

Value name	**PluginsAW**
Data type:	**REG_SZ** (string)

Then assign the following path as the value data:

C:\Program Files\Microsoft Office\plugins.aw

Register a CHM file

You can instruct the Custom Installation Wizard to register a CHM file while Office XP is installing, or you can register the CHM file manually after installation. Both of these methods require adding a new registry entry as part of the following subkey:

HKEY_LOCAL_MACHINE\Software\Microsoft\Windows\HTML Help

Value name:	"**<CHM file name>**"
Data type:	**REG_SZ** (string)

Use the CHM file name as the value name and the path where the CHM file resides as the value data. For example, if you create a new CHM file called Plugins.chm and place it in the C:\Program Files\Microsoft Office folder, add a new value entry called **Plugins.chm** and assign the following path as its value data:

C:\Program Files\Microsoft Office

Enable an AW file with a system policy

If you have already deployed Office XP, you can use a system policy to change the registry settings on all the computers in your organization at one time. From the **Default User** icon, navigate to the **Custom Answer Wizard database path** policy in the **Miscellaneous** category for each Office application. Set the policy to checked and enter the path and file name to the **Custom Answer Wizard database path** box.

> **Note** The System Policy Editor allows you to define one AW file per Office application. If you need to add more than one AW file, you must create a separate registry entry for each new file by using the Windows Registry Editor. Then you distribute the new registry entries by using either a configuration maintenance file (CMW file) or profile settings file (OPS file).

Linking the Answer Wizard to the Web

Help on the Web, a feature in Microsoft Office XP, connects users to information about Office XP on the Microsoft Office Web site. You can disable Help on the Web or customize it to point to a site on your intranet. You can also use Help on the Web to collect user feedback to improve your custom Answer Wizard files and custom Help topics.

Using and expanding Help on the Web

You can use the Help on the Web feature to extend built-in Help and technical support for users. This is a valuable option when users are not satisfied by the Help topics the Answer Wizard provides to a query.

Users typically gain access to Help on the Web through a link provided by the Office Assistant. When a user asks the Office Assistant a question, the Answer Wizard returns a list of Help topics, which includes the link **None of the above, look for more Help on the Web** as the last entry in the list.

Clicking this link connects users to a feedback form, where they can comment on their search. When they submit the feedback form, they are redirected to the Microsoft Office Web site, and their search is automatically repeated on the latest Office content. A list of Microsoft Knowledge Base articles relating to their search is displayed. When they click the **Send and go to the Web** button, their comments are collected and sent to Microsoft, where support engineers evaluate the data and use it to improve both Answer Wizard Help topics and the Microsoft Office Web site.

You can customize the Help on the Web link to redirect users to a site on your intranet instead, especially if your users do not have access to the World Wide Web. When users click **None of the above, look for more Help on the Web**, they could be redirected to an intranet site that includes a list of frequently asked questions (FAQs) relating to their search topic.

To redirect the Help on the Web URL link, change the Feedback URL. You can also customize the **None of the above...** text in the Office Assistant and the third paragraph in the Feedback form in the **Find Help Topics** topic. If you prefer not to use the Help on the Web feature at all, you can disable the link.

The following examples show you a few of the many ways you can customize Help on the Web to suit your needs:

- Direct users to a static page on an intranet Web site

    If you do not want to create a custom Active Server Pages (ASP) file, create a static Web page with a list of FAQs and a telephone number or an e-mail address users can use to contact your organization's support staff.

    To implement this solution, create the Web page, delete the third paragraph in the **Finding Help Topics** topic (feedback dialog text), and supply the static Web page address as the Feedback URL.

- Collect user questions to create or expand custom Help files

    This method requires that you create an ASP file.

    If you are considering creating a Help system in the future, you can collect current user questions without redirecting users to an external Web site. Later, you can implement a custom Help system with these questions to Help you refine an AW file.

    If you have already created custom Help and AW files for your organization, tracking user questions and comments can help you find ways to expand your custom Help. By using user created questions, you can research and write more topics and fine-tune your AW file for your custom Help, as well as supplement the online Help system for Office XP.

    To implement this solution, create an ASP file to log user questions and comments. Change the feedback button label from **None of the above...** to "Send us comments about your search," and change the third paragraph in the **Finding Help Topics** topic (feedback dialog text) to inform users that their comments are going to be sent to you. Change the Feedback URL to point to the ASP file you created, and the system will begin recording all submitted questions.

- Redirect searches to an intranet site

    This method requires that you create an ASP file.

    You can instruct Help on the Web to search for information from your intranet rather than the Microsoft Office Web site.

    To redirect users to your Web site, create an ASP file to search your organization's Web site. Change the feedback button label **None of the above...** text in the Office Assistant and the third paragraph in the **Finding Help Topics** topic (feedback dialog text) to tell users where their browsers are being redirected. Update the Feedback URL to point to your ASP file.

- Send questions to your support staff

    This method requires that you create an ASP file.

    You can use a custom ASP file for handling user questions. For example, users can fill in the feedback form with pertinent questions and comments. The system can automatically route the form to your support staff. After the form is submitted, users are redirected to a Web page with FAQs or are provided a link to a Web site they can use to search for more information.

Customizing Help on the Web

You can customize Help on the Web by changing any of the following items:

- Text in the Office Assistant
- Feedback dialog text in the Help pane
- Feedback URL

You can also disable Help on the Web if you do not want to make this feature available to users.

Customize text in the Office Assistant

You can customize the feedback button label text **None of the above, look for more Help on the Web**. For example, you can change the text to **Look for more Help on our local support Web site**.

You can change this text with either a system policy or with the Custom Maintenance Wizard.

To change the text in the Office Assistant with a policy

1. In the System Policy Editor, double-click the **Default User** icon.
2. Expand (click the plus (+) sign) the **Microsoft Office XP** node.
3. Expand the **Assistant** node.
4. Expand the **Help on the Web** node.
5. Set the **Feedback button label** check box to checked.
6. In the **Settings for Feedback button label** work area, type the text you want to use.

   Note The maximum number of characters for the feedback button label is 255 characters.

To change the text in the Office Assistant with the Custom Maintenance Wizard

1. Start the Custom Maintenance Wizard.
2. Open the MSI for the edition of Office you want to customize.
3. Navigate to the **Change Office User Settings** page.
4. Expand (click the plus (+) sign) the **Common Office Settings** node.
5. Select the **Assistant / Help on the Web** option.
6. Enter the text you want in the **Feedback button label** text box.
7. Save the CMW file.

Customize text in Finding Help Topics topic

You can customize the feedback dialog text (third paragraph of the topic) in the **Finding Help Topics** Help topic. By default, the following text appears in the middle of the Help topic, just below the repeated user question:

> Click the **Send and go to the Web** button below to launch Microsoft Internet Explorer and send your question to a site that provides further assistance. You can switch back to Help at any time.

You can change the text of this paragraph with either a system policy or with the Custom Maintenance Wizard.

To change the text in the Help window with a policy

1. In the System Policy Editor, double-click the **Default User** icon.
2. Expand (click the plus (+) sign) the **Microsoft Office XP** node.
3. Expand the **Assistant** node.
4. Expand the **Help on the Web** node.
5. Set the **Feedback dialog text** check box to checked.
6. In the **Settings for Feedback dialog text** work area, type the text you want to use.

   Note The maximum number of characters for the feedback dialog text is 255 characters.

To change the text in the Help window with the Custom Maintenance Wizard

1. Start the Custom Maintenance Wizard.
2. Open the MSI for the edition of Office you want to customize.
3. Navigate to the **Change Office User Settings** page.
4. Expand (click the plus (+) sign) the **Common Office Settings** node.
5. Select the **Assistant / Help on the Web** option.
6. Enter the text you want in the **Feedback dialog text** text box (or leave it blank).
7. Save the CMW file.

Customize the Feedback URL

By default, the Feedback URL in the Office Assistant points to the Microsoft Office Web site.

You can change this URL to an intranet Web site if you prefer by using the System Policy Editor or the Custom Maintenance Wizard.

To change the Feedback URL with a policy

1. In the System Policy Editor, double-click the **Default User** icon.
2. Expand (click the plus (+) sign) the **Microsoft Office XP** node.
3. Expand the **Assistant** node.
4. Expand the **Help on the Web** node.
5. Set the **Feedback URL** check box to checked.
6. In the **Settings for Feedback URL** work area, type the URL you want to use.

   Note The maximum number of characters for the feedback URL is 255 characters.

To change the Feedback URL with the Custom Maintenance Wizard

1. Start the Custom Maintenance Wizard.
2. Open the MSI for the edition of Office you want to customize.
3. Navigate to the **Change Office User Settings** page.
4. Expand (click the plus (+) sign) the **Common Office Settings** node.
5. Select the **Assistant / Help on the Web** option.
6. Enter the URL you want in the **Feedback URL** text box.
7. Save the CMW file.

Customizing the Answer Wizard Feedback form

When a user clicks **None of the above, look for Help on the Web** in the Office Assistant, the user is presented with a feedback form. This form is for entering a comment about the problem the user is experiencing and the type of Help topic the user expects the Assistant to return. If the user chooses to submit their comments, they are directed to the Microsoft Office Web site, where a search for applicable information is automatically run again using the user's original question.

If you want to redirect information to your organization's support staff, you can customize the feedback form and create a custom Active Server Pages (ASP pages) file to handle the information from the form.

To customize the feedback form, change the following three options in the sample Answiz.asp file.

Option	Description
F_log=1	Set to **0** to disable logging of users' questions. Default is **1**.
f_redirect_to_MS=1	Set to **0** to disable sending of information to the Microsoft Office Web site. Default is **1**.
Where_if_not_MS="alert.htm"	Set to the URL of the page you want users to see after they submit the feedback form. This option is valid only if you have set the redirect option to **0**.

Toolbox The Office Resource Kit includes a sample ASP file named Answiz.asp for customizing the Answer Wizard feedback form. This sample file is installed by default when you run the Office Resource Kit Setup program. For more information, see "Supplemental Documentation" in the Toolbox.

The following is an example of the Answiz.asp file.

```
<%
response.expires = 0

f_log = 1
f_redirect_to_MS = 1
where_if_not_MS = "alert.htm"
```

```
APP = request.form("app")           ' used
UQ = request.form("UQ")             ' used
UD = request.form("UD")             ' not used
IAP = request.form("IAP")           ' not used
HLCID = request.form("HLCID")       ' not used
OPC = request.form("OPC")           ' not used
OCC = request.form("OCC")           ' not used

if f_log = 1 then
    app=mid(app,11)
    what_tl_log=APP & ":" & UQ
    what_to_log=mid(what_to_log,1,80)
    response.appendToLog(what_to_log)
end if

if f_redirect_to_MS = 1 then
    redirloc = "http://www.Microsoft.com/office/"
    redirloc = redirloc&"redirect/fromOffice10/answerwizard.asp"

    public buffer
    public buff2
    quote = chr(34)
    LF = chr(10) & chr(13) ' carriage return and line feed

    function bufferwrite(x)
        buffer=buffer & x
    End Function

    buffer=""

    bufferwrite("<form action-" & redirloc & " method=post name=f>" & LF)
    for each i in request.form
    buff2=" name=" & quote & i & quote & " value=" & quote & _
    request.form(i) & quote
        bufferwrite("<input type=hidden" & buff2 & ">" & LF)
    next

bufferwrite("</form>")
    bufferflush
    %>
    <script language=javascript for=window event=onLoad()>
        <!--f.submit();-->
```

```
    </script>
    <%
else
    response.redirect(where_if_not_MS)
end if
%>
```

Disabling Office on the Web

Office on the Web is a portal to the Internet for more information about Office. This feature allows users the option of examining information about Office that may not have made it into the product documentation, issues about Office that have recently been discovered, or new enhancements or updates you can download. Some administrators do not like users having access to the Internet from any portion of Office and prefer to disable it.

If you want to disable the Office on the Web Help option, you use a system policy or the Custom Maintenance Wizard to do so. To disable Office on the Web with a policy setting, select the **Help | Office on the Web** option in the **Disable command bar buttons and menu items** policy for each application.

> **Note** The Office on the Web feature is automatically disabled if a default Web browser is not installed on the user's computer, or if a feedback URL is not defined in the Windows registry.

To redirect or disable Office on the Web for all Office applications with a policy

1. In the System Policy Editor, double-click the **Default User** icon.
2. Expand (click the plus (+) sign) the **Microsoft Office XP** node.
3. Expand the **Help | Office on the Web** node.
4. Set the **Office on the Web URL** check box to checked.
5. Under **Settings for Office on the Web URL** work area, set the **Office on the Web URL** text box to the URL you want to use (or leave it blank).

To redirect or disable Office on the Web for all Office applications from the Custom Maintenance Wizard

1. Start the Custom Maintenance Wizard.
2. Open the MSI for the edition of Office you want to customize.
3. Navigate to the **Change Office User Settings** page.
4. Expand (click the plus (+) sign) the **Common Office Settings** node.
5. Select the **Help | Office on the Web** option.
6. Enter an intranet web URL in the **Office on the Web URL** text box (or leave it blank).
7. Save the CMW file.

PART 4

Worldwide Deployment

Chapter 12   Planning an International Deployment   363

Chapter 13   Deploying Office Internationally   373

Chapter 14   Upgrading International Installations   407

Chapter 15   Maintaining International Installations   425

Chapter 16   Preparing Users' Computers for International Use   443

CHAPTER 12

Planning an International Deployment

You can install, customize, and maintain a single version of Microsoft Office XP throughout your multinational organization. The plug-in language features of Office allow users in foreign locales to continue working in their own languages. Alternatively, you can deploy a localized version of Office for each language-speaking area.

In this chapter

Preparing for an International Deployment   363

International Deployment Scenarios   365

Localized Versions of Office XP   370

Preparing for an International Deployment

The core functionality of Microsoft Office XP and the plug-in language features of the Microsoft Office Multilingual User Interface Pack (MUI Pack) enable users worldwide to run the Office XP user interface and online Help in the users' own languages, and to create documents in many other languages.

Office XP offers a wide range of multilingual deployment options from which to choose, depending upon your organization's needs.

Office language versions and editing tools

To take full advantage of the international features that support Microsoft Office XP, you can deploy one of the following additional language resources:

- Microsoft Office Multilingual User Interface Pack (MUI Pack)
- Microsoft Office Proofing Tools
- Localized version of Microsoft Office XP

For administrators, the core functionality of Office XP allows you to deploy a single version of Office for your users, regardless of the users' language-speaking area. You can then customize Office to include local language capabilities, or to allow users to select their own language settings. Or, depending on your organization's needs, you can install only Proofing Tools for reading and editing text.

After you have installed Office, you can deploy Proofing Tools or Multilingual User Interface Pack files separately. By developing an integrated deployment plan, however, you can install either of these products at the same time that you install Office XP.

> **Note** The Multilingual User Interface Pack Setup program is available in English only. However, the Setup program for Office Proofing Tools is available in Brazilian Portuguese, English, French, German, Italian, and Spanish.

In addition to the multilingual capabilities of Office XP and the Multilingual User Interface Pack, Office XP is also localized in many different languages. The localized versions are based on the same international core as Office XP and the MUI Pack, but they provide additional language-specific functionality in minor areas such as right-click menus.

Office Proofing Tools

Office Proofing Tools includes spelling and grammar checkers, thesauruses, AutoCorrect lists, Input Method Editors — all the tools users need to create and edit Office documents in more than 30 languages.

Proofing tools are also included in the MUI Pack. The Office Proofing Tools product is available separately. Unlike the Multilingual User Interface Pack, Office Proofing Tools works with localized versions of Office XP.

You can install Proofing Tools for one or more languages on users' computers. Each language set that you install allows a user to create and edit documents in that language by using tools such as spelling or grammar checkers and the AutoCorrect list.

Hard-disk space requirements for Proofing Tools vary by language. Proofing Tools for most languages requires about 20 MB of hard-disk space in addition to what Office requires. However, Asian languages require as much as 120 MB of hard-disk space in addition to what Office requires, to include the necessary fonts and Input Method Editors (IMEs).

You install Proofing Tools when your users need to read and edit documents in one or more other languages while continuing to use a standardized language for the user interface and Help text in their Office applications. It is not necessary to deploy the full Multilingual User Interface Pack unless your users also require different languages for the user interface or Help text.

Office Multilingual User Interface Pack

The Microsoft Office Multilingual User Interface Pack includes files for displaying the Office user interface and online Help in several languages. The MUI Pack is designed to enhance the English version of Office XP; it does not work with localized versions of Office XP.

Although Office is localized into specific language versions, with the MUI Pack, Office provides combined support for those languages in a single product. Office XP with the Multilingual User Interface Pack is built on core code that you can run internationally. Language-specific user interface and Help text are stored separately, primarily in dynamic-link library (DLL) files. These features "plug in" to the core Office XP code; your users can install and run these features when they need them.

This plug-in language capability means that you can install English Office XP with the Multilingual User Interface Pack on your computer, but view the Office XP user interface and Help in another language. You can even view Help in a specific language, while displaying the user interface in English. For example, you may want to keep the user interface standardized across your organization, yet let each region display localized Help content.

You can customize your Office installation to include MUI Pack files for several languages. You can then specify different user interface and Help text languages for different groups of users in your organization, or allow users to set their own language.

Localized versions of Office XP

The Multilingual User Interface Pack lets you change the user interface and Help to any of dozens of languages, and provides proofing tools for more than 80 languages. However, using Office XP with the Multilingual User Interface Pack is not the same as using a localized version of Office XP.

Because not all features have plug-in language capability, Office XP is localized in many languages for users who want to use all Office features in their own language. Localized versions of Office XP are compatible with Office XP with the Multilingual User Interface Pack; that is, users of one language version can easily share documents created in other language versions. However, MUI Packs must be installed on English Office XP, not on localized versions of Office.

International Deployment Scenarios

The powerful multilingual features of Microsoft Office XP give you a lot of flexibility in configuring Office for international users.

You can deploy Proofing Tools or the Office Multilingual User Interface Pack files separately after you install Office. If you develop an integrated deployment plan, however, you can deploy either of these products to users at the same time that you deploy Office XP.

Examples of multilingual installations

You can install different combinations of Office language versions and language-specific tools, based on the needs of your international organization. Some of these combinations are described in the following table.

If you want to...	Install the following language version and tools
Deploy a single version of Office internationally for your organization and allow different users to work with a user interface and Help in their own language (regardless of the language used in their documents).	English Office XP with one MUI Pack
Deploy a single version of Office internationally for your organization and allow users to work in one or more user interface and Help languages (regardless of the language used in their documents). Allow users to view and edit documents in other languages.	English Office XP with several MUI Packs
Standardize on an English user interface for your organization, and allow users to view documents in other languages.	English Office XP only
Standardize on an English user interface, and provide viewing and editing capabilities in other languages.	English Office XP and Office Proofing Tools
Provide users with fully localized functionality in all Office applications in a single language, and allow them to view documents in other languages.	Localized versions of Office XP for one language
Provide users with fully localized functionality in all Office applications, and allow them to view and edit documents in other languages.	Localized versions of Office XP for one language and Office Proofing Tools

Typical scenarios for multilingual deployment include the following:

- Mimic a localized version using the MUI Pack.

  Deploy English Office XP along with the MUI Pack package (MSI file) and System Files Update files for an additional language.

- Use English as a standard user interface, but provide Help text in native languages.

  Deploy English Office XP along with the MUI Pack MSI file that adds additional Help files in another language.

- Provide a multilingual version of Office on one computer.

    For example, setting up a computer to be used by traveling users from different countries. Deploy English Office XP along with MUI Pack MSI files for each required language.

- Read and edit text in another language.

    Deploy Office XP (an English or localized version) along with the proofing tools for the required language or languages.

- Use a fully localized version of Office with no English text.

    Install a localized version of Office XP. Localized versions provide a limited number of additional localized features, such as language-specific right-click menus.

Notes   One advantage of deploying a global version of Office plus a MUI Pack is that you can use the Custom Installation Wizard to establish a standard version of Office for all of your sites. If you do use the Custom Installation Wizard to configure Office for an international deployment, you must make sure that all language configurations are enabled through the core Office installation and the Custom Installation Wizard — not the MUI Pack. For example, while customizing the Office MSI you would configure settings such as the default Help language and the languages enabled for editing. During installation, these settings will be applied to the Office applications. When you modify the MSI file for a MUI Pack with the Custom Installation Wizard, the language configuration options are not available.

To effectively install a MUI Pack with Office, the MUI Pack installation should be chained to Office Setup. By chaining the MUI installation, you can ensure that the Office settings will be applied first, and that MUI Pack will be installed before Office is started for the first time. (Starting Office without a MUI Pack installed will cause the language settings to revert to their default state.) For information on chaining installations through Setup, see "Including Additional Packages in the Office Installation" in Chapter 5, "Installing and Customizing Office."

Deployment process strategies

In addition to determining the type of multilingual installation that suits your users, consider how you will deploy Office and multilingual tools to your organization. Depending on the structure of your organization and the languages that you need, you can adopt one of several different strategies for deploying Office internationally.

Centralized or local deployment

You can deploy language-specific custom installations from a centralized administrative source. Or you can customize Office, then distribute your customized version to your international administrative departments, allowing each department in a subsidiary to customize the installation for its own language-speaking area.

Deploying Office from a central administrative source

If your organization is centralized, where one administrative group deploys Office to the entire organization, you can make all the customizations your users need at your headquarters and deploy directly to users internationally. In this scenario, you customize the Multilingual User Interface Pack and create a custom installation of Office for each language-speaking area.

For example, if you were deploying Office and the MUI Pack to users in the United States and Canada, you might deploy Office as follows:

- For English-speaking users in the United States, install only proofing tools from the MUI Pack, and enable languages for editing as needed.

- For Spanish-speaking users in the United States, install Spanish language features from the MUI Pack, leave the installation language set at U.S. English, set the user interface and Help language to Spanish, and enable Spanish for editing (English is automatically enabled for editing if the installation language is English).

- For users in English-speaking Canadian provinces, set the installation language to Canadian English, and enable Canadian French and Canadian English for editing.

- For users in Québec, install French language features from the MUI Pack, set the installation language to Canadian French, set the user interface and Help language to French, and enable Canadian French and Canadian English for editing.

Deploying Office at local subsidiaries

If your organization's administrative resources are distributed internationally, each local subsidiary can modify the standard installation for local users.

In this case, a central corporate administrative group supplies each local office with a standard Windows Installer transform (MST file) with the installation language set to English. Local administrators customize the MUI Pack, select language settings, and modify the transform for their language-speaking area.

For example, if you are a site administrator in Hong Kong, you might customize the corporate deployment as follows:

- Install Traditional Chinese language features on users' computers and set Simplified Chinese language features so that they are installed the first time users activate the features.

- Set English or Traditional Chinese as the language for the user interface and online Help, set the installation language to Pan-Chinese, enable Simplified Chinese and Traditional Chinese and U.K. English for editing.

- Customize Office applications for Hong Kong users.

    For example, add a button to the toolbar in Microsoft Word for converting between Simplified Chinese and Traditional Chinese.

Note For Traditional Chinese user interface and executable mode, users must be running a Traditional Chinese version of Microsoft Windows, or Microsoft Windows 2000 with the system locale of Hong Kong or Taiwan.

One or multiple administrative installation points

You can use a single centralized administrative installation point for Office, the Multilingual User Interface Pack, or Proofing Tools. Or you can deploy Office from one installation point, and deploy one or more MUI Packs (or Proofing Tools) from additional installation points. It might be easier to manage deployment from a single administrative installation point. However, there are scenarios in which using multiple installation points is a preferred method.

For example, suppose you are deploying several different sets of languages to groups in different parts of your organization. In this scenario, you might choose to use different installation points for these groups to avoid using large amounts of hard-disk space when you replicate a single administrative installation point image to multiple locations around the world.

Note The MUI Packs include System Files Update files. If you choose to deploy MUI Packs from a separate administrative installation point, you must manually copy the System Files Update files to your Office installation point or do an administrative install of the Multilingual User Interface Pack to the same location of the administrative install of Office but choosing to install only the System Files Update.

Install with or after Office XP

You can chain installations of the Multilingual User Interface Pack or Proofing Tools with your Office XP installation. Or you can deploy Office first, and deploy other multilingual features later.

For example, if you are ready to deploy Office XP right away but the MUI Pack for a particular language is not yet available, you might choose to proceed with your Office deployment and then deploy the additional MUI Pack when it becomes available.

To learn more about options for coordinating your installation of language resources with your Office deployment, see "Deploying Office with the Multilingual User Interface Pack" in Chapter 13, "Deploying Office Internationally."

Install using Systems Management Server or Windows 2000 IntelliMirror

Systems Management Server and Windows 2000 IntelliMirror provide flexible and powerful software for deploying software. You can choose to deploy Office with MUI Packs or Proofing Tools by using either SMS or IntelliMirror.

Note By default, Office must be installed before MUI Pack files are installed. However, when you deploy with Systems Management Server and Windows 2000 IntelliMirror, you cannot specify the order in which components are installed. To prevent installation errors, you set a property (**CHECKINSTALLORDER**) when you configure your Office installation that allows Office and MUI Pack files to be installed in any order.

See also

You can provide multilingual user interface and Help text to Office users by installing one or more MUI Packs. For more information about configuring an Office Multilingual User Interface Pack to meet the needs of your organization, see "Deploying Office with the Multilingual User Interface Pack" in Chapter 13, "Deploying Office Internationally."

You can allow users to edit and proof documents by installing Proofing Tools. For more information about making Proofing Tools available to users in your organization, see "Installing Proofing Tools" in Chapter 13, "Deploying Office Internationally."

Fully localized versions of Office provide limited additional language localization over using the Multilingual User Interface Pack with Office. For more information about installing a fully localized version of Office for your users, see "Localized Versions of Office XP" in Chapter 12, "Planning an International Deployment."

Localized Versions of Office XP

Deploying Microsoft Office XP with the Office Multilingual User Interface Pack (MUI Pack) gives you the advantage of having a single installation of Office for your entire international organization. However, due to limitations of some plug-in language features, you might decide to deploy localized versions of Office XP in some language-speaking areas.

To install a localized version of Office XP you follow the same procedure as installing any other Office SKU. For example, you can customize your installation by creating a transform with the Custom Installation Wizard.

Office profiles and multiple languages

Office user profiles generated by the Profile Wizard are independent of the operating system — including operating systems in other languages. For example, a profile settings file (OPS file) created on Microsoft Windows 98 (U.S. English version) can be restored to a computer with Windows 2000 (Japanese version).

However, Office user profiles are specific to a particular Office language version. For example, if you create an OPS file in the U.S. English version of Office XP, it cannot be restored to a computer with the German version of Office XP installed. There is some overlap between language families. For example, you can restore a U.S. English Office profile to an English or Australian version of Office XP.

This Office language limitation exists because the different Office versions include localized folder names for the folders that contain the Office user profile information.

Advantages to installing localized versions of Office

Installing a localized version of Office XP has its advantages. For instance, the user interface of some features in Office XP with the Multilingual User Interface Pack cannot be changed. If it is important that users run these features in the users' own language, you can deploy a localized version of Office to these users. Localized versions of Office XP are based on the same international core as Office XP with the Multilingual User Interface Pack, so users can exchange documents between language versions of Office XP with no loss of data.

There are some differences between running Office XP with the Multilingual User Interface Pack and running a localized version of Office. For example:

- Office XP with the Multilingual User Interface Pack cannot switch the user interface language of Excel add-ins, some OCX controls, and some Help elements (such as dialog boxes and the **Contents** tab).
- In Office XP with the Multilingual User Interface Pack, shortcuts on the **Start** menu are not localized.
- Localized versions of Office include localized right-click menus.

> **Toolbox** Information about which Office features cannot have the language of the user interface switched is available in the Excel workbook Intlimit.xls. Intlimit.xls is installed by default when you run the Office XP Resource Kit Setup program. For more information about installing Intlimit.xls, see "Supplemental Documentation" in the Toolbox.

Disadvantages to installing localized versions of Office

There are some drawbacks to deploying localized versions of Office rather than building around a standard version. With separate versions, you need separate procedures for deployment, support, and administration. Also, localized versions do not usually support the ability to switch the language of the user interface.

However, some localized versions of Office XP provide limited ability to switch the language of the user interface. You can switch the language of the user interface to English in the following localized versions of Office XP:

- Arabic
- Hebrew
- Pan-Chinese
- Simplified Chinese

- Traditional Chinese
- Japanese
- Korean
- Thai

In the Arabic version of Office XP, you can also switch the user interface to French. In the Pan-Chinese (Hong Kong) version, you can switch most Office XP applications to Simplified Chinese (except for Microsoft Outlook and Microsoft FrontPage) if the user is running Microsoft Windows NT.

Depending on your needs, you can deploy a localized version of Office XP in selected language-speaking areas. For example, you might deploy Office XP with the Multilingual User Interface Pack everywhere except Japan, where you deploy the Japanese version of Office XP.

See also

There are some limitations to installing a localized version of Office on a computer with an operating system that uses a different language. For more information about these limitations, see "Choosing an Operating System" in Chapter 16, "Preparing Users' Computers for International Use."

CHAPTER 13
Deploying Office Internationally

Deploying Microsoft Office XP with the Office Multilingual User Interface Pack is more straightforward than deploying earlier versions. For instance, the process of including one or more Office XP MUI Packs with your Office deployment is made easier by the following — separate MUI Pack files, and options in Setup for chaining installations. The topics in this chapter describe the basic customization and installation procedures for multilingual installations, as well as provide detailed steps for several more complex scenarios.

In this chapter

Deploying Office with the Multilingual User Interface Pack   373

Sample Customizations for Office with the Multilingual User Interface Pack   389

Installing Proofing Tools   398

Customizing Language Features   401

Deploying Office with the Multilingual User Interface Pack

Plug-in language capability in Microsoft Office XP is provided by the Office Multilingual User Interface Pack (MUI Pack). You have great flexibility in customizing and installing the language files your organization needs. For example, you can customize Office to install with MUI Pack files by chaining your installation, or you can customize and install language files after deploying Office. In addition, although the MUI Pack and Office XP are installed from different CDs, each can be deployed from the same or a different administrative installation point.

MUI Pack components and installation process

Office XP and its language components give you flexibility in how you deploy Office and the Multilingual User Interface Pack for your organization. For example, you can create a separate administrative installation point for the MUI Pack, or multiple installation points for different groups of languages. Or you can include Office and MUI Pack files on the same installation point.

The Office Multilingual User Interface Pack comes with its own setup program. Each language has its own package (MSI file) and can be customized individually. When you install the MUI Pack, you can make language files available to users on demand, instead of copying files to users' computers; or you can choose to copy the language files to users' hard disks. The MUI Pack works with Windows Installer to install the necessary files only when users run Office XP with a particular language configuration.

You can also choose to let users customize their own installation of language files, selecting from the language files that you make available on the administrative installation point.

MUI Pack components

The MUI Pack for Office XP has the following components:

- MUI Packs (Lpk.msi files)

  There is one package (MSI file) per language.

- Multilingual User Interface Pack Wizard (Lpkwiz.msi)

  Used by Multilingual User Interface Pack Setup, this wizard file allows users to choose languages from the administrative installation point to install on their computers.

- Multilingual User Interface Pack Setup (Lpksetup.exe)

  You use this setup program with the **/a** option to copy languages you select to create an administrative installation point. Users can also deploy MUI Packs themselves by running this program to call the Multilingual User Interface Pack Wizard.

- System Files Update (Osp.msi)

  This contains required Office XP system and shared files for different languages.

By using these components, you can create a customized multilingual deployment suited to your organization's needs.

Locale Identifiers for each language

In some deployment scenarios, you must know the locale identifier (LCID) for a language in order to install the correct MUI Pack. Multilingual User Interface Packs are installed on the administrative installation point under folder names by their corresponding locale identifier.

The following table lists languages for which the Office Multilingual User Interface Pack includes MUI Packs; it also lists the corresponding locale identifiers.

Language	Locale identifier (LCID)
Arabic	1025
Basque	1069
Bulgarian	1026
Catalan	1027
Chinese (Simplified)	2052
Chinese (Traditional)	1028
Croatian	1050
Czech	1029
Danish	1030
Dutch	1043
English (U.S.)	1033
Estonian	1061
Finnish	1035
French	1036
Galician	1110
German	1031
Greek	1032
Gujarati	1095
Hebrew	1037
Hindi	1081
Hungarian	1038
Iberian Portuguese	2070
Indonesian	1057
Irish	2108
Italian	1040
Japanese	1041

Language (cont'd)	Locale identifier (LCID)
Kannada	1099
Korean	1042
Latvian	1062
Lithuanian	1063
Marathi	1102
Norwegian (Bokmal)	1044
Polish	1045
Portuguese (Brazilian)	1046
Punjabi	1094
Romanian	1048
Russian	1049
Serbian (Latin)	2074
Slovak	1051
Slovenian	1060
Spanish	3082
Swedish	1053
Tamil	1097
Telugu	1098
Thai	1054
Turkish	1055
Ukranian	1058
Urdu	1056
Vietnamese	1066
Welsh	1106

Overview of the deployment process

Your deployment process will depend on whether you install the Multilingual User Interface Pack with or after installing Office and other options.

Note Be sure that your client machines have the proper language support for MUI Pack installation before you deploy MUI Packs. For example, ensure that the proper fonts are installed on users' machines. For more information about preparing client machines for a multilingual environment, see Chapter 16, "Preparing Users' Computers for International Use."

In general, follow these steps to deploy the Multilingual User Interface Pack:

1. Create an administrative installation point for Office XP.

2. Create an administrative installation point for the MUI Pack files you will deploy in your installation (this can be the same location as the Office installation point).

3. Customize your MUI Pack installation.

   Create a customized transform for Office, for individual MUI Packs, or for both. For an Office transform, you can include language settings stored with other Office settings in an Office profile settings file (OPS file), if you choose, as well as language settings you select in the Custom Installation Wizard. For a MUI Pack transform, you can customize feature states and setup properties.

   Note that language settings — such as the Help language and installed version of Microsoft Office — cannot be set when customizing individual MUI Pack installations. Instead, customize these settings when you deploy Office.

4. Configure Setup.ini to chain the installation of one or more languages with your Office deployment

5. Deploy Office to your users, together with selected MUI Packs (if you choose).

   Note that while Office usually must be installed on users' computers before the MUI Pack files, you can turn off this requirement by using the Setup property **CHECKINSTALLORDER**. You specify this option when you cannot ensure the deployment order for the components being installed. These circumstances might apply to deployments that use Microsoft Windows® 2000 IntelliMirror® technology or Systems Management Server.

6. Install one or more MUI Packs (possibly in addition to MUI Packs you have already installed with Office) by using a separate Setup.ini customization or by allowing users to choose MUI Packs with the MUI Pack Wizard.

   Note When you install Office XP with the Multilingual User Interface Pack, or when you install individual MUI Packs, all corresponding Office 2000 MultiLanguage Pack files on users' computers are deleted by default. If you plan to keep some Office 2000 applications, however, you can retain the Office 2000 language packs. Specify **KEEPLPK9=1** in Setup.ini or in a transform for each Office XP MUI pack that you install. To retain Office 2000 Proofing Tools, specify **KEEPPTK9 = 1**.

Create an administrative installation point for the MUI Pack

You run the Multilingual User Interface Pack Setup program (Lpksetup.exe) in administrative mode to install the MUI Pack to an administrative installation point located on the server.

The Multilingual User Interface Pack consists of language files on multiple CDs. If you want to use languages on different CDs, you must run Lpksetup.exe separately for each CD you need. You can add language files to an existing administrative installation point by specifying the same location each time.

The procedure below assumes that you create an administrative installation point on a computer using Microsoft Windows 2000. You can, instead, create an administrative installation point on a computer using the Microsoft Windows NT®, Microsoft Windows 98, or Microsoft Windows Millennium Edition (Windows Me) operating systems. However, the computer used to create the admin image must have the correct code page (or pages) installed that corresponds to the MUI Packs that you are copying to the installation point. Otherwise, only the languages that are supported by the system will be copied. If you are creating an admin image for multiple languages that use different code pages, use a Windows NT or Windows 2000 computer. (Windows 98 and Windows Me support only one code page at a time.)

> **Note** System Files Update files are automatically copied to the installation point with the MUI Pack files. However, if you choose to create an installation point for your MUI Pack files that is separate from Office, you must manually copy the additional languages' System Files Update files to your Office installation point to ensure that the client computer receives the System Files Update files that match the language of the operating system.

To create an administrative installation point for the Multilingual User Interface Pack

1. Create a share on a network server for the administrative installation point.

    The folder must be at least one level below the top level: for example, \\server\share\office. Also, the share must be large enough to store the resources for the languages that you need. Multilingual User Interface Pack disk-space requirements are approximately 150 MB to 350 MB per MUI Pack.

2. On a computer running Windows 2000, with write access to the share, connect to the server share.

    Note that you can create an administrative installation point on a computer using the Microsoft Windows NT®, Microsoft Windows 98, or Microsoft Windows Millennium Edition (Windows Me) operating systems. However you may need to take special steps to ensure you have the correct code page, as described earlier.

3. On the **Start** menu, click **Run**, and then click **Browse** to locate the Multilingual User Interface Pack CD.

4. On the Multilingual User Interface Pack CD, select **Lpksetup.exe** and click **Open**.
5. On the command line, following **Lpksetup.exe**, type **/a** and click **OK**.
6. When prompted by Lpksetup.exe, enter the organization name you want to define for all users who install the Multilingual User Interface Pack from administrative installation point, then click **Next**.
7. Enter the server and the share that you created and click **Next**.

    Note that if you want to install only the System Files Update files for the languages available on this CD, select the check box before clicking **Next**.

8. On the **Available Languages** page, choose the languages you want to include on this installation point.

    Note that languages that are not available on the current CD will appear dimmed on this page. You can add languages from other CDs to the same administrative installation point by running **Lpksetup.exe /a** with additional MUI Pack CDs and specifying the same network server location.

Customize MUI Pack language options

You can customize your Office XP deployment with the Multilingual User Interface Pack to include specific language settings, and to specify which languages you want to deploy. You can specify language settings as part of your Office customization, or modify settings after installing Office and the Multilingual User Interface Pack.

When you deploy MUI Packs customized in an Office transform as part of your Office deployment, you can include language settings stored with other Office settings in an Office profile settings file (OPS file), if you choose, as well as language settings you select in the Custom Installation Wizard. For a MUI Pack transform, you can only customize feature states and Setup properties.

> **Note** If you want to enforce certain language settings and not allow users to change them, you can specify settings for users with system policies. In the Office policies template (Office1.adm), specify policies under Language Settings. For more information about using system policies, see "How to Set System Policies" in Chapter 9, "Using System Policies."

Include language settings in an Office transform

You can define language settings when you create a custom Office transform as part of your Office XP deployment. You can save and apply the language settings in two ways: by using a profile settings file (OPS file) created with the Office Profile Wizard, or by specifying language settings in the Custom Installation Wizard directly when customizing Office.

Save language settings in an OPS file

When you run Office to specify language settings and user preferences, you can use the Profile Wizard to store the settings in an OPS file. The OPS file becomes part of a customized installation of Office. Because the choice of editing languages affects the functionality of certain applications, you can create unique OPS files for different groups of users based on the languages they are using.

In general, follow these steps to configure and capture language settings by using the Office Profile Wizard.

1. Install Office on the test machine, along with the Multilingual User Interface Pack files for the languages you want to install.
2. Customize the Office environment and language settings.
3. Save the settings in an OPS file by using the Office Profile Wizard.

    Note The Office Profile Wizard stores and retrieves Office XP customizations. By using the Profile Wizard, you can create and deploy a standard user profile when you deploy Office XP so that all of your users start off with the same settings. For more information about the Profile Wizard and OPS files, see "Using the Office Profile Wizard" in Chapter 8, "Maintaining an Installation."

Install Office and the MUI Pack on a test computer

Install Microsoft Office on a test computer by using Office Setup (Setup.exe) on the CD for your edition of Office. Then install the MUI Pack files that you want to customize by using the MUI Pack Setup (Lpksetup.exe) program. The MUI Pack Setup program starts the Multilingual User Interface Pack Setup Wizard, which will step you through installing the MUI Pack files that you choose. You can specify language settings (such as the Help language) during the Multilingual User Interface Pack Setup installation, or by using the Language Settings tool after Office and the MUI Packs have been installed.

Capture settings in an OPS file

Typically, most users creating multilingual documents rarely work with more than three languages. Limiting the number of editing languages results in a user interface that is less cluttered and allows Office applications to run efficiently for particular languages.

You can specify the following language settings for users:

- **Install Language**: Sets defaults for Office applications and documents. Also called the default version of Office.
- **User Interface Language**: Determines language used by menus and dialogs.
- **Help Language**: Determines language used for end-user Help.
- **Editing Languages**: Exposes functionality for editing documents in those particular languages.

You set these values for your installation on your test computer, then save them with other settings to customize users' computers.

To capture language feature settings by using the Microsoft Office Profile Wizard

1. Click **Start, Programs, Microsoft Office Tools**.
2. In the **Microsoft Office Language Settings** page, click the **Enabled Languages** tab.
3. Select the languages to use for user interface, online Help, and editing.

   Users can change these default settings later by running the Language Settings utility themselves (unless system policies are in place that enforce settings).
4. Set the value of **Default version of Microsoft Office** to the installation language you want for your users.
5. Start Office, and specify any additional user settings.
6. Start the Office Profile Wizard and save your settings in an OPS file.

You then include the OPS file in the Custom Installation Wizard when you create a transform that is applied when Office XP is installed.

Specify language settings with the Custom Installation Wizard

Instead of — or in addition to — using an OPS file to specify and save language customizations, you can specify language settings in the Custom Installation Wizard. Your customizations are then saved in a transform (MST file).

To specify language settings in the Custom Installation Wizard

1. In the Custom Installation Wizard, on the **Change Office User Settings** page, click **Microsoft Office XP (user)**.
2. Navigate the tree under **Language Settings**, and select the language options that you want for your deployment.

   For example, to set the user interface language, click **User Interface**, then double-click **Display menus and dialog boxes in**. In the **Display menus and dialog boxes in Properties** dialog, click **Apply Changes**, and then choose a language from the drop-down menu.

   Note The settings you specify in the **Change Office User Settings** page take precedence over settings you include in an OPS file in the same transform.

Create a MUI Pack transform

You might choose to install additional MUI Packs after Office, or to install all MUI Packs separately from Office. You create a MUI Pack transform when you want to customize the way that a particular MUI Pack is installed. An advantage of deploying MUI Packs with Office is that you can customize language settings in your Office transform, which you cannot do with a MUI Pack transform.

Settings you can customize in a MUI Pack transform are:

- Features states
- Setup properties

> **Note** You customize default language settings in your Office deployment. You cannot include these settings in a MUI Pack transform. If you have already deployed Office, you can modify language settings by using the Custom Maintenance Wizard with Office.

If you are deploying Office with the Multilingual User Interface Pack using Windows 2000 IntelliMirror, you must include a separate transform for each MUI Pack, in which you set the **CHECKINSTALLORDER** Setup property to **False**. By using IntelliMirror for your deployment, you cannot guarantee the order in which components are installed, so MUI Packs might be installed before Office. Usually, this is disallowed. However, by setting this property, MUI Packs can be installed on a user's computer even if Office is not yet installed.

> **Note** When you deploy Office XP and the Multilingual User Interface Pack with SMS, you can specify the **CHECKINSTALLORDER** Setup property in individual MUI Pack transforms, or provide the property as a command-line option.

To customize feature states and Setup properties in a transform for a MUI Pack

1. In the Custom Installation Wizard, on the **Open MSI File** page, enter (or browse to) the name of the MSI file for the MUI Pack you want to customize.

2. On the **Set Feature Installation States** page, open **Office Shared Features**.

3. By opening **International Support**, you can choose installation states for fonts (for example, for **Japanese Font**).

4. By opening **Proofing Tools**, you can choose installation states for proofing tools available in the Multilingual User Interface Pack.

5. On the **Modify Setup Properties** page, choose or add Setup properties that you want to include in the MUI Pack transform.

   To modify an existing property, click the property, then click **Modify**. For example, click **NOFEATURESTATEMIGRATION**, then click **Modify**. Select **Do not match feature states during installation** from the drop-down menu, then click **OK**.

   > **Note** If you make any changes in the transform for a MUI Pack, you must specify **NOFEATURESTATEMIGRATION** property as **Do not match feature states during installation** for the transform to take effect.

   Or click **Add** and enter a property name and value. For example, enter **CHECKINSTALLORDER** in the **Name** field and **False** in the **Value** field, then click **OK**.

Specify language-specific feature installation states

When you select language-specific features on the **Set Feature Installation States** page, keep in mind the following:

- If your users work with a right-to-left language (Arabic, Hebrew, Farsi, or Urdu) and their operating system can support right-to-left text, install the Bidirectional Support feature on users' computers.

- If your users work with Asian, Georgian, Armenian, Hindi or Tamil text and they are not running a matching language version of Windows, install the Japanese, Korean, Traditional Chinese, Simplified Chinese, Georgian, Armenian, Hindi, or Tamil fonts on users' computers. These features are included under **Office Shared**, **International Support**.

- If your users need a full Unicode font — for example, if they are working with Access datasheets that include languages that use more than one code page — install the Universal font on users' computers.

    Note For users running a non-Asian version of Windows NT that is earlier than version 4.0 SP 6a, do not install more than two of the Asian or Universal font choices. These fonts include many characters and might not display properly if more than two of them are installed on a computer running earlier versions of Windows NT 4.0.

Allow users to choose languages to install

Users can use the MUI Pack Wizard to select their own languages to install from the languages you make available by including them on an administrative installation point. Users gain access to the wizard by double-clicking Lpksetup.exe on the administrative installation point. This starts the MUI Pack Wizard (Lpkwiz.msi), which steps users through choosing the languages they want installed on their computers.

The MUI Pack Wizard does not have a silent mode. It is used interactively to install MUI Packs on a user's computer.

> **Note** Although the Multilingual User Interface Pack Wizard is named with an .msi extension, it does not behave like a typical MSI file. For example, you cannot advertise it, and you cannot customize it by using the Custom Installation Wizard or the Custom Maintenance Wizard.

To manually choose the MUI Pack languages to install

1. On the administrative installation point, click on Lpksetup.exe to start the Multilingual User Interface Pack Wizard.

2. On the **Available Languages** page, choose the languages you want to install.

3. On the **Choose the current languages to use** page, specify the language settings for the languages.

   If you choose **Auto Select**, no changes are made to the current settings.

4. On the **Choose the type of installation you need** page, choose **Install Now**, or select another install type.

Customize and install the MUI Pack with an Office installation

If you know the language requirements of your organization at the time that you are deploying Office, it is straightforward to install MUI Packs at the same time by chaining your MUI Pack installation with your Office installation.

To chain your MUI Pack installation, first install the MUI Packs on your administrative installation point. Then use the Setup INI Customization Wizard (Iniwiz.exe) to add a section for each MUI Pack that you want to chain with your Office installation.

You can create a separate transform for each language to select the language-specific features you want to be available for your users. For example, in a transform specific to an individual MUI Pack, you can change feature states, specify additional server, and modify or add properties. However, you must customize language settings (such as specifying the user interface language) in the Custom Installation Wizard with other Office settings and save them in your Office transform.

> **Toolbox** The Setup INI Customization Wizard allows you to easily customize a Setup.ini file for your Office deployment. The Setup INI Customization Wizard is installed by default when you run the Office Resource Kit Setup program. For more information, see "Setup INI Customization Wizard" in the Toolbox.

There are two properties that you might want to set for your chained installation with MUI Packs:

- The **CHECKINSTALLORDER** property allows the MUI Pack files to be installed before Office is installed. Set this property to **False** when the installation order for a chained deployment cannot be determined in advance; for example, with SMS or Windows IntelliMirror deployments.

- Office Multilingual User Interface Pack Setup automatically matches MUI Pack feature installation states to the corresponding features in the core English version of Office. If you specify different installation states for MUI Pack features in a transform, you must set the **NOFEATURESTATEMIGRATION** property to **Do not match feature states during installation** to override the default matching behavior.

To customize Setup.ini to chain MUI Pack packages to your Office installation

1. Start the Setup INI Customization Wizard and enter the path to your Office XP administrative installation point.

2. On the **Select MSI and EXE files to include in your INI file** page, select the check boxes next to the packages that you want to include in your custom INI file, or click **Browse** to add packages from another location, and then click **Next**.

3. On the **Specify options for each package in your INI file** page, select the chained package you want to customize and specify the options you want for that package. For each package you can specify an MST file and unique display settings, as well as additional property values.

   If you are deploying using SMS or Windows 2000 IntelliMirror, select each package, click **Advanced Properties**, enter the property **CHECKINSTALLORDER**, and set it to **False**.

   If you want to maintain feature state settings for one or more of your MUI Packs, select each package, enter the property **NOFEATURESTATEMIGRATION**, and set it to **True**.

4. Click **Next**.

Customize and install the MUI Pack after an Office installation

You can install the MUI Pack packages after your Office installation, rather than chaining the installation with Office. If you create an administrative installation point that includes the Multilingual User Interface Pack, you can simplify and control the deployment process. For example, you can standardize installation of language resources for all the users in your organization.

As with a combined Office and the Multilingual User Interface Pack scenario, you can configure language settings in your Office transform. If you want to change the language settings after you install the MUI Packs, you use the Custom Maintenance Wizard.

> **Note** Another option is for users to configure their own language settings. This option is available, for example, if users run the MUI Pack Wizard to choose and install the languages they select over the network from the MUI Pack administrative installation point.

Customize and install additional MUI Packs after Office

You might chain one or more MUI Packs with your Office deployment, or install Office without any MUI Packs. Then, later, you can chain together the deployment of additional MUI Packs.

Suppose you want to deploy the French, Spanish, and Vietnamese Language Packs after your initial deployment of Office.

To chain packages, you customize the Setup INI file for one of the MUI Packs by using the Setup INI Customization Wizard (Iniwiz.exe). (A Setup.ini file is included in each MUI Pack folder.) Although you can modify Setup.ini manually in Notepad, the wizard provides a convenient interface for adding and customizing chained packages.

> **Toolbox** The Setup INI Customization Wizard allows you to easily customize a Setup.ini file. The Setup INI Customization Wizard is installed by default when you run the Office Resource Kit Setup program. For more information, see "Setup INI Customization Wizard" in the Toolbox.

To customize Setup to chain additional language features to an Office deployment

1. Start the Setup INI Customization Wizard and enter the path to the folder for one of the MUI Packs on your administrative installation point.

   For example, to use the folder for the French Language Pack files, you might enter:

   \\server1\share\office\1036

2. On the **Select MSI and EXE files to include in your INI file** page, select the check boxes next to the packages that you want to include in your custom INI file, or click **Browse** to add packages from another location, and then click **Next**.

   In this example, to include Spanish (3082) and Vietnamese (1066) in addition to French, you might select:

   \\server1\share\office\3082\Lpk.msi

   and

   \\server1\share\office\1066\Lpk.msi

   Use the **Search Directory for More MSIs...** button to list all the MSI files in a directory tree.

3. On the **Specify options for each package in your INI file** page, select the chained package you want to customize and specify the options you want for that package. For each package, you can specify an MST file and unique display settings, as well as additional property values.

Users can now install this group of MUI Packs by running the Setup command line in the French Language Pack folder. For example:

```
\\server1\share\office\1036\setup.exe /qb-
```

Modify Office language settings

After Microsoft Office has been deployed, you might want to change the language settings you originally deployed with Office. In this case, you modify your Office installation with the Custom Maintenance Wizard.

To change language settings for an Office installation

1. Start the Custom Maintenance Wizard.
2. On the **Open the MSI File** page, specify the Office MSI file. For example:

   \\server1\share\office\proplus.msi
3. On the **Change Office User Settings** page, click **Microsoft Office XP (User)**.
4. Navigate the tree under **Language Settings**, and select the language options that you want for your deployment.

   For example, to enable additional editing languages for the MUI Packs you are installing, click **Enabled Languages**, then select French, Vietnamese, and Spanish in the right-hand pane.

After saving the customizations, apply the CMW file to users' computers. For example:

\\server1\share\office\maintwiz.exe /c Langupdate.cmw

> **Toolbox** The Custom Maintenance Wizard allows you to modify an existing Office installation. The Help file included with the wizard includes details about how to make changes to your installation. The Custom Maintenance Wizard is installed by default when you run the Office Resource Kit Setup program. For more information, see "Custom Maintenance Wizard" in the Toolbox.

Allow users to install additional MUI Packs

You can also allow users to install individual MUI Packs over the network from an administrative installation point.

To install MUI Pack files on a single computer

1. On the Multilingual User Interface Pack installation point that contains the languages you want to install (or from the CD that includes the MUI Packs you want to install), run Lpksetup.exe to start the MUI Pack Wizard.
2. On the **Available Languages** page, choose the languages you want to install.
3. On the **Choose the current languages to use** page, specify the language settings for the languages.

   If you choose **Auto Select**, no changes are made to the current settings.
4. On the **Choose the type of installation you need** page, choose **Install Now**, or select another installation type.

Use Systems Management Server to deploy Office and the MUI Pack

Systems Management Server provides a flexible and powerful tool for deploying software. You can deploy Office with the Multilingual User Interface Pack or Proofing Tools with Systems Management Server. First, customize your Office installation by using the Custom Installation Wizard to create transforms for Office and the multilingual features you are deploying. Then deploy Office by creating SMS Packages and distributing them to selected clients.

You cannot control the order in which components are deployed with Systems Management Server. Because of this, you must set the **CHECKORDER** property to **FALSE** when configuring your Office deployment. This allows the Multilingual User Interface Pack files to be installed even if Office is not.

For more information on using SMS for software deployment, see the Microsoft Systems Management Server Web site at http://www.microsoft.com/smsmgmt/default.asp.

Use Windows 2000 IntelliMirror to deploy Office with the MUI Pack

Windows 2000 IntelliMirror provides a software deployment and systems management solution designed to support Windows 2000 clients.

By default, Office must be installed before MUI Pack files are installed. However, when you deploy with Systems Management Server and Windows 2000 IntelliMirror, you cannot specify the order in which components are installed. To prevent installation errors, you set a property (**CHECKINSTALLORDER**) when you configure your Office installation. This property allows Office and MUI Pack files to be installed in any order.

For more information on deploying Office with IntelliMirror, see "Using Windows 2000 Software Installation" in Chapter 6, "Deploying on Windows 2000."

See also

In addition to specifying language features and providing support for international users, you can customize many other aspects of your Office installation. For more information about customizing Office with the Custom Installation Wizard, see "Customizing the Office Installation" in Chapter 5, "Installing and Customizing Office."

You can use the Office Profile Wizard to save language-related settings to a file you distribute as part of a custom installation of Office. For more information about the Profile Wizard and profile settings files (OPS files), see "Using the Office Profile Wizard" in Chapter 8, "Maintaining an Installation."

Sample Customizations for Office with the Multilingual User Interface Pack

You can customize your deployment of Microsoft Office XP with the Office Multilingual User Interface Pack for separate language-speaking areas, or for different groups of users with combinations of language resource requirements. In addition, you can use chaining to deploy MUI Pack files together with Office, or you can install language files separately later, after you have deployed Office. Sample deployment procedures for these scenarios are included in this section.

Customize the MUI Pack installation for one language-speaking area

You might require just one MUI Pack for the users in your organization. Customizing and deploying Office XP with the Multilingual User Interface Pack for one language-speaking area is straightforward: you create an Office transform and customize Setup.ini for your users. In the Office transform, you specify the customized language settings for your users. In the Setup.ini file, you chain the MUI Pack to the Office installation.

In this example, suppose you want to install Office with the Japanese Language Pack from a single administrative installation point.

> **Note** For more information about creating an administrative installation point for Office, see "Creating an Administrative Installation Point" in Chapter 5, "Installing and Customizing Office."

After you have created your administrative installation point for Office, add the MUI Pack file that you plan to deploy.

To add a MUI Pack to an administrative installation point

1. Insert the CD that contains the MUI Pack that you want to install.

   In this example, insert the CD with the Japanese Language Pack.

2. On the **Start** menu, click **Run**, and then click **Browse** to locate the MUI Pack CD.

3. On the MUI Pack CD, select **Lpksetup.exe** and click **Open**.

4. On the command line, following **Lpksetup.exe**, type **/a** and click **OK**.

5. When prompted by Lpksetup.exe, enter the organization name you want to define for all users who install the MUI Pack files from this administrative installation point and click **Next**.

6. Enter the server and the share for your Office administrative installation point and click **Next**.

   Or, if you have decided to store your MUI Pack administrative images in a different location, enter that location here.

   The share must be large enough to store the resources for the language that you need in addition to the Office XP files. MUI Pack disk-space requirements are approximately 150 MB to 350 MB per MUI Pack.

7. On the **Available Languages** page, choose a language (in this example, **Japanese**).

   Note Languages that are not available on the current CD will appear dimmed on this page. You can add languages from other CDs to the same administrative installation point by running **Lpksetup.exe /a** with additional MUI Pack CDs and specifying the same network server location.

You can include language feature customizations for the MUI Pack in your Office transform. For example, in this scenario, you might set the Installation Language to Japanese.

To create an Office transform with language settings for Japanese

1. Start the Custom Installation Wizard.

2. On the **Open MSI File** page, enter (or browse to) the MSI file name for your Office installation (for example, Proplus.msi) from the administrative installation point for Office:

   \\server1\share\office\Proplus.msi

3. On the **Select the MST File to Save** page, enter the name of the MST file you are creating; for example:

   \\server1\share\office\OfficeWithJapanese.mst

4. On the **Set Feature Installation States** page, under **Microsoft Office**, **Office Share Features**, **International Support**, choose to install the Japanese fonts (only if the computer you are installing Office on is not running the Japanese version of Windows).

5. On the **Change Office User Settings** page, click **Microsoft Office (User)**.

6. Navigate the tree under **Language Settings** to **Enabled Languages**.

7. Double-click **Installed version of Microsoft Office** to open the **Properties** page for this setting.

8. Click **Apply changes**, then select **Japanese** from the **Installed version of Microsoft Office** drop-down menu.

9. Click **OK**.

Now you chain the Japanese Language Pack to your Office installation. To chain packages, you customize the Office Setup.ini file by using the Setup INI Customization Wizard (Iniwiz.exe). Although you can modify Setup.ini manually in Notepad, the wizard provides a convenient interface for adding and customizing chained packages.

> **Toolbox** The Setup INI Customization Wizard allows you to easily customize a Setup.ini file for your Office deployment. The Setup INI Customization Wizard is installed by default when you run the Office Resource Kit Setup program. For more information, see "Setup INI Customization Wizard" in the Toolbox.

To chain the Japanese Language Pack with your Office deployment

1. Start the Setup INI Customization Wizard and enter the path to your Office XP administrative installation point.

2. On the **Select MSI and EXE files to include in your INI file** page, select the check boxes next to the packages that you want to include in your custom INI file, or click **Browse** to add packages from another location, and then click **Next**. In this example, you might select:

   \\server1\share\office\1041\Lpk.msi

3. On the **Specify options for each package in your INI file** page, select the chained package you want to customize and specify the options you want for that package.

   If you will not be installing the Office XP package before the MUI Pack, select **Advanced Properties** and enter the property **CHECKINSTALLORDER**, setting it to **False**, and then click **Next**.

Users can now install Office with the Japanese Language Pack by using the following command line:

```
\\server1\share\Office\setup.exe /q
TRANSFORMS=\\server1\share\office\OfficeWithJapanese.mst
```

Use chaining to deploy multiple MUI Packs with Office

What if you need to deploy two languages with Office? With the Office XP Setup program and the chaining capabilities provided by Setup.ini, you can easily include multiple languages with your Office XP installation.

For example, suppose you want to install French and Polish language features on the user's computer at the same time that you deploy Office. French language features are installed from one CD disk, and Polish language features from another CD.

The sequence of tasks in this situation is as follows:

1. Create an administrative installation point for the core Office product (English).

2. Use Lpksetup.exe to copy the French and Polish Language Packs to the same administrative installation point.

3. Use the Custom Installation Wizard with the Office package (MSI file) and customize language settings for French and Polish, then save the transform with a name (for example, OfficeFrPo.mst).

4. Use the Setup INI Customization Wizard to add sections to chain installations of the French and Polish Language Packs.

After you have created your administrative installation point for Office, add the MUI Pack files that you plan to deploy.

> **Note** For more information about creating an administrative installation point for Office, see "Creating an Administrative Installation Point" in Chapter 5, "Installing and Customizing Office."

To add MUI Packs to an administrative installation point

1. Insert the CD that contains the French Language Pack.
2. On the **Start** menu, click **Run**, and then click **Browse** to locate the MUI Pack CD.
3. On the MUI Pack CD, select **Lpksetup.exe** and click **Open**.
4. On the command line, following **Lpksetup.exe**, type **/a** and click **OK**.
5. Enter the server and the share for your Office administrative installation point and click **Next**.

   The share must be large enough to store the resources for the languages that you need, in addition to the Office XP files. MUI Pack disk-space requirements are approximately 150 MB to 350 MB per MUI Pack.

6. On the **Available Languages** page, choose **French** and click **Install**.

   Note that languages that are not available on the current CD will appear dimmed on this page.

7. Insert the CD that contains the Polish Language Pack.
8. Run **Lpksetup.exe** with the **/a** option again.
9. On the **Available Languages** page, choose **Polish** and click **Install**.

Now customize your Office transform to include language settings for French and Polish.

To create an Office transform with language settings for French and Polish

1. Start the Custom Installation Wizard.
2. On the **Open MSI File** page, enter (or browse to) the MSI file name for your Office installation (for example, Proplus.msi) from the administrative installation point for Office:

   \\server1\share\office\Proplus.msi

3. On the **Select the MST File to Save** page, enter the name of the MST file you are creating; for example:

   \\server1\share\office\OfficeWithFrPo.mst

4. On the **Change Office User Settings** page, click **Microsoft Office (User)**.

5. Navigate the tree under **Language Settings**, and set the language features you want for this deployment.

   For example, you might choose to enable editing for both languages. Open **Enabled Languages**, and click **Show controls and enable editing for**. In the languages shown in the right-hand pane, open **French**, click **Apply changes**, then click **Check to turn setting on**. Click **OK**. Follow the same steps for enabling **Polish**.

Now you chain the French and Polish Language Packs to your Office installation. To chain packages, you customize the Office Setup.ini file by using the Setup INI Customization Wizard (Iniwiz.exe). Although you can modify Setup.ini manually in Notepad, the wizard provides a convenient interface for adding and customizing chained packages.

> **Toolbox** The Setup INI Customization Wizard allows you to easily customize a Setup.ini file for your Office deployment. The Setup INI Customization Wizard is installed by default when you run the Office Resource Kit Setup program. For more information, see "Setup INI Customization Wizard" in the Toolbox.

To chain the French and Polish Language Packs with your Office deployment

1. Start the Setup INI Customization Wizard and enter the path to your Office XP administrative installation point.

2. On the **Select MSI and EXE files to include in your INI file** page, select the check boxes next to the packages that you want to include in your custom INI file, or click **Browse** to add packages from another location, and then click **Next**.

   1036 is the LCID for French and 1045 is the LCID for Polish. So in this example, you might select:

   \\server1\share\office\1036\Lpk.msi

   and

   \\server1\share\office\1045\Lpk.msi

3. On the **Specify options for each package in your INI file** page, select the chained package you want to customize and specify the options you want for that package.

   If you will not be installing the Office XP package before the MUI Pack, select **Advanced Properties** and enter the property **CHECKINSTALLORDER**, setting it to **False**, and then click **Next**.

Users can now install Office with these MUI Packs by specifying the Office transform in the Setup command line:

```
\\server1\share\Office\setup.exe /q
TRANSFORMS=\\server1\share\Office\OfficeFrPo.mst
```

From a user's perspective, deployment proceeds in the following uninterrupted sequence:

1. Office Setup installs Office, as specified in the OfficeFrPo.mst transform.
2. When Office installation is complete, Office Setup runs MUI Pack Setup to install the French Language Pack, as specified in the Setup.ini file.
3. When the French Language Pack installation is complete, Office Setup runs MUI Pack Setup to install the Polish Language Pack, as specified in the Setup.ini file.

At the end of the process, the user has English Office installed with French and Polish language features enabled. By running the Microsoft Office Language Settings utility from the **Start** menu, users can switch the user interface and Help language of Office to English, French, or Polish.

Deploy different language resources for groups of users

In many organizations, you must install different language resources for different groups of users. In this case, you create separate Office transforms, separate MUI Packs transforms, and a customized Setup.ini for each group to perform the following functions:

- In each Office transform, you specify the customized language settings for a group of users.
- In each MUI Pack transform, you define customizations, such as setting setup properties.
- In the Setup.ini file, you chain the languages to the Office installation.

For example, you might have one group of users that speaks French but needs to edit documents in German. You might have a second group of users that speaks Russian but needs to edit in Hungarian. In this scenario, you customize two sets of Office and MUI Pack transforms, along with the corresponding Setup.ini files, one set for each group of users.

First, you create an administrative installation point on the server to deploy Office in each configuration:

- Core Office (English) plus the French Language Pack and German proofing tools from the German Language Pack
- Core Office (English) plus the Russian Language Pack and Hungarian proofing tools from the Hungarian Language Pack

You can use the same administrative installation point, or two separate installation points.

Using the same administrative installation point for two Office installations

If you choose to use the same administrative installation point for two Office installations, you must take steps to ensure that the correct Setup INI file is used for each installation. First, you specify two different Setup.ini files to use, one for each deployment. Then you have two options for using the appropriate Setup.ini file for an installation: using the **/settings** option for Setup.exe or use two copies of Setup.exe with names that correspond to the correct Setup.ini file.

For example, suppose you have two Setup.ini files, SetupFra.ini, and SetupGer.ini. In this situation, choose one of these two methods for installation:

- Use **/settings** to specify which Setup.ini file to use on the Setup.exe command line you provide to your users. For example:

    Setup.exe /settings SetupFra.ini, and

    Setup.exe /settings SetupGer.ini

- Copy Setup.exe to match the Setup.ini file names, then direct users to run the appropriate Setup program file. For example:

    SetupFra.exe will by default use SetupFra.ini.

    SetupGer.exe will by default use SetupGer.ini.

Next, you customize Office transforms for each group of users. You also customize separate transforms by using the MUI Pack MSI files to include proofing tools that provide additional language editing capabilities.

Finally, you create a customized Setup.ini for each group of users to chain the MUI Pack installation with the Office deployment for that group.

Choices for installing proofing tools

You can choose to install proofing tools from the Office Proofing Tools product instead of using the proofing tools included in the Multilingual User Interface Pack. Office Proofing Tools can be chained to your Office installation just as individual MUI Packs can. However, your installation is not as scalable if you choose to use Office Proofing Tools instead of installing the proofing tools included in the Multilingual User Interface Pack.

For example, suppose you install proofing tools for a language from Office Proofing Tools and then decide to include proofing tools for another language later. Proofing Tools includes all languages in a single MSI file. When you install the proofing tools for the first language, you might choose to disable installation for all the other proofing tools in the MSI file. In this case, to later deploy proofing tools for another language, you must use the Custom Maintenance Wizard to change the feature state for the additional proofing tools.

For example, you create the Office transform for the French-speaking group as described in this procedure.

To create an Office transform with language settings for French and German

1. Start the Custom Installation Wizard.
2. On the **Open MSI File** page, enter (or browse to) the MSI file name for your Office installation (for example, Proplus.msi) from the administrative installation point for Office:

    \\server1\share\office\Proplus.msi

3. On the **Select the MST File to Save** page, enter the name of the MST file you are creating; for example:

   \\server1\share\office\OfficeWithFrGr.mst

4. On the **Change Office User Settings** page, click **Microsoft Office (User)**.

5. Navigate the tree under **Language Settings** to **Enabled Languages**.

6. Double-click **Installed version of Microsoft Office** to open the **Properties** page for this setting.

7. Click **Apply changes**, then select **French** from the **Installed version of Microsoft Office** drop-down menu.

8. Click **OK**.

9. Click **Show controls and enable editing for**.

10. In the languages shown in the right-hand pane, open **French**, click **Apply changes**, then click **Check to turn setting on**.

11. Click **OK**.

12. Follow steps 9 through 11 again with German.

13. Next, customize a transform to select the proofing tools from the German Language Pack.

To create a transform for German proofing tools from the German Language Pack

1. Start the Custom Installation Wizard.

2. On the **Open MSI File** page, enter (or browse to) the German Language Pack MSI file:

   \\server1\share\office\1031\Lpk.msi

3. On the **Select the MST File to Save** page, enter the name of the MST file you are creating; for example:

   \\server1\share\office\1031\LPKGermanPT.mst

4. On the **Select Feature Installation States** page, choose **Not Available** for all features.

   (You can alternately specify **Not Available, Hidden, Locked**.)

5. Navigate to **Office Shared Features**, **Proofing Tools**, and click **German**, then choose the install state (for example, **Run from My Computer**).

After you have created the custom transforms, you modify Setup.ini to install Office and the French Language Pack, as well as the transform to install the German proofing tools. To chain packages, you customize the Office Setup.ini file by using the Setup INI Customization Wizard (Iniwiz.exe). Although you can modify Setup.ini manually in Notepad, the wizard provides a convenient interface for adding and customizing chained packages.

Toolbox The Setup INI Customization Wizard allows you to easily customize a Setup.ini file for your Office deployment. The Setup INI Customization Wizard is installed by default when you run the Office Resource Kit Setup program. For more information, see "Setup INI Customization Wizard" in the Toolbox.

To customize Setup to chain additional language features to an Office deployment

1. Start the Setup INI Customization Wizard and enter the path to your Office XP administrative installation point.

2. On the **Select MSI and EXE files to include in your INI file** page, select the check boxes next to the packages that you want to include in your custom INI file, or click **Browse** to add packages from another location, and then click **Next**.

    1036 is the LCID for French, and 1031 is the LCID for German. So in this example, you might select:

    \\server1\share\office\1036\Lpk.msi

    and

    \\server1\share\office\1031\Lpk.msi

3. On the **Specify options for each package in your INI file** page, select the chained package you want to customize and specify the options you want for that package.

    For each package you can specify an MST file and unique display settings, as well as additional property values.

4. In this example, specify the MST file for the German Language Pack:

    \\server1\share\office\1031\LPKGermanPT.mst

    If you will not be installing the Office XP package before the MUI Pack, select **Advanced Properties** and enter the property **CHECKINSTALLORDER**, setting it to **False**, and then click **Next**.

The French-speaking group installs Office by using the following command line:

```
\\server1\share\Office\setup.exe /q
TRANSFORMS=\\server1\share\office\OfficeWithFrench.mst
```

The French-speaking group ends up with a French user interface and Help system with both French and German editing tools enabled.

The basic procedures for deploying to Russian-speaking users are identical, substituting the appropriate languages. Then the Russian-speaking group installs Office by using the following command line:

```
\\server1\share\Office\setup.exe /q
TRANSFORMS=\\server1\share\office\OfficeWithRussian.mst
```

This group ends up with a Russian user interface and Help system with both Russian and Hungarian editing tools enabled.

Installing Proofing Tools

The Microsoft Office Proofing Tools product includes spelling and grammar checkers, thesauruses, and AutoCorrect lists that help users create and edit Office documents in more than 30 languages. Proofing tools for all languages are included on a single CD, but you can install the tools for only the languages that users need.

In addition, proofing tools are included in the Office Multilingual User Interface Pack.

Hard-disk space requirements for Proofing Tools vary by language. Proofing tools for most languages requires about 20 MB of hard-disk space in addition to what Office requires. However, Asian languages require as much as 120 MB of hard-disk space in addition to what Office requires — including the necessary fonts and Input Method Editors (IMEs).

You can install Office Proofing Tools at the same time that you deploy Microsoft Office XP, or separately from Office.

Installing Office Proofing Tools separately from Office

When you install Proofing Tools separately from Office, you can install Proofing Tools for one user or all users in your organization. When you customize for all users at once, you can deploy Proofing Tools customized in a standard way for everyone. This simplifies your deployment and allows you to control the deployment process.

To install Proofing Tools on a single computer

1. On the Office Proofing Tools CD, run Setup.exe.
2. On the **Select Feature Installation States** page, select the languages you want to install and set the appropriate installation states.
3. Click **Install**.

To install Proofing Tools throughout your organization, you create an administrative installation point on a server by running Setup.exe with the **/a** command-line option. All users in your organization can then install Proofing Tools from this location.

You can customize the installation by using the Custom Installation Wizard to create a transform (MST file) that includes settings for the language features you want users to install. If users install Proofing Tools over the network using the transform, they will receive your customizations.

Using a transform, you can omit a language feature from the installation by setting the feature to **Not Available, Hidden, Locked** on the **Set Feature Installation States** page of the wizard. Users cannot change the installation state of a feature marked as **Not Available, Hidden, Locked** during Setup, nor can they add or remove the feature later by using **Add/Remove Programs** in Control Panel.

Toolbox The Office XP Resource Kit includes the Custom Installation Wizard, which is installed by default when you run the Office Resource Kit Setup program. For more information, see "Custom Installation Wizard" in the Toolbox.

To create a transform to customize a Proofing Tools installation

1. Start the Custom Installation Wizard.
2. When prompted for an MSI file, enter (or browse to) the Ptk.msi file from the administrative installation point.
3. On the **Set Feature Installation States** page, select the languages you want to install and set the appropriate installation states.

   Note If Office is already installed, the installation states for Proofing Tools that you install will match the installation states of the Office installation.

For your customizations to be applied when users run Setup from the administration installation point, Setup must be instructed to use your custom transform. You can use the **TRANSFORMS=** command-line option to specify this transform, or you can specify the transform in Setup.ini.

For example, users might use the following command line:

`\\server1\Proof\setup.exe /q TRANSFORMS=\\server1\Proof\Proof.mst`

Or you could add the following entry to your Setup.ini file:

`[MST]`
`MST1=Proof.mst`

Tip To install only a few languages, set the installation state of the entire **Microsoft Office Proofing Tools** feature in the transform to **Not Available**. Then expand the feature tree, select the languages you want, and set them to another installation state.

Installing Office Proofing Tools with Office

If you deploy language resources from Office Proofing Tools at the same time that you deploy Office XP, you can chain the installations together so that they are installed on a user's computer during the same operation.

To do this, you create a custom Setup.ini file for Office Setup that includes the MSI package for Proofing Tools. You can use the Setup INI Customization Wizard to update the Setup.ini file to include Proofing Tools, or you can modify your Setup.ini file manually.

Toolbox The Setup INI Customization Wizard allows you to easily customize a Setup.ini file for your Office deployment. The Setup INI Customization Wizard is installed by default when you run the Office Resource Kit Setup program. For more information, see "Setup INI Customization Wizard" in the Toolbox.

To include Proofing Tools in your Office installation

1. Start the Setup INI Customization Wizard and enter the path to your Office XP administrative installation point.

2. On the **Select MSI and EXE files to include in your INI file** page, select the check boxes next to the packages that you want to include in your custom INI file, or click **Browse** to add packages from another location, and then click **Next**. In this example, you might select:

   \\server1\share\office\Ptk.msi

3. On the **Specify options for each package in your INI file** page, select the chained package you want to customize and specify the options you want for that package. For each package you can specify an MST file and unique display settings, as well as additional property values.

Alternatively, you can manually edit your Setup.ini file on your Office administrative installation point. For example, you could add a section similar to the following:

```
[ChainedInstall_1]
Path=PTK.MSI
CmdLine=TRANSFORMS=Proof.MST
TaskType=msi
IgnoreReturnValue=0
Reboot=0
```

This example assumes that your Proofing Tools administrative image is in the same folder as your Office administrative image.

> **Tip** If your Proofing Tools administrative image is located in the same folder as your Office administrative image, you should specify all paths as relative paths as in the above example. Using a relative path will allow you to copy your administrative image to new servers later, if necessary, without updating the INI file to use the new server name. If your Proofing Tools administrative image is located in a different folder (and possibly different server) than your Office administrative image, you should specify paths as absolute paths (for example, \\server1\proof\ptk.msi).

Now users can install Office and Proofing Tools together by running Office Setup. Office Setup runs Proofing Tools after the Office installation is complete.

> **Note** This chaining technique does not work when deploying by using Windows 2000 IntelliMirror technology, since IntelliMirror does not use Setup technology for installation. See "Using Windows 2000 Software Installation" in Chapter 6, "Deploying on Windows 2000" for information on deploying Office with IntelliMirror.

See also

You may need to provide Proofing Tools in one language while including MUI Pack support in another language for a group of users. For more information about customizing your Office deployment with different combinations of language resources for different users, see "Deploying Office with the Multilingual User Interface Pack" in Chapter 13, "Deploying Office Internationally."

You have customization options when you install Proofing Tools together with Office. For more information about chained deployments, see "Including Additional Packages in the Office Installation" in Chapter 5, "Installing and Customizing Office."

For more information about using the Custom Installation Wizard to create transforms, see "Customizing the Office Installation" in Chapter 5, "Installing and Customizing Office."

Customizing Language Features

When a Microsoft Office XP application starts up for the first time on a user's computer, Office XP chooses default language settings that are appropriate for the language version of Office you are installing and the operating system language on the computer. However, you can configure these language settings yourself rather than letting Office select default settings. You have several choices for customizing language settings. You can:

- Set a value in the Windows registry before any Office applications are started.
- Configure language settings in a transform, by specifying language settings in the Custom Installation Wizard.
- Modify language settings on a user computer through the Microsoft Office Language Settings utility.

The language features you can specify include the:

- Install Language: Sets language defaults for Office applications and documents.
- User Interface Language: Determines the language used for end-user Help.
- Help Language: Determines the language used to display menus and dialogs.
- Editing languages: Exposes functionality to edit documents in those particular languages.
- In addition, some applications use the SKU language setting to determine some behavior. This language setting is based on the original SKU that was installed and cannot be modified.

Note Administrators can elect to disable the Taiwanese date format in Office XP by configuring the Disable Taiwan Calendar setting through the Custom Installation Wizard during deployment, or through the Custom Maintenance Wizard after deployment. To change this setting, go to the **Change Office User Settings** page in the appropriate wizard. Under **Microsoft Office XP (user)**, navigate the tree to **Language Settings**. Select **Other**, then double-click the setting for **Disallow Taiwanese calendar** to open the **Disallow Taiwanese calendar Properties** dialog box. Select **Apply Changes**, then click **OK** to configure the new setting.

Setting values in the Languages Resources subkey

The first time any Office application runs after Office is installed, Office creates the following subkey in the Windows registry:

HKEY_CURRENT_USER\Software\Microsoft\Office\10.0\Common\LanguageResources

When Office applications run, they read value entries in the LanguageResources subkey to determine language-related default behavior. For example:

- Microsoft Word checks locale ID (LCID) value entries and turns on its language auto-detection feature for languages that are enabled for editing.

- Word checks the **InstallLanguage** value entry to determine how to create its initial Normal.dot file.

Instead of letting Office create the LanguageResources subkey, you can set language settings in the Custom Installation Wizard and deploy them as part of your Office XP installation. If Office detects that the language settings are already defined (in the LanguageResources subkey), Office will not override the existing settings when an Office application starts for the first time.

Customizing the installation language

When users start an Office application, the application reads an installation language setting in the Windows registry to determine certain default language-based behavior. For example, this setting is checked to set the default spelling checker for Microsoft Outlook® and to determine how to create the initial Normal.dot file for Microsoft Word.

Office initializes language settings when an Office application first runs on the user's computer. In the LanguageResources subkey, Office creates a value entry named **InstallLanguage** with a value equal to the locale ID (LCID) for the installation language of Office. For example, if the value of **InstallLanguage** is **1041**, the installation language is Japanese. In this case, Normal.dot in Word is based on Japanese settings, and Office applications run with Japanese settings as their default.

To view a table mapping languages to their corresponding locale ID numbers, see "Deploying Office with the Multilingual User Interface Pack" in Chapter 13, "Deploying Office Internationally."

Office automatically sets the installation language to correspond to the language version of the operating system. You can customize the installation language for foreign offices, however, so that Office runs with defaults that match foreign locations.

> **Note** If you plan to select an installation language for your Office deployment (rather than let Office choose the installation language based on the language version of the operating system), it is best to make your selection before you install Office. It is possible to change the installation language afterwards, but you will lose customizations. For example, you will lose macros added to Normal.dot, buttons added to toolbars, and so on.

To customize users' default installation language (or other language feature choices) during deployment, you can use one of two methods: use the Microsoft Office Language Settings utility to select languages, and then capture the settings by using the Profile Wizard (described later in this topic); or, specify language settings on the **Change Office User Settings** page in the Custom Installation Wizard.

To customize the installation language when deploying Office

1. In the Custom Installation Wizard, go to the **Change Office User Settings** page and click **Microsoft Office (User)**.
2. Navigate the tree under **Language Settings** to **Enabled Languages**.
3. Double-click **Installed version of Microsoft Office** to open the **Properties** page for this setting.
4. Click **Apply changes**, then select a language from the **Installed version of Microsoft Office** drop-down menu.
5. Click **OK**.

You can specify other language feature settings under **Language Settings** as well, such as choosing languages to be enabled for editing.

Configuring language-specific defaults

In addition to using the installation language setting, Office XP also configures language-related defaults, such as number format, to match the user locale of the operating system. If you want Office to use defaults based on the installation language regardless of the user locale, you can set the value of **LangTuneUp** in the LanguageResources subkey to **ON**. (To prevent Office from using the defaults, set the value of **LangTuneUp** to **PROHIBITED**.)

System Policy Tip You can use system policies to prevent Office from adjusting defaults to the user locale for any group of users in your organization. In the System Policy Editor, set the **Microsoft Office XP\Language Settings\Other\Do not adjust defaults to user's locale** policy. For more information about using system policies settings with Office, see "How to Set System Policies" in Chapter 9, "Using System Policies."

For example, if your organization is based in the United States and you want to standardize settings internationally, you can deploy Office with the **InstallLanguage** entry set to **1033** (U.S. English) and the **LangTuneUp** entry set to **ON**. Users would get the same set of defaults regardless of their user locale.

An advantage of preventing Office from configuring to the user locale is that macros are more compatible internationally when all settings are consistent. A disadvantage of setting the **LangTuneUp** entry to **ON** is that, if you are upgrading from a previous localized version of Office, you cannot migrate user settings from a language version that differs from the Office XP installation language.

Notes Users who read and enter Asian characters in Office documents must have the corresponding Asian fonts available on their computers in order for the characters to display properly. Typically, the installation language on a user's computer matches the language used in the documents. In this case, Office uses the appropriate Asian font, regardless of the value of the **LangTuneUp** registry subkey.

If a user needs to open documents that require Asian fonts not supported by the installation language, however, setting the **LangTuneUp** registry subkey to **ON** may prevent the user from being able to view the fonts of the non-default language. If you need to enable your computers to support multiple Asian language locales, you will need to set the value of **LangTuneUp** to **Prohibited**, not **ON**, for these installations.

Customizing languages for the user interface, online Help, and editing

Office XP allows users to choose different languages for displaying menus and dialog box text, Help text, and for editing documents. To customize users' default language choices during deployment, you can use one of two methods: use the Microsoft Office Language Settings utility to select languages, and then capture the settings by using the Profile Wizard; or, specify language settings on the **Change Office User Settings** page in the Custom Installation Wizard (as described earlier in this topic).

To select language settings

1. On the **Start** menu, point to **Programs**, and then point to **Microsoft Office Tools**.
2. Click **Microsoft Office Language Settings**, and then click the **User Interface** tab.

    Note that the **User Interface** tab is available only if the MUI Pack has been installed.

3. In the **Display menus and dialogs in** box, select the user interface language.

4. In the **Display Help in** box, select a language for online Help.

   If you do not specify a language in the Display Help in box, the online Help language defaults to the language that you selected as the user interface language.

5. Click the **Enabled Languages** tab, and select languages that you want to be available for editing documents.

6. In the **Default version of Microsoft Office** box, select the Office installation language (optional), which sets the installation language.

   Note that if the installation language of Office is English, French, German, Norwegian, or Serbian, selecting the local variety of the language makes utilities such as spelling checkers more useful.

After selecting language settings in the Microsoft Office Language Settings tool, you can capture the settings by using the Office Profile Wizard to save an OPS file. Then you can deploy the settings to your users when you deploy Office by including the OPS file in your custom Office transform. If you want to make additional changes to the settings after you have captured the settings in the OPS file, you can make modifications on the **Change Office User Settings** page of the Custom Installation Wizard (as described earlier in this topic).

Enabling languages without the Multilingual User Interface Pack

The options on the **User Interface** tab in the Microsoft Office Language Settings dialog box include all the languages installed from the Multilingual User Interface Pack. However, the **options on the Enabled Languages** tab include all the languages supported by Office, regardless of what is installed from the Multilingual User Interface Pack.

Consequently, you can enable functionality for working with certain languages regardless of whether the MUI Pack is installed. For example, by selecting Korean as an editing language, you enable Asian and Korean features in Word regardless of whether Korean proofing tools from the MUI Pack are available.

If you installed Microsoft Office Proofing Tools instead of the MUI Pack, Office uses Proofing Tools for the languages you enable for editing.

System Policy Tip You can use system policies to specify default language settings for any group of users in your organization. In the System Policy Editor, set the **Microsoft Office XP\Language Settings\User Interface** policies to determine user interface languages. To determine editing languages, set the **Microsoft Office XP\Language Settings\Enabled Languages\Show controls and enable editing for** policies. For more information about using system policy settings with Office, see "How to Set System Policies" in Chapter 9, "Using System Policies."

When you set system policies for the user interface and online Help, be sure the languages you select are supported by users' operating system. Note that:

- In Microsoft Windows 2000, most languages are supported for the user interface and online Help.
- In English and European versions of Microsoft Windows 98, Microsoft Windows Millennium Edition (Windows Me), and Microsoft Windows NT 4, users can run the user interface and online Help in English and all European languages.
- In Greek, Asian and right-to-left language (Arabic, Hebrew) versions of Windows 98, Windows Me, and Windows NT 4, users can run the user interface and online Help in English or the language of their operating system.

Note Users running an Arabic version of Windows 98, Windows Me, and Windows NT 4 can also select French as their user interface and online Help language.

See also

Each Office application uses language settings differently for making changes in user interfaces and other language-specific areas of the application. For more information, see "Managing Language Settings for Each Application" in Chapter 16, "Maintaining International Installations."

You can change the installation language or other language settings after you have installed Office. For more information, see "Changing Language Settings" in Chapter 16, "Maintaining International Installations."

CHAPTER 14

Upgrading International Installations

Microsoft Office XP and the Office Multilingual User Interface Pack allow international users to upgrade easily from previous versions of Office with MultiLanguage Pack or localized versions of Office. Migration of user settings from previous localized versions, Unicode support, and multilingual features of Office XP make for a smooth international upgrade, whether your organization makes the transition in stages or all at once.

In this chapter

Upgrading Your MultiLanguage Pack Installation   407

Upgrading with Input Method Editors   408

Sharing Files Across Language Versions   409

Upgrading Your MultiLanguage Pack Installation

It is a straightforward process to upgrade an existing Microsoft Office 2000 MultiLanguage Pack installation to use the Microsoft Office Multilingual User Interface Pack. To successfully migrate an installation, ensure that all previous MultiLanguage Pack files are deleted. Then install the MUI Pack files.

To upgrade an existing MultiLanguage Pack installation during your Office XP installation, first customize your Office transform to remove existing MultiLanguage Pack files. In the Custom Installation Wizard, on the **Remove Previous Versions** page, click **Remove the following versions of Microsoft Office applications**. Then select Microsoft Office 2000 MultiLanguage Pack.

If you are upgrading an existing MultiLanguage Pack installation after you have deployed Office XP, you must use another method (such as using the Office Removal Wizard) to ensure that all the existing MultiLanguage Pack files have been removed from users' computers before you install the Multilingual User Interface Pack.

After ensuring that previous versions of the MultiLanguage Pack have been removed, you can customize and install one or more MUI Packs.

See also

Procedures for various MUI Pack deployment scenarios are included in "Sample Customizations for Office with the Multilingual User Interface Pack" in Chapter 13, "Deploying Office Internationally."

You can use the Office Removal Wizard to remove applications or files after completing your initial Office installation. For more information about using the Removal Wizard, see "Removing Applications or Features After Installation" in Chapter 8, "Maintaining an Installation."

Upgrading with Input Method Editors

The Microsoft Office Multilingual User Interface Pack now includes Input Method Editors (IMEs) for the languages that you choose to install. If your organization uses IMEs, you can install and use any of the updated IMEs supplied with the Office Multilingual User Interface Pack (MUI Pack). If your organization uses a Global Input Method Editor instead, you can now use the editors provided with the MUI Pack or download the new replacement editor that works with Office XP.

Upgrading to Office XP with the Multilingual User Interface Pack could result in multiple Input Method Editors on your users' computers. Existing IMEs are not uninstalled by the Office installation process, but instead are unregistered from the Active keyboard during Office XP Setup. If Office XP is uninstalled later, on East Asian computers the older IMEs will become available again automatically.

To migrate with language-specific IMEs, install the MUI Pack languages that your organization needs. The corresponding IMEs will be installed automatically with the languages.

> **Note** If your users have Microsoft Windows® 2000, they must enable the language for the IME before installing the IME. To do this, go to Regional Options in Control Panel. Under the **Language settings for the system** area in the **General** tab, choose the language of the IME. This process will install the appropriate language support files.

If you currently use a Global Input Method Editor instead of a language-specific IME in your organization's environment, be aware that the Global Input Method Editor is no longer supported. If you install the MUI Pack, you no longer need a Global Input Method Editor.

If you choose to use a Global Input Method Editor in your organization (instead of installing the MUI Pack), you must download the new equivalent to the Global Input Method Editor, called the Web Downloadable Input Method Editor. Download and install this file before you update to Office XP. To download the Input Method Editor from the World Wide Web, see the Microsoft Office Web site at http://office.microsoft.com.

Sharing Files Across Language Versions

Just as file compatibility affects how users share files between numbered versions of Microsoft Office, file compatibility also affects how users share files across different language versions of Office — for example, sharing files from the Japanese version of Microsoft Office 95 with files from Microsoft Office XP with the Multilingual User Interface Pack (MUI Pack). Several strategies are available to help you share files across language versions of Office.

Sharing Office files across language versions

When all users in an international organization have upgraded to Microsoft Office XP, sharing files across languages is easy, whether the files are from Office XP with the Multilingual User Interface Pack or from localized versions of Office XP. Even during a gradual upgrade to Office XP, you can still share files with older localized versions of Office.

If you are upgrading gradually to Office XP, you can save Office XP files in formats that allow users of previous localized versions of Office to open the files, yet preserve the Office XP multilingual features. These file formats vary by Office application and are not the same as the formats used by previous localized versions. So, if you save Office XP files in the format of the previous localized version, multilingual features of Office XP are lost.

For example, Microsoft Word 2002, Microsoft Excel 2002, and Microsoft PowerPoint 2002 can display multiple Asian languages in the same file. When these files are saved in versions of Office earlier than Office 2000, the multi-Asian language feature is lost and only one of the languages is displayed properly.

Unicode® allows you to share multilingual files between Office XP and Office 2000 or Office 97 without any loss of text. Older versions of Office might not properly display multilingual text from an Office XP file, because versions of Office prior to 97 are based on code pages, not Unicode. For more information about Unicode and how it supports multilingual documents in Office, see "Unicode Support and Multilingual Documents" in Chapter 15, "Maintaining International Installations."

Your operating system can determine whether you can display Asian or right-to-left text (such as Arabic, Hebrew, Farsi, or Urdu) between different versions of Office.

To display a right-to-left language, you must be running a right-to-left language version of your operating system. To display Asian languages, note the following:

- Office XP and Office 2000 provide files — including fonts — that extend an operating system's ability to support Asian languages.
- The Office 97 Asian support files — including fonts — extend an operating system's ability to support Asian languages.

- To display or edit Asian text in an older version of Office (earlier than Office 97), you must run a language version of the operating system that matches the Asian language with which you want to work.

Sharing Access database files across language versions

Microsoft Access 2002 can open databases created in any previous localized version of Access. For some languages, Access 2002 users who are running Microsoft Windows NT® 4.0 might need to install language support available with Windows NT 4.0.

> **Note** Users of previous localized versions of Access cannot open Access 2002 databases.

Opening databases from previous localized versions in Access 2002

Because the default file format in Access 2002 is the same as in Access 2000, all Access 2000 database users can share databases with Access 2002 users. However, if you are using Access 97 or earlier and only part of your organization is upgrading to Access 2002, you might want to leave existing databases in the format of your previous version of Access so that all users can open the databases.

If you are using Access 2002 and want to open databases in Access 97 or earlier, you might not be able to open the older databases if the language version of your operating system differs from the operating system on the computer used to create the database. Access databases are saved in a particular sort order, and the default sort order matches the sort order used by the operating system on the computer used to create the database.

For example, a database created in Access 95 on a computer running the Arabic version of Microsoft Windows 95 uses the Arabic sort order by default and cannot be opened on a computer running the English version of Microsoft Windows 95/98 or the English version of Windows NT 4.0.

> **Note** Microsoft Windows 2000 includes international sort order support for multiple languages. Users running Access 2002 on Windows 2000 can open databases from previous versions of Access in the native sort order.

There are two ways to work around the difficulty of opening older databases. One solution is to install national language support (NLS) files that extend the ability of the operating system to support additional sort orders. The other solution is to recompact the database by using a sort order that is supported by multiple operating systems.

Supporting the default sort order on Windows NT 4.0

In Windows NT 4.0, you can install a MUI Pack for the operating system that includes NLS files that support the default sort order of the database.

To install MUI Pack files to support database sort order

1. At your installation source for Windows NT 4.0, go to the Langpack folder.
2. Right-click on the .inf file for the language you want, and then click **Install**.

Using the General sort order on Windows 98

In Windows 98, you cannot add the NLS files that support foreign language sort orders. Instead, you must compact the database by using a sort order that is supported by the operating systems on all computers concerned. The most commonly supported sort order is General.

The General sort order allows users running a variety of language versions of Windows 98 to open a database. However, this might not work well for your organization if you store data in Spanish and Asian languages, which do not support the General sort order. For such databases, it might be preferable to convert the database to the Access 2000 file format.

For example, Access 2002 users running the English version of Windows 98 might need to open an Access 95 database that originated on a computer running the Japanese version of Windows 95. In this scenario, it might be better to convert the database to the Access 2000 file format than to attempt to share it across language versions of the operating system.

> **Note** For a list of languages that support the General sort order, see Access Help.

To compact the original database by using the General sort order

1. Open the database in the original, localized version of Access.

   You must open the database on a computer running the same language version of the operating system as was used to create the database, or you can open the database on a computer running Windows NT 4.0 or Windows 2000 with language support for the original sort order.

2. Change the sort order to **General**, and recompact the database.

   Steps for changing sort order and compacting the database vary with different versions of Access. For more information, see Access Help.

Opening forms and reports from previous localized versions

Access 2002 can open and read the English- and European-language content of forms and reports from any previous localized version of Access. However, if the database is based on a code page other than Latin 1 (code page 1252), and if you are using Access 2000 with an English or a Western European version of the operating system, some text might be rendered incorrectly.

For example, a database created in Access 95 on the Greek version of Windows 95 is based on the Greek code page. When an Access 2002 user running the English version of Windows 98 opens the database, the operating system maps code points to the new code page, so some Greek characters might appear as accented European characters, question marks, open boxes, or other unintelligible characters.

Converting databases from previous localized versions of Access

If Access 2002 users do not need to share a database from a previous localized version of Access with users of the older version, convert the database to the Access 2000 file format. If the database was saved in the default sort order on a computer running a non-English version of the operating system, convert it by opening it in Access 2002 and saving it in the Access 2000 file format. Access converts the data to Unicode.

Using the original language sort order

When you convert an older database to the Access 2000 file format, Access uses the sort order to determine which code page to use for converting the data to Unicode. Access 2002 associates the General sort order with the Western European code page, so if non-Western European data is stored in the General sort order, the data is corrupted when Access 2002 converts it.

Therefore, if the older database is based on a non-English version of the operating system, and it is saved in the General sort order, you must recompact it in the original language sort order before converting it to the Access 2000 file format. Otherwise, Access 2002 cannot properly convert the data to Unicode.

To convert a localized database to the Access 2000 file format

1. Open the database in the original, localized version of Access.

   You must open the database on a computer running the same language version of the operating system as that used to create the database, or you can open the database on a computer running Windows NT 4.0 or Windows 2000 with language support for the original sort order.

2. Change the sort order to match the language of the operating system, and recompact the database.

   Note that the steps for changing sort order and compacting the database vary with different versions of Access. For more information, see Access Help.

3. Start Access 2002, but do not open the database.

4. On the **Tools** menu, point to **Database Utilities**, point to **Convert Database**, and then click **To Current Access Database Version**.

5. In the **Database to Convert From** dialog box, select the database you want to convert, and click **Convert**.

Specifying the code page for the General sort order

If you do not have the necessary language version of the operating system, or if the data in the older database is in a language that had no sort order in earlier versions of Access, you can still convert the database to the Access 2000 file format.

For example, databases in earlier versions of Access that are based on Vietnamese, Farsi, or a Baltic version of the operating system (Estonian, Latvian, or Lithuanian) default to the General sort order because previous versions of Access did not support sort orders for those languages. To convert these databases, you must create a registry entry to prevent Access 2002 from corrupting the non-Western European data.

To convert non-Western European databases that use the General sort order

1. If you are converting an Access version 1.*x* or 2.0 database, go to the following registry subkey:

    HKEY_LOCAL_MACHINE\Software\Microsoft\Jet\4.0\Engines\Jet 2.x

    – or –

    If you are converting an Access 95 or 97 database, go to the following registry subkey:

    HKEY_LOCAL_MACHINE\Software\Microsoft\Jet\4.0\Engines\Jet 3.x

2. In the Jet 2.x or Jet 3.x subkey, create a new value entry named **ForceCp** and set the value to **ANSI** to use the computer's default code page.

    You can specify a different code page by setting the value to the code page number, such as **1257** for Windows Baltic Rim.

3. Convert the database to the Access 2000 file format.

4. Delete the **ForceCP** value entry from the registry so that Access 2002 reverts to using the sort order of a database to determine the code page.

Removing conflicting data to solve indexing problems

Access 2002 upgrades some sort orders so that they differ from previous versions of Access. In the new sorting, characters that were considered different in older databases might be considered the same in Access 2002. As a result, the converted database might contain conflicting data, making it impossible to create a unique index for some tables. To create a unique index on the affected tables, you must remove the conflicting data.

A similar problem might occur when changing the sort order of a database. Characters might be different in one language but equivalent in another language. For example, the Western European lowercase *i* and uppercase *I* are considered equivalent when sorting alphabetically. But in Turkish a lowercase *i* might be dotted or not dotted, and the two *i* characters are not considered equivalent when sorting alphabetically in Turkish. Because they are considered equivalent in the General sort order, however, these characters can create conflicting data when you upgrade a Turkish database to the Access 2000 file format.

Sharing Excel workbooks across language versions

In Excel 2002, you can open and edit any workbook created in a previous localized version of Excel, regardless of the language, provided the operating system supports the language of the file. For example, you can use Excel 2002 to open and edit a Korean Excel 2000 file on a Korean system. If you need to share files across languages (for example, opening a Korean Excel workbook on a Spanish system), it is recommended that you use Windows 2000 with its robust support for multiple languages.

Users of Excel 2002 and previous localized versions can share workbooks as follows. In Excel 2002, you can open and save:

- Localized Excel 5/95 files only on same language operating system (since these files do not use Unicode).

    On Windows 2000, this requires that the **Default System Locale** be set to the same language of the operating system.

- Any Excel 97 or Excel 2000 file without language limitations as long as the operating system includes support for the characters and fonts.

- European, Asian, and Complex Script (Hebrew, Arabic, Thai, and Vietnamese) files in the Excel 97/2000 format on any operating system that supports these languages.

Platform support for multilingual file sharing

Windows 2000 provides the best support for organizations with requirements for multilingual file sharing. In Windows 2000, you can enable support for multiple languages or even change your code page through the **Default System Locale** setting. If you must open and edit Excel workbooks in multiple languages on the same machine, it is recommended that you use the Windows 2000 operating system on your computer.

To view an Excel file in a different language from your default language on Windows 2000, simply ensure that the other language is enabled on your system. The proper characters are displayed when you open, edit, and save the file. This works for all Unicode Excel versions (Excel 97 and later, including Excel 2002).

Multilingual file sharing with non-Unicode files

Sharing multilingual files that do not support Unicode is problematic. Non-Unicode files include Excel files created in versions earlier than Excel 97 (including Excel 5 and Excel 95), files saved in one of these earlier formats, or Lotus files, for example. Opening these files on a computer with a different language will not work, even if the operating system on the computer is Windows 2000.

There are several work-arounds for this. For example, you can set up your computer to perform a dual boot, configuring the second boot to use the appropriate language for the multilingual file. However, you must own a copy of Windows in each language that you wish to use for booting your computer.

With Windows 2000, there is an easier solution. You can change the code page to the other language by modifying the **Default System Locale**, then reboot your system. Now you can view and edit the non-Unicode file that was created in another language.

Sharing FrontPage files across language versions

Microsoft FrontPage® 2002 allows you to work with more languages and characters than you can with previous versions. FrontPage now has full Unicode support and recognizes more HTML 4.0 character entity references than do previous versions. However, file names and URLs are still dependent on operating system language support. To ensure that all users can access files on a FrontPage server, it is recommended that ASCII file names be used.

Character entity references make up a set of HTML characters that are represented by easy-to-remember mnemonic names. For example, the character entity reference **å** specifies a lowercase *a* topped by a ring. It's easier to remember **å** than it is to remember **&229;**.

In Microsoft FrontPage 2002, you can open and edit any document created in FrontPage 2000, FrontPage 98, or FrontPage 97, regardless of the language used in the document, provided the operating system supports the language of the file.

> **Note** FrontPage 2002 and Internet Explorer 5 encode URLs in UTF-8, a Unicode format. To use FrontPage 2002 to edit FrontPage-based webs that include non-ASCII URLs, you must either have a Web server that supports UTF-8 or turn off UTF-8 encoding.

The enhanced language features in FrontPage 2002 affect file sharing between FrontPage 2002 and previous versions in the following ways:

- In a folder list or view in FrontPage 2002, folder and file names are displayed correctly regardless of your default language.

    However, to open or save files, the code page of the file name must match the default system code page of the operating system. For example, to save a file with a Japanese name, the default system code page must be Japanese. This does not affect the content of the document, just the file name.

- If you use FrontPage 2002 to create a document in some languages, such as Thai, you cannot open or edit that document in FrontPage 97 or FrontPage 98.

    If you try to open it, both FrontPage 97 and FrontPage 98 display an error message.

- If you use FrontPage 2002 to create a document that contains a Unicode character, such as **Β** for the Greek capital letter beta, you cannot display that character in FrontPage 2000 or earlier versions.

    If you save the document in a version of FrontPage earlier than FrontPage 2002, the Unicode character is deleted.

- If you use FrontPage 2002 to create a document that contains an HTML 4.0 character entity reference, then you cannot edit that character in FrontPage 2000 or earlier versions.

    The character entity reference appears as **δ** and is not deleted if you save the document in a version earlier than FrontPage 2002.

Exchanging Outlook messages across language versions

Enhancements in Microsoft Outlook® 2002 make it easier to exchange Outlook messages across language versions. You can enable multilingual display support for Outlook, and you can specify auto-select outbound encoding for all mail messages. As in Outlook 2000, Outlook 2002 supports Unicode in the body of mail messages.

Enabling multilingual display support for Outlook

There are two ways to enable Outlook to display content in multiple languages — through Office Setup or the operating system. Please note that multilingual support has to be installed on both the sending and receiving sides of an e-mail exchange to ensure full functionality.

The first way to install multilingual support is through Office Setup. Some of the files are automatically installed as part of the System Files Update if they are not already present on your system. Font support may have to be added manually by following these steps:

1. Rerun Setup, and then select **Add/Remove components**.
2. Expand the **Office Shared Features** section, and then under **International Support**, make sure that the font corresponding to the desired language is installed locally.
3. Select **OK** to apply the changes.

The second way to install multilingual support is through the operating system.

Installing multilingual support for Windows 2000 users

1. In Control Panel, double-click **Regional Options**.
2. Click the **General** tab.
3. In the list shown under **Language settings for the system**, select the check boxes next to the languages you want to use for sending and receiving messages.
4. Click **OK**.

    Note A system reboot is required after installing the support files.

Installing multilingual support for users of Windows 98, Windows 98 SE, and Windows Millennium Edition

1. In Control Panel, double-click **Add/Remove Programs**.
2. Click the **Windows Setup** tab.
3. Select **Multilanguage Support** from the list and click **Details**.
4. From the list of languages shown, select the language you want to use for sending and receiving messages.

   Note that a system reboot may be necessary after installing the support files.

   Note Windows cannot be enabled for some languages by following the above procedure — for example, non-Asian versions cannot be enabled for Asian languages. For those cases, please follow the steps described under the first method of installing multilingual support.

Outlook data that is not in the body of the message — such as Contacts, Tasks, and the To and Subject lines of messages — are limited to characters defined by the system code page. Such characters might be unintelligible for a recipient whose operating system uses a different code page.

Specifying character encoding

In addition to enabling multilingual display support for Outlook, you can specify the character encoding (also known as the code page) of the message being sent.

It is recommended that you rely on the new Auto-Select Outbound Encoding feature, which Microsoft has introduced with Outlook 2002. This feature is automatically switched on when you have Internet Explorer 5.5 or higher installed. Auto-Select Outbound Encoding scans the entire text of outgoing messages to determine a minimal popular encoding capable of representing all characters and optimized that the majority of the receiving e-mail programs can interpret and render the content.

You can also manually select an encoding that supports the characters being sent and that the recipient's e-mail application can interpret. For example, if all users' e-mail applications support multilingual Unicode data, Unicode (UTF-8) encoding is an excellent choice, since it supports a big range of characters in different scripts.

> **Notes** An Outlook 2002 user's default **Preferred encoding for outgoing messages** is the Internet encoding that corresponds to the user's Windows code page. For example, **Japanese (JIS)** encoding for a Japanese Windows code page, **Western European (ISO)** encoding for a Western European Latin1 code page, or **Cyrillic (KOI8-R)** encoding for a Cyrillic code page.
>
> The active Windows code page of your operating system is defined by your system locale. On Windows 2000 it can be set in **Regional Options** in Control Panel by selecting the **Set Default** button, which opens the **Select System Locale** dialog.

To enable Auto-Select Outbound Encoding in Outlook 2002

1. On the **Tools** menu, click **Options**, then click the **Mail Format** tab.
2. Click **International Options**, and activate the **Auto-Select encoding for outgoing messages** check box.
3. Select a character encoding in the **Preferred encoding for outgoing messages** box.

   This encoding is used by Auto-Select Outbound encoding in cases where more than one minimal popular encoding can represent all the text. If you prefer, you can manually specify the character encoding.

To manually specify character encoding in Outlook 2002

1. On the **Tools** menu, click **Options**, then click the **Mail Format** tab.
2. Click **International Options**, and deactivate the **Auto-Select encoding for outgoing messages** check box.
3. Select a character encoding in the **Preferred encoding for outgoing messages** box.

   This encoding is now used for all messages you create, regardless of the text (characters) you type into them. Note that the **Auto-Select encoding for outgoing messages** check box is only available if you have Internet Explorer 5.5 or higher installed.
4. If you want message flags and Forward and Reply headers to be in English, select the **Use English for message flags** and **Use English for message headers on replies and forwards** check boxes.

   If you clear these check boxes, message flags and headers match the language of the Outlook user interface, and e-mail applications that run in another language might not display the text properly.

> **System Policy Tip** You can use a system policy to set character encoding for Outlook 2002 messages. You set these policies in **Microsoft Outlook 2002\Tools | Options\Mail Format\International Options**. For more information about using system policies with Office applications, see "How to Set System Policies" in Chapter 9, "Using System Policies."

When you click **Send To** on the **File** menu in Office applications to create e-mail messages, the content of the message is saved in HTML format. The **Preferred encoding for outgoing messages** setting in Outlook determines the character encoding for the message, or if Auto-Select Outbound Encoding is activated, Outlook automatically selects an appropriate encoding.

When you do not want to rely on Auto-Select Outbound Encoding, you can manually set the encoding of mail messages by picking an appropriate encoding from the Format.Encoding list. If you do rely on the Auto-Select Encoding feature, Outlook will always show **Auto-Select** in the Format.Encoding menu and will not allow users to manually overwrite the option.

Sharing PowerPoint presentations across language versions

Just as with non-localized versions of Microsoft PowerPoint®, localized PowerPoint 2000 can open and read PowerPoint 2002 presentations directly, but localized PowerPoint 95 must have the PowerPoint 97 converter for PowerPoint 95 installed, or PowerPoint 2002 presentations must be saved in PowerPoint 97-2002 & 95 format.

PowerPoint 4.0 users can open PowerPoint 2002 presentations if they install the PowerPoint 97 converter for PowerPoint 4.0.

Users of PowerPoint 2000 and previous localized versions can share presentations as follows:

- In PowerPoint 2000, you can open and edit any presentation created in a previous localized version of PowerPoint, regardless of the language, provided the operating system supports the language of the file.
- In localized PowerPoint 97, you can open and edit PowerPoint 2002 presentations, regardless of the language, provided the operating system supports the language of the file.
- In localized PowerPoint 95, in addition to an operating system that supports the language of the file, you need the following to open PowerPoint 2002 presentations:

    You must have the PowerPoint 97 converter for PowerPoint 95 converter installed.

    – or –

    The file must be in PowerPoint 97-2002 & 95 format.

- In localized PowerPoint 4.0, in addition to an operating system that supports the language of the file, you must have the PowerPoint 97 converter for PowerPoint 4.0 installed to open PowerPoint 2002 presentations.

Opening presentations from previous localized versions in PowerPoint 2002

When you open PowerPoint 95 or PowerPoint 4.0 presentations in PowerPoint 2002, PowerPoint 2002 converts the text to Unicode. Because PowerPoint 2000 and PowerPoint 97 both support Unicode, PowerPoint 2002 does not need to convert PowerPoint 97 or PowerPoint 2000 text.

PowerPoint 2002 can display English and European text in presentations from any language version of PowerPoint 2000, PowerPoint 97, PowerPoint 95, and PowerPoint 4.0. If PowerPoint 2002 users have enabled the appropriate language in Microsoft Office Language Settings, PowerPoint 2002 can display text in any language provided the operating system supports the language of the file.

> **Note** Some unknown characters might appear when you open an English or European-language version of PowerPoint 95 or PowerPoint 4.0 presentation in the Korean, Simplified Chinese, or Traditional Chinese versions of PowerPoint 2002. To correct this problem, click **Options** on the PowerPoint 2002 **Tools** menu, and then click the **Asian** tab. Clear the **Convert font-associated text** check box.

Opening PowerPoint 2002 presentations in localized PowerPoint 2000 and PowerPoint 97

PowerPoint 2002 files containing Unicode surrogate pairs will in most cases display correctly if you have the appropriate language support installed on your computer. Editing these characters, however, will not work correctly. PowerPoint 2002 files containing Hindi characters will in most cases display individual characters correctly if you have the appropriate language support installed on your computer. Layout for the Hindi text in PowerPoint 2000 might be different than it is in PowerPoint 2002, and editing will not work correctly.

Localized versions of PowerPoint 2000 can display PowerPoint 2002 text as shown in the following table.

This language version of PowerPoint 2002...	...can display text in these languages
U.S./European, Asian, right-to-left language (Arabic, Hebrew)	English, European, Asian, right-to-left language (Arabic, Hebrew)
Thai	Thai, English, European, Asian, right-to-left language (Arabic, Hebrew)
Vietnamese	Vietnamese, English, European, Asian, right-to-left language (Arabic, Hebrew)

Opening PowerPoint 2002 presentations in localized PowerPoint 97

PowerPoint 97 can directly open and read PowerPoint 2002 presentations. However, to display Asian or right-to-left (Arabic, Hebrew, Farsi, or Urdu) text that doesn't match the language version of PowerPoint 97, you must have the appropriate language support installed on your computer.

For Asian text, you can install the Office 97 Asian support files, but for right-to-left text, you must use a compatible right-to-left language version of PowerPoint 97.

The layout for the Hindi text in PowerPoint 97 might be different than it is in PowerPoint 2002, and editing will not work correctly.

Localized versions of PowerPoint 97 can display PowerPoint 2002 text as shown in the following table.

This language version of PowerPoint 97	Can display text in these languages
U.S./European	English, European, Asian (Asian requires the Office 97 Asian support files)
Asian	English, European, matching Asian and nonmatching Asian (nonmatching Asian requires Office 97 Asian support files)
Right-to-left language (Arabic, Hebrew)	English, European, and a compatible right-to-left language

Note The layout for Asian text in PowerPoint 97 and PowerPoint 2000 might be different than it is in PowerPoint 2002.

Opening PowerPoint 2002 presentations in localized PowerPoint 95 and PowerPoint 4.0

Depending on the language, PowerPoint 95 can open and read PowerPoint 2002 presentations by using the PowerPoint 97 converter for PowerPoint 95 or if the presentations are saved in the PowerPoint 97-2002 & 95 format. Similarly, PowerPoint 4.0 can open and read PowerPoint 97, PowerPoint 2000, and PowerPoint 2002 presentations by using the PowerPoint 97 converter for PowerPoint 4.0, depending on the language.

Note The PowerPoint 97 converter for PowerPoint 4.0 cannot be used with Asian versions of PowerPoint 4.0. Therefore, users of Asian versions of PowerPoint 4.0 cannot open PowerPoint 2002 presentations.

Localized versions of PowerPoint 95 and PowerPoint 4.0 can display PowerPoint 2002 text as shown in the following table.

This language version of PowerPoint 4.0/95	Can display text in these languages
U.S./European	English, European
Asian (PowerPoint 95 only)	English, European, and the matching Asian language
Right-to-left language (Arabic, Hebrew) (PowerPoint 95 only)	English, European, and a compatible right-to-left language

Sharing Publisher files across language versions

Microsoft Publisher 2002 can open and read publications created in any localized version of Publisher. However, previous localized versions of Publisher cannot open Publisher 2002 publications.

Publisher 2002 supports editing right-to-left text (for languages such as Arabic, Hebrew, Farsi, and Urdu) on versions of Windows that support right-to-left display and processing. Some right-to-left text as well as some formatting may not be preserved when saving a publication in an earlier version of Publisher if the version does not support editing right-to-left text.

When you use Publisher 2002 to open documents composed in Publisher 97 or earlier, Publisher converts the text to Unicode. Because Publisher 2002, Publisher 2000, and Publisher 98 all support Unicode, Publisher 2002 does not need to convert the text for documents created in those later versions.

Sharing Word documents across language versions

Each new version of Word can successfully open more language versions from older releases of Word. For example, English Word 2000 can open Asian Word 6.0-95 files correctly — something that English Word 97 cannot do. English Word 2002 now correctly opens and handles all legacy documents, including Thai Word 6.0-2000 documents, as well as Hindi/Tamil documents created in South Asian Word 2000.

Users of previous versions of Word can also share documents with Word 2002 users. Just as with non-localized versions, localized Word 97 can open and read Word 2002 documents directly, but localized Word 95 or Word 6.0 must have the Word 97-2002 converter installed, or the Word 2002 documents must be saved in Rich Text Format (RTF).

RTF allows you to exchange multilingual documents between Microsoft Office versions. In Office XP (as well as Office 2000 and Office 97), RTF files support Unicode and also allow Word 95 and Word 6.0 to use all Unicode characters that occur in single-byte code pages. As long as the Word 95 or Word 6.0 user does not save the file, the complete Unicode content of the document is preserved when the RTF file is reopened in Word 2002 (as well as in Word 2000 and Word 97).

> **Toolbox** The Office XP Resource Kit includes a spreadsheet that shows how documents are handled when they are opened in different versions of Word or different languages. The file Multilpk.xls is installed by default when you run the Office Resource Kit Setup program. For more information, see "Supplemental Documentation" in the Toolbox.

Opening documents from previous localized versions in Word 2002

When you open Microsoft Word 95 or 6.0 documents in Word 2002, Word 2002 converts the text to Unicode. Because Word 2002, Word 2000, and Word 97 all support Unicode, these versions do not need to convert text when documents are opened in another version.

Word 2002 can display English and European-language text in documents from any language version of Word 97, Word 95, and Word 6.0. Word 2002 can display text in any language provided the operating system supports the language of the file, except for Unicode-only languages, such as Hindi, Georgian, and Armenian.

Opening Word 2002 documents in localized Word 2000

Word 2000 can directly open and read Word 2002 documents. The file format is essentially unchanged. However, there are a few new features in Word 2002 that are not accessible in Word 2000 (for example, new table styles).

Opening Word 2002 documents in localized Word 97

Word 97 can directly open and read Word 2002 documents. However, to display Asian or right-to-left (Arabic, Hebrew, Farsi, or Urdu) text that doesn't match the language version of Word 97, you must have the appropriate language support installed on your system.

For Asian text, you can install the Office 97 Asian support files, but for right-to-left text, you must use a compatible right-to-left language version of Word 97.

Localized versions of Word 97 can display Word 2002 text as shown in the following table.

This language version of Word 97	Can display text in these languages
U.S./European	English, European, and Asian (Asian requires the Office 97 Asian support files)
Asian	English, European, matching Asian, and non-matching Asian (non-matching Asian requires the Office 97 Asian support files)
Right-to-left language (Arabic, Hebrew)	English, European, and a compatible right-to-left language

Note The layout for Asian text in Word 97 might be different than it is in Word 2002.

Opening Word 2002 documents in localized Word 95 and Word 6.0

Depending on the language, Word 95 and Word 6.0 can open and read Word 2002 documents by using the Word 97-2002 converter, or Word 95 and Word 6.0 can open and read Word 2002 documents that are saved in RTF.

Localized versions of Word 95 and Word 6.0 can display Word 2002 text as shown in the following table.

This language version of Word 6.0/95	Can display text in these languages
U.S./European	English, European
Asian	English, European, and the matching Asian language
Right-to-left language (Arabic, Hebrew)	English, European, and a compatible right-to-left language

Running macros from previous localized versions of Word

When Word 2002 opens older localized documents, it converts WordBasic to Visual Basic® for Applications (VBA) and translates the commands to English. Converted macros use the form WordBasic.732. However, strings — including user-created strings and WordBasic strings — are not translated. If a command is a WordBasic command, the language of the arguments accepted by that command can be either English or the localized language.

In Word 2002, Word 2000, and Word 97, you can write macros that work in all language versions of Word 2002, Word 2000, and Word 97. Be sure to use enumerations in your VBA code, and do not refer to objects by the names used in the user interface, because these names are different in each language version.

See also

The Unicode standard provides unique character values for every language that Office supports and makes it even easier to share multilingual documents. For more information, see "Unicode Support and Multilingual Documents" in Chapter 15, "Maintaining International Installations."

You can use the Microsoft Office Language Settings tool to enable languages for editing. For more information, see "Customizing Language Features" in Chapter 13, "Deploying Office Internationally."

For some languages, you need to have an operating system and fonts that allow you to display and edit the text. For more information, see Chapter 16, "Preparing Users' Computers for International Use."

CHAPTER 15

Maintaining International Installations

Microsoft Office XP makes it straightforward to upgrade your international installation by enabling you to migrate your settings and customize your international deployment. Office XP is flexible in multilingual environments. For example, Office support of Unicode allows users who work in different language versions of Office to use the same documents. You can further customize your installation — for example, by changing language settings — as needs change for users in your organization.

In this chapter

Unicode Support and Multilingual Documents   425

Taking Advantage of Unicode Support   427

Changing Language Settings   431

Removing Multilingual User Interface Files   433

Managing Language Settings for Each Application   433

Unicode Support and Multilingual Documents

Sharing documents in a multilingual environment can be challenging when the languages involved span multiple Microsoft Windows code pages. However, using the Unicode® character encoding standard overcomes many of these challenges.

Without Unicode, systems typically use a code page–based environment, in which each script has its own table of characters. Documents based on the code page of one operating system rarely travel well to an operating system that uses another code page. In some cases, the documents cannot contain text that uses characters from more than one script.

For example, if a user running the English version of the Microsoft Windows® 98 operating system with the Latin code page opens a plain text file created in the Japanese version of Windows 98, the code points of the Japanese code page are mapped to unexpected or nonexistent characters in the Western script, and the resulting text is unintelligible.

The universal character set provided by Unicode overcomes this problem. In Microsoft Office XP, all applications are capable of using Unicode.

Scripts and code pages

Multilingual documents can contain text in languages that require different scripts. A single script can be used to represent many languages.

For example, the Latin or Roman script has character shapes — glyphs — for the 26 letters (both uppercase and lowercase) of the English alphabet, as well as accented (extended) characters used to represent sounds in other Western European languages.

The Latin script has glyphs to represent all of the characters in most European languages and a few others. Other European languages, such as Greek or Russian, have characters for which there are no glyphs in the Latin script; these languages have their own scripts.

Some Asian languages use ideographic scripts that have glyphs based on Chinese characters. Other languages, such as Thai and Arabic, use scripts that have glyphs that are composed of several smaller glyphs or glyphs that must be shaped differently depending on adjacent characters. These scripts are referred to throughout the documentation as complex scripts.

A common way to store plain text is to represent each character by using a single byte. The value of each byte is a numeric index — or code point — in a table of characters; a code point corresponds to a character in the default code page of the computer on which the text document is created. For example, a byte value of decimal 65 (the code point for which is the decimal value 65) might represent the capital letter "A" on a machine with Western European code page.

A table of characters grouped together is called a code page. For single-byte code pages, each code page contains a maximum of 256 byte values; because each character in the code page is represented by a single byte, a code page can contain as many as 256 characters.

One code page with its limit of 256 characters cannot accommodate all languages because all languages together use far more than 256 characters. Therefore, different scripts use separate code pages. There is one code page for Greek, another for Cyrillic, and so on.

In addition, single-byte code pages cannot accommodate Asian languages, which commonly use more than 5,000 Chinese-based characters. Double-byte code pages were developed to support these languages.

One drawback of the code page system is that the character represented by a particular code point depends on the specific code page on which it was entered. If you do not know which code page a code point is from, you cannot determine how to interpret the code point unambiguously. This can cause problems when a text document is shared between users on different computers.

For example, unless you know which code page it comes from, the code point 230 might be the Greek lowercase zeta (ς) the Cyrillic lowercase zhe (ж), or the Western European (æ). All three characters have the same code point (230), but the code point is from three different code pages (1253, 1251, and 1252, respectively). Users exchanging documents between these languages are likely to see incorrect characters.

Unicode: a worldwide character set

Unicode was developed to create a universal character set that can accommodate all known scripts. Unicode uses a unique, two-byte encoding for every character; so in contrast to code pages, every character has its own unique code point. For example, the Unicode code point of lowercase zeta (ζ) is the hexadecimal value 03B6, lowercase zhe (ж) is 0436, and the diphthong (æ) is 00E6.

Unicode 2.0 defines code points for approximately 40,000 characters. More definitions were added in Unicode 2.1 and Unicode 3.0. Built-in expansion mechanisms in Unicode allow for more than one million characters to be defined, which is more than sufficient for all known scripts.

Currently in the Microsoft Windows operating systems, the two systems of storing text — code pages and Unicode — coexist. However, Unicode-based systems are replacing code page–based systems. For example, Microsoft Windows NT® 4, Microsoft Windows 2000, Microsoft Office 97 and later, Microsoft Internet Explorer 4.0 and later, and Microsoft SQL Server™ 7.0 and later all support Unicode.

Taking Advantage of Unicode Support

Microsoft Office XP is based on an international character encoding standard — Unicode — that allows users upgrading to Office XP to more easily share documents across languages. Unicode support in Office XP also allows users to read international documents created in any previous versions of Office.

Office XP also provides the conversion tables necessary to convert code page–based data to Unicode and back again for interaction with previous applications. Because Office XP provides fonts to support many languages, users can create multilingual documents with text from multiple scripts.

Unicode support in Office XP means that users can copy multilingual text from Office 97 documents and paste it into any Office XP document, and the text is displayed correctly. Conversely, multilingual text copied from any Office XP document can be pasted into a document created in any Office 97 application (except Microsoft Access and Microsoft Outlook).

In addition to document text, Office XP supports Unicode in other areas, including document properties, bookmarks, style names, footnotes, and user information. Unicode support in Office XP also means that you can edit and display multilingual text in dialog boxes. For example, you can search for a file by a Greek author's name in the **Open** dialog box.

Outlook 2002 supports Unicode in the body of mail messages. However, Outlook data — such as Contacts, Tasks, and the **To** and **Subject** lines of messages — is limited to characters defined by the user's code page.

> **Note** Microsoft Windows NT 4.0 and Microsoft Windows 2000 provide full support for Unicode. Some support is provided in Microsoft Windows 98.

Using Unicode values in Visual Basic for Applications

The Microsoft Visual Basic® for Applications environment does not support Unicode. Only text supported by the operating system can be used in the Visual Basic Editor or displayed in custom dialog boxes or message boxes.

You can use the **ChrW**() function to manipulate text outside the code page. The **ChrW**() function accepts a number that represents the Unicode value of a character and returns that character string.

Using local language file names

In Windows 98 and Windows Millennium Edition (Windows Me), Unicode characters in file names are not supported, but they are supported in Windows NT and Windows 2000. In Windows 98 and Windows Me, file names must use characters that exist in the code page of the operating system.

If users in your organization share files between language versions of Windows, they should use ASCII characters (unaccented Latin script) to ensure that the file names can be used in any language version of the operating system.

In Office XP, all applications (except Microsoft FrontPage® and Outlook) now support opening and saving files with Unicode file names, using **File | Open** in the application or by double-clicking the file name in Windows Explorer.

> **Note** While Microsoft Excel can open and save files with Unicode file names, it cannot save a new file using characters in the name that do not exist in the current system code page.

Printing and displaying Unicode text

Not all printers can print characters from more than one code page. In particular, printers that have built-in fonts might not have characters for other scripts in those fonts. Also, new characters such as the euro currency symbol might be missing from a particular font.

Although the Office applications contain many workarounds to enable printing on such printers, it is not possible in all cases. If text is not printing correctly, updating the printer driver might fix the problem. If the latest driver does not fix the problem, you can look for an option in the printer driver options called "download soft fonts" or "print TrueType as graphic." Change this setting and try printing again.

If the text still does not print correctly, you can create a registry entry that works around the printing problems of most printers; the printing quality, however, might be lowered.

To set the registry so that extended characters are printed correctly

1. Go to the following registry subkey:

   HKEY_CURRENT_USER\Software\Microsoft\Office\10.0\Word\Options

2. Add a new value entry named **NoWideTextPrinting** and set its value to **1**.

Compressing files that contain Unicode text

Office XP stores text in a form of Unicode called "UTF-16." Unicode characters are encoded in two bytes (or very rarely, four bytes) rather than what is used in non-Unicode systems (i.e. a single byte, or in a mixture of one and two bytes in some Asian languages). Generally, Office XP files with multilingual text are similar in size to Office 97 or 2000 files. However, Office XP files may be 30 to 50 percent larger than files created in previous, non-Unicode versions of Office (Office 95 and earlier).

> **Note** If a file contains text from only English or Western European languages, there is little or no increase in file size because Office XP applications can compress the text.

When Microsoft Word 2002 users open and save an English or Western European file from a previous, non-Unicode version of Word (a version earlier than Office 2000), Word converts the contents to Unicode. The first time the file is saved, Word analyzes the file and notes regions that can be compressed, resulting in a file that is temporarily twice the size of the original file. The next time the file is saved, Word performs the compression, and file size returns to normal.

For Microsoft PowerPoint® files, text is typically a small percentage of file size, so Unicode does not significantly increase file size.

Copying multilingual text

You can use the Clipboard to copy multilingual text from one Office application to another. Text from the Clipboard in RTF, HTML, and Unicode formats can successfully be pasted into Office applications.

Multilingual text in RTF, HTML, and Unicode

When you copy text from an Office XP document, the RTF or HTML formatting data, as well as the Unicode text data, is stored on the Clipboard. This allows applications that do not support Unicode but do support data in multiple code pages to accept RTF text from the Clipboard, which retains some of the multilingual content. For example, both Word 95 and Word 6.0 accept multilingual Word 2002 text from the Clipboard as RTF format (as well as Word 2000 and Word 97 text).

All language versions of Word 95 and Word 6.0 can display text in most European languages. However, Asian and right-to-left language versions cannot display other Asian or right-to-left languages. Also, English and European versions of Word 6.0 and Word 95 cannot display any Asian or right-to-left text properly.

Word 97 can accept RTF and Unicode text from the Clipboard and display content in all European and most Asian languages. Word 2000 accepts HTML as well, and properly handles all Asian and right-to-left content.

Access 2000, Access 2002, Excel 2000, and Excel 2002 all support copying multilingual Unicode, RTF, or HTML text to the Clipboard. However, Access and Excel cannot accept RTF content. They can accept HTML-formatted text or Unicode text from the Clipboard instead.

Multilingual code page–based single-byte text

In some rare conditions, users may paste single-byte (ANSI) text into an Office XP document that is encoded in a code page that is different from the one their operating system uses. If this occurs, depending on the application they are pasting into they may get unintelligible characters in their document. This problem occurs because Office cannot determine which code page to use to interpret the single-byte text.

For example, you might paste text from a non-Unicode text editor that uses fonts to indicate which code page to use. If the text editor supplies only RTF and single-byte text, the font (and code page) information is lost when the text is pasted in an application that does not accept RTF (for example, Excel). Instead, the application uses the operating system's code page, which maps some characters' code points to unexpected or nonexistent characters.

Troubleshooting corrupt text results with older multilingual files

There may be occasions when a user cannot successfully use Office XP to open a file created on an older system. There are several possible scenarios that can create this problem, and for each situation there are steps you can take to work around the issues.

- The document is a pre-Office 97 document that was created using some incorrectly made TrueType® fonts.

  For example, a document that looked fine in Word 95 can be opened in Word 2002, and the document text is converted to a mixture of characters from Western Europe. This situation occurs because the fonts used in the Word 95 document were marked internally as Western European, and the text data was therefore converted to Unicode Western European text. There are a few other variations on this problem involving symbol fonts; but in all cases you can try one of the following solutions to correct the problem:

    - Change the fonts that display the incorrect characters.
    - Use the "broken fonts add-in" that ships with Office XP. In Word, install the add-in. Then, under the **Tools** menu, click **Fix Broken Text**.

- The document is a pre-Office 97 document created under a "shell" program designed to enable English Windows to support Chinese or other Asian language.

    For example, Chinese Star, RichWin, and TwinBridge. In this case, try one of the following solutions:

    - If you open the document in Word, ensure that the correct Chinese language is enabled by checking the setting in the Microsoft Office Language Settings tool (go to **Start | Programs | Microsoft Office Tools | Microsoft Office Language Settings**). Start Word, and go to **Tools | Options | General**. Set the value of the option **English Word 6/95 documents** to the appropriate setting — for example, **Contain Asian text**.
    - If you open the document in PowerPoint, go to **Tools | Options | Asian**. Locate the option **convert from font-associated text**, and set the language correctly.

- The document is HTML, and the encoding of the file is not marked correctly in the file.

    In this case, with the document currently open, go to **Tools | Options | General**, and click **Web Options**. Click the **Encoding** tab, then change the encoding to open the file with different values until the characters in the file are shown correctly.

Changing Language Settings

You can use a language in an Office application that is different from the current installation language by enabling other languages for applications to use, or by changing the installation language.

All Microsoft Office XP applications use the installation language setting to determine language-related default behavior. The installation language setting is the locale ID (LCID) assigned to the value entry **InstallLanguage**, which Office Setup creates in the following registry subkey:

HKEY_CURRENT_USER\Software\Microsoft\Office\10.0\Common\LanguageResources

For example, if the value of **InstallLanguage** is **1041** (Japanese), Microsoft Word creates its initial Normal.dot file based on Japanese settings and automatically enables commands for Asian text layout.

Enabling other languages through Microsoft Office language settings, instead of changing the installation language, is preferred because you will retain your custom settings. Some custom settings are lost when you change the installation language. For example, when you change the installation language, your Normal.dot file is replaced, and any customizations saved to Normal.dot are lost. Other settings are reset to default values as well.

For a complete list of how language settings are used by Office applications, see "Managing Language Settings for Each Application" in Chapter 15, "Maintaining International Installations."

> **Note** If you change any language setting, including the installation language, you must restart applications before the updated language is available.

When you enable languages for editing, you turn on language-specific features in Office XP applications rather than changing the underlying installation language.

For example, Word automatically detects the language a user is typing based on the languages that the user enables for editing. If features for proofing tools are installed, Word uses the spelling checker, AutoCorrect list, and so on for the languages it detects.

Some Office XP applications also display commands and dialog box options based on enabled languages. For example, if you enable an Asian language in Word, you can configure Asian text layout in the **Format** menu.

To enable additional languages

1. Click **Start, Programs, Microsoft Office Tools**.
2. In the **Microsoft Office Language Settings** dialog, click the **Enabled Languages** tab.
3. Click the check boxes for the languages you wish to enable, then click **OK**.

   If you choose to change the installation language instead of enabling additional languages, you make that change on this tab as well.

To change the installation language value

1. Click **Start, Programs, Microsoft Office Tools**.
2. In the **Microsoft Office Language Settings** dialog, click the **Enabled Languages** tab.
3. Change the value of **Default version of Microsoft Office** to the default language.
4. Close any open Office applications, and start (or restart) the application you want to use.

You can establish new language settings for users throughout your organization by using the Custom Maintenance Wizard. To deploy new language settings, in the Custom Maintenance Wizard click **Microsoft Office (User)** on the **Change Office User Settings** page. Navigate the tree under **Language Settings** and update the settings. Then save the configuration maintenance file (CMW file) and deploy it to your users.

Note that when you set the **Installed Version of Microsoft Office** using the Custom Maintenance Wizard, some applications — Word, Microsoft PowerPoint, and Microsoft Outlook — will automatically update default settings (such as the default paper size) to correspond with the language you selected.

In addition to deploying new language settings to users, you can establish a required installation language value for users by setting a system policy.

To require a specific installation language for users

1. In the System Policy Editor or Group Policy Editor, go to the **User Configuration** branch.
2. Locate the policy **Administrative Templates\Microsoft Office XP\Language Settings\Enabled Languages\Installed version of Microsoft Office**.
3. Double-click this policy to see a list of languages, and then select the language you want to enforce as the installation language on users' computers.

See also

You can deploy Office XP so that its default settings are based on a particular language. For more information about customizing language features when deploying Office XP with the Multilingual User Interface Pack, see "Deploying Office with the Multilingual User Interface Pack" in Chapter 13, "Deploying Office Internationally."

You can customize language settings for your international deployment. For more information about setting language options, see "Customizing Language Features" in Chapter 13, "Deploying Office Internationally."

In most situations, you can gain access to, or change, language settings by using the language name. However, in some cases, you need to know the locale ID of a language. A table of all locale IDs and their corresponding languages is in "Deploying Office with the Multilingual User Interface Pack" in Chapter 13, "Deploying Office Internationally."

Removing Multilingual User Interface Files

In a busy international organization, a user might need a set of Microsoft Office Multilingual User Interface Pack (MUI Pack) features for a particular language installed on a computer for short-term use. When a user no longer needs to work with files in that language, or if a traveling user moves on, these MUI Pack files remain on the computer, taking up hard-disk space.

You can remove these Multilingual User Interface Pack files, if you prefer.

To remove Office Multilingual User Interface Pack files

1. In Control Panel, double-click the **Add/Remove Programs** icon, and then double-click the name of the Multilingual User Interface Pack file that you want to remove.

2. Click **Add or Remove Features**, select the Multilingual User Interface Pack features you want to remove, and then click **Not Available**.

3. Click **Update Now**.

Managing Language Settings for Each Application

Microsoft Office XP stores language settings in the LanguageResources subkey of the Windows registry. Office sets default language settings when an Office application runs for the first time after being installed. You can also specify or change language settings rather than let Office use default settings.

When Office applications run, they look up entries in the LanguageResources subkey to determine language-related default behavior. You can determine the effects on an Office application of changing a language setting by reviewing the information in this topic.

How language settings affect Office applications

Although each Office XP language setting has a specific purpose, Office applications reference these settings to change application behavior in different ways. In general, these settings define application behavior as follows:

- **Install Language**: Sets defaults for Office applications and documents.
- **User Interface Language**: Determines language used by menus and dialogs.
- **Help Language**: Determines language used for end-user Help.
- **Editing Languages**: Exposes functionality for editing documents in those particular languages.

Office XP sets these four language categories by default. However, you can specify or change the settings. For more information about changing language settings, see "Changing Language Settings" in Chapter 15, "Maintaining International Installations."

In addition, some applications use the SKU language setting to determine some behavior. This language setting is based on the original Office SKU that was installed and cannot be modified.

How Office applications use language settings

Each Office application can interpret language settings differently in determining language-related default behavior specific to that application.

Word

Microsoft Word 2002 uses language settings as described below.

Install Language

- Determines which Normal.dot file is used. If you have a customized Normal.dot template, your changes are lost when you modify the Install Language setting.
- Determines which Toolbar registry is used.
- Determines which preferences settings registry is used.
- Determines which bullets and numbering preset gallery is used.

User Interface Language

- Has no effects other than to change the language of the user interface.

Help Language

- Has no effects other than to change the language of Help text.

Editing Languages:

- Exposes additional user interface.
- Used by Language AutoDetect to narrow possibilities to detect languages.

SKU Language

- Is not used by Word 2002.

Excel

Microsoft Excel 2002 uses language settings as described below.

Install Language

- Controls whether Excel supports features specific for working primarily with East Asian content.
- If an East Asian install language is enabled, offers additional East Asian features (such as phonetic info, non-Gregorian calendar parsing, and string functions), different assumptions (more country-specific fallbacks for font handling), different default number formats, and Visual Basic for Applications backwards compatibility with native language versions of Excel.

  An East Asian install language should be chosen only if the primary language to be used is Asian.

  With any install language, Excel supports Input Method Editors and East Asian fonts. However, an East Asian install language is more aggressive in choosing fonts and defaults that match native language versions of Excel.

User Interface Language

- Has no effects other than to change the language of the user interface.

Help Language

- Has no effects other than to change the language of Help.

Editing Languages

- Is not used by Excel 2002.

SKU Language

- Is not used by Excel 2002.

PowerPoint

Microsoft PowerPoint 2002 uses language settings as described below.

Install Language

- When used with East Asian values, has the following effects:
    - Sets the default state of the Input Method Editor to "on."
    - Adds "composite" font structure to the **Format | Font** dialog and default East Asian font values.
    - Adds toolbar buttons.
    - Turns on and sets linguistic feature defaults.

      For example, setting the Installation Language to Japanese causes PowerPoint to use Asian rules for controlling first and last characters.
    - Affects font list sorting in the font lists (in the font toolbar control on the formatting toolbar, as well as the **Format | Font** dialog).
    - Converts backslash to a Yen when Install Language is Japanese.
- When set to a language that has bidirectional values, has the following effects:
    - Adds "composite" font structure to the **Format | Font** dialog and default bidirectional fonts.
    - Determines the default text direction behavior and default view orientation behavior.
    - Sets the default state of the Auto-Keyboard switching option to "on"; otherwise, the default state is "off."
- Changes Design Template behavior depending upon the Install Language value.

  You can create Design Templates with a single set of defaults (a "global" template). Based on the Install Language, PowerPoint uses plug-in user interface support to insert the correct text defaults in the template.
- Affects the default behavior of the document.

  For example, if the language is set to an East Asian language, a presentation will have East Asian defaults. This includes default fonts, East Asian typography rules, and so on.
- Used as the tie-breaker in certain cases to manage font conversion for East Asian (but not Japanese) text in PowerPoint 4.0 files.
- Determines vertical underline behavior for East Asian languages.

  For example, with Chinese (either Traditional or Simplified), the vertical underline is on the left, and for Korean or Japanese, the vertical underline is on the right.
- Determines the default language used for date formats and the types of calendars available.

- Used as the default language tag for text when converting previous presentations (PowerPoint 3.0 and 4.0, and PowerPoint 95) that did not have a language tag.
- Determines if font names for East Asian fonts are handled by using their English name or their localized name.

    When the Installation Language is set to an East Asian language, PowerPoint expects East Asian font names to be localized. When the Installation Language is set to a non-East Asian language, PowerPoint expects East Asian font names to be in English.

- Determines the success of displaying non-ANSI characters during file sharing operations with others using older versions of PowerPoint.

    For example, setting the Install Language to Greek allows Greek characters written on the Slide Master to be saved in PowerPoint 95 format. The Greek PowerPoint 95 user can view and edit the Greek characters correctly. The presentation can then be opened again in PowerPoint 2002 with the Greek characters included properly on the slide master.

- Helps to fix language variation conflicts (for example, French vs. French/Canadian) in Content Templates when those templates are opened in **File | New** or by the AutoContent Wizard.
- Used as the default text language for new text objects on new presentations if the user has not set the default language in **Tools | Language**.
- Used as a tie-breaker for determining the text language identifier (LID) for Language Autodetect integration with plain-text pasting.
- Determines which localized bullet schemes appear in the **Format | Bullets and Numbering** dialog.
- Causes Blank.pot (if it exists) to be renamed to Oldblank.pot when Installation Language changes.
- If the Installation Language or the system locale is set to Japanese, lists the JIS paper sizes in the **File | Page Setup** dialog.
- Determines the order of font slots displayed in the **Format|Font** dialog.

    If the Installation Language is set to an East Asian language, the font list displays East Asian fonts first in the list.

- Determines the correct defaults for Style Checker options for East Asian and some European languages.

    The defaults are set as follows:

    - The correct value for Slide Title Style is **Sentence case (0x01)** instead of **"Title case" (0x04)**.

        Languages affected: Brazilian Portuguese, Czech, Danish, Dutch, Finnish, French, French/Canadian, Greek, Hungarian, Iberian Portuguese, Italian, Norwegian, Polish, Russian, Spanish (Modern Sort), Swedish.

- The correct value for **Number of fonts should not exceed: is 0x04** instead of 0x03.

    Languages affected: Japanese, Korean, Traditional Chinese, and Simplified Chinese

- The correct value for **Body punctuation** is **0x00** instead of **0x01**.

    Languages affected: Korean, Traditional Chinese, Simplified Chinese (but not Japanese)

User Interface Language

- Has no effects other than to change the language of the user interface

Help Language

- Has no effects other than to change the language of the Help text.

Editing Languages

- If enabled, may expose additional user interface in PowerPoint.

    For example, these languages add extra controls to the user interface:

    - East Asian (Traditional Chinese, Simplified Chinese, Japanese, and Korean)
    - Complex Scripts (including bidirectional languages, such as Arabic and Hebrew, and other Complex Scripts languages, such as Thai and Hindi)

- Influences font association conversions if Traditional Chinese, Simplified Chinese, and Korean editing languages are set.

- If you enable editing languages other than code page 1252 languages (that is, code pages for languages that are not in the Western European code page) and you are creating Presentation Broadcast lobby pages, then the lobby pages will use Numeric Character References (NCRs) for the text.

    For example, if you enable Greek (code page 1253) and you create lobby pages, the lobby pages will use NCRs for the text.

- If enabled, causes date formats for those languages to appear in the **Insert | Date and Time** dialog.

    Note Setting East Asian editing languages does not influence Input Method Editor default startup behavior and does not change document defaults.

SKU Language

- The SKU Language LCID is used as a parameter in the URL that procures the Viewer from the Microsoft Office Web site using the Pack and Go Wizard.

System locale

- Used as a tie-breaker in determining text language identifiers for Language Autodetect integration with plain-text pasting.

- Determines which fonts should not be embedded during font embedding operations, preventing the default fonts typically used in that locale from being embedded.

Access

Microsoft Access 2002 uses language settings as described below.

Install Language

- Used to expose Japanese-specific properties and enable wizards specific to East Asian languages.
- Sets the default speller dictionary language according to the Install Language setting.

User Interface Language

- Makes Japanese and other East Asian wizards available when the user interface language (or the operating system language) is the corresponding East Asian language.

Help Language

- Has no effects other than to change the language of the Help text.

Editing Languages

- Is not used by Access 2002.

SKU Language

- Is not used by Access 2002.

System Locale

- Used to determine default datasheet fonts and default sort order for the database.

Outlook

Microsoft Outlook 2002 uses language settings as described below.

Install Language

- Determines default speller in **Tools | Options | Spelling**.

User Interface Language

- Has no effects other than to change the language of the user interface.

Help Language

- Has no effects other than to change the language of the Help text.

Editing Languages

- Makes additional Mail encodings available.
- Makes additional property page available in **Tools | Options** with miscellaneous RTL and Bidi calendar settings (for Arabic and Hebrew).

SKU Language

- Is not used by Outlook.

FrontPage

Microsoft FrontPage 2002 uses language settings as described below.

Install Language

- Is not used by FrontPage.

User Interface Language

- Changes the language of the user interface text.
- Determines the language of the templates FrontPage loads for a new page or Web site.

Help Language

- Changes the language of the Help text.
- Changes the language for other files linked to from inside FrontPage (such as Microsoft Office Web site files).

Editing Languages

- Exposes additional user interface.

SKU Language

- Is not used by FrontPage.

Default System Code Page

- Determines which character set will be supported for opening and saving since FrontPage does not support Unicode file names.

User Locale

- Sets the default speller.

Input Locale

- Used to determine the language and encoding of a page.

In general, when the page language is different from the input locale, FrontPage uses language settings to span that difference with language information.

Publisher

Microsoft Publisher 2002 uses language settings as described below.

Install Language

- Enables helpful pointers (cursors).
- Allows Japanese crop marks.
- Affects the default justification options that appear in Publisher menus and on the formatting toolbar.
- Adjusts Input Method Editor (IME) status to text flow.
- If set to an East Asian language, controls whether an IME is enabled.
- Sets date and time format for print marks.
- Sets default business card size.
- Sets default font size, paragraph alignment, tab stop, bullet font, and bullet characters.
- Used as the Language Control Identifier (LCID) applied to text in some cases where the text file format does not contain language information.
- Used as a tie-breaker for some features when multiple East Asian languages are installed.

   Determines the defaults for some text formatting preferences, including East Asian hanging punctuation default and character-spacing control (CSC) default.
- Controls the exposure of Simplified Chinese–named font sizes.

Editing Language

- Controls the exposure of East Asian formatting features (such as Ruby and Text Direction).
- Enables East Asian proofing tools.
- Enables East Asian font and formatting properties in the font dialog.
- Enables complex Script features and options.

User Interface Language

- Sets language for Publisher wizards, font schemes, and color schemes.

   Japanese-specific wizards are only available with a Japanese user interface.

Help Language

- Has no effect other than to change the language of the Help text.

Web locale

- Has no functionality specific to Publisher.

SKU language

- Has no functionality specific to Publisher.

System locale

- Has no functionality specific to Publisher.

User locale

- Changes the Calendar format.

Input locale

- Default input locale determines the default text language for new text frames.
- As the user types, current input locale/keyboard is used to assign language to text.

CHAPTER 16

Preparing Users' Computers for International Use

All of the international features of Microsoft Office XP work on Microsoft Windows 98, Microsoft Millennium Edition (Windows Me), Microsoft Windows NT 4.0, and Microsoft Windows 2000. However, some of these operating systems are better suited to handling multiple languages. You can also set up browsers, fonts, and printers to take better advantage of international features.

In this chapter

Choosing an Operating System   443

Choosing a Web Browser   449

Administering Fonts   451

Printing Documents   455

Choosing an Operating System

The Microsoft Windows® 98, Microsoft Windows Millennium Edition (Me), Microsoft Windows NT® 4.0, and Microsoft Windows 2000 operating systems support international features of Microsoft Office XP. However, if your users work with a set of different languages that includes Asian languages, Indic languages, or right-to-left languages, then Windows 2000 provides the best support for displaying and editing documents and for changing the language of the user interface.

> **Toolbox**   Information about the languages supported by each operating system and the limitations of that support is included in the Microsoft Excel spreadsheet Wwsuppt.xls, which is installed by default when you run the Office Resource Kit Setup program. For more information, see "Supplemental Documentation" in the Toolbox.

Displaying the user interface in other languages

The ability of Office XP to display the user interface and online Help in some languages depends on the capabilities of the operating system. Windows 98 and Windows Me provide fairly broad support within a single language category. Windows NT 4.0 has more flexibility, and Windows 2000 provides support for all possible Office user interface languages.

For example, on a computer running the English version of Windows 98 or Windows Me, Microsoft Word can display the user interface in any European language. On a computer running Windows NT 4.0, Word can also display the user interface in Asian languages, and on Windows 2000, Word supports right-to-left languages.

Some code pages provide support for groups of languages; other code pages provide support for only a single language. Therefore, make sure a user's system locale (which governs the code page of the user's computer) is set to a locale that supports the primary language the user needs.

> **Note** Only Windows NT 4.0 and Windows 2000 support changing the system locale. With Windows 98 and Windows Me, users must run the appropriate localized version of the operating system.

For example, if your users work primarily in Japanese, set their system locale to Japanese (or have them run a Japanese version of Windows 98). If your users work primarily in French, their system locale can be any Western European system locale (or they can run any Western European version of Windows 98).

The tables included below provide guidelines for getting the best support for displaying the Office XP user interface and online Help in Microsoft Access, Excel, Microsoft PowerPoint, and Word when your users run Windows 98, Windows Me, or Windows NT 4.0.

The following table contains guidelines for getting the best support for displaying the Office XP user interface and online Help in Windows 98 and Windows Me.

Users running this language version of Windows 98 or Windows Me	Can display the user interface and online Help in these languages
English, Western European, or Eastern European	English, Western European, and Eastern European
Asian	English and the matching Asian
Right-to-left (Arabic or Hebrew)	English, Western European, Eastern European, and the matching right-to-left language

The following table contains guidelines for getting the best support for displaying the Office XP user interface and online Help in Windows NT 4.0.

Users running this language version of Windows NT 4.0	Can display the user interface and online Help in these languages
English, Western European, or Eastern European	English, Western European, Eastern European, and Asian
Asian	English, Western European, Eastern European, and Asian
Right-to-left (Arabic or Hebrew)	English, Western European, Eastern European, and the matching right-to-left language

The following table contains guidelines for getting the best support for displaying the Office XP user interface and online Help in Windows 2000.

Users running this language version of Windows 2000	Can display the user interface and online Help in these languages
Any	English, Western European, Eastern European, Asian, and right-to-left languages

Note Eastern European languages are supported by the Central European, Baltic Rim, Cyrillic, Greek, and Turkish code pages.

Limitations of displaying the user interface in other languages

For some applications and features in Office XP, the native code page of the operating system must support the user interface language. For these applications and features, text in the user interface — such as menus and dialog text in Microsoft Outlook® or file names in Binder — must be supported by the operating system's system code page.

When you use Microsoft FrontPage®, Outlook, and some Office features (such as Binder and the Office XP Shortcut Bar), you can change the user interface language to any language that is supported by the system code page of your operating system.

When you change the user interface to a language that does not have code page support, Outlook and FrontPage display the user interface in English.

Toolbox Some Office features do not allow you to change the language of the user interface or online Help. Information about those features is available in the Microsoft Excel workbook Intlimit.xls, which is installed by default when you run the Office Resource Kit Setup program. For more information, see "Supplemental Documentation" in the Toolbox.

Displaying online Help in other languages

When you change the online Help language in Office XP, the Help content is displayed in the new language, but the Help user interface is still displayed in the Office user interface language. However, some elements of the Help user interface (such as the **Contents** tab, the **Options** menu, and toolbar ScreenTips) are always in the language version of the Office SKU that was installed.

Furthermore, when you change the Help content language, the language must have code page support from your operating system. Otherwise, the Help topics listed in the **Contents** tab will be unintelligible. In this case, you can use the **Answer Wizard** and **Index** tabs to find Help topics. However, if you want to use these tabs, you must display online Help in a language that the Answer Wizard supports.

> **Note** Windows 2000 supports all languages used by Office XP.

If you change the Help language to a language that is not supported by the Answer Wizard, the language must have code page support. In this case, Help displays the **Full Text Search** tab to allow you to find Help topics.

The Answer Wizard supports the following languages:

Arabic	Finnish	Norwegian
Chinese (Simplified)	French	Polish
Chinese (Traditional)	German	Portuguese (Brazilian)
Czech	Hebrew	Portuguese (Iberian)
Danish	Italian	Russian
Dutch	Japanese	Spanish
English	Korean	Swedish
		Thai

> **Note** For the Thai language, only the Answer Wizard index is localized.

Displaying documents in other languages

Users running Office XP can display documents in a wider range of languages than they can use for the Office XP user interface and online Help. For example, German users running Office XP on the German language version of Windows 98 can view Japanese documents even though they cannot switch to a Japanese user interface.

All language versions of Windows 2000 support displaying documents in all languages. The following table provides guidelines for getting the best support for displaying Office XP documents in Windows 98 or Windows NT 4.0.

Users running this language version of Windows 98, Windows Me, or Windows NT 4.0	Can display documents in these languages
English, Western European, Eastern European, or Asian (including Thai and Vietnamese)	All languages, except right-to-left and Indic
Right-to-left (Arabic or Hebrew)	All languages, except Thai, Vietnamese, and Indic

Note Eastern European languages are supported by the Central European, Baltic Rim, Cyrillic, Greek, and Turkish code pages. The Indic languages supported include Devanagari-based languages (Hindi, Konkani, Marathi, Nepali, and Sanskrit) and Tamil.

Editing documents in other languages

Typically, if a user's operating system prevents the display of a certain language, users are not able to edit documents in that language. However, in the case of Asian documents, even though users can display documents, they might not be able to edit them without a special editing interface.

Input of Asian characters requires an Input Method Editor (IME). The Microsoft Office Multilingual User Interface Pack provides IMEs for Japanese, Korean, Simplified Chinese, and Traditional Chinese. The IMEs allow users to edit Asian text in Office applications, regardless of the language version of their operating system. Microsoft Office Proofing Tools also includes Input Method Editors.

Limitations for entering content in Outlook in other languages

There are two main types of content that users can type in Outlook: plain text and rich text. Text typed in a plain text area cannot be saved and retrieved in a language that is not supported by the default code page set on the user's computer. For example, text entered in most fields in a Contact entry (such as the contact name or telephone number) are plain text. They cannot have special formatting (for instance, bold or italics), and they cannot be saved and retrieved in a language that is not supported by the default code page.

Other text-entry areas support rich text – for example, the message body of an e-mail message. Rich text support is provided in several ways (for instance, by using RTF or HTML), and supports formatting, links, and so on. Rich text areas also support text entry and retrieval for languages that are not supported by the default code page on the user's computer.

Adding international support to Windows 98 and Windows Me

If your international organization includes Windows 98 or Windows Me users who work with Office XP documents in several languages, you can add international capabilities to the operating system. Adding multilingual support allows users to display foreign language characters that Windows 98 and Windows Me do not otherwise support, and adding keyboard support allows users to input characters not found on the U.S. keyboard.

To add multilingual support

1. In Control Panel, double-click **Add/Remove Programs**, and then click the **Windows Setup** tab.
2. Select the **Multilanguage Support** check box.
3. To install support for selected languages, double-click **Multilanguage Support** and then select the languages you want.

   Note Support for right-to-left languages can be added only to a right-to-left language version of Windows 98 and Windows Me.

To enter text in a given language, users need to use the appropriate keyboard layout.

To add keyboard support

1. In Control Panel, double-click **Keyboard**, and on the **Language** tab, click **Add**.
2. In the **Add Language** dialog box, choose a setting from the **Language** list.
3. To change the keyboard layout for a language, click the **Properties** button, and in the **Language Properties** dialog box, choose a setting from the **Keyboard layout** list.
4. To enable switching between keyboards by clicking an indicator on the taskbar, select the **Enable indicator on taskbar** check box.

See also

- Windows NT 4.0 and Windows 2000 provide multilingual support, but you must select the keyboard layout you want to use. For information about adding keyboard support, see online Help for the appropriate operating system.
- The Office Web site provides a keyboard layout program, Visual Keyboard, that makes it easier for users to type languages not represented on the physical keyboard. For information about the Visual Keyboard, see the Microsoft Office Web site at http://www.officeupdate.microsoft.com.

Choosing a Web Browser

The Web browser installed on users' computers can affect how well Microsoft Office XP supports switching to different user interface languages. In addition, browsers that support Unicode® allow users to create multilingual Web pages.

Supporting multilingual dialog boxes

Microsoft Internet Explorer 5 allows Microsoft Office XP applications to display certain dialog boxes in any user interface language that the operating system supports. Dialog boxes such as **New** and **Open** from the **File** menu depend on the code page of the operating system to display text.

A minimum installation of Internet Explorer 5 allows users to switch to different user interface languages regardless of the code page. Without Internet Explorer 5, users might see meaningless characters in dialog boxes after changing user interface languages.

> **Note** If users are switching between languages that use the same code page — for example, all Western European languages — they do not need to install Internet Explorer 5 to display all dialog boxes properly.

If you want users to be able to change their user interface language across code pages, but you do not want a full-featured installation of Internet Explorer 5 on users' computers, you can customize Office Setup with a minimum installation of Internet Explorer 5.

To customize Office Setup with a minimum installation of Internet Explorer 5

- In the **Customize IE5 Installation Options** page of the Office Custom Installation Wizard, select the **Upgrade to Internet Explorer 5** option, and in the **Internet Explorer 5 upgrade mode** box, select **Minimum**.

> **Note** After installing Internet Explorer 5, users must turn Microsoft Active Desktop® off before they can change their user interface language.

Using Unicode in multilingual Web pages

Unicode allows users to create multilingual Web pages that not only use multiple scripts but also produce smaller files that are easy to parse on your intranet. You need Internet Explorer 4.01 or later, or Netscape Navigator 4.03 or later for your browser to interpret Unicode Web pages. If you want to maintain compatibility with earlier browsers, avoid using Unicode.

> **Note** The Unicode format commonly used on the Internet is called Universal Character Set Transformation Format 8-bit (UTF-8). UTF-8 is the only Unicode format that is commonly supported by Web browsers and by Microsoft FrontPage Server Extensions.

You can set Office XP applications to save the current HTML document in Unicode.

To save an HTML document in Unicode in Office XP applications

1. Click **Tools**, **Options**.
2. On the **General** tab, click **Web Options**.
3. On the **Encoding** tab, in the **Save this document as** list, select **Unicode (UTF-8)**.

> **Note** To save HTML documents in the Unicode format by default, select the **Always save Web pages in the default encoding** check box in the **Web Options** dialog box.

Using Unicode in multilingual URLs

In addition to allowing users to create HTML documents in UTF-8 encoding, Office XP and Internet Explorer 5 can send UTF-8 encoded URLs to Web servers.

UTF-8 encoding allows users to use URLs that include non-ASCII characters, regardless of the language of the user's operating system and browser, or the language version of Office. Without UTF-8 encoding, a user's Web server must be based on the same code page as that of the user's operating system in order for the Web server to interpret non-ASCII URLs. However, for a Web server to interpret UTF-8 encoded URLs, the Web server must have UTF-8 support.

> **Note** To use UTF-8 encoded URLs, you must have Microsoft Internet Information Server (IIS) 4.0 or later or another Web server that supports UTF-8.

If your organization has code page–based Web servers that do not support UTF-8, and you have non-ASCII URLs, you should turn off UTF-8 URL encoding in Internet Explorer 5. Otherwise, when users try to use a UTF-8–encoded URL that includes non-ASCII characters, the code page–based Web server that does not support UTF-8 cannot interpret the URL.

To prevent sending URLs in UTF-8 encoding

1. In Internet Explorer 5, on the **Tools** menu, click **Internet Options**.
2. In the **Internet Options** dialog box, click the **Advanced** tab.
3. Under **Browsing**, clear the **Always send URLs as UTF-8** check box.

See also

Documents that use Unicode are easier to share among users who work in different languages. For more information about Unicode, see "Unicode Support and Multilingual Documents" in Chapter 15, "Maintaining International Installations."

To display localized server messages, you must install a localized version of Microsoft FrontPage Server Extensions. For information about the latest release of FrontPage Server Extensions in a particular language, see the Microsoft FrontPage Web site at http://www.microsoft.com/frontpage/.

To display localized messages for servers running SharePoint™ Team Services from Microsoft, you must install a localized version of SharePoint Team Services. For information about the latest release of Microsoft's SharePoint Team Services in a particular language, see the SharePoint Team Services Web site. Information about the SharePoint Team Services Web site is available in this topic on the Office Resource Kit Web site at http://www.microsoft.com/office/ork.

Administering Fonts

Microsoft Office XP provides fonts that allow users to view and edit documents in different languages, across different scripts. Some of these fonts are installed with Office XP; others are available in the Microsoft Office Multilingual User Interface Pack (MUI Pack). Some international fonts supplied with Office XP might update Microsoft Windows fonts that users already have.

Understanding how Office XP uses fonts for different languages can help you administer fonts for users across your international organization.

International fonts included with Office XP

The Office Multilingual User Interface Pack includes fonts necessary for working with the international features of Office. These additional fonts allow you to:

- Display the user interface and online Help in various languages.
- Display text in various languages — in an existing document or text that you enter — including languages that require Input Method Editors (IMEs).

   Note The Multilingual User Interface Pack also includes IMEs that work with Internet Explorer as well as Office XP applications.

In addition to the fonts in the Multilingual User Interface Pack, which support particular character sets, Office XP also includes a complete Unicode font, which supports all characters in all of the languages supported by Office. This Unicode font is especially useful when you cannot apply multiple fonts — for example, when you work with multilingual data in Microsoft Access data tables.

The following table lists the fonts provided by the Multilingual User Interface Pack, along with the code pages and the languages they support.

Font (file)	Code page	Supported languages
BatangChe (BatangCh.ttf), Gulim (Gulim.ttf)	1250, 1251, 1252, 1253, 1254, 1257, 949	All European languages, Korean
MingLiu (Mingliu.ttf)	932, 936, 950	English, Simplified Chinese, Traditional Chinese, Japanese
MS UI Gothic (Msuigoth.ttf)	1250, 1251, 1252, 1253, 1254, 1257, 932	All European languages, Japanese

The following table lists the fonts provided by Office XP, along with the code pages and the languages that the fonts support.

Font (file)	Code page	Supported languages
Arial Unicode MS (Arialuni.ttf)	All	All
Batang (Batang.ttf)	250, 1251, 1252, 1253, 1254, 1257, 949	Most European languages, Korean
PMingLiu (PMingliu.ttf)	932, 936, 950	English, Simplified Chinese, Traditional Chinese, Japanese
MS Mincho (Msmincho.ttf)	1250, 1251, 1252, 1253, 1254, 1257, 932	Most European languages, Japanese
SimSun (Simsun.ttf)	936	English, Simplified Chinese, Traditional Chinese
Georgian and Armenian Font (Sylfaen.ttf)	1250, 1251, 1252, 1253, 1254, 1257, Unicode	Most European languages, Georgian, Armenian
Hindi Font (Mangal.ttf)	(Unicode)	Hindi
Tamil Font (Latha.ttf)	(Unicode)	Tamil

Updating Windows fonts to big fonts

Many of the fonts that are included with Microsoft Windows 98, Microsoft Windows NT 4.0, and Microsoft Windows 2000 are stored as big font files. The big font files include glyphs for multiple character sets and accommodate many languages. Big font files include Tahoma, which is the default Office XP user interface font for all languages except Asian languages. When you install Office XP, Office updates existing Windows fonts to big fonts and installs additional fonts.

The following is a list of big fonts that Office Setup installs or updates:

- Arial
- Arial Black
- Arial Bold
- Arial Narrow
- Bookman Old Style
- Courier New
- Garamond
- Impact
- Tahoma
- Times New Roman
- Trebuchet (Central and Eastern European languages only)
- Verdana®

Installing fonts that support multiple languages

If your users frequently share documents or e-mail messages across different scripts, you can install fonts that support those scripts.

In most cases, Office Setup automatically installs or updates fonts to display characters in multiple scripts. For example, a document formatted in the Arial font can display Western European, Cyrillic, Turkish, Baltic, Central European, Greek, Arabic, or Hebrew text.

For Asian languages or Unicode characters, however, you must install the appropriate fonts on users' computers.

> **Important** Do not change the default user interface font. The Office XP user interface is designed to fit Tahoma and certain Asian fonts. Using a different user interface font might truncate user interface labels in some languages.

Installing Asian fonts

Office XP provides Asian fonts for four languages: Japanese, Korean, Simplified Chinese, and Traditional Chinese. If users need to edit or read documents in these languages, they must install the appropriate Asian fonts.

To install Asian fonts

1. On the **Set Feature Installation States** page in the Custom Installation Wizard, select the **Office Tools\International Support** feature.

2. For each of the Asian fonts you want to use, select the font, and set the installation state to **Run from My Computer**.

Installing Indic fonts

The Indic languages supported in Office XP include Devanagari-based languages (Hindi, Konkani, Marathi, Nepali, and Sanskrit) and Tamil. If users need to edit or read documents in these languages, they must install the appropriate Indic fonts.

To install Indic fonts

1. On the **Set Feature Installation States** page in the Custom Installation Wizard, select the **Office Tools\International Support** feature.

2. For each of the Indic fonts you want to use, select the font, and set the installation state to **Run from My Computer**.

Installing the Unicode font

Some documents, such as Access data tables, can display only one font at a time. But these documents can display multilingual text in more than one script if you use the Unicode font. The Unicode font provided by Office XP allows users to input and display characters across scripts and across code pages that support the various scripts.

Installing a Unicode font on users' computers has some disadvantages. First, the Unicode font file is much larger than font files based on code pages. Second, some characters might look different from their character equivalents in code pages. For these reasons, do not use the Unicode font as your default font. However, if your users share documents across many different scripts, the Unicode font might be your best choice.

To install the Unicode font

1. On the **Set Feature Installation States** page in the Custom Installation Wizard, select the **Office Tools\International Support** feature.

2. Select the **Universal Font** feature, and set the installation state to **Run from My Computer**.

See also

You can install a utility that adds code-page information to the properties shown when you right-click a font file in Windows 98, Windows NT 4.0, or Windows 2000. For more information about the font properties extension utility, see the Microsoft Typography Web site at http://www.microsoft.com/typography/.

Printing Documents

Using the international features of Microsoft Office XP in documents creates some special requirements for printing. You must ensure that your printers are configured for the correct paper size and for font substitution.

Specifying the correct paper size

Many printers allow you to load both A4 and letter-size paper. If users in Europe exchange documents with users in the United States, having both A4 and letter-size paper in your printers accommodates everyone's documents.

Even if your printers are stocked only with the paper commonly used in your part of the world, most Office documents are printed with no loss of text. Microsoft Word documents and Microsoft PowerPoint presentations are automatically scaled to fit the printer's default paper size. Microsoft Outlook messages are printed according to locally defined default print parameters. Microsoft FrontPage documents are printed according to the browser's page layout settings.

> **Note** For Microsoft Publisher documents, users must open documents and manually change the paper size. For Microsoft Access reports, users must open a report, manually change the paper size, close the report, reopen the report, and then print.

In some circumstances, you might not want documents scaled to fit the printer's default paper size. For example, if your printer has A4 set as its default paper size but the printer also has letter-size paper, then Word cannot detect that both sizes are available. Because the printer can supply the correct size paper, you might want to turn off the resizing option that is available in Word.

> **System Policy Tip** You can use a system policy to turn off the **Allow A4/Letter paper resizing** option on the **Print** tab (**Options** menu) in Word. In the System Policy Editor, set the **Microsoft Word 2002\Tools | Options\Print\Printing options\Allow A4/Letter paper resizing** policy. For more information about the System Policy Editor, see Chapter 9, "Using System Policies."

Setting TrueType fonts to print correctly

To display characters in multiple scripts, Office uses big fonts. In addition to being bold or italic, big fonts can also be Cyrillic, Greek, or one of several other scripts.

However, big fonts are also TrueType® fonts, and many laser printers substitute built-in printer fonts when printing documents that use TrueType fonts. Built-in printer fonts cannot render text in multiple scripts, so characters in other scripts do not print properly.

For example, your laser printer might substitute its own internal version of Arial, which accommodates only Western European characters. Word uses the big font version of Arial to display Greek and Russian characters in documents, but if users print those documents, the Greek and Russian characters are printed as unintelligible Western European character strings.

To work around the problem, set the option in your printer driver to send TrueType fonts as graphics.

> **Tip** Some non-Asian printers cannot properly print Asian documents because the size of the Asian font is too large for the printer's memory. You might need to install additional memory in these printers.

See also

Unicode might affect the way that Office XP documents are printed. For information about Office XP support of Unicode, see "Taking Advantage of Unicode Support" in Chapter 15, "Maintaining International Installations."

PART 5

Messaging

Chapter 17   Planning for Outlook   459

Chapter 18   Deploying Outlook   467

Chapter 19   Special Outlook Deployment Scenarios   481

Chapter 20   Upgrading to Outlook 2002   503

Chapter 21   Maintaining an Outlook Installation   523

Chapter 22   Administering Outlook Security   535

CHAPTER 17

Planning for Outlook

A close review of your organization's messaging needs will help you plan the optimal Microsoft Outlook 2002 deployment. Among the configuration and installation choices you will make are deciding which e-mail messaging server to use with Outlook, and timing your Outlook deployment to best suit your organization's needs.

In this chapter

Planning an Outlook Deployment   459

Choosing Among E-mail Servers   463

Determining When to Install Outlook   463

Planning an Outlook Deployment

Every organization's messaging environment is unique. For example, one organization might be upgrading to Microsoft Outlook® 2002 messaging and collaboration client, while another might be installing Outlook for the first time; one needs services for roaming users, another needs support for different languages. A close review of your organization's messaging needs will help you plan the optimal Outlook 2002 deployment.

Determining your organization's needs

Your organization's messaging environment will help shape your Outlook 2002 deployment. Factors to consider include whether you are upgrading Outlook, installing the application for the first time, planning for roaming or remote users, or choosing a combination of these and other factors.

Upgrade or initial installation

If you are upgrading to Outlook 2002 from an earlier version of Outlook, consider whether you will migrate previous settings, modify user profiles, and use new customization options.

If you are deploying Outlook on client computers for the first time, each user will need an Outlook profile to store information about e-mail messaging server connections and other important Outlook settings. You can define profile settings for your users by using the Custom Installation Wizard.

If you need to migrate data from another messaging application, importers are provided in Outlook (for example, for Eudora Lite) that might be helpful.

Collaboration Data Objects dependencies

If you use Collaboration Data Objects, this feature must be installed to run locally, not on demand. Use the **Set Feature Installation States** page in the Custom Installation Wizard to specify the install state as **Run from My Computer**.

Remote and roaming users

Special customizations are required if you are deploying Outlook to remote users or roaming users, and setting up Outlook for multiple users on the same computer.

When you are deploying to remote users, ensure that features are not set to install over the network as they are needed, since users may be using slow access lines. Use the **Set Feature Installation States Tree** page in the Custom Installation Wizard to specify the installation state for Outlook features as **Run from My Computer.** For features that you are not deploying, you can set the feature state to **Not Available, Hidden, Locked**.

Roaming users should have the same messaging environment on each computer to which they roam. This includes the type and version of operating system, version of Outlook, and the Outlook installation location on the computer.

For multiple users sharing the same computer, use the Windows logon features on the computer's operating system to manage user logon verification. Also, make sure that each user runs the same version of Outlook so that shared file conflicts do not arise. This conflict can happen when one version of Outlook attempts to write a file to a file folder location that is shared by other versions of Outlook also used on the computer.

Multilingual requirements

Microsoft Office XP provides broad support for deploying in international or multilingual environments. Office products such as the Office Multilingual User Interface Pack and Office Proofing Tools help multilingual groups work with and edit files in a variety of languages and provide support for localized Help and user interfaces.

Outlook 2002 includes enhanced Unicode® support to help multilingual organizations seamlessly exchange messages and other information across languages in local areas.

Outlook 2002 and Terminal Services

With Microsoft Terminal Services, you install a single copy of Microsoft Outlook 2002 on a Terminal Services computer. Then, instead of running Outlook locally, multiple users connect to the server and run Outlook from there.

To achieve the best results when you use Outlook with Terminal Services, pay close attention to how you customize your Outlook configuration. Note that Outlook may be part of an environment that includes other applications provided on the same Terminal Services computer.

Client and messaging server platforms

Some deployment customization decisions for Outlook 2002 depend on which version of Microsoft Exchange Server you are using. If you currently use Exchange Server as your messaging server and have not upgraded to Exchange 2000, consider timing your Exchange Server upgrade with your deployment timing for Outlook 2002. While Outlook 2002 works well with earlier versions of Exchange, you may gain the greatest benefit by combining Outlook 2002 with Exchange 2000.

Choosing when and how to install Outlook 2002

You have options for when and how you install Outlook 2002. For example, consider whether it would be best for your organization to:

- Install or upgrade Outlook in stages (for different groups of users) or at one time.
- Install Outlook as a stand-alone application.
- Install Outlook before, with, or after Office XP.

Each organization has a different environment and might make different choices about timing Outlook 2002 upgrades. For example, you might have a messaging group that is responsible for upgrading Outlook and a separate group that plans deployment for other Office applications. In this case, it might be simpler to upgrade Outlook separately from the rest of Office, rather than attempting to coordinate deployment between the two groups.

Customizing Outlook settings and profiles

You can customize your Outlook installation to handle Outlook user settings and profiles in several ways. For instance, you can:

- Capture Outlook settings in an Office profile settings file (OPS file), then include the OPS file in a transform (MST file) that is applied during Setup.
- Specify Outlook user settings in the Custom Installation Wizard.
- Specify options for managing new and existing Outlook profiles in the Custom Installation Wizard.

For example, you can allow Outlook users to migrate their current profiles and settings while defining default profiles and settings for new Outlook users. Or you can modify existing profiles as well as establishing new default profiles for new Outlook users.

After you customize Outlook using these options, you save your choices — along with other installation preferences — in a transform (MST file) that is applied during Setup. Later, you can update settings and profile information by using the Custom Maintenance Wizard.

Migrating data

In your Outlook deployment, you might choose to migrate data from other mail clients to Outlook.

If your organization currently uses a different mail client, you might need to migrate data from that program to Outlook 2002. If you need to migrate data from another messaging application, importers are provided in the product (for example, for Eudora Lite) that might be helpful in your situation.

Assessing your organization's security needs

Outlook 2002 provides enhanced security features for sending and receiving secure e-mail messages over the Internet or local intranet. You can customize features in your Outlook 2002 deployment to set security options appropriate for your organization.

You can also implement additional security features. For example, you can provide security labels that match your organization's security policy. An Internal Use Only label might be implemented as a security label to apply to mail that should not be sent or forwarded outside of your company.

See also

You can configure a number of options when deploying Outlook 2002. For more information about Outlook configuration choices, see "Options for Installing Outlook" in Chapter 18, "Deploying Outlook."

The Office Customization Wizard provides a straightforward way to configure and install Outlook 2002. For more information about Outlook configuration choices, see "Customizing an Outlook Installation" in Chapter 18, "Deploying Outlook."

You can stage your Outlook 2002 deployment to install Outlook with Office, before Office, or after Office, depending on the needs of your organization. For more information about staging an Outlook deployment, see "Installing Before or After Office" in Chapter 19, "Special Outlook Deployment Scenarios."

Careful planning can help your upgrade to a new release of Outlook go smoothly. For more information about planning an Outlook upgrade, see "Planning an Upgrade" in Chapter 20, "Upgrading to Outlook 2002."

Planning and implementing an appropriate security plan for your organization is key to a successful Outlook installation. For more information about security in Outlook 2002, see Chapter 22, "Administering Outlook Security."

Choosing Among E-mail Servers

Microsoft Outlook 2002 can be used with a wide variety of e-mail servers and services. The primary e-mail servers and services supported by Outlook include:

- The Simple Mail Transfer Protocol (SMTP)
- The Post Office Protocol version 3 (POP3)
- The Internet Mail Access Protocol version 4 (IMAP4)
- The Messaging Application Program Interface (MAPI), which includes servers such as Microsoft Exchange Server, Lotus Domino/Notes Server, and Lotus cc:Mail server

Outlook can also be used with a number of other messaging and information sources, including Hewlett-Packard OpenMail and Banyan Intelligent Messaging. Use of these additional service providers is made possible by the way that Outlook uses the MAPI extensibility interface. If users want to use the Contacts, Tasks, and Calendar features in a stand-alone configuration, they can also use Outlook without an e-mail server.

See also

You can configure Microsoft Exchange Server settings for Outlook profiles as part of your Outlook 2002 deployment. For more information about using the Custom Installation Wizard to customize Outlook profiles, see "Customizing an Outlook Installation" in Chapter 18, "Deploying Outlook."

Determining When to Install Outlook

You can install Microsoft Outlook 2002 before, with, or after an installation of other Microsoft Office XP applications. You can also deploy Outlook in stages for different users at different times. Each installation strategy has its own requirements, as well as advantages and disadvantages.

Installing Outlook with Office

You can install Outlook 2002 as a part of your overall upgrade to Office XP. Outlook is included in all editions of Office XP.

Installing Outlook with Office is recommended because it is the simplest installation strategy — you avoid the extra steps involved in customizing separate application installations.

Installing Outlook before Office

Choosing to install Outlook 2002 before you deploy other Office XP applications might be preferred in the following circumstances:

- When you want to test custom solutions that rely on previous versions of Microsoft Word or Microsoft Excel before you install current versions of those Office applications.
- When your messaging support group has the resources to install Outlook now, but the desktop applications support group must wait to install the rest of Office.

If you choose to install Outlook 2002 before you install Office XP, you can do so by:

- Installing the stand-alone version of Outlook from its own administrative installation point.

    Later, you can create a separate administrative installation point for Office and direct users to upgrade to Office from there.

- Installing the stand-alone version of Outlook from the same administrative installation point from which you plan to deploy Office.

    With this method you must rename the Setup program files for Office or Outlook to prevent the files from being overwritten.

- Running Office Setup to install only Outlook.

    Later, you can run the Custom Maintenance Wizard to install the rest of Office.

Advantages to installing before Office

If you deploy Outlook 2002 promptly, users can begin using new features without waiting for testing or technical support to become available for a complete upgrade to Office.

Disadvantages to installing before Office

Installing Outlook before you install the rest of Office has several disadvantages:

- When you deploy the other Office applications later on, you must customize the installation process in order to preserve your original Outlook settings.
- You cannot use the WordMail editor in Outlook 2002 until Microsoft Word 2002 has also been installed.
- If you use separate administrative installation points for Outlook and Office, you must also allow for more hard-disk space, because the files common to all of Office are duplicated on the server.
- If you use the same administrative installation point for Outlook and Office, you must take extra steps to manage multiple versions of the Setup files or to modify installation options.

Installing Outlook after Office

You can wait to install Outlook until after you have installed Office XP. For example, if any of the following scenarios describes your organization, you might consider delaying your deployment of Outlook:

- You plan to coordinate your Outlook deployment with a future upgrade of Microsoft Exchange Server.
- You want to convert Lotus Notes to a Microsoft Exchange Server solution before you upgrade to Outlook.
- Your desktop support group has the resources to upgrade to Office now, but the messaging support group must wait to deploy Outlook.

If you choose to install Outlook after you have installed Office XP, you can do so by:

- Installing the stand-alone version of Outlook from a separate administrative installation point.
- Installing the stand-alone version of Outlook from the same administrative installation point from which you installed Office.

    With this method you must rename the Setup program files (for Office or Outlook) to prevent the original files from being overwritten.

- Running Office Setup to install Office but exclude Outlook.

    Later, you can use the Custom Maintenance Wizard to install Outlook.

Advantages to installing after Office

In many organizations, it makes sense to coordinate an Outlook deployment with an upgrade of a mail server, rather than with an upgrade of other desktop applications.

Disadvantages to installing after Office

When you install Office without Outlook, you must explicitly change default Setup settings in the Custom Installation Wizard so that previous versions of Outlook are not removed from users' computers.

Regardless of when or how you install Outlook separately from Office, you must take extra steps to manage duplicate files, multiple versions of the Setup files, or customizations to the installation process.

Staging an Outlook deployment

Some groups in your organization might be ready to upgrade to Outlook immediately, while other groups might need more time to prepare or find additional resources. A situation like this, or one of the following conditions, might be best managed by a staged deployment of Outlook:

- Your normal policy is to stage upgrades to ensure a smooth rollout of new software throughout your organization.
- You have remote systems support groups (for example, in regional sales offices) that require relative autonomy in scheduling upgrades for their areas.
- Some groups want to wait until after a project deadline before making changes to their local computers.
- You have limited resources for staging and upgrading systems throughout your organization.

Advantages to staging a deployment

Staging your Outlook deployment gives you more flexibility in managing your upgrading resources. In addition, pilot users immediately become familiar with the new features and productivity enhancements of Outlook 2002.

Having users on different versions of Outlook within an organization does not pose any significant technical problems. Outlook 2002 users can communicate seamlessly with users of Outlook 2000 and Office XP.

Disadvantages to staging a deployment

You must take into account the logistics of scheduling and managing a staged deployment. Your organization might also encounter extra overhead to support users on different versions of the same product.

See also

Specific procedures can help you successfully deploy Outlook before or after you install Office. For more information about implementing a staged deployment of Outlook, see "Installing Before or After Office" in Chapter 19, "Special Outlook Deployment Scenarios."

CHAPTER 18

Deploying Outlook

Tools provided with Microsoft Office XP allow you to control how Microsoft Outlook 2002 is installed for your users. By using the Custom Installation Wizard, you can customize your Outlook deployment to include new or modified default Outlook profiles as well as other settings. In addition, you can create or modify profiles by using the Outlook profile file (PRF file).

In this chapter

Options for Installing Outlook   467

Customizing an Outlook Installation   470

Customizing Profiles with an Outlook Profile File   477

Options for Installing Outlook

Microsoft Outlook® 2002, like other Microsoft Office XP applications, takes advantage of the Office Custom Installation Wizard to control how Outlook 2002 is installed on users' computers. The Custom Installation Wizard allows you to include custom settings and profile configurations for Outlook 2002 in a transform (MST file) that is applied when Outlook is installed from an administrative installation point.

Outlook features that can be customized with the Custom Installation Wizard

Microsoft Outlook 2002 uses the same installation tools as your other Microsoft Office XP applications, including the Custom Installation Wizard. When you customize an Outlook 2002 installation with the wizard, you can do the following:

- Specify installation states for the Outlook features.
- Specify Outlook user settings.
- Specify how to set user profile information — create a profile, modify a profile, or use an existing profile file (PRF file) — or choose to use existing profile settings.
- Configure profile and account information, including Microsoft Exchange server connections.

- Remove existing information services.
- Optionally export your profile settings to a PRF file (for advanced scenarios).
- Customize other settings to apply during the installation process.

Note To function correctly, Outlook 2002 requires that Internet Explorer 4.01 or later is installed on the client computers.

After your initial installation, you can use the Office Custom Maintenance Wizard to modify and deploy customizations for your installation.

Specifying installation states for Outlook features

As with the other Office XP applications, you can specify where and when specific features of Outlook 2002 or all of Outlook 2002 is installed. You can use the **Set Feature Installation States** page in the Custom Installation Wizard to set feature installation states for Outlook 2002.

For example, for the feature **Microsoft Outlook for Windows**, you might set the feature installation state to **Run from My Computer**. In this case, all Outlook features are installed on the user's local hard disk. Or you might choose to set some features to be installed locally (with **Run from My Computer**), and others to install when the user first gains access to the feature (**Installed on First Use**). Another common option (**Not Available, Hidden, Locked**) is to set some features to not be installed, and to not even appear in the feature tree if users change the installation state of the parent feature.

Specifying Outlook user settings

There are two ways to customize Outlook user settings for your installation:

- You can specify default Office settings for users by using the Office Profile Wizard.

    In this case, you install Office on a test machine and customize Office with the defaults you select, including Outlook options, and capture those settings in an profile settings file (OPS file). Then you include the OPS file in a transform on the **Customized Default Application Settings** page in the Custom Installation Wizard.

    Note While using the Office Profile Wizard is an efficient way to save most Outlook settings, not all options are captured by the wizard. For more information about settings that are not captured by the Office Profile Wizard, see "Locating and Configuring Outlook Settings" in Chapter 21, "Maintaining an Outlook Installation."

- You can also customize Outlook user settings individually on the **Change Office User Settings** page in the Custom Installation Wizard.

    This requires stepping through the options tree and setting each option individually. This option might be more time-consuming than capturing settings with the Office Profile Wizard, especially if you have a large number of user settings to specify.

Notes Several Outlook settings that would otherwise have been included on the **Change Office User Settings** page are customized instead on the **Change Outlook: Change Default Settings** page. These options are:

- Migration option: Choosing to convert Personal Address Books to Outlook Address Books.
- Default settings for e-mail defaults: Specifying defaults for the Outlook e-mail editor and for the default format of e-mail messages.

One approach for specifying user settings is to customize an Outlook installation on a test machine and capture the settings with the Office Profile Wizard. Then specify the OPS file in the Custom Installation Wizard to establish a basic installation configuration. Finally, adjust additional settings by using the **Change Office User Settings** page in the Custom Installation Wizard.

If you have just a few Outlook user settings to specify and you are not already using the Office Profile Wizard to capture other Office settings, it may be more efficient to find and set the user options in the Custom Installation Wizard without using an OPS file.

Customizing Outlook profiles

The Outlook pages in the Custom Installation Wizard provide options for creating Outlook profiles or modifying the settings in existing Outlook profiles. For example, you can keep all existing Outlook user profiles and specify a default configuration for new Outlook user profiles.

Your options for configuring profiles include:

- Specifying Exchange server connections.
- Defining account information, such as adding POP3 or LDAP accounts.
- Saving the profile configuration information in an Outlook profile file (PRF file), once you have configured user profiles to meet your organization's needs.

See also

Detailed information about using the Office Profile Wizard to save user options is available. For more information about the Office Profile Wizard and OPS files, see "Using the Office Profile Wizard" in Chapter 8, "Maintaining an Installation."

Outlook settings and profile information can be viewed and modified in different ways, depending on the specific type of setting or option. For more information about Outlook settings, see "Locating and Configuring Outlook Settings" in Chapter 21, "Maintaining an Outlook Installation."

Customizing an Outlook Installation

Like the rest of Microsoft Office XP, a Microsoft Outlook 2002 installation is highly customizable. By using the Office Custom Installation Wizard, you can specify which features you want installed, whether they should run from the local hard disk or the network, how to customize profiles, and so forth.

Specify installation states for Outlook 2002 features

You can specify installation states for many features in Outlook 2002 when you customize your Office XP installation.

To set installation states for Outlook 2002 features

1. Start the Custom Installation Wizard.
2. On the **Set Feature Installation States** page, click the plus sign (+) next to **Microsoft Outlook for Windows** to expand the feature tree.
3. Click the down arrow next to the feature you want to set, and then select the installation state to use for that feature.

    For example, you might not want users to install Collaboration Data Objects, if your organization does not use this feature. In this case, you click the down arrow, then choose **Not Available, Hidden, Locked** in the menu listed. After deployment, users will not be able to see Collaboration Data Objects as an Outlook feature that they could install.

Specify user settings

If you have specified settings using the Office Profile Wizard and saved those settings in a profile settings file (OPS file), you can specify the file on the **Customize Default Application Settings** page of the Custom Installation Wizard. You can also specify user settings on the **Change Office User Settings** page. These settings will override choices that are specified in the OPS file.

If you want current user settings to migrate for all users, select the check box next to **Migrate user settings** on the **Customize Default Application Settings** page. If you choose to migrate user settings, other customizations to user settings that you specify — including those in an OPS file or selections you make on the **Change Office User Settings** page — will not override existing user settings.

Customize Outlook profile creation and modification

Microsoft Outlook 2002 uses profiles to store information about users' e-mail servers, where their Outlook information is stored (on the server or in a local file), and other options.

Configuring how Outlook handles creating default profiles

When users install Outlook 2002 on a clean computer, the Outlook Profile Wizard assists them in creating a profile the first time they start Outlook. If a user is upgrading from a previous version of Outlook or Microsoft Exchange Client, Outlook 2002 detects the existing profile on the user's computer and uses that profile instead of creating a new one.

Outlook profile configurations affect how e-mail messages are sent and received. Because profiles are so important, the process to create profiles can be automated — saving users from having to create profiles through the Outlook Profile Wizard. You can use the Office Custom Installation Wizard to create profiles automatically for your users during installation, or to modify existing profiles.

After your initial Outlook deployment, you can modify how Outlook manages profile creation by using the Custom Maintenance Wizard to update the original profile configuration information you specified in your transform.

Configuring how Outlook handles existing and new profiles

The Outlook pages in the Custom Installation Wizard provide options for creating Outlook profiles or modifying the settings in existing Outlook profiles. Your options for how to handle Outlook profile settings are shown on the **Customize Default Profile** page:

- **Use existing profiles**

    If an Outlook profile exists, use that profile. If an Outlook profile is not found, the Outlook Profile Wizard takes the user through creating a profile.

- **Modify Profile**

    This is the typical scenario. Users who have an Outlook profile are migrated to Outlook 2002. Settings you define in the Custom Installation Wizard automatically create new default user profiles for users who have no profile when Outlook first runs.

- **New Profile**

    This option is less common, because current Outlook users will get new profiles. This option creates a new default user profile for all users. Existing profiles remain on the user's computer but are not the default profiles used by Outlook.

- **Apply PRF**

    As an option, you can save Outlook profile settings in an Outlook profile file (PRF file). To import these settings the next time you run the Custom Installation Wizard, enter the file name here.

Note that with both **Modify Profile** and **New Profile** options, you can define new Exchange Server connections for new and existing users.

Defining and customizing an Outlook 2002 profile file (PRF file)

A simple way to create a PRF file that is compatible with Outlook 2002 is to step through the Custom Installation Wizard to specify Outlook profile settings. Then, when prompted, export the settings to a PRF file.

You can modify this PRF file in a text editor to include other customizations. For example, you may have profile customizations in a PRF file from an earlier version of Outlook that you want to incorporate in your Outlook 2002 deployment. Manually editing the Outlook 2002 PRF file gives you maximum flexibility for customizing your Outlook profile settings.

Now you can use the PRF file to define Outlook user profile options. For example, in the Custom Installation Wizard on the **Customize Default Profile** page, select **Apply PRF** and enter the name of the file.

For more information about creating and using PRF files, see "Customizing Profiles with an Outlook Profile File" in Chapter 18, "Deploying Outlook."

To choose how to customize Outlook profiles in the Custom Installation Wizard

1. In the Custom Installation Wizard, on the **Outlook: Customize Default Profile** page, click the option for how you choose to customize your users' profile information — **Modify Profile**, **New Profile**, or **Apply PRF**.

    Note that if you select **Modify Profile** or **New Profile**, you are prompted to specify user profile settings in subsequent pages of the wizard. If you choose **Apply PRF**, the settings in your PRF file establish the profile customizations for the transform.

    If you select **Modify Profile**, Outlook uses the default name for Outlook profiles, Microsoft Outlook, to save the profile information for users without an existing profile.

2. If you select **New Profile**, enter a profile name for saving the new user profile information.

3. If you select **Apply PRF**, enter (or browse to) the name of the PRF file to use.

Configure Exchange settings for user profiles

You have several options for configuring Microsoft Exchange Server connections for users (including not configuring connection information). You can make configuration changes for new Exchange users and for existing users.

- For users who do not have an Exchange Server connection configured, you can specify a user name and server name, as well as offline settings.
- For users with an existing Exchange Server connection, you can keep that connection or replace the current Exchange Server configuration with a new one.

To specify Exchange settings for Outlook user profiles in the Custom Installation Wizard

1. In the Custom Installation Wizard, on the **Outlook: Specify Exchange Settings** page, click Configure an Exchange Server connection.

    Note that if you chose **New Profile** on the previous page, this configuration will apply to all Outlook users.

2. Use the default %UserName% variable setting for the user's logon name.

    You can choose to use another system variable name if, for example, you have a separate user name for Outlook access. Then specify the Exchange server name.

    Note that on Microsoft Windows® 98 and Microsoft Windows Millennium Edition (Windows Me), UserName is not defined by default. If this variable is not set on user's computers, the Windows NT® domain logon name will be used here (if %UserName% is specified for the logon name on this page).

3. Enter the name of an Exchange server on your network.

    This will be replaced with the specific Exchange server for each individual user when Outlook first starts.

4. Click on **More Settings...** to configure offline settings, then click **OK**.

5. Select **Overwrite existing Exchange settings if an Exchange connection exists** to use the Exchange Server connection you have defined for all users.

    This only applies when modifying a profile. If you are defining new default profiles, the one you define will be used for all users.

6. Click **Next**.

Add and customize accounts for Outlook user profiles

You can add account definitions to Outlook user profiles. For example, you might create a POP3 e-mail account or configure an Internet Directory Service (LDAP) to add to user profiles.

To add and customize Outlook accounts

1. In the Custom Installation Wizard, on the **Outlook: Add Accounts** page, select **Customize additional Outlook profile and account information**.

2. To create a new account for user profiles, click **Add**.

3. Select an account from the list, and click **Next**.
4. Follow the directions shown to configure the account.

   The additional information required varies depending on the account type that you choose.
5. When you click **Finish**, the account appears in the table on the **Outlook: Add Accounts** page.

   When an account is added, the column **If Account Exists** is populated with one of two values: **Do Not Replace** or **Replace**. This applies only when you have chosen to modify user profiles (**Modify Profiles**).
6. To modify an account you have created, click on the account name in the list and then click **Modify**.
7. To delete an account you have created, click on the account name in the list and then click **Delete**.
8. In the **Deliver new mail to the following location field**, <default> is displayed.

   With this option, new mail is delivered to a user's existing default mail delivery location. For new users, <default> means that mail is delivered to the server. To change the location for new mail delivery, click the drop-down arrow and click a new location.

   Note that if you have not added any accounts to the profile, no additional locations are displayed in the drop-down.
9. When you are finished adding and modifying accounts, click **Next**.

Remove extra mail accounts and export user profile settings

If you are modifying user profiles, you can choose to remove extra mail accounts for Lotus cc: Mail or Microsoft Mail from your users' profiles.

To remove extra mail accounts

- In the Custom Installation Wizard, on the **Outlook: Remove Accounts and Export Settings** page, click the check boxes to select the accounts you want to remove from user profiles.

Also, you can choose to save to a PRF file the current Outlook user profile settings that you have configured in the previous four pages in the Custom Installation Wizard. This is optional and does not affect your user profile customizations.

> **Note** Any changes you make after exporting the current settings will not be updated in the exported PRF file.

To save Outlook user profile settings to a PRF file

1. In the Custom Installation Wizard, on the **Outlook: Remove Accounts and Export Settings** page, click the **Export Profile Settings** button.

2. Enter (or browse to) the file name and location for the PRF file and click **Save**.

    Later, you can manually edit this file (for example, using Notepad) to make changes not available through the Custom Installation Wizard.

3. Click **Next**.

    Note This process is a fast way of creating a PRF file for use in your deployment. Create your preliminary configuration by specifying Outlook options in the Custom Installation Wizard, then export the settings. After saving the file, open it with a text editor and make any additional changes you choose. For more information about working with PRF files, see "Customizing Profiles with an Outlook Profile File" in Chapter 18, "Deploying Outlook."

Customize default migration and e-mail settings

In addition to configuring Outlook user profile information, you can specify whether to migrate all users' Personal Address Book data. You can also specify default e-mail settings - the default settings for the editor Outlook will use in composing messages, and for the message format in which Outlook will send messages.

To set Outlook migration option and default settings

1. In the Custom Installation Wizard, on the **Outlook: Customize Default Settings** page, you can select the check box to have users' Personal Address Books converted to an Outlook Address Book when Outlook first runs.

2. Next, choose the **Outlook default settings** option. Set the Outlook default e-mail editor by clicking the drop-down arrow and choosing an option.

3. Set the Outlook default e-mail format by clicking the drop-down arrow and choosing an option.

4. Click **Next** to continue setting options for your Office transform.

    Note If you selected **Migrate user settings** on the **Customize Default Application Settings** page, then users' current settings will override what you specify on this page. If you did not select **Migrate user settings**, your selections here will override users' current settings.

Specify registry key settings

If there are registry key settings that you want to include in your Outlook deployment, you can specify them on the **Add/Remove Registry Entries** page of the Custom Installation Wizard.

For example, you might want to reset folder names for all users when you deploy Outlook to synchronize users' folder names to the User Interface Language of their version of Outlook. This could be useful, for example, if a corporate-wide process has initialized new mailboxes before new users have started Outlook for the first time. In this case, the mailboxes will end up with default folders in the language of the server. (Note that users can, instead, specify the **/resetfoldernames** option on the Outlook.exe command line to synchronize the folder names on their computers.)

To reset folder names when deploying Outlook

1. In the Custom Installation Wizard, go to the **Add/Remove Registry Entries** page.
2. Click **Add** to add a registry entry for **ResetFolderNames**.
3. On the **Add/Modify Registry Entry** page, select or type the following:
   - Under **Root:**, select **HKEY_CURRENT_USER**.
   - Under **Data type:**, select **Dword**.
   - In the **Key:** field, type **Software/Microsoft/Office/10.0/Outlook/Setup**.
   - In the **Value name:** field, type **ResetFolderNames**.
   - In the **Value data:** field, type **1**.

   Any non-zero value will cause Outlook to synchronize the user's folder names to the User Interface Language of Outlook.
4. Click **OK** to save the entry.

See also

The Custom Installation Wizard offers a wide range of configuration options for defining and modifying user profiles. For more information about creating and using PRF files, see "Customizing Profiles with an Outlook Profile File" in Chapter 18, "Deploying Outlook."

Customizing Profiles with an Outlook Profile File

The Outlook profile file (PRF file) allows you to quickly create MAPI profiles for Outlook users. The PRF file is a text file with syntax that Microsoft Outlook uses to generate a profile. By using a PRF file, you can set up new profiles for users or modify existing profiles without affecting other aspects of your Outlook (or Microsoft Office) installation. You can also manually edit a PRF file to customize Outlook to include services that are not included in the Custom Installation Wizard user interface.

Enhanced PRF file features in Outlook 2002

Outlook 2002 improves PRF file functionality and processing by including an enhanced file format, new options for specifying additional services, and better verification for account settings.

The Outlook 2002 PRF file format combines the features included in the two previous PRF file formats. One format was designed for the Outlook tool Newprof.exe. The second format worked with the Modprof.exe tool for Outlook 2000.

In addition, with the Outlook 2002 PRF file, you can specify services to remove from Outlook profiles, or to define new services to add.

In addition to file format changes, Outlook 2002 improves PRF file processing in these ways:

- Outlook 2002 PRF files are now executable, so you can update profiles by double-clicking the file name to run the file directly.
- When Outlook processes the PRF file, Outlook verifies that services that should be unique are not added more than once, and that services that cannot be duplicated have unique account names.

Most MAPI services can be added only once to a profile. The exceptions to this rule include providers for POP, IMAP, PST (personal store folder), and LDAP.

Using Outlook 98 and Outlook 2000 PRF files

You may already have a PRF file from an earlier version of Outlook that you want to update and use with Outlook 2002. If you have a PRF file from Outlook 98 or Outlook 2000 that includes Corporate or Workgroup settings only, you can import the file into the Custom Installation Wizard to specify profile settings for your transform.

If your earlier PRF file specifies Internet Only settings, create a new PRF file using the Custom Installation Wizard, then export the settings to a PRF file. The new PRF file can now be used to configure profile settings in your transform, or used to customize Outlook profiles through other methods (such as starting the file directly on a user's computer).

Creating and updating PRF files

To create an Outlook 2002 PRF file, you can configure profile settings in the Custom Installation Wizard, and then export the settings to a PRF file. This process creates a new Outlook 2002 PRF file with your specifications.

You can also specify profile settings by editing an existing PRF file manually using a text editor. This existing PRF file might be one that you created by using the Custom Installation Wizard, or a PRF file from a previous version of Outlook.

Creating PRF files in the Custom Installation Wizard

A straightforward way to create a PRF file with Outlook 2002 profile settings is to customize the settings in the Custom Installation Wizard, and then export the settings to a PRF file.

To create a PRF file in the Custom Installation Wizard

1. In the Custom Installation Wizard, on the **Outlook: Customize Default User Profile** page, select how you want to customize profiles for your users.

   To specify settings to be included in a PRF file, choose **Modify Profile** or **New Profile**, then click **Next**.

2. On the next three pages, customize profile information such as configuring Exchange server connections and adding accounts.

3. On the **Outlook: Remove Accounts and Export Settings** page, click **Export Profile Settings**, then when prompted, enter (or browse to) a file name and location.

Manually editing PRF files

If your organization requires special modifications to Outlook profiles — for example, if you want to add a new service that is not included in the Custom Installation Wizard — you can edit the PRF file. Use a text editor such as Notepad to edit your older PRF file, or a new PRF file created with the Custom Installation Wizard. Make your changes or additions, and then save the file.

The main functional areas in the Outlook 2002 PRF file include:

- A section specifying actions to take, such as creating new profiles, modifying existing profiles, overwriting existing profiles, and so on.
- Sections with organization-specific customizations, including server names, configurations to deploy, and so on.
- Sections that map information specified in earlier parts of the file to registry key settings.

The PRF file includes detailed comments for each section, describing existing settings and options for modifying the file with your updates. The file includes eight sections:

- Section 1: Profile defaults
- Section 2: A list of MAPI services to be added to the profile.
- Section 3: A list of Internet accounts to be created.
- Section 4: Default values for each service.
- Section 5: Settings values for each Internet account.
- Section 6: Mapping for profile properties.
- Section 7: Mapping for Internet account properties.
- Section 8: A list of MAPI services to be removed from the profile.

To allow each service definition to be customized individually, default variables and values in Section 4 can be duplicated under the separate headings (Service1, Service2, and so on) for each service in the profile. Section 6 also groups variables under each service definition, so, for example, some services can be defined as unique (UniqueService is Yes) while others are not (UniqueService is No).

You typically do not modify existing entries in sections 6 and 7. These sections define mappings for information defined elsewhere in the file to registry key settings. However, if you define new services in the PRF file, you must add the appropriate mappings for those services to sections 6 and 7.

The following table lists accounts that are unique, and how Outlook determines if a new account of the same type can be added. Keep this information in mind when you add providers in the PRF file. Outlook verifies that unique services are not added more than once, and that other services do not collide (for example, that all POP accounts have unique names).

Account	Unique account?	Method for determining collisions when adding new account
POP	No	Account name
IMAP	No	Account name
Hotmail®/HTTP	No	Account name
PST	No	Full path to PST (including file name)
Outlook Address Book	Yes	Existence of account
Personal Address Book	Yes	Existence of account
LDAP	No	Account name
Exchange	Yes	Existence of provider

Configuring Outlook user profiles by using a PRF file

You can use a PRF file in several ways to update Outlook 2002 profiles:

- Import the PRF file in the Custom Installation Wizard or Custom Maintenance Wizard to specify profile settings in a transform, and then include the transform when you deploy or update Outlook.

- Specify the PRF file as a command-line option for Outlook.exe. For example:

    outlook.exe /importprf \\server1\share\outlook.prf

- Launch the PRF file directly on users' computers by double-clicking the file.

- Set a registry key to trigger Outlook to import the PRF file when Outlook starts up and include the registry key in your transform.

    In the HKEY_CURRENT_USER\Software\Microsoft\Office\10.0\Outlook\Setup subkey, set the value of ImportPRF to a string value that specifies the name and path of the PRF file. For example, set **ImportPRF** to **\\server1\share\outlook.prf**.

See also

For more information about customizing Outlook profiles by using the Custom Installation Wizard, see "Customizing an Outlook Installation" in Chapter 18, "Deploying Outlook."

CHAPTER 19

Special Outlook Deployment Scenarios

Microsoft Office XP gives you considerable flexibility when you are installing Microsoft Outlook 2002 in unique environments or with special configurations. You can ensure that Outlook installs quietly and does not prompt the user when Outlook starts for the first time. You can configure Outlook for Terminal Server environments or roaming scenarios. In addition, you can control whether Outlook is deployed before, with, or after Office.

In this chapter

Ensuring a Quiet Installation and Startup   481

Installing in a Terminal Services Environment   484

Installing Before or After Office   485

Configuring Outlook for Roaming Users   497

Ensuring a Quiet Installation and Startup

Like the other Microsoft Office XP applications, Microsoft Outlook® 2002 prompts users for information during installation — such as the installation location — and for information when a user first starts the application — such as Outlook profile information, account migration, etc.

If you prefer to install Outlook 2002 without any user prompts, you can use Setup options to ensure a quiet installation, just as with any other Office XP application. In addition, you can use settings in the Custom Installation Wizard to configure your installation to prevent most user prompts when Outlook 2002 first runs.

Ensuring automatic user profile creation

You can make sure that users are not prompted to enter profile information themselves when Outlook 2002 first starts by giving them a default Outlook profile.

To configure a default profile for users, choose one of the following options on the **Outlook: Customize Default Profile** page of the Custom Installation Wizard:

- **New Profile:** Customize a new default profile for all Outlook users.

    Existing profiles are saved, but the new profile that you have defined becomes the default profile for all users.

- **Modify Profile:** Define changes to existing default profiles and create default profiles for new Outlook users.

    Outlook uses the customizations you specify to create default profiles for users who do not have a profile.

Avoiding user prompts due to Personal Address Book conversions and Send Receipts option

Unless you specify certain configuration information when you customize your deployment, users might be prompted when Outlook first runs to choose options for these features: Personal Address Book migration and Send Receipts options.

Most required Outlook migration happens automatically when Outlook 2002 starts on a user's computer for the first time. In general, users see a dialog box that shows progress as their account information and user data are migrated, but they are not prompted to enter any information. However, if you do not specify how Personal Address Book conversion should be managed, users may be prompted to choose a conversion option.

If you want to avoid user prompts regarding account conversion when Outlook starts for the first time, specify how Personal Address Book conversion will be managed by setting an option in the Custom Installation Wizard.

To prevent user prompting for Personal Address Book account conversion

1. In the Custom Installation Wizard, go to the **Outlook: Customize Default Settings** page.
2. Clear the check box next to **Convert Personal Address Book (PAB file) to an Outlook Address Book**.

    By clearing this option, Outlook does not import an existing PAB file into a Contacts folder when Outlook is first run, and the user is not asked to import the file.

Controlling Read Receipt settings

With Outlook 2002, users can now specify a default response to e-mail messages that arrive with a return receipt request. Users can set an option to always send return receipt (when one is requested), to never send a return receipt, or to be prompted about sending a response when a return receipt is requested. When Outlook 2002 first starts, users are prompted to specify one of these options to set as the default.

Administrators may need to implement a default setting for read receipts, depending upon the policies of their organizations. An organization may want to enforce the sending of read receipts as a way of ensuring accountability, for example, or they may want to turn off the option as a way of managing privacy. Either option can be set at the initial deployment of Outlook 2002.

If you want to avoid user prompts for specifying read receipt options when Outlook starts for the first time, specify a default read receipt response option for users by setting an option in the Custom Installation Wizard.

To prevent user prompting to specify a default read receipt response

1. In the Custom Installation Wizard, on the **Change Office User Settings** page, click **Microsoft Outlook 2002**.
2. Navigate the tree to **Tools | Options**, **Preferences**, **E-mail Options**, **Tracking Options**.
3. Double-click **Options** to open the **Options Properties** dialog.
4. Click **Apply Changes**, then choose an option in the **When Outlook is asked to respond to a read receipt request** drop-down menu.
5. Click **OK**.

User prompts caused by other messaging clients

If a messaging client other than Outlook — such as Outlook Express or a third-party client — is defined on the user's computer, there are special circumstances in which a user may be prompted for input when Outlook 2002 starts. The following scenarios with other messaging clients may result in user prompts when Outlook 2002 first runs:

- A user has a non-Outlook client installed that is defined as the default messaging client after Outlook 2002 is installed, but before Outlook 2002 is run for the first time.

    In this case, when Outlook starts, the user is asked if Outlook 2002 should be the default client.

- A user has a non-Outlook client installed with multiple accounts defined.

    When Outlook starts, the user is prompted to choose one of the accounts to import to Outlook 2002.

See also

The Custom Installation Wizard offers a wide range of configuration options for defining and modifying user profiles. For more information about your options for configuring Outlook profiles, see "Customizing an Outlook Installation" in Chapter 18, "Deploying Outlook."

Outlook 2002 supports the same Setup command-line options that the other Office 2000 applications support. These options can be set to prevent any prompts from appearing during installation. For more information about ensuring a quiet installation of Office applications, including Outlook, see "Customizing How Setup Runs" in Chapter 5, "Installing and Customizing Office."

Installing in a Terminal Services Environment

By using Windows Terminal Services, you can use Microsoft Outlook 2002 without having to upgrade every computer in your organization. Users can work in the latest Microsoft Office XP environment even when their computers have limited hard-disk space, memory, or processing speed.

Windows Terminal Services allows you to run Microsoft Windows–based programs on a server and display them remotely on client computers. For example, you can install a single copy of Microsoft Outlook 2002 on a Windows Terminal Services computer. Then, instead of running Outlook locally, multiple users can connect to the server and run Outlook from there.

To provide the best Outlook experience for your users in a Terminal Services environment, pay special attention to managing Outlook features that might adversely affect performance.

Using WordMail with Terminal Services

Outlook 2002 and Microsoft Word 2002 can both use a large amount of memory on the Terminal Services computer. If Outlook users use WordMail as their e-mail editor, this can affect the number of users that you can serve simultaneously in a Terminal Services environment. Although the default editor for Outlook 2002 is WordMail, you can set a different default editor as part of your customized Outlook deployment.

You set the default Outlook editor in the **Message format** section of the **Tools | Options | Mail Format** menu. You can customize these settings in a test installation of Office, then capture your settings by using the Office Profile Wizard. The settings will be saved to a profile settings file (OPS file) that you can include with a transform (MST file) or configuration maintenance file (CMW file).

Or you can use the **Outlook: Customize Default Settings** page in the Custom Installation Wizard or the Custom Maintenance Wizard to set the default e-mail editor.

After configuring the default editor for Outlook, install Outlook with the customization file (MST file or CMW file) that includes this new setting.

Unlocking registry settings

By default, Windows Terminal Services clients do not have write access to the registry on the Windows Terminal Services computer. To run some Outlook features, you might need to give users write access to some keys and subkeys. For example:

- To allow users use of custom MAPI forms for Outlook 2002, unlock the subtree HKEY_CLASSES_ROOT\CLSID.

- To allow users use of Schedule+ resources, unlock the subkey HKEY_LOCAL_MACHINE\Software\Microsoft\Schedule+\Application.

See also

The Office Customization Wizard provides a straightforward way to configure and install Outlook 2002. For more information about Outlook configuration choices, see "Customizing an Outlook Installation" in Chapter 18, "Deploying Outlook."

Installing Before or After Office

Although it is usually simpler to deploy all of Microsoft Office XP at once, your organization might benefit from a staged deployment of some Office applications. For example, you might choose to install Microsoft Outlook 2002 before Office XP, allowing users to benefit immediately from enhancements in Outlook 2002. Or, you might upgrade Outlook 2002 after you have installed Office XP and upgraded your messaging server to Microsoft Exchange 2000 Server.

Installing Outlook before or after Office is one example of staging the deployment of an Office application. However, you can use the methods described here to install any Office application before or after installing the rest of Office.

Options for installing Outlook before Office

When you install Outlook 2002 over the network by using an administrative installation point, you can use one of the following methods to install Outlook before you install Office:

- Install the stand-alone version of Outlook from the same or a different administrative installation point from which you plan to install Office.

- Run Office Setup to install only Outlook, then rerun Office Setup in maintenance mode to install the rest of Office when you are ready.

Installing a stand-alone version of Outlook before Office

One way to install Outlook 2002 before Office XP is to use an Office XP CD along with a stand-alone version of Outlook. With this option, you can choose to use one administrative installation point for Outlook and Office, or separate installation points.

Choosing whether to use one or more administrative installation points

When you use the stand-alone version to install Outlook, you can create two administrative installation points — one for Office, the other for Outlook — or you can deploy the stand-alone version of Outlook from the same administrative installation point from which you deploy Office. Each scenario has unique benefits, depending on your deployment plans.

You might choose to use separate installation points, for example, if two different groups in your organization will be deploying Office and Outlook, respectively. In this scenario, you use Office XP plus a stand-alone copy of Microsoft Outlook 2002.

Separate administrative installation points can be in different folders on one network server, or they can be on separate servers. Users install Outlook from one administrative installation point, and install the rest of Office later from the second administrative installation point. In this scenario, files that are common among all Office applications are duplicated on each administrative installation point.

Another method for deploying Outlook before Office is to create a single administrative installation point that includes both Outlook and Office. You create the initial administrative installation point by running Setup with the **/a** command-line option from the stand-alone Outlook version. Then you install the rest of Office from the Office XP disc into the same folder structure.

This method saves disk space because files that are common among all Office applications are shared on the single administrative installation point. Because Outlook and Office use the same names for two Setup files (Setup.exe and Setup.ini), however, you must rename the files to avoid overwriting the unique Outlook and Office versions.

> **Important**   When users set Outlook and another Office application to **Run from Network** from separate administrative installation points, Microsoft Windows® operating systems load two copies of the shared Mso.dll file if both Outlook and another Office application are being used. Mso.dll uses approximately 5 MB of memory each time it is loaded. Having the administrative images in the same location avoids this additional memory requirement.

Installing Outlook from the stand-alone Outlook version

The process for installing Outlook from a stand-alone version includes these steps:

- Creating an administrative installation point for the stand-alone version of Outlook.
- Customizing your Outlook deployment.
- Saving your customizations in a transform.
- Installing Outlook with the custom transform on users' computers.

Note As part of an initial Outlook customization, you can capture and include settings in a profile settings file (OPS file). To do this, install Outlook on a test computer, and then make any desired changes to the Outlook settings and environment. When you capture your customizations by running the Office Profile Wizard and creating an OPS file, be sure to include only Outlook settings. Then include the OPS file in the Custom Installation Wizard when you create the transform for installing Outlook.

To install Outlook by using a stand-alone Outlook 2002 version

1. Using the stand-alone Outlook 2002 version, run **Setup.exe** with the **/a** command-line option.

2. When prompted for the server location, enter a unique folder for Outlook on a network server. For example:

   \\server1\software\outlook

   –or–

   Enter the same folder that you will use for your Office deployment. For example:

   \\server1\software\office

3. Use the Custom Installation Wizard to create a transform that references the Outlook MSI file in the root of this administrative installation point, and that specifies the appropriate Outlook configuration for your users.

   For example, you can include an OPS file for Outlook (if you created one), specify Outlook settings, and configure user profiles in the Custom Installation Wizard. Save the transform in the same folder as the Setup settings file.

4. If you are using the same administrative installation point that you will use for your Office deployment, rename the Setup files to prevent these files from being overwritten when you install the rest of Office.

   In the root folder of the administrative installation point, rename Setup.exe and Setup.ini. Use consistent file names and the appropriate file name extensions. For example, OlkSetup.exe and OlkSetup.ini. (If you created the administrative image from the Microsoft Select CD subscription, the files have already been renamed for you.)

5. Edit the Outlook Setup settings file (INI file) to specify the transform that you created.

   For example, you might add the following line under the [MST] section:

   `MST1=Outlook.mst`

   You must remove the comment marker (;) from the [MST] header line so that the transform is read correctly.

6. Direct users to install Outlook from this administrative installation point by using Outlook Setup.

Installing Office after installing a stand-alone version of Outlook

When you deploy the rest of Office, you can use the same administrative installation point or create a new location for your Office files. If you use the same administrative installation point as Outlook, then you must make sure that the Outlook Setup files have been renamed so the Office Setup files do not overwrite them. Then you customize your Office deployment, save the customizations in a transform, and direct users to install the rest of Office XP from the Office administrative installation point.

> **Note** As part of an initial Office customization, you can capture and include settings in an OPS file. To do this, install Office on a test computer, and then make any desired changes to the Office settings and environment. When you capture your customizations by running the Office Profile Wizard and creating an OPS file, be sure to exclude Outlook settings. Then include the OPS file in the Custom Installation Wizard when you create the transform for installing Outlook.

To install Office after installing stand-alone Outlook

1. Using an Office XP CD, run **Setup.exe** with the **/a** command-line option.

2. When prompted for the server location, enter a folder on the network server. For example:

   \\server1\software\office

3. Use the Custom Installation Wizard to create a transform to customize Office for your deployment.

   As part of your customization, on the **Set Feature Installation States** page, set **Microsoft Outlook for Windows** to **Not Available, Hidden, Locked**. In addition to customizing options for other Office applications, you can optionally fine-tune your Outlook customizations in this transform as well. When you are finished, save the transform in the same folder as the Setup settings file.

4. To specify this transform when you install Outlook, start the Setup INI Customization Wizard.

5. On the **Specify options for each package in your INI file** page, select the Outlook MSI file and specify your transform in the **Transform (MST file) to apply during installation** box.

   The Setup INI Customization Wizard adds the following entry to the INI file:
   ```
   [MST1]
   MST1=Office.mst
   ```

   Note that if you elect to edit the INI file manually, you must remove the comment marker (;) from the [MST] header line so that the transform is read correctly.

6. Direct users to install Office from the administrative installation point.

Using installation options to install Outlook before Office

Another way to stage your deployment of Outlook 2002 and Office XP is to install Outlook first from an Office XP SKU that includes Outlook. Then you can configure Office to be installed by using the Custom Maintenance Wizard and changing installation options to install the rest of Office. In this case, you use a single administrative installation point for both installations.

Issues to consider

If you are upgrading from an earlier version of Office, there are several issues to consider when using this method for installing Outlook 2002 before Office XP. First, if you plan to use the Office Profile Wizard to capture Office settings, you must configure these settings and include the OPS file when creating the Custom Installation Wizard transform to deploy Outlook. The Custom Maintenance Wizard does not allow you to include an OPS file.

Also, when you deploy Office XP by using the Custom Maintenance Wizard, you limit your options for easily removing earlier versions of other Office applications. When you deploy Outlook 2002 by using the Custom Installation Wizard, you can choose to remove earlier versions of Outlook while leaving other existing Office applications. However, when you deploy Office by using the Custom Maintenance Wizard, you cannot specify to remove older versions of Office applications. However, you can use the Office Removal Wizard to remove files instead.

Start by running Setup with the **/a** option to copy Office files to your administrative installation point. When prompted for the server location, enter a folder on a network server. For example:

\\server1\software\office

Then follow these steps to install Outlook and other Office applications in stages:

First, you use the Custom Installation Wizard to create a transform that includes any Outlook and Office customizations you might have. Then, install Outlook using that transform.

When you want to install the rest of Office, you use the Custom Maintenance Wizard. You can include both Office and Outlook customizations in the second installation.

> **Notes** As part of an initial Outlook customization, you can capture and include settings in an OPS file. To do this, install Outlook on a test computer, and then make any desired changes to the Outlook settings and environment. When you capture your customizations by running the Office Profile Wizard, be sure to include only Outlook settings.
>
> Optionally, you can install all of Office on the test machine and capture settings for other Office XP applications as well as Outlook. In this case, capture all customizations when you run the Office Profile Wizard to create an OPS file.
>
> Then include the OPS file in the Custom Installation Wizard when you create the transform for installing Outlook.

To install Outlook by using the Office XP CD

1. Start the Custom Installation Wizard and open the Office XP package (MSI file).

2. On the **Remove Previous Versions** page, click **Remove the following versions of Microsoft Office applications**.

3. In the table of applications, for each Office application except Microsoft Outlook, click the application name, then click the **Details...** button.

   Clear all the check boxes to retain the current versions of the application on users' computers, then click **OK**. Repeat for each application.

4. On the **Set Feature Installation States** page, set all Microsoft Office applications in the feature tree to **Not Available**.

5. Set the **Microsoft Outlook for Windows** feature to **Run from My Computer**.

   You can also install shared Office tools, converters, or other features that support your Outlook installation.

6. Configure any other installation options, then complete the transform.

   For example, you can specify Outlook profile information.

7. To specify this transform when you install Outlook, start the Setup INI Customization Wizard.

8. On the **Specify options for each package in your INI file** page, select the Outlook MSI file and specify your transform in the **Transform (MST file) to apply during installation** box.

   The Setup INI Customization Wizard adds the following entry to the INI file:
   ```
   [MST1]
   MST1=Office.mst
   ```

   Note that if you elect to edit the INI file manually, you must remove the comment marker (;) from the [MST] header line so that the transform is read correctly.

9. Instruct users to install Outlook by running Setup from this administrative installation point.

10. Later, use the Custom Maintenance Wizard to install additional Office applications and to modify existing Office installations (including your Outlook installation) throughout your organization after your initial deployment.

Similar to the Custom Installation Wizard, the Custom Maintenance Wizard reads the Office XP package (MSI file) and records your changes in a configuration maintenance file (CMW file). To add Office applications to your initial Outlook installation, you create a CMW file with the appropriate configuration, and then run the Custom Maintenance Wizard on users' computers.

> **Toolbox** The Office XP Resource Kit includes the Custom Maintenance Wizard, which is installed by default when you run the Office Resource Kit Setup program. For more information, see "Custom Maintenance Wizard" in the Toolbox.

Options for installing Outlook after Office

When you install Microsoft Outlook 2002 over the network by using an administrative installation point, you can use one of the following methods to install Outlook after you install Office:

- Run Office Setup to install Office applications except for Outlook, then rerun Office Setup in maintenance mode to install Outlook when you are ready.

   In this case, you use the same administrative installation point for both Office and Outlook.

- Install Office applications, excluding Outlook, first, then install Outlook from the Outlook 2002 stand-alone version.

   In this case, you can choose to install Outlook from its own administrative installation point or from the same administrative installation point from which you installed Office.

Issues to consider

Using a stand-alone version of Outlook to install Outlook separately from Office has the advantage of allowing you to remove the previous version of Outlook at deployment. Since you are installing two separate SKUs, you can use the Custom Installation Wizard to create two transforms, one for each deployment. In each transform, you can specify to remove earlier versions of the applications. For example, when you deploy Outlook, you can specify in the transform to remove earlier versions of Outlook when Outlook 2002 is installed.

In contrast, if you deploy Office and then Outlook from the Office CD, you can use a customized transform with only your Office deployment. When you deploy Outlook by using the Custom Maintenance Wizard, you cannot specify to remove older versions of Outlook. The Office Removal Wizard can be used to remove previous versions of Office applications.

Installing Outlook after Office is one example of staging your deployment of Office applications. However, you can use the methods described here to install any Office application after installing the rest of Office.

Using installation options to install Outlook after Office

One way to stage your deployment of Outlook 2002 and Office XP is to install Office first from an Office XP SKU and customize your installation to exclude Outlook. Then, later, you can configure Outlook to be installed by using the Custom Maintenance Wizard and changing installation options to install just Outlook. In this case, you use a single administrative installation point for both installations.

Issues to consider

If you are upgrading from an earlier version of Office, there are several issues to consider when using this method for installing Office XP before Outlook 2002. First, if you plan to use the Office Profile Wizard to capture Outlook settings, you must configure these settings and include the OPS file when creating the Custom Installation Wizard transform to deploy Office. The Custom Maintenance Wizard does not allow you to include an OPS file.

Also, when you deploy Outlook 2002 by using the Custom Maintenance Wizard, you limit your options for easily removing earlier versions of Outlook software. When you deploy Office XP by using the Custom Installation Wizard, you can choose to remove earlier versions of Office while leaving existing Outlook software. However, when you deploy Outlook by using the Custom Maintenance Wizard, you cannot specify to remove older versions of Outlook. However, you can use the Office Removal Wizard to remove files instead.

Start by using Setup with the **/a** option to copy Office files to your administrative installation point. When prompted for the server location, enter a folder on a network server. For example:

\\server1\software\office

Then follow these steps to install Office XP and Outlook 2002 in stages:

- First, you use the Custom Installation Wizard to create a transform that is used to install Office but excludes Outlook. You include Office customizations in the transform (and, optionally, customizations for Outlook). You then install Office XP using the transform.

- Then, later, you use the Custom Maintenance Wizard to install Outlook 2002. You can include both Outlook and Office customizations in the second installation.

> **Note** As part of an initial Outlook customization, you can capture and include settings in an OPS file. To do this, install Outlook on a test computer, and then make any desired changes to the Outlook settings and environment.

To install Office from the Office XP CD, excluding Outlook 2002

1. Start the Custom Installation Wizard and open the Office XP package (MSI file).

2. On the **Remove Previous Versions** page, click **Remove the following versions of Microsoft Office applications**.

3. In the table of applications, click on **Microsoft Outlook**, then click the **Details...** button to open a dialog box.

   Clear the check box next to the version of Outlook you want to retain on each user's computer, then click **OK**.

4. On the **Set Feature Installation States** page, set the **Microsoft Outlook for Windows** feature to **Not Available, Hidden, Locked**.

5. Set all other Microsoft Office applications in the feature tree (that you want to be installed) to **Run from My Computer**.

6. Configure any other installation options, then complete the transform.

7. To specify this transform when you install Outlook, start the Setup INI Customization Wizard.

8. On the **Specify options for each package in your INI file** page, select the Outlook MSI file and specify your transform in the **Transform (MST file) to apply during installation** box.

   The Setup INI Customization Wizard adds the following entry to the INI file:

   ```
   [MST1]
   MST1=Office.mst
   ```

   Note that if you elect to edit the INI file manually, you must remove the comment marker (;) from the [MST] header line so that the transform is read correctly.

9. Instruct users to install Office by running Setup from the administrative installation point.

10. Later, use the Custom Maintenance Wizard to install Outlook and to modify any existing Office installations throughout your organization.

Similar to the Custom Installation Wizard, the Custom Maintenance Wizard reads the Office XP package (MSI file) and records your changes in a configuration maintenance file (CMW file). To add Outlook 2002 to your initial Office XP installation, you create a CMW file with the appropriate configuration and then run the Custom Maintenance Wizard on users' computers.

> **Toolbox** The Office XP Resource Kit includes the Custom Maintenance Wizard, which is installed by default when you run the Office Resource Kit Setup program. For more information, see "Custom Maintenance Wizard" in the Toolbox.

Installing a stand-alone version of Outlook after Office

Another way to install Outlook 2002 after Office XP is to use an Office XP CD along with a stand-alone version of Outlook. With this option, you can choose to use one administrative installation point for Outlook and Office, or separate installation points.

Choosing whether to use one or more administrative installation points

When you use a stand-alone version to install Outlook, you can create two administrative installation points — one for Office, the other for Outlook — or you can deploy the stand-alone version of Outlook from the same administrative installation point from which you install Office. Each scenario has unique benefits, depending on your deployment plans.

You might choose to use separate installation points, for example, if two different groups in your organization will be used to install Office and Outlook, respectively. These administrative installation points can be in different folders on one network server, or they can be on separate servers. Users install Office from one administrative installation point, and install Outlook later from the second administrative installation point. In this scenario, files that are common among all Office applications are duplicated on each administrative installation point.

Another method for deploying Outlook after Office is to create a single administrative installation point that includes both Outlook and Office. You create the initial administrative installation point by running Setup with the **/a** command-line option from the Office XP CD. Then you install Outlook from the stand-alone Outlook version into the same folder structure.

This method saves disk space because files that are common among all Office applications are shared on the single administrative installation point. Because Outlook and Office use the same names for Setup files, however, you must rename these files to avoid overwriting the unique Outlook and Office versions:

- Setup.exe
- Setup.ini

> **Important** When users set Outlook and another Office application to **Run from Network** from separate administrative installation points, Windows loads two copies of the shared Mso.dll file if both Outlook and another Office application are being used. Mso.dll uses approximately 5 MB of memory each time it is loaded. Having the administrative images in the same location avoids this additional memory requirement.

Excluding Outlook when installing Office applications from an Office CD

The process for excluding Outlook when installing Office applications from an Office CD includes these steps:

- Copying Office files to an administrative installation point.
- Customizing your Office deployment to exclude Outlook.
- Saving your customizations in a transform.
- Installing Office with the custom transform on users' computers.

> **Note** As part of an initial Office customization, you can capture and include custom settings in an OPS file. To do this, install Office on a test computer, and then make any desired changes to the Office settings and environment. When you capture your customizations by running the Office Profile Wizard and creating an OPS file, be sure to exclude Outlook settings. Then include the OPS file in the Custom Installation Wizard when you create the transform for installing Office.

To install Office from the Office XP CD, excluding Outlook 2002

1. Using an Office XP CD, run **Setup.exe** with the **/a** command-line option.
2. When prompted for the server location, enter a folder on the network server.

   For example:

   \\server1\software\office

3. If you are using the same administrative installation point that you will use for your Outlook deployment, rename the Setup files to prevent these files from being overwritten when you install Outlook.

   In the root folder of the administrative installation point, rename Setup.exe and Setup.ini. Use consistent file names and the appropriate file name extensions. For example, OffSetup.exe and OffSetup.ini. (If you created the administrative image from the Microsoft Select CD subscription, the files have already been renamed for you.)

4. Start the Custom Installation Wizard and open the Office XP package (MSI file).
5. On the **Remove Previous Versions** page, click **Remove the following versions of Microsoft Office applications**.
6. In the table of applications, click on **Microsoft Outlook**, then click the **Details...** button to open a dialog box.

    Clear the check box next to the version of Outlook you want to retain on users' computer, then click **OK**.
7. On the **Set Feature Installation States** page, set the **Microsoft Outlook for Windows** feature to **Not Available, Hidden, Locked**.
8. Set all other Microsoft Office applications in the feature tree (that you want to be installed) to **Run from My Computer**.
9. Configure any other installation options, then complete the transform.
10. To specify this transform when you install Outlook, start the Setup INI Customization Wizard.
11. On the **Specify options for each package in your INI file** page, select the Outlook MSI file and specify your transform in the **Transform (MST file) to apply during installation** box.

    The Setup INI Customization Wizard adds the following entry to the INI file:
    ```
    [MST1]
    MST1=Office.mst
    ```
    Note that if you elect to edit the INI file manually, you must remove the comment marker (;) from the [MST] header line so that the transform is read correctly.
12. Instruct users to install Office by running Setup from the administrative installation point.

Installing a stand-alone version of Outlook after installing Office

When you deploy Outlook from a stand-alone Outlook version, you can use the same administrative installation point as Office or create a new location for your Outlook files. If you use the same administrative installation point as Office, then you must make sure that the Office Setup files have been renamed so the Outlook Setup files do not overwrite them. Then you customize your Outlook deployment, save the customizations in a transform, and direct users to install Outlook from the Office administrative installation point.

> **Note** As part of an initial Outlook customization, you can capture and include settings in an OPS file. To do this, install Outlook on a test computer, and then make any desired changes to the Outlook settings and environment. When you capture your customizations by running the Office Profile Wizard and creating an OPS file, be sure to include only Outlook settings. Then include the OPS file in the Custom Installation Wizard when you create the transform for installing Outlook.

To install Outlook after Office by using a stand-alone Outlook 2002 version

1. Using the stand-alone Outlook 2002 version, run **Setup.exe** with the **/a** command-line option.

2. When prompted for the server location, enter a unique folder for Outlook on a network server. For example:

   \\server1\software\outlook

   –or–

   Enter the same folder that you used for your Office deployment. For example:

   \\server1\software\office

   Note that if you use the same folder as you used for Office deployment, make sure that the Office Setup files (Setup.exe and Setup.ini) have been renamed before you copy files for Outlook. For example, you might rename the Office Setup files to OffSetup.exe and OffSetup.ini. Otherwise, the Outlook Setup files will overwrite the existing Office Setup files.

3. Use the Custom Installation Wizard to create a transform in which you specify the appropriate Outlook configuration for your users.

   For example, you can include an OPS file for Outlook (if you created one), specify Outlook settings, and configure user profiles. Save the transform in the same folder as the Setup settings file.

4. If you are using the same administrative installation point that you used for your Office deployment, optionally rename the Outlook Setup files to make it clearer which Setup files belong to which installation.

   To do this, in the root folder of the administrative installation point, rename Setup.exe and Setup.ini. Use consistent file names and the appropriate file name extensions. For example, OlkSetup.exe and OlkSetup.ini. (If you created the administrative image from the Microsoft Select CD subscription, the files have already been renamed for you.)

5. Edit the Outlook Setup settings file (INI file) to specify the transform that you created.

   For example, you might add the following line under the [MST] section:

   MST1=Outlook.mst

   You must remove the comment marker (;) from the [MST] header line so that the transform is read correctly.

6. Direct users to install Outlook from the administrative installation point using the Outlook Setup.exe file.

See also

There are a number of considerations to examine when choosing the timing of your Outlook deployment. For more information about the advantages and disadvantages of staging an Outlook installation, see "Determining When to Install Outlook" in Chapter 17, "Planning for Outlook."

The Office Customization Wizard provides a straightforward way to configure and install Outlook 2002. For more information about Outlook configuration choices, see "Customizing an Outlook Installation" in Chapter 18, "Deploying Outlook."

You can use the Office Removal Wizard to remove applications after completing your initial Office installation. For more information about using the Removal Wizard, see "Removing Applications or Features After Installation" in Chapter 8, "Maintaining an Installation."

Configuring Outlook for Roaming Users

Roaming users move between different computers on a network. With Microsoft Office XP, these users can move between computers without changing the way that they work. Their documents and their application settings for Outlook and other Office applications travel with them, along with any system preferences.

You can help ensure a smooth roaming experience for Outlook users in your organization by following several recommended strategies and configuration options.

Recommended strategies for Outlook roaming

Roaming with Outlook 2002 works only between computers that are set up with the same operating system and the same versions of software. The following recommendations will ensure a smooth roaming experience for users:

- Roam between platforms on the same version of the same operating system.

    For example, Microsoft Windows 2000 to Microsoft Windows 2000, Windows 98 to Windows 98, and so on. Supported platforms are Windows 2000, Microsoft Windows Millennium Edition (Windows Me), Microsoft Windows 98, and Microsoft Windows NT® 4.0 Service Pack 6a.

- Ensure that the same operating system language version is installed on all computers that users roam between.

- Ensure that the same language version and release version of Outlook are installed on all computers that users roam between.

- Install Outlook on all computers for roaming users as per-computer.

    Installing as per-user is also possible but is not recommended.

- Install Outlook in the same location on all computers that will be used for roaming users.

Upgrading roaming users to Outlook 2002

If your organization already has roaming configured for Outlook users, you can ensure a smooth transition when you upgrade to Outlook 2002 by following the guidelines mentioned in this section.

Users can only roam between computers running the same version of Outlook. If you have roaming users on an older version of Outlook, be sure to upgrade all users and computers in a single area (such as a domain) at the same time. New features in Outlook 2002 are not available to users with Outlook 2000 profiles, which can create confusion for users roaming in an environment with a mix of Outlook versions.

Setting up roaming users with Outlook 2002

To set up roaming for users in Outlook 2002, you first decide how to manage users' data so the information they need is available to them as they roam. Then you configure user profiles for roaming by using the network Primary Domain Controller (PDC) computer.

Managing folder locations

To ensure that a user's e-mail messages and other Outlook information roam with the user, you might need to take special steps to configure Outlook folder locations.

For example, suppose the users in your organization receive mail in an Inbox located on their Microsoft Exchange server. They can view new mail when they roam without taking special steps. However, perhaps users also need access to a personal file folder (for example, to read mail that has been transferred off of the messaging server). In this case, you can put the files that contain this data on a network share.

When you enable roaming and specify a network share for roaming files, certain files and folders automatically roam with users. That is, the files are available for them on the network location when they roam to use different computers. Files and folders in the following locations (on the local computer) roam with users (with the exception of one folder, noted below):

- On Windows 2000: \Documents and Settings\%UserName%
- On Windows NT 4.0: \Winnt\Profiles\%UserName%
- On Windows 98: \Windows\Profiles\%UserName%
- On Windows Me: \Windows\Profiles\%UserName%
- On Windows 2000 after upgrading from Windows NT 4.0: \Winnt\Profiles\%UserName%

(%UserName% is replaced by the user's logon name on the computer.)

The one folder that does not roam with users in the default roaming scenario is the Local Settings folder under %UserName%. This exception affects Outlook users because, by default, the file folders for some Outlook services are created in this non-roaming folder.

Service name	File extension
Personal Folders (PST)	.pst
Personal Address Book (PAB)	.pab

Because the files reside in a non-roaming directory, Outlook can see and open them only on the local computer (on which the files were created). To allow users to use PST or PAB files while roaming, you can place the files on a network share.

There are several ways to place files on a network share. For example:

- You can set the file location to a network share for new services that you create in the Custom Installation Wizard or Custom Maintenance Wizard.

  You do this when you create a custom transform for deploying or updating Outlook. For example, you can add a PST file for all Outlook users and specify the location of a network share. This allows users to move e-mail messages to the PST file, and those messages will be available to them when they roam.

- You can notify roaming users to relocate local folders to a network share.

  Users can move folders by using the Outlook user interface. This is good choice for users who have existing Outlook files that must be accessible to them on other computers.

Another option is to relocate the files into a roaming folder on the user's local computer. However, these personal files can become large. The advisability of relocating the files depends on network speed and traffic, as well as the number of users who roam in your organization. Typically, placing PST and PAB files in folders that roam with users is not recommended.

Configuring Windows NT servers for roaming users

Setting up roaming user profiles for a Windows NT–based network involves two steps on the server side:

1. Create a shared Profiles folder on the server to store roaming user profiles.
2. Configure client user profiles to point to the shared Profiles folder.

   Note Use a file server rather than your Primary Domain Controller (PDC) to store user profiles. Using a file server helps you balance the workload without straining the resources on your PDC.

After you update the profile information to point to that shared folder, the profile is retrieved automatically when the user logs on, and updated automatically when the user logs off. This retrieving and updating process is called reconciling the user profile.

Create a Profiles folder on the server

The Profiles folder stores all your roaming user profiles on an NTFS-formatted disk drive on the server. Make sure your roaming users have full control permissions to their subfolders so they can update their profiles whenever the profiles change. However, do not give users access to any subfolders other than their own.

> **Note** Do not create the Profiles folder in the %Systemroot% directory on your server. If you use %Systemroot%\Profiles, the client computer uses the local profile instead of the server copy.

Next, you update all your client user profiles on the Windows PDC server. The procedures vary depending on the version of Windows you use on your PDC server.

Configure client user profiles on Windows NT 4.0

If the operating system on your Primary Domain Controller (PDC) is Windows NT 4.0, use this procedure to configure profile information for each of the users in your organization who will roam.

To configure profile information for each roaming user on Windows NT 4.0

1. On a Windows NT 4.0 PDC server, click **Start**, point to **Programs**, point to **Administrative Tools (Common)**, and then click **User Manager for Domains**.
2. In the list of user names, double-click a user name.
3. In the **User Properties** box, click **Profile**.
4. In the **User Profile Path** box, type the full path to the Profiles folder you created (for a Windows NT client or a Windows 2000 client).

   – or –

   Under **Home Directory**, in the **Local Path** box, type the full path to the Profiles folder you created (for a Windows 98 or Windows Me client).

   For example: \\Server\Subfoldername\Profiles

Repeat steps 2 through 4 for each user that you are configuring for roaming. When you have finished, these users can use other computers to gain access to Outlook with their existing Outlook profile configuration and settings.

Configure client user profiles on Windows 2000

If the operating system on your Primary Domain Controller (PDC) is Windows 2000, use this procedure to configure profile information for each of the users in your organization who will roam.

To configure profile information for each roaming user on Windows 2000

1. On a Windows 2000 PDC server, click **Start**, point to **Programs**, point to **Administrative Tools**, and then click **Active Directory Users and Computers**.
2. In the console tree, expand the domain node, then click the folder where users are located (typically the **Users** folder).
3. In the list of user names, click to select a user name.
4. Right-click and select **Properties**.
5. In the **Profile** tab, in the **Profile Path** edit box under **User Profile**, type the full path to the Profiles folder you created (for a Windows NT client or a Windows 2000 client). For example:

   \\server\share\Profiles

   – or –

   In the **Profile** tab, under **Home Folder**, go to the **Connect** area. In the **To:** box, type the full path to the user folder in the Profiles folder you created (for a Windows 98 or Windows Me client). For example:

   \\server\share\Profiles\Username

Repeat steps 3 through 5 for each user that you are configuring for roaming. When you have finished, these users can use other computers to gain access to Outlook with their existing Outlook profile configuration and settings.

See also

You have considerable flexibility in configuring and deploying Outlook 2002. For more information about using the Custom Installation Wizard to create a custom transform for deploying Outlook 2002, see "Customizing an Outlook Installation" in Chapter 18, "Deploying Outlook."

CHAPTER 20

Upgrading to Outlook 2002

Microsoft Outlook 2002 users can exchange e-mail messages and scheduling data with users of previous versions of Microsoft e-mail and calendar applications, as well as interact with users of other applications. However, previous versions of Outlook or other applications do not support all Outlook 2002 features. As you plan your upgrading strategy, consider when and how you will take advantage of new features — and also consider differences between Microsoft Office XP and earlier versions of Office applications.

In this chapter

Planning an Upgrade   503

Upgrading from Previous Versions   504

Upgrading From Older Versions of Messaging Clients   505

Upgrading from Schedule+   509

Sharing Information with Other Versions or Applications   511

Upgrading to Outlook 2002 Security   520

Reverting to a Previous Installation   522

Planning an Upgrade

Because Microsoft Outlook® 2002 is compatible with earlier versions of Outlook and can share files with other Microsoft e-mail and calendar applications, upgrading strategies typically involve only preparation and distribution issues. When you decide how you want your upgrade to proceed, and you identify the applications required, upgrading to Outlook 2002 is a simple process.

Before you start the upgrade process, you must make the following general decisions:

- Decide which browser you want to use.
- Decide which security settings you want for your users.
- If you use Microsoft Exchange 5.5 as your messaging server, decide whether to upgrade to Exchange 2000 before deploying Outlook 2002.

Note that before upgrading to any new release, it is wise to create a backup copy of your existing data. This task prevents you from permanently losing data during the upgrade process.

Part 5 Messaging

> **Tip** Although Microsoft Office 2000 works with Microsoft Internet Explorer 4.0, it is recommended that you upgrade to Internet Explorer 5.5, which is included with Microsoft Office XP. Because of the offline capabilities of Internet Explorer 5.5, it is much easier for Outlook 2002 users to download and store any folder home pages so that they can be modified offline.

You can easily upgrade to Outlook 2002 from previous Microsoft e-mail and calendar applications. You can install Outlook 2002 over a Microsoft Outlook 97, Microsoft Outlook 98, or Microsoft Outlook 2000 installation. Like other Office XP applications, Outlook 2002 migrates user settings stored in the registry. In addition, if a Messaging Application Programming Interface (MAPI) profile already exists on a user's computer, your Outlook 2002 deployment can be configured to continue to use the profile.

As an administrator, you can plan upgrade strategies for the following scenarios:

- A one-time upgrade to Outlook 2002.
- A gradual upgrade to Outlook 2002.

If you plan a gradual upgrade, keep in mind that Outlook users might need to exchange e-mail messages and scheduling data with users of other Microsoft e-mail and calendar applications, which can complicate support issues.

See also

You can deploy Outlook separately from the rest of Office XP. For more information, see "Determining When to Install Outlook" in Chapter 17, "Planning for Outlook."

Upgrading from Previous Versions

When you upgrade to Microsoft Outlook 2002 from an earlier version of Outlook, you must make choices about configuring Outlook user profiles, and you must be aware of fax and forms changes.

Choosing e-mail support in Outlook 2002

You can configure a variety of Outlook 2002 e-mail services by using the Custom Installation Wizard to define user profiles, then save your customizations in a transform (MST file). For example, you can define Microsoft Exchange Server connections, add POP3 accounts, or specify other e-mail support.

When you create a transform for Outlook, you also have several choices for keeping, creating, or modifying user profiles. For example, you can choose to create new default profiles for new Outlook users and keep existing profiles for current Outlook users.

Choosing fax support in Outlook 2002

Integrated fax support is no longer provided in Microsoft Outlook. However, you can use third-party MAPI fax providers or Microsoft Windows® fax support.

WinFax is uninstalled by Outlook 2002. However, the viewer is left so users can still view faxes already received.

Supporting forms in Outlook 2002

Previous versions of Microsoft Exchange Client and Outlook (earlier than Outlook 2000) install runtime files for Electronic Forms Designer, which allows users to design 16-bit custom forms that run without error.

Outlook 2002 does not install Electronic Forms Designer runtime files. If your organization requires Electronic Forms Designer support, you must install Electronic Forms Designer manually.

Note You do not need to install Electronic Forms Designer runtime support on all your computers. However, users with computers that have never had Outlook or Exchange Client installed must install Electronic Forms Designer runtime support if you deploy EFP-based forms on those computers, and users want to use the forms.

See also

The Office Customization Installation Wizard provides a straightforward way to configure and install Outlook 2002. For more information about Outlook configuration choices, see "Customizing an Outlook Installation" in Chapter 18, "Deploying Outlook."

Upgrading From Older Versions of Messaging Clients

Microsoft Outlook 2002 provides a convenient upgrade path from Microsoft Exchange Client and Microsoft Mail $3.x$ for Windows. By upgrading to use Outlook as your messaging client, you can provide improved features and better integration with other Office applications.

Upgrading from Microsoft Exchange Client

Because both Microsoft Outlook 2002 and Microsoft Exchange Client are MAPI-compatible applications, Outlook can completely replace Exchange Client. Except for changes in the user interface and other features, you can continue working with e-mail messages in Outlook in the same way that you work with e-mail messages in Exchange Client.

Outlook 2002 uses the same profile and other configuration information, and Outlook can use all Exchange Client extensions and custom forms. Because of this compatibility, users can exchange e-mail messages, and they can share public folders with Exchange Client users. Some exceptions are described in the following sections.

> **Toolbox**   Outlook is not designed to run on the same computer as Exchange Client, but the Office Resource Kit includes the SwitchForms utility that allows you to run both Outlook and Exchange Client on the same computer. For more information about installing SwitchForms, see the Microsoft Office 97/98 Resource Kit Web site at http://www.microsoft.com/office/ork/home.htm.

Unless you specify a profile, when you run Outlook 2002 for the first time, it uses the default e-mail profile to open your Personal Address Book (PAB) and personal folders, and it connects to the Exchange server and any other services that you specify in that profile.

Whether you configure the profile to deliver e-mail messages to the Inbox on the Exchange Server or to the Inbox in personal folders, Outlook 2002 continues to accept new e-mail in the same Inbox folder. After you install Outlook, you work with the same Inbox, Outbox, Sent Items, Deleted Items, and any other personal folders used by the Microsoft Exchange Client profile.

> **Tip**   To make the new user interface of Outlook 2002 look more like the Exchange Client user interface, you can view the Outlook folder list by using the **Folder List** command (**View** menu). Later, you can choose to hide the folder list and then use the Outlook Bar exclusively for quick access to Outlook functions and Microsoft Windows folders.

Outlook 2002 starts with the same profile configuration as Exchange Client, except that a new information service is added to the Outlook 2002 default profile. This allows Outlook and any other Messaging Application Programming Interface (MAPI) applications to use the Outlook Contacts folder as an e-mail address book. Outlook 2002 can also do the following:

- Recognize any folder views you define.
- Maintain the read or unread message status.

> **Note**   The Microsoft Office Resource Kit for Office 97/98 provides additional upgrading and file-sharing information for Microsoft Exchange Client, including information about Exchange Client folders and views, client forms, and extensions. For more information, see Microsoft Office 97/98 Resource Kit Web site at http://www.microsoft.com/office/ork/home.htm. For more information, see Microsoft Office 97/98 Resource Kit Web site.

Upgrading from Microsoft Mail 3.*x* for Windows

Microsoft Outlook 2002 provides all the features of Microsoft Mail 3.*x* for Windows, and it provides many additional features, such as:

- Integrated calendar functions with contact, journal, and task items
- Multiple views of messages
- Custom view capabilities

- Message handling rules
- Custom form creation
- Advanced printing options

> **Note** Because Outlook 2002 runs only on Microsoft Windows 98, Microsoft Windows Millennium Edition, Microsoft Windows NT® Workstation 3.51 or later, and Microsoft Windows 2000, Microsoft Mail 3.*x* for Windows users running Windows 3.11 or Windows for Workgroups must upgrade to a new version of Windows before upgrading to Outlook 2002.

Outlook 2002 can serve as a complete replacement for Microsoft Mail 3.*x* for Windows. Except for changes in the user interface and other features, you can work with e-mail in Outlook in the same way that you work with Microsoft Mail 3.*x* for Windows.

Outlook 2002 uses the same MSMail.ini file and other configuration information; and Outlook can use all Microsoft Mail 3.*x* for Windows add-ins and custom forms. This means that you can share information with Microsoft Mail 3.*x* for Windows users by sending e-mail back and forth or by making messages available in shared folders. However, Outlook 2002 e-mail messages might not appear the same to users of Microsoft Mail 3.*x* for Windows.

> **Tip** To make the Outlook user interface look more like the user interface of Microsoft Mail 3.*x* for Windows, you can view the Outlook folder list by using the **Folder List** command (**View** menu). Later, you can choose to hide the folder list and then use the Outlook Bar exclusively for quick access to Outlook features and Windows folders.

Importing Microsoft Mail files

After Outlook is installed, you must import the contents of the Microsoft Mail File (MMF). The MMF stores your e-mail messages, attachments, and personal address book (PAB). You can store the MMF in the post office folder in the MMF directory, or you can move the MMF to your hard disk or a network location.

If the MMF is in the post office, you must first connect to the post office with Microsoft Mail 3.*x* for Windows, and you then move the MMF either to your hard disk or to an accessible network location before importing the contents by using Outlook.

To move the MMF from the post office to a hard disk

1. On the Microsoft Mail 3.*x* for Windows **Mail** menu, click **Options**.
2. Click **Server**.
3. Click **Local**, and then enter a file name for your MMF.
4. After the MMF is on your hard disk or stored on a network server, you can import its contents to an Outlook personal folder.

To import the MMF to a personal folder in Outlook

1. On the Outlook **File** menu, click **Import and Export**.
2. Select **Import from another program or file**, and then click **Next**.
3. In the **Select file type to import from** box, select **Microsoft Mail File (.mmf)**, and then click **Next**.
4. In the **File name** box, enter the name of the MMF to import, and then click **Open**.
5. Enter the password (if requested), and then select both the **Import messages** and **Import personal address book entries** check boxes.
6. To store messages in existing personal folders, click **Put the messages into existing Personal Folders**, and then click the folder you want.

    – or –

    To create a new personal folders store, click **Put the messages into new Personal Folders**, and then enter the path name. To display the new folders in the folder list, click **Display new Personal Folders**. Outlook creates the new personal folders and adds them to your profile.

    Outlook imports the messages and PAB entries from the MMF.

If you have used multiple information services such as AT&T or CompuServe for e-mail messages, you might have multiple PAB files in the MMF. When you import the MMF with the **Import and Export** command, you can choose which PABs to import.

When you import an MMF, consider the following:

- If there is a network failure, Outlook retries the network connection four times in the first two seconds, and then repeats this process every 10 minutes. A message is displayed during the 10-minute retry period.
- Any errors while importing the MMF are logged to a file in the client directory with the same file name as the MMF and the file name extension .log. You can view the .log file in Notepad or any other text editor.

Note When you begin using Outlook, there is no easy way to transfer new messages back to an MMF or a mailbag file. You can copy the messages to a shared folder, and then you can retrieve them with your old client. However, this does not guarantee privacy.

Avoiding duplicate e-mail messages

In Microsoft Mail, you can keep a copy of all of the e-mail messages in your Inbox in the post office on the server. If you migrate to Microsoft Exchange Server, these messages might be duplicated because during migration the Inbox in the post office is copied to your Microsoft Exchange Server folders, and you also import the messages from the local MMF by using Outlook.

To avoid duplicate messages, on the Microsoft Mail 3.*x* for Windows **Mail** menu, click **Options**. In the **Server** dialog box, clear the **Copy Inbox on Postoffice for Dialin Access** check box.

Migrating to Microsoft Exchange Server

If you plan to migrate your workgroup from Microsoft Mail 3.*x* to Microsoft Exchange Server, upgrading to Outlook 2002 is a good intermediate step because Outlook works with both e-mail applications. Microsoft Mail 3.*x* users can use Outlook 2002 while they continue to work with Microsoft Mail 3.*x* post office.

Later, when you upgrade the post office to Microsoft Exchange Server, these users only need to change their profiles to continue to use Outlook. This allows you to manage the upgrade of the user interface and the upgrade of the e-mail system separately.

The process of migrating users from Microsoft Mail 3.*x* post offices to Microsoft Exchange Server involves more than upgrading e-mail client software, and it is beyond the scope of the Microsoft Office XP Resource Kit. The Microsoft Exchange Server CD contains a document that takes you through all the planning and implementation steps necessary to migrate users from Microsoft Mail 3.*x* to Microsoft Exchange Server. The document title is "Migrating from Microsoft Mail for PC Networks," and you can find it on the Microsoft Exchange Server CD in Migrate\Docs\Msmailpc.doc.

This document discusses upgrading Microsoft Mail 3.*x* users to Exchange Client, and the information also applies to Outlook, because you can use Outlook as a direct replacement for Exchange Client. Review this document thoroughly if you plan to move your workgroup to Microsoft Exchange Server.

See also

You have a wide range of options for customizing Outlook 2002 installation for your users. For more information about Outlook customization features, see "Customizing an Outlook Installation" in Chapter 18, "Deploying Outlook."

You can install Outlook 2002 separately from the rest of Office XP. For more information, see "Determining When to Install Outlook in Chapter 17, "Planning for Outlook."

Upgrading from Schedule+

When you upgrade to use the scheduling features in Microsoft Outlook 2002, users can continue to use the same basic scheduling features as Microsoft Schedule+ applications, plus benefit from improved functionality.

Microsoft Outlook 2002 includes all the features of Microsoft Schedule+ 7.*x* and Microsoft Schedule+ 1.0, including appointments, events, contacts, and tasks. Outlook also provides the following features that are not available in Schedule+:

- Integrated e-mail functions with journal and note items
- Additional views for calendar, contact, and task information

- Advanced custom view capabilities
- Task delegation

Except for changes in the user interface and other features, you can work with your calendar, contact, and task information in Outlook in the same way that you work with them in Schedule+. You can also freely exchange free/busy information with Schedule+ users. (Note that when Outlook 2002 and Schedule+ 1.0 share information, Outlook uses Schedule+ 7.x to read and interpret Schedule+ 1.0 data.) However, you cannot retain Schedule+ as your primary calendar while using Outlook 2002 for e-mail and other functions.

Importing a Schedule+ data file

To upgrade to Outlook 2002 from Schedule+, install Outlook 2002, and then import the Schedule+ data file. (Schedule+ is not removed from your computer.)

> **Note** Outlook uses the Schedule 7.x application to import the Schedule+ 1.0 CAL file. If Schedule+ 7.x is not installed on your computer, Outlook does not give you the option to import a Schedule+ 1.0 CAL file.

To import a Schedule+ 7.x SCD file or a Schedule+ 1.0 CAL file

1. On the Outlook **File** menu, click **Import and Export**, and then click **Import from Schedule+ or another program or file**.

2. In the **Select file type to import from** box, click **Schedule+ 7.x** or **Schedule+ 1.0**.

3. In the **File to import** box, enter the SCD or CAL file name, or click **Browse** to find the file.

   This dialog box also includes several options for dealing with entries in the data file that duplicate entries you already have in your Outlook Calendar, Contacts, or Tasks folders.

4. To replace duplicate entries in your Outlook folder with Schedule+ entries, click **Replace duplicates with items imported**.

   –or–

   To allow duplicate entries to be imported, click **Allow duplicates to be created**.

   –or–

   To avoid importing duplicate entries, click **Do not import duplicate items**.

5. If requested, enter the password for the schedule file.

6. In **The following actions will be performed** box, select the items you want to import and their destination folders.

   To change the destination folder for an item type, click **Change Destination**. To alter the way Schedule+ fields are imported into Outlook, click **Map Custom Fields**.

By default, Outlook imports Schedule+ information into the following Outlook folders:

- Appointments and events are imported into the Calendar folder.
- Contact data is imported into the Contacts folder.
- Task data is imported into the Tasks folder.

The Schedule+ data file is not modified or deleted during the import process. You can import schedule files at any time after Outlook is installed using the **Import and Export** command (**File** menu).

> **Note** The Covey Seven Habits tool in Schedule+ 7.*x* is not included in Outlook. In addition, because its object model is very different, Outlook does not recognize Automation (formerly OLE Automation) interfaces in Schedule+ 7.*x*.

See also

You can install Outlook 2002 separately from the rest of Microsoft Office XP. For more information on staging an Outlook deployment, see "Installing Before or After Office" in Chapter 19, "Special Outlook Deployment Scenarios."

Sharing Information with Other Versions or Applications

Microsoft Outlook 2002 users can exchange e-mail messages and scheduling data with users of previous versions of Microsoft e-mail and calendar applications, as well as interact with users of other applications. However, previous versions of Outlook or other applications do not support all Outlook 2002 features.

Sharing information with previous versions of Outlook

Microsoft Outlook 2002 shares information seamlessly with Microsoft Outlook 97, Microsoft Outlook 98, and Microsoft Outlook 2000. Outlook 2002 has the same storage formats, Messaging Application Programming Interface (MAPI) profiles, and message formats. Consequently, in general you can upgrade gradually to Outlook 2002 without losing e-mail and other message functionality.

There are a few exceptions, described in the following sections.

Offline folder file format

The offline folder file (OST file) in Outlook 97 version 8.03 is different in Outlook 2002, Outlook 2000, and Outlook 98. When you upgrade to Outlook 2002 from versions of Outlook 97 prior to version 8.03, you must recreate the OST file.

HTML-based e-mail

In addition to Rich Text Format (RTF) and plain text (ASCII) format, Outlook 2002, Outlook 2000, and Outlook 98 support HTML-based e-mail. This format allows users to send messages in HTML format.

Outlook 97 supports only RTF and plain text format, but Outlook 2002 converts and stores HTML in RTF so that Outlook 97 users can read the messages. However, the original HTML might not be displayed correctly in RTF.

Online meetings

Outlook 2002 supports online meetings, which can be hosted by using Microsoft NetMeeting® conferencing software or Microsoft Windows NT Server NetShow™ Services. Online meeting requests made by using the Outlook 2002 NetMeeting or NetShow Services features appear as in-person meeting requests to Outlook 97, Outlook 98, and Outlook 2000 users.

If your organization includes Outlook 97, Outlook 98, or Outlook 2000 users, and you schedule an online meeting by using Outlook 2002, you must identify the meeting format in the content of the message as either NetMeeting or NetShow Services.

Stationery and custom signatures

When you upgrade to Outlook 2002, the Outlook 98 Stationery feature is moved to a new location. Outlook 98 and Outlook 2000 user signatures are preserved in Outlook 2002.

Sharing information with Microsoft Exchange Client

Microsoft Outlook 2002 recognizes all Microsoft Exchange Client message properties. Although Outlook users can share information with Microsoft Exchange Client users, Microsoft Exchange Client users might not be able to view or use portions of Outlook 2002 messaging information.

When you install and run Outlook, it recognizes and opens all the Exchange Client e-mail folders defined in the mail profile. Outlook 2002 also creates the Outlook-specific folders: Calendar, Contacts, Journal, Notes, and Tasks.

Outlook 2002 recognizes and maintains all specified folder views in Exchange Client, including custom views. While Outlook can create more advanced custom views than Exchange Client, Outlook and Exchange Client can share public folders that might include custom views.

Limitations when exchanging messages

In a mixed environment, it is recommended that Outlook users be aware that their coworkers who use Microsoft Exchange Client cannot take full advantage of many Outlook 2002 messaging features, including an enhanced standard message form, extended message properties, and folder-level privacy.

Enhanced standard message form

Microsoft Exchange Client users who view messages created in Outlook 2002 see the messages in the Microsoft Exchange Client standard message form, which does not support the advanced features of the Outlook standard message form, such as message expiration. As a result, some of the information in an Outlook message might not be viewable to Microsoft Exchange Client users.

Extended message properties

When a Microsoft Exchange Client user opens an Outlook 2002 message, extended Outlook message properties, such as voting buttons are ignored because they are not recognized by Microsoft Exchange Client. This means that some messages created in Outlook might appear different to Microsoft Exchange Client users. However, Outlook recognizes all Microsoft Exchange Client message properties.

Private items

When an Outlook 2002 user marks an item (such as an e-mail or calendar item) as "Private," other Outlook users cannot view the item. However, Microsoft Exchange Client users can view the item if they have been granted folder access privileges for the folder where the item is stored. Because Outlook folder-level privacy is absolute, the workaround for this functionality difference is to have Outlook users put private items in a separate folder, which they do not share or for which they have set restrictions.

Non-table views

Microsoft Exchange Client users can display Outlook 2002 table views — views that consist only of rows and columns — if the **Automatically generate Microsoft Exchange views** check box is selected in the **Folder Properties** dialog box for the Outlook folder. However, Microsoft Exchange Client cannot display Outlook non-table views (such as the day, week, and month views in the calendar), or card, icon, and timeline views.

When Outlook and Microsoft Exchange Client users access the same set of public folders, Microsoft Exchange Client users cannot display any non-table views created by Outlook users.

Saved views

Outlook 2002 and Microsoft Exchange Client use different formats to create saved views. Outlook supports both formats, so Outlook users can use any Microsoft Exchange Client view. By contrast, Microsoft Exchange Client does not support the Outlook format, so Microsoft Exchange Client cannot use Outlook views.

Outlook users can choose to maintain two copies of all saved table views in a folder automatically — one copy in Outlook format and one copy in Microsoft Exchange Client format. This workaround enables Microsoft Exchange Client users to use Outlook forms, although any Outlook-specific view features, such as formula fields, are not included in the Microsoft Exchange Client copy.

Custom field types

Microsoft Exchange Client users cannot view Outlook 2002 custom field types, such as formula and combination fields.

Attachments

Outlook 2002 can open attachments or objects within e-mail messages created by Microsoft Exchange Client users, and Exchange Client users can likewise open attachment or objects in Outlook 2002 messages. Both Outlook and Microsoft Exchange Client users can attach one message to another message.

Outlook users can also attach other Outlook items (such as a contact) to a message. However, Microsoft Exchange Client users receive these items as text-only attachments.

Sending and receiving vCards

Outlook 2002 allows users to send and receive contact information by using the Internet standard vCard format. Microsoft Exchange Client does not support this feature.

Using public folders

Outlook 2002 supports all of the custom public folder view features of Microsoft Exchange Server. In fact, Microsoft Exchange Server does not distinguish between Outlook and Microsoft Exchange Client when users open a public folder. For this reason, Outlook and Microsoft Exchange Client users can gain access to a common set of public folders.

Using other messaging and collaboration features

Some interoperability differences between Outlook 2002 and Microsoft Exchange Client features go beyond the basic capabilities of exchanging e-mail messages and using public folders.

Rules

Microsoft Exchange Client users use the Inbox Assistant to manage rules. By contrast, Outlook 2002 includes an enhanced Rules Wizard. The Outlook Rules Wizard allows users to manage Inbox Assistant rules (server-side rules) in addition to their Outlook rules (client-side rules). The Rules Wizard also allows users to convert Inbox Assistant rules into Outlook rules.

Each time that the Rules Wizard is started, it checks for active Inbox Assistant rules on the user's computer. If any Inbox Assistant rules exist, the Rules Wizard gives the user the option to convert them automatically to Outlook rules. After an Inbox Assistant rule has been converted to an Outlook rule, users can modify the Outlook rule by using the Rules Wizard.

Forms

Forms created by using the Outlook 2002 forms design environment can be used only by Outlook users. Forms created by using Electronic Forms Designer can be used by both Outlook and Microsoft Exchange Client users. Forms implemented using Exchange Server 5.5 HTML interfaces can be used by Outlook, but not by Microsoft Exchange Client. Developers can create forms by using the tool that is appropriate for the mix of operating systems in a specific organization.

Microsoft Exchange Server provides an alternative means of creating forms to use in collaborative applications. It does this by using Active Server Pages (ASP pages) and the Microsoft Exchange Collaboration Data Objects (CDO) interface to script forms that are displayed as HTML in a Web browser. Outlook supports Microsoft Exchange Server HTML forms. These features provide Microsoft Exchange sites with an option for developing electronic forms that can be deployed across all operating systems.

WordMail

To use WordMail as their Outlook 2002 editor, Outlook 2002 users must have Word 2002 installed. However, Outlook 2002 users can receive and read e-mail messages composed with other versions of Word.

Voting

By using Outlook 2002, users can easily create and send ballot messages to other Outlook users, and then they can track the voting responses automatically in Outlook. An Outlook user specifies the voting choices when creating the message and then sends the message to other users. When recipients using Outlook receive a voting message, the selections they can vote for appear as buttons in the Outlook message However, when Microsoft Exchange Client users receive voting messages from Outlook users, they receive only the text of the Subject line and the body of the voting message. No voting buttons are displayed.

Microsoft Exchange Client preview pane

Outlook 2002 has a built-in preview pane. The Microsoft Exchange Client preview pane is not compatible with Outlook.

Task delegation

When an Outlook 2002 user delegates a task to a user who is running Microsoft Exchange Client, the recipient receives only an e-mail message that lists the description of the task, start and end dates, and other information as text in the body of the message.

> **Toolbox** The Microsoft Office Resource Kit for Office 97/98 provides additional file sharing information for Microsoft Exchange Client, including information about using public folders, converting rules to use with the Rules Wizard, and exchanging forms. For more information, see *Microsoft Office Resource Kit for Office 97/98*.

Sharing information with Microsoft Schedule+

Microsoft Outlook 2002 users and users of all previous versions of Microsoft Schedule+ can share calendar and group scheduling information such as calendar free/busy status information, and meeting request messages. However, Schedule+ users might not be able to view or use some Outlook 2002 message or calendar features.

For most organizations, viewing free/busy status and exchanging meeting requests are essential scheduling tasks. Outlook 2002 and Schedule+ share information completely in both of these key areas.

Exchanging meeting requests

Outlook 2002 and Schedule+ 1.0 and Schedule+ 7.x users can freely exchange meeting messages across the Microsoft Windows and Macintosh operating environments. Although Outlook 2002 users and Schedule+ 1.0 users can freely exchange meeting requests and responses, Schedule+ 1.0 does not recognize the advanced features of Outlook such as attachments, the meeting location field, and recurring meetings. As a result, when a Schedule+ 1.0 user receives a meeting message from an Outlook user, Schedule+ 1.0 ignores any Outlook-specific message features it does not recognize. For example, if an Outlook user sends a recurring meeting request to a Schedule+ 1.0 user, the Schedule+ user receives only the first meeting request.

Viewing free/busy status

When users publish their free/busy status, other users can view the free/busy status in Meeting Planner. By having appropriate permission, Outlook 2002 and Schedule+ 7.x and Schedule+ 1.0 users can view each other's free/busy status. Permission is not needed to view the free/busy status of other users.

In addition to designating free/busy status, Outlook 2002 users can designate tentative and out-of-office status that other Outlook users can view. However, when Schedule+ users view an Outlook calendar, tentative status appears as free status, and out-of-office status appears as busy status.

Outlook differs slightly from Schedule+ in how it handles unpublished free/busy status. When Schedule+ users choose not to publish their free/busy status, other Schedule+ users can still view the free/busy status in Meeting Planner — provided they have read permission. However, when Outlook users choose not to publish their free/busy status, no one can view their free/busy status in Meeting Planner, but they can open calendars to view unpublished free/busy status, provided they have read permission to the user's calendar.

Viewing free/busy details

Outlook 2002 users on Microsoft Exchange Server can view the free/busy details of Schedule+ users who are on Microsoft Exchange Server, but they cannot view the details of users on Microsoft Mail Server. Schedule+ 7.x users can view the free/busy details of Outlook users when all users are on Microsoft Exchange Server, and the necessary Windows 16-bit or 32-bit driver is installed. Schedule+ 1.0 users cannot view free/busy details for Outlook users.

Outlook users who have Read Only permission for other user calendars can see when those users are free or busy, and they can view the details of scheduled appointments and activities in Meeting Planner.

Delegating e-mail messages and scheduling tasks

In Outlook 2002, you can give others permission to read or modify your folders, and you can delegate your e-mail messages and scheduling tasks to other users. Delegates can create, send, and reply to messages; and they can request meetings and delegate tasks on your behalf.

A delegate relationship requires that both users run the same scheduling client. For example, Outlook users can be delegates only for other Outlook users. Outlook users who want to participate in delegate relationships must keep all their primary folders, such as Calendar and Inbox, on the server instead of on their local computers.

Schedule+ 7.x users can designate other users to be their delegate owners. As a delegate owner, a user has all the capabilities of a delegate and can also designate additional delegates for the owner's schedule. Like Schedule+ 7.x users, Outlook folder owners can enable their delegates to give other users the necessary permission for gaining access to the owner's folders. However, Outlook does not allow a delegate to designate additional delegates for the owner's folders. To designate a delegate in Outlook, you must be logged on as the folder (account) owner.

Using direct booking

Outlook 2002 users with the appropriate permission can use the direct booking feature to book appointments directly into an Outlook or Schedule+ Calendar. However, Schedule+ 1.0 and Schedule+ 7.x users cannot book appointments directly into Outlook 2002 Calendars.

With direct booking, no meeting request is actually sent to a user or resource such as a conference room. The client software of the meeting organizer adds the meeting directly to the resource calendar. If the direct booking fails for an Outlook 2002 user, the user is informed, and no meeting request is sent. If the direct booking fails for a Schedule+ user, a meeting request is sent. If no one responds to the meeting request, the resource is not booked.

Because a directly booked resource is unlikely to receive many meeting requests, you are not required to assign a delegate to the resource or to have a continuously running computer logged into the account of the resource to process incoming meeting requests. However, if a user sends a meeting request to the resource instead of booking an appointment, the meeting request is not noticed until a user logs on to the account of the resource. With appropriate permission, an Outlook user can open the Calendar of a resource and modify it directly — if necessary.

> **Note** A Schedule+ user can read the calendar of an Outlook user, but cannot add to it or edit it — regardless of the permissions that the Outlook user grants.

Working with tasks

Outlook 2002 gives users new task features that are not available in Schedule+ 7.*x* or Schedule+ 1.0. For example, Outlook provides additional views for task items, making it easier for users to manage tasks in a way that best suits their needs. Also, Outlook enables users to delegate tasks to other users. When Outlook users delegate a task to other Outlook users, all of the task information (such as start date, end date, and status) is sent as a special task request message to the recipients, who can add it to their own task lists automatically.

After Outlook 2002 is installed, users can import their Schedule+ 7.*x* or Schedule+ 1.0 task data at any time by using the **Import and Export** command on the Outlook **File** menu. By default, Outlook imports Schedule+ task information into the Outlook Tasks folder. Users can choose to ignore or replace any duplicate entries encountered during the import process.

Working with contacts

Outlook 2002 provides a Contacts feature that helps users keep their business and personal contact information up to date. Although Schedule+ 7.*x* includes some contact features, many of the Outlook contact management enhancements, such as additional contact views, are not available in Schedule+ 7.*x*.

The enhanced Contacts feature enables Outlook users to include e-mail addresses with their contacts. Outlook users can import all Schedule+ 7.*x* contacts, as well as contacts stored in Microsoft Exchange Client personal address books (PABs). In addition, Outlook users can maintain contacts as their personal e-mail address books, so they do not need to maintain contact names and e-mail addresses in two separate places.

After installing Outlook 2002, users can import their Schedule+ contact data at any time by using the **Import and Export** command on the Outlook **File** menu. By default, Outlook imports Schedule+ contact information into the Outlook Contacts folder. Users can choose to ignore or replace any duplicate entries encountered during the import process. The Outlook Import Wizard also imports Microsoft Exchange Client PABs.

Sharing information with Microsoft Project

Microsoft Project 2000 and Microsoft Project 98 can work with Microsoft Outlook 2002 to provide task scheduling for your users. Microsoft Project users can assign tasks to Outlook 2002 users. When the Outlook recipients accept the tasks, Microsoft Project adds the tasks to Outlook Tasks automatically. Users can also create Outlook reminders from within Microsoft Project 2000, and they can add Microsoft Project 2000 and 98 items to the Outlook Journal.

To use the workgroup features of Microsoft Project with Outlook 2002, you must configure Microsoft Project for a workgroup. These workgroup configurations allow team members to view the custom e-mail messages, such as team status reports, generated in Microsoft Project. Project managers can use the TeamAssign feature to send custom e-mail messages, and to assign project tasks to the team members who receive messages in the Outlook Inbox.

After each team member accepts a task and sends the response to the project manager, the task is logged automatically in the Outlook Task list of the team member. Project tasks are grouped under a new category that corresponds to the project name. Each team member can keep track of the task status in the Outlook Task list.

Microsoft Project adds a new menu command called **New TeamStatus Report** to the Outlook **Tasks** menu. This feature allows team members to generate and submit TeamStatus reports without waiting for the project manager to ask for them.

When the team member chooses the **New TeamStatus Report** command, a custom TeamStatus e-mail message is created and stored in the Outlook Inbox. If the team member is tracking the task status in the task list, the status information is added automatically to the TeamStatus report. Users can just open the report and send it to the project manager. In addition, they can use the TeamStatus message to track the task status, and to save and store the message in the Inbox until they are ready to submit it to the project manager.

> **Notes** You must configure Microsoft Project 2000 and Microsoft Project 98 for workgroups before you can take advantage of the interactions between Microsoft Project and Outlook 2002. For more information, see:
>
> - "Install the Workgroup Message Handler" in the Microsoft Project 2000 online document C:\Program Files\Microsoft Office\Office\1033\Prjsetup.htm.
> - "Install the Workgroup Message Handler" in the Microsoft Project 98 online document C:\Program Files\Microsoft Office\Office\Setup.wri.

Upgrading to Outlook 2002 Security

If you are upgrading from a version of Microsoft Outlook earlier than Outlook 2000, the first time a user attempts to read or send secure e-mail messages, Microsoft Outlook 2002 triggers a security upgrade feature. To upgrade from Outlook 97 or Exchange Client to Outlook 2002 security, the user's security file (EPF file) must exist on the computer, and the user must know the password. To upgrade from Outlook 98 security, the user must know the Digital ID password. (Users upgrading from Outlook 2000 already have the updated security features.)

During the upgrade process, a Digital ID name is generated for the security keys of each user, which includes one signing key and one encryption key. The user must select a password to associate with the Digital ID name.

The Outlook 2002 upgrade feature attempts to save the security information in a secure store. If the EPF file cannot be found, or the user cannot remember the password, the upgrade feature can be canceled.

If you are using Microsoft Exchange Advanced Security, you can recover the security keys (that is, enroll again) by asking for a new security token from the administrator. The upgrade process must occur before you are security-enabled to send and receive secure e-mail messages.

If you are using Microsoft Certificate Server, or a public Certification Authority such as VeriSign™, Inc., and you forget your password, the following restrictions occur:

- You cannot gain access to your keys.
- You cannot read encrypted e-mail messages sent to you previously.
- You must re-enroll to get new Digital IDs.

The following procedure describes how Outlook 2002 users can enroll in security by using Microsoft Exchange Key Management Server (KMS). Before you begin this procedure, contact the system administrator for a security token. The request for security enrollment uses this token.

To enroll in security or obtain a certificate using Microsoft Exchange KMS

1. On the **Tools** menu, click **Options**, and then click the **Security** tab.
2. Click **Get a Digital ID**, select **Set up Security for me on the Exchange Server**, and then click **OK**.
3. In the **Digital ID name** box, type the name you want to use; in the **Token** box, type your security token, and then click **OK**.

   A message is sent to Microsoft Exchange KMS. After you receive a reply, Outlook 2002 attempts to store your security keys in the secure store.

4. Select a password for your Digital ID.

    You are prompted for the password every time you gain access to the keys. However, you can choose to have Outlook 2002 remember the password for a limited period of time.

5. Click **OK** to save your changes.

6. To add the certificate to the Root Store, click **Yes**.

    The dialog box provides the required information about the certificate. If you click **No**, you experience problems when you attempt to read and send secure messages, and you must repeat the entire enrollment process.

The following procedure describes how Outlook 2002 users can enroll in security by using public certificate authorities.

To enroll in security or obtain a certificate by using external certificate authorities

1. On the **Tools** menu, click **Options**, and then click the **Security** tab.

2. Click **Get a Digital ID**, select **Get a S/MIME certificate from an external Certification Authority**, and then click **OK**.

    A Microsoft Web page provides information about obtaining a certificate. The page lists a number of certificate authorities.

3. Select the link to the certificate authority that you want to use to obtain a certificate.

    While your Web browser is storing your certificate and keys on your computer, you might be prompted to select the security level to associate with your keys.

4. When prompted, select a password for your Digital ID.

    You are prompted for the password every time you gain access to the keys. However, you can choose to have Outlook 2002 remember the password for a limited period of time.

5. To add this certificate to the Root Store, click **Yes**.

    While storing the certificates, you might be prompted to save the root certificate. The dialog box provides the required information about the certificate. If you click **No**, you experience problems when you attempt to read and send secure messages. When you experience such problems, contact your certification authority to install another copy of the root certificate.

After the certificate and keys are installed, Outlook can access and use them.

See also

There are several options to choose from when you set up security for your Outlook 2002 users. For more information about Outlook security, see "Outlook 2002 Security Model" in Chapter 22, "Administering Outlook Security."

Reverting to a Previous Installation

In some circumstances, you may need to go back to a previous installation of Microsoft Outlook after upgrading to Microsoft Outlook 2002. To do this, you first remove Outlook 2002, then re-install your previous version of Outlook. You may need to also recreate your Outlook profile.

To remove Outlook 2002

1. On the **Start** menu, point to **Settings**, and then point to **Control Panel**.
2. Click **Add/Remove Programs**.
3. Click **Microsoft Outlook 2002** in the list of programs, and then click **Add/Remove**.
4. When prompted, choose to **Remove Outlook**.

When you have removed Outlook 2002, reinstall your previous version of Outlook following the process for your organization.

Outlook 2002 creates a backup copy of existing profiles when it first runs. After you reinstall your previous version of Outlook, the backup profile works with Outlook just as it did before you upgraded to Outlook 2002.

However, under some circumstances, you must recreate your Outlook profile. For example, POP3 and IMAP e-mail services cannot be used after reverting to a previous Outlook installation. In this case, create a new profile and add the services.

To recreate your Outlook profile after reinstalling a previous version of Outlook

1. On the **Start** menu, point to **Run**, and then enter **Outlook /cleanprofile**.
2. When Outlook starts up, it prompts you for the required information to create a new profile.

CHAPTER 21

Maintaining an Outlook Installation

With enhanced support for updating profiles and other settings, Microsoft Outlook 2002 makes it easier for administrators to manage Outlook installations. Automatic messaging encoding provides additional benefits — less configuration work for administrators and a better experience for users.

In this chapter

Updating Outlook Profiles   523

Locating and Configuring Outlook Settings   526

Using Automatic Message Encoding   529

Unicode Support   532

Updating Outlook Profiles

You can create or modify Microsoft Outlook® user profiles when you deploy Outlook 2002 by using the Custom Installation Wizard. If you need to update Outlook profile information after installing Outlook 2002, you have two main choices:

- Use the Custom Maintenance Wizard to reconfigure profile settings and apply a configuration maintenance file (CMW file) with these settings to your users' installations.

- Update profile information in an Outlook profile file (PRF file), and distribute the file to your users.

    When Outlook imports the PRF file, user profile settings are updated.

If you are making other changes to Microsoft Office settings at the same time that you want to modify Outlook profile information, or you are making substantial or complicated changes to Outlook profiles, using the Custom Maintenance Wizard to update users might be the best choice.

On the other hand, if you saved a PRF file with your users' Outlook profile configurations when you installed Outlook, and you are making minor changes, updating the profiles by distributing a new PRF file might be the simplest strategy. Another advantage to updating Outlook profile settings by using a PRF file is that other Office settings cannot be inadvertently modified.

Using the Custom Maintenance Wizard to modify Outlook profiles

The Custom Maintenance Wizard offers the same Outlook profile configuration options that are available in the Custom Installation Wizard. You can choose to modify existing profiles, add new profiles (for all users), or import an existing PRF file.

To use the Custom Maintenance Wizard to update your users' Outlook profiles, you will need to copy the Custom Maintenance Wizard (Maintwiz.exe) to the administrative installation point. Instructions for performing this task are included in the Help file provided with the program.

Note that, unlike the Custom Installation Wizard, which uses a transform to specify customizations through Setup.exe, the Custom Maintenance Wizard is run from, and applies a customized configuration maintenance file to, users' computers.

Updating Outlook profiles in the Custom Maintenance Wizard

You can use the Custom Maintenance Wizard to update Outlook profile information after you have deployed Outlook. The Outlook profile customization pages are identical in the Custom Maintenance Wizard and the Custom Installation Wizard. (However, note that you cannot use an Office profile settings file (OPS file) to define Office settings in the Custom Maintenance Wizard.)

For example, if you want to change users' default delivery location for messages from a PST file to the Exchange server, you can use the Custom Maintenance Wizard to reconfigure Exchange connections.

To change the default message delivery location to users' Exchange server

1. In the Custom Maintenance Wizard, on the **Outlook: Customize Default Profile** page, click **Modify Profile**, then click **Next**.

2. On the **Outlook: Specify Exchange Settings** page, specify **Configure an Exchange Server Connection**.

3. Specify a server name.

   This step will ensure that new Outlook users have the appropriate configuration as well as existing users.

4. On the **Outlook: Add Accounts** page, choose **Customize additional Outlook profile and account information**.

5. From the drop-down list, choose **Exchange Server**.

6. Save the CMW file and deploy it to your users.

Deploying updated Outlook profiles to users

After you create the Custom Maintenance Wizard maintenance file, you deploy it to your users to update their Outlook profiles.

First, ensure that the Custom Maintenance Wizard executable files and the configuration maintenance file you are deploying are available to the users on the administrative installation point (or any file server to which users can gain access).

Then provide a command line such as the following:

`\\share\office\Maintwiz updateprof.cmw /cq`

The **/c** option ensures that the changes are "committed." The **/q** option prevents dialogs from being presented to the users during the update.

Using a PRF file to modify Outlook profiles

Another option for updating users' Outlook profiles is to edit an existing Outlook profile file (PRF file), and distribute the file to users. When Outlook imports the file on a user's computer, the user's profile is updated with the new settings you have specified.

You update a PRF file by editing it in a simple text editor, such as Notebook. The PRF file contains detailed comments to guide you in making appropriate changes. All of the customizations that are available through pages in the Custom Maintenance Wizard can be made manually by editing the file.

In addition, you can add custom features to users' Outlook profiles by editing the file. For example, if you need to add a new messaging service for your users that is not provided in the Custom Maintenance Wizard, you can make manual changes to the PRF file to add the service.

After you have made changes to the PRF file, you can use it to update Outlook profiles in several ways. For example, you can provide it to users by making it available on a network share. Then, since the PRF file is executable, users can update their profiles by simply double-clicking the file name.

> **Note** A fast way to create a PRF file for use in your deployment is to create your preliminary configuration by specifying Outlook options in the Custom Installation Wizard, then export the settings. After saving the file, open it with a text editor and make any additional changes you choose. For more information about working with PRF files, see "Customizing Profiles with an Outlook Profile File" in Chapter 18, "Deploying Outlook." For more information about working with PRF files, see Customizing Profiles with an Outlook Profile File.

See also

The Custom Installation Wizard offers a wide range of configuration options for defining and modifying user profiles. For more information about your options for configuring Outlook profiles, see "Customizing an Outlook Installation" in Chapter 18, "Deploying Outlook."

Complete details on modifying user profile information by editing and distributing a PRF file are provided in "Customizing Profiles with an Outlook Profile File" in Chapter 18, "Deploying Outlook."

Locating and Configuring Outlook Settings

The tools provided with Microsoft Office XP help you install Microsoft Outlook with the best configuration for your organization, and help you update and maintain your Outlook installation to meet changing needs.

Most Outlook 2002 settings can be configured by using the Custom Installation Wizard and maintained by using the Custom Maintenance Wizard. You can also install Outlook on a test computer, then customize and capture the settings by using the Office Profile Wizard. Those settings can then be distributed to users' computers. Or, you can set system policies to enforce specific settings to maintain a more uniform environment.

There are some exceptions to how settings are normally specified and maintained. For example, some options cannot be captured by the Office Profile Wizard.

Most common settings to configure

The following table shows common Outlook 2002 settings that you might specify, and when and how you can set them.

Groups of settings to set:	At initial deployment (by using the Custom Installation Wizard and Office Profile Wizard). Set by using:	To update deployment (by using the Custom Installation Wizard and Office Profile Wizard). Set by using:	To maintain a specific environment (Group Policy Editor, System Policy Editor). Set in policy template:
Location of Outlook binary files	Custom Installation Wizard feature tree	Custom Maintenance Wizard feature tree	N/A
Tools | Options E.g. Specify WordMail as Outlook editor	• OPS file in Custom Installation Wizard • **Change Office User Settings** in Custom Installation Wizard • **Outlook: Customize Default Settings** in Custom Installation Wizard	• OPS file (for stand-alone) in Custom Maintenance Wizard • **Change Office User Settings** page in Custom Maintenance Wizard • **Outlook: Customize Default Settings** page in Custom Maintenance Wizard	Outlk10.adm — includes most of these options. Office10.adm — includes settings common to all of Office XP
MAPI profile E.g. Microsoft Exchange connection, define PST files, and so on	Custom Installation Wizard Outlook profile configuration pages	Custom Maintenance Wizard Outlook profile configuration pages	Outlk10.adm

Settings not captured by the Office Profile Wizard

Most Outlook settings are captured in an Office profile settings file (OPS file) when you use the Office Profile Wizard to customize an Outlook installation. By design, the Profile Wizard excludes some settings, including user-specific information such as the user name and Most Recently Used file list (**File** menu).

For example, the Profile Wizard does not capture the following Microsoft Outlook 2002 settings:

- Profile settings, including mail server configuration
- Storage settings, such as default delivery location and personal folder files (PST files)
- E-mail accounts and directories (**Tools|Options|Mail Setup|E-mail Accounts**)
- Send/Receive groups (**Tools|Options|Mail Setup|Send/Receive**)
- Customized views; for example, the fields displayed in the Inbox or another folder.
- Outlook Bar shortcuts
- Auto-archive options set for a particular folder, which you set by right-clicking the folder, clicking **Properties**, and choosing options in the **AutoArchive** tab
- Delegate options (**Tools|Options|Delegates**)

In addition, the following Outlook 2002 settings are not captured in an OPS file:

- **Send Immediately when connected** check box (**Tools|Options|Mail Setup**)
- **When forwarding a message** option (**Tools|Options|Preferences|E-mail Options**)
- **Mark my comments with** option (**Tools|Options|Preferences|E-mail Options**)
- **Request secure receipt for all S/MIME signed messages** check box (**Tools|Options|Security**)
- **Show an additional time zone** check box (**Tools|Options|Preferences|Calendar Options|Time Zone**)
- **Automatically decline recurring meeting requests** check box (**Tools|Options|Preferences|Calendar Options|Resource Scheduling**)
- **Automatically decline conflicting meeting requests** check box (**Tools|Options|Preferences|Calendar Options|Resource Scheduling**)
- **Automatically accept meeting requests and process cancellations** check box (**Tools|Options|Preferences|Calendar Options|Resource Scheduling**)

Settings that cannot be centrally administered

Most Outlook 2002 options are customizable using Office tools or the Windows registry. The Outlook settings that cannot be configured using these methods include:

- Other Outlook settings that are stored in user-specific locations such as:
  - Outlook Bar shortcuts
  - Most Recently Used (MRU) lists
  - View information, such as specific columns that are displayed for a user's Inbox or PST file
  - Delegate information specified in the **Tools | Options**, **Delegates** tab
- The options specified in **E-mail Accounts** and **Send/Receive Groups** in the **Tools | Options**, **Mail Setup** tab.

Using Automatic Message Encoding

Microsoft Outlook now automatically selects an optimal encoding for outgoing mail messages. This feature increases the likelihood that when you send a message with Outlook 2002, the receiver will see all the characters rendered properly, even if they run older e-mail programs.

Outlook scans the entire text of the outgoing message to determine a minimal popular encoding for the message. Outlook selects an encoding that is capable representing all of the characters and that is optimized so that the majority of the receiving e-mail programs can interpret and render the content properly.

This table shows a few examples of how this works.

If the message contains these characters:	Outlook selects this encoding:
English (ASCII) text (A-Z, a-z)	US-ASCII
German (Latin 1) text (A-Z, a-z and Umlauts)	Western European (ISO)
Greek text (A-Z, a-z and Greek characters)	Greek (ISO)
Japanese text (A-Z, a-z, Hiragana, Katakana, Kanji)	Japanese (JIS)
Multilingual text (different scripts)	Unicode® (UTF-8)

This works for users sending Internet mail through the POP/SMTP or IMAP transport, or for messages sent through Microsoft Exchange Server 5.5 SP 1 or higher.

> **Note** This Outlook feature requires that users sending the message have Microsoft Internet Explorer 5.5 installed.

With previous versions of Outlook, users had to manually overwrite format encoding to choose the most appropriate encoding for an individual message. Users are no longer required to do this.

Disabling Auto-Select outbound encoding

Microsoft Outlook automatically enables Auto-Select outbound encoding once Internet Explorer 5.5 or higher is installed. You can disable Auto-Select outbound message encoding with a registry key. For the following subkey, set **Autodetect_CodePageOut** to **0**:

HKEY_CURRENT_USER\Software\Microsoft\Office\10.0\Outlook\Options\MSHTML\International

The value is a **DWORD**.

If the registry subkey is not found, if there is no value set for the registry subkey, or if the value is set to **1**, Auto-Select is enabled (as long as Internet Explorer 5.5 is installed on the user's computer).

To set this value through the user interface, go to the **Tools |Options**, **Mail Format** tab. In the **Message format:** section, click **International Options**, then select **Auto-Select encoding for outgoing messages**.

Setting default encoding for outbound messages

You can set a registry key to establish a default encoding for outbound e-mail messages. This encoding is used for all outbound messages if Auto-Select encoding is not enabled. This encoding is also used as the preferred encoding if the Auto-Select encoding algorithm finds multiple suitable encodings for the message. By default, Outlook sets preferred encoding to a popular Internet encoding corresponding to the active Windows code page of the user's computer. For example, Outlook specifies Western European (ISO) when running on Western European Latin1 Windows code page 1252.

For example, to set the default code page to be used for message encoding to "Western European (ISO)":

HKEY_CURRENT_USER\Software\Microsoft\Office\10.0\Outlook\Options\MSHTML\International**Default_CodePageOut=00006faf**

This value is a **DWORD**. (See the table in the next section for a list of encodings and corresponding code pages.)

To set this value through the user interface, go to **Tools**, **Options**, **Mail Format**. In the **Message format:** section, click **International Options**. Then, in the drop-down list for **Preferred encoding for outgoing messages**, select the encoding that you prefer.

Outlook encoding support

Outlook supports the following encodings when sending and receiving e-mail messages.

> **Note** For Auto-Select encoding to work properly, you must make sure that appropriate international support (NLS files and fonts) is installed on users' computers. For more information about enabling international support, see Chapter 16, "Preparing Users' Computers for International Use."

By default, Auto-Select considers for detection all encodings marked "Yes" in the table below. All encodings in the list below are valid values to set as the "Preferred encoding for outgoing messages" by using the registry subkey (described above) Default_CodePageOut.

Name	Character set	Code page	Auto-Select?
Arabic (ISO)	ISO-8859-6	28596	
Arabic (Windows)	Windows-1256	1256	Yes
Baltic (ISO)	ISO-8859-4	28594	Yes
Baltic (Windows)	Windows-1257	1257	
Central European (ISO)	ISO-8859-2	28592	Yes
Central European (Windows)	Windows-1250	1250	
Chinese Simplified (GB2312)	GB2312	936	Yes
Chinese Simplified (HZ)	HZ-GB-2312	52936	
Chinese Traditional (Big5)	Big5	950	Yes
Cyrillic (ISO)	ISO-8859-5	28595	
Cyrillic (KOI8-R)	KOI8-R	20866	Yes
Cyrillic (KOI8-U)	KOI8-U	21866	
Cyrillic (Windows)	Windows-1251	1251	Yes
Greek (ISO)	ISO-8859-7	28597	Yes
Greek (Windows)	Windows-1253	1253	
Hebrew (ISO-Logical)	ISO-8859-8-I	38598	

Name (cont'd)	Character set	Code page	Auto-Select?
Hebrew (Windows)	Windows-1255	1255	Yes
Japanese (EUC)	EUC-JP	51932	
Japanese (JIS)	ISO-2022-JP	50220	Yes
Japanese (JIS-Allow 1 byte Kana)	ISO-2022-JP	50221	
Japanese (Shift-JIS)	Shift-JIS	932	
Korean	KS_C_5601-1987	949	Yes
Korean (EUC)	EUC-KR	51949	
Latin 3 (ISO)	ISO-8859-3	28593	
Latin 9 (ISO)	ISO-8859-15	28605	
Thai (Windows)	Windows-874	874	Yes
Turkish (ISO)	ISO-8859-9	28599	Yes
Turkish (Windows)	Windows-1254	1254	
Unicode (UTF-7)	UTF-7	65000	
Unicode (UTF-8)	UTF-8	65001	Yes
US-ASCII	US-ASCII	20127	Yes
Vietnamese (Windows)	Windows-1258	1258	Yes
Western European (ISO)	ISO-8859-1	28591	Yes
Western European (Windows)	Windows-1252	1252	

Unicode Support

In an increasingly interconnected world, organizations frequently need to communicate and share data with multilingual audiences inside and outside of the organizations. This can be a challenge if several code pages are needed to support all languages that are required for collaboration. However, an international character encoding standard — Unicode — allows users to more easily share documents across languages.

As in Microsoft Outlook 2000, Microsoft Outlook 2002 supports Unicode only in the body of mail messages. Outlook data — such as Contacts, Tasks, and the To and Subject lines of messages — is limited to characters defined by the current system code page of the user's computer.

The Outlook 2002 user interface also does not implement Unicode but uses languages that are supported by the current system code page. (Note that the English user interface is supported on any system code page.)

Note that Terminal Services allows only one system code page to be configured per computer. This means, for example, that the Chinese and Greek user interfaces cannot be supported for different users of the same Terminal Services server. To provide user interfaces for a multilingual user community that spans multiple code pages, you may need to implement multiple Terminal Services servers with different system code pages. However, some related locales share a single code page (for example, most West European locales share a single code page). Also, many East European locales require only a small set of code pages.

See also

For more information about how code pages work and how Unicode provides better support for multilingual organizations, see "Unicode Support and Multilingual Documents" in Chapter 15, "Maintaining International Installations."

For more information about using Unicode in other Office XP applications, see "Taking Advantage of Unicode Support" in Chapter 15, "Maintaining International Installations."

CHAPTER 22

Administering Outlook Security

Microsoft Outlook 2002 provides enhanced security features for sending and receiving secure e-mail messages over the Internet or local intranet.

In this chapter

Outlook 2002 Security Model   535

Secure E-mail Messaging   546

Outlook 2002 Security Model

Microsoft Outlook® 2002 provides enhanced security features for sending and receiving secure e-mail messages over the Internet or local intranet.

Overview of the Outlook 2002 security model

Outlook 2002 supports S/MIME v3 security, which allows users to exchange secure e-mail messages with other S/MIME e-mail clients over the Internet, as well as within an organization.

The Outlook 2002 security model helps to ensure the security of Outlook e-mail messages by using public key encryption to send and receive signed and encrypted e-mail messages. This feature includes digital signing, which allows users to verify the identity of senders and the integrity of messages; and message encryption, which protects the contents of messages from being read by anyone except their intended recipients. Users can exchange signed and encrypted e-mail messages with other e-mail clients that support S/MIME.

E-mail messages encrypted by the user's public key can be decrypted using only the associated private key. When a user sends an encrypted e-mail message, the recipient's certificate (public key) is used to encrypt it; likewise, when a user reads an encrypted e-mail message, Outlook 2002 uses the user's private key to decrypt it.

Several new security features that are optional in Outlook 2000 Service Release 1 are standard in Outlook 2002. These features include support for security labels and signed receipts, which allow you to provide more secure e-mail communications within your organization and to customize security to your requirements. The new features also meet standards for secure e-mail messaging with other organizations.

With Outlook 2002 security profiles are configured automatically. Outlook 2002 also includes greater flexibility for customizing security settings. You can use registry settings to customize controls on secure messages to match your organization's security policies. These settings are listed in the table at the end of this topic.

Digital certificates

S/MIME features rely on digital certificates, which associate the user's identity with a public key. The associated private key is saved in a secure store on the user's computer. The combination of a certificate and private key is called a Digital ID. Outlook 2002 fully supports X.509v3 standard digital certificates, which must be created by a certificate authority.

Outlook 2002 supports public World Wide Web-based enrollment to certificate authorities such as VeriSign™ and Microsoft Certificate Server. Outlook 2002 also works with Microsoft Exchange Key Management Server to provide an integrated X.509v3-based public key infrastructure for corporate users. The sender only needs an X.509v3 certificate and private key to exchange digitally signed e-mail messages. For encrypted e-mail messages, the sender must also have each recipient's certificate.

Certificates can be exchanged by including them in a signed message. Certificates are stored in each Outlook user's Contacts. Microsoft Exchange Key Management Server automatically stores each user's certificate in the Global Address Book so that encrypted e-mail messages can be sent to other users in the organization. You can also add a default encryption certificate from another source to the Global Address List.

When you update digital certificates or other security profile information, users do not have to change their settings.

Security labels and signed receipts

Users can attach custom security labels to messages. Labels are created by each organization and made available to users.

A security label lets you add information to the message header about the sensitivity of the message content. The label can also restrict which recipients can open, forward, or send the message. You define one or more security policies for your organization and implement them programmatically. For example, an Internal Use Only label might be implemented as a security label to apply to mail that should not be sent or forwarded outside of your company.

Users can also send secure receipt requests with messages to verify that the recipients recognize the user's digital signature. When the message is received and saved (even if it is not yet read) and the signature is verified, a receipt is returned to the user's Inbox. If the user's signature is not verified, no receipt is sent.

> **Note** Using secure receipts and custom security labels requires the Microsoft Windows® 2000 or an upgraded version of other versions of Windows operating systems.

See also

- Public key cryptography can help you maintain secure e-mail systems. For more information about the use of public key cryptography in Outlook, search for "Outlook 98 Security White paper" on the Knowledge Base Search page of the Microsoft Product Support Services Web site at http://search.support.microsoft.com/kb/c.asp.

- S/MIME is based on RSA Labs Public Key Cryptography Standard documents. These documents were consolidated in the Internet Engineering Task Force process to become the Internet standard S/MIME. For more information, see the S/MIME Central Web site at http://www.rsa.com/smime/.

- Microsoft Exchange Key Management Server version 5.5 issues keys for Microsoft Exchange Server security only. Microsoft Exchange Key Management Server 5.5, Service Pack 1 supports both Exchange security and S/MIME security. For more information, see the *Microsoft Exchange Server version 5.5 Resource Guide* in the *Microsoft BackOffice Resource Kit, Second Edition*.

Working with security keys and certificates

Occasionally, you must renew, import, or export a set of security keys and digital certificates. For example, you might need to change computers and take your Digital ID (the combination of your certificate and public and private encryption key set) with you. Or you might need to get someone's public security key in order to send them encrypted e-mail messages. Outlook provides ways to manage your security keys and certificates so that you can keep your e-mail messages secure.

Components for your Digital ID are stored in the Windows registry on your computer. The key set is encrypted using a password that you supply. If you use more than one computer, you must copy your Digital ID to each computer that you use.

> **Tip** Make a copy of your Digital ID for safekeeping. You can protect the file that contains the copy by encrypting it and by using a password.

Storing digital certificates

Certificates can be stored in three locations:

- Microsoft Exchange Global Address Book
- Lightweight Directory Access Protocol (LDAP) directory service
- Windows registry

Microsoft Exchange Global Address Book

Users who enroll in Exchange Advanced Security have their certificates stored in the Global Address Book. Alternatively, users can open the Global Address Book by using their LDAP provider.

Only certificates generated by Microsoft Exchange Server Advanced Security or by Microsoft Exchange Key Management Server are automatically published in the Global Address Book. However, externally generated certificates can be manually published to the Global Address Book.

LDAP directory service

External directory services, certificate authorities, or other certificate servers may publish their users' certificates through an LDAP directory service. Outlook 2002 allows access to these certificates through LDAP directories.

Windows registry

If a user imports another user's certificate into Outlook 2002 (for example, by adding a contact or importing a file), the certificate is stored in the registry. It cannot be shared or published to a directory service directly.

Obtaining other users' certificates

In order to exchange secure e-mail messages with another user, you must have that user's public key. You gain access to the public key through the user's certificate. There are three ways to obtain another user's certificate:

- Digitally signed e-mail messages
- Directory services, such as the Exchange Global Address Book
- Imported files

Obtain a certificate from a digitally signed e-mail message

When you receive a signed message from someone whose certificate you want to save, you can right-click the sender's name on the **To** line and then click **Add to Contacts**. The address information is saved in your Contacts, and the sender's certificate is saved in the registry.

> **Note** If you export a Contacts list, the corresponding certificates are not included. You must add the certificates from a received e-mail message on each computer that you use.

Obtain a certificate from a directory service

Using a standard LDAP server, you can automatically retrieve another user's certificate from an LDAP directory when you send an encrypted e-mail message. To gain access to a certificate this way, you must be enrolled in S/MIME security and you must have a Digital ID for your e-mail account.

Or you can obtain certificates from the Global Address Book. To do this, you must be enrolled in Exchange Advanced Security.

Obtain a certificate from a file

You can request that another user export a certificate to a file. To import this certificate provided by another user, click the **Import/Export Digital ID** button on the **Security** tab in the **Options** dialog box (**Tools** menu). You can also use the **Import** button on the **Certificates** tab in a contact item in your Contacts folder.

Renewing keys and certificates

A time limit is associated with each certificate and private key. When the keys given by the Microsoft Exchange Key Management Server approach the end of the designated time period, Outlook displays a warning message and offers to renew the keys. Outlook sends the renewal message to the server on your behalf.

Setting consistent security options for all users in the workgroup

You can control many aspects of the Outlook 2002 security features to properly configure messaging security and encryption for your organization's needs. To control these features, you specify settings in the Windows registry or through policies. For example, you can use Windows registry settings to require a security label on all outgoing mail or to disable publishing to the Global Address List.

> **Note** A number of Outlook security registry settings have an equivalent setting on the **Security** tab in the **Options** dialog box (**Tools** menu). You can use the Windows registry to change these settings. However, setting the value in the user interface does not create or set the equivalent setting in the Windows registry.

The following table lists the Windows registry settings that you can configure for your custom installation. You add these value entries in the HKEY_CURRENT_USER\Software\Policies\Microsoft\Office\10.0\Outlook\Security subkey.

Value name	Value data (Data type)	Description	Corresponding UI option
AlwaysEncrypt	0, 1 (DWORD)	When you set the value to **1**, all outgoing messages are encrypted. Default is **0**.	**Encrypt contents** check box
AlwaysSign	0, 1 (DWORD)	When you set the value to **1**, all outgoing messages are signed. Default is **0**.	**Add digital signature** check box
ClearSign	0, 1 (DWORD)	When you set the value to **1**, Clear Signed is used for all outgoing messages. Default is **0**.	**Send clear text signed message** check box
RequestSecureReceipt	0, 1 (DWORD)	When you set the value to **1**, secure receipts are requested for all outgoing messages. Default is **0**.	**Request secure receipt** check box
ForceSecurityLabel	0, 1 (DWORD)	When you set this value to **1**, a label is required on all outgoing messages. (Note that the registry setting does not specify which label.) Default is **0**.	None
ForceSecurityLabelX	ASN encoded BLOB (Binary)	This value entry specifies whether a user-defined security label must be present on all outgoing signed messages. String can optionally include label, classification, and category. Default is no security label required.	None
SigStatusNoCRL	0, 1 (DWORD)	Set to **0** means a missing CRL during signature validation is a warning. Set to **1** means a missing CRL is an error. Default is **0**.	None

Value name (con't)	Value data (Data type)	Description	Corresponding UI option
SigStatusNoTrustDecision	0, 1, 2 (DWORD)	Set to **0** means that a No Trust decision is allowed. Set to **1** means that a No Trust decision is a warning. Set to **2** means that a No Trust decision is an error. Default is **0**.	None
PromoteErrorsAsWarnings	0, 1 (DWORD)	Set to **0** to promote Error Level 2 errors as errors. Set to **1** to promote Error Level 2 errors as warnings. Default is **0**.	None
PublishtoGalDisabled	0, 1 (DWORD)	Set to **1** to disable the Publish to GAL button. Default is **0**.	**Publish to GAL** button
FIPSMode	0, 1 (DWORD)	Set to **1** to put Outlook into FIPS 140-1 mode. Default is **0**.	None
WarnAboutInvalid	0, 1, 2 (DWORD)	Set to **0** to display the **Show and Ask** check box (Secure E-mail Problem point dialog box). Set to **1** to always show the dialog box. Set to **2** to never show the dialog box. Default is **2**.	**Secure E-mail Problem** point dialog box
DisableContinueEncryption	0, 1 (DWORD)	Set to **0** to show the Continue Encrypting button on final Encryption Errors dialog box. Set to **1** to hide the button. Default is **0**.	**Continue Encrypting** button on final **Encryption Errors** dialog box

Value name (con't)	Value data (Data type)	Description	Corresponding UI option
RespondtoReceiptRequest	0, 1, 2, 3 (DWORD)	Set to **0** to always send a receipt response and prompt for a password if needed. Set to **1** to prompt for a password when sending a receipt response. Set to **2** to never send a receipt response. Set to **3** to enforce sending a receipt response. Default is **0**.	None
NeedEncryptionString	String	Displays the specified string when the user tries unsuccessfully to open an encrypted message. Can provide information about where to enroll in security. Default string is used unless value entry is set to another string.	Default string
Options	0, 1 (DWORD)	Set to 0 to show a warning dialog box when a user attempts to read a signed message with an invalid signature. Set to **1** to never show the warning. Default is **0**.	None.
MinEncKey	40, 64, 128, 168 (DWORD)	Set to the minimum key length for an encrypted e-mail message.	None.
RequiredCA	String	Set to the name of the required certificate authority.	None.

Value name (con't)	Value data (Data type)	Description	Corresponding UI option
EnrollPageURL	String	URL for the default certificate authority (internal or external) from which you wish your users to obtain a new digital ID. Note: set in HKEY_CURRENT_USER\Software\Microsoft\Office\9.0\Outlook\Security subkey if you do not have administrator privileges on the user's computer.	**Get Digital ID** button in **Security** | **Options**

The following table lists additional Windows registry settings that you can use for your custom configuration. These settings are contained in the HKEY_CURRENT_USER\Software\Microsoft\Cryptography\SMIME\SecurityPolicies\Default subkey.

Value name	Value data (Data type)	Description	Corresponding UI option
ShowWithMultiLabels	0, 1, (DWORD)	Set to **0** to attempt to display a message when the signature layer has different labels set in different signatures. Set to **1** to prevent display of message. Default is **0**.	None
CertErrorWithLabel	0, 1, 2 (DWORD)	Set to **0** to process a message with a certificate error when the message has a label. Set to **1** to deny access to a message with a certificate error. Set to **2** to ignore the message label and grant access to the message. (The user still sees a certificate error.) Default is **0**.	None

The following table lists additional Windows registry settings that you can use for your custom configuration. These settings are contained in the HKEY_CURRENT_USER\Software\Microsoft\Cryptography\Defaults\Provider subkey.

Value name	Value data (Data type)	Description	Corresponding UI option
MaxPWDTime	0, number (DWORD)	Set to **0** to remove user's ability to save a password (user is required to enter a password each time a key set is required). Set to a positive number to specify a maximum password time in minutes. Default is **999**.	None
DefPWDTime	Number (DWORD)	Set to the default value for the amount of time a password is saved.	None

When you specify a value for **PromoteErrorsAsWarnings**, note that potential Error Level 2 conditions include the following:

- Unknown Signature Algorithm
- No Signing Certification Found
- Bad Attribute Sets
- No Issuer certificate found
- No CRL Found
- Out of Date CRL
- Root Trust Problem
- Out of Date CTL

When you specify a value for **EnrollPageURL**, use the following parameters to send information about the user to the enrollment Web page.

Parameter	Placeholder in URL string
User display name	%1
SMTP e-mail name	%2
User interface language ID	%3

For example, to send user information to the Microsoft enrollment Web page, set the EnrollPageURL entry to the following value, including the parameters:

www.microsoft.com/ie/certpage.htm?name=%1&email=%2&helplcid=%3

If the user's name is Jeff Smith, his e-mail address is someone@microsoft.com, and his user interface language ID is 1033, then the placeholders are resolved as follows:

www.microsoft.com/ie/certpage.htm?name=Jeff%20Smith&email=someone@microsoft.com&helplcid=1033

> **System Policy Tip** You can use system policies to set security levels in Outlook. In the System Policy Editor, set the **Required Certificate Authority, Minimum encryption settings, S/MIME interoperability with external clients,** and **Outlook Rich Text in S/MIME messages** policies under **Microsoft Outlook 2002\Tools | Options\Security\Cryptography**. For more information about the System Policy Editor, see Chapter 9, "Using System Policies."

Setting security for Outlook Folder Home Pages

In Microsoft Outlook 2002, you can associate a Web page with any personal or public folder. These Folder Home Pages use the following security modes:

- Use zone security and allow script access to Outlook object model
- Use zone security only

Use zone security and allow script access to Outlook object model

This mode, which is the default for Outlook 2002, gives scripts on a Web page access to the Outlook object model and also ensures that the Outlook Today ActiveX® control is running continuously. For all other aspects of the Web page, the appropriate Microsoft Internet Explorer zone security settings are used.

For example, if the Internet Explorer zone security settings specify that ActiveX controls are not allowed to run, then no ActiveX controls run for a Folder Home Page except the Outlook Today ActiveX control.

Access to the object model allows scripts to manipulate all of the user's Outlook information on the computer. The primary security ramification of this mode is that it allows anyone who creates a public folder for a home page to include scripts that can manipulate data in user mailboxes. Although it provides the opportunity to create powerful public folder applications, access to the object model also exposes users to some security risks.

Use zone security only

Zone security mode is activated directly through the Windows registry or indirectly through a system policy. In this mode, scripts on the Web page do not have access to the Outlook object model, and the Outlook Today ActiveX control is subject to the same Internet Explorer zone security settings as all other ActiveX controls.

For example, if the Internet Explorer zone security settings specify that ActiveX controls are not allowed to run, then the Outlook Today ActiveX control does not run on the computer.

> **System Policy Tip**   You can tighten security by using a system policy to disable Folder Home Pages for all of your users. In the System Policy Editor, in the **Microsoft Outlook 2002\Miscellaneous\Folder Home Pages for Outlook special folders** category, select the **Disable Folder Home Pages** policy and then select **Disable Folder Home Pages for all folders** in the **Settings for Disable Folder Home Pages** area. For more information about the System Policy Editor, see Chapter 9, "Using System Policies."

Secure E-mail Messaging

For secure e-mail messaging in your organization, use encrypted e-mail messages and install Microsoft Outlook 2002 with appropriate privileges for users to take advantage of security functionality.

Encryption strengths for secure e-mail messaging

There are two classes of encryption key strengths available from Microsoft: High (128-bit) and Low (40-bit).

> **Note**   For signing, the Digital Signature Key lengths for High and Low encryption are RSA 1024-bit and RSA 512-bit, respectively.

Microsoft Office XP includes a technology that determines whether the user's installation is capable of 128-bit encryption operations. Microsoft provides 128-bit encryption capabilities in Microsoft Internet Explorer 3.02, Internet Explorer 4.*x*, Internet Explorer Service Packs, Microsoft Windows NT® 4.0, and Windows NT 4.0 Service Packs. Windows Installer tests these programs for certified 128-bit encryption capabilities during Office XP Setup.

If your system already has 128-bit encryption capabilities, Office XP installs new 128-bit encryption components during Setup. Systems that do not already have 128-bit encryption capabilities receive 40-bit encryption components.

Installation modes and feature options for secure e-mail messaging

To get full security functionality in Microsoft Outlook 2002 under Windows NT 4.0 or Windows 2000, you must install Outlook 2002 with local administrative rights or with elevated privileges. (Full security functionality is automatically included with Windows 98.)

With full e-mail security, users can perform the following tasks:

- Read S/MIME V2 encrypted e-mail messages
- Send S/MIME V2 encrypted e-mail messages
- Read S/MIME V2 digitally signed e-mail messages
- Send S/MIME digitally signed e-mail messages
- Enroll in public S/MIME security
- Enroll in MS Exchange Advanced Security
- Read Exchange 4.0/5.0 secure e-mail messages
- Send Exchange 4.0/5.0 secure e-mail messages

Without administrative rights on Microsoft Windows NT 4.0 or Microsoft Windows 2000, e-mail security functionality is degraded to limited security or no security, depending on the circumstances.

With limited e-mail security, users can perform the following tasks:

- Read S/MIME V2 encrypted e-mail messages
- Send S/MIME V2 encrypted e-mail messages
- Read S/MIME V2 digitally signed e-mail messages
- Send S/MIME digitally signed e-mail messages
- Enroll in public S/MIME security

With no e-mail security features, users can only read S/MIME V2 digitally signed e-mail messages; no other e-mail security features are available.

See also

If you are installing Outlook 2002 on client computers for users who do not have local administrative rights, you can give them elevated privileges for the installation. For more information about using elevated privileges in Office installations, see "Installations That Require Elevated Privileges" in Chapter 4, "Overview of Setup."

Appendix

Contents

Toolbox   551

APPENDIX

Toolbox

The Microsoft Office XP Resource Kit contains tools that help you to customize, configure, and deploy Office XP within your organization. If you have the Office XP Resource Kit CD or an Enterprise edition of Office XP, you can install the core tools and support documents through one integrated Setup program. The tools are also available separately from the download site of the Office Resource Kit Web site.

In the Toolbox

Answer Wizard Builder   552

CMW File Viewer   552

Corporate Error Reporting   553

Custom Installation Wizard   553

Custom Maintenance Wizard   554

HTML Help Workshop   555

MST File Viewer   556

OEM Tools   556

Office Converter Pack   558

OPS File Viewer   558

Outlook Security Features Administrative Package   559

Package Definition Files   559

PowerPoint Viewer   560

Profile Wizard   560

Removal Wizard   561

Setup INI Customization Wizard   562

Supplemental Documentation   562

System Policy Editor and Templates   565

Appendix Toolboz

Answer Wizard Builder

The Answer Wizard Builder enables you to create your own Answer Wizard content to address questions specific to your organization. Users sometimes submit queries to the Answer Wizard (the intelligence engine behind the Office Assistant) that the Answer Wizard cannot answer because the question is unique to your situation. A user might ask for the path to a printer on your local network, for example, or ask for the location of a form on your intranet.

You can use the Answer Wizard Builder utility to add custom Help content to any application that uses the Office Assistant. However, the Answer Wizard Builder will only work on a computer that has Microsoft Office XP installed

Install the Answer Wizard Builder

The Answer Wizard Builder is automatically installed on your computer when you install the Office Resource Kit. To locate the tool, click the **Start** button, point to **Programs**, point to **Microsoft Office Tools**, point to **Microsoft Office XP Resource Kit Tools**, and then click **Answer Wizard Builder**.

The Answer Wizard Builder can also be downloaded from the Toolbox on the Office Resource Kit Web site at http://www.microsoft.com/office/ork.

See also

For more information about the Answer Wizard Builder, see "Making Custom Help Content Accessible" in Chapter 11, "Creating Custom Help."

CMW File Viewer

The CMW File Viewer (CMWView.exe) enables you to view the changes that a configuration maintenance file (CMW file) makes to a user's computer. This viewer also provides a list of all possible changes the Custom Maintenance Wizard can make through a CMW file.

To use the CMW File Viewer, you must supply the path and file name of the CMW file you created with the Custom Maintenance Wizard. The CMW File Viewer is not a separate application — instead, it reads the CMW file and creates a plain-text file, which is displayed by the Notepad text editor.

Install the CMW File Viewer

The CMW File Viewer is automatically installed on your computer when you install the Office Resource Kit. To locate the tool, click the **Start** button, point to **Programs**, point to **Microsoft Office Tools**, point to **Microsoft Office XP Resource Kit Tools**, and then click **CMW File Viewer**.

When the CMWView dialog box is displayed, search for the CMW file you want to view. When you have selected the file, click the **Open** button to display the text file created by the CMW File Viewer.

The CMW File Viewer can also be downloaded from the Toolbox on the Office Resource Kit Web site at http://www.microsoft.com/office/ork.

Corporate Error Reporting

Corporate Error Reporting is a tool that administrators can use to manage the cabinet files created by DW.exe. Corporate Error Reporting allows organizations to redirect crash reports to a local file server instead of submitting the information directly to Microsoft crash-reporting servers over the Internet. When enough crash entries are collected, administrators can review the information and submit only the crash data they think is useful to Microsoft.

With Corporate Error Reporting, administrators can review what types of crashes users are experiencing the most. The information can then be used in educating users on how to avoid problems or produce work-arounds to potential crash situations.

Install Corporate Error Reporting

The Corporate Error Reporting tool is automatically installed on your computer when you install the Office Resource Kit. To locate the tool, click the **Start** button, point to **Programs**, point to **Microsoft Office Tools**, point to **Microsoft Office XP Resource Kit Tools**, and then click **Corporate Error Reporting**.

Corporate Error Reporting can also be downloaded from the Toolbox on the Office Resource Kit Web site at http://www.microsoft.com/office/ork.

See also

For more information about Corporate Error Reporting, see "Reporting Office Application Crashes" in Chapter 8, "Maintaining an Installation."

Custom Installation Wizard

The Custom Installation Wizard enables you to record changes to the master installation in a Windows Installer transform (MST file), without altering the original package (MSI file). Because the original package is never altered, you can create a different transform for every installation scenario you need. When you run Setup with both the package and the transform, Windows Installer applies the transform to the original package, and Setup uses your altered configuration to perform the installation.

By using the Custom Installation Wizard, you can also create a transform that runs additional Setup programs, such as the Profile Wizard, at the end of the Microsoft Office XP installation. If you run the Microsoft Internet Explorer Administration Kit from within the Custom Installation Wizard, you can customize the way Office Setup installs Internet Explorer 5.

For Office XP, the Custom Installation Wizard has been updated to include the following features:

- An improved user interface and enhancements to the Help system
- New installation states (**Not Available, Hidden, Locked**)
- The ability to add and remove files with a transform
- Improved navigation for Outlook customization pages and the ability to create an Outlook PRF file
- Enhanced security customization, including the ability to choose whether or not to install Visual Basic for Applications

Install the Custom Installation Wizard

The Custom Installation Wizard is automatically installed on your computer when you install the Office Resource Kit. To locate the tool, click the **Start** button, point to **Programs**, point to **Microsoft Office Tools**, point to **Microsoft Office XP Resource Kit Tools**, and then click **Custom Installation Wizard**.

The Custom Installation Wizard can also be downloaded from the Toolbox on the Office Resource Kit Web site at http://www.microsoft.com/office/ork.

See also

For more information about the Custom Installation Wizard, see "Customizing the Office Installation" and other topics in Chapter 5, "Installing and Customizing Office."

Custom Maintenance Wizard

The Custom Maintenance Wizard enables you to make changes to a Microsoft Office XP installation after the initial deployment. Using the Custom Maintenance Wizard, you can modify almost every feature that you can set in the Custom Installation Wizard — including default user settings, security levels, Outlook settings, and registry keys.

The Custom Maintenance Wizard works by creating a configuration maintenance file (CMW file) based on the Windows Installer package (MSI file) used in the Office XP installation. To apply the changes to a client computer, you run the Custom Maintenance Wizard from a command line on the client computer, specifying the customization file that contains the changes you want to apply.

Install the Custom Maintenance Wizard

The Custom Maintenance Wizard is automatically installed on your computer when you install the Office Resource Kit. To locate the tool, click the **Start** button, point to **Programs**, point to **Microsoft Office Tools**, point to **Microsoft Office XP Resource Kit Tools**, and then click **Custom Maintenance Wizard**.

The Custom Maintenance Wizard can also be downloaded from the Toolbox on the Office Resource Kit Web site at http://www.microsoft.com/office/ork.

See also

For more information about the Custom Maintenance Wizard, see "Changing Feature Installation States" in Chapter 8, "Maintaining an Installation."

HTML Help Workshop

You can use the HTML Help Workshop to create Help topics that provide information and assistance specific to your organization. You can also integrate those topics with the Microsoft Office XP Help system, or combine them with custom Answer Wizard databases to create a complete assistance solution.

Also included in the Office Resource Kit are two cascading style sheets that you can use to build your own custom Help topics using Microsoft styles. The style sheets, Office10.css and Startpag.css, must be used with Internet Explorer 4.0 or later.

Install the HTML Help Workshop

The HTML Help Workshop must be installed separately from the other applications — it is not installed by the Office Resource Kit Setup program. To install the HTML Help Workshop, run Htmlhelp.exe from the \Files\PFiles\ORKTools\ORK10\Tools\Htmlhelp\ folder on the Office Resource Kit CD. If you are installing HTML Help Workshop from an Office Enterprise Edition CD, the path is \ORK\Files\PFiles\ORKTools\ORK10\Tools\Htmlhelp\. The style sheets (Office10.css and Startpag.css) are included in the same folder as the Htmlhelp.exe application.

The HTML Help Workshop can also be downloaded from the Toolbox on the Office Resource Kit Web site at http://www.microsoft.com/office/ork.

Appendix Toolboz

MST File Viewer

The MST File Viewer (MSTView.exe) enables you to view customizations a transform (MST file) makes to a user's computer. Transforms are created by using the Custom Installation Wizard.

To use the MST File Viewer, you must supply it with the path and file name of the MST file you created with the Custom Installation Wizard. The MST File Viewer is not a separate application — instead, it reads the MST file and creates a plain-text file containing readable content. The information is then displayed through the Notepad text editor.

Install the MST File Viewer

The MST File Viewer is automatically installed on your computer when you install the Office Resource Kit. To locate the tool, click the **Start** button, point to **Programs**, point to **Microsoft Office Tools**, point to **Microsoft Office XP Resource Kit Tools**, and then click **MST File Viewer.**

When you run the tool, the Windows Installer Transform Viewer dialog box is displayed. You then need to specify both a Windows Installer base package (MSI file) and the transform you want to view (MST file). After you have selected the files, click **View Transform** to display the text file created by the MST File Viewer.

OEM Tools

The OEM tools are support utilities designed for original equipment manufacturers (OEMs) that enable you to reset the initial installation information after Microsoft Office XP has been installed on a computer.

Tool	Description
Addbinrg.exe	Called by the Oem.bat file to reset the company name and user name for the installation.
Audit.reg	Enables an OEM to avoid the registration and product key dialogs on the first run of any Office application. The file can be run from a command line or Windows Explorer to set audit mode. To set the computer back to normal state, run the Oem.bat file.
Oem.bat	The core tool of this set, Oem.bat enables you to change the CD key, change the user and company name, force the EULA to show at the first start of any Office application, exit audit mode, and reset user data.
Srclist.exe	Called by the Oem.bat file to reset the installation source to the CD. Requires the product code of the MSI you want to reset as an argument.

Information about using the Office XP OEM tools is available on the Office Resource Kit Web site.

Install the OEM Tools

The OEM Tools must be installed separately from the other applications — they are not installed by the Microsoft Office Resource Kit Setup program. To install the OEM Tools, you extract the separate tools files from the compressed Ork.cab file and copy them to your computer.

Information on using the Oem.bat file is also contained within the file itself. You can use Notepad or another plain-text editor to view the contents.

The OEM Tools can also be downloaded from the Toolbox on the Office Resource Kit Web site at http://www.microsoft.com/office/ork.

Office Converter Pack

The Microsoft Office Converter Pack bundles together a collection of file converters and filters that can be deployed to users. The Converter Pack can be useful to organizations that use Microsoft Office XP in a mixed environment with previous versions of Office, including Office for the Macintosh, or other Office-related productivity applications. Many of these converters and filters have been previously available, but they are packaged together here for convenient deployment.

You can customize the Office Converter Pack to deploy any number of these converters that your organization needs. You can also choose to deploy them with no user interaction or full user interaction, or you can include the converters with your deployment of Office XP.

Install the Office Converter Pack

The Office Converter Pack must be installed separately from the other applications — it is not installed by the Office Resource Kit Setup program. To install the Office Converter Pack, run Setup.exe from the \Files\PFiles\ORKTools\ORK10\Tools\Ocp\ folder on the Office Resource Kit CD. If you are installing the Office Converter Pack from an Office Enterprise Edition CD, the path is \ORK\Files\PFiles\ORKTools\ORK10\Tools\Ocp\.

The Office Converter Pack can also be downloaded from the Toolbox on the Office Resource Kit Web site at http://www.microsoft.com/office/ork.

OPS File Viewer

The OPS File Viewer (OPSView.exe) enables you to view changes that an Office profile settings file (OPS file) makes to a user's computer. This viewer also provides a list of all possible changes that the Office Profile Wizard can make to a user's computer through an OPS file.

To use the OPS File Viewer, you must supply the path and file name of an OPS file you created with the Profile Wizard. The viewer is not a separate application — instead, it reads the OPS file and creates a plain-text file, which is displayed by the Notepad text editor.

Install the OPS File Viewer

The OPS File Viewer is automatically installed on your computer when you install the Office Resource Kit. To locate the tool, click the **Start** button, point to **Programs**, point to **Microsoft Office Tools**, point to **Microsoft Office XP Resource Kit Tools**, and then click **OPS File Viewer.**

When the **OPSView** dialog box is displayed, search for the OPS file you want to view. When you have selected the file, click the **Open** button to display the text file created by the OPS File Viewer.

The OPS File Viewer can also be downloaded from the Toolbox on the Office Resource Kit Web site at http://www.microsoft.com/office/ork.

Outlook Security Features Administrative Package

If your organization is using Microsoft Outlook® 98/2000/2002 with a server that has server-side security, such as Microsoft Exchange Server, you can customize the security features to meet your organization's needs. For example, you can control the types of attached files blocked by Outlook, modify the Outlook Object Model warning notifications, and specify user- or group-security levels.

The Outlook Security Features Administrative Package consists of four files, packaged into one self-extracting executable. When you run the executable, the following files are copied to a location you specify:

- OutlookSecurity.oft, an Outlook template that enables you to customize the security settings on the Microsoft Exchange server.
- Readme.doc, a document that provides information on the values and settings available in the template and describes how to deploy the new settings on Exchange Server.
- Hashctl.dll, the file for the Trusted Code control, a tool used by the template to specify trusted COM add-ins.
- Comdlg32.ocx, a control that provides a user interface for selecting the trusted COM add-in.

Install the Outlook Security Features Administrative Package

The Outlook Security Features Administrative Package must be installed separately from the other applications — it is not installed by the Office Resource Kit Setup program. To install the Outlook Security Features Administrative Package, run Admpack.exe from the \Files\PFiles\ORKTools\ORK10\Tools\Admpack\ folder on the Office Resource Kit CD. If you are installing the Outlook Security Features Administrative Package from an Office Enterprise Edition CD, the path is \ORK\Files\PFiles\ORKTools\ORK10\Tools\Admpack\. This executable will copy the four administrative files to a location you specify on your computer.

The Outlook Security Features Administrative Package can also be downloaded from the Toolbox on the Office Resource Kit Web site at http://www.microsoft.com/office/ork.

Package Definition Files

The package definition files (SMS format) are used by Microsoft Systems Management Server to install Office remotely. For Microsoft Office XP, the package definition files have been consolidated into two core files: Off2002.SMS, which covers all product suites, and LPK2002.SMS, which covers the Office Multilingual User Interface Packs. Office XP supports only Microsoft Systems Management Server 2.0.

Install the package definition files

The package definition files are automatically installed on your computer when you install the Office Resource Kit. To locate the files, click the **Start** button, point to **Programs**, point to **Microsoft Office Tools**, point to **Microsoft Office XP Resource Kit Tools**, and then click **Package Definition Files**. The computer will then display a folder containing the files.

The package definition files can also be downloaded from the Toolbox on the Office Resource Kit Web site at http://www.microsoft.com/office/ork.

See also

For more information about using System Management Server to deploy package definition files, see "Distributing Office to Users' Computers" in Chapter 5, "Installing and Customizing Office."

PowerPoint Viewer

The Microsoft PowerPoint 97/2000/2002 Viewer enables you to share PowerPoint 97, PowerPoint 2000, or PowerPoint 2002 presentations with users who do not have PowerPoint installed on their systems. The PowerPoint Viewer allows users to view and print PowerPoint presentations, but it does not allow them to edit the presentations.

Install the PowerPoint Viewer

The PowerPoint Viewer must be installed separately from the other applications — it is not installed by the Office Resource Kit Setup program. To install the PowerPoint Viewer, run Ppview97.exe from the \Files\PFiles\ORKTools\ORK10\Tools\Pptview\ folder on the Office Resource Kit CD. If you are installing the PowerPoint Viewer from an Office Enterprise Edition CD, the path is \ORK\Files\PFiles\ORKTools\ORK10\Tools\Pptview\.

The PowerPoint Viewer can also be downloaded from the Toolbox on the Office Resource Kit Web site at http://www.microsoft.com/office/ork.

Profile Wizard

The Profile Wizard helps you to create and distribute a default user profile, including standard locations for files and templates. Using the Profile Wizard, you can preset options so that users don't have to customize their settings. You can also change default values to match your organization's needs or to ensure that users have access to shared templates. When you deploy a standard user profile, all of your users start with the same Office configuration.

When you save an Office user profile, you create an Office profile settings file (OPS file). You can include your OPS file in a Windows Installer transform (MST file) to distribute the settings when Microsoft Office XP is deployed. You can also use the Profile Wizard to help back up and restore user-defined settings from one computer to another.

Install the Profile Wizard

The Profile Wizard is automatically installed on your computer when you install the Office Resource Kit. To locate the tool, click the **Start** button, point to **Programs**, point to **Microsoft Office Tools**, point to **Microsoft Office XP Resource Kit Tools**, and then click **Profile Wizard**.

The Profile Wizard can also be downloaded from the Toolbox on the Office Resource Kit Web site at http://www.microsoft.com/office/ork.

See also

For more information about the Profile Wizard, see "Customizing User-defined Settings" in Chapter 5, "Installing and Customizing Office."

Removal Wizard

Although version removal functionality is built into Microsoft Office XP Setup and the Custom Installation Wizard, a stand-alone version of the Removal Wizard is included as well. You can use this tool to exert a detailed level of control over which files to remove and which to retain. For example, if you are upgrading gradually to Office XP, you can use the Removal Wizard to remove previously installed versions of the specific applications you choose to upgrade.

The Removal Wizard can detect and remove Microsoft Office 4.x, Office 95, Office 97, and Office 2000, as well as MultiLanguage Packs and individual Office applications. A companion file list allows you to review and edit the detailed list of files that can be removed. The Removal Wizard does not remove documents or other user files from the computer.

Install the Removal Wizard

The Removal Wizard is automatically installed on your computer when you install the Office Resource Kit. To locate the tool, click the **Start** button, point to **Programs**, point to **Microsoft Office Tools**, point to **Microsoft Office XP Resource Kit Tools**, and then click **Removal Wizard**.

The Removal Wizard can also be downloaded from the Toolbox on the Office Resource Kit Web site at http://www.microsoft.com/office/ork.

See also

For more information about the Removal Wizard, see "Customizing Removal Behavior" in Chapter 5, "Installing and Customizing Office."

Setup INI Customization Wizard

The Setup INI Customization Wizard (Iniwiz.exe) provides a convenient user interface for creating or modifying custom Setup settings files. The wizard automatically enters the settings that you select into the correct section of the settings file, and it creates a command line that includes the **/settings** option and specifies your custom INI file.

Before you can use the Setup INI Customization Wizard, you must create a Microsoft Office XP administrative installation point. Your custom INI file must be based on an existing INI file, such as the Setup.ini file for Office XP.

Install the Setup INI Customization Wizard

The Setup INI Customization Wizard is automatically installed on your computer when you install the Office Resource Kit. To locate the tool, click the **Start** button, point to **Programs**, point to **Microsoft Office Tools**, point to **Microsoft Office XP Resource Kit Tools**, and then click **Setup INI Customization Wizard**.

The Setup INI Customization Wizard can also be downloaded from the Toolbox on the Office Resource Kit Web site at http://www.microsoft.com/office/ork.

See also

For more information about the Setup INI Customization Wizard, see "Customizing the Office Installation" in Chapter 5, "Installing and Customizing Office."

Supplemental Documentation

The Microsoft Office XP Resource Kit includes a collection of supplemental documents that provide detailed information on such areas as registry settings, international configurations, and the Office XP file list.

The supplemental documents are installed by default when you run the Office Resource Kit Setup program. Setup organizes the documents into four folders, accessible with the rest of the Office Resource Kit components from the Windows Start menu. The documents are also available for download from the Office Resource Kit Web site.

Appendix Toolbox

The following tables list the documents and other files available from each of the folders.

Customizable Alerts

The Customizable Alerts folder contains sample and support files you can use to create or extend custom error messages.

Document file name	Description
Alert.asp	Sample ASP page for an error message
Alert.htm	Sample HTML page for an error message
Alert2.asp	Sample ASP page with a response form
Alert2a.asp	Sample ASP page with embedded JavaScript
Aspscrpt.xls	Spreadsheet used to create or update ASP scripts
Errormsg.xls	ID numbers for all error message in Office 2000
Fishng2.jpg	Sample image in JPG format
Fr_bkg.gif	Sample image in GIF format
Nyi.htm	Sample HTML page for a "Not yet implemented" error

The Customizable Alerts documents are automatically installed on your computer when you install the Office Resource Kit. To locate the documents, click the **Start** button, point to **Programs**, point to **Microsoft Office Tools**, point to **Microsoft Office XP Resource Kit Documents**, and then click **Customizable Alerts**. The computer will then display a folder containing the files and documents.

Help On the Web

The Help on the Web folder contains samples and other files you can use to customize the Answer Wizard feedback form.

Document file name	Description
Answiz.asp	Sample Help Desk ASP file
Answiz.htm	Sample Help Desk HTM file
Fishng2.jpg	Sample image in JPG format
Fr_bkg.gif	Sample image in GIF format
Nyi.htm	Sample HTML page for a "Not yet implemented" error
Posredir.inc	Sample INC file (for use with Answiz.asp)

Appendix Toolboz

The Help On the Web documents are automatically installed on your computer when you install the Office Resource Kit. To locate the documents, click the **Start** button, point to **Programs**, point to **Microsoft Office Tools**, point to **Microsoft Office XP Resource Kit Documents**, and then click **Help On the Web**. The computer will then display a folder containing the files and documents.

International Information

The International Information folder contains reference files that provide information on international versions of Office XP.

Document file name	Description
Intlimit.xls	Lists the limitations of plug-in language compatibility by component.
Multilpk.xls	Lists components of the Multilingual User Interface Pack and the Proofing Tools Kit by language.
Wwfeatre.xls	Lists the effect of various language settings on each Office application.
Wwsuppt.xls	Lists support, by language of operating system, of different language features of Office applications.

The International Information documents are automatically installed on your computer when you install the Office Resource Kit. To locate the documents, click the **Start** button, point to **Programs**, point to **Microsoft Office Tools**, point to **Microsoft Office XP Resource Kit Documents**, and then click **International Information**. The computer will then display a folder containing the files and documents.

Office Information

The Office folder contains a variety of support files such as the product file list, comprehensive registry key list, and list of all entry points to the Web from within Office XP applications.

Document file name	Description
Cfgquiet.ini	Contains default settings for the Microsoft Office Server Extension log file.
Filelist.xls	Lists all files provided with Office XP.
Formats.doc	Lists supported data formats and installed OLE DB providers.
Presbrod.xls	Lists and describes registry entries that can be set on client computers to specify default values and restrictions for using Presentation Broadcasting.

Document file name (cont'd)	Description
IE5feats.xls	Lists the Office XP features that degrade when used with previous versions of Microsoft Internet Explorer.
Opc.doc	Explains the syntax in files used by the Removal Wizard so that administrators can customize the removal of applications.
Regkey.xls	Lists default registry key values.
Setupref.doc	Lists Office Setup command-line options, properties, and settings file formats.
Stopword.doc	Contains the list of words not indexed by the Find Fast utility.
Webent.xls	Lists all entry points to the Web from within Office and describes how to disable them.

The Office Information documents are automatically installed on your computer when you install the Office Resource Kit. To locate the documents, click the **Start** button, point to **Programs**, point to **Microsoft Office Tools**, point to **Microsoft Office XP Resource Kit Documents**, and then click **Office Information**. The computer will then display a folder containing the files and documents.

System Policy Editor and Templates

The System Policy Editor enables you to use templates provided with the Office XP Resource Kit to enforce system policies globally for users of Office on a network. By using system policies, an administrator can quickly enforce a user configuration on users' computers when users, groups, or computers log on to the network.

The Microsoft Office policy templates (ADM files) describe all of the policy settings you can set for Office. These ADM files can be used with the System Policy Editor and Group Policy snap-in tools in Microsoft Windows® operating systems to apply policies to users' computers.

Install the System Policy Editor

The System Policy Editor is automatically installed on your computer when you install the Office Resource Kit. To locate the tool, click the **Start** button, point to **Programs**, point to **Microsoft Office Tools**, point to **Microsoft Office XP Resource Kit Tools**, and then click **System Policy Editor**.

The policy templates (ADM files) are installed in the \Windows\INF folder on your computer.

The System Policy Editor and templates can also be downloaded from the Toolbox on the Office Resource Kit Web site at http://www.microsoft.com/office/ork.

See also

For more information about the System Policy Editor, see "Understanding System Policies" in Chapter 9, "Using System Policies."

Glossary

A

access control list (ACL)   Contains a list of userids or groups and their security permissions. Identifies who can update, modify, or delete an object on a computer or resource on the network.

Active Server Pages (ASP pages)   Technology that allows Web developers to combine scripts and HTML code to create dynamic Web content and Web-based applications.

administrative installation point   Network share from which users install Office. Created by running Setup with the **/a** command-line option; contains all the Office files.

administrative rights   Highest level of permissions that can be granted to an account in Windows NT User Manager. An administrator can set permissions for other users and create groups and accounts within the domain. Required to install the System Files Update.

advertise   Windows Installer method for making an application available to the user without installing it. When the user attempts to use the application for the first time, the application is installed and run. Applications can be advertised by using the **/jm** command-line option (Windows NT 4.0 and Windows 2000) or by using IntelliMirror software installation (Windows 2000 only). *See also* assign, publish.

assign   Method of installing an application when using Windows 2000 Group Policy support. An administrator assigns the application to a user, group, or computer. When the application is selected for the first time, Windows Installer installs the application. Assigning places a shortcut for the assigned application in the **Start** menu. *See also* advertise, publish.

automatic recovery   See rollback.

B   *No Entries*

C

cache   A special memory subsystem in which frequently used data values, such as files that are made available for use offline, are duplicated for quick access.

certificate   Set of data issued by a certificate authority to completely identify an entity; issued only after that authority has verified the entity's identity.

certificate authority   A mutually trusted organization that issues certificates. Before issuing a certificate, the certificate authority requires you to provide identification information. Versign, Inc. is a recognized certificate authority.

chaining, chained package   Method used to include additional packages in an Office XP installation; chained packages are specified in the Setup settings file.

character entity reference   A set of HTML characters that are represented by easy-to-remember mnemonic names.

character set A grouping of alphabetic, numeric, and other characters that have some relationship in common. For example, the standard ASCII character set includes letters, numbers, symbols, and control codes that make up the ASCII coding scheme. See also code page.

child feature A subordinate feature in the Office feature tree; contained within a parent feature. Setting an installation state for a parent feature can affect the installation state of a child feature.

clear text Unencrypted, non-machine dependent, ASCII text in readable form.

CMW file A file created by the Custom Maintenance Wizard. *See also* configuration maintenance file.

code page Ordered set of characters in which a numeric index (code point) is associated with each character of a particular writing system. There are separate code pages for different writing systems, such as Western European and Cyrillic. *See also* Unicode.

code point Numeric value in Unicode encoding or in a code page; corresponds to a character. In the Western European code page, 132 is the code point for the letter ä; however, in another code page, the code point 132 might correspond to a different character.

complex script Writing system based on characters that are composed of multiple glyphs or whose shape depends on adjacent characters. Thai and Arabic use complex scripts. *See also* glyph.

configuration maintenance file A CMW file created by the Custom Maintenance Wizard; applies changes to feature installation states and other settings after Office is installed.

configuration property Also known as configuration variable, a property that allows an administrator to control SharePoint Team Services settings.

digital certificate File issued by a certificate authority. Can be used to verify the user's identity for digitally signed or encrypted e-mail messages. Associates the user's identity with a public encryption key.

D

Digital ID Combination of a digital certificate and a public and private encryption key set.

digital signature Confirms that an e-mail message, macro, or program originated from a trusted source who signed it. Also confirms that the message, macro, or program has not been altered.

Document library A folder where a collection of files is stored, and the files often use the same template. Each file in a library is associated with user-defined information that is displayed in the content listing for that library.

E

elevated privileges In Windows 2000 and Windows NT 4.0, a method of granting administrator rights to an installation program to modify system areas of the Windows registry or password-secured folders of a hard disk. Can be accomplished by logging on with administrator rights, advertising the program, giving administrator rights to all Windows Installer programs, or using Systems Management Server. *See also* advertise.

encryption Method used to scramble the content of a file or data packet to make the data unreadable without the decryption key.

encryption, 128-bit High level of encryption. Uses a 128-bit key to scramble the contents of a file or data packet to make the data unreadable without the decryption key.

encryption, 40-bit Low level of encryption. Uses a 40-bit key to scramble the contents of a file or data packet to make the data unreadable without the decryption key.

F

file allocation table (FAT) Common file format of file cataloging for DOS and Windows operating systems; physical method of storing and accessing files from a hard disk. The FAT contains a list of all files on the physical or logical drive.

File Folder Tree A folder tree structure where crash-reporting data from DW.exe is reported. Used as an intermediate storage area so that administrators can review the data before it is submitted to Microsoft.

FrontPage Server Extensions A set of programs and scripts that support authoring in Microsoft FrontPage and extend the functionality of a Web server.

FTP File Transfer Protocol. Protocol used to gain remote access to a Web server.

G

glyph Shape of a character as rendered by a font. For example, the italic "a" and the roman "a" are different glyphs representing the same alphabetical character.

Group Policy In Windows 2000, allows administrators to manage users' computer configuration, including installation and maintenance of Office XP applications. You use Group Policy to define configurations for groups of users and computers, and you can specify settings for registry-based policies, security, software installation, scripts, folder redirection, and remote installation services.

H

home page Main page of a Web site. Usually has hyperlinks to other pages, both within and outside the site. One Web site can contain many home pages. For example, the Microsoft home page contains a Products home page, which contains other home pages.

host The main computer in a system of computers connected by communications links.

hyperlink Colored and underlined text or a graphic that you click to go to a file, a location in a file, an HTML page on the World Wide Web, or an HTML page on an intranet. Hyperlinks can also go to newsgroups and to Gopher, Telnet, and FTP sites.

I

ideographic script Writing system that is based on characters of Chinese origin, where the characters represent words or syllables that are generally used in more than one Asian language.

input locale Sets what language is currently being entered and how to display it. Usually used in reference to the keyboard, code page, and font configuration of an operating system. *See also* user locale.

Input Method Editor (IME) Software utility that converts keystrokes to characters in an ideographic script (Korean, Chinese, Japanese, and so on).

installation language Locale ID (LCID) assigned to the value entry **InstallLanguage** in the Windows registry. Also called the default version of Office. This entry, along with other language settings, determines default behavior of Office applications.

installation state The installation setting applied to an Office XP application or feature; determines whether a feature is installed locally, run from the network, installed on demand, not installed, or not available to users.

IntelliMirror In Windows 2000, a set of tools and technologies that allow administrators to manage users' computer configurations by policy. IntelliMirror includes a software installation and maintenance feature that can be used to install and manage Office XP.

Internet The World Wide Web.

intranet An internal Web site for an organization.

J

JavaScript A cross-platform, World Wide Web scripting language. JavaScript code is inserted directly into an HTML page. JavaScript makes it possible to build Java programs.

K

keypath A file or registry entry listed as part of a component or feature of Office. If missing, triggers a reinstall of that component.

L

LAN Local area network. A computer network technology designed to connect computers separated by a short distance. A LAN can be connected to the Internet and used for intranet Web sites.

local administrators group The group of users who have permission to perform administrative tasks on the local server computer. The permissions for this group are set by using the administration tools for the operating system.

locale ID (LCID) A 32-bit value defined by Windows that consists of a language ID, sort ID, and reserved bits. Identifies a particular language. For example, the LCID for English is 1033 and the LCID for Japanese is 1041.

M

maintenance mode Configuration mode of an operating system for installing, updating, or removing applications.

MSDE Microsoft Data Engine (also known as Microsoft SQL Server 2000 Desktop Engine). A data store based on Microsoft SQL Server technology, but designed and optimized for use on smaller computer systems, such as a single user computer or a small workgroup server.

MSI file *See also* package.

MST file *See also* transform.

N

network place A folder on a network file server, Web server, or Exchange 2000 server. Create a shortcut to a network place to work with files there. Some network places, such as document libraries, have features not available with local folders.

NLS files National Language Support files. Files that extend the ability of the operating system to support multilingual features.

NTFS file system (NTFS) Designed exclusively for use with the Windows NT operating system. NTFS allows for stronger security and more flexible file management methods than does FAT. *See also* file allocation table (FAT).

O

Office user profile A collection of user-defined options and settings captured by the Office Profile Wizard in an OPS file and applied to another computer.

OPS file A file created by the Office Profile Wizard. *See also* Office user profile.

P

package (MSI file) In Windows Installer, a relational database that contains all the information necessary to install a product. The MSI file associates components with features and contains information that controls the installation process.

plug-in language features User interface, online Help, and editing tools that users can install with Office XP to run Office in the users' own language, and to create documents in many other languages.

private key One of a pair of keys used for encryption. A message encrypted with the public key must be decrypted with the private key. Part of a Digital ID.

public key One of a pair of keys used for encryption. A message encrypted with the public key must be decrypted with the private key. Part of a Digital ID.

publish A method of advertising an application by using Windows 2000 Group Policy support. A published application is not advertised with shortcuts or **Start** menu icons. Instead, the application is configured to be installed the first time another application requests it, such as when double-clicking a .doc file from Windows Explorer. *See also* advertise, assign.

Q

quiet installation Also known as unattended installation. An installation run by using the **/q** command-line option that runs without generating any user prompts.

R

right File and folder-level permissions that allow access to a Web site.

roaming user User who uses more than one computer on a regular basis. Works at multiple sites using multiple computers. *See also* traveling user.

roaming user profiles Account information established for roaming users, usually within a given domain of a network. Automatically configures the computer when the user logs on.

role A named group of user rights. Users are assigned to roles when they are added to a Web site based upon SharePoint Team Services.

rollback A method used by Windows Installer to recover from a failed install. Similar to the rollback definition used in SQL. Consists of storing files, folders, and registry settings marked for deletion in a hidden temporary folder. If a serious error is encountered during the installation of new software, the files, folders, and registry settings are returned to their previous settings (as if the attempted installation never happened).

S

script In character sets, a set of characters from a particular writing system, such as Arabic, Cyrillic, Hebrew, or Latin.

scripting language A programming language designed specifically for Web site programming. Examples include JavaScript and VBScript.

Secure Multipurpose Internet Mail Extensions (S/MIME) Method of security that allows users to exchange encrypted and digitally signed messages with any S/MIME-compliant mail reader. Messages are encrypted or digitally signed by the sending client and decrypted by the recipient.

Secure Sockets Layer A proposed open standard that was developed by Netscape Communications for establishing a secure communications channel to prevent the interception of critical information, such as credit card numbers.

security labels An Outlook feature that allows you to add information to a message header about the sensitivity of the message content. The label can also restrict which recipients can open, forward, or send the message.

Setup settings file An INI file, such as Setup.ini, read by Setup.exe at the start of the installation process; contains properties that control the installation process.

signed receipts A message receipt that verifies that the recipients recognize the user's digital signature.

SMTP mail server An e-mail server that uses the Simple Mail Transfer Protocol. SMTP is available with Windows NT Server 4.0 and Windows 2000 Server.

SQL Server A network or Web server that uses the standardized query language protocol for requesting information from a database. More commonly, a computer with an installed configuration of Microsoft SQL Server with a configured database that is available from a network location.

system locale In Windows NT and Windows 2000, the setting that determines the code page and default input locale. *See also* input locale, user locale, code page.

T

transform (MST file) In Windows Installer, a relational database that contains information about components, features, and Setup properties. A transform is based on a particular package and contains the modifications to apply to that package during installation. You use the Custom Installation Wizard to create transforms for Office XP.

traveling user Uses more than one computer on a regular basis, often a portable computer the user takes to different locations. Traveling users might have different language requirements or need access to different configurations of the same application (local or remote). *See also* roaming user.

U

Unicode Universal character set designed to accommodate all known scripts. Unlike most code pages, Unicode uses a unique two-byte encoding for every character, also known as double byte character set (DBCS). Unicode is a registered trademark of Unicode, Inc.

URL Uniform Resource Locator. An address that specifies a protocol (such as HTTP or FTP) and a location of an object, document, World Wide Web page, or other destination on the Internet or an intranet. Example: http://www.microsoft.com/.

user locale Setting that determines formats and sort orders for date, time, currency, and so on. Also known as regional settings. *See also* input locale.

V

VBScript (Visual Basic Scripting Edition) A subset of the Visual Basic for Applications programming language optimized for Web-related programming. As with JavaScript, code for VBScript is embedded in HTML documents.

vCard The Internet standard for creating and sharing virtual business cards.

virtual server A virtual computer that resides on an HTTP server but appears to the user as a separate HTTP server. Several virtual servers can reside on one computer, each capable of running its own programs and each with individualized access to input and peripheral devices. Each virtual server has its own domain name and IP address and appears to the user as an individual Web site or FTP site.

W

Web query In Microsoft Excel, a query that retrieves data stored on your intranet or the Internet.

Web server A computer that hosts Web pages and responds to requests from browsers. Also known as an HTTP server, a Web server stores files whose URLs begin with http://.

Windows Installer shortcut An application shortcut that supports Windows Installer install-on-demand functionality. On Windows NT 4.0, requires the Windows Desktop Update. *See also* assign, publish, and advertise.

X *No Entries*

Y *No Entries*

Z *No Entries*

Index

A

Access
- file-level security 298
- language version
  - converting databases 412–413
  - forms and reports 411–412
  - general Office considerations 409–410
  - language settings 439
  - opening databases from previous versions 410–411
  - Windows 2000 sort order 410
  - Windows 98 sort order 411
  - Windows NT 4.0 sort order 410–411
- macro security level 291
- paper size for printing documents 455
- record locking in shared databases 43, 44
- removing VBA 305
- runtime packages 58
- upgrading database files 47, 51

access control
- system policy access 237
- Windows registry access
  - locked by Terminal Services 308
  - Outlook considerations 308, 485
  - security considerations 306
  - setting permissions 307

Access10.adm file
- environment variables 265
- policy settings 256–257
- templates in Resource Kit 241

Accessrt.msi file 59

Active Directory 165–167

ActiveX controls
- accessing system services 296
- application security level 296
- defined as macro 309
- list of trusted sources *See* trusted sources
- more security options *See* macro security
- Office Web Components controls 58, 81–82
- Outlook Folder Home Pages security 545–546
- overview 295
- safe mode 316
- safety standards 297
- security entries in registry 315–316
- security settings 295–296
- signing 296–297
- trusted by application or Internet Explorer 293
- trusted if registered 296

Add/Remove Programs
- customizing user interface 98
- elevated privileges 214
- installing hidden applications 201
- removing MUI Packs 433
- removing Outlook 522
- working with published software 169–170

Addbinreg.exe tool 557

add-ins, Excel 4 macros 311–312

add-ins, trusting installed 293, 314–315

address book
- file formats 51
- storing certificates in 536, 538

Microsoft Office XP Resource Kit 575

administrative installation point
    advantages of using 77–78
    configuration maintenance file 80
    copying to custom Office CD 150
    creating
        for MUI Pack 378–379
        for Office deployment 78–79
        for Office Web Components 81
        for Outlook 486–487, 493–496
    laptop installations 79
    Office file locations 79
    Office service releases 157–159
    read access 79
    replicating 80
    Setup.exe location 79
    single point for two installations 394
    single vs. multiple 369
Admpack.exe file 559
advertising Office
    advantages 191
    chained installations 132
    Office package or single application 191
    setting up 148–149
    SQL Server 2000 Desktop Engine 81
    System Files Update 192
    when to use 75
    Windows Desktop Update 190
    Windows Installer shortcuts 190
Alert.asp file 331, 333, 563
Alert.htm file 331, 563
Alert2.asp file 331, 333, 335, 563
Alert2a.asp file 331, 333, 335, 563
AlwaysEncrypt policy 282
AlwaysSign policy 283

Answer Wizard
    adding questions for topics 349–350
    AW file
        building 350
        deploying Help 352
        location 350, 351
        registry entry 352
        system policy 353
    creating Help systems *See* custom Help
    creating project 348–349
    enabling custom Help 350–351
    excluding topics 341
    Help on the Web link
        extending 354–355
        feedback button label 356
        feedback dialog text 356–357
        feedback form 358–360
        redirecting 357–358
        sample and support files 563
    languages supported 446
    overview 347–348
    topic styles 346
Answer Wizard Builder
    installing 552
    what's new 17
Answiz.asp file 358, 563
Answiz.htm file 563
anti-virus software 309
Application object, AutomationSecurity method 311
applications
    changing installation state *See* installation states
    crash data *See* Corporate Error Reporting tool

applications *(continued)*
    deploying *See* deploying Office XP
    Internet Explorer dependencies 65
    policies *See* system policies
    preventing users from installing 205
    preventing users from running 320
    removing
        tools for 205
        using Add/Remove Programs 214
        using installation states 202–206
        using wizard *See* Removal Wizard
    repairing 195–197
    running on server *See* Terminal Services
    user interface control *See* system policies
Artisoft LANtastic network support 44
Asian languages
    Access language settings 439
    Clipboard formats 429
    default user display font 453
    disk space 364, 398
    displaying user interface in 444
    editing documents in 447
    Excel installation language 435
    font size and printing 455, 456
    ideographic scripts 426
    Input Method Editor 447
    installing fonts 454
    LangTuneUp registry entry 404
    language version compatibility
        Access databases 411, 413
        Excel workbooks 414
        general Office considerations 409–410
        PowerPoint presentations 420–421
        Word documents 423
    multiple Asian languages 404
    operating system support 443, 444–445, 447
    PowerPoint language settings 436–438
    Publisher language settings 441
    single-byte code pages 426
    troubleshooting 430–431
Aspscrpt.xls file 332, 563
assigning Office
    customizing using transform 170
    deployment scenarios 171–172
    elevated privileges 72, 75
    Group Policy
        and Active Directory 166–167
        guidelines for using 179
        setting 172–178
    installation conflicts 168
    installation requirements 163
    limitations of assigning 186
    preliminary steps 172
    to computers 167, 168
    to users 167, 168–169
    Windows IntelliMirror technologies 147
Audit.reg tool 557
Authenticode 296
author name, document privacy 304
AutomationSecurity method 311
Auto-Select character encoding 417–418, 529–532

B

background save policy 268
BackOffice Server Web site 20
Banyan Intelligent Messaging 463
Banyan network support 42
big fonts 453, 455
broken fonts add-in 430

C

CAL files, importing to Outlook 510–511
cascading style sheets for Help 346, 555
CD for distributing Office 149–151
certificates
    accepting as trusted 293
    ActiveX controls 296–297
    added to registry 294
    checking for revoked 282, 292
    checking macros for 309, 310–311
    digital signatures 292
    maintaining trusted sources 292–295
    Microsoft Corporation 293, 313–314
    opening signed macros 293
    Outlook messaging
        default certificate 536
        Digital ID 537
        getting certificate of sender 538–539
        getting personal certificate 520–521
        renewing certificate 539
        security model 535–537
        storing certificates 537
    preventing users from trusting 314
    requirements for trusted sources 292
    Selfcert.exe 291–292
    trusted by application vs. Internet Explorer 293
    trusting installed executables 293, 314–315
    VeriSign 297, 309
Cfgquiet.ini file 564
character entity references 415

CHM files
    See also custom Help
    compared to HTML Help 342–344
    deleting topics 341
    deploying 352
    enabling Help 350
    registering 351, 353
    topic file location for compiling 347
    updating content 345
ClearSign policy 283
clip art on Media Content CD 134
Clip Organizer policy template 263
Clipboard, multilingual text 429–430
CMW File Viewer 17, 552–553
Cnvpck16.exe 48
code pages
    Access forms and reports 411–412
    admin images for MUI Packs 378
    characters used in file names 428
    code points 425–427
    database compatibility 411–413
    displaying in font properties 455
    Excel workbook compatibility 414, 415
    fonts 452
    for Indic and Eastern European languages 447
    FrontPage compatibility 415, 445
    Help search language 446
    included in MUI Packs 452
    included in Office 452
    Internet Explorer language support 449
    Outlook
        message formats 447
        message header text 417, 418
        setting default code page 530–531
        setting for message 417
        using unsupported code page 445

Index

code pages *(continued)*
    printing text 428–429
    scripts 425–426
    sharing multilingual documents 425–428
    system locale setting 444
    Terminal Services and system code pages 533
    text copied using Clipboard 429–430
    Unicode conversion 427
    user interface language 445
    Word documents 422
code signing *See* macro security
Collaboration Data Objects 460
collaboration features
    encrypted documents 298
    new Office features 23–24
    Web sites based on SharePoint Team Services 21–22
command bars
    disabling commands and buttons 246, 252, 270–272
    disabling document password command 253
    disabling shortcut keys 246–247, 276–279
    item control IDs 272–275
    locking down user interface 251–252
    preventing changes to 252
Common.adm file 242, 317
communities on the Web 23
company name, specifying 79, 80
compressing files containing Unicode text 429
Conf.adm file 317
conferencing software in Outlook 512
Config.pol file 238, 250
configuration maintenance file
    applied if user settings reset to default 229
    based on MSI file used to install Office 198
    installation language policy 236
    specifying 199
    storing on installation point 80

converting file formats
    Access databases 51
    Excel, Word, PowerPoint documents 47
    installing converters 48–50
    Office 95 documents 47
    Office 97 documents 47
    Office Converter Pack 558
    Office upgrade considerations 47
Convpack.exe 48
Convpack.ini file 48
copying multilingual text 429–430
Corporate Error Reporting tool
    client configuration 215, 216, 221
    configuring server 216
    enabling tracking 222
    File Folder Tree 216–218
    installing 553
    internal crash-reporting server URL 221
    log files 222
    Office deployment settings 102
    overview 214–215
    registry entries
        DWFileTreeRoot 215, 219, 221
        DWNeverUpload 223
        DWNoExternalURL 222
        DWNoFileCollection 222
        DWNoSecondLevelCollection 222
        DWReporteeName 223
        DWTracking 222
        DWURLLaunch 223
        setting 221
    security considerations 220
    sending data to Microsoft 224
    sending data to server 220
    server requirements 216

Corporate Error Reporting tool *(continued)*
   system policies
      configuring 218–219, 221
      NoExternalURL 222
      NoFileCollection 222
      NoSecondLevelCollection 222
      policy template 237
      Tracking policy 222
      URLLaunch policy 223
crash.log 222
crashes *See* Corporate Error Reporting tool
cryptography policies, Outlook 282–287
custom applications
   deploying with Office 108
   removing 138, 207
custom error messages
   activating 336–338
   ASP file
      creating 331–332
      generating 332–333
      location on server 331
      sample script 333–335
      writing script 335–336
   CGI script 329
   creating and implementing 329
   disabling 339–340
   multilingual environments 330
   Office XP Setup 102
   overview 327–330
   sample and support files 563
   Web page with Help text 331

custom Help
   Answer Wizard
      adding questions 349–350
      AW file location 350, 351
      building AW file 350
      project file 348–349
      registry entry 352
      system policy 353
   converting WinHelp files 344–345
   creating topics 341–342, 344–345
   deploying 352–354
   enabling 350–351
   file formats 343–344
   Help on the Web
      extending 354–355
      feedback button label 356
      feedback dialog text 356–357
      feedback form 358–360
      redirecting feedback URL 357–358
      sample and support files 563
   ignoring individual topics 341
   Office on the Web, disabling 360
   overview 341–342, 347
   registry entries 352–354
   style sheets 346, 555
   topic file location 347
Custom Installation Wizard
   chained installations 131
   conflicting Setup properties 94
   creating transform containing OPS file 119
   customizing assigned software 170

Custom Installation Wizard (*continued*)
    customizing Outlook deployment
        creating PRF file 478
        default mail editor 484
        Exchange Server settings 473
        feature installation states 470
        overview 467–468
        setting registry entries 476
        specifying PRF file 472
        suppressing user prompts 481–483
        user profiles 469, 471–475
        user settings 468, 470, 475
    customizing published software 170
    customizing shortcuts
        adding shortcuts 110
        modifying default settings 109–110
        overview 109
        removing shortcuts 110
        shortcuts from previous versions 111–112
        Windows Installer shortcuts 110–111
    customizing user settings
        Outlook settings 124–125
        setting values 124
        ways of 114–116
    deploying custom files with Office 108–109
    deploying custom Help 352
    disabling command bar items 246
    embedding OPS files in transforms 226
    hiding Office features at Setup 105
    installing the wizard 554
    macro security settings
        ActiveX controls 295–296, 315–316
        applications you can configure 290
        implementing trusted sources 126, 294, 295
        location in registry 312–313
        preventing users from trusting certificates 314
        security level 291, 314–315
        trusting Microsoft certificates 313–314
    migrating user settings 119, 184–185
    option to remove applications 207
    overview 553–554
    replicating administrative image 80
    running Office Profile Wizard 226–228
    running programs during Setup 131
    setting default installation states 103–104
    setting registry values in transform 126–127
    Setup user interface options 94, 97
    specifying client installation path 102
    specifying organization name 79
    System Files Update options 101
    user language settings
        setting for MUI Pack 382
        setting for Office 381
        setting installation language 403
        Windows registry subkey 402
    what's new 10
Custom Maintenance Wizard
    changing user settings 128, 202–203
    CMW File Viewer 552–553
    configuration maintenance file 80
    customizing Help on the Web 356, 357, 358
    deploying custom Help 352
    disabling command bar items 246
    disabling Office on the Web 360
    installing 555
    installing Office in staged deployment 489–490
    language options 386–387, 431, 432, 433
    log file 200

Custom Maintenance Wizard *(continued)*
  macro security settings
    ActiveX controls 295–296, 315–316
    applications you can configure 290
    implementing trusted sources 295
    preventing user from trusting certificates 314
    security level 291, 314–315
    trusting Microsoft certificates 313–314
  Outlook
    installing after Office 491–493
    setting default mail editor 484
    updating profiles 523–525
  overview 554
  quiet mode 200
  running on users' computers 199
  setting installation states
    configuration maintenance file 198–199
    hidden applications 201–202
    Leave Unchanged setting 201
    parent/child features 201
    removing features 205–206
    states that cannot be reversed 200, 201, 202
    updating client 199–200
  what's new 13
custom templates, installing 108, 114
Customizable Alerts folder 563

D

database file formats 51
date format, Taiwanese 402

default computer profile
  creating 238
  macro security
    applications you can configure 294
    protecting trusted source list 294
    security setting registry nodes 313
  setting policies
    for all computers 244
    for specific applications 204
    opening policy template 238
default user profile
  creating 238
  macro security
    applications you can configure 294
    security setting registry nodes 313
  setting policies
    for all users 244
    for specific applications 204
    opening policy template 238
deleting MUI Packs 433
deleting programs *See* removing applications and features
deploying custom Help 352–354
deploying FrontPage Server Extensions 82–83
deploying Media Content 134
deploying MUI Packs
  administrative installation point 378–379
  advertising Office 148
  chained installations 133, 384, 391
  default installation states 68, 106, 107
  default Setup properties 67
  elevated privileges 73
  example scenarios
    different languages for groups 394–397
    multiple languages 391–394
    proofing tools 394–396
    single language 389–391

deploying MUI Packs *(continued)*
    including in hard-disk image 151
    installation language 403
    installation steps 376–377
    language deployment strategies
        administrative installation points 369
        centralized deployment 367–368
        chained deployment 369
        examples 365–367
        local deployment 368
        Office language configurations 363–365
        Systems Management Server 369
        Windows 2000 IntelliMirror 369
    language settings
        Custom Installation Wizard 381
        defining in Office transform 379–381
        enforcing on client 379
        modifying on client 386–387
        OPS files 380–381
        user interface language 404–406
        ways to define 379
    locale identifier 374–376
    Lpk.msi files 61
    Office packages 58
    overview 373
    preparing clients 377
    remotely using SMS 559–560
    running MUI Pack Wizard
        administrative installation point 387
        MUI Pack Setup 67
        Office XP Setup 61
    System Files Update
        copied to installation point 374
        multiple language versions 83
        Osp.msi file 378
    transforms
        chained installations 384
        creating 390, 392, 395
        installing fonts 383
        language settings 379–381
        Lpkwiz.msi file 383
        specifying in Setup.ini 391
        using MUI Pack transform 381–383
        using Office transform 379–381
    upgrading from previous versions 407–408
    user input for languages to install 383
    using IntelliMirror 369, 388
    using SMS 369, 388
    with Office deployment 384–385, 391–394
    with Office installed 385–386
deploying Office XP
    administrative installation point
        advantages of using 77–78
        configuration maintenance file 80
        creating 78–79
        file locations 79
        read access for users 79
        replicating 80
        Setup.exe location 79
        single vs. multiple 369
    advertising software *See* advertising Office
    assigning software *See* assigning Office
    chained installations
        Custom Installation Wizard 131
        elevated installation 132
        IntelliMirror software installation 132
        restarting computer 132
    custom CD 149–151
    customization methods 83–84
    hard-disk image 151–154, 165
    installation language setting 403

Index

deploying Office XP *(continued)*
    Internet Explorer *See* Internet Explorer
    laptop users 79
    MSDE 2000 80–81
    Office Resource Kit 83
    Office XP Web Components 81–82
    Outlook *See* deploying Outlook 2002
    packages *See* packages
    profile settings file *See* OPS files
    publishing applications *See* publishing Office
    Remote OS Installation 154–155
    repairing installations 195–197
    running programs at Office installation 131
    service releases *See* deploying service releases
    transforms *See* transforms
    using IntelliMirror *See* IntelliMirror software installation
    using Setup *See* Setup (Office XP)
    using SMS 155–156, 559–560
    ways of 141
    Windows 2000 advantages 163, 165
    Windows NT environment *See* Windows NT 4.0
deploying Office XP Web Components 81–82
deploying Outlook 2002
    after Office XP
        deployment considerations 465, 491
        stand-alone version 493–496
        using installation options 491–493
    before Office XP
        deployment considerations 464, 485
        stand-alone version 486–488
        using installation options 489–490
    Custom Installation Wizard features 467–468

deployment planning
    Collaboration Data Objects 460
    multiple users on computer 460
    profiles 461
    remote or roaming users 460
    staged deployments 466, 485, 491
    Terminal Services 460–461
    user settings 461
    when to install 461, 463
Exchange Server connections 472–473
feature installation states 468, 470
full security functionality 547–548
Internet Explorer version 468, 504
migrating Personal Address Book 475
PRF files
    creating 478, 525
    editing entries 478–479
    from previous versions 477
    overview 472, 477
    saving profile settings in 474
    specifying file to apply 472
    updating user profiles 480, 525
quiet installation 481–484
read receipt response setting 482
registry settings 476
reverting to previous installation 522
Security Features Administrative Package 559
settings file name 486
staged deployments 485
synchronizing folder names 476
Terminal Services environments 484–485

Index

deploying Outlook 2002 *(continued)*
    upgrade considerations
        conferencing software 512
        Electronic Forms Designer 505
        e-mail services 504
        Exchange Client 505–506
        fax support 505
        installing Outlook before Office 489
        MAPI profiles 504
        Microsoft Mail 506–509
        offline folders 512
        overview 503
        Schedule + 509–511
        security file (EPF file) 520–521
        stationery 512
    upgrade considerations
        user settings 504
        user signatures 512
    user profiles
        default 471–472, 481
        Exchange Server settings 472–473
        initial profile 471
        mail accounts 473–475
        updating 523
        ways to configure 469
    user settings
        capturing with Office Profile Wizard 468
        migrating current 470
        resolving conflicting values 116
        setting default 475
        setting in transform 124–125
        setting using Custom Installation Wizard 468
        specifying profile settings file 470
        ways to set 468–469
    with Office XP 463
deploying Proofing Tools
    administrative installation point 398–399
    default feature installation states 107
    disk space requirements 398
    language deployment strategies
        administrative installation points 369
        centralized deployment 367–368
        chained deployment 369
        examples 365–367
        local deployment 368
        Office language configurations 363–365
    on single computer from CD 398
    overview 364, 398
    setting installation states 398
    Setup languages 364
    specifying languages to install 399
    Systems Management Server 369
    transform 398–399
    user interface language settings 404–406
    Windows 2000 IntelliMirror 369
    with MUI Pack using transform 382
    with Office deployment 399–401
deploying service releases
    administrative installation point 157–159
    administrative updates 156
    installing on client
        administrative updates 159–161
        customizing installation 160
        stand-alone computers 161–162
        synchronizing clients 160
        using IntelliMirror 160
    Software Installation snap-in 181
    staged deployments 157
    updating stand-alone computers 156
    upgrade decision 156
deploying SharePoint Team Services 22, 82–83
deploying SQL Server 2000 Desktop Engine 80–81

Detect and Repair command 196
Developer edition system requirements 36–39
dialog boxes
    disabling dialog box options 253
    multilingual 449
Digital OpenVMS networks 43
Digital Pathworks networks 43
digital signatures
    See also certificates
    ActiveX controls 296–297
    opening signed macros 293
    trusted sources 292–293
    user signatures 304
DisableContinueEncryption policy 286
disk space requirements
    administrative installation point share 78
    Office XP Developer 38
    Office XP Professional 33
    Office XP Small Business 31
    Office XP Standard 29
    Professional with FrontPage 35
    Proofing Tools 398
    Windows registry 29
documents
    collaboration features
        encrypted documents 298
        Web sites based on SharePoint Team Services 21–22
        what's new 23–24
    converting *See* converting file formats
    multilingual *See* languages, multilingual documents
    opening on Web 255

passwords
    Access 298
    Excel workbooks 298–301
    hard-coding 298
    overview 297–298
    PowerPoint presentations 303
    preventing users from applying 251, 253
    setting options 303–304
    Word documents 301–302
privacy options 304
security features 289–290
DW.exe *See* Corporate Error Reporting tool
DWFileTreeRoot registry entry
    File Folder Tree 215
    running DW.exe 221
    specifying server 219–220
DWNeverUpload registry entry 223
DWNoExternalURL registry entry 222
DWNoFileCollection registry entry 222
DWNoSecondLevelCollection registry entry 222
DWReporteeName registry entry 223
DWTracking registry entry 222
DWURLLaunch registry entry 223

E

Electronic Forms Designer 505, 515
e-mail software requirements 29
encrypting document files *See* file encryption
encrypting mail *See* Outlook, secure messaging
End User License Agreement, displaying 557
Enterprise edition system requirements 39–40
environment variables 230, 264
environment variables in system policies 247–248
EPF file, upgrading 520–521

error messages
    custom *See* custom error messages
    sample and support files 563
Errormsg.xls file 329, 563
Excel
    file formats
        converting from previous versions 47
        installing converters 48–50
        Office 95 documents 47
        Office 97 documents 47
    languages
        language settings 435
        version compatibility 409, 414–415
    macro virus protection
        See also macro security
        Excel 4 macros 311–312
        overview 308–308
        security levels 291, 309–310
        trusted sources 293
        types of macros 309
    securing workbooks
        encryption routines 299
        file protection levels 298
        passwords 297–301
        protecting specific elements 299–300
        read-only recommended 298
    Unicode characters in file names 428
Excel10.adm file
    environment variables 265
    policy settings 257
    templates included in Resource Kit 241
Exchange Client
    sharing data with Outlook 512–516
    upgrading security file (EPF file) 520–521
    upgrading to Outlook 505–506
Exchange Global Address Book, storing certificates in 536, 538

Exchange Key Management Server
    enrolling in security 520
    publishing certificates in address book 538
    using certificates 536
    version support 537
Exchange Server
    configuring user connections 472–473
    migrating from Microsoft Mail 509
Exchange Server Advanced Security 520, 538
extended characters registry entry 428
extending Help *See* custom Help

F

fax support in Outlook 505
feature states *See* installation states
federal release features 282
file encryption
    Access files 298
    document collaboration 298
    document password required 297
    Excel workbooks 299
    overview 297–298
    PowerPoint presentations 303
    setting options 303–304
    Word documents 301
file format converters
    Access databases 51
    Excel, Word, PowerPoint 47
    installing converters 48–50
    Office 95 documents 47
    Office 97 documents 47
    Office Converter Pack 558
    Outlook 51
    upgrading applications 47
Filelist.xls file 59, 564

files
- converting *See* converting file formats
- data files *See* documents
- encrypting *See* file encryption
- file size and Unicode text 429
- language version compatibility *See* languages
- list of all Office files (Filelist.xls) 564
- log *See* log files
- macro viruses *See* macro security
- supplemental documentation 562–565
- Unicode characters in file names 428
- updating in System folder 59
- updating system *See* System File Upgrade

FIPSMode policy 285
folder for installing Office 102
folder locations for roaming users 498–499
fonts
- font properties extension 455
- installing MUI Pack *See* deploying MUI Packs
- international
  - big fonts 453, 455
  - default user interface font 453
  - included with Office 451–452
  - installing 453–455
  - printing 428–429, 455–456
  - troubleshooting 430–431
  - TrueType fonts 455–456
  - Unicode font 454
- TrueType 430

ForceSecurityLabel policy 284
Formats.doc 564
Fp10.adm file 241, 258

FrontPage
- character entity references 415
- language support
  - language settings 440
  - unsupported code page 445
  - version compatibility 409, 415–416
- macros, types of 309
- paper size for printing documents 455

FrontPage Server Extensions
- localized server messages 450
- operating system support 82
- system requirements 35
- Unicode support 449

FTP Network Access Suite 3.0 support 43

G

Gal10.adm file 241, 263
Global Address Book, storing certificates 536, 538
glyphs, code page scripts 426
Gpedit.msc file 239
grammar checking tools 398
graphics filters 47–50, 558
Group Policy
- assigning or publishing Office
  - guidelines 179
  - overview 165–167
  - setting policies 172–178
  - starting Software Installation snap-in 172
- deploying product upgrades 181–183
- deploying service releases 181
- distributing policy file 250
- elevated installation privileges policy 74
- policy configurations 240
- policy states 243

Group Policy *(continued)*
    policy templates
        loading 239–240
        overview 241–242
        Windows 2000 template 239
    Registry.pol files 244
    setting policies 244, 245
    shared Office policies 242
    starting 239
    templates in Office Resource Kit 241
    tools for setting policies 241
    unmanaged Office installations 179
    upgrading Office 2000 183–185

H

hard-disk image 151–154, 165
hardware requirements *See* system requirements
Hashctl.dll file 559
Help
    custom *See* custom Help
    display language
        Answer Wizard language 446
        configuring for deployment 404–406
        English-only requirements 445
        operating system support 443–445
        system locale setting 444
        system policies 405–406
        topic content 446
        user interface 446
Help on the Web
    customizing link *See* Answer Wizard
    disabling access 254–255, 360
    system policy 356, 357
Help on the Web folder 563–564
Hewlett Packard OpenMail 463

hidden applications and features
    installing by user 201
    Not Available, Hidden, Locked installation state 200, 205
    preventing user from installing 201, 205–206
    unhiding 202
Hide installation state 104–105, 202
High encryption 546
hits.log file 222
HTML character entity references 415
HTML documents, saving in Unicode 449
HTML formatting, copying 429–430
HTML Help Workshop
    converting WinHelp files 344–345
    creating Help topics 344–345
    installing 555
    overview 341–342
    style sheets 346, 555
Hyperlink command, disabling 246, 247

I

IBM network support 43
ideographic scripts 426
IE5Feats.xls file 65, 565
IME *See* Input Method Editors
importing MMF files in Outlook 507–508
importing Schedule+ data in Outlook 510–511
Indic languages
    code page 447
    installing fonts 454
    operating system support 443
input locale
    FrontPage language settings 440
    list of locale identifiers 374–376
    Publisher language settings 442
    Windows registry entry 402

Input Method Editors
- included in MUI Pack 447
- installed by default 58
- Internet Explorer compatibility 451
- Office XP Proofing Tools 364, 447
- upgrading 407–408
- Web Downloadable Input Method Editor 408

installation language
- Access 439
- changing 431, 432
- enforcing 432
- Excel 435
- macro compatibility 404
- Office deployment 403
- Office language settings 434
- Outlook 439
- overview 402
- PowerPoint 436–438
- Publisher 441
- registry entry 431, 433
- Word 434

installation states
- CMW file for changing 198–199
- default 103, 106–108
- disabling Installed on First Use 105–106
- disabling Run from Network 105–106
- hiding features in Setup 104–105, 201–202
- install-on-demand, Windows NT 190–192
- interactive Setup 103
- irreversible 200, 201, 202
- MSI file to use 198

MUI Packs 68
- parent/child feature or application 104, 201
- registry entries for install on demand 74
- removing features or applications 205–206
- setting during Custom installation (Setup) 145
- setting for assigned or published software 170
- setting using Custom Installation Wizard 103–104
- Terminal Services considerations 106, 108
- updating on client 199–200
- ways to set 197–198

Installed on First Use installation state
- advertising Office 190
- child feature state 201
- disabling 105–106, 200, 201
- enabling under Windows NT 192
- Office deployment settings 104

installing features on demand 72, 74
installing hidden applications 201
installing international fonts 453–455
installing Internet Explorer
- administrative installation point 83
- custom installation using transform 92
- default installation 27
- minimum installation 449
- Office Setup process 65–67

installing MSDE 80
installing Office *See* deploying Office XP
installing Office Converter Pack 48
installing Office Resource Kit tools
- all tools 83
- Answer Wizard Builder 552
- CMW File Viewer 552–553
- Corporate Error Reporting tool 553
- Custom Installation Wizard 553–554
- Custom Maintenance Wizard 555

installing Office Resource Kit tools *(continued)*
    HTML Help Workshop 555
    MST File Viewer 556
    OEM Tools 556–557
    OPS File Viewer 558
    Outlook Security Features Administrative Package 559
    PowerPoint Viewer 560
    Profile Wizard 560–561
    Removal Wizard 561
    Setup INI Customization Wizard 562
    SMS package definition files 559–560
    supplemental tools 8
    System Policy Editor 565–566
    tools installed by default 6
installing System Files Update 64–65
installing Windows Desktop Update 192
installing Windows Installer 58
installing Windows multilingual support 448
InstallLanguage registry entry 402–403, 431, 433
Instlr11.adm file
    policy settings 263
    System Policy Editor 242
    templates included in Resource Kit 241
Instmsi.exe file 56, 70
Instmsiw.exe file 56, 70
IntelliMirror software installation
    Active Directory directory service 165–167
    assigning Office *See* assigning Office
    chained installations 132
    deploying languages 369, 388
    deploying product upgrades 181–183
    deploying service releases 160, 181
    Group Policy options 165–167
    installing and maintaining Office 147
    limitations 186
    Office deployment requirements 163
    Office deployment scenarios 171–172
    overview 164–165
    publishing Office *See* publishing Office
    SQL Server 2000 Desktop Engine 81
    unmanaged Office installations 179–181
    upgrading Office 2000 183–185
    ways to deploy Office 167–168
International Information folder 564
Internet
    opening documents on 255
    Web *See* Web pages, *See* Web pages
Internet Explorer
    administrative installation point 83
    certificate revocation check 292
    customizing by using transform 92
    default installation 27
    determining installed version 60–61
    e-mail encryption strength support 547
    international fonts 451
    list of trusted sources 293
    minimum installation 449
    Office requirements 27–28
    Office Setup installation process 65–67
    Office software dependencies 65
    Outlook Folder Home Pages security zone 545–546
    Outlook requirements 468, 504
    security setting inheritance 309
    Unicode support 449
    user interface language dependencies 449
    UTF-8 URL encoding 450
    Windows Desktop Update included 191
    Windows NT version 190, 191
Intlimit.xls file 371, 445, 564

J *No Entries*

K

key codes 278–281
keyboard layout 448
keyboard shortcuts
    disabling 246–247, 253, 276–278
    key codes 278–281
keypath resources, missing or corrupt 196
Keypath.xls file 196

L

LangTuneUp registry entry 403–404
language policies
    enforcing installation language 236
    optimizing language configuration 236
    user interface defaults 405–406
    user locale 404
languages
    advertising 75
    components installed by default 58–59
    customizable settings 401
    default language settings 401
    deployment strategies
        administrative installation points 369
        centralized deployment 367–368
        chained deployment 369
        examples 365–367
        local deployment 368
        MUI Packs 364–365
        Office language configurations 363–365
        Proofing Tools 364
        Systems Management Server 369
        Windows 2000 IntelliMirror 369

editing language
    enabling 431–432
    Excel 438
    FrontPage 440
    Office language settings 434
    Outlook 439
    Publisher 441
    Word 435
FrontPage considerations 445
Input Method Editors 447, 451
installation language
    changing 431, 432
    enforcing 432
    macro compatibility 404
    Office deployment 403
    overview 402
    registry entry 431, 433
installing MUI Packs *See* deploying MUI Packs
installing Proofing Tools *See* deploying Proofing Tools
international fonts
    big fonts 453, 455
    included with Office 451–452
    installing 453–455
    TrueType fonts 455–456
keyboard layout 448
language packs *See* MUI Packs
language settings
    Access 439
    configuring 404–406
    Excel 435
    FrontPage 440
    Outlook 439
    overview 433
    PowerPoint 436–438
    Publisher 441–442
    Word 434–435

Languages *(continued)*
    localized Office *See* localized versions of Office
    localized server messages 450
    multilingual documents
        copying text 429–430
        displaying 446–447
        displaying Unicode text 428
        editing 447
        file size and Unicode text 429
        font support 451
        page size 455
        printing 428–429, 455–456
        Proofing Tool features 364
        saving in Unicode 449
        scaling to paper size 455
        sharing across languages 425–427
        troubleshooting 430–431
        Unicode characters in file names 428
        Unicode features 427
    multilingual URLs 450
    multilingual Web pages 449–450
    operating system support
        document language 446–447
        installing in Windows 98 or Me 448
        user interface language 443–445
    Outlook
        code page support 445
        folder names 476
        language settings 439
        message encoding 530–531
        message format 447
        multilingual messages 416–417
    preventing changes to settings 404
    registry entries 402
    settings based on user locale 403–404
    System Files Update language 83

    Unicode format *See* Unicode
    user interface language
        default font 453
        dialog boxes 449
        English-only requirements 445
        FrontPage templates 440
        Internet Explorer dependencies 449
        limitations 371
        online Help 446
        operating system 443–445
        PowerPoint 439, 441
        system code page support 445
        system locale setting 444
        system policies 405–406
    user profiles 128, 370
    version compatibility
        Access databases 410–413
        Asian languages 409
        Excel workbooks 414–415
        FrontPage documents 415–416
        language version considerations 409
        PowerPoint presentations 419–421
        Publisher files 421
        Unicode 409
        Word documents 422–424
    Web browser considerations 449
LANtastic network support 44
LCIDs (locale identifiers)
    language settings based on locale 403–404
    list of 374–376
    Windows registry entry 402
LDAP directory service 538
licensing for Terminal Services 18
licensing programs for Office 18
locale identifiers *See* LCIDs
localized server messages 451

localized versions of Office
- benefits and drawbacks 371–372
- installing 370
- language configuration scenarios 366
- language resources in Office 363
- multilingual Office scenarios 366
- Proofing Tools compatibility 364
- user profile compatibility 370
- using with MUI Pack 365
- version compatibility
  - Access databases 410–413
  - Asian languages 409
  - considerations 409–410
  - Excel workbooks 414–415
  - FrontPage documents 415–416
  - PowerPoint presentations 419–421
  - Publisher files 421
  - Word documents 422–424
- vs. using MUI Packs 370

locking Office features during Setup 104–105

locking Windows registry
- effect on Outlook 308
- security considerations 306
- Terminal Services 308
- unlocking 485
- using regedt32.exe 307

log files
- Office Setup 69
- Removal Wizard 141
- Setup.ini settings 56
- Windows Installer 69, 99–101

Lotus cc Mail accounts, removing 474
Low encryption 546
Lpk.msi file 61, 67, 85, 374
LPK2002.sms file 559

Lpksetup.exe
- administrative installation points 67
- administrative mode 378
- MUI Pack components 374
- running 378

Lpkwiz.msi file 58, 61, 68

M

macro security
- ActiveX *See* ActiveX controls
- anti-virus software 309
- applications you can configure 290, 294
- default security level 291
- differences between applications 308
- elevated privileges security risk 75
- Excel 4 macros 311–312
- inherited Internet Explorer settings 309
- opening signed macros 293
- Outlook Folder Home Pages 545–546
- overview 290–291
- preventing user from trusting certificates 314
- revoked certificates 292
- Selfcert.exe certificates 291–292
- setting security level
  - application Security key 314–315
  - AutomationSecurity method 311
  - overview 291
  - security level descriptions 309–310
  - system policies 294, 312–316
  - transform 125
- trusting executables *See* trusted sources

macros
- Excel 4 311–312
- installation language compatibility 404
- previous localized versions of Word 424
- types of 309

Index

Makecert.exe 291
managed state 179–181
mapping network drives, restricting 320
Media Content 134
memory requirements
    Developer edition 37
    Office XP Professional 32–33
    Office XP Small Business 30–31
    Office XP Standard 28
    Professional with FrontPage 35
menu bars
    controlling MRU file list 269–270, 321
    disabling commands
        predefined commands 270–272
        standard commands 252
        system policies 246
    disabling document password command 253
    disabling shortcut keys 246–247, 276–279
    display language *See* languages
    getting list of all Word commands 281
    item control IDs 272–275
    locking down user interface 251–252
    preventing changes to 252
messages
    error *See* custom error messages
    localized server messages 450
    logging Setup messages 99–101
    suppressing in Office XP Setup 95
    suppressing in Outlook Setup 481–483
Microsoft BackOffice Server Web site 20
Microsoft Data Engine (MSDE) 58, 80
Microsoft Exchange Client
    sharing data with Outlook 512–516
    upgrading security file (EPF file) 520–521
    upgrading to Outlook 505–506
Microsoft Exchange Global Address Book, storing certificates 536, 538

Microsoft Exchange Key Management Server
    enrolling in security 520
    publishing certificates in address book 538
    using certificates 536
    version support 537
Microsoft Exchange Server
    configuring user connections 472–473
    migrating from Microsoft Mail 509
Microsoft Exchange Server Advanced Security 520, 538
Microsoft Mail
    removing account from profile 474
    upgrading to Outlook 506–509
Microsoft NetMeeting 512
Microsoft Office Converter Pack 558
Microsoft Office XP Media Content 134
Microsoft Product Support Services Web site 19
Microsoft Project, sharing data with Outlook 519
Microsoft Schedule + 509–511, 516–518
Microsoft SQL Server 2000 Desktop Engine (MSDE 2000) 80–81
Microsoft Systems Management Server
    deploying MUI Packs 388
    installing Office on client 155–156
    installing package definition files 559–560
Microsoft TechNet Web site 20
Microsoft Terminal Services *See* Terminal Services
Microsoft Volume Licensing program 18
Microsoft Windows NT Server NetShow Services 512
Microsoft Windows Web site 20
MMF files, importing in Outlook 507–508
MRU file list 269–270, 321
MSDE 2000, installing 80–81
MSI files *See* packages
Msi.dll file 57
Msiexec.exe file 57, 63, 64

MST File Viewer tool 17, 556
MST files *See* transforms
MUI Pack Wizard
    installing 61
    MUI Pack components 374
    Office administrative image 68
    running manually 383, 387
MUI Packs
    advertising 75
    code pages included 452
    compatibility with localized Office 364, 365
    components 374
    deployment strategies
        administrative installation points 369
        centralized deployment 367–368
        coordinating with Office deployment 369
        installing using SMS 369
        local deployment 368
    fonts included 451–452
    Input Method Editors provided 447
    installing *See* deploying MUI Packs, *See* deploying MUI Packs
    modifying client language settings 386–387
    multilingual Office scenarios 366
    overview 364–365
    removing 433
    Setup.ini file properties 384–385
    System Files Update 369
    using with localized Office 365
    vs. localized Office 370, 371–372
    vs. Office XP Proofing Tools 364, 395
Multilpk.xls file 564

My Computer
    hiding drives 318–319
    removing Places Bar 322
My Network Places
    hiding drives 318–319
    preventing drive mapping 320
    removing Entire Network 319
    removing Places Bar 322

N

national language support files 410
NeedEncryptionString policy 287
NetMeeting 512
Netscape Navigator Unicode support 449
NetShow Services 512
network clients
    operating systems supported 41–44
    Terminal Services requirements 46
network connections, user restrictions 320
network servers
    administrative installation points 41
    operating system support 41–44
    Terminal Services requirements 45–46
network share for roaming folders 498
Newprof.exe tool 477
Normal.dot language 402, 403, 431
Not Available installation state 104, 205
Not Available, Hidden, Locked installation state
    Office deployment settings 104
    preventing feature installation 105, 201, 205
    ways to set 200
Novell network support 42
Ntconfig.pol file 238, 250

O

Oclean.dll file 135, 210, 213
Oclncore.opc file
 custom shortcut clean-up 113–112
 directory location 208, 213
 file structure 210–212
 loading 209
 modifying 212
 overview 209
 Removal Wizard component files 135
Oclncust.opc file
 custom removal routines 141
 directory location 208, 213
 file structure 210–212
 loading 209
 modifying 212–213
 overview 209
Oclnintl.opc file
 directory location 210
 loading 209
 Removal Wizard components 135
OEM tools 556–557
Off2002.sms file 559
Offcln.exe file 135, 210, 213
Office 2000 managed installations 183–185
Office 2000 MultiLanguage Pack 407
Office Converter Pack 48–50, 558
Office Custom Installation Wizard *See* Custom Installation Wizard
Office Custom Maintenance Wizard *See* Custom Maintenance Wizard
Office Developer Web site 20
Office documents *See* documents
Office Information folder 564–565
Office on the Web
 disabling access 254–255, 360
 Office solutions and support sites 19–20

Office Profile Wizard
 adding OPS file to transform 226
 applying user settings 204, 226–228
 capturing user settings 226
 conflicting user settings 116
 creating OPS file 118–119, 229–230
 customizing 123–124
 excluded Outlook settings 527
 implementing trusted sources 293, 294–295
 INI file descriptions 225
 installing 561
 multilingual user profiles 370
 overview 117, 225, 560
 removing files and registry settings 214
 resetting user settings to defaults 226, 228–229
 running after Office deployment 227
 running after Office is installed 123
 running during Office Setup 119–122
 Save My Settings Wizard 14, 225
 staged deployments 231
 starting 225
 user information not captured 117–118
 ways to customize user settings 114–116
 what's new 14
Office Sites Worldwide Web site 20
Office Tools on the Web
 application object model misuse 324
 bad code posted on site 325
 bad frame on a page 325
 data exchange privacy 324
 denial of service attacks 324–325
 security considerations 323, 325
 VBA removed from Office 305
 Web portal redirection 323, 325

Office XP
    deploying *See* deploying Office XP
    licensing 18
    requirements *See* system requirements
    service releases *See* deploying service releases
Office XP Media Content 134
Office XP Resource Kit
    installing *See* installing Office Resource Kit tools
    list of tools 6–8
    Ork.msi package 59
    supplemental documentation 562–565
    Web site 19
    what's new
        Answer Wizard Builder 17
        Corporate Error Reporting 14
        Custom Installation Wizard 10
        Custom Maintenance Wizard 13
        Office Profile Wizard 14
        Removal Wizard 16
        Save My Settings Wizard 14
        Setup INI Customization Wizard 15
        Setup.exe 15
        System Policy Editor 17
        tools for troubleshooting 17
        Windows Installer 16
Office XP Web Components
    deploying 81–82
    MSI file 58
Office10.adm file
    Corporate Error Reporting tool settings 237
    environment variables 253, 264
    overview 242
    setting descriptions 256
    templates included in Resource Kit 241
    Windows registry node 244

Office10.css file 346, 555
offline folder files, upgrading 512
online communities 23
online Help *See* Help
online meetings 512
OPC files
    customizing for Removal Wizard 141
    Office Setup process 138
    running Removal Wizard 213
    used with Removal Wizard and Setup 135
Opc.doc file 112, 564
operating systems supported
    network servers and clients 41–44
    runtime applications 37
    Windows versions 27, 28
OPS File Viewer tool 17, 558
OPS files
    adding to transform 118, 119, 226, 227
    applying settings 204, 226–228
    capturing language settings 405
    configuring client for crash reporting 216, 221
    configuring user settings 526–528
    conflicting user settings 116
    creating 118–119, 229–230
    customizing Outlook deployment 487
    excluding settings for staged deployments 231
    hard-disk image for distributing Office 152
    INI section descriptions 231–233
    installation language compatibility 128
    language settings 380–381
    localized Office version compatibility 370
    migrated user settings 119
    operating system compatibility 128
    Outlook deployment 470

OPS files *(continued)*
    Outlook user settings 468, 469
    resetting user settings to defaults 226, 228–229
    running Profile Wizard at Setup 119–122
    setting security options 125–126
    uninstalled application settings in registry 117
    user information not captured 117–118
    user interface language settings 404
    ways to customize user settings 114–116

OPW10adm.ini file
    editing 123
    excluding settings 231
    generic profile settings file 229
    INI section descriptions 231–233
    Office Profile Wizard INI files 225
    removing registry settings 214

OPW10usr.ini file
    excluding settings 231
    INI section descriptions 231–233
    Office Profile Wizard INI files 225

organization name, specifying 79, 80
Ork.msi file 58
Osp.msi file
    called by Setup 64
    MUI Pack components 374
    packages included with Office 58
    System Files Update components 59
    ways to customize 85

OST files, upgrading Outlook 512

Outlk10.adm file
    cryptography policies 282–287
    policies settings 258–259
    templates included in Resource Kit 241

Outlook
    configuring user settings 526–529
    deploying *See* deploying Outlook
    enrollment Web page 544
    Exchange Client on same computer 506
    exchanging data
        Exchange Client 512–516
        Microsoft Project 519
        previous versions of Outlook 511–512
        Schedule + 516–518
    Folder Home Page security zone 545–546
    language support
        See also languages
        code page support 445
        enabling multilingual messages 416–417
        folder names 476
        language settings 439
        message format 447
    macro virus protection
        See also macro security
        available security levels 309–310
        overview 308–309
        setting security level 291
        setting trusted sources 293
        types of macros 309
    mail servers supported 463
    message delivery location 524
    message encoding
        Auto-Select 417–418, 529–532
        character encoding setting 417–418
        setting default 530–531
        supported encodings 531
    migrating to Exchange Server 509
    paper size for printing messages 455
    removing 522

Outlook *(continued)*
   roaming users
      configuration considerations 497
      Digital ID 537
      folder locations 498–499
      setting options 498
      user profiles 499–501
      Windows 2000 user profiles 500
      Windows NT user profiles 499–500
   secure messaging
      certificates, getting 520–521
      cryptography policies 282–287
      digital certificates 536, 537–539
      Digital ID 536
      Digital Signature Key lengths 547
      encryption key strengths 546–547
      Exchange Key Management Server 536, 537
      full security functionality 547–548
      getting certificate of sender 538–539
      initial security configuration 520–521
      managing security components 537
      Outlook security model 535–537
      reading encrypted messages 547–548
      registry settings 539–545
      roaming users 537
      RSA Labs Public Key Cryptography Standard 537
      secure receipt requests 536
      Security Features Administrative Package 559
      security labels 536
      upgrading security file 520
   Terminal Services considerations 308
   Unicode support 417, 532–533
   updating profiles 523–525
   upgrading file formats 47, 51
   WordMail editor 484, 515
Outlook Today ActiveX control 545
OutlookSecurity.oft file 559
Owc10.msi file 59, 81
Ows.msi file 59

P

package definition files (SMS) 559–560
packages
   advertising Office 148
   assigning Office 147
   chaining
      chained package defaults 127–128
      elevated installations 132
      Media Content packages 134
      MUI Packs 133, 384–386
      overview 129
      Proofing Tools package 399–401
      setting up in Setup.ini 67, 93, 129–131
   customizable 85
   default Setup property values 86
   FrontPage Server Extensions package 82
   included with Office 58
   installing on client 63
   installing Windows Desktop Update 192
   multiple 93
   new file format 12
   not included in Office core package 58
   Office core package 58, 67
   Office service releases 156, 157
   product upgrades 181, 183
   publishing Office 147
   setting values using transform 91
   SharePoint Team Services package 82
   specifying in Setup.ini 56
   System Files Update package 59
   Windows Installer files 57
paper size for printing 455

Index

passwords
    Access databases 298
    command changes in Office XP 303–304
    Digital ID in Outlook 520–521
    Excel workbooks 298–301
    hard-coding 298
overview 297–298
    PowerPoint presentations 303
    preventing users from applying 251, 253
    Word documents 301–302
permissions
    access to system policies 237
    for installing Office 72
    Windows registry
        security considerations 306
        set by Terminal Services 308
        setting permissions 307
Personal Address Book, migrating 475, 499
Policies subkey, locking 237, 248
Posredir.inc file 563
PowerPoint
    controlling MRU file list 269–270
    file formats
        converting from previous versions 47
        installing converters 48–50
        Office 95 documents 47
        Office 97 documents 47
    language settings 436–438
    language version compatibility
        backward compatibility 420–421
        files from previous versions 419–420
        general Office considerations 409
        sharing presentations 419

macro virus protection
    See also macro security
    available security levels 309–310
    overview 308–309
    setting security level 291
    setting trusted sources 293
    types of macros 309
paper size for printing documents 455
protecting presentations
    file encryption routines 303
    file protection levels 303
    forgotten passwords 303
    passwords 297–298, 303
    read-only recommended 303
PowerPoint Viewer 560
Ppt10.adm file
    environment variables 253, 266
    policies settings 260
    templates included in Resource Kit 241
PRF files
    creating 478, 525
    editing entries 478–479
    from previous versions 477
    overview 472, 477
    saving profile settings in 474
    specifying file to apply 472
    updating user profiles 480, 523, 525
printing documents 428–429, 455–456
private properties in Setup 68
Pro.msi file 58
Product Support Services Web site 19
Professional edition of Office
    MSI file 58
    system requirements 32–34, 39
Professional with FrontPage edition
    MSI file 58
    system requirements 34–36, 39

Microsoft Office XP Resource Kit   601

Index

profile settings files *See* OPS files
Profile Wizard *See* Office Profile Wizard
Project, sharing data with Outlook 519
PromoteErrorsAsWarnings policy 284
proofing tools (MUI Pack)
    adding to MUI Pack transform 395
    compatibility with localized Office 364
    installation example 394–396
    vs. Office XP Proofing Tools product 395
Proofing Tools (Office XP Proofing Tools)
    adding package to Setup settings file 399–400
    compatibility with localized Office 364
    deploying *See* deploying Proofing Tools
    disk space requirements 364, 398
    multilingual Office scenarios 366
    overview 364
    specifying transform in Setup 399
    vs. MUI Pack proofing tools 395
Proplus.msi file 58, 85
protecting documents
    Excel workbooks 298–301
    overview 297–298
    password option locations 303–304
    personal information privacy 304
    PowerPoint presentations 303
    Word documents 301–302, 306
PST file formats 51
Pub10.adm file
    environment variables 254, 267
    policies settings 261
    templates included in Resource Kit 241
public folders and Exchange Client 514
public properties in Setup 68

Publisher
    language settings 441–442
    language version compatibility 409, 421
    paper size for printing documents 455
    setting macro security level 291
    types of macros 309
publishing Office
    customizing using transform 170
    deployment scenarios 171–172
    elevated privileges 72, 75
    Group Policy and Active Directory structures 166–167
    guidelines for using Group Policy 179
    installation requirements 163
    installing published software on client 169–170
    overview 147
    preliminary steps 172
    setting Group Policy 172–178
PublishToGALDisabled policy 285

Q

QFE (quick fix engineering) fixes 181

R

record locking in shared Access databases 43, 44
regional language settings *See* languages
Registry Editor 307
registry, Windows *See* Windows registry
Registry.pol file 244, 250
Regkey.xls file 564
reinstalling applications 195–197
Remote OS Installation 154–155, 165

Removal Wizard
- command-line options 139–140, 208–209
- component files 135
- customizing in OPC file 138
- customizing in transform 138
- error reporting 209
- error-checking 140
- executables 210
- files to remove detected by Setup 136–137
- installing 561
- log file 208
- log file for OPC file testing 141
- modes 207
- overview 135, 206–207
- removing Small Business Tools 137
- running
    - as stand-alone 138–139
    - from OPC file 141, 213
    - using shortcut or batch file 213
    - with Office Setup 135
- template files
    - administrative installation point 213
    - file descriptions 209–210
    - loading 209
    - modifying 212–213
    - structure 210–212
- ways to customize 137
- what's new 16

removing applications and features
- Add/Remove Programs 214
- effect on customized user settings 200
- installation state options 202–206
- MUI Packs 433
- Office 2000 MultiLanguage Pack 407
- Outlook 522
- preventing reinstallation 205
- tools for 205
- using Office Profile Wizard 214
- using Removal Wizard *See* Removal Wizard
- Visual Basic for Applications 305–306

renewing digital certificates 539
repairing applications 195–197
reporting crashes *See* Corporate Error Reporting tool
RequestSecureReceipt policy 283
Reset010.ini file 226, 228
resolving conflicting user settings 116
RespondToReceiptRequests policy 286
restarting computer after chained installation 132
revoked certificates 282, 292
routing error messages *See* custom error messages
RSA Labs Public Key Cryptography Standard 537
RTF text, copying 429–430
Run all from My Computer installation state 103
Run all from Network installation state 104
Run from My Computer installation state
- child features 201
- installing hidden features 201
- Office deployment settings 103

Run from Network installation state
- child features 201
- disabling 105–106, 200, 201
- installing hidden features 201
- Office deployment settings 103

runtime applications, Windows 95 support 37

S

Save My Settings Wizard
    applying settings from OPS file 227
    Office Profile Wizard 225
    overview 14
    starting 225
    workgroup strategies 23
scaling documents to paper size 455
Schedule + 509–511, 516–518
scripts
    code page 425–426
    Outlook object model access 545–546
security
    document passwords *See* passwords
    Office security features 289–290
    Outlook *See* Outlook
    removing VBA 305–306
    setting in transform 125–126
    trusted sources *See* trusted sources
    virus protection *See* macro security
    Windows registry access control 306–308
Selfcert.exe certificates 291–292
server messages, localized 450
service releases *See* deploying service releases
Setup (MSDE 2000) 80
Setup (MUI Pack) *See* deploying MUI Packs
Setup (Office XP Web Components) 81
Setup (Office XP)
    administrative mode
        creating installation point 78–79
        excluding Outlook 494
        files not installed by default 80
    advertising programs *See* advertising Office
    assigning programs *See* assigning Office
    chained installation
        chained package defaults 127–128
        elevated privileges 132
        IntelliMirror software installation 132
        Media Content packages 134
        MUI Packs 133, 384–386
        overview 129
        Proofing Tools package 399–401
        required restart 132
        running programs during Setup 131
        setting up in Setup.ini 67, 93, 129–131
    command-line options 63, 68–69, 86–88
    creating hard-disk image 151–153
    customizing user interface
        custom text and buttons 97–98
        overview 95–96
        quiet installation 96
        setting options 95, 96–97
    displaying Remove Applications 207
    elevated privileges
        administrator rights 73
        chained installations 132
        registry entry 74
        SMS script for enabling 75
        system policy 73–75
        ways to enable 72
        when required 72
    error messages, custom 102
    hidden applications 201
    installation folder on client 102
    installing additional files 108, 109, 131
    installing Converter Pack 48
    installing Internet Explorer
        administrative installation point 83
        custom installation using transform 92
        default installation 27
        installation process 65–67
        minimum installation 449

Setup (Office XP) *(continued)*
- installing languages *See* deploying MUI Packs
- installing multilingual support for Outlook 416
- installing Office on client
  - batch file with command-line options 142
  - Custom installation 145
  - default installation 144–145
  - end-user license agreement 143
  - from administrative installation point 142
  - initialization 62
  - installation folder 145
  - installation mode 143–144
  - installing packages 63, 67
  - Internet Explorer files 65–67
  - keeping previous versions 146
  - log files 56, 69
  - MUI Packs 61
  - Office CD product key 143
  - overview 55, 61–62, 70
  - passing properties 68–69
  - quiet mode 142
  - required restarts 69
  - running programs after installation 67
  - running Windows Installer 57
  - Setup options and properties 63
  - starting Setup 62
  - updating system files 64–65, 142–143
  - upgrading Windows Installer 58
  - user information 143
  - user prompts 142
  - ways of 141
  - Web server path 63
- installing service releases 161

installing shortcuts
- adding shortcuts 110
- modifying default settings 109–110
- overview 109
- removing shortcuts 110
- shortcuts from previous versions 111–112
- Windows Installer shortcuts 110–111

installing stand-alone Outlook 487
log files 99–101
maintenance mode
- changing installation states 214
- customizing 98
- repairing applications 196

migrating user settings 119
Outlook and Office file names 486, 488
properties
- conflicting 94
- default values 86
- overview 85
- passing to Windows Installer 68, 86
- public and private 68
- Setupref.doc file 86
- ways to set 94

publishing Office 72, 75
quiet mode
- command-line option 86
- configuring user interface 96
- customizing installation 91
- files removed from previous versions 136
- installing System Files Update 143
- selecting features to install 103
- specifying in Setup settings file 88
- switching to full interface 97

removing previous versions *See* Removal Wizard

Setup (Office XP) *(continued)*
    resolving conflicting options 94
    running 62
    running Profile Wizard 119–122
    running programs at Office installation 131
    setting installation states *See* installation states
    Setup settings file *See* Setup.ini file
    Setup.exe file location 79
    specifying organization name 79
    specifying product ID 79
    specifying transform to apply 93
    transforms *See* transforms
    updating system files *See* System Files Update
    upgrading Windows Installer 58
    user input to select features to install 103
    what's new 15
    when to publish software 170
    Windows Installer 57–58
Setup (Proofing Tools) *See* deploying Proofing Tools
Setup INI Customization Wizard
    configuring chained installations 130–131
    creating custom settings file 89–91
    installing 562
    setting up MUI Packs 384–385
    Setup user interface options 97
    specifying transform 93
Setup.ini file
    chaining packages
        configuring 130–131
        MUI Packs 61, 384–386
        Proofing Tools package 399–400
        settings 129–130
        syntax 67

    client installation path setting 102
    creating custom 89–91
    distributing custom 91
    Dw.exe property 102
    entering property names 68
    installing Proofing Tools 399
    location on administrative installation point 56
    MSDE 2000 80
    multiple administrative installation points 394
    multiple settings files
        different groups of users 91
        on single installation point 394
        specifying file to use 91
    new sections 56–57
    Office XP Web Components 82
    Outlook and Office settings file names 486
    overview 56, 88–89
    passing Setup properties 68
    removing Small Business Tools 137
    Setup display properties 95–98
    Setup error message properties 102
    specifying settings file to use
        logon script or package 91
        Settings command 63, 91
        shortcuts on administrative installation point 87
    specifying transform 56, 57, 93
    syntax 88
    System Files Update properties 60, 101
    when read by Setup.exe 63
Setupref.doc file
    location 565
    Setup properties 86
    Windows Installer command-line options 63

Index

SharePoint Team Services
    installing 22
    localized server messages 451
    MSI file 58, 82
    operating system support 82
    overview 21–22
    system requirements 35
shortcut keys
    disabling 246–247, 253, 276–278
    key codes 278–281
shortcuts installed with Office
    adding shortcuts 110
    advertising Office 148
    modifying default settings 109–110
    overview 109
    removing 110
    shortcuts from previous versions 111–112
    Windows Installer shortcuts 110–111, 191
signatures, Outlook 512
signing code *See* certificates
signing Outlook messages 282–285
SigStatusNoCRL policy 284
Small Business edition of Office
    MSI file 58
    system requirements 30–32, 39
Small Business Tools, removing 137
Smbus.msi file 58
SMS *See* Systems Management Server
software dependencies *See* system requirements
Software Installation snap-in *See* IntelliMirror software installation
speech recognition software requirements
    Office XP Developer 39
    Office XP Small Business 32
    Office XP Standard 30
    Professional with FrontPage 36
spell checking tools 398
SQL Server 2000 Desktop Engine 80–81

SqlRun01.msi file 59, 80
Srclist.exe tool 557
Standard edition of Office
    package (MSI file) 58
    system requirements 28–30, 39
Standard.msi file 58
Startpag.css file 346, 555
stationery, Outlook 98 512
Stopword.doc file 565
style sheets for Help content 346, 555
subscription programs for Office 18
Sun Microsystems networks 43
SwitchForms utility for Exchange Client 506
System Files Update
    adding to Setup settings file 93
    advertising Office 148
    custom installation options 63, 101
    elevated privileges 73
    installing Internet Explorer 60–61, 65–67, 83
    installing on users' computers 64–65, 142–143
    installing Windows Desktop Update 192
    language 83
    MUI Pack deployment 369, 374, 378
    overview 59–60
    Setup /spforce option 66
    Setup.ini section 57
    when not required 59
    Windows NT environments 72, 190
system locale
    Access language settings 439
    list of locale identifiers 374–376
    PowerPoint language settings 438
    used by code page 444
    Windows registry entry 402

system policies
    access control 237
    Corporate Error Reporting policies
        configuring 218–219, 221
        NoExternalURL 222
        NoFileCollection 222
        NoSecondLevelCollection 222
        policy template 237
        Tracking policy 222
        URLLaunch policy 223
    enabling install with elevated privileges 73–75
    enforcing Office installation language 432
    environment variables 247–248, 264–267
    error message policies 336, 338–340
    how to set
        complex policies 270
        for users or computers 240, 244–246
        overview 240–243
        simple policies 267
        using Group Policy snap-in 241
        using System Policy Editor 238
    language policies
        enforcing installation language 236
        user interface defaults 405–406
        user locale 404
    macro security policies
        ActiveX controls 315–316
        location in registry 312–313
        Office.adm template 312
        preventing user from trusting certificates 314
        setting security level 294, 314–315
        trusting Microsoft certificates 313–314
    multiple versions of Office 237, 248
    operating system considerations 238
    Outlook messaging
        character encoding policy 418
        cryptography policies 282–287
        policy templates 258–259
        security labels 536
        security settings 539–545
    overview 235–237
    paper resizing option in Word 455
    policy file name and location 238
    policy states 239, 242–243
    policy templates
        Access 256–257
        Clip Organizer 263
        Corporate Error Reporting tool 237
        created for Group Policy 242
        Excel 257
        exclamation points in 249
        finding policies 249–250
        FrontPage 258
        loading 238–240
        Office 256
        Office Resource Kit 241
        Outlook 258–259, 559
        overview 241–242
        PowerPoint 260
        Publisher 261
        Windows 242, 317–318
        Windows Installer 263
        Word 262–263
    shared between programs 242

Index

system policies *(continued)*
- System Policy Editor *See* System Policy Editor
- updating on client 240
- user interface policies
  - Answer Wizard file path 353
  - background saves in Word 268
  - Detect and Repair command 196
  - disabling command bar items 246–247, 252, 270–275
  - disabling dialog box options 253
  - disabling password protection 253
  - disabling recently used file list 321, 323
  - disabling shortcut keys 253, 276–281
  - disabling Web links 254–255
  - Help on the Web policy 356, 357
  - hiding drives 318–319
  - hiding Entire Network 319
  - locking command bars 252
  - locking Office configuration 251–252
  - MRU file list 269–270
  - Office on the Web 360
  - opening documents on Web 255
  - operating system environment 316–317
  - preventing users from running programs 320
  - removing Run command 318
  - removing Shut Down command 319–320
  - restricting browsing in dialog boxes 322–323
  - restricting network connections 320–321
  - shared between applications 256

Windows registry settings
- application Security key 314–315
- finding policy values 249–250
- Policies node 313–314
- Policies subkey structure 248–249
- security setting nodes 312–313
- setting default 128
- Software subkey 237, 248
- updating client 248

System Policy Editor
- *See also* system policies
- changing user settings 204
- Default Computer profile 238, 244
- Default User profile 238, 244
- installing 565–566
- policy file
  - adding users and computers 244
  - creating 238
  - distributing 250
  - location 238
  - name 238
  - updating 248
- setting policies
  - enforcing policy setting 239
  - environment variables 247–248, 264–267
  - for computers 244–245
  - for groups 245–246
  - for users 244–245
  - loading templates 238, 250
  - overview 238
  - policy configurations 240
  - policy states 239, 242–243
  - using templates 241–242
- shared Office policies 242
- tools for setting policies 241
- updating client registry 248

Microsoft Office XP Resource Kit 609

System Policy Editor *(continued)*
    what's new 17
    Windows templates 242
system requirements
    Enterprise editions 39–40
    Internet Explorer version 27–28
    network operating system support 41–44
    Office deployment using Windows 2000 163
    Office XP Developer 36–39
    Office XP Professional 32–34, 39
    Office XP Small Business 30–32, 39
    Office XP stand-alone applications 40–41
    Office XP Standard 28–30, 39
    Professional with FrontPage 34–36, 39
    Terminal Services 45–46
    Windows NT 189
    Windows versions supported 27, 28
System.adm file 317
Systems folder file updates 59
Systems Management Server
    deploying MUI Packs 388
    installing Office on client 155–156
    installing package definition files 559–560

T

Taiwanese date format 402
team collaboration
    encrypted documents 298
    new Office features 23–24
    Web sites based on SharePoint Team Services 21–22
TechNet Web site 20
templates
    custom, deploying with Office 108, 114
    included in Resource Kit 241
    Normal.dot language (Word) 402, 403, 431
    policy templates *See* system policies
    removing 205
    trusting installed 293, 314–315

temporary files, deleting 136
Terminal Services
    feature installation state settings 106, 108
    installing Outlook 460–461, 484–485
    license requirements 44
    locking Windows registry 308
    one system code page per computer restriction 533
    Outlook memory considerations 484
    overview 44, 308
    registry locking and Outlook 308, 485
    system requirements 45–46
    Web site 18
text converters 47–50, 558
toolbars
    disabling buttons 246, 252, 270–272
    disabling shortcut keys 246–247, 276–279
    item control IDs 272–275
    locking down user interface 251–252
    preventing changes to 252
transforms
    adding OPS file 118
    adding Profile Wizard 120
    adding registry values 126–127
    advertising Office 75, 148
    assigning Office 147, 170
    configuring client for crash reporting 216, 221
    customizing Removal Wizard 138
    customizing Setup error messages 102
    customizing Setup maintenance mode 98
    customizing user settings
        adding OPS file 119
        adding settings 124
        migrating previous settings 119
        Outlook settings 124–125
        resolving conflicting values 116
        ways of 114–116

transforms *(continued)*
    default features installed with Office 144
    default installation state 103
    deploying custom files with Office 108–109
    deploying Outlook 504
    displaying Remove Applications in Setup 207
    embedded OPS files 226, 227
    for MUI Pack *See* deploying MUI Packs
    for Proofing Tools 398–399
    for System Files Update 59
    Help files 352
    hiding applications and features 105, 201, 202
    implementing trusted sources 294
    installing Windows Desktop Update 192, 197
    modifying OPS files 119
    MST File Viewer 556
    overview 91–92
    publishing Office 147, 170
    resolving conflicting Setup properties 94
    running with Office Setup 67
    setting security options 125–126
    Setup user interface options 94
    specifying in Setup.ini 56, 57
    specifying multiple 93
    specifying organization name 79
    specifying transform to use 93
    Windows Installer packages 57, 57
troubleshooting applications
    crashes *See* Corporate Error Reporting tool
    repairing applications 195–197
troubleshooting multilingual text 430–431
TrueType fonts 430, 455–456
Trusted Code control 559

trusted sources
    accepting certificates 293
    adding to list of 293
    digital signature requirement 292
    Internet Explorer list of 293
    Microsoft Corporation 293, 313–314
    opening signed macros 293
    overview 292
    preventing changes to list of 294
    preventing user from trusting 314
    registry entries 294, 313–314
    removing sources from list of 293
    revoked certificates 292
    Selfcert.exe macros 292
    setting in transform 126
    setting up on client 294–295
    trusting installed programs 293, 314–315
    viewing list of 293

U

Unicode
    character encoding code points 427
    code page conversion 427
    code points 427
    converting databases to 412–413
    copying text 429–430
    displaying text 428
    file names 428
    file size 429
    getting Unicode value of character 428
    installing Unicode font 383, 454
    multilingual Web pages 449–450
    Outlook message character encoding 417
    overview 427
    previous versions of FrontPage files 415
    printing text 428–429
    saving HTML documents 449

Index

Unicode *(continued)*
    sharing documents across language versions 409
    sharing multilingual documents 425–428
    troubleshooting text 430–431
    using in Outlook 532–533
    UTF-8 encoded URLs 450
    VBA environment 428
    Word documents converted automatically 429
uninstalling applications *See* removing applications and features
uninstalling Visual Basic for Applications 305–306
UNIX NFS client support 43
unlocking registry 485
unmanaged Office installations 179–181
upgrading documents *See* converting file formats
upgrading Internet Explorer 60, 65–66
upgrading MUI Packs 407–408
upgrading Office
    future upgrades in Windows 2000 181–183
    managed installations 183–185
    service releases *See* deploying service releases
upgrading Outlook *See* deploying Outlook, upgrade considerations
upgrading Windows Installer 58, 70
URLs, multilingual 450
UseCRLChasing policy 282
user information, specifying for Setup 143
user interface display language
    default font 453
    dialog boxes 449
    English-only requirements 445
    FrontPage templates 440
    Internet Explorer dependencies 449

    limitations 371
    online Help 446
    operating system 443–445
    PowerPoint 439, 441
    system code page support 445
    system locale setting 444
    system policies 405–406
user interface for Office XP Setup
    custom text and buttons 97–98
    overview 95–96
    quiet installation 96
    setting options 95, 96–97
user interface policies
    Answer Wizard file path 353
    background saves in Word 268
    Detect and Repair command 196
    disabling command bar items 246–247, 252, 270–275
    disabling dialog box options 253
    disabling password protection 253
    disabling recently used file list 321, 323
    disabling shortcut keys 253, 276–281
    disabling Web links 254–255
    Help on the Web policy 356, 357
    hiding drives 318–319
    hiding Entire Network 319
    locking command bars 252
    locking Office configuration 251–252
    MRU file list 269–270
    Office on the Web 360
    opening documents on Web 255
    operating system environment 316–317
    preventing users from running programs 320
    removing Run command 318
    removing Shut Down command 319–320

user interface policies *(continued)*
    restricting browsing in dialog boxes 322–323
    restricting network connections 320–321
    shared between applications 256
    Windows policy templates 317–318
user locale
    FrontPage language settings 440
    language settings based on 403–404
    list of locale identifiers 374–376
    Publisher language settings 442
    registry entry for identifier 402
user profiles
    installing with Office 119–123
    multiple Office languages 370
    Outlook *See* deploying Outlook
user settings
    capturing *See* Office Profile Wizard
    conflicting 116
    effect of reinstalling Office 200
    hard-disk image for distributing Office 152
    installation language compatibility 128, 404
    migrating using Setup 119
    migrating using Windows 2000 184–185
    Outlook
        capturing with Profile Wizard 468, 527
        commonly-used settings 527
        migrating current 470
        setting default 475
        setting in transform 124–125
        setting using Custom Installation Wizard 468
        specifying profile settings file 470
        ways to set 468–469, 526

running Profile Wizard after Setup 123
running Profile Wizard at Setup 119–122
    setting in transforms *See* transforms
    setting using system policies 128, 204
    tools for updating 202–204
    updating using Custom Maintenance Wizard 128, 203
    ways to customize 114–116
user signatures, Outlook 512
USERNAME environment variable 230
USERPROFILE environment variable 230
UTF-16 character encoding 429
UTF-8 encoded URLs 415, 450
UTF-8 format 449

V

vCards in Exchange Client 514
VeriSign Certificate Authority 297, 309
viruses *See* macro security
Visual Basic for Applications
    removing 305–306
    Unicode characters 428
Visual Keyboard 448
Volume Licensing program 18

W

WarnAboutInvalid policy 285
Web browser Unicode support 449
Web Downloadable Input Method Editor 408
Web pages
    BackOffice Server site 20
    communities on the Web 23
    development tools 24–25
    disabling links from applications 252, 254–255
    Microsoft Office home page 19
    Microsoft Product Support Services site 19
    Microsoft TechNet site 20
    Microsoft Web platforms 25

Web pages *(continued)*
- Microsoft Windows site 20
- multilingual 449–450
- new team collaboration features 23–24
- Office Developer Web site 20
- Office on the Web site
  - disabling access 254–255, 360
  - Office solutions and support sites 19–20
- Office Resource Kit Web site 19
- Office Sites Worldwide Web site 20
- Office Tools on the Web site
  - application object model misuse 324
  - bad code posted on site 325
  - bad frame on a page 325
  - data exchange privacy 324
  - denial of service attacks 324–325
  - security considerations 323, 325
  - VBA removed from Office 305
  - Web portal redirection 323, 325
- opening documents on 255
- Outlook Folder Home Pages security zone 545–546
- Terminal Services 18
- Web sites based on SharePoint Team Services 21–22

Webent.xls file 565

Windows 2000
- assigning Office 75
- FrontPage Server Extensions support 82
- Group Policy snap-in *See* Group Policy
- installing Internet Explorer 83
- Internet Explorer version 60–61
- language support
  - Asian languages 443
  - big fonts 453
  - document language 446–447
  - Excel workbooks 414
  - installing for Outlook 416
  - international sort order 410
  - keyboard layout 448
  - limitations 443
  - Office user interface language 444–445
- limitations of using for deployment 186
- locking down Office 251, 307
- locking Policies subkey 237
- Ntconfig.pol policy file 238, 250
- Outlook roaming user profiles 500
- permissions for running Setup 72
- Registry.pol 250
- Remote OS Installation 154–155
- required for Outlook security features 536
- roaming folder 498
- running Removal Wizard 139
- SharePoint Team Services support 82
- Software Installation snap-in *See* IntelliMirror software installation
- System Files Update not installed 59
- Unicode characters in file names 428
- user interface system policies
  - disabling recently used file list 321, 323
  - hiding drives 318–319
  - hiding Entire Network 319
  - policy templates 317–318
  - preventing users from running programs 320
  - removing Run command 318
  - removing Shut Down command 319–320
  - restricting file browsing in dialog boxes 322–323
  - restricting network connections 320–321

Windows 2000 Terminal Services *See* Terminal Services

Windows 95 runtime application support 37

Windows 98
    automatic repair feature 197
    Config.pol policy file 238
    creating environment variables 248
    installing Internet Explorer 83
    language support
        Access database sort orders 411
        Asian languages 443
        big fonts 453
        document language 446–447
        installing 448
        installing for Outlook 417
        limitations 443
        Office user interface language 443–444
    locking down Office 251
    roaming folder 498
    Unicode characters in file names 428
    updating system files 59
    upgrading Internet Explorer 60, 65–66
    upgrading Windows Installer 70
Windows Desktop Update
    advertising Office 148
    included with Internet Explorer 191
    installing 192
    required for automatic repair 197
    Windows NT environments 190, 191
Windows Explorer
    hiding drives in 318–319
    preventing network drive mapping 320
    removing Entire Network from 319
    removing Places Bar 322
Windows Installer
    application repair 196–197
    called by Setup 63–64, 67
    command-line options 63
    elevated privileges 73–75
    installing features on demand from CD 74

installing Internet Explorer 65–67
installing shortcuts 110–111
installing System Files Update 64–65
log files 56, 69, 99–101
Office service releases
    administrative installation point setup 157–159
    deployment process 156
    specifying package 157
    updating client 159
overview 57–58
packages *See* packages
passing Setup properties 68
registry entries for install on demand 74
Remove Applications page 207
resolving conflicting user settings 116
running from Add/Remove Programs 205, 214
running from Custom Maintenance Wizard 199
Setup.ini section 56
system policies 242, 263
transforms *See* transforms
upgrading 58
what's new 16
Windows NT environments
    installing advertised software 190
    support for shortcuts 191
    Windows Desktop Update 190
Windows Millennium (Windows Me)
    installing Internet Explorer 83
    Internet Explorer version 60–61
    language support
        Asian languages 443
        document language 446–447
        installing 417, 448
        limitations 443
        Office user interface language 443–444

Windows Millennium (Windows Me) *(continued)*
    roaming folder 498
    System Files Update not installed 59
    Unicode characters in file names 428
Windows NT 4.0
    automatic repair feature 197
    e-mail encryption strength support 547
    font installation limitations 383
    FrontPage Server Extensions support 82
    installing Internet Explorer 83
    Internet Explorer version 28
    language support
        Asian languages 443
        big fonts 453
        document language 446–447
        installing NLS files for Access 410–411
        keyboard layout 448
        limitations 443
        Office user interface language 443–445
    locking down Office 251, 307
    locking Policies subkey 248
    Ntconfig.pol policy file 238
    Office deployment considerations
        advertising Office 192
        elevated privileges 190
        implementing install-on-demand 192
        Internet Explorer version 190, 191
        Service Pack 6a 189
        specific issues 189, 190
        System Files Update 190
        Windows Desktop Update 192
        Windows Installer shortcuts 191
    Outlook roaming folder 498
    Outlook roaming user profiles 499–500
    permissions for running Setup 72
    permissions for system policies 237
    running Removal Wizard 139
    Unicode characters in file names 428
    upgrading files
        Internet Explorer 60, 65–66
        system files 59, 72
        Windows Installer 58, 70
    user interface system policies
        hiding drives 318–319
        hiding Entire Network 319–320
        policy templates 317
        preventing users from running programs 320
        removing Shut Down command 319–320
        restricting network connections 320–321
Windows NT Server NetShow Services 512
Windows NT Terminal Server 308
Windows registry
    access control
        locked by Terminal Services 308
        Outlook affected by 308, 485
        security considerations 306
        setting permissions 307
        unlocking 485
    changing using Custom Maintenance Wizard 203
    controlling access to Policies subkey 237
    custom error messages
        activating 336–338
        disabling 339–340
    custom Help file entries 352–353
    disk space requirements 29
    DW.exe entries *See* Corporate Error Reporting tool
    exporting sections 127
    extended characters entry 428
    Keypath.xls file 196

Windows registry *(continued)*
    LanguageResources subkey
        changing using Custom Installation Wizard 402
        created automatically 402
        InstallLanguage entry 402–403, 431, 433
        LangTuneUp entry 403–404
    Outlook entries
        default message encoding 530
        folder name setting 476
        secure messaging components 537, 538
        security settings 539–545
        setting during deployment 476
    policies *See* system policies
    removing entries using Profile Wizard 214
    repairing application entries 195–197
    security entries
        application Security key 314–315
        common Security key 315–316
        Excel 4 macros 311–312
        location of 312–313
        security level 125
        trusted source list 293, 294, 313–314
    using transform to set entries 126–127
    Windows Installer entries 74
Windows Terminal Services *See* Terminal Services
Windows.adm file 242
WinFax 504
WinHelp, converting to HTML 344–345
Winnt.adm file 242, 317

Word
    allowing background saves 268
    file formats
        converting documents to Unicode 429
        converting from previous versions 47
        installing converters 48–50
        Office 95 documents 47
        Office 97 documents 47
    language
        language settings 434–435
        Normal.dot language 402, 403, 431
        troubleshooting multilingual text 430–431
    language version compatibility
        general Office considerations 409–410
        macros 424
        opening documents in different versions 422–423
        requirements 422
    macro virus protection
        See also macro security
        available security levels 309–310
        overview 308–309
        setting security level 291
        setting trusted sources 293
        types of macros 309
    paper size for printing documents 455

Word *(continued)*
    protecting documents
        document passwords 301–302
        file protection levels 301
        forgotten passwords 302
        macros in templates *See* macro security
        passwords 297–298
        privacy options 304
        read-only recommended 301
        Save properties moved 306
        specific elements in 301
    WordMail editor in Outlook 484, 515

Word10.adm file
    environment variables 254, 267
    policy settings 262–263
    templates included in Resource Kit 241

WordMail editor in Outlook 484, 515

Workflow Service system requirements 38

workgroup collaboration
    encrypted documents 298
    new Office features 23–24
    Web sites based on SharePoint Team Services 21–22

Wwfeatre.xls file 564

Wwsuppt.xls file 443, 564

X

xlm macros 311

Y *No Entries*

Z

zone security, Outlook Folder Home Pages 545

Microsoft® TechNet
Insights and Answers for IT Professionals

Receive a 5% discount on a new TechNet or TechNet Plus Subscription now!

TechNet is the essential resource for IT Professionals that evaluate, deploy, maintain, and support Microsoft products. When you join, you'll receive a shipment of information-packed CDs or DVDs, that includes Microsoft product resource kits, service packs, Knowledge Base articles, updated drivers and patches, important technical information, and more.

Every month we'll send you updates so that you have the latest information you need to be successful. A TechNet Plus Subscription includes early beta release software that will help you stay ahead of the game. Be one of the first to receive Microsoft operating system, server, and desktop application software.

pricing:

TechNet Single User License u.s.	$299
TechNet Single Server License u.s.	$699
TechNet *Plus* Single User License u.s.	$449
TechNet *Plus* Single Server License u.s.	$849

To order online: visit http://technetbuynow.one.microsoft.com/.
To order by phone: call (800) 344-2121, ext. 3517
6:30 A.M. to 5:30 P.M. (Pacific time).

www.microsoft.com/technet

Microsoft

Ready solutions for the IT administrator

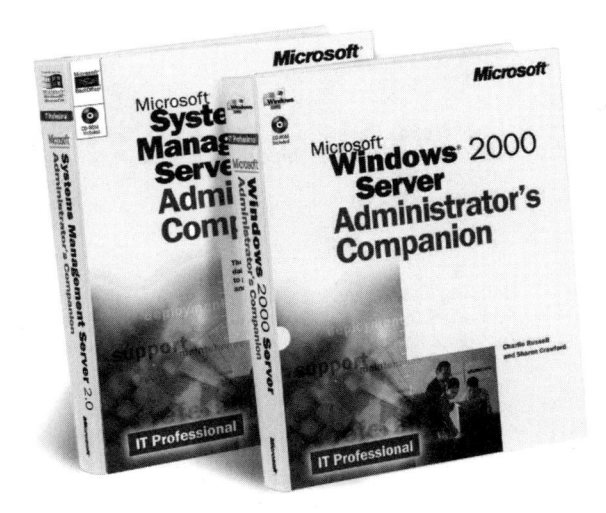

Keep your IT systems up and running with the ADMINISTRATOR'S COMPANION series from Microsoft. These expert guides serve as both tutorials and references for critical deployment and maintenance of Microsoft products and technologies. Packed with real-world expertise, hands-on numbered procedures, and handy workarounds, ADMINISTRATOR'S COMPANIONS deliver ready answers for on-the-job results.

Microsoft® SQL Server™ 2000 Administrator's Companion
U.S.A. $59.99
Canada $86.99
ISBN   0-7356-1051-7

Microsoft Exchange 2000 Server Administrator's Companion
U.S.A. $59.99
Canada $86.99
ISBN   0-7356-0938-1

Microsoft Windows® 2000 Server Administrator's Companion
U.S.A. $ 69.99
Canada $ 107.99
ISBN   1-57231-819-8

Microsoft Systems Management Server 2.0 Administrator's Companion
U.S.A. $59.99
Canada $92.99
ISBN   0-7356-0834-2

Microsoft Press® products are available worldwide wherever quality computer books are sold. For more information, contact your book or computer retailer, software reseller, or local Microsoft Sales Office, or visit our Web site at mspress.microsoft.com. To locate your nearest source for Microsoft Press products, or to order directly, call 1-800-MSPRESS in the United States (in Canada, call 1-800-268-2222).

Prices and availability dates are subject to change.

Microsoft®
mspress.microsoft.com

In-depth. Focused.
And
ready for work.

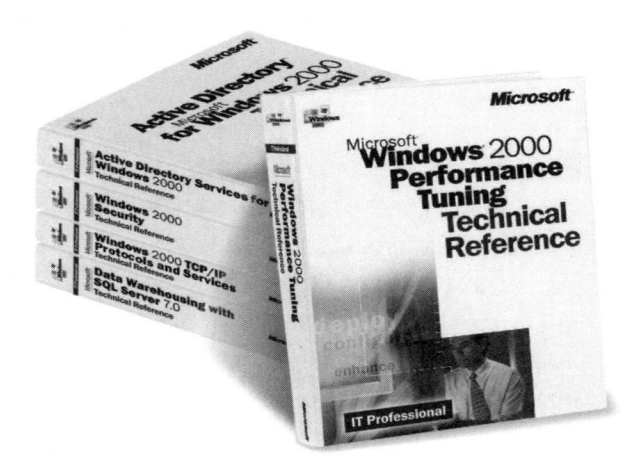

Data Warehousing with Microsoft® SQL Server™ 7.0 Technical Reference
U.S.A. $49.99
Canada $76.99
ISBN 0-7356-0859-8

Microsoft SQL Server 7.0 Performance Tuning Technical Reference
U.S.A. $49.99
Canada $76.99
ISBN 0-7356-0909-8

Building Applications with Microsoft Outlook® 2000 Technical Reference
U.S.A. $49.99
Canada $72.99
ISBN 0-7356-0581-5

Microsoft Windows NT® Server 4.0 Terminal Server Edition Technical Reference
U.S.A. $49.99
Canada $72.99
ISBN 0-7356-0645-5

Microsoft Windows® 2000 TCP/IP Protocols and Services Technical Reference
U.S.A. $49.99
Canada $76.99
ISBN 0-7356-0556-4

Active Directory™ Services for Microsoft Windows 2000 Technical Reference
U.S.A. $49.99
Canada $76.99
ISBN 0-7356-0624-2

Microsoft Windows 2000 Security Technical Reference
U.S.A. $49.99
Canada $72.99
ISBN 0-7356-0858-X

Microsoft Windows 2000 Performance Tuning Technical Reference
U.S.A. $49.99
Canada $72.99
ISBN 0-7356-0633-1

Get the technical drilldown you need to deploy and support Microsoft products more effectively with the MICROSOFT TECHNICAL REFERENCE series. Each guide focuses on a specific aspect of the technology—weaving in-depth detail with on-the-job scenarios and practical how-to information for the IT professional. Get focused—and take technology to its limits—with MICROSOFT TECHNICAL REFERENCES.

Microsoft Press® products are available worldwide wherever quality computer books are sold. For more information, contact your book or computer retailer, software reseller, or local Microsoft Sales Office, or visit our Web site at mspress.microsoft.com. To locate your nearest source for Microsoft Press products, or to order directly, call 1-800-MSPRESS in the United States (in Canada, call 1-800-268-2222).

Prices and availability dates are subject to change.

Microsoft®
mspress.microsoft.com

Get a **Free** e-mail newsletter, updates, special offers, links to related books, and more when you

register on line!

Register your Microsoft Press® title on our Web site and you'll get a FREE subscription to our e-mail newsletter, *Microsoft Press Book Connections.* You'll find out about newly released and upcoming books and learning tools, online events, software downloads, special offers and coupons for Microsoft Press customers, and information about major Microsoft® product releases. You can also read useful additional information about all the titles we publish, such as detailed book descriptions, tables of contents and indexes, sample chapters, links to related books and book series, author biographies, and reviews by other customers.

Registration is easy. Just visit this Web page and fill in your information:

http://mspress.microsoft.com/register

Microsoft®

Proof of Purchase

Use this page as proof of purchase if participating in a promotion or rebate offer on this title. Proof of purchase must be used in conjunction with other proof(s) of payment such as your dated sales receipt—see offer details.

Microsoft® Office XP Resource Kit
0-7356-1403-2

CUSTOMER NAME

Microsoft Press, PO Box 97017, Redmond, WA 98073-9830

Microsoft License Agreement

(*Microsoft Office XP Resource Kit* Book Companion CD)

IMPORTANT-READ CAREFULLY: This End-User License Agreement ("EULA") is a legal agreement between you (either an individual person or a single legal entity, who will be referred to in this EULA as "You") and the Licensor for the Microsoft software technology that displays this EULA, including any associated media, printed materials and electronic documentation (the "Software"). The Software also includes any software updates, add-on components, web services and/or supplements that the Licensor may provide to You or make available to You after the date You obtain Your initial copy of the Software to the extent that such items are not accompanied by a separate license agreement or terms of use. By installing, copying, downloading, accessing or otherwise using the Software, You agree to be bound by the terms of this EULA. If You do not agree to the terms of this EULA, do not install, access or use the Software. For purposes of this EULA, the term "Licensor" refers to Microsoft Corporation, except in the event that You acquired the Software as a component of a Microsoft software product originally licensed from the manufacturer of your computer system or computer system component, then "Licensor" or refers to such hardware manufacturer. By installing, copying, downloading, accessing or otherwise using the Software, You agree to be bound by the terms of this EULA. If You do not agree to the terms of this EULA, Licensor is unwilling to license the Software. In such event, You may not install, copy, download or otherwise use the Software.

SOFTWARE LICENSE

The Software is protected by intellectual property laws and treaties. The Software is licensed, not sold.

1. **GRANT OF LICENSE.** This EULA grants You the following rights:
   - **Installation and Use.** If You licensed the Software from Your hardware manufacturer, You may install and use one (1) copy of the Software. If You licensed the Software from Microsoft, You may install and use an unlimited number of copies of the Software.
   - **Reproduction and Distribution.** If You licensed the Software from Microsoft, You may reproduce and distribute an unlimited number of copies of the Software provided that each copy is a true and complete copy, including all copyright and trademark notices, and is accompanied by a copy of this EULA.

2. **DESCRIPTION OF OTHER RIGHTS AND LIMITATIONS.**
   - **Limitations on Reverse Engineering, Decompilation, and Disassembly.** You may not reverse engineer, decompile, or disassemble the Software, except and only to the extent that such activity is expressly permitted by applicable law notwithstanding this limitation.
   - **Trademarks.** This EULA does not grant You any rights in connection with any trademarks or service marks of Licensor or its suppliers.
   - **No rental, leasing or commercial hosting.** You may not rent, lease, lend or provide commercial hosting services to third parties with the Software.
   - **Support Services.** Licensor may provide You with support services related to the Software ("Support Services"). Use of Support Services is governed by the policies and programs described in the user manual, in "online" documentation, or in other materials from the support services provider. Any supplemental software code provided to You as part of the Support Services are considered part of the Software and subject to the terms and conditions of this EULA. You acknowledge and agree that Licensor may use technical information You provide to Licensor as part of the Support Services for its business purposes, including for product support and development. Licensor will not utilize such technical information in a form that personally identifies You. For Software licensed from the hardware manufacturer, please refer to the manufacturer's support number and address provided in Your hardware documentation.
   - **Termination.** Without prejudice to any other rights, Licensor or its suppliers may terminate this EULA if You fail to comply with the terms and conditions of this EULA. In such event, You must destroy all copies of the Software and all of its component parts.

3. **INTELLECTUAL PROPERTY RIGHTS.** All title and intellectual property rights in and to the Software (including but not limited to any images, photographs, animations, video, audio, music, text, and "applets" incorporated into the Software), the accompanying printed materials, and any copies of the Software are owned by Licensor or its suppliers. All title and intellectual property rights in and to the content that is not contained in the Software, but may be accessed through use of the Software, is the property of the respective content owners and may be protected by applicable copyright or other intellectual property laws and treaties. This EULA grants You no rights to use such content. If this Software contains documentation that is provided only in electronic form, you may print one copy of such electronic documentation. You may not copy the printed materials accompanying the Software. All rights not specifically granted under this EULA are reserved by Licensor and its suppliers.

4. U.S. GOVERNMENT LICENSE RIGHTS. All Software provided to the U.S. Government pursuant to solicitations issued on or after December 1, 1995 is provided with the commercial license rights and restrictions described elsewhere herein. All Software provided to the U.S. Government pursuant to solicitations issued prior to December 1, 1995 is provided with RESTRICTED RIGHTS as provided for in FAR, 48 CFR 52.227-14 (JUNE 1987) or DFAR, 48 CFR 252.227-7013 (OCT 1988), as applicable.

5. EXPORT RESTRICTIONS. You acknowledge that the Software is subject to U.S. export jurisdiction. You agree to comply with all applicable international and national laws that apply to the Software, including the U.S. Export Administration Regulations, as well as end-user, end-use and destination restrictions issued by U.S. and other governments. For additional information, see <http://www.microsoft.com/exporting/>.

6. APPLICABLE LAW.
If you acquired this Software in the United States, this EULA is governed by the laws of the State of Washington. If you acquired this Software in Canada, unless expressly prohibited by local law, this EULA is governed by the laws in force in the Province of Ontario, Canada; and, in respect of any dispute which may arise hereunder, you consent to the jurisdiction of the federal and provincial courts sitting in Toronto, Ontario. If this Software was acquired outside the United States, then local law may apply.

7. LIMITED WARRANTY
NOTE: IF YOU LICENSED THE SOFTWARE FROM A HARDWARE MANUFACTURER AS A COMPONENT OF A MICROSOFT SOFTWARE PRODUCT, PLEASE REFER TO THE LIMITED WARRANTIES, LIMITATION OF LIABILITY, AND OTHER SPECIAL PROVISION APPENDICES PROVIDED WITH OR IN SUCH OTHER MICROSOFT SOFTWARE PRODUCT. SUCH LIMITED WARRANTIES, LIMITATIONS OF LIABILITY AND SPECIAL PROVISIONS ARE AN INTEGRAL PART OF THIS EULA AND SHALL SUPERSEDE ALL OF THE WARRANTIES, LIMITATIONS OF LIABILITY AND OTHER SPECIAL PROVISIONS SET FORTH BELOW.

FOR SOFTWARE LICENSED FROM MICROSOFT CORPORATION, THE FOLLOWING SECTIONS APPLY:

LIMITED WARRANTY FOR SOFTWARE ACQUIRED IN THE US AND CANADA. Microsoft warrants that the SOFTWARE will perform substantially in accordance with the accompanying materials for a period of ninety (90) days from the date of receipt.

If an implied warranty or condition is created by your state/jurisdiction and federal or state/provincial law prohibits disclaimer of it, you also have an implied warranty or condition, BUT ONLY AS TO DEFECTS DISCOVERED DURING THE PERIOD OF THIS LIMITED WARRANTY (NINETY DAYS). AS TO ANY DEFECTS DISCOVERED AFTER THE NINETY (90) DAY PERIOD, THERE IS NO WARRANTY OR CONDITION OF ANY KIND. Some states/jurisdictions do not allow limitations on how long an implied warranty or condition lasts, so the above limitation may not apply to you.

Any supplements or updates to the SOFTWARE, including without limitation, any (if any) service packs or hot fixes provided to you after the expiration of the ninety (90) day Limited Warranty period are not covered by any warranty or condition, express, implied or statutory.

LIMITATION ON REMEDIES; NO CONSEQUENTIAL OR OTHER DAMAGES. Your exclusive remedy for any breach of this Limited Warranty is as set forth below. Except for any refund elected by Microsoft, YOU ARE NOT ENTITLED TO ANY DAMAGES, INCLUDING BUT NOT LIMITED TO CONSEQUENTIAL DAMAGES, if the SOFTWARE does not meet Microsoft's Limited Warranty, and, to the maximum extent allowed by applicable law, even if any remedy fails of its essential purpose. The terms of Section 11 below ("Exclusion of Incidental, Consequential and Certain Other Damages") are also incorporated into this Limited Warranty. Some states/jurisdictions do not allow the exclusion or limitation of incidental or consequential damages, so the above limitation or exclusion may not apply to you. This Limited Warranty gives you specific legal rights. You may have others which vary from state/jurisdiction to state/jurisdiction.

YOUR EXCLUSIVE REMEDY. Microsoft's and its suppliers' entire liability and your exclusive remedy shall be, at Microsoft's option from time to time exercised subject to applicable law, (a) return of the price paid (if any) for the Software, or (b) repair or replacement of the Software, that does not meet this Limited Warranty and that is returned to Microsoft with a copy of your receipt. You will receive the remedy elected by Microsoft without charge, except that you are responsible for any expenses you may incur (e.g. cost of shipping the Software to Microsoft). This Limited Warranty is void if failure of the Software has resulted from accident, abuse, misapplication, abnormal use or a virus. Any replacement Software will be warranted for the remainder of the original warranty period or thirty (30) days, whichever is longer. Outside the United States or Canada, neither these remedies nor any product support services offered by Microsoft are available without proof of purchase from an authorized international source. To exercise your remedy, contact: Microsoft, Attn. Microsoft Sales Information Center/One Microsoft Way/Redmond, WA 98052-6399, or the Microsoft subsidiary serving your country.

LIMITED WARRANTY FOR SOFTWARE ACQUIRED OUTSIDE THE US AND CANADA. FOR THE LIMITED WARRANTIES AND SPECIAL PROVISIONS PERTAINING TO YOUR PARTICULAR JURISDICTION, PLEASE REFER TO YOUR WARRANTY BOOKLET INCLUDED WITH THIS PACKAGE OR PROVIDED WITH THE SOFTWARE PRINTED MATERIALS.

8. DISCLAIMER OF WARRANTIES. THE LIMITED WARRANTY THAT APPEARS ABOVE IS THE ONLY EXPRESS WARRANTY MADE TO YOU AND IS PROVIDED IN LIEU OF ANY OTHER EXPRESS WARRANTIES (IF ANY) CREATED BY ANY DOCUMENTATION OR PACKAGING. EXCEPT FOR THE LIMITED WARRANTY AND TO THE MAXIMUM EXTENT PERMITTED BY APPLICABLE LAW, MICROSOFT AND ITS SUPPLIERS PROVIDE THE

SOFTWARE AND SUPPORT SERVICES (IF ANY) *AS IS AND WITH ALL FAULTS*, AND HEREBY DISCLAIM ALL OTHER WARRANTIES AND CONDITIONS, EITHER EXPRESS, IMPLIED OR STATUTORY, INCLUDING, BUT NOT LIMITED TO, ANY (IF ANY) IMPLIED WARRANTIES, DUTIES OR CONDITIONS OF MERCHANTABILITY, OF FITNESS FOR A PARTICULAR PURPOSE, OF ACCURACY OR COMPLETENESS OR RESPONSES, OF RESULTS, OF WORKMANLIKE EFFORT, OF LACK OF VIRUSES AND OF LACK OF NEGLIGENCE, ALL WITH REGARD TO THE SOFTWARE, AND THE PROVISION OF OR FAILURE TO PROVIDE SUPPORT SERVICES. ALSO, THERE IS NO WARRANTY OR CONDITION OF TITLE, QUIET ENJOYMENT, QUIET POSSESSION, CORRESPONDENCE TO DESCRIPTION OR NON-INFRINGEMENT WITH REGARD TO THE SOFTWARE.

9. **EXCLUSION OF INCIDENTAL, CONSEQUENTIAL AND CERTAIN OTHER DAMAGES.** TO THE MAXIMUM EXTENT PERMITTED BY APPLICABLE LAW, IN NO EVENT SHALL MICROSOFT OR ITS SUPPLIERS BE LIABLE FOR ANY SPECIAL, INCIDENTAL, INDIRECT, OR CONSEQUENTIAL DAMAGES WHATSOEVER (INCLUDING, BUT NOT LIMITED TO, DAMAGES FOR LOSS OF PROFITS OR CONFIDENTIAL OR OTHER INFORMATION, FOR BUSINESS INTERRUPTION, FOR PERSONAL INJURY, FOR LOSS OF PRIVACY, FOR FAILURE TO MEET ANY DUTY INCLUDING OF GOOD FAITH OR OF REASONABLE CARE, FOR NEGLIGENCE, AND FOR ANY OTHER PECUNIARY OR OTHER LOSS WHATSOEVER) ARISING OUT OF OR IN ANY WAY RELATED TO THE USE OF OR INABILITY TO USE THE SOFTWARE, THE PROVISION OF OR FAILURE TO PROVIDE SUPPORT SERVICES, OR OTHERWISE UNDER OR IN CONNECTION WITH ANY PROVISION OF THIS EULA, EVEN IN THE EVENT OF THE FAULT, TORT (INCLUDING NEGLIGENCE), STRICT LIABILITY, BREACH OF CONTRACT OR BREACH OF WARRANTY OF MICROSOFT OR ANY SUPPLIER, AND EVEN IF MICROSOFT OR ANY SUPPLIER HAS BEEN ADVISED OF THE POSSIBILITY OF SUCH DAMAGES.

10. **LIMITATION OF LIABILITY AND REMEDIES.** NOTWITHSTANDING ANY DAMAGES THAT YOU MIGHT INCUR FOR ANY REASON WHATSOEVER (INCLUDING, WITHOUT LIMITATION, ALL DAMAGES REFERENCED ABOVE AND ALL DIRECT OR GENERAL DAMAGES), THE ENTIRE LIABILITY OF MICROSOFT AND ANY OF ITS SUPPLIERS UNDER ANY PROVISION OF THIS EULA AND YOUR EXCLUSIVE REMEDY FOR ALL OF THE FOREGOING (EXCEPT FOR ANY REMEDY OF REPAIR OR REPLACEMENT ELECTED BY MICROSOFT WITH RESPECT TO ANY BREACH OF THE LIMITED WARRANTY) SHAL BE LIMITED TO THE GREATER OF THE AMOUNT ACTUALLY PAID BY YOU FOR THE SOFTWARE OR U.S. $5.00. THE FOREGOING LIMITATIONS, EXCLUSIONS AND DISCLAIMERS (INCLUDING SECTIONS 7, 8, AND 9 ABOVE) SHALL APPLY TO THE MAXIMUM EXTENT PERMITTED BY APPLICABLE LAW, EVEN IF ANY REMEDY FAILS ITS ESSENTIAL PURPOSE.

11. **ENTIRE AGREEMENT.** This EULA (including any addendum or amendment to this EULA which is included with the Software) is the entire agreement between you and Microsoft relating to the Software and the support services (if any) and they supersede all prior or contemporaneous oral or written communications, proposals and representations with respect to the Software or any other subject matter covered by this EULA. To the extent the terms of any Microsoft policies or programs for support services conflict with the terms of this EULA, the terms of this EULA shall control.

Si vous avez acquis votre produit Microsoft au CANADA, la garantie limitée suivante vous concerne :
GARANTIE LIMITÉE

Microsoft garantit que le Produit fonctionnera conformément aux documents inclus pendant une période de 90 jours suivant la date de réception.

Si une garantie ou condition implicite est créée par votre État ou votre territoire et qu'une loi fédérale ou provinciale ou État en interdit le déni, vous jouissez également d'une garantie ou condition implicite, MAIS UNIQUEMENT POUR LES DÉFAUTS DÉCOUVERTS DURANT LA PÉRIODE DE LA PRÉSENTE GARANTIE LIMITÉE (QUATRE-VINGT-DIX JOURS). IL N'Y A AUCUNE GARANTIE OU CONDITION DE QUELQUE NATURE QUE CE SOIT QUANT AUX DÉFAUTS DÉCOUVERTS APRÈS CETTE PÉRIODE DE QUATRE-VINGT-DIX JOURS. Certains États ou territoires ne permettent pas de limiter la durée d'une garantie ou condition implicite de sorte que la limitation cidessus peut ne pas s'appliquer à vous.

Tous les suppléments ou toutes les mises à jour relatifs au Produit, notamment, les ensembles de services ou les réparations à chaud (le cas échéant) qui vous sont fournis après l'expiration de la période de quatre-vingt-dix jours de la garantie limitée ne sont pas couverts par quelque garantie ou condition que ce soit, expresse ou implicite.

LIMITATION DES RECOURS; ABSENCE DE DOMMAGES INDIRECTS OU AUTRES. Votre recours exclusif pour toute violation de la présente garantie limitée est décrit ciaprès. Sauf pour tout remboursement au choix de Microsoft, si le Produit ne respecte pas la garantie limitée de Microsoft et, dans la mesure maximale permise par les lois applicables, même si tout recours n'atteint pas son but essentiel, VOUS N'AVEZ DROIT À AUCUNS DOMMAGES, NOTAMMENT DES DOMMAGES INDIRECTS. Les modalités de la clause «Exclusion des dommages accessoires, indirects et de certains autres dommages » sont également intégrées à la présente garantie limitée. Certains États ou territoires ne permettent pas l'exclusion ou la limitation des dommages indirects ou accessoires de sorte que la limitation ou l'exclusion cidessus peut ne pas s'appliquer à vous. La présente garantie limitée vous donne des droits légaux spécifiques. Vous pouvez avoir d'autres droits qui peuvent varier d'un territoire ou d'un État à un autre. VOTRE RECOURS EXCLUSIF. L'obligation intégrale de Microsoft et de ses fournisseurs et votre recours exclusif seront, selon le choix de Microsoft de temps à autre sous réserve de toute loi applicable, a) le remboursement du prix payé, le cas échéant, pour le Produit ou b) la réparation ou le remplacement du Produit qui ne respecte pas la présente garantie limitée et qui est retourné à Microsoft avec une copie de votre reçu. Vous recevrez la compensation choisie par Microsoft, sans frais, sauf que vous êtes responsable des dépenses que vous pourriez engager (p. ex., les frais d'envoi du Produit à Microsoft). La présente garantie limitée est nulle si la défectuosité du Produit est causée par un accident, un usage abusif, une mauvaise application, un usage anormal ou un virus. Tout Produit de remplacement sera garanti pour le reste de la période de garantie initiale ou pendant trente (30) jours, selon la plus longue entre ces deux périodes. À l'extérieur des États-Unis ou du Canada, ces recours ou l'un quelconque des services de soutien technique offerts par Microsoft ne sont pas disponibles sans preuve d'achat d'une source internationale autorisée. Pour exercer votre recours, vous devez communiquer avec Microsoft et vous adresser au Microsoft Sales Information Center/One Microsoft Way/Redmond, WA 98052-6399, ou à la filiale de Microsoft de votre pays.

DÉNI DE GARANTIES. La garantie limitée mentionnée ci-dessus constitue la seule garantie expresse qui vous est donnée et remplace toutes autres garanties expresses (s'il en est) mentionnées dans un document ou sur un emballage. Sauf en ce qui a trait à la garantie limitée et dans la mesure maximale permise par les lois applicables, le Produit et les services de soutien technique (le cas échéant) sont fournis *TELS QUELS ET AVEC TOUS LES DÉFAUTS* par Microsoft et ses fournisseurs, lesquels par les présentes dénient toutes autres garanties et conditions expresses, implicites ou en vertu de la loi, notamment (le cas échéant) les garanties, devoirs ou conditions implicites de qualité marchande, d'adaptation à un usage particulier, d'exactitude ou d'exhaustivité des réponses, des résultats, des efforts déployés selon les règles de l'art, d'absence de virus et de négligence, le tout à l'égard du Produit et de la prestation des services de soutien technique ou de l'omission d'une telle prestation. PAR AILLEURS, IL N'Y A AUCUNE GARANTIE OU CONDITION QUANT AU TITRE DE PROPRIÉTÉ, À LA JOUISSANCE OU LA POSSESSION PAISIBLE, À LA CONCORDANCE À UNE DESCRIPTION NI QUANT À UNE ABSENCE DE CONTREFAÇON CONCERNANT LE PRODUIT.

EXCLUSION DES DOMMAGES ACCESSOIRES, INDIRECTS ET DE CERTAINS AUTRES DOMMAGES. DANS LA MESURE MAXIMALE PERMISE PAR LES LOIS APPLICABLES, EN AUCUN CAS MICROSOFT OU SES FOURNISSEURS NE SERONT RESPONSABLES DES DOMMAGES SPÉCIAUX, CONSÉCUTIFS, ACCESSOIRES OU INDIRECTS DE QUELQUE NATURE QUE CE SOIT (NOTAMMENT, LES DOMMAGES À L'ÉGARD DU MANQUE À GAGNER OU DE LA DIVULGATION DE RENSEIGNEMENTS CONFIDENTIELS OU AUTRES, DE LA PERTE D'EXPLOITATION, DE BLESSURES CORPORELLES, DE LA VIOLATION DE LA VIE PRIVÉE, DE L'OMISSION DE REMPLIR TOUT DEVOIR, Y COMPRIS D'AGIR DE BONNE FOI OU D'EXERCER UN SOIN RAISONNABLE, DE LA NÉGLIGENCE ET DE TOUTE AUTRE PERTE PÉCUNIAIRE OU AUTRE PERTE DE QUELQUE NATURE QUE CE SOIT) SE RAPPORTANT DE QUELQUE MANIÈRE QUE CE SOIT À L'UTILISATION DU PRODUIT OU À L'INCAPACITÉ DE S'EN SERVIR, À LA PRESTATION OU À L'OMISSION D'UNE TELLE PRESTATION DE SERVICES DE SOUTIEN TECHNIQUE OU AUTREMENT AUX TERMES DE TOUTE DISPOSITION DU PRÉSENT EULA OU RELATIVEMENT À UNE TELLE DISPOSITION, MÊME EN CAS DE FAUTE, DE DÉLIT CIVIL (Y COMPRIS LA NÉGLIGENCE), DE RESPONSABILITÉ STRICTE, DE VIOLATION DE CONTRAT OU DE VIOLATION DE GARANTIE DE MICROSOFT OU DE TOUT FOURNISSEUR ET MÊME SI MICROSOFT OU TOUT FOURNISSEUR A ÉTÉ AVISÉ DE LA POSSIBILITÉ DE TELS DOMMAGES.

LIMITATION DE RESPONSABILITÉ ET RECOURS. Malgré les dommages que vous puissiez subir pour quelque motif que ce soit (notamment, tous les dommages susmentionnés et tous les dommages directs ou généraux), l'obligation intégrale de Microsoft et de l'un ou l'autre de ses fournisseurs aux termes de toute disposition du présent EULA et votre recours exclusif à l'égard de tout ce qui précède (sauf en ce qui concerne tout recours de réparation ou de remplacement choisi par Microsoft à l'égard de tout manquement à la garantie limitée) se limite au plus élevé entre les montants suivants : le montant que vous avez réellement payé pour le Produit ou 5,00 $US. Les limites, exclusions et dénis qui précèdent (y compris les clauses ci-dessus), s'appliquent dans la mesure maximale permise par les lois applicables, même si tout recours n'atteint pas son but essentiel.

La présente Convention est régie par les lois de la province d'Ontario, Canada. Chacune des parties à la présente reconnaît irrévocablement la compétence des tribunaux de la province d'Ontario et consent à instituer tout litige qui pourrait découler de la présente auprès des tribunaux situés dans le district judiciaire de York, province d'Ontario.

Au cas où vous auriez des questions concernant cette licence ou que vous désiriez vous mettre en rapport avec Microsoft pour quelque raison que ce soit, veuillez contacter la succursale Microsoft desservant votre pays, dont l'adresse est fournie dans ce produit, ou écrivez à : Microsoft Sales Information Center, One Microsoft Way, Redmond, Washington 98052-6399.

PN 097-0002296

System Requirements

To use the *Microsoft Office XP Resource Kit* tools and documentation you need a computer that meets the following requirements:

Processor   Pentium 133-MHz or higher processor required for all operating systems.

Operating system   Microsoft Windows 98, Microsoft Windows 98 Second Edition, Windows Millennium Edition, Microsoft Windows NT 4.0 with Service Pack 6 or greater, or Microsoft Windows 2000. The recommended operating system is Windows 2000 Professional.

On systems running Windows NT 4.0 with Service Pack 6, the version of Internet Explorer must be upgraded to at least Microsoft Internet Explorer 4.01 with Service Pack 1.

Microsoft Office XP   An Enterprise Edition of Microsoft Office XP is required to run many of the tools included with the Office XP Resource Kit. The documentation can be viewed with Internet Explorer 4.01 or greater or a compatible browser.

Memory   Memory requirements depend upon the operating system used with the computer. Operating system RAM requirements assume default Windows installations; running additional utilities or applications may require additional RAM.

- For Windows 98 and Windows 98 Second Edition, 24 MB of RAM.
- For Windows Me and Windows NT Workstation or Server 4.0 or later, 32 MB of RAM.
- For Windows 2000 Professional, 64 MB of RAM recommended minimum. For Windows 2000 Server or Advanced Server, 256 MB of RAM recommended minimum.

Hard-disk space   A minimum of 55 MB of RAM is recommended.

Registry space   Under Windows NT and Windows 2000, at least 4 MB of space must be available in the registry.

Disk drives   CD-ROM drive.

Monitor   VGA or higher-resolution monitor; Super VGA recommended.

Pointing device   Microsoft Mouse, Microsoft IntelliMouse, or compatible pointing device.

Internet   Some Internet functionality may require Internet access via a 14,400 or higher baud modem and payment of a separate fee to a service provider; local charges may apply.